The Rational Expectations Revolution

The Rational Expectations Revolution

Readings from
the Front Line

edited by
Preston J. Miller

The MIT Press
Cambridge, Massachusetts
London, England

This book was set in Palatino by Asco Trade Typesetting Ltd., Hong Kong, and was printed and bound in the United States of America.

Library of Congress Cataloging-in-Publication Data

The Rational expectations revolution : readings from the front line / edited by
  Preston J. Miller.
    p.   cm.
  Includes bibliographical references and index.
  ISBN 0-262-13297-4.—ISBN 0-262-63155-5 (pbk.)
  1. Rational expectations (Economic theory) 2. Macroeconomics. I. Miller, Preston J.
HB172.5.R38   1994
339—dc20   93-5815
                                                                         CIP

Contents

Contributors

S. Rao Aiyagari
Research Department
Federal Reserve Bank of
Minneapolis

V. V. Chari
J. L. Kellogg Graduate
School of Management
Northwestern University
and
Research Department
Federal Reserve Bank of
Minneapolis

Lawrence J. Christiano
Department of Economics
Northwestern University
and
Research Department
Federal Reserve Bank of
Minneapolis

Michael R. Darby
Graduate School of Management
University of California, Los
Angeles

Gary D. Hansen
Department of Economics
University of Pennsylvania
and
Department of Economics
University of California, Los
Angeles

Finn E. Kydland
Graduate School of Industrial
Administration
Carnegie Mellon University

Robert E. Lucas, Jr.
Department of Economics
University of Chicago

Preston J. Miller
Research Department
Federal Reserve Bank of
Minneapolis

Edward C. Prescott
Department of Economics
University of Minnesota
and
Research Department
Federal Reserve Bank of
Minneapolis

Arthur J. Rolnick
Research Department
Federal Reserve Bank of
Minneapolis

Thomas J. Sargent
Hoover Institution
Stanford University
and
Department of Economics
University of Chicago
and
Research Department
Federal Reserve Bank of
Minneapolis

Lawrence H. Summers
Under Secretary of the Treasury
for International Affairs

Neil Wallace
Department of Economics
University of Minnesota
and
Research Department
Federal Reserve Bank of
Minneapolis

Warren E. Weber
Research Department
Federal Reserve Bank of
Minneapolis

Randall Wright
Department of Economics
University of Pennsylvania
and
Research Department
Federal Reserve Bank of
Minneapolis

Acknowledgments

I thank Ed Green, Ed Prescott, Art Rolnick, and Tom Sargent for their comments on the general introduction, and I especially appreciate the detailed criticisms and suggestions on that introduction and on the chapter introductions given by Ellen McGrattan, Neil Wallace, and Chuck Whiteman. Kathy Rolfe and Martie Starr deserve credit for making my discussion more readable. Any views expressed herein are those of the authors and not necessarily those of the Federal Reserve Bank of Minneapolis or the Federal Reserve System.

Introduction

Over the last 20 years, macroeconomic theory has undergone a revolution which moved monetary and budget policymaking from a physical setting to a human one. Somewhat by chance, the Minneapolis Federal Reserve Bank found itself on the front line. This volume contains papers written during the revolution and published primarily in a research journal, the *Federal Reserve Bank of Minneapolis Quarterly Review*. The papers describe the roots and development of the revolutionary school of thought that has become known as *rational expectations*. This volume takes readers from the beginnings to the present and is intended to provide an understanding of that school's current research strategy and its positions in current economic debates.

Before the revolution, macroeconomic policymaking was viewed as an engineering problem. Guiding the economy is similar to guiding a rocket ship—or so I was taught in the 1960s. A macroeconomic policymaker's goal was to keep the economy on a full employment, noninflationary path, similar to an engineer's goal of keeping a rocket ship on its course. The policymaker had policy tools to control, such as tax rates or base money, similar to an engineer's levers and dials. The policymaking problem was posed as adjusting the tools based on new information about the economy's position and the economic environment to best keep the economy on its full employment, noninflationary path. This was similar to the engineer's problem of adjusting the levers and dials based on new information about the rocket ship's position and external conditions to best keep the rocket ship on its course.

Macroeconomic engineering made some major strides in the 1960s. Macroeconomists devised better control systems: better models to represent the path of the economy and better feedback rules to inform policymakers how to adjust their policy tools based on new information. The models were extended to dynamic, stochastic representations of the economy, and advances were made in deriving optimal policy rules in these models.

In the early 1970s, a research team at the Minneapolis Fed (composed of John Kareken, Thomas Muench, Thomas Sargent, and Neil Wallace) was using the engineering paradigm to determine the optimal FOMC policy in the context of an estimated model, when Robert Lucas, then at Carnegie Mellon and now at the University of Chicago, sent the team a draft of his now-famous "Expectations and the Neutrality of Money" and later his "Econometric Policy Evaluation: A Critique." (See Chapter 1 in this volume.) The team quickly recognized that the engineering paradigm was fundamentally flawed and that a revolution in thought was required.

The engineering paradigm requires that the relationships which determine how the economy moves over time be invariant to changes in policy rules. That is, in order for an economic model to indicate how outcomes for goal variables, such as real growth and inflation, depend on the rules for setting the policy variables, the model's relationships cannot change whenever the rules change. Yet, Lucas' papers indicated that economic relationships in the macroeconometric models then in use would be expected to change when relevant policy rules changed. Thus, economic models that were attempting to represent human behavior were fundamentally different from engineering models that were attempting to capture the movement of inanimate objects.

The reasoning behind what is now known as the *Lucas critique* is straightforward. The relationships in a macroeconometric model can be considered as aggregates of individual and firm decision rules. Those rules are solutions to agents' problems of maximizing utility or profits in a dynamic, stochastic setting. The maximization is done subject to individuals being bound by their budget constraints and firms being bound by their minimal cost constraints. The decisions of individuals and firms then will depend on expectations of future policy actions that affect their budgets or costs. A change in policy rules changes agents' expectations of future policy actions, thus changing their constraints and the way their decisions are related to current information. The changes in agents' decision rules then produce changes in the coefficients of aggregate relationships in macroeconometric models.

Although the ramifications of the Lucas critique are now quite clear, they were not when it first appeared. Macroeconomists had to come to grips with two questions: What did the Lucas critique say about the way analysis was then conducted? And what new directions should the theory take?

At the time, many macroeconomists took the view that while there may be some validity to the Lucas critique, it was just one of many criticisms of macroeconometric models and probably was not quantitatively significant. They argued that the relationships in traditional macroeconometric models are intended to represent aggregations of individual decision rules, and they made the analogy to static supply and demand curves to argue that these relationships would remain invariant to most relevant policy changes.

The economists in the Minneapolis Fed's research team took a more extreme view. Their classical backgrounds, their familiarity with Lucas' work, and their active involvement at the time in macroengineering led them to argue that the Lucas critique was fatal and that new approaches had to be developed. They argued that the analogy to static demand and supply curves does not hold up in dynamic, stochastic environments. A revolution in macroeconomic thought was called for. These revolutionary economists became associated with the *rational expectations* school of macroeconomics. Those who maintained the usefulness of the traditional macroeconometric policy analysis were associated with the *Keynesian* view.

The chapters in the first section of this volume (Chapters 1–3) discuss in a somewhat general way why traditional Keynesian macroeconometric policy analysis could not be patched up and how it had to be changed. The rational expectations school required changes in three key areas:

• The *policy goal* had to be stated in terms of the welfare of individuals and not in terms of macro variables such as inflation and output. This way policies could be evaluated in terms of the efficiency and income distributions associated with their implied outcomes.

• *Models* had to be built from the ground up (general equilibrium), explicitly describing the economic environment and the optimization problems of the economic agents, and not built on assumed aggregate relationships. Only in this way could invariance be plausibly argued.

• Policies had to be defined as rules which describe how policy variables are set based on available information and not defined as one-time actions. In rational expectations models, only *policy rules* can be evaluated, since agents' decisions depend not just on policy actions taken today but also on actions agents expect to be taken in the future.

The first three chapters emphasize the differences in policymaking when the process being controlled represents the decisions of humans rather than the movements of inanimate objects.

It is one thing to criticize existing theory; it is quite another to replace it. The revolution required redoing almost everything: formulating tractable general equilibrium models, empirically parameterizing the models, and evaluating alternative policy rules in the context of these models.

The chapters in the second section of this volume (Chapters 4–10) construct and use simple, tractable general equilibrium models to analyze monetary and budget policies in a closed economy (with no foreign trade). These chapters include several important results:

• Monetary and budget policy changes can have real effects in general equilibrium models. Although rational expectations initially was associated with policy neutrality, these papers show that the association need not hold.

• Monetary or budget policy changes can affect different groups (such as lenders and debtors, the old and the young) differently. The welfare effects of alternative policies then cannot be simply characterized by macroeconomic variables, such as real output or inflation.

• Monetary and budget policies cannot be made independently. For instance, it may not be possible over a sustained period to run high budget deficits to stimulate the economy while maintaining low money growth to control inflation.

This last result was perhaps the most important. It contradicted the Keynesian view of the time, which suggested that the government could arbitrarily choose the mix of policies to effect a desired outcome.

Chapters in the third section (Chapters 11–13) consider monetary and budget policies in an open economy. Their method was essentially to extend the models for closed economies by introducing foreign economies that resemble the domestic economy and have their own monetary and budget policies. A central issue raised in this section is what kinds of exchange rate regimes are feasible. One key finding is that exchange rates are indeterminate under a floating regime when there are no financial restrictions or capital controls. Another is that under feasible regimes, the effects of changes in one country's monetary and budget policies spill over into foreign economies, so some policy coordination among countries may be desirable.

The analysis and policy findings described so far focus on the longer-run. But in order to take on the traditional Keynesian theory, the rational expectations economists had to provide defensible general equilibrium models of the business cycle. After all, business cycles and countercyclical policymaking were the primary focus of traditional Keynesian macroeconomics. One simple approach that has proven remarkably successful was pioneered in part by Finn Kydland and Edward Prescott. That approach is to model business cycles as the result of shocks that impinge in a neoclassical growth model.

The chapters in the fourth section of this volume (Chapters 14–19) describe the new real business cycle theory. The theory's success is not universally accepted, however. One chapter in this section (Chapter 15) describes a skeptic's criticisms, while another (Chapter 19) describes an alternative general equilibrium model of the business cycle that emphasizes "psychic" as opposed to "real" causes.

Finally, the rational expectations economists had to devise new statistical methods to be consistent with the new theories. One approach involves system estimation with cross-equation restrictions. Although the approach has been widely used, it is only generally described in the first section. A second approach involving calibration receives more attention in this volume. It is briefly described in the fourth section. In the fifth section, Chapters 20 and 21 explain how calibration is done and illustrate how theory and empirical observations interact in quantitative general equilibrium models.

Back in the 1960s macroeconomic policymaking seemed much simpler. Rocket ships, unlike people, do not have minds of their own. But a big problem arose in the 1970s as models based on the engineering paradigm seemed to break down. This is what gave the Lucas critique so much force. The revolution in thought and the reconstruction of models to ground them more firmly in the theory of human behavior have been difficult. Perhaps the new knowledge and direction represented by the articles collected in this volume will lead to better policies.

I

The Rational Expectations Approach to Macroeconomic Policymaking

The first two chapters in this section, by Lucas and Sargent and by Sargent, argue that the traditional macroeconometric approach to policy analysis is flawed, and they describe in general terms how policy analysis should be conducted. The third chapter, by Chari, discusses the policy concern of time inconsistency—something that was not even present in the old analysis.

Likening the old analysis to guiding a rocket ship, as was done in the introduction, needs some explanation. Nowhere in the first two chapters do the authors use that analogy. In fact, they state that the traditional analysis was based on economic models composed of estimated aggregate demand and supply relationships. On the surface the authors seem just to argue that the traditional macroeconometric models were not very good and new ones would be better. The argument is much more subtle, however, and on reflection is consistent with the rocket ship analogy.

The basic flaw the authors find in traditional macroeconometric models is the failure to account for human behavior. The models did not allow agents' decisions, which implicitly generate the aggregate demand and supply relationships, to adjust to policy changes.

This point can be illustrated simply with an example. Suppose an agent maximizes utility over a two-period horizon where income and the interest rate are taken as given:

$$\max U(c_1, c_2)$$

subject to

$$c_1 + \frac{c_2}{1 + r} = y_1 + \frac{y_2}{1 + r},$$

where

c_i is consumption in period i, $i = 1, 2$

y_i is income in period i, $i = 1, 2$, and

r is the rate of interest between periods.

Suppose that this problem generates a linear demand schedule for first-period consumption, a *consumption function*:

$$\hat{c}_1 = a + br + dy_1 + ey_2,$$

where $\hat{c}_1$ is demand for c_1 and a, b, d, and e are constants. Suppose further that for given policies, y_2 is some multiple of y_1:

$$y_2 = hy_1,$$

where h is the multiple.

The composite of these two relationships would be included in traditional macroeconometric models since demand would have to be expressed in terms of observables rather than unknown future values like y_2:

$$\hat{c}_1 = a + br + fy_1,$$

where

$$f \equiv d + eh.$$

Now suppose a policy change, such as a tax cut, caused a change in y_1 to y_1' and, more importantly, a change in the relationship between y_2 and y_1; that is, $y_2' = h'y_1'$. The agent's maximization problem suggests that the consumption function now will be given by

$$\hat{c}_1 = a + br + f'y_1',$$

where

$$f' = d + eh'.$$

Yet the traditional macroeconometric models maintained that the consumption function would be given by

$$\hat{c}_1 = a + br + fy_1'.$$

Thus, while the effect of the policy change on y_1 would be incorporated into the model, the effect of the change on consumption would be incorrect. The old coefficient f would be used incorrectly in place of f'. Hence, in traditional macroeconometric models, agents were not able to respond to a change in policies that altered the relationship between y_2 and y_1. Like rocket ships, they could not respond today to a change in policy controls that would definitely occur tomorrow.

For policy analysis, the traditional macroeconometric models were used to describe the laws of motion of the economy in much the same way as an engineering model would describe the laws of motion of a rocket ship. The economic policymaker, like the engineer, was assumed to be playing a game against nature, because the economic agents in the model could not react (adjust their decision rules) to the policymaker's moves. The new analysis changed the policy game to one against other players, where the other players, the private agents, are allowed to adjust to the moves of the policymaker.

Perhaps the unifying idea of the three chapters in this section is that economic policy analysis must permit the agents in economic models to adjust to changes in policies in accordance with the agents' best interests. This idea is behind the argument of the first two chapters that traditional macroeconometric policy analysis is flawed and must be replaced with an analysis based on models that explicitly describe the decision-making problems of individual agents. This idea is behind the prescription of a new econometric approach, and it is what gives rise to the time inconsistency problem described in the third chapter.

To understand how the time inconsistency problem can arise, consider the case of monetary policy. Suppose that the best monetary policy, after the behavioral responses of private agents have been taken into account, is to pursue zero inflation for all time. In the current period, the monetary policymaker announces this policy, and agents base their decisions on this policy. The next period, however, the policymaker may have an incentive to deviate from the zero inflation policy. Since agents have built the zero inflation expectation into their decisions, the policymaker could improve the current period's outcome by temporarily boosting demand and inflation. The policymaker could assure that future outcomes are not made worse by promising to never trick agents again. But, of course, when the next period arrives, the policymaker will want to break that promise.

Clearly, rational agents cannot be tricked consistently or systematically. They will take into account the *time inconsistency problem*: the incentive of the policymaker to deviate from the best policy. Thus, the best policy may not be attainable unless there is some mechanism for committing the policy authority to that policy. If there is no commitment mechanism, the best policy is in a sense second best: it must be chosen from the set of policies that are time consistent. Because of the time inconsistency problem, rules that tie the hands of economic policymakers can be welfare improving.

The chapters in this section provide an overview of what the rational expectations revolution entailed. They describe what rational expectations economists thought was wrong with the traditional approach, how they proposed to replace that approach, and why the new approach led to new policy concerns.

1

After Keynesian Macroeconomics

Robert E. Lucas, Jr., and Thomas J. Sargent

For the applied economist, the confident and apparently successful application of Keynesian principles to economic policy which occurred in the United States in the 1960s was an event of incomparable significance and satisfaction. These principles led to a set of simple, quantitative relationships between fiscal policy and economic activity generally, the basic logic of which could be (and was) explained to the general public and which could be applied to yield improvements in economic performance benefitting everyone. It seemed an economics as free of ideological difficulties as, say, applied chemistry or physics, promising a straightforward expansion in economic possibilities. One might argue as to how this windfall should be distributed, but it seemed a simple lapse of logic to oppose the windfall itself. Understandably and correctly, noneconomists met this promise with skepticism at first; the smoothly growing prosperity of the Kennedy-Johnson years did much to diminish these doubts.

We dwell on these halcyon days of Keynesian economics because without conscious effort they are difficult to recall today. In the present decade, the U.S. economy has undergone its first major depression since the 1930s, to the accompaniment of inflation rates in excess of 10 percent per annum. These events have been transmitted (by consent of the governments involved) to other advanced countries and in many cases have been amplified. These events did not arise from a reactionary reversion to outmoded, "classical" principles of tight money and balanced budgets. On the contrary, they were accompanied by massive government budget deficits and high rates of monetary expansion, policies which, although bearing an admitted risk of inflation, promised according to modern Keynesian doctrine rapid real growth and low rates of unemployment.

Reprinted from the *Federal Reserve Bank of Minneapolis Quarterly Review*, Spring 1979.

That these predictions were wildly incorrect and that the doctrine on which they were based is fundamentally flawed are now simple matters of fact, involving no novelties in economic theory. The task now facing contemporary students of the business cycle is to sort through the wreckage, determining which features of that remarkable intellectual event called the Keynesian Revolution can be salvaged and put to good use and which others must be discarded. Though it is far from clear what the outcome of this process will be, it is already evident that it will necessarily involve the reopening of basic issues in monetary economics which have been viewed since the thirties as "closed" and the reevaluation of every aspect of the institutional framework within which monetary and fiscal policy is formulated in the advanced countries.

This paper is an early progress report on this process of reevaluation and reconstruction. We begin by reviewing the econometric framework by means of which Keynesian theory evolved from disconnected, qualitative talk about economic activity into a system of equations which can be compared to data in a systematic way and which provide an operational guide in the necessarily quantitative task of formulating monetary and fiscal policy. Next, we identify those aspects of this framework which were central to its failure in the seventies. In so doing, our intent is to establish that the difficulties are *fatal*: that modern macroeconomic models are of *no* value in guiding policy and that this condition will not be remedied by modifications along any line which is currently being pursued. This diagnosis suggests certain principles which a useful theory of business cycles must have. We conclude by reviewing some recent research consistent with these principles.

Macroeconometric Models

The Keynesian Revolution was, in the form in which it succeeded in the United States, a revolution in method. This was not Keynes' (1936)[1] intent, nor is it the view of all of his most eminent followers. Yet if one does not view the revolution in this way, it is impossible to account for some of its most important features: the evolution of macroeconomics into a quantitative, *scientific* discipline, the development of explicit statistical descriptions of economic behavior, the increasing reliance of government officials on technical economic expertise, and the introduction of the use of mathematical control theory to manage an economy. It is the fact that Keynesian theory lent itself so readily to the formulation of explicit econometric models which accounts for the dominant scientific position it attained by the 1960s.

Because of this, neither the success of the Keynesian Revolution nor its eventual failure can be understood at the purely verbal level at which Keynes himself wrote. It is necessary to know something of the way macroeconometric models are constructed and the features they must have in order to "work" as aids in forecasting and policy evaluation. To discuss these issues, we introduce some notation.

An econometric model is a system of equations involving a number of endogenous variables (variables determined by the model), exogenous variables (variables which affect the system but are not affected by it), and stochastic or random shocks. The idea is to use historical data to estimate the model and then to utilize the estimated version to obtain estimates of the consequences of alternative policies. For practical reasons, it is usual to use a standard linear model, taking the structural form[2]

$$A_0 y_t + A_1 y_{t-1} + \cdots + A_m y_{t-m} = B_0 x_t + B_1 x_{t-1} + \cdots + B_n x_{t-n} + \varepsilon_t \quad (1)$$

$$R_0 \varepsilon_t + R_1 \varepsilon_{t-1} + \cdots + R_r \varepsilon_{t-r} = u_t, R_0 \equiv I. \quad (2)$$

Here y_t is an $(L \times 1)$ vector of endogenous variables, x_t is a $(K \times 1)$ vector of exogenous variables, and ε_t and u_t are each $(L \times 1)$ vectors of random disturbances. The matrices A_j are each $(L \times L)$; the B_j's are $(L \times K)$, and the R_j's are each $(L \times L)$. The $(L \times L)$ disturbance process u_t is assumed to be a serially uncorrelated process with $Eu_t = 0$ and with contemporaneous covariance matrix $Eu_t u_t' = \Sigma$ and $Eu_t u_s' = 0$ for all $t \neq s$. The defining characteristic of the exogenous variables x_t is that they are uncorrelated with the ε's at all lags so that $Eu_t x_s'$ is an $(L \times K)$ matrix of zeros for all t and s.

Equations (1) are L equations in the L current values y_t of the endogenous variables. Each of these structural equations is a behavioral relationship, identity, or market clearing condition, and each in principle can involve a number of endogenous variables. The structural equations are usually not regression equations[3] because the ε_t's are in general, by the logic of the model, supposed to be correlated with more than one component of the vector y_t and very possibly one or more components of the vectors $y_{t-1}, \ldots, y_{t-m}$.

The structural model (1) and (2) can be solved for y_t in terms of past y's and x's and past shocks. This reduced form system is

$$y_t = -P_1 y_{t-1} - \cdots - P_{r+m} y_{t-r-m} + Q_0 x_t + \cdots + Q_{r+n} x_{t-n-r} + A_0^{-1} u_t \quad (3)$$

where[4]

$$P_s = A_0^{-1} \sum_{j=-\infty}^{\infty} R_j A_{s-j}$$

$$Q_s = A_0^{-1} \sum_{j=-\infty}^{\infty} R_j B_{s-j}.$$

The reduced form equations are regression equations, that is, the disturbance vector $A_0^{-1} u_t$ is orthogonal to $y_{t-1}, \ldots, y_{t-r-m}, x_t, \ldots, x_{t-n-r}$. This follows from the assumptions that the x's are exogenous and that the u's are serially uncorrelated. Therefore, under general conditions the reduced form can be estimated consistently by the method of least squares. The population parameters of the reduced form (3) together with the parameters of a vector autoregression for x_t

$$x_t = C_1 x_{t-1} + \cdots + C_p x_{t-p} + a_t \tag{4}$$

where $Ea_t = 0$ and $Ea_t \cdot x_{t-j} = 0$ for $j \geqslant 1$ completely describe all of the first and second moments of the (y_t, x_t) process. Given long enough time series, good estimates of the reduced form parameters—the P_j's and Q_j's —can be obtained by the method of least squares. All that examination of the data by themselves can deliver is reliable estimates of those parameters.

It is not generally possible to work backward from estimates of the P's and Q's alone to derive unique estimates of the structural parameters, the A_j's, B_j's, and R_j's. In general, infinite numbers of A's, B's, and R's are compatible with a single set of P's and Q's. This is the identification problem of econometrics. In order to derive a set of estimated structural parameters, it is necessary to know a great deal about them in advance. If enough prior information is imposed, it is possible to extract estimates of the A_j's, B_j's, R_j's implied by the data in combination with the prior information.

For purposes of *ex ante* forecasting, or the unconditional prediction of the vector $y_{t+1}, y_{t+2}, \ldots$ given observation of y_s and x_s, $s \leqslant t$, the estimated reduced form (3), together with (4), is sufficient. This is simply an exercise in a sophisticated kind of extrapolation, requiring no understanding of the structural parameters, that is, the *economics* of the model.

For purposes of *conditional* forecasting, or the prediction of the future behavior of some components of y_t and x_t *conditional* on particular values of other components, selected by policy, one needs to know the structural parameters. This is so because a change in policy necessarily alters some of the structural parameters (for example, those describing the past behavior of the policy variables themselves) and therefore affects the reduced form parameters in a highly complex way (see the equations defining P_s and Q_s above). Unless one knows which structural parameters remain invariant as policy changes and which change (and how), an econometric model is of no value in assessing alternative policies. It should be clear that this is true regardless of how well (3) and (4) fit historical data or how well they perform in unconditional forecasting.

Our discussion to this point has been highly general, and the formal considerations we have reviewed are not in any way specific to *Keynesian* models. The problem of identifying a structural model from a collection of economic time series is one that must be solved by anyone who claims the ability to give quantitative economic advice. The simplest Keynesian models are attempted solutions to this problem, as are the large-scale versions currently in use. So, too, are the monetarist models which imply the desirability of fixed monetary growth rules. So, for that matter, is the armchair advice given by economists who claim to be outside the econometric tradition, though in this case the implicit, underlying structure is not exposed to professional criticism. Any procedure which leads from the study of observed economic behavior to the quantitative assessment of alternative economic policies involves the steps, executed poorly or well, explicitly or implicitly, which we have outlined.

Keynesian Macroeconometrics

In Keynesian macroeconometric models structural parameters are identified by the imposition of several types of a priori restrictions on the A_j's, B_j's, and R_j's. These restrictions usually fall into one of the following three categories:[5]

(a) A priori setting of many of the elements of the A_j's and B_j's to zero.

(b) Restrictions on the orders of serial correlation and the extent of cross-serial correlation of the disturbance vector ε_t, restrictions which amount to a priori setting of many elements of the R_j's to zero.

(c) A priori classifying of variables as exogenous and endogenous. A relative abundance of exogenous variables aids identification.

Existing large Keynesian macroeconometric models are open to serious challenge for the way they have introduced each type of restriction.

Keynes' *General Theory* was rich in suggestions for restrictions of type (a). In it he proposed a theory of national income determination built up from several simple relationships, each involving a few variables only. One of these, for example, was the "fundamental law" relating consumption expenditures to income. This suggested one "row" in equations (1) involving current consumption, current income, and *no other* variables, thereby imposing many zero-restrictions on the A_i's and B_j's. Similarly, the liquidity preference relation expressed the demand for money as a function of only income and an interest rate. By translating the building blocks of the Keynesian theoretical system into explicit equations, models of the form (1) and (2) were constructed with many theoretical restrictions of type (a).

Restrictions on the coefficients R_i governing the behavior of the error terms in (1) are harder to motivate theoretically because the errors are by definition movements in the variables which the *economic* theory cannot account for. The early econometricians took standard assumptions from statistical textbooks, restrictions which had proven useful in the agricultural experimenting which provided the main impetus to the development of modern statistics. Again, these restrictions, well-motivated or not, involve setting many elements in the R_i's equal to zero, thus aiding identification of the model's structure.

The classification of variables into exogenous and endogenous was also done on the basis of prior considerations. In general, variables were classed as endogenous which were, as a matter of institutional fact, determined largely by the actions of private agents (like consumption or private investment expenditures). Exogenous variables were those under governmental control (like tax rates or the supply of money). This division was intended to reflect the ordinary meanings of the words *endogenous*—"determined by the [economic] system"—and *exogenous*—"affecting the [economic] system but not affected by it."

By the mid-1950s, econometric models had been constructed which fit time series data well, in the sense that their reduced forms (3) tracked past data closely and proved useful in short-term forecasting. Moreover, by means of restrictions of the three types reviewed above, their structural parameters A_i, B_j, R_k could be identified. Using this estimated structure, the models could be simulated to obtain estimates of the consequences of different government economic policies, such as tax rates, expenditures, or monetary policy.

This Keynesian solution to the problem of identifying a structural model has become increasingly suspect as a result of both theoretical and statistical developments. Many of these developments are due to efforts of researchers sympathetic to the Keynesian tradition, and many were advanced well before the spectacular failure of the Keynesian models in the 1970s.[6]

Since its inception, macroeconomics has been criticized for its lack of foundations in microeconomic and general equilibrium theory. As was recognized early on by astute commentators like Leontief (1965, disapprovingly) and Tobin (1965b, approvingly), the creation of a distinct branch of theory with its own distinct postulates was Keynes' conscious aim. Yet a main theme of theoretical work since the *General Theory* has been the attempt to use microeconomic theory based on the classical postulate that agents act in their own interests to suggest a list of variables that belong on the right side of a given behavioral schedule, say, a demand schedule for a factor of production or a consumption schedule.[7] But from the point of view of identification of a given structural equation by means of restrictions of type (a), one needs reliable prior information that certain variables should be excluded from the right-hand side. Modern probabilistic microeconomic theory almost never implies either the exclusion restrictions suggested by Keynes or those imposed by macroeconometric models.

Let us consider one example with extremely dire implications for the identification of existing macro models. Expectations about the future prices, tax rates, and income levels play a critical role in many demand and supply schedules. In the best models, for example, investment demand typically is supposed to respond to businesses' expectations of future tax credits, tax rates, and factor costs, and the supply of labor typically is supposed to depend on the rate of inflation that workers expect in the future. Such structural equations are usually identified by the assumption that the expectation about, say, factor prices or the rate of inflation attributed to agents is a function only of a few lagged values of the variable which the agent is supposed to be forecasting. However, the macro models themselves contain complicated dynamic interactions among endogenous variables, including factor prices and the rate of inflation, and they generally imply that a wise agent would use current and many lagged values of many and usually most endogenous and exogenous variables in the model in order to form expectations about any one variable. Thus, virtually any version of the hypothesis that agents act in their own interests will contradict the identification restrictions imposed on expectations formation. Further, the restrictions on expectations that have been used to achieve identification are entirely arbitrary and have not been derived from any deeper assumption reflecting first principles about economic behavior. No general first principle has ever been set down which would imply that, say, the expected rate of inflation should be modeled as a linear function of lagged rates of inflation alone with weights that add up to unity, yet this hypothesis is used as an identifying restriction in almost all existing models. The casual treatment of expectations is not a peripheral problem in these models, for the role of expectations is pervasive in them and exerts a massive influence on their dynamic properties (a point Keynes himself insisted on). The failure of existing models to derive restrictions on expectations from any first principles grounded in economic theory is a symptom of a deeper and more general failure to derive behavioral relationships from any consistently posed dynamic optimization problems.

As for the second category, restrictions of type (b), existing Keynesian macro models make severe a priori restrictions on the R_j's. Typically, the R_j's are supposed to be diagonal so that cross-equation lagged serial correlation is ignored, and also the order of the ε_t process is assumed to be short so that only low-order serial correlation is allowed. There are at present no theoretical grounds for introducing these restrictions, and for good reasons there is little prospect that economic theory will soon provide any such grounds. In principle, identification can be achieved without imposing any such restrictions. Foregoing the use of category (b) restrictions would increase the category (a) and (c) restrictions needed. In any event, existing macro models do heavily restrict the R_j's.

Turning to the third category, all existing large models adopt an a priori classification of variables as either strictly endogenous variables, the y_t's, or strictly exogenous variables, the x_t's. Increasingly it is being recognized that the classification of a variable as exogenous on the basis of the observation that it could be set without reference to the current and past values of other variables has nothing to do with the econometrically relevant question of how this variable has *in fact* been related to others over a given historical period. Moreover, in light of recent developments in time series econometrics, we know that this arbitrary classification procedure is not necessary. Christopher Sims (1972) has shown that in a time series context the hypothesis of econometric exogeneity can be tested. That is, Sims showed that the hypothesis that x_t is strictly econometrically exogenous in (1) necessarily implies certain restrictions that can be tested given time series on the y's and x's. Tests along the lines of Sims' ought to be used routinely to check classifications into exogenous and endogenous sets of variables. To date they have not been. Prominent builders of large econometric models have even denied the usefulness of such tests. (See, for example, Ando 1977, pp. 209–10, and L. R. Klein in Okun and Perry 1973, p. 644.)

Failure of Keynesian Macroeconometrics

There are, therefore, a number of theoretical reasons for believing that the parameters identified as structural by current macroeconomic methods are not in fact structural. That is, we see no reason to believe that these models have isolated structures which will remain invariant across the class of interventions that figure in contemporary discussions of economic policy. Yet the question of whether a particular model is structural is an empirical, not a theoretical, one. If the macroeconometric models had compiled a record of parameter stability, particularly in the face of breaks in the stochastic behavior of the exogenous variables and disturbances, one would be skeptical as to the importance of prior theoretical objections of the sort we have raised.

In fact, however, the track record of the major econometric models is, on any dimension other than very short-term unconditional forecasting, very poor. Formal statistical tests for parameter instability, conducted by subdividing past series into periods and checking for parameter stability across time, invariably reveal major shifts. (For one example, see Muench et al. 1974.) Moreover, this difficulty is implicitly acknowledged by model builders themselves, who routinely employ an elaborate system of add-factors in forecasting, in an attempt to offset the continuing drift of the model away from the actual series.

Though not, of course, designed as such by anyone, macroeconometric models were subjected to a decisive test in the 1970s. A key element in all Keynesian models is a trade-off between inflation and real output: the higher is the inflation rate, the higher is output (or equivalently, the lower is the rate of unemployment). For example, the models of the late 1960s predicted a sustained U.S. unemployment rate of 4 percent as consistent with a 4 percent annual rate of inflation. Based on this prediction, many economists at that time urged a deliberate policy of inflation. Certainly the erratic "fits and starts" character of actual U.S. policy in the 1970s cannot be attributed to recommendations based on Keynesian models, but the inflationary bias on average of monetary and fiscal policy in this period should, according to all of these models, have produced the lowest average unemployment rates for any decade since the 1940s. In fact, as we know, they produced the highest unemployment rates since the 1930s. This was econometric failure on a grand scale.

This failure has not led to widespread conversions of Keynesian economists to other faiths, nor should it have been expected to. In economics as in other sciences, a theoretical framework is always broader and more flexible than any particular set of equations, and there is always the hope that if a particular specific model fails, one can find a more successful model based on roughly the same ideas. The failure has, however, already had some important consequences, with serious implications for both economic policymaking and the practice of economic science.

For policy, the central fact is that Keynesian policy recommendations have no sounder basis, in a scientific sense, than recommendations of non-Keynesian economists or, for that matter, noneconomists. To note one consequence of the wide recognition of this, the current wave of protectionist sentiment directed at "saving jobs" would have been answered ten years ago with the Keynesian counterargument that fiscal policy can achieve the same end, but more efficiently. Today, of course, no one would take this response seriously, so it is not offered. Indeed, economists who ten years ago championed Keynesian fiscal policy as an alternative to inefficient direct controls increasingly favor such controls as supplements to Keynesian policy. The idea seems to be that if people refuse to obey the equations we have fit to their past behavior, we can pass laws to make them do so.

Scientifically, the Keynesian failure of the 1970s has resulted in a new openness. Fewer and fewer economists are involved in monitoring and refining the major econometric models; more and more are developing alternative theories of the business cycle, based on different theoretical principles. In addition, more attention and respect are accorded to the theoretical casualties of the Keynesian Revolution, to the ideas of Keynes' contemporaries and of earlier economists whose thinking has been regarded for years as outmoded.

No one can foresee where these developments will lead. Some, of course, continue to believe that the problems of existing Keynesian models can be resolved within the existing framework, that these models can be adequately refined by changing a few structural equations, by adding or subtracting a few variables here and there, or perhaps by disaggregating various blocks of equations. We have couched our criticisms in such general terms precisely to emphasize their generic character and hence the futility of pursuing minor variations within this general framework. A second response to the failure of Keynesian analytical methods is to renounce analytical methods entirely, returning to judgmental methods.

The first of these responses identifies the quantitative, scientific goals of the Keynesian Revolution with the details of the particular models developed so far. The second renounces both these models and the objectives they were designed to attain. There is, we believe, an intermediate course, to which we now turn.

Equilibrium Business Cycle Theory

Before the 1930s, economists did not recognize a need for a special branch of economics, with its own special postulates, designed to explain the business cycle. Keynes founded that subdiscipline, called *macroeconomics*, because he thought explaining the characteristics of business cycles was impossible within the discipline imposed by classical economic theory, a discipline imposed by its insistence on adherence to the two postulates (a) that markets clear and (b) that agents act in their own self-interest. The outstanding facts that seemed impossible to reconcile with these two postulates were the length and severity of business depressions and the large-scale unemployment they entailed. A related observation was that measures of aggregate demand and prices were positively correlated with measures of real output and employment, in apparent contradiction to the classical result that changes in a purely nominal magnitude like the general price level were pure unit changes which should not alter real behavior.

After freeing himself of the straightjacket (or discipline) imposed by the classical postulates, Keynes described a model in which rules of thumb, such as the consumption function and liquidity preference schedule, took the place of decision functions that a classical economist would insist be derived from the theory of choice. And rather than require that wages and prices be determined by the postulate that markets clear—which for the labor market seemed patently contradicted by the severity of business depressions—Keynes took as an unexamined postulate that money wages are sticky, meaning that they are set at a level or by a process that could be taken as uninfluenced by the macroeconomic forces he proposed to analyze.

When Keynes wrote, the terms *equilibrium* and *classical* carried certain positive and normative connotations which seemed to rule out either modifier being applied to business cycle theory. The term *equilibrium* was thought to refer to a system at rest, and some used both *equilibrium* and *classical* interchangeably with *ideal*. Thus an economy in classical equilibrium would be both unchanging and unimprovable by policy interventions. With terms used in this way, it is no wonder that few economists regarded equilibrium theory as a promising starting point to understand business cycles and design policies to mitigate or eliminate them.

In recent years, the meaning of the term *equilibrium* has changed so dramatically that a theorist of the 1930s would not recognize it. An economy following a multivariate stochastic process is now routinely described as being in equilibrium, by which is meant nothing more than that at each point in time, postulates (a) and (b) above are satisfied. This development, which stemmed mainly from work by K. J. Arrow (1964) and G. Debreu (1959a), implies that simply to look at any economic time series and conclude that it is a disequilibrium phenomenon is a meaningless observation.

Indeed, a more likely conjecture, on the basis of recent work by Hugo Sonnenschein (1973), is that the general hypothesis that a collection of time series describes an economy in competitive equilibrium is *without content*.[8]

The research line being pursued by some of us involves the attempt to discover a particular, econometrically testable equilibrium theory of the business cycle, one that can serve as the foundation for quantitative analysis of macroeconomic policy. There is no denying that this approach is counterrevolutionary, for it presupposes that Keynes and his followers were wrong to give up on the possibility that an equilibrium theory could account for the business cycle. As of now, no successful equilibrium macroeconometric model at the level of detail of, say, the Federal Reserve-MIT-Penn model has been constructed. But small theoretical equilibrium models have been constructed that show potential for explaining some key features of the business cycle long thought inexplicable within the confines of classical postulates. The equilibrium models also provide reasons for understanding why estimated Keynesian models fail to hold up outside the sample over which they have been estimated. We now turn to describing some of the key facts about business cycles and the way the *new classical* models confront them.

For a long time most of the economics profession has, with some reason, followed Keynes in rejecting classical macroeconomic models because they seemed incapable of explaining some important characteristics of time series measuring important economic aggregates. Perhaps the most important failure of the classical model was its apparent inability to explain the positive correlation in the time series between prices and/or wages, on the one hand, and measures of aggregate output or employment, on the other. A second and related failure was its inability to explain the positive correlations between measures of aggregate demand, like the money stock, and aggregate output or employment. Static analysis of classical macroeconomic models typically implied that the levels of output and employment were determined independently of both the absolute level of prices and of aggregate demand. But the pervasive presence of positive correlations in the time series seems consistent with causal connections flowing from aggregate demand and inflation to output and employment, contrary to the classical neutrality propositions. Keynesian macroeconometric models do imply such causal connections.

We now have rigorous theoretical models which illustrate how these correlations can emerge while retaining the classical postulates that markets clear and agents optimize (Phelps 1970 and Lucas 1972, 1975). The key step in obtaining such models has been to relax the ancillary postulate used in much classical economic analysis that agents have perfect information. The new classical models still assume that markets clear and that agents optimize; agents make their supply and demand decisions based on real variables, including perceived relative prices. However, each agent is assumed to have limited information and to receive information about some prices more often than other prices. On the basis of their limited information—the lists that they have of current and past absolute prices of various goods—agents are assumed to make the best possible estimate of all of the relative prices that influence their supply and demand decisions.

Because they do not have all of the information necessary to compute perfectly the relative prices they care about, agents make errors in estimating the pertinent relative prices, errors that are unavoidable given their limited information. In particular, under certain conditions, agents tend temporarily to mistake a general increase in all absolute prices as an increase in the relative price of the good they are selling, leading them to increase their supply of that good over what they had previously planned. Since on average everyone is making the same mistake, aggregate output rises above what it would have been. This increase of output above what it would have been occurs whenever this period's average economy-wide price level is above what agents had expected it to be on the basis of previous information. Symmetrically, aggregate output decreases whenever the aggregate price turns out to be lower than agents had expected. The hypothesis of *rational expectations* is being imposed here: agents are assumed to make the best possible use of the limited information they have and to know the pertinent objective probability distributions. This hypothesis is imposed by way of adhering to the tenets of equilibrium theory.

In the new classical theory, disturbances to aggregate demand lead to a positive correlation between unexpected changes in the aggregate price level and revisions in aggregate output from its previously planned level. Further, it is easy to show that the theory implies correlations between revisions in aggregate output and unexpected changes in any variables that help determine aggregate demand. In most macroeconomic models, the money supply is one determinant of aggregate demand. The new theory can easily account for positive correlations between revisions to aggregate output and unexpected increases in the money supply.

While such a theory predicts positive correlations between the inflation rate or money supply, on the one hand, and the level of output, on the other, it also asserts that those correlations do not depict tradeoffs that can be exploited by a policy authority. That is, the theory predicts that there is no way that the monetary authority can follow a systematic activist policy and achieve a rate of output that is on average higher over the business cycle than what would occur if it simply adopted a no-feedback, X-percent rule of the kind Friedman (1948) and Simons (1936) recommended. For the theory predicts that aggregate output is a function of current and past unexpected changes in the money supply. Output will be high only when the money supply is and has been higher than it had been expected to be, that is, higher than average. There is simply no way that on average over the whole business cycle the money supply can be higher than average. Thus, while the theory can explain some of the correlations long thought to invalidate classical macroeconomic theory, it is classical both in its adherence to the classical theoretical postulates and in the nonactivist flavor of its implications for monetary policy.

Small-scale econometric models in the standard sense have been constructed which capture some of the main features of the new classical theory. (See, for example, Sargent 1976a.)[9] In particular, these models incorporate the hypothesis that expectations are rational or that agents use all available information. To some degree, these models achieve econometric identification by invoking restrictions in each of the three categories (a), (b), and (c). However, a distinguishing feature of these "classical" models is that they also rely heavily on an important fourth category of identifying restrictions. This category (d) consists of a set of restrictions that are derived from probabilistic economic theory but play no role in the Keynesian framework. These restrictions in general do not take the form of zero restrictions of the type (a). Instead they typically take the form of cross-equation restrictions among the A_j, B_j, C_j parameters. The source of these restrictions is the implication from economic theory that current decisions depend on agents' forecasts of future variables, combined with the implication that these forecasts are formed optimally, given the behavior of past variables. The restrictions do not have as simple a mathematical expression as simply setting a number of parameters equal to zero, but their economic motivation is easy to understand. Ways of utilizing these restrictions in econometric estimation and testing are rapidly being developed.

Another key characteristic of recent work on equilibrium macroeconometric models is that the reliance on entirely a priori categorizations (c) of variables as strictly exogenous and endogenous has been markedly reduced, although not entirely eliminated. This development stems jointly from the fact that the models assign important roles to agents' optimal forecasts of future variables and from Christopher Sims' (1972) demonstration that there is a close connection between the concept of strict econometric exogeneity and the forms of the optimal predictors for a vector of time series. Building a model with rational expectations necessarily forces one to consider which set of other variables helps forecast a given variable, say, income or the inflation rate. If variable y helps predict variable x, the Sims' theorems imply that x cannot be regarded as exogenous with respect to y. The result of this connection between predictability and exogeneity has been that in equilibrium macroeconometric models the distinction between endogenous and exogenous variables has not been drawn on an entirely a priori basis. Furthermore, special cases of the theoretical models, which often involve side restrictions on the R_j's not themselves drawn from economic theory, have strong testable predictions as to exogeneity relations among variables.

A key characteristic of equilibrium macroeconometric models is that as a result of the restrictions across the A_j's, B_j's, and C_j's, the models predict that in general the parameters in many of the equations will change if there is a policy intervention that takes the form of a change in one equation that describes how some policy variable is being set. Since they ignore these cross-equation restrictions, Keynesian models in general assume that all other equations remain unchanged when an equation describing a policy variable is changed. We think this is one important reason Keynesian models have broken down when the equations governing policy variables or exogenous variables have changed significantly. We hope that the new methods we have described will give us the capability to predict the consequences for all of the equations of changes in the rules governing policy variables. Having that capability is necessary before we can claim to have a scientific basis for making quantitative statements about macroeconomic policy.

So far, these new theoretical and econometric developments have not been fully integrated, although clearly they are very close, both conceptually and operationally. We consider the best currently existing equilibrium models as prototypes of better, future models which will, we hope, prove of practical use in the formulation of policy.

But we should not understate the econometric success already attained by equilibrium models. Early versions of these models have been estimated and subjected to some stringent econometric tests by McCallum (1976), Barro (1977, 1978b), and Sargent (1976a), with the result that they do seem able to explain some broad features of the business cycle. New and more sophisticated models involving more complicated cross-equation restrictions are in the works (Sargent 1978). Work to date has already shown that equilibrium models can attain within-sample fits about as good as those obtained by Keynesian models, thereby making concrete the point that the good fits of the Keynesian models provide no good reason for trusting policy recommendations derived from them.

Criticism of Equilibrium Theory

The central idea of the equilibrium explanations of business cycles sketched above is that economic fluctuations arise as agents react to unanticipated changes in variables which impinge on their decisions. Clearly, any explanation of this general type must imply severe limitations on the ability of government policy to offset these initiating changes. First, governments must somehow be able to foresee shocks invisible to private agents but at the same time be unable to reveal this advance information (hence, defusing the shocks). Though it is not hard to design theoretical models in which these two conditions are assumed to hold, it is difficult to imagine actual situations in which such models would apply. Second, the governmental countercyclical policy must itself be unforeseeable by private agents (certainly a frequently realized condition historically) while at the same time be systematically related to the state of the economy. Effectiveness, then, rests on the inability of private agents to recognize systematic patterns in monetary and fiscal policy.

To a large extent, criticism of equilibrium models is simply a reaction to these implications for policy. So wide is (or was) the consensus that *the* task of macroeconomics is the discovery of the particular monetary and fiscal policies which can eliminate fluctuations by reacting to private sector instability that the assertion that this task either should not or cannot be performed is regarded as frivolous, regardless of whatever reasoning and evidence may support it. Certainly one must have some sympathy with this reaction: an unfounded faith in the curability of a particular ill has served often enough as a stimulus to the finding of genuine cures. Yet to confuse a possibly functional faith in the existence of efficacious, reactive monetary and fiscal policies with scientific evidence that such policies are known is clearly dangerous, and to use such faith as a criterion for judging the extent to which particular theories fit the facts is worse still.

There are, of course, legitimate questions about how well equilibrium theories can fit the facts of the business cycle. Indeed, this is the reason for our insistence on the preliminary and tentative character of the particular models we now have. Yet these tentative models share certain features which can be regarded as essential, so it is not unreasonable to speculate as to the likelihood that *any* model of this type can be successful or to ask what equilibrium business cycle theorists will have in ten years if we get lucky.

Four general reasons for pessimism have been prominently advanced:

(a) Equilibrium models unrealistically postulate cleared markets.

(b) These models cannot account for "persistence" (serial correlation) of cyclical movements.

(c) Econometrically implemented models are linear (in logarithms).

(d) Learning behavior has not been incorporated in these models.

Cleared Markets

One essential feature of equilibrium models is that all markets clear, or that all observed prices and quantities are viewed as outcomes of decisions taken by individual firms and households. In practice, this has meant a conventional, competitive supply-equals-demand assumption, though other kinds of equilibria can easily be imagined (if not so easily analyzed). If, therefore, one takes as a basic "fact" that labor markets do not clear, one arrives immediately at a contradiction between theory and fact. The facts we actually have, however, are simply the available time series on employment and wage rates plus the responses to our unemployment surveys. Cleared markets is simply a principle, not verifiable by direct observation, which may or may not be useful in constructing successful hypotheses about the behavior of these series. Alternative principles, such as the postulate of the existence of a third-party auctioneer inducing wage rigidity and uncleared markets, are similarly "unrealistic," in the not especially important sense of not offering a good description of observed labor market institutions.

A refinement of the unexplained postulate of an uncleared labor market has been suggested by the indisputable fact that long-term labor contracts with horizons of two or three years exist. Yet the length per se over which contracts run does not bear on the issue, for we know from Arrow and Debreu that if *infinitely* long-term contracts are determined so that prices and wages are contingent on the same information that is available under the assumption of period-by-period market clearing, then precisely the same price-quantity process will result with the long-term contract as would occur under period-by-period market clearing. Thus equilibrium theorizing provides a way, probably the only way we have, to construct a *model* of a long-term contract. The fact that long-term contracts exist, then, has *no* implications about the applicability of equilibrium theorizing.

Rather, the real issue here is whether actual contracts can be adequately accounted for within an equilibrium model, that is, a model in which agents are proceeding in their own best interests. Stanley Fischer (1977), Edmund Phelps and John Taylor (1977), and Robert Hall (1978a) have shown that some of the nonactivist conclusions of the equilibrium models are modified if one substitutes for period-by-period market clearing the imposition of long-term contracts drawn contingent on restricted information sets that are exogenously imposed and that are assumed to be independent of monetary and fiscal regimes. Economic theory leads us to predict that the costs of collecting and processing information will make it optimal for contracts to be made contingent on a small subset of the information that could possibly be collected at any date. But theory also suggests that the particular set of information upon which contracts will be made contingent is not immutable but depends on the structure of costs and benefits of collecting various kinds of information. This structure of costs and benefits will change with every change in the exogenous stochastic processes facing agents. This theoretical presumption is supported by an examination of the way labor contracts differ across high-inflation and low-inflation countries and the way they have evolved in the U.S. over the last 25 years.

So the issue here is really the same fundamental one involved in the dispute between Keynes and the classical economists: Should we regard certain superficial characteristics of existing wage contracts as given when analyzing the consequences of alternative monetary and fiscal regimes? Classical economic theory says no. To understand the implications of long-term contracts for monetary policy, we need a model of the way those contracts are likely to respond to alternative monetary policy regimes. An extension of existing equilibrium models in this direction might well lead to interesting variations, but it seems to us unlikely that major modifications of the implications of these models for monetary and fiscal policy will follow from this.

Persistence

A second line of criticism stems from the correct observation that if agents' expectations are rational and if their information sets include lagged values of the variable being forecast, then agents' forecast errors must be a serially uncorrelated random process. That is, on average there must be no detectable relationships between a period's forecast error and any previous period's. This feature has led several critics to conclude that equilibrium models cannot account for more than an insignificant part of the highly serially correlated movements we observe in real output, employment, unemployment, and other series. Tobin (1977, p. 461) has put the argument succinctly:

One currently popular explanation of variations in employment is temporary confusion of relative and absolute prices. Employers and workers are fooled into too many jobs by unexpected inflation, but only until they learn it affects other prices, not just the prices of what they sell. The reverse happens temporarily when inflation falls short of expectation. This model can scarcely explain more than transient disequilibrium in labor markets.

So how can the faithful explain the slow cycles of unemployment we actually observe? Only by arguing that the natural rate itself fluctuates, that variations in unemployment rates are substantially changes in voluntary, frictional, or structural unemployment rather than in involuntary joblessness due to generally deficient demand.

The critics typically conclude that the theory only attributes a very minor role to aggregate demand fluctuations and necessarily depends on disturbances to aggregate supply to account for most of the fluctuations in real output over the business cycle. "In other words," as Modigliani (1977) has said, "what happened to the United States in the 1930's was a severe attack of contagious laziness."

This criticism is fallacious because it fails to distinguish properly between *sources of impulses* and *propagation mechanisms*, a distinction stressed by Ragnar Frisch ([1933] 1965) in a classic paper that provided many of the technical foundations for Keynesian macroeconometric models. Even though the new classical theory implies that the forecast errors which are the aggregate demand impulses are serially uncorrelated, it is certainly logically possible that propagation mechanisms are at work that convert these impulses into serially correlated movements in real variables like output and employment. Indeed, detailed theoretical work has already shown that two concrete propagation mechanisms do precisely that.

One mechanism stems from the presence of costs to firms of adjusting their stocks of capital and labor rapidly. The presence of these costs is known to make it optimal for firms to spread out over time their response to the relative price signals they receive. That is, such a mechanism causes a firm to convert the serially uncorrelated forecast errors in predicting relative prices into serially correlated movements in factor demands and output.

A second propagation mechanism is already present in the most classical of economic growth models. Households' optimal accumulation plans for claims on physical capital and other assets convert serially uncorrelated impulses into serially correlated demands for the accumulation of real assets. This happens because agents typically want to divide any unexpected changes in income partly between consuming and accumulating assets. Thus, the demand for assets next period depends on initial stocks and on unexpected changes in the prices or income facing agents. This dependence makes serially uncorrelated surprises lead to serially correlated movements in demands for physical assets. Lucas (1975) showed how this propagation mechanism readily accepts errors in forecasting aggregate demand as an impulse source.

A third likely propagation mechanism has been identified by recent work in search theory. (See, for example, McCall 1965, Mortensen 1970, and Lucas and Prescott 1974.) Search theory tries to explain why workers who for some reason are without jobs find it rational not necessarily to take the first job offer that comes along but instead to remain unemployed for awhile until a better offer materializes. Similarly, the theory explains why a firm may find it optimal to wait until a more suitable job applicant appears so that vacancies persist for some time. Mainly for technical reasons, consistent theoretical models that permit this propagation mechanism to accept errors in forecasting aggregate demand as an impulse have not yet been worked out, but the mechanism seems likely eventually to play an important role in a successful model of the time series behavior of the unemployment rate.

In models where agents have imperfect information, either of the first two mechanisms and probably the third can make serially correlated movements in real variables stem from the introduction of a serially uncorrelated sequence of forecasting errors. Thus theoretical and econometric models have been constructed in which in principle the serially uncorrelated process of forecasting errors can account for any proportion between zero and one of the steady-state variance of real output or employment. The argument that such models must necessarily attribute most of the variance in real output and employment to variations in aggregate supply is simply wrong logically.

Linearity

Most of the econometric work implementing equilibrium models has involved fitting statistical models that are linear in the variables (but often highly nonlinear in the parameters). This feature is subject to criticism on the basis of the indisputable principle that there generally exist nonlinear models that provide better approximations than linear models. More specifically, models that are linear in the variables provide no way to detect and analyze systematic effects of higher than first-order moments of the shocks and the exogenous variables on the first-order moments of the endogenous variables. Such systematic effects are generally present where the endogenous variables are set by risk-averse agents.

There are no *theoretical* reasons that most applied work has used linear models, only compelling technical reasons given today's computer technology. The predominant technical requirement of econometric work which imposes rational expectations is the ability to write down analytical expressions giving agents' decision rules as functions of the parameters of their objective functions and as functions of the parameters governing the exogenous random processes they face. Dynamic stochastic maximum problems with quadratic objectives, which produce linear decision rules, do meet this essential requirement—that is their virtue. Only a few other functional forms for agents' objective functions in dynamic stochastic optimum problems have this same necessary analytical tractability. Computer technology in the foreseeable future seems to require working with such a class of functions, and the class of linear decision rules has just seemed most convenient for most purposes. No issue of principle is involved in selecting one out of the very restricted class of functions available. Theoretically, we know how to calculate, with expensive recursive methods, the nonlinear decision rules that would stem from a very wide class of objective functions; no new econometric principles would be involved in estimating their parameters, only a much higher computer bill. Further, as Frisch and Slutzky emphasized, linear stochastic difference equations are a very flexible device for studying business cycles. It is an open question whether for explaining the central features of the business cycle there will be a big reward to fitting nonlinear models.

Stationary Models and the Neglect of Learning

Benjamin Friedman and others have criticized rational expectations models apparently on the grounds that much theoretical and almost all empirical work has assumed that agents have been operating for a long time in a stochastically stationary environment. Therefore, agents are typically assumed to have discovered the probability laws of the variables they want to forecast. Modigliani (1977, p. 6) put the argument this way:

At the logical level, Benjamin Friedman has called attention to the omission from [equilibrium macroeconomic models] of an explicit learning model, and has suggested that, as a result, it can only be interpreted as a description not of short-run but of long-run equilibrium in which no agent would wish to recontract. But then the implications of [equilibrium macroeconomic models] are clearly far from startling, and their policy relevance is almost nil.

But it has been only a matter of analytical convenience and not of necessity that equilibrium models have used the assumption of stochastically stationary shocks and the assumption that agents have already learned the probability distributions they face. Both of these assumptions can be abandoned, albeit at a cost in terms of the simplicity of the model. (For example, see Crawford 1973 and Grossman 1975.) In fact, within the framework of quadratic objective functions, in which the "separation principle" applies, one can apply the Kalman filtering formula to derive optimum linear decision rules with time-dependent coefficients. In this framework, the Kalman filter permits a neat application of Bayesian learning to updating optimal forecasting rules from period to period as new information becomes available. The Kalman filter also permits the derivation of optimum decision rules for an interesting class of nonstationary exogenous processes assumed to face agents. Equilibrium theorizing in this context thus readily leads to a *model* of how process nonstationarity and Bayesian learning applied by agents to the exogenous variables lead to time-dependent coefficients in agents' decision rules.

While models incorporating Bayesian learning and stochastic nonstationarity are both technically feasible and consistent with the equilibrium modeling strategy, we know of almost no successful applied work along these lines. One probable reason for this is that nonstationary time series models are cumbersome and come in so many varieties. Another is that the hypothesis of Bayesian learning is vacuous until one either arbitrarily imputes a prior distribution to agents or develops a method of estimating parameters of the prior from time series data. Determining a prior distribution from the data would involve estimating initial conditions and would proliferate nuisance parameters in a very unpleasant way. Whether these techniques will pay off in terms of explaining macroeconomic time series is an empirical matter: it is not a matter distinguishing equilibrium from Keynesian macroeconometric models. In fact, no existing Keynesian macroeconometric model incorporates either an economic model of learning or an economic model in any way restricting the pattern of coefficient nonstationarities across equations.

The macroeconometric models criticized by Friedman and Modigliani, which assume agents have caught on to the stationary random processes they face, give rise to systems of linear stochastic difference equations of the form (1), (2), and (4). As has been known for a long time, such stochastic difference equations generate series that "look like" economic time series. Further, if viewed as structural (that is, invariant with respect to policy interventions), the models have some of the implications for countercyclical policy that we have described above. Whether or not these policy implications are correct depends on whether or not the models are structural and not at all on whether the models can successfully be caricatured by terms such as "long-run" or "short-run."

It is worth reemphasizing that we do not wish our responses to these criticisms to be mistaken for a claim that existing equilibrium models can satisfactorily account for all the main features of the observed business cycle. Rather, we have simply argued that no sound reasons have yet been advanced which even suggest that these models are, as a class, *incapable* of providing a satisfactory business cycle theory.

Summary and Conclusions

Let us attempt to set out in compact form the main arguments advanced in this paper. We will then comment briefly on the main implications of these arguments for the way we can usefully think about economic policy.

Our first and most important point is that existing Keynesian macroeconometric models cannot provide reliable guidance in the formulation of monetary, fiscal, or other types of policy. This conclusion is based in part on the spectacular recent failures of these models and in part on their lack of a sound theoretical or econometric basis. Second, on the latter ground, there is no hope that minor or even major modification of these models will lead to significant improvement in their reliability.

Third, *equilibrium* models can be formulated which are free of these difficulties and which offer a different set of principles to identify structural econometric models. The key elements of these models are that agents are rational, reacting to policy changes in a way which is in their best interests privately, and that the impulses which trigger business fluctuations are mainly unanticipated shocks.

Fourth, equilibrium models already developed account for the main qualitative features of the business cycle. These models are being subjected to continued criticism, especially by those engaged in developing them, but arguments to the effect that equilibrium theories are in principle unable to account for a substantial part of observed fluctuations appear due mainly to simple misunderstandings.

The policy implications of equilibrium theories are sometimes carica-tured, by friendly as well as unfriendly commentators, as the assertion that "economic policy does not matter" or "has no effect."[10] This implication would certainly startle neoclassical economists who have successfully applied equilibrium theory to the study of innumerable problems involving important effects of fiscal policies on resource allocation and income distri-bution. Our intent is not to reject these accomplishments but rather to try to *imitate* them or to extend the equilibrium methods which have been applied to many economic problems to cover a phenomenon which has so far resisted their application: the business cycle.

Should this intellectual arbitrage prove successful, it will suggest impor-tant changes in the way we think about policy. Most fundamentally, it will focus attention on the need to think of policy as the choice of stable rules of the game, well understood by economic agents. Only in such a setting will economic theory help predict the actions agents will choose to take. This approach will also suggest that policies which affect behavior mainly because their consequences cannot be correctly diagnosed, such as mone-tary instability and deficit financing, have the capacity only to disrupt. The deliberate provision of misinformation cannot be used in a systematic way to improve the economic environment.

The *objectives* of equilibrium business cycle theory are taken, without modification, from the goal which motivated the construction of the Keynesian macroeconometric models: to provide a scientifically based means of assessing, quantitatively, the likely effects of alternative economic policies. Without the econometric successes achieved by the Keynesian models, this goal would be simply inconceivable. However, unless the now evident limits of these models are also frankly acknowledged and radically different new directions taken, the real accomplishments of the Keynesian Revolution will be lost as surely as those we now know to be illusory.

Notes

A paper presented at a June 1978 conference sponsored by the Federal Reserve Bank of Boston and published in its *After the Phillips Curve: Persistence of High Inflation and High Unemployment*, Conference Series No. 19. Edited for publication in the *Quarterly Review*.

The authors acknowledge helpful criticism from William Poole and Benjamin Friedman.

1. Author names and years refer to the works listed at the end of this volume.

2. Linearity is a matter of convenience, not principle. See *Linearity* section of the paper.

3. A regression equation is an equation to which the application of ordinary least squares will yield consistent estimates.

4. In these expressions for P_s and Q_s, take matrices not previously defined (for example, any with negative subscripts) to be zero.

5. These three categories certainly do not exhaust the set of possible identifying restrictions, but they're the ones most identifying restrictions in Keynesian macroeconometric models fall into. Other possible sorts of identifying restrictions include, for example, a priori knowledge about components of Σ and cross-equation restrictions across elements of the A_j's, B_j's, and C_j's, neither of which is extensively used in Keynesian macroeconometrics.

6. Criticisms of the Keynesian solutions of the identification problem along much the following lines have been made in Lucas 1976, Sims 1980, and Sargent and Sims 1977.

7. Much of this work was done by economists operating well within the Keynesian tradition, often within the context of some Keynesian macroeconometric model. Sometimes a theory with optimizing agents was resorted to in order to resolve empirical paradoxes by finding variables omitted from some of the earlier Keynesian econometric formulations. The works of Modigliani and Friedman on consumption are good examples of this line of work; its econometric implications have been extended in important work by Robert Merton. The works of Tobin and Baumol on portfolio balance and of Jorgenson on investment are also in the tradition of applying optimizing microeconomic theories for generating macroeconomic behavior relations. In the last 30 years, Keynesian econometric models have to a large extent developed along the line of trying to model agents' behavior as stemming from more and more sophisticated optimum problems.

   Our point here is certainly not to assert that Keynesian economists have completely foregone any use of optimizing microeconomic theory as a guide. Rather, it is that, especially when explicitly stochastic and dynamic problems have been studied, it has become increasingly apparent that microeconomic theory has very damaging implications for the restrictions conventionally used to identify Keynesian macroeconometric models. Furthermore, as emphasized long ago by Tobin (1965b), there is a point beyond which Keynesian models must suspend the hypothesis either of cleared markets or of optimizing agents if they are to possess the operating characteristics and policy implications that are the hallmarks of Keynesian economics.

8. For an example that illustrates the emptiness at a general level of the statement that employers are always operating along dynamic stochastic demands for factors, see the remarks on econometric identification in Sargent 1978. In applied problems that involve modeling agents' optimum decision rules, one is impressed at how generalizing the specification of agents' objective functions in plausible ways quickly leads to econometric underidentification.

   A somewhat different class of examples comes from the difficulties in using time series observations to refute the view that agents only respond to unexpected changes in the money supply. In the equilibrium macroeconometric models we will describe, predictable changes in the money supply do not affect real GNP or total employment. In Keynesian models, they do. At a general level, it is impossible to discriminate between these two views by observing time series drawn from an economy described by a stationary vector random process (Sargent 1976b).

9. Dissatisfaction with the Keynesian methods of achieving identification has also led to other lines of macroeconometric work. One line is the index models described by Sargent and Sims (1977) and Geweke (1977). These models amount to a statistically precise way of implementing Wesley Mitchell's notion that a small number of common influences explain the covariation of a large number of economic aggregates over the business cycle. This low dimensionality hypothesis is a potential device for restricting the number of parameters to

be estimated in vector time series models. This line of work is not entirely atheoretical (but see the comments of Ando and Klein in Sims 1977), though it is distinctly un-Keynesian. As it happens, certain equilibrium models of the business cycle do seem to lead to low dimensional index models with an interesting pattern of variables' loadings on indexes. In general, modern Keynesian models do not so easily assume a low-index form. See the discussion in Sargent and Sims 1977.

10. A main source of this belief is probably Sargent and Wallace 1975, which showed that in the context of a fairly standard macroeconomic model, but with agents' expectations assumed rational, the choice of a reactive monetary rule is of no consequence for the behavior of real variables. The point of this example was to show that within precisely that model used to rationalize reactive monetary policies, such policies could be shown to be of no value. It hardly follows that all policy is ineffective in all contexts.

2

Rational Expectations and the Reconstruction of Macroeconomics

Thomas J. Sargent

Fans of the National Football League may well have observed the following behavior by the Houston Oilers during the 19— season. At home against Kansas City, when confronted with a fourth down in its own end of the field, Houston punted 100 percent of the time. The next week, at St. Louis, in the same situation, Houston punted 93 percent of the time. The following week at Oakland, again in that situation, Houston again punted 100 percent of the time, as it did the subsequent week at home against San Diego, and so on and on for the rest of the season. In short, on the basis of the time series data, Houston has a tendency to punt on fourth downs in its own territory, no matter what team it plays or where.

Having observed this historical record, suppose it is our task to predict how Houston will behave in the future on fourth and long in its own territory. For example, suppose that next week Houston is to play an expansion team at Portland that it has never played before. It seems safe to predict that Houston will punt on fourth downs in its own territory at Portland. This sensible prediction is not based on any understanding of the game of football, but rather on simply extrapolating a past behavior pattern into the future.

In many cases, we would expect this method of prediction to work well. However, for precisely those cases in which predictions are most interesting, the extrapolative method can be expected to break down. For instance, suppose that the Commissioner of the National Football League announced a rule change, effective next Sunday, which gave a team six downs in which to make a first down. Would we still expect Houston to punt on fourth down? Clearly not; at least no one familiar with the game of football would.

What this example indicates is that historical patterns of human behavior often depend on the rules of the game in which people are participating.

Reprinted from the *Federal Reserve Bank of Minneapolis Quarterly Review*, Summer 1980.

Since much human behavior is purposeful, it makes sense to expect that it will change to take advantage of changes in the rules. This principle is so familiar to fans of football and other sports that it hardly bears mentioning. However, the principle very much deserves mentioning in the context of economic policy because here it has been routinely ignored—and with some devastating results.[1] Adherents of the theory of rational expectations believe, in fact, that no less than the field of macroeconomics must be reconstructed in order to take account of this principle of human behavior. Their efforts to do that involve basic changes in the ways economists formulate, simulate, and predict with econometric models. They also call for substantial changes in the ways economic policymakers frame their options.[2]

Models Must Let Behavior Change with the Rules of the Game

In order to provide quantitative advice about the effects of alternative economic policies, economists have constructed collections of equations known as *econometric models*.[3] For the most part, these models consist of equations that attempt to describe the behavior of economic agents— firms, consumers, and governments—in terms of variables which are assumed to be closely related to their situations. Such equations are often called *decision rules* since they describe the decisions people make about things like consumption rates, investment rates, and portfolios as functions of variables that summarize the information people use to make those decisions. For all of their mathematical sophistication, econometric models amount to statistical devices for organizing and detecting patterns in the past behavior of people's decision making, patterns which can then be used as a basis for predicting their future behavior.

As devices for extrapolating future behavior from the past under a given set of rules of the game, or government policies, these models appear to have performed well.[4] They have not, however, when the rules have changed. In formulating advice for policymakers, economists have routinely used these models to predict the consequences of historically unprecedented, hypothetical government interventions that can only be described as changes in the rules of the game. In effect, the models have been manipulated in a way which amounts to assuming that people's patterns of behavior do not depend on those properties of the environment that government interventions would change. The assumption has been, that is, that people will act under the new rules just as they have under the old, so that even under new rules past behavior is still a reliable guide to future behavior.

Econometric models used in this way have not been able to accurately predict the consequences of historically unparalleled interventions.[5] To take one painful recent example, standard Keynesian and monetarist econometric models built in the late 1960s failed to predict the effects on output, employment, and prices that were associated with the unprecedented large deficits and rates of money creation of the 1970s.

Recent research has been directed at building econometric models that take into account that people's behavior patterns will vary systematically with changes in government policies or the rules of the game.[6] Most of this research has been conducted by adherents of the so-called hypothesis of rational expectations. They model people as making decisions in dynamic settings in the face of well-defined constraints. Included among these constraints are laws of motion over time that describe such things as the taxes that people must pay and the prices of the goods that they buy and sell. The hypothesis of rational expectations is that people understand these laws of motion. The aim of the research is to build models that can predict how people's behavior will change when they are confronted with well-understood changes in ways of administering taxes, government purchases, aspects of monetary policy, and the like.

The Investment Decision as an Example

A simple example will serve to illustrate both the principle that decision rules depend on the laws of motion that agents face and the extent that standard macroeconomic models have violated this principle. Let k_t be the capital stock of an industry and τ_t be a tax rate on capital. Let τ_t be the first element of z_t, a vector of current and lagged variables including those that the government considers when it sets the tax rate on capital. We have $\tau_t \equiv e^T z_t$, where e is the unit vector with unity in the first place and zeros elsewhere.[7] Let a firm's optimal accumulation plan require that capital acquisitions obey[8]

$$k_t = \lambda k_{t-1} - \alpha \sum_{j=0}^{\infty} \delta^j E_t \tau_{t+j} \qquad \begin{matrix} \alpha > 0 \\ 0 < \lambda < 1 \\ 0 < \delta < 1 \end{matrix} \qquad (1)$$

where $E_t \tau_{t+j}$ is the tax rate at time t which is expected to prevail at time $(t + j)$.

Equation (1) captures the notion that the demand for capital responds negatively to current and future tax rates. However, equation (1) does not become an operational investment schedule or decision rule until we specify how agents' views about the future, $E_t \tau_{t+j}$, are formed. Let us suppose that the actual law of motion for z_t is

$$z_{t+1} = Az_t \qquad (2)$$

where A is a matrix conformable with z_t.[9] If agents understand this law of motion for z_t, the first element of which is τ_t, then their best forecast of τ_{t+j} is $e^T A^j z_t$. We impose rational expectations by equating agents' expectations $E_t \tau_{t+j}$ to this best forecast. Upon imposing rational expectations, some algebraic manipulation implies the operational investment schedule

$$k_t = \lambda k_{t-1} - \alpha e^T (I - \delta A)^{-1} z_t. \qquad (3)$$

In terms of the list of variables on the right-hand side, equation (3) resembles versions of investment schedules which were fit in the heyday of Keynesian macroeconomics in the 1960s. This is not unusual, for the innovation of rational expectations reasoning is much more in the ways equations are interpreted and manipulated to make statements about economic policy than in the look of the equations that are fit. Indeed, the similarity of standard and rational expectations equations suggests what can be shown to be true generally: that the rational expectations reconstruction of macroeconomics is not mainly directed at improving the statistical fits of Keynesian or monetarist macroeconomic models over given historical periods and that its success or failure cannot be judged by comparing the R^2's of reconstructed macroeconomic models with those of models constructed and interpreted along earlier lines.

Under the rational expectations assumption, the investment schedule (3) and the laws of motion for the tax rate and the variables that help predict it (2) have a common set of parameters, namely, those of the matrix A. These parameters appear in the investment schedule because they influence agents' expectations of how future tax rates will affect capital. Further, notice that all of the variables in z_t appear in the investment schedule, since via equation (2) all of these variables help agents forecast future tax rates. (Compare this with the common econometric practice of using only current and lagged values of the tax rate as proxies for expected future tax rates.)

The fact that (2) and (3) share a common set of parameters (the A matrix) reflects the principle that firms' optimal decision rule for accumulating capital, described as a function of current and lagged state and information variables, will depend on the constraints (or laws of motion) that firms face. That is, the firm's pattern of investment behavior will respond systematically to the rules of the game for setting the tax rate τ_t. A widely understood change in the policy for administering the tax rate can be represented as a change in the first row of the A matrix. Any such change in the tax rate regime or policy will thus result in a change in the investment schedule (3). The dependence of the coefficients of the investment schedule on the environmental parameters in A is reasonable and readily explicable as a reflection of the principle that agents' rules of behavior change when they encounter changes in the environment in the form of new laws of motion for variables that constrain them.

To illustrate this point, consider two specific tax rate policies. First consider the policy of a *constant* tax rate $\tau_{t+j} = \tau_t$ for all $j \geqslant 0$. Then $z_t = \tau_t$, $A = 1$, and the investment schedule is

$$k_t = \lambda k_{t-1} + h_0 \tau_t \tag{4}$$

where

$$h_0 = -\alpha/(1 - \delta).$$

Now consider an *on-again, off-again* tax rate policy of the form $\tau_t = -\tau_{t-1}$. In this case $z_t = \tau_t$, $A = -1$, and the investment schedule becomes

$$k_t = \lambda k_{t-1} + h_0 \tau_t \tag{5}$$

where now

$$h_0 = -\alpha/(1 + \delta).$$

Here the investment schedule itself changes as the policy for setting the tax rate changes.

Standard econometric practice has not acknowledged that this sort of thing happens. Returning to the more general investment example, the usual econometric practice has been roughly as follows. First, a model is typically specified and estimated of the form

$$k_t = \lambda k_{t-1} + h z_t \tag{6}$$

where h is a vector of free parameters of dimension conformable with the vector z_t. Second, holding the parameters h fixed, equation (6) is used to predict the implications of alternative paths for the tax rate τ_t. This procedure is equivalent to estimating equation (4) from historical data when $\tau_t = \tau_{t-1}$ and then using this same equation to predict the consequences for capital accumulation of instituting an on-again, off-again tax rate policy of the form $\tau_t = -\tau_{t-1}$. Doing this assumes that a single investment schedule of the form (6) can be found with a single parameter vector h that will remain fixed regardless of the rules for administering the tax rate.[10]

The fact that equations (2) and (3) share a common set of parameters implies that the search for such a regime-independent decision schedule is misdirected and bound to fail. This theoretical presumption is backed up by the distressing variety of instances in which estimated econometric models have failed tests for stability of coefficients when new data are added. This problem cannot be overcome by adopting more sophisticated and more general lag distributions for the vector h, as perhaps was hoped in the 1960s.

General Implications

The investment example illustrates the general presumption that the systematic behavior of private agents and the random behavior of market outcomes both will change whenever agents' constraints change, as when government policy or other parts of the environment change. To make reliable statements about policy interventions, we need dynamic models and econometric procedures which are consistent with this general presumption. Foremost, we need a new and stricter definition of the class of parameters that can be regarded as *structural*. The body of doctrine associated with the simultaneous equations model in econometrics properly directs the attention of the researcher beyond reduced form parameters to the parameters of structural equations which are meant to describe those aspects of people's behavior that remain constant across a range of hypothetical environments. Although such structural parameters are needed to analyze an interesting class of policy interventions, most often included among them have been parameters of equations describing the rules of choice for private agents. Consumption functions, investment schedules, and demand functions for assets are all examples of such rules of choice. In dynamic settings, regarding the parameters of these rules of choice as structural or invariant under policy interventions violates the principle that optimal decision rules depend on the environment in which agents believe they are operating.

If parameters of decision rules cannot be regarded as structural or invariant under policy interventions, deeper objects that can must be sought. The best that can be hoped for is that parameters characterizing private agents' preferences and technologies will not change when changes in economic policy change the environment. If dynamic econometric models were formulated explicitly in terms of the parameters of preferences, technologies, and constraints, in principle they could be used to predict the effects on observed behavior of changes in policy rules. In terms of our investment example with equations (2) and (3), the idea would be to estimate the free parameters of the model $(\lambda, \alpha, \delta, A)$. With these estimates, economists could predict how the investment schedule would change if different A's occurred.[11]

Policymakers Must Choose Among Alternative Rules, Not Isolated Actions

These ideas have implications not only for theoretical and econometric practices, but also for the ways in which policymakers and their advisers think about the choices confronting them. In particular, the rational expectations approach directs attention away from particular isolated actions and toward choices among feasible rules of the game, or repeated strategies for choosing policy variables. While Keynesian and monetarist macroeconomic models have been used to try to analyze what the effects of isolated actions would be, it is now clear that the answers they have given have necessarily been bad, if only because such questions are ill-posed.

In terms of our investment example, by selecting different values for the first row of A, we can analyze the effects on current and subsequent investment of switching from one well-understood policy for setting the tax rate to another—that is, we can analyze the effects of different *strategies* for setting the tax rate. However, we cannot analyze the effects on current and subsequent investment of alternative *actions* consisting of different possible settings for the tax rate τ_t at a particular point in time $t = \bar{t}$. For in order to make predictions, we must specify agents' views about the law of motion A, and this is not done when we simply consider actions consisting of alternative settings for τ_t at one isolated point in time. This idea is so widely accepted as to be uncontroversial among decision theorists (and football fans); but even today practicing macroeconomists usually ignore it.

To take a concrete example, in the United States there was recently interest in analyzing what would happen to the rate of domestic extraction of oil and gas if the tax on profits of oil producers increased a lot on a particular date. Would supply go up or down if the tax were raised to X percent on July 1? The only scientifically respectable answer to this question is "I don't know." Such a rise in the oil-profits tax rate could be interpreted as reflecting one of a variety of different tax strategies (A matrices), each with different implications for current and prospective extraction of oil.

For example, suppose that oil companies had reason to believe that the increase in the tax is temporary and will be repealed after the election. In that case, they would respond by decreasing their rate of supply now and increasing it later, thus reallocating their sales to periods in which their shareholders get a larger share of profits and the government a smaller share. Yet suppose that oil companies believed that the increase in the tax rate on July 1 is only the beginning and that further increases will follow. In that case, the response to the tax rate increase would be the reverse: to increase supply now and decrease it later in order to benefit companies' shareholders. This example illustrates that people's views about the government's strategy for setting the tax rate are decisive in determining their responses to any given actions and that the effects of actions cannot be reliably evaluated in isolation from the policy rule or strategy of which they are an element.

What policymakers (and econometricians) should recognize, then, is that societies face a meaningful set of choices about alternative economic policy regimes. For example, the proper question is not about the size of tax cut to impose now in response to a recession, but about the proper strategy for repeatedly adjusting tax rates in response to the state of the economy, year in and year out. Strategic questions of this nature abound in fiscal, monetary, regulatory, and labor market matters. Private agents face the problem of determining the government regime under which they are operating, and they often devote considerable resources to doing so. Whether governments realize it or not, they do make decisions about these regimes. They would be wise to face these decisions deliberately rather than ignore them and pretend to be able to make good decisions by taking one seemingly unrelated action after another.

Notes

This paper is based on remarks prepared for the September 1980 International Symposium of the Hosei University in Tokyo, Japan.

1. Charles Whiteman and Ian Bain are responsible for impressing upon me the many parallels between football and macroeconomics.

2. This is the message of Lucas 1976.

3. Lucas and Sargent [in Chapter 1 in this volume] provide a brief explanation of econometric models and their uses in macroeconomics.

4. This evidence is cited by Litterman (1979) and his references.

5. Sims (1980) and Lucas (1976) describe why econometric models can perform well in extrapolating the future from the past, assuming no changes in rules of the game, while performing poorly in predicting the consequences of changes in the rules.

6. For an example of such research and extensive lists of further references, see L. Hansen and Sargent 1980 and Lucas and Sargent 1981.

7. Here T denotes matrix transposition.

8. The investment schedule (1) can be derived from the following dynamic model of a firm. A firm chooses sequences of capital to maximize

$$E_0 \sum_{t=0}^{\infty} \beta^t \left\{ f_1 k_t - \frac{f_2}{2} k_t^2 - f_3 k_t \tau_t - \frac{d}{2} (k_t - k_{t-1})^2 \right\} \tag{*}$$

where $f_1, f_2, f_3, d > 0$; $0 > \beta > 1$; and E_0 is the mathematical expectation operator conditioned on information known at time 0. The maximization is subject to (k_{t-1}, τ_t) being known at the time t. Maximization problems of this kind are analyzed in Sargent 1979. The parameters λ, α, and δ can be shown to be functions of f_1, f_2, f_3, and d.

9. The eigenvalues of A are assumed to be less than δ^{-1} in absolute value.

10. This is analogous to assuming that Houston's propensity to punt on fourth down does not depend on the number of downs per series determined by the NFL rules.

11. As claimed in note 8, the parameters $(\lambda, \alpha, \delta)$ can be shown to be functions of the parameters (f_1, f_2, f_3, d) of the present value function being maximized in (*).

3

Time Consistency and
Optimal Policy Design

V. V. Chari

The standard framework for economic policy design consists of a model to predict how people will behave under alternative policies and a criterion to compare the outcomes of alternative policies. Given a model, the policy design problem is to use the model to choose the best policy under the criterion.

Although this process seems straightforward, in practice solving the design problem is far from simple. The main difficulty is developing models that accurately predict private behavior under alternative policies. In most situations, people's current decisions depend on their expectations of future policies, and forecasting how these expectations will change in response to current policy changes is a difficult task. For example, investment decisions depend on investors' expectations of future after-tax rates of return. If investors expect future returns to be high, then they'll invest more today; if low, then less today. Consequently, policy designers can't predict how investment will respond to a tax cut today unless they know how people's expectations of future tax rates have changed as a result of the cut.

Lucas (1976) suggests an elegant way around this problem of forecasting changes in expectations following policy changes. He argues that although people's decisions vary systematically with their expectations of future policies, it is reasonable to suppose that *some* features of the economy do not change even if current and expected future policies change. For example, people don't make decisions arbitrarily; rather, their decisions are made to maximize their objective functions, given current and expected future policies.

It is now standard practice to suppose that private agents' objective functions do not change when policy changes. If policy designers know the objective functions people seek to maximize and their expectations of

Reprinted from the *Federal Reserve Bank of Minneapolis Quarterly Review*, Fall 1988.

future policies, they can predict people's decisions for each policy. Because objective functions don't change with policy changes, historical data can be used to estimate them (as, for instance, in L. Hansen and Sargent 1980). And the expectations of future policies can easily be predicted in situations where the government chooses an entire *sequence* of policies today (or possibly, *rules* describing policy choices in various contingencies) and people believe those policies will be implemented in the future. Such a sequence of policies is called a *policy regime*. Given a policy regime, private agents' objective functions are used to compute their optimal decisions. Then the policy criterion is applied to compare the outcomes of alternative regimes, and the best policy regime is selected. This procedure has its origins in the public finance tradition stemming from Ramsey (1927), so I call the best sequence of policies *Ramsey policies* and the associated outcomes *Ramsey outcomes*.[1]

Suppose, then, that policymakers have chosen a Ramsey policy regime. At some future date, suppose the policymakers ask whether it is wise to continue with that regime. To reevaluate, they calculate the optimal policies in precisely the same way they had done at the original date. If the optimal policies chosen at the future date coincide with the original plan, the policymakers will stick to that plan, and the policy regime is *time consistent*.[2] If, however, the policymakers want to renege on the original plan, the policies of the regime are *time inconsistent*.

In a series of graphic examples, Kydland and Prescott (1977), Calvo (1978), and Fischer (1980) show that Ramsey policies are often time inconsistent. Their examples suggest that time inconsistency problems arise when people's current decisions depend on expectations of future policies and their current choices affect future opportunity sets. Since their decisions have been made by the time the future date arrives, the government often has an incentive to renege on the Ramsey policies. If Ramsey policies are time inconsistent, people realize that these policies will not be followed in the future. But Ramsey policies are computed under the assumption that people believe they will be carried out. If people expect a different set of future policies, the Ramsey policies may no longer be optimal.

The problem of time inconsistency can be illustrated quite simply in a model where the only sources of government revenue are proportional taxes on capital and labor income. Suppose the government chooses a sequence of tax rates for current and future periods and then evaluates outcomes assuming people believe that this sequence will be carried out. If the government wants to maximize the welfare of consumers, how should it choose the sequence of tax rates? To solve this problem, the government needs to know how capital and labor will respond. The stock of capital changes slowly over time, since investment is only a small fraction of the stock; however, people can change their labor supplies relatively quickly. Furthermore, the key determinant of investment decisions is the after-tax return expected in the future, whereas the current after-tax wage rate is the key variable for labor supply decisions. So the government's best policy for current tax rates is to tax capital at high rates and labor at low rates. As a result of this policy, capital supply decisions aren't affected very much and labor supply is stimulated. For future tax rates, the government's best policy is to lower rates on capital to stimulate investment, and to raise the rest of the needed revenues with higher rates on labor.

But what will the government do when that future date arrives? At that point the government has an incentive to tax capital income heavily, since the investments that created the capital stock have already been made, and to tax labor lightly to increase work effort. The Ramsey policies are therefore time inconsistent.

Of course, people recognize this incentive to renege. Since they know that the government cannot commit to its policies, people rationally choose low levels of investment because they expect high future tax rates on capital income. Consequently, the procedure of designing a once-and-for-all policy sequence is useful only in environments where the government can commit to such policies, or—to use the terminology of Chari, Kehoe, and Prescott (1989)—in environments where a *commitment technology* is available. When the government commits to a policy regime, by definition it cannot change policies in the future, and the time inconsistency of the Ramsey policies is therefore irrelevant. In such situations it is appropriate to refer to the Ramsey policies and outcomes as a *Ramsey equilibrium.*

In many situations it is implausible to think that a commitment technology is available. Governments often make policy choices sequentially, with no ability to commit to future policies. What can be said about policies and outcomes in such situations? Suppose that at each date, the policies are chosen to maximize society's welfare taking into account, exactly as in the Ramsey problem, that private agents respond optimally. Since the policies must maximize society's welfare at each date, the policies are *sequentially rational* for the government. Optimal behavior by private agents requires that they forecast future policies as being sequentially rational for the government. A sequence of private outcomes and policy rules satisfying optimality by private agents and sequential rationality in policy choice is a *sustainable equilibrium.*[3] The associated policy rules and outcomes are referred to as *sustainable policies* and *sustainable outcomes.*

In this paper I develop two classic models to illustrate the time inconsistency of Ramsey policies and to show how sustainable policies and outcomes can be computed. The first is a model of capital taxation and the second, a model of default on government debt. In the capital taxation model, investment decisions depend on expected tax rates. In the default model, decisions to purchase government debt depend on expectations of future default. In both models, once private decisions are made, people are vulnerable to policy changes.

I consider both finite and infinite horizon versions of the models. I show that when the horizon is finite, Ramsey policies and sustainable policies are quite different: the Ramsey policies yield higher welfare than the sustainable ones. Thus, if a commitment technology is available, it should certainly be used to prevent governments from deviating from the Ramsey policies. If a commitment technology is not available, then the best that can be done is the sustainable policies. When the horizon is infinite, the set of sustainable policies and outcomes is much larger. In fact, it is sometimes possible to sustain even Ramsey policies in equilibrium. Essentially this works because people believe that if the government has followed the Ramsey policies in the past, it will continue to do so. If, however, the government ever deviates, then people believe the government will revert to finite horizon sustainable policies. The government, faced with these beliefs, has no incentive to renege. Such policies are called *trigger strategies*, since small changes in one player's decision trigger large changes by other players.[4]

Although the result that the Ramsey policies are sometimes sustainable is appealing, the use of trigger strategies to support such policies implies that people's beliefs about future policies change drastically in response to even small policy changes. In fact, discontinuous changes in beliefs are necessary to support Ramsey policies as equilibria. This discontinuity suggests a difficulty in designing good policies: A policy change that policymakers view as desirable might lead the public to expect a change in the policy regime, thereby inducing undesirable outcomes.

In this sense, these results reinforce the Lucas critique of econometric policy evaluation. Lucas argues that models used for policy evaluation must take into account how people's expectations change in response to policy changes. Given the *practical* difficulties in forecasting how people's expectations change when current policy changes, Lucas (1980b) suggests that economists can give reliable policy advice only in situations where the rules determining policy are well understood by the public. I argue that there are also *theoretical* reasons why forecasting people's expectations after policy changes may be difficult. These theoretical reasons arise from the fact that in many sustainable equilibria, people's beliefs about out-of-equilibrium actions are critical in sustaining equilibrium actions. Since out-of-equilibrium actions, by definition, will never be observed, it is often impossible to use historical data to deduce these beliefs.

One way the government can forestall this problem of deducing beliefs is to undertake policy changes only after extensive public debate. Such debate has the advantage of educating policymakers about people's expectations and people about the proposed policy. In that case, the difficult problem of forecasting how people's expectations will change in response to current policy changes no longer needs to be solved.

The Capital Taxation Model

Kydland and Prescott (1977, 1980) first analyzed the time inconsistency of capital taxation. Fischer (1980) constructed a particularly simple capital taxation model to illustrate the time inconsistency problem. In this section, I consider a version of Fischer's model, modified along the lines of Chari and Kehoe (1990). Initially, I consider a one-period version of the model.

A Single-Period Version

Consider an economy with a large number of identical consumers and a government. Consumers make decisions at two distinct points in time, the *first stage* and the *second stage*. At the first stage, consumers are endowed with w units of a consumption good from which they consume c_1 units and store k units. A storage technology transforms the stored units into Rk units at the second stage. In addition, consumers can work at the second stage. The marginal product of labor is 1, so if a consumer works l units, output at the second stage is l. The government must finance G units per capita in spending at the second stage. Revenues are raised from proportional taxes on capital and labor. The tax rates on capital and labor are denoted by δ and τ, respectively. Thus, a consumer's second-stage income is $(1 - \delta)Rk + (1 - \tau)l$.

Each consumer's preferences over consumption and labor[5] are denoted by a utility function $U(c_1 + c_2, l)$. Each consumer seeks to maximize the value of this function, given the tax rates δ and τ. I write this problem as follows: choose (c_1, k, c_2, l) to solve[6]

$$\max U(c_1 + c_2, l) \tag{1}$$

subject to

$$c_1 + k \leqslant w \tag{2}$$

$$c_2 \leqslant (1 - \delta)Rk + (1 - \tau)l. \tag{3}$$

The constraints to this programming problem say that first-stage consumption and savings cannot exceed the consumer's endowment, and second-stage consumption cannot exceed after-tax earnings on capital and wages.

The government in turn must meet its expenditure requirements. Let K and L denote the per capita input of capital and labor in the economy. Then the government must meet a budget constraint of the form

$$G \leqslant \delta RK + \tau L. \tag{4}$$

That is, government spending cannot exceed tax revenues from capital and labor.

I assume that government spending G is large enough so that labor must always be taxed.[7] The government uses a social welfare function to compare the outcomes of various policies. In this world with identical consumers, a natural objective for the government is to maximize the welfare of each consumer. The social welfare function is given by $U(C_1 + C_2, L)$, where C_1 and C_2 denote per capita levels of consumption at the first and second stages and where L denotes labor supply.

With Commitment

I model the government's ability to commit to a policy plan by assuming that it chooses policies *before* consumers make their first-stage decisions. A *policy*, denoted by π, is simply a choice of tax rates (δ, τ). Given a policy, consumers respond optimally by solving problem (1). Denote the resulting aggregate choices for each policy by

$$F(\pi) = (C_1(\pi), K(\pi), C_2(\pi), L(\pi)). \tag{5}$$

A *Ramsey equilibrium* is a policy π and an aggregate choice $F(\pi)$ which have the properties that for every policy, consumers choose their decisions by solving problem (1) and, given the aggregate choice functions, the government's policy maximizes its utility subject to its budget constraint.

Notice that consumers' decisions are required to be optimal for each policy. Had I required their decisions to be optimal only at the government's chosen policy, absurd outcomes could be part of an equilibrium, including *any* policy that satisfies the government's budget constraint. Consider, for example, a choice function F for consumers that specifies optimal behavior at some arbitrary policy π^* and zero labor supply otherwise. The government, confronted with this function, optimally chooses the policy π^*. Obviously, such an aggregate choice function is not a rational response by consumers to policies other than π^*. Thus, a Ramsey equilibrium imposes rationality at every point where a consumer must make a decision.

The Ramsey policies and outcomes are easy to characterize. The tax on labor distorts labor supply decisions. The *social* return to work is the sum of the private return and the return to the government. Since each unit of labor supply yields one unit of the good, the social return is unity. But consumers care only about the private return, which is $1 - \tau$. This divergence between social and private returns causes consumers' labor supply decisions to be distorted.[8] As a result, the government would like to set tax rates on labor as low as possible.

Yet the government must find some way to raise enough revenues to finance its consumption. Suppose it sets the tax rate on capital so high that $(1 - \delta)R < 1$. The after-tax return to saving is then so low that consumers rationally consume their entire first-stage endowments. Hence, no revenues are raised from capital taxation. Suppose, now, that the government sets the tax rate on capital at a low enough level that $(1 - \delta)R > 1$. Then consumers save their entire endowments and continue to do so as long as $(1 - \delta)R \geqslant 1$. The government therefore raises the tax rate on capital until consumers are just indifferent between consumption and saving, that is, to the point where $(1 - \delta)R = 1$. It raises the rest of the needed revenues by labor taxation. Thus, the Ramsey capital tax rate is set so that $(1 - \delta)R = 1$ (or $\delta = 1 - 1/R$), and consumers save their entire endowments.

Without Commitment
I model the inability to commit by assuming that the government sets its policy *after* private agents have made their first-stage decisions. The government seeks to maximize the same utility function as in the Ramsey problem. To see how the government solves its problem, it is useful to start with the second-stage decisions of consumers. Given their first-stage decisions and government policy, consumers rationally make their consumption and labor supply decisions by maximizing their utility functions. This maximization induces aggregate choice functions at the second stage. Given these functions and first-stage decisions, the government in turn chooses its policies optimally. These optimal policies are then used to solve for the consumers' first-stage decisions. A *sustainable equilibrium* consists of a first-stage decision by consumers, a government policy, and a second-

stage decision function which together satisfy two conditions: consumers' maximization problems at each stage and the government's maximization problem.

Notice that consumers' second-stage decisions must be described as a function. This requirement is imposed because the government must be able to evaluate the outcomes of alternative policies. Consumers, however, view the government's policies as a fixed pair of tax rates, since no single consumer perceives that a person's own actions have any effect on the government's policy. Thus, consumers behave competitively, whereas the government does not.

It is easy to describe sustainable equilibrium outcomes in this model. First, I claim that aggregate savings will be zero. The supporting argument is by contradiction. Suppose aggregate savings are not zero. By an argument parallel to the Ramsey case, the government should tax capital fully, since this policy reduces the need to resort to the distorting labor tax. Anticipating that capital income will be fully taxed, consumers choose not to save at all. Since savings are zero, the government must raise all the needed revenues through distorting labor taxation. In short, consumers rationally anticipate the government's policy, and the government chooses its policies rationally, given consumers' first-stage decisions.

I now show that the government's utility is strictly higher in the Ramsey equilibrium than in the sustainable equilibrium. In the environment with commitment, it is *feasible* for the government to choose a tax rate on capital of unity and the same tax rate on labor as in the sustainable equilibrium. If it chose these policies, consumers would choose not to save at all, and the outcomes would coincide with those in the sustainable equilibrium. Therefore, in an environment with commitment, the government can always realize at least the utility level of the sustainable equilibrium. Since the government chooses a different set of policies in the environment with commitment than in the one without, it is clearly better off in the Ramsey equilibrium.

It is also clear that the Ramsey policies are time inconsistent. Since the Ramsey policies specify low tax rates on capital, consumers save their entire endowments. If the government could change its policies in midstream, it would have every incentive to tax capital fully to reduce reliance on labor taxation. So Ramsey policies make sense only if the government can commit to them. In other words, the Ramsey policies are not sustainable in a world without commitment.

Note, furthermore, that the time inconsistency problem does not arise because the government's preferences changed in midstream. In fact, in this example the government is a benevolent one that seeks to do well by its citizens. Rather, the problem arises because capital, once put in place, cannot readily be reconverted into consumption. Since consumers have already committed to their decisions, even a benevolent government has an incentive to renege on the very policies that led to the capital accumulation. This incentive, then, is the source of the time inconsistency problem. Given a government's inability to commit, the best that policymakers can choose is the sustainable equilibrium.

Multiperiod Versions

A natural extension of Fischer's capital taxation model involves allowing consumers to make decisions over many periods. So I now consider a finite repetition of the single-period model just discussed. For simplicity, I do not allow capital to accumulate between periods. Thus, within each period, consumers face exactly the same problem as in (1). The consumers' utility functions are given by

$$\sum_{t=0}^{T} \beta^t U(c_{1t} + c_{2t}, l_t) \tag{6}$$

where T is the length of the horizon, β is a discount factor between zero and one, and (c_{1t}, c_{2t}, l_t) is consumption at the first and second stages and labor supply in period t. The government's utility function is the same as each consumer's.

With Commitment
When a commitment technology is available, the government chooses an entire sequence of policies. Thus, before consumers make their decisions, the government chooses tax rates for every period. Since this problem is simply a finite repetition of the single-period problem, the Ramsey policies and outcomes are also finite repetitions of the single-period Ramsey policies and outcomes: In each period, consumers save their entire first-stage endowments and the government sets the tax rate on capital to make the after-tax return on capital equal to one.

Without Commitment
What if a commitment technology is not available? Then how is a sustainable equilibrium defined? Since consumers' beliefs about future policies may well depend on current policies, a policy choice in any period must now be thought of as a *function* of past policies. Given a sequence of policy func-

tions, one for every period, consumers make their decisions optimally. Thus, the consumers' maximization problems can be solved to generate a sequence of consumers' aggregate choice functions that also depend on the history of past policies. The government chooses policies to maximize its objective function, given these aggregate choice functions. A sustainable equilibrium consists of sequences of policy functions and aggregate choice functions that solve, respectively, the government's maximization problems and consumers' maximization problems at each date and for every history. (A precise mathematical definition of sustainable equilibrium is given in Appendix A.)

What can be said about sustainable policies and outcomes? The answer depends on whether the horizon is finite or infinite. First, consider the finite horizon problem. It will be useful to proceed from the last period, T. Clearly, the problem here is identical to a single-period problem. Thus, sustainable equilibrium policies and outcomes coincide with those in the single-period case, and this result holds *regardless* of past policies and outcomes. Now consider the problem at $T - 1$. Since what happens in this next-to-last period has no effect on outcomes in the final period, none of the government's policy choices can have any effect on consumers' beliefs about policies in period T. Rational consumers realize that in the last period, the government will follow the single-period sustainable policy. So the problems faced by both governments and consumers reduce to the single-period problem, as do the resulting policies and outcomes. By the same line of reasoning, it is clear that in every period, sustainable policies and outcomes are identical to those in the single-period problem.

Second, consider a situation where the horizon is infinite. Since there is no last period, the finite horizon argument doesn't apply. However, if repeated forever, the single-period sustainable policies and outcomes are also equilibrium outcomes with an infinite horizon. Suppose consumers believe that no matter what the government chooses today, it will choose single-period sustainable policies forever in the future. Given these beliefs, the government's problem reduces to the static single-period problem. Clearly, the best policy, given these beliefs, is to tax capital fully. Recognizing this as the best policy, consumers at the first stage choose not to save, and the result is the static sustainable outcome. This outcome, however, is not a unique equilibrium.

Consider the following set of beliefs held by consumers. They believe that as long as the government has chosen Ramsey policies in the past, it will continue to do so; but if the government has ever deviated, it will tax capital fully from then on. Now consider the problem faced by the government when consumers have saved their entire endowments. It can choose to tax capital at higher rates than the Ramsey plan. In doing so, it realizes a gain in the current period, but it knows that consumers will never again save in the future. Therefore, it would suffer a utility loss in all subsequent periods. If future utility is not discounted too much, the current gain is more than offset by the future losses. Thus, the government is induced to tax capital at the Ramsey rates.

Note that the beliefs of consumers are rational. If the government has taxed capital heavily in the past, given consumers' beliefs about future policies, the best policy for the government is to tax capital heavily today. However, if the government has not deviated in the past, it realizes that deviating will trigger a bad outcome. Therefore, it rationally chooses not to tax capital heavily. In both situations, consumers' expectations are fulfilled.

At this point a reasonable question to ask is, Why aren't Ramsey policies sustainable when the horizon is finite but long? They aren't sustainable because consumers' beliefs that Ramsey policies will be chosen in the future are irrational. Consumers realize that in the last period, for example, it will never be rational for the government to pursue Ramsey policies. Thus, their beliefs are pinned down in the last period and, by backward induction, in all previous periods.[9]

Some Implications

The capital taxation example offers some implications for policy design. In the equilibria that support Ramsey policies, consumers' beliefs necessarily change sharply in response to some kinds of small policy changes. If beliefs did not change sharply, the Ramsey policies could not be supported. For example, suppose consumers believe that Ramsey policies will be followed in the future if the current capital tax rate is slightly higher than the Ramsey rate. Correctly anticipating no utility loss in future periods, the government would then deviate to a higher tax rate. This incentive to deviate remains in all periods. Recall, though, that at the Ramsey rate, consumers were just indifferent about their consumption and savings decisions. With a higher tax rate, they will choose not to save at all. Consequently, these beliefs do not constitute an equilibrium. To support Ramsey policies as part of an equilibrium, consumers must anticipate large changes in future policies in response to small changes in current policy. This discontinuity in beliefs implies that it is dangerous for policymakers to suppose small policy changes will always have small effects on the economy's operating characteristics.

It should also be pointed out that there are many sustainable outcomes in the infinite horizon version of this model. To take an extreme example, suppose the government chooses Ramsey policies in even periods and the single-period sustainable policies in odd periods. Consumers expect that any deviation in an even period will be followed by deviations in all subsequent even periods. Again, with sufficiently little discounting, the even-odd policy is sustainable. An observer of this economy might suggest that the government has taxed capital fully in the past (in odd periods) without noticeable harm; therefore, a tax in a current even period should do no harm. Obviously, the consequences will be disastrous: consumers will never save and the economy is pushed into a bad outcome. The point here is that it is often difficult to discern from past data how expectations will respond to current policy changes.

The model also illustrates the advantages of instituting delays in implementing policies. For example, suppose that policies are implemented with a one-period lag. At the second stage of a period t, the government chooses policies that are implemented in $t + 1$. It is not possible for the government to commit to policies for periods $t + 2$, $t + 3$, and so on. In such a situation, even though a commitment technology is not available, the outcomes are the same as in the Ramsey equilibrium. Since the policies are, in effect, chosen before private agents have made their savings decisions, the government optimally chooses to tax capital at rates low enough to induce investment. Because delays in implementing policies allow the government to take account of the effect of the policy on current decisions, they help in resolving the time inconsistency problem. Of course, the result that the outcomes with delays coincide with the Ramsey equilibrium depends on the special repetitive structure of the model, and this result would be altered by allowing for capital accumulation from one period to the next. Nevertheless, the essential message—that delays in implementing policies result in better outcomes—still holds. Such delays are a particularly easy form of partial commitment. For example, the requirement that two-thirds of U.S. state legislatures must approve constitutional amendments delays implementation and helps resolve time inconsistency problems.

The Debt and Default Model

I turn now to a model of debt and default to analyze a second problem in time consistency—the problem of default on the public debt. (Prescott 1977 was the first to address this issue in the time consistency literature.) I introduce this example for two reasons: First, it has substantive interest in its own right. Second, it illustrates more vividly than the capital taxation example the problem of using historical data to deduce consumers' beliefs following policy changes.

The Role of Public Debt

The public debt serves an important role by smoothing fluctuations in tax revenues over time. If the government could never issue debt, the budget would then have to be balanced in each period. A balanced budget would be undesirable, since government spending fluctuates over time—thanks to wars and varying needs for public services. For example, to balance the budget during a war, tax rates must be intolerably high, reducing work effort precisely when needed most. By issuing debt, the government can keep wartime tax rates relatively low. Of course, in the ensuing peacetime, taxes have to be raised to pay off the debt. The higher peacetime taxes reduce work effort, but this reduction is the cost of relatively low wartime taxes.

Consider the problem facing the government when it inherits a large public debt and current government spending is low. Tax revenues must be used to pay off the public debt. These taxes distort private decisions, particularly those about labor supply. If the government defaulted on the debt, tax rates could be lowered and the size of the economic pie increased. People, of course, recognize this incentive, so they will not buy debt issued in wartime if they believe the government will default. Thus, the benefits of tax smoothing are lost. Clearly, in this case a commitment technology is valuable. Given the government's ability to commit, a promise not to default in the future is credible. But what if a commitment technology is not available? In that case an important source of discipline for the government is that if it defaults, people may be unwilling to buy debt in the future. As a result, the government can't finance future wars by issuing debt, and this outcome may then deter the government from defaulting on the current debt.[10] I explore this possibility in the model.

The Economy

Consider an economy populated by a large number of identical people who live from period 0 through T (where T is possibly infinite). In each period, a nonstorable consumption good is produced from labor. One unit of labor input produces one unit of the good. Part of the output is used for government consumption and the remainder is available for private consumption. The per capita level of government consumption G_t is exogenously given and varies over time. The national income identity is

$$C_t + G_t = L_t \tag{7}$$

where C_t and L_t denote per capita private consumption and labor input.

The government raises revenues from a proportional tax on labor income. The tax rate in period t is denoted by τ_t. Thus, after-tax income is given by $(1 - \tau_t)L_t$. The government also issues public debt in the form of one-period discount bonds with a face value of one unit of the consumption good. To accommodate the possibility of default, I assume the government can levy a tax on the outstanding debt. The tax rate on debt is denoted by δ_t. If the tax rate on debt equals unity, the government is said to have *defaulted* on the debt. Of course, the price of the discount bonds issued in the current period depends on market interest rates and the public's expectations of future taxes on debt. Denote the price of new debt in period t by q_t. In each period the government faces a budget constraint of the form

$$\tau_t L_t + q_t B_{t+1} = G_t + (1 - \delta_t)B_t \tag{8}$$

where B_t is the public debt outstanding in period t. The left side of (8) gives the revenues raised from taxation and the sale of new debt, and the right side gives expenditures on government consumption and retirement of outstanding debt. The price of new debt issues is determined by

$$q_t = (1 - \delta_{t+1})/(1 + {}_tr_{t+1}) \tag{9}$$

where ${}_tr_{t+1}$ is the one-period interest rate between t and $t + 1$ and δ_{t+1} is the tax rate expected to prevail in $t + 1$. For example, if a 60 percent tax rate is anticipated, the discount bond is equivalent to a tax-exempt bond with a face value of 40 cents.

The preferences of consumers over consumption and labor are given by

$$\sum_{t=0}^{T} \beta^t U(C_t, L_t). \tag{10}$$

I assume that in addition to government debt, consumers can borrow and lend among themselves in default-free, single-period discount bonds. The consumer's budget constraint at some date t is given by

$$C_t + D_{t+1}/(1 + {}_tr_{t+1}) + q_t B_{t+1} = (1 - \tau_t)L_t + (1 - \delta_t)B_t + D_t \tag{11}$$

where B_t is the stock of government debt and D_t the stock of private debt held by the consumer. The terminal conditions are that $B_{T+1} = D_{T+1} = 0$.

Given a sequence of one-period interest rates and a sequence of tax rates, the consumer makes consumption, labor supply, and debt-holding decisions to maximize the utility function, subject to the budget constraints. Since the consumption good is nonstorable, market clearing requires that the net quantity of private debt be zero and that government debt issues be held willingly.

I denote the sequence of tax rates by

$$\pi = (\delta_t, \tau_t)_{t=0}^T. \tag{12}$$

Given a policy π, a *competitive equilibrium* is a sequence of consumption, labor supply, and debt-holding decisions $(C_t, L_t, B_{t+1}, D_{t+1})_{t=0}^T$ and a sequence of one-period interest rates $(_t r_{t+1})_{t=0}^T$ that meet the following conditions:

- Consumers' decisions maximize (10) subject to (11), where q_t is defined in (9), given the sequence of interest rates and B_0, D_0.
- The debt market clears; that is, $D_t = 0$ for all t.

For future reference, it is convenient to denote the policy-induced competitive equilibrium decisions of consumers by the function $F(\pi)$ and the sequence of equilibrium interest rates by the function $r(\pi)$.

The policy instruments available to the government are its tax policies. As in the capital taxation model, the government chooses these instruments to maximize the welfare of the representative consumer, which is given by

$$\sum_{t=0}^T \beta^t U(C_t, L_t). \tag{13}$$

With Commitment
In an environment with commitment, the government first chooses its policies for all periods. Consumers then make their decisions, taking the policies and market interest rates as given. The interest rates in turn are determined by market-clearing conditions. The government chooses the policy that maximizes its utility subject to its budget constraints (8), given the competitive equilibrium functions $F(\pi)$ and $r(\pi)$. Such a policy and the policy-induced competitive equilibrium functions constitute a *Ramsey equilibrium*.

At least two features of the Ramsey equilibrium deserve comment. First, as Chari and Kehoe (1988) show, attention can be restricted to equilibria where the government does not tax the debt in periods 1 through T. If there is any positive debt outstanding at period 0, it is best to default on that debt. Note that this immediately raises the possibility that Ramsey policies are time inconsistent. Second, Lucas and Stokey (1983) show that in any two periods where government spending is the same, the government chooses the same tax policies. In fact, this result also generalizes to situations where government spending fluctuates stochastically over time. This result is somewhat surprising. (A detailed exposition of how this result is reached appears in Appendix B.)

Here I provide some intuition for their result: Consumers prefer smooth rather than variable streams of consumption and labor supply over time. Now consider any two periods with the same value of government spending. By choosing the same policy on both dates, the government equates consumption as well as labor supply on those dates. Consumers prefer such an outcome and, therefore, so does the government. (Note that on any two dates with unequal levels of government spending, the national income identity implies that both consumption and labor supply cannot be equated on those dates.) The result that policies should be the same even if government spending fluctuates stochastically follows from the same type of reasoning. Barro (1979), Aschauer (1988), and others argue that increases in government consumption that are expected to last for a long time should be accompanied by higher tax rates than increases that are viewed as temporary. This model, in contrast, suggests the policies should be the same in both situations.[11]

Without Commitment

I turn now to an environment without commitment. For simplicity, I assume that the government can never own claims on consumers, so the government's debt is never negative. In a finite horizon model, the backward induction technique used in the capital taxation example immediately implies that the government's budget is necessarily balanced period by period. Consumers realize that in the final period, the government will default on any outstanding debt. Consequently, the market price of new debt issues in $T - 1$ is necessarily zero, and no revenues can be gained from issuing new debt. Hence in $T - 1$, the government finds it best to default on the debt it inherits. Backward induction implies that the government's budget is always balanced. However, in a Ramsey equilibrium the ability to issue debt allows for tax smoothing. Labor taxes can be lowered in periods of high government spending and raised in periods of low government spending. Thus, work effort is stimulated when most needed. Consumers and the government are therefore better off in a Ramsey equilibrium than in a sustainable equilibrium. But Ramsey policies are not sustainable without commitment. If the government inherits positive debt, it will default. Recognizing this incentive to default, consumers will not buy any debt issued by the government. As a result, the only sustainable outcome is a balanced budget.

The common perception is that governments do not default because they fear they will be permanently denied access to financial markets. This intuition is confirmed by examining the infinite horizon version of the model. As in the capital taxation example, an equilibrium outcome has the government's budget being balanced in every period. This equilibrium is sustained by consumers' beliefs that the government will always default. Again, as in the taxation example, better equilibria can be sustained. If consumers believe that a current default signals defaults forever in the future, then they will be unwilling to purchase new debt issues in the event of a default. The government, realizing this, does not default because it loses the tax-smoothing benefits obtained from debt sales forever in the future. So with sufficiently little discounting of the future, the government rationally chooses not to default.

Some Implications

Consider the implications of this analysis for policy design. Suppose that the economy is in an infinite horizon equilibrium with Ramsey outcomes supported by consumers' beliefs, as just discussed. An analyst, understanding the effect of tax distortions, points out the burden caused by public debt and suggests that the government default on the debt and then never do so again. Clearly, the resulting outcomes will be bad: the government is forced to balance its budget in all succeeding periods. It is also clear that most people would immediately point out the possibility that debt would never be bought again, so the analyst's recommendation is likely to go unheeded. In slightly more sophisticated contexts, however, it is more difficult to discern erroneous analysis of this kind.

To see the difficulty in discerning this kind of faulty analysis, consider a variation on the debt and default model. Suppose government spending fluctuates stochastically over time. For simplicity, suppose that the economy is either in wartime or peacetime and that these states are equally likely. Government spending is high in war and low in peace, and the government can issue single-period discount bonds to smooth tax revenues.

Consider the policy design problem in an environment with commitment. Suppose at date 0 the economy is in wartime with no inherited debt. What do the Ramsey policies look like? The government runs a deficit in the current period. It must also form a contingency plan describing what it will do tomorrow if the war continues or if peace breaks out. If the government runs a deficit today, it will clearly run a surplus tomorrow in peacetime. What if the war continues? Surprisingly, it turns out that the best policy is to default on the debt. By following such a policy, the outstanding stock of debt is zero if the war continues and positive in peacetime. This policy ensures that distorting taxes do not have to be raised to pay off the debt when it is necessary to raise taxes to finance the war effort. Consumers are willing to buy debt issued in wartime at an appropriate price because there's a 50-50 chance they'll get their money back.[12]

Now consider the same problem in an environment without commitment. Again, with sufficiently little discounting, it is possible to construct consumers' beliefs that support Ramsey policies as equilibria. Defaults on the debt in wartime are part of the Ramsey policy. Consumers rationally anticipate such defaults and do not change their beliefs after defaults occur. However, defaults in peacetime trigger expectations of defaults in all future peacetimes, and the government loses the benefits of tax smoothing in the future.[13] An analyst observing such a history of policies and outcomes may be tempted to argue that past defaults have led to no change in the public's willingness to buy debt. Therefore, a current default, even in peacetime, should have no effect on the willingness to buy debt. The result of this recommendation is that the public never again buys debt. The government will be forced to balance its budget in every succeeding period. Clearly, such outcomes are undesirable.

This variation on the debt and default model shows that if policy analysis fails to consider the public's expectations that supported a particular equilibrium in the past, the analysis may lead to erroneous recommendations for the future. However, as mentioned earlier, such expectations are difficult to discern from past data. A solution—one already suggested by the capital taxation example—is to undertake policy changes only after public debate. Such debate has the advantages of educating the public about proposed policies and the policymakers about the public's responses.

The Policy Implications Summarized

From the two examples presented in this paper, three main policy implications emerge: First, the use of economic models to compare policy regimes is likely to be most effective in situations where commitment is possible. If societies can commit to policy rules, say through constitutions or other devices, they should do so while recognizing and resisting the incentives to renege in the future. If such a commitment technology is not available, policy choices that ignore how policies will be chosen in the future and, particularly, that ignore people's expectations of future policies—these policy choices will yield poor results. I have also argued that delays in implementing policies are equivalent to a form of limited commitment and are therefore desirable.

Second, expectations of future policies often depend critically on the history of past policies. For instance, is it best to default on the outstanding debt? Often, if the expectations of private agents about future policies are ignored, the answer is yes. In this situation it may be obvious that the effect of current policies on the public's expectations of future policies should be considered. In particular, there is a real possibility that the government will have to borrow at prohibitively high rates in the future if it defaults today. In other situations, the answer is less obvious. For instance, should an investment tax credit be instituted during a recession? If such a tax credit is instituted, the next recession might well be more severe as investors wait for a tax credit to be instituted or expanded. Consequently, policy prescriptions should take into account how changes in current policies affect expectations of future policies. A major difficulty here, of course, is that it is often impossible to deduce from the available data how these expectations will change. Given this difficulty, one possible method of evaluating policy regimes is to consider only the long-run or average operating characteristics of the economy under each regime. This criterion rules out the short-term gains that are at the heart of the time consistency problem.

Third, both examples have a bearing on the debate over rules versus discretion. Should policymakers be bound to rules prescribing their actions? Or should policies be changed whenever policymakers think it desirable? Friedman (1960) argues that policymakers and economists simply do not know enough about the economy to use discretion wisely. Lucas (1980b, p. 205) also argues that rules are preferable:

Our ability as economists to predict the responses of agents rests, in situations where expectations about the future matter, on our understanding of the stochastic environment agents believe themselves to be operating in. In practice, this limits the class of policies the consequences of which we can hope to assess in advance to policies generated by fixed, well understood, relatively permanent rules. . . .

Kydland and Prescott (1977) extend the argument further by suggesting that discretionary management would lead to time consistent outcomes inferior to the preferable Ramsey rules. Therefore, if a commitment technology is available, it should be used.

I have argued, here, that if a commitment technology is not available, policy recommendations that ignore the effect of history on people's ex-

pectations will yield inferior outcomes. Apart from the practical considerations emphasized by Lucas, there are theoretical reasons why economists
can offer reliable policy advice only in situations where policies are generated by well-understood, relatively permanent rules. Because historical data
cannot provide information about consumers' beliefs about future policies
following out-of-equilibrium actions, it is often illusory to think that economists can forecast changes in expectations following a policy change.
Therefore, policy regimes should be viewed as institutions that are subject
to change only after extensive public debate. This standpoint diminishes
the role of economists as day-to-day managers, but enhances their role as
designers of arrangements and constitutions.

Appendix A: More About the Capital Taxation Model

In this appendix I develop the infinite horizon capital taxation model. For
a formal development, see Chari and Kehoe 1990.

I make explicit the role of history in affecting people's expectations
about the course of future policies. I start by considering the problem of a
consumer at some date t. Suppose this consumer expects a sequence of
tax rates, denoted by (δ_s^e, τ_s^e), for periods $s = t, t + 1, \ldots$. The consumer
chooses consumption, savings, and labor supply to solve the problem

$$\max \sum_{s=t}^{\infty} \beta^s U(c_{1s} + c_{2s}, l_s) \tag{A1}$$

subject to

$$c_{1s} + k_s = w \tag{A2}$$

$$c_{2s} = R(1 - \delta_s^e)k_s + (1 - \tau_s^e)l_s \tag{A3}$$

for $s = t, t + 1, \ldots$.

I now describe how the expectations of future policies in problem (A1)
are formed. Since consumers' expectations may be affected by past policies,
I define the *history of the economy* H_t at date t to be the record of all
government policies up to and including t:

$$H_t = (\pi_s)_{s=0}^t. \tag{A4}$$

Consumers expect the government to follow a policy plan σ, which
specifies government policies as a function of the history. For example,
$\sigma_t(H_{t-1})$ specifies consumers' beliefs at the first stage of date t about the
policies that will be chosen at t, given that the policies in the history H_{t-1}

have been chosen in the past. Beliefs about future policies are inductively generated. For example, at the first stage of period t, consumers believe that the history the government confronts in period $t + 1$ will be given by $(H_{t-1}, \sigma_t(H_{t-1}))$. The resulting policy will be given by $\sigma_{t+1}(H_{t-1}, \sigma_t(H_{t-1}))$. The same procedure can be used to derive consumers' expectations about policies in all subsequent periods. Of course, consumers could be wrong in their expectations. In such a case, they continue to use the policy plan σ to form expectations of future policies, given this new history.

At each date, the government maximizes its utility by choosing its current policy. Such a policy choice has two effects: first, it affects labor supply and second-stage consumption decisions in the current period; second, because it is now part of the history H_t, it affects consumers' expectations of future policies and their future decisions. The government must form expectations of how private decisions will be affected. Denote these expectations by functions $(C_{1t}(H_{t-1}), K_t(H_{t-1}), C_{2t}(H_t), L_t(H_t))$, which I call consumers' *contingency plans*. The government's problem at date t, given a history H_{t-1}, is

$$\max \sum_{s=t}^{\infty} \beta^s U(C_{1s}(H_{s-1}) + C_{2s}(H_s), L_s(H_s)) \tag{A5}$$

subject to

$$C_{1s}(H_{s-1}) + K_s(H_{s-1}) = w \tag{A6}$$

$$C_{2s}(H_s) = R(1 - \delta_s)K_s(H_{s-1}) + (1 - \tau_s)L_s(H_s) \tag{A7}$$

where the histories are induced from H_{t-1} by the chosen policies. Notice that by its policy choice, the government can affect histories and thereby expectations, but consumers assume that the evolution of the histories is beyond their control.

A *sustainable equilibrium* is a policy plan for the government and contingency plans for consumers such that for every history, the following conditions are met:

• Consumers' contingency plans solve problem (A1), given the policy plan.

• Given consumers' contingency plans, the government's policy plan solves problem (A5).

The set of sustainable outcomes is completely characterized by Chari and Kehoe (1990). They show that the worst sustainable equilibrium (in terms of utility) is an infinite repetition of the single-period sustainable equilibrium. They also establish that with sufficiently little discounting, the Ramsey policies are sustainable. The plans supporting such outcomes specify that the government should follow Ramsey policies as long as these policies have been followed in the past. Consumers' contingency plans specify that for such histories, they should save their entire endowments. If the government has ever deviated from the Ramsey policies, consumers' plans specify that they save nothing. Given such plans, the government chooses optimally to continue the Ramsey policies in each period.

Appendix B: Computing Ramsey Policies for the Debt and Default Model

In this appendix, I show how to compute the Ramsey policies for the debt and default model. I also show that taxes on labor supply are the same on any two dates with the same level of government spending.

It is convenient to collapse the sequence of budget constraints faced by consumers into a single budget constraint. Let P_t denote the price at date 0 for delivery of one unit of the consumption good at date t. I can then represent the one-period interest rate between t and $t + 1$ as

$$P_{t+1}/P_t = 1/(1 + {}_tr_{t+1}). \tag{B1}$$

Of course, $P_0 = 1$. Alternatively, P_{t+1}/P_t can be thought of as the price of a default-free, single-period discount bond at t. Then, the consumer's budget constraint (11) can be written as

$$C_t + (P_{t+1}/P_t)D_{t+1} + [P_{t+1}(1 - \delta_{t+1})/P_t]B_{t+1}$$
$$= (1 - \tau_t)C_t + (1 - \delta_t)B_t + D_t. \tag{B2}$$

Multiplying (B2) by P_t, adding across dates 0 through T, and using the terminal conditions that $B_{T+1} = D_{T+1} = D_0 = 0$, I get

$$\sum_{t=0}^{T} P_t C_t = \sum_{t=0}^{T} P_t(1 - \tau_t)L_t + (1 - \delta_0)B_0. \tag{B3}$$

The consumer maximizes the utility function (10) subject to (B3). The first-order conditions to this problem are (B3),

$$\beta^t U_c(C_t, L_t) = \lambda P_t \tag{B4}$$

and

$$\beta^t U_l(C_t, L_t) = -\lambda P_t(1 - \tau_t) \tag{B5}$$

where λ is the Lagrange multiplier associated with (B3).

For the government's budget constraints, I repeat the same process as for the consumer, collapsing the sequence of budget constraints (8) to get a single constraint given by

$$\sum_{t=0}^{T} P_t(\tau_t L_t) = \sum_{t=0}^{T} P_t G_t + (1 - \delta_0) B_0. \tag{B6}$$

The government maximizes its utility function subject to (B6). Unlike the consumer, the government does not take prices as given. It recognizes that the prices and consumers' decisions are implicitly given by the first-order conditions (B3)–(B5) and the national income identity (7). Substituting the consumers' first-order conditions into (B6), using the national income identity, and rearranging gives the government's budget constraint:

$$\sum \beta^t [C_t U_c(C_t, L_t) + L_t U_l(C_t, L_t)] = (1 - \delta_0) B_0. \tag{B7}$$

The government maximizes the utility function (13) subject to (B7) and the national income identity (7). Let μ denote the Lagrange multiplier on (B7), and let v_t denote the Lagrange multipliers on (7). The first-order conditions for the government's maximization problem are

$$\beta^t U_c + \mu \beta^t (U_c + C_t U_{cc} + L_t U_{cl}) - v_t = 0 \tag{B8}$$

and

$$\beta^t U_l + \mu \beta^t (U_l + C_t U_{cl} + L_t U_{ll}) + v_t = 0 \tag{B9}$$

where, for convenience, I have suppressed the time subscripts on the partial derivatives. Adding (B8) and (B9) and rearranging, I get

$$(1 + \mu)/\mu = [C_t(U_{cc} + U_{cl}) + L_t(U_{ll} + U_{cl})]/(U_c + U_l). \tag{B10}$$

The left side of (B10) is independent of the date and the value of government spending. Consequently, for any two dates with the same government spending, choosing the same values of consumption and labor supply solves (B10). Hence, the policies for any two such dates must be the same.

Notes

The models presented in this paper and most of the results were developed in collaboration with Patrick J. Kehoe, assistant professor of economics at the University of Minnesota and visitor at the Minneapolis Fed's Research Department. Kehoe should not, however, be held responsible for any misstatements, errors, or opinions expressed here.

1. Frank Plumpton Ramsey (1903–30), a brilliant British mathematical economist, first posed and solved the problem of designing optimal excise tax rates in an economy with many goods (see Ramsey 1927). A government requires a fixed amount of revenue raised by

excise taxes on the goods. Given the taxes, prices and quantities are determined in a competitive equilibrium. The government's problem is to choose tax rates to maximize the welfare of consumers. It turns out that this problem is formally equivalent to choosing tax rates on labor over time. (The intuition behind this equivalence is as follows: think of labor at each date as a different good and interest rates as the relative prices of the goods.)

2. Robert H. Strotz introduced the issue of time consistency (see Strotz 1955–56). He considered the problem of a decision maker whose tastes change over time, showing that this person might have an incentive to change a planned course of action. It is easy to show, as Strotz did, that if a person's tastes remain unchanged over time, a course of action that initially maximizes the objective function continues to do so at all future dates. The remarkable feature of the modern literature on time consistency is that tastes do not change; rather, the time inconsistency problem, as discussed in my paper, arises because there is more than one decision maker.

3. This terminology is borrowed from Chari and Kehoe (1988, 1990) and Chari, Kehoe, and Prescott (1989). *Sustainability* requires that decisions be optimal at each date they are made. It is closely related to the notions of *subgame perfection* (see Selten 1975) and *sequential equilibrium* (see Kreps and Wilson 1982) in game theory. *Sustainable equilibrium* extends these ideas to environments with anonymous, competitive private agents (see Chari and Kehoe 1990 for details).

4. An extensive literature in game theory uses trigger strategies to describe equilibrium outcomes in infinite horizon environments. See J. Friedman 1971, Fudenberg and Maskin 1986, Green 1980, Green and Porter 1984, and Abreu 1988. In the macroeconomics literature, Barro and Gordon 1983 was the first to use trigger strategies.

5. Usually, preferences are described over consumption and leisure. Since the sum of leisure and labor must equal the fixed endowment of time available, the two representations are equivalent.

6. In this problem, if the tax rate on capital is set so that $(1 - \delta)R = 1$, consumers are indifferent about how much to save, because $c_1 + c_2$ is independent of the saving decision. I assume that in such a case, consumers save their entire endowments.

7. Formally, this requires that $G > Rw$, so even if consumers save their entire endowments, a tax on labor is necessary.

8. This distortion can be understood by contrasting the environment in the text with one where lump-sum taxes are available. A tax is *lump sum* if it is unrelated to any economic activity. Thus, if each consumer had to pay G units to the government regardless of the consumer's other decisions, every extra unit of labor would give consumption of one unit, which is the social return.

9. Because this result depends sensitively on the horizon being infinite, it may well be questioned on the grounds that it is sheer vanity to suppose humanity is immortal. However, there is every reason to question the finite horizon result, especially when the horizon is long, rather than the infinite horizon result. Kreps and others (1982) show that introducing a tiny element of strategic uncertainty can overturn the finite horizon results. For example, suppose there is an infinitesimally small probability that the government will irrationally choose Ramsey policies in the last period. Then in a finite but long horizon model, every government has an incentive to develop a reputation for choosing Ramsey policies. Kreps and others show that no matter how small this probability, as long as it is positive, good outcomes are sustainable in economies with finite but long horizons.

10. In stable democracies, explicit default on the public debt seems unlikely. However, unanticipated inflation serves, in effect, as a partial default on nominal obligations. Furthermore, as shown here, the incentive to default may be low in infinite horizon economies.

11. There are two reasons for the different policy implications. First, Lucas and Stokey (1983) consider a richer class of government policies. In particular, they allow for state-contingent debt, which has returns depend on the level of government consumption. For example, debt issued in wartime should have the feature that the return on the debt is low if the war continues and high if the war ends. The stock of outstanding debt is then low when government spending stays high, and the debt level is low when the outlook is for low government spending. Lucas and Stokey argue that this policy could be implemented by high inflation rates during wartime and a deflation after a war. Second, Barro (1979) and Aschauer (1988) implicitly assume that the interest rate is constant, independent of government policy. One rationalization of this assumption is that consumers and the government can borrow in the world market at constant interest rates. The problem with this rationalization is that in such an environment, consumption and labor supply are constant in every period, independent of the level of government consumption. This prediction clearly goes against the facts.

12. Note that this state-contingent default is equivalent to state-contingent debt. If the government sold debt that promised payment in peacetime and no payment in wartime, the outcomes would be the same.

13. Grossman and Van Huyck (1988) make a similar argument.

II

Monetary and Budget Policy Analysis in Closed Economies

The chapters in this section use tractable general equilibrium models to analyze the effects of national monetary and budget policies in closed economies. The authors had to take stands on two basic issues:

- How should monetary and budget policies be defined?
- Why do agents hold money?

While the definition of policies seems a mundane issue, it is crucial in understanding the effects of policy changes studied in alternative models. Let us in general call a monetary policy change *expansionary* if it results in an increased quantity of money. Many studies in the economics literature define an expansionary monetary policy as a *helicopter drop*; that is, money is distributed to individuals as if dropped from a helicopter, with no other changes in policies.

The definition of monetary policy is different for the chapters in this section. In order to clearly describe the difference, let us assume the existence of separate monetary and budget authorities. The budget authority sets tax rates and determines expenditures except for interest payments on the debt. The budget authority is assumed to issue bonds if the budget (including interest payments) is in deficit and to retire bonds if it is in surplus. The monetary authority is assumed to conduct open market operations by exchanging (base) money and government bonds. For example, an open market purchase of bonds takes bonds out of the market and replaces them with currency or bank reserves. At a point in time in these models, budget policy determines the total debt of the government—the sum of bonds and money—while monetary policy determines the mix of debt—the ratio of bonds to money.

An expansionary monetary policy thus is defined differently in this section's chapters than in much of the literature. Here it is defined as an increase in the quantity of money with the total debt of the government held fixed. In other studies that consider helicopter drops, it is defined as an increase in the quantity of money with an equal increase in the total debt of the government. Thus, according to this section's chapters, a helicopter drop is both a budget policy change and a monetary policy change. The budget policy change is an increase in government transfers financed by the issue of bonds. The monetary policy change is the purchase of those bonds in exchange for base money. This difference in policy experiments must be kept in mind when comparing the effects of monetary policy changes in different models.

In this section's models, money and bonds are assumed to be *fiat*, having no intrinsic value and not being explicitly backed by the assets or tax revenues of the government. So before one can explain why agents hold money, one must explain why agents hold any fiat debt—either non—interest-bearing money or interest-bearing bonds. The device used to give fiat debt value in these models is to assume an economic structure in which some desirable transactions would not be possible without the debt. That is, if individuals had only goods or their private debt to offer in trade, they frequently would not be able to find sellers of the good they desire who would accept their means of payment. This is referred to in the literature as an *absence of a double coincidence of wants*. In these economic structures, however, the fiat debt could serve as a medium of exchange, which would create a double coincidence of wants. Sellers would accept the fiat debt in payment since they would be assured that they could use it to purchase the goods they desire.

An economic structure that simply gives this medium of exchange function to fiat debt is the *overlapping generations model*. In the simplest version of this model, people live for two periods, with a new generation born each period. In any one period, two generations of like individuals exist: the old and the young. In the model, welfare-improving trades would have the young in each period provide some goods to the existing old. These trades cannot be carried out privately, however, because there is a complete absence of a double coincidence of wants. If the young privately gave goods to the old, they would want to be repaid in the next period; that is, they would want to make a private loan. But the old will not be around in the next period; hence, they cannot repay the loans.

With fiat debt, in effect, trades across generations can be made. When fiat debt has value, the current young are willing to sell goods to the old in exchange for the old's holdings of this debt. The debt is carried over to the next period, by which time the current young have aged to become the next period's old. Then similar transactions are carried out between the old and the young. By accepting the fiat debt, the young pass goods on to the old. Thus, without fiat debt, no trades are possible; with it, some beneficial trades are. This is what gives fiat debt value in the models in this section.

Even when there is a rationale for individuals to hold and value fiat debt, there still must be an explanation for why they hold non–interest-bearing money when interest-bearing bonds are available. Chapter 4 on legal restrictions by Wallace addresses this issue. Wallace argues that government restrictions which prevent some types of financial exchanges are an important part of the explanation. Without any restrictions, Wallace argues, financial intermediaries would arise which issue private money backed 100 percent by safe government securities. This private money would be a perfect substitute for government money. It would be issued until the profit from an extra dollar put into circulation, the interest rate earned on the bonds backing the private dollar, was just equal to the cost of intermediation. But in this case, Wallace reasons, the interest rate on government securities would be much lower than what we actually observe. That is because intermediation costs for similar activities, such as those performed by mutual funds, are actually very low. So Wallace argues that *legal restrictions*, which prevent some types of transactions in order to increase the demand for the government's money, are needed to explain why people hold both money and bonds when bonds significantly dominate in rate of return.

Why do governments impose such restrictions? Wallace suggests that it allows them to implicitly tax poor and wealthy individuals at different rates. Another possible explanation is that it gives the government two policy instruments. Money can be used to stabilize the price level over time, while bonds can be used to smooth tax rates over time.

In Chapter 5, on unpleasant choices, Wallace examines the effects of monetary policy in an overlapping generations model with legal restrictions. The restrictions are taken to be reserve requirements against savings, where the reserves must be held in the form of money. These restrictions impose a real friction. Because of them, changes in monetary policy have real effects, such as causing changes in the real interest rate, and they affect different groups of individuals differently, such as causing opposite changes in the welfare of lenders and borrowers. Any change in monetary policy then is unpleasant, because it adversely affects the welfare of some group in society.

The next three chapters take up the topic of unpleasant monetarist arithmetic, in which authors question the independence of monetary and budget policies. In Chapter 6, Sargent and Wallace use an overlapping generations model with legal restrictions to derive the implication that an initially nonaccommodating monetary policy in the face of an easing budget policy can be inflationary. This result is what is known as *unpleasant monetarist arithmetic*. Sargent and Wallace show that if the government permanently increases its budget deficit net of interest and if the real interest rate exceeds the economy's real growth rate, the monetary authority must accommodate eventually by purchasing the debt in exchange for money. If it doesn't, the interest expense on the debt will multiply and eventually exceed the government's capacity to tax. Sargent and Wallace show that it can be less inflationary, even in the short run, if the monetary authority accommodates sooner rather than later.

Darby, in Chapter 7, shows that the unpleasant arithmetic need not follow when the real interest rate is less than the real growth rate. In this case, bonds bring more resources into the government than the government pays out. Thus, the government can finance increased deficits with bond issue alone. Moreover, Darby points out that in recent U.S. history the real interest rate on government debt has in fact been below the economy's real growth rate.

In Chapter 8, Miller and Sargent reply to Darby that although historically the real interest rate has been below the economy's growth rate, higher budget deficits, such as those projected then for the 1980s, might still require monetary accommodation. Miller and Sargent base their analysis on an overlapping generations model with legal restrictions and physical capital in which the real rate of return on capital is variable and determined by factors within the model. Their analysis suggests that even when the real interest rate is initially below the economy's growth rate, higher budget deficits may not be sustainable with bond issue alone for two reasons:

1. The higher deficits may exceed the revenue-raising capacity of the bonds.

2. The higher deficits may raise interest rates enough so that after the budget policy change the real interest rate exceeds the economy's growth rate.

When initially published, these three papers as a group brought attention to the issue of policy independence. They also led analysts to examine the projected growth of government debt relative to the growth in the economy to determine the sustainability of current federal budget and monetary policies.

In Chapter 9, Aiyagari illustrates why government policies that shift the burden of taxes over time, such as temporary budget deficits or social security, have real effects in standard overlapping generations models and not in many other models found in the literature. The key is how individuals are linked over time. If people lived forever, an assumption made in many models, the types of policies mentioned above would have no real effects because people could adjust their savings to offset the changes over time in their taxes. In overlapping generations models, people don't live forever, so they cannot always perfectly offset tax changes. Aiyagari shows, however, that when parents make bequests to their children or when children give gifts to their parents, the generations of a family are linked into a dynasty that behaves, in an economic sense, like a person who lives forever. With generations linked completely, Aiyagari shows that temporary deficit financing and social security have no real effects.

The last chapter of this section, Chapter 10, is different from the rest. Rather than just explaining what current policies and their effects are, an exercise in *positive economics*, Chari and Miller propose what policies should be, an exercise in *normative economics*. They attempt to apply many of the ideas and concepts contained in the earlier chapters in this volume, including

- The need to express policies in terms of rules.
- The need to implement mutually consistent monetary and budget policies.
- The desirability of binding the actions of policymakers.

Chari and Miller also draw on general principles from modern public finance theory, such as having users pay for services and having taxes smoothed over time.

4

A Legal Restrictions Theory of the Demand for "Money" and the Role of Monetary Policy

Neil Wallace

In this paper, I discuss a simple theory that explains the coexistence of alternative assets, some of which have significantly higher yields or returns than others.[1] The theory attributes such a paradoxical pattern of returns among assets to legal restrictions on private intermediation, an example being the widespread prohibition against private bank note issue. As I will show, this theory has as an almost immediate implication that monetary policy—central bank asset exchanges accomplished through open market operations or discount window lending—matters only in the presence of binding legal restrictions on private intermediation.[2]

In the first section, I describe obvious instances of paradoxical rate-of-return patterns and argue that these would disappear under laissez-faire—that is, in the absence of legal restrictions on private intermediation. The implication for monetary policy—that monetary policy under laissez-faire does not affect anything, not even the price level—is explained in the second section. In the third section, I discuss whether legal restrictions ought to be imposed. Although I do not arrive at a recommendation, I do discuss some of the considerations that are relevant to arriving at one.

Legal Restrictions and the Coexistence of High- and Low-Return Assets

An obvious instance of a paradoxical pattern of returns among assets is the coexistence of, on the one hand, U.S. Federal Reserve notes (U.S. currency) and, on the other hand, interest-bearing securities that are default-free. By default-free, I mean that these securities, with complete certainty, entitle their owner to a stated amount of currency at some future date. Examples

Reprinted from the *Federal Reserve Bank of Minneapolis Quarterly Review*, Winter 1983.

of such securities are U.S. savings bonds and Treasury bills. Our first task is to identify the features of these securities that prevent them from playing the same role in transactions as Federal Reserve notes. For if they could play that role, then it is hard to see why anyone would hold non—interest-bearing currency instead of the interest-bearing securities.

U.S. savings bonds, although issued in various and small denominations, are nonnegotiable. U.S. Treasury bills are negotiable and, until recently, were bearer securities, but they have always been issued in large denominations, for the most part in $10,000 denominations. I now argue that non-negotiability in the case of savings bonds and large denomination in the case of bearer Treasury bills are *necessary* to explain why they cannot be substituted for Federal Reserve notes as alternative forms of currency.

Consider what would happen if the Treasury started issuing bearer Treasury bills in small denominations—perhaps, $20s, $50s, and $100s. To be precise, suppose each such bill when issued says that the Treasury will pay the bearer at a date one year from the issue date or thereafter x dollars of Federal Reserve notes, where x is either 20, 50, or 100. Let us say that these bills are distinguishable from Federal Reserve notes because they are red, not green, but that they are the same physical size as Federal Reserve notes (and do not smell too much worse or have other obnoxious but inessential characteristics). If such bills were to coexist with Federal Reserve notes, then would they sell at a discount (so that they bear interest) or would they sell at par (and not bear interest)?

If these bills and Federal Reserve notes were to coexist, then they would sell at par and be used interchangeably with Federal Reserve notes in the same way that Lincoln and Indianhead pennies coexisted and were used interchangeably. To see this, consider what would happen at a date very close to the maturity date of the bills. If the bills were selling at a discount at such a date, then everyone would prefer them to Federal Reserve notes because the bills would surely appreciate and the Federal Reserve notes would not. But if everyone chose the bills, then the Federal Reserve notes would not be held, and the two would not coexist. Therefore, at a date sufficiently close to the maturity date of the bills, the bills would sell at par if they and Federal Reserve notes were to coexist. Now consider a somewhat earlier date. Since this date bears the same relationship to the first date we considered as the latter did to the maturity date and since we have concluded that the bills would sell at par at the date near maturity, we can apply the argument used above to the earlier date. Our conclusion is the same: small-denomination bearer Treasury bills would sell at par if they and Federal Reserve notes were to coexist. Repeated application of this argument—considering dates further and further from the maturity date of the bills and nearer and nearer to their issue date—shows that these bills would sell at par at every date.[3] Note, moreover, that if these small-denomination Treasury bills were selling at par, then there would be no incentive to turn them in at their maturity date; they would continue to circulate.

U.S. savings bonds differ from these hypothetical small-denomination Treasury bills only because they are very far from being bearer securities; they are nonnegotiable. Until very recently, when they ceased being bearer securities, U.S. Treasury bills differed only in their large denomination. That is why I claim that nonnegotiability in the case of savings bonds and large denomination in the case of bearer Treasury bills are necessary in order to explain how Federal Reserve notes can coexist with these securities while they bear substantial interest.

Our next task is to consider whether nonnegotiability and large denomination are *sufficient* for explaining the coexistence paradox. These features do explain why an individual with $10 or $20 in Federal Reserve notes does not switch them into savings bonds or Treasury bills even when those securities bear substantial interest. However, nonnegotiability and large denomination are not sufficient to explain the rate-of-return paradox because by themselves they fail to rule out arbitrage by financial institutions between such interest-bearing securities and small-denomination bearer notes. To see this, let us focus on denomination and begin with an analogy involving large and small packages of butter.

Suppose, for example, that we observe butter in one-pound packages selling for $1 per pound and butter in one-hundred-pound packages selling for 25 cents per pound. Is it an adequate explanation of this spread in prices per pound to say that individual households buy one-pound packages because they may not have or want to devote $25 to buying butter and they may not be able to transport or store one-hundred-pound packages? Obviously, such reasons are not adequate if there are sufficiently inexpensive ways to convert large packages into small packages and if there is free entry into the business of converting large packages into small packages.

If there is free entry into the business of converting large packages of butter into small packages, then the least costly technique for doing this sets an upper bound on the spread between prices per pound of large and small packages—that is, an upper bound on the quantity discount. Explanations of an observed quantity discount along the lines of individual households having small refrigerators are relevant only if barriers of one sort or another prevent the use of the least costly means or if individual

Some Applications of the Legal Restrictions Theory

The legal restrictions theory described in this article has been applied to many issues in monetary theory and policy. A list and brief descriptions of some of these applications follow.

International Monetary Systems

Kareken and Wallace (1978b, 1981) and Wallace [in Chapter 11] apply the legal restrictions theory to exchange rate systems. In a system of freely floating exchange rates among fiat currencies issued by different countries, legal restrictions that inhibit substitution among the currencies are necessary in order for exchange rates to be determined. Absent such restrictions, no natural forces determine exchange rates.

Multiple Government Liabilities

Most governments impose legal restrictions on private intermediaries and issue a variety of liabilities—for example, currency and bonds. Bryant and Wallace (1984) rationalize both in terms of price discrimination. Legal restrictions create separate markets for the different liabilities by preventing arbitrage among them; the composition of government liabilities determines relative sales by the government in the separated markets. Bryant and Wallace display circumstances in which these devices permit the levying of a discriminatory inflation tax that is preferable to the levying of a uniform inflation tax.

The Real Bills Doctrine

This doctrine asserts that the quantity of money ought to vary with the needs of trade and that it will vary appropriately if private credit markets are allowed to function without interference. Sargent and Wallace (1982) offer a defense of this much-criticized doctrine.

Commodity Money

Sargent and Wallace (1983) model commodity money as one of several of the storable goods (capital goods) in a growth model. Among the topics addressed are the nature of the inefficiency of commodity money; the validity of quantity-theory predictions for commodity money systems; the circumstances under which one commodity emerges naturally as the commodity money; and the role of inside money (money backed by private debt) in commodity money systems.

household use of large packages is, in effect, the least costly way of carrying out such conversion. The latter seems unlikely.

Similar considerations apply in the case of the spread between the rate of return on Federal Reserve notes and that on default-free securities. In particular, consider a financial intermediary that does nothing but buy default-free securities—for example, U.S. Treasury bills—and issue bearer notes in small denominations with maturities that coincide with those of the default-free securities it holds. Such an intermediary is perfectly hedged so that, fraud aside, its bearer notes are as safe as the securities it holds as backing for them. It follows that such an activity gives rise to the same situation that prevails if the Treasury itself issues small-denomination bearer securities. If we suppose that, as part of its business, this intermediary takes actions that prevent fraud, then we conclude, exactly as we did for small-denomination bearer securities issued by the Treasury, that the bearer notes issued by such intermediaries would sell at par and be used interchangeably with Federal Reserve notes if the two were to coexist.

Since the revenue for this intermediation business comes from buying default-free securities at a discount and issuing bearer notes at par, in an equilibrium with free entry the discount on default-free securities like Treasury bills must be small enough so that it is not profitable to expand this activity. That is the case when the discount is just sufficient to cover the costs of engaging in the business. In other words, in a laissez-faire system in which Federal Reserve notes and default-free securities like Treasury bills coexist, the yield or nominal rate of return on the latter is bounded above by the least costly way of operating such a financial intermediation business.

Rough estimates of the magnitude of this cost can be inferred from two sources: the cost of operating financial intermediaries in existing intermediary activities and the cost to the U.S. Treasury and Federal Reserve of issuing and maintaining the stock of Federal Reserve notes. Many financial intermediaries—common stock and money market mutual funds—operate at spreads of 1 percent or less. There is no reason to expect that the cost of intermediating securities like Treasury bills into bearer notes would be much different from the cost of operating these intermediaries. This view is buttressed by the fact that, for all but the smallest denominations, the cost to the Treasury and Federal Reserve of maintaining Federal Reserve currency is a small fraction of 1 percent of the outstanding stock. These observations suggest that our hypothetical intermediary could operate with a discount that is close to zero and, hence, suggest that the upper bound on nominal interest rates on safe securities under laissez-faire would be close to zero.

Thus far my argument says that if Federal Reserve notes and default-free securities like Treasury bills coexist under laissez-faire, then nominal interest rates are close to zero. But they may not coexist. Laissez-faire means, among other things, no reserve requirements, no capital controls of the sort recently put into effect in Mexico, and so on. In other words, laissez-faire means the absence of legal restrictions that tend, among other things, to enhance the demand for a government's currency. Thus, the imposition of laissez-faire would almost certainly reduce the demand for government currency. It could even reduce it to zero. A zero demand for a government's currency should be interpreted as the abandonment of one monetary unit in favor of another—for example, the abandonment of the dollar in favor of one ounce of gold. Thus, my prediction of the effects of imposing laissez-faire takes the form of an either/or statement: either nominal interest rates go to zero or existing government currency becomes worthless.

While these possibilities seem extreme, they are not unfamiliar to economists. They match almost completely two possibilities described by Samuelson (1947, p. 123):

It is true that in a world involving no transaction friction and no uncertainty, there would be no reason for a spread between the yield on any two assets, and hence there would be no difference in the yield on money and on securities. Hicks concludes, therefore, that securities will not bear interest but will accommodate themselves to the yield on money. It is equally possible and more illuminating to suppose that under these conditions money adjusts itself to the yield of securities. In fact, in such a world securities themselves would circulate as money and be acceptable in transactions; demand bank deposits would bear interest, just as they often did in this country in the period of the twenties. And if money could not make the adjustment, as in the case of metal counters which Aristotle tells us are barren, it would pass out of use, wither away and die, become a free good.

What is added in my discussion is the claim that the only significant frictions are those created by legal restrictions. Moreover, uncertainty seems not to be relevant because the hypothetical note-issuing intermediary described above is perfectly hedged.[4]

Legal Restrictions and Monetary Policy

In this section, let us make an additional assumption, which has already been hinted at above—namely, that a common and constant average-cost technology for the production and distribution of small-denomination bearer notes is available to the government and to potential private sector intermediaries. In terms of our butter analogy, this says that the government has neither a technological advantage nor a technological disadvantage relative to the private sector when it comes to converting large packages into small packages and that the cost per unit of producing small packages from large ones does not depend on the number produced. Under this assumption, my argument is that central bank intermediation activities, apart from outright credit subsidies, have no significant effects under laissez-faire.

In order to be concrete, I will discuss central bank intermediation in terms of an open market purchase of Treasury bills. This results in the private sector holding fewer bills and more Federal Reserve notes. Under laissez-faire, the equilibrium adjustment is a contraction in the scale of operations of private note-issuing intermediaries, a contraction that exactly offsets the open market purchase. If it is costly in terms of resources to carry out this private intermediation, then the contraction frees some resources—paper, people to run the presses, and so on. With technological symmetry between the private sector and the government, these are precisely the resources the government needs in order to provide and maintain the larger outstanding stock of government currency. In other words, under laissez-faire and technological symmetry, the open market purchase does no more than change the location from the private sector to the government of a given quantity of an economic activity, the production of small-denomination bearer notes. Nothing else is affected, neither interest rates nor the price level nor the level of economic activity. A similar argument applies to open market sales.[5]

Matters are very different under binding legal restrictions on private intermediation. Let us discuss what would happen in terms of our butter analogy. Suppose the government has a legal monopoly on the business of converting large packages into small ones. Then much depends on the scale at which it chooses to operate. Under our assumptions, if the government chooses the output level that would have been produced in the absence of the legal monopoly, then the legal restriction does not matter. If it chooses a lower level of output, then it makes the legal restriction binding. An obvious measure of bindingness is the observed spread in prices per pound of small and large packages. How much greater is the observed spread than that which would obtain under laissez-faire?

The Federal Reserve does, of course, have a legal monopoly on the issue of small-denomination bearer notes in the United States. By its choice of an open market and discount window strategy, it determines how binding this legal restriction turns out to be. The appropriate measure of bindingness is the observed discount on Treasury bills. This corresponds exactly to the observed quantity discount on large packages of butter.

An important qualification is that the central bank not conduct its intermediation activities so as to incur losses. In terms of our butter analogy, if the government sells small packages at a price that does not permit it to cover costs, then even with free entry the government's operations clearly matter. To consider an intermediation example, suppose the central bank is allowed to incur losses and does so by granting both safe and risky loans at the laissez-faire interest rate on safe loans. Then, since risky loans would not otherwise be available at that rate, the central bank's lending has significant effects.

Thus, for a central bank constrained not to incur losses on average, our conclusion is that its intermediation matters if and only if there exist profitable arbitrage opportunities that the private sector cannot exploit because of legal restrictions.

The most objectionable of the assumptions used to obtain this result may be the constant-cost assumption. The provision of small-denomination bearer notes may be a decreasing average-cost activity, perhaps because the cost of inhibiting counterfeiting of the notes of a particular issuer does not increase in proportion to the value of the notes outstanding. If note issue is a decreasing cost activity, then the least costly way of providing small-denomination bearer notes is by way of a single supplier. Moreover, if there are decreasing average costs, then we cannot conclude that an open market operation under laissez-faire simply shifts the location of a given activity between the government and the private sector. We can, however, continue to conclude that under laissez-faire the cost structure for providing small-denomination bearer notes implies an upper bound on nominal interest rates on default-free securities when these and non–interest-bearing currency coexist. Also, we can continue to conclude that the degree to which legal restrictions are binding is to be judged by the magnitude of such interest rates.

Why Impose Legal Restrictions?

So far, nothing has been said about what legal restrictions, if any, ought to be imposed and what central bank intermediation strategy ought to be followed. Although I will not arrive at a recommendation, I will discuss some of the presumed costs and benefits of legal restrictions on private intermediation.

Legal restrictions on private intermediation give rise to costs that are similar to those that accompany barriers to trade in other contexts: resources tend to be misallocated under binding restrictions. For example, consider a prohibition on private note issue. If this prohibition is binding, then some borrowers face higher interest rates on loans than they would if they, directly or through "banks," were able to borrow by issuing small-denomination bearer notes. The prohibition puts a barrier between borrowers and lenders and, hence, inhibits the carrying out of some beneficial intertemporal trade.

The same point can be made in a slightly different way. We are familiar with proposals that urge that the quantities of certain private sector liabilities be controlled—for example, proposals that urge that the quantity of private bank notes should be zero or that the quantity of deposits subject to check should grow at some prescribed rate. But what is so special about deposits subject to check and private bank notes? They are particular private credit instruments. If it makes sense to control their quantities, why not those of other credit instruments? For example, most economists would not favor a proposal to constrain the dollar volume of mortgages on single family residences to grow at a prescribed rate. Almost certainly, most would say that it is a necessary feature of a well-functioning credit system that the number of mortgages be determined in the market and not be set administratively. But if this is right for one set of private credit instruments, why is it not right for all? No satisfactory answer has ever been given.

One presumed benefit of legal restrictions that has played a prominent role in prior discussions rests on the notion that it would be much more difficult to control the price level were it not for restrictions on credit instruments like private bank notes and checking deposits. Since some forms of private debt are better substitutes than others for government currency—or, under a gold standard, gold coins—this notion may be valid. In particular, if there is a variable demand for forms of credit that under laissez-faire would compete closely with government currency or gold coins, then it can happen that the price level would be more variable under laissez-faire than under legal restrictions that limit or prohibit the issue of such forms of private debt.[6] Given that such restrictions, when they are binding, misallocate resources, it follows that there can be a trade-off between achieving price level stability and achieving efficient resource allocation through credit markets.

However, this tradeoff presents a problem only if we accept price level stability as a goal, as an end in itself. That it should be a goal is not obvious. Although widely espoused as a goal, there exist no complete arguments leading to the conclusion that people are on average better off the more stable the price level, *given* the steps that have to be taken to attain greater stability of the price level. On the contrary, as Sargent and Wallace (1982) argue, the restrictions that make greater price level stability possible hurt some people and benefit others, while on average, in a certain sense, making all worse off.

I suspect that those who espouse price level stability as a goal do so partly because they think it is easy to attain; all that is needed is the right open market or intermediation strategy on the part of the central bank. That view, however, ignores what I argued above, namely, that central bank intermediation matters only in the presence of binding legal restrictions. Without such restrictions, it is no easier to achieve price level stability than it is to achieve stability of some relative price.

There is another potential benefit from legal restrictions on private intermediation that is less easy to dismiss. Such restrictions help governments tax asset holdings. Most legal restrictions on private intermediation have been and are the result of governments trying to enhance the demand for their liabilities. In general, such restrictions make it easier for governments to borrow and to tax by inflation. The fact that the restrictions misallocate resources is not decisive since the same can be said of virtually all taxes that are levied.

Finally, it should be noted that the above discussion does not deal with the transition from one set of restrictions to another. As with any major change in policy regime, substantial wealth redistribution may accompany alterations in legal restrictions on private intermediation.

Concluding Remarks

The theory I have described does two things. At a positive level, it suggests that we explain paradoxical rate-of-return patterns by way of legal restrictions on the kinds of assets and liabilities that the private sector can hold and issue. At a normative level, it suggests that we consider the consequences of alternative legal restrictions on the financial system in much the same way as we consider restrictions on trade in other contexts and, in particular, that we not be content with describing those consequences only in terms of their effects on variables like the price level and interest rates.

Notes

An earlier version of this paper was prepared for a November 1982 conference on interest rate deregulation and monetary policy sponsored by the Federal Reserve Bank of San Francisco.

1. Hicks (1935) views this coexistence as the main puzzle facing monetary theory. He says (p. 5), "This, as I see it, is really the central issue in the pure theory of money. Either we have to give an explanation of the fact that people do hold money when rates of interest are positive, or we have to evade the difficulty somehow."

2. See Fama 1980 and Hall 1982 for other discussions of the legal restrictions theory. Some other applications of the theory are listed in the box in this article.

3. Liberty Bonds, which were issued during World War I as bearer securities in denominations as small as $50, actually seem to have circulated as currency from time to time. In August 1918, the secretary of the treasury, William Gibbs McAdoo, complained that merchants were accepting Liberty Bonds in exchange for merchandise (*New York Times*, August 23, 1918).

On September 20, 1920, Theodore Hardee, the director of the Treasury Department's Government Savings Organization for the Twelfth District, sent a statement from the secretary of the treasury entitled "On the Evils of Exchanging Merchandise for Liberty Bonds" to the Commonwealth Club in San Francisco. The statement began: "It has been brought to my attention that numbers of merchants throughout the country are offering to take Liberty Loan Bonds at par, or even in some cases at a premium, in exchange for merchandise."

4. Some readers may wonder whether the coexistence in the U.S. of non—interest-bearing checking accounts and interest-bearing Treasury bills is an important counterexample to the claim that rate-of-return disparities are to be explained by legal restrictions. It is not, because government regulations and subsidies—interest ceilings, reserve requirements, zero marginal-cost check clearing by the Federal Reserve, and the failure to tax income in the form of transaction services—explain the way checking account services have been priced. In the absence of these forms of government interference, most observers predict that checking accounts would pay interest at the market rate with charges levied on a per transaction basis. (Note that under such pricing of demand deposit services, there would be no reason to distinguish the part of wealth that is subject to transfer by check from the part that is not, and checking accounts, whether distinguishable or not, could not be treated as part of the "cash" of inventory models of money demand. See, for example, Baumol 1952 and Tobin 1956.)

5. The result that central bank intermediation does not matter under laissez-faire also holds for central bank exchanges of Federal Reserve notes for other assets—risky mortgages, risky commercial loans, or common stock. It is a straightforward extension of a well-known finding in corporate finance called the Modigliani-Miller theorem. (See Stiglitz 1969 and Wallace 1981.)

6. For a complete example that exhibits this possibility, see Sargent and Wallace 1982.

5 Some of the Choices for Monetary Policy

Neil Wallace

Almost daily, the Federal Reserve is offered conflicting advice about how to conduct monetary policy. Some people, such as the members of the Shadow Open Market Committee, advise the Fed to gradually slow the growth of money and let interest rates take care of themselves. Others, such as foreign central bankers, advise the Fed to lower interest rates and let money grow as it may. And still others, such as the *Wall Street Journal* and various supply-siders, advise the Fed to stabilize commodity prices and pay little attention to either money growth or interest rates.

Though conflicting, the advice the Fed receives seems to be based on a common view that choosing a monetary policy is a technical problem. The presumption seems to be that there is a unique best policy for the Fed to follow and the Fed's problem is to find it. Those advising the Fed seem to see their task as convincing the Fed that their particular analysis is the right one.

This attitude is somewhat hard to understand. Most economists agree that the choice of a government policy should be based on an analysis of how individual welfare is affected and that in general any policy choice results in both gainers and losers. How, then, can those advising the Fed argue that one particular monetary policy is best? Do they think they have found a policy that will benefit everyone and harm no one? Or are they arguing for a policy which they recognize will help some and hurt others but which reflects their personal judgment about how the interests of different groups should be weighted?

Considering the state of monetary policy analysis, this ambiguity is perhaps not surprising. Until recently, economists have simply not been able to build models which describe how individual welfare is affected by

Reprinted from the *Federal Reserve Bank of Minneapolis Quarterly Review*, Winter 1984.

alternative monetary policies. Most of the models economists use to analyze monetary policies only consider how the Fed's actions affect certain
aggregate features of the economy; they do not directly describe what
happens to the individuals who make up the economy.

This paper describes a simple model which provides a coherent analysis
of how monetary policy affects people in different circumstances.[1] The
model is populated by three types of agents: borrowers, lenders, and people who hold assets valued in terms of the current price level (nominally
denominated assets, like currency). A government is assumed to run a permanent budget deficit which it finances by issuing fiat money and bonds.
The monetary policy problem in this model is how to choose paths of
money and bonds to finance this deficit.

The model demonstrates that different policy choices affect the three
types of people differently. In a situation like that in the United States
today—where the government has a large prospective deficit and is a net
debtor and where the real interest rate is high—the model says a more
accommodative monetary policy would raise the price level but lower rates
of inflation and real interest.[2] Such an outcome, the model says, would
make the holders of nominally denominated assets worse off and borrowers better off, while lenders could be made either better or worse off.

The particular implications of the model for alternative monetary policies should be viewed cautiously, for they probably could be altered by
reasonable changes in assumptions. What cannot be easily altered, however, is the message that the Fed's task as it selects a monetary policy is a
difficult one—to weigh conflicting interests.

The Model

Here I describe, in detail, the people and the government in my model
economy, how they behave, and precisely what I mean by *monetary policy*.

The People

The people in this model live only two periods. At each date t (where t is
an integer) a new generation—generation t—of two-period–lived people
appears. Thus, members of generation t are in this economy at t and $t + 1$
only, and at any date t, the population consists of the members of generation $t - 1$ (who are old at t) and the members of generation t (who are
young at t).

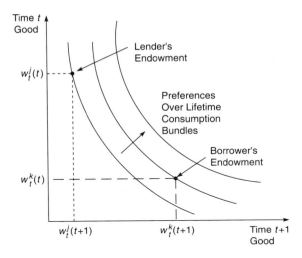

Figure 5.1
The Preferences and Endowments of Borrowers and Lenders in Generation t

At each date, only one good exists. The good that exists at date t is called the time t good. Each member of generation t has preferences about the amounts of the time t good and the time $t + 1$ good that she or he would like to consume in a lifetime (preferences about lifetime consumption bundles). I represent such preferences by an *indifference curve* map of the kind shown in Figure 5.1. Any combination of amounts of time t and time $t + 1$ goods is on some indifference curve (even though I have shown only some of the curves). Each individual member of generation t is indifferent among bundles of the two goods on the same indifference curve, and (because people prefer more goods to less) each prefers bundles on higher indifference curves (in the direction of the arrow) to bundles on lower indifference curves.

Each member of generation t also has an income stream (an endowment) consisting of some amounts of the time t good and the time $t + 1$ good, denoted $w_i^j(t)$ and $w_i^j(t + 1)$, respectively, for member j of generation t. I assume that these goods cannot be produced and, in particular, that the time t good cannot be stored to produce the time $t + 1$ good. In other words, unless member j engages in some sort of trade, she or he is stuck with the endowment as a lifetime consumption bundle.

To keep things simple, I assume that different generations are identical and that there is a limited kind of diversity within each generation. Each generation consists of two groups of people. Members of one group, whom I call *lenders* (or savers), are identical and have preferences and endowments that lead them to want to lend (or save) at most rates of return. Members of the other group, whom I call *borrowers* (or dissavers), are also identical and have preferences and endowments that lead them to want to borrow (or dissave) at most rates of return. As Figure 5.1 shows, lenders are heavily endowed with the time t good and borrowers with the time $t + 1$ good, so trades of the two goods between the two groups are natural.

I now describe competitive desired trades of the two goods by lenders and borrowers at various terms of trade (or rates of exchange). I denote these terms of trade r_t, which represents the price of the time t good in units of the time $t + 1$ good. Equivalently, r_t is the discount factor for computing the value at time t of the time $t + 1$ good; thus, time t wealth of member j of generation t in units of the time t good is $w_t^j(t) + [w_t^j(t + 1)/r_t]$. (Think of r_t as the gross real rate of interest, *gross* because it is 1 plus the real rate of interest.) The total trades lenders desire as a group at each r_t can be represented by a *market supply curve* of the time t good, a curve which describes the desired saving, or lending, of the group heavily endowed with the time t good. I denote this supply curve $S(r)$. Similarly, the total trades borrowers desire as a group at each r_t can be represented by a *market demand curve* for the time t good, a curve which describes the desired dissaving, or borrowing, of the group heavily endowed with the time $t + 1$ good. I denote this demand curve $D(r)$.

To find the $S(r)$ curve, I begin with one of the identical lenders. Figure 5.2 shows how much of the time t good one lender wants to trade when r_t has a particular value. The straight line is the upper boundary of all affordable bundles, the lender's *budget*, implied by that value of r_t. Assuming that the lender behaves competitively, as a price taker, her or his supply of the time t good at the particular value of r_t is the difference between how much of the good the lender has (the lender's endowment) and how much of the good the lender wants to consume (the lender's preferred consumption bundle) at that value of r_t. When faced with different values of r_t, the lender can afford different combinations of the two goods; for a higher r_t, for example, the lender's budget line tilts as in Figure 5.3. This changes the lender's preferred consumption bundle and so her or his desired trades. By facing the lender with different values of r_t, then, I can trace out how the lender's supply of the time t good depends on r_t. Since all lenders are identical, the $S(r)$ curve is simply the number of lenders in any generation times the supply of the time t good of the individual lender at each r_t. The

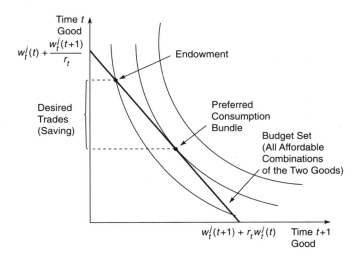

Figure 5.2 For a Particular r_t

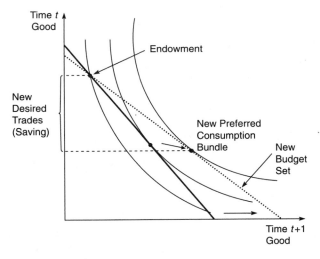

Figure 5.3 For a Higher r_t

Figures 5.2 and 5.3
A Lender's Supply of the Time t Good

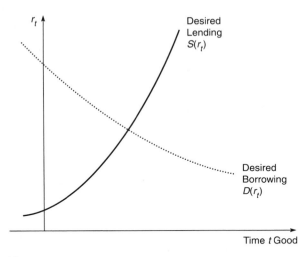

Figure 5.4
Market Supply of and Demand for the Time *t* Good

$D(r)$ curve is obtained from an analogous examination of borrowers. Examples of the resulting $S(r)$ and $D(r)$ curves are shown in Figure 5.4.

Because generations are identical in this economy, the $S(r)$ and $D(r)$ curves describe competitive desired trades of lenders and borrowers in every period. The first date (the current date or the date when a policy is chosen) is, however, special. At $t = 1$, the population of the economy consists of the members of generation 0 (the old) and the members of generation 1 (the young). The $S(r)$ and $D(r)$ curves describe the behavior of the members of generation 1 and successive generations. But those curves do not describe the behavior of generation 0 at $t = 1$. The members of generation 0 are assumed to initially own among them some time 1 good and some assets, like currency, that are valued in terms of the current price level (nominally denominated assets) which they offer to sell in order to be able to consume more of the time 1 good. Members of generation 0 act competitively to maximize their individual consumption of this good—that is, they supply all their assets at whatever is the market price (perfectly inelastically).

From this description of the economy's three groups of people, I can deduce how the well-being of the members of each group is affected by the value of currency and the rates of return they face. The members of generation 0, the old at the first date, are better off the higher the value at time 1 of their assets because the higher is that value (the lower the price level) the greater is the amount of time 1 consumption they can obtain. From Figure 5.3, it is clear that lenders are better off the higher the rate of return that they face and that borrowers are better off the lower the rate of return at which they can borrow. (As the rate of return changes, the budget line pivots on the endowment point, which lets the individuals reach a higher or lower indifference curve, or level of preferred consumption.) My task in this paper is to show how these rates of return and the initial value of currency—and so these three groups of people—are affected by the choice of a government policy.

The Government

Since I want to analyze monetary policy, I take as given the government's fiscal policy as measured by the path of the real deficit net of interest. More precisely, I take as given real government expenditures and real taxes (and, hence, their difference), with interest payments excluded from expenditures. The requirement that any such deficit be financed can be represented by the cash flow constraint of the combined fiscal and monetary authority (comparable to the Treasury and the Federal Reserve in the United States):

$$G_t = p_t(H_{t+1} - H_t) + p_t(P_t B_{t+1} - B_t) \qquad (1)$$

for all $t \geq 1$. Here G_t, measured in units of the time t good, is the government's real deficit net of interest payments. On the right side of equation (1) are two terms, each corresponding to a way of financing this deficit: the first term is the value in terms of good t of the government's addition to the outstanding monetary base (new fiat money) and the second term is the value of its addition to its outstanding debt (new fiat bonds). Specifically, the variables on the right side of (1) are defined this way:

$H_t =$ the monetary base (or high-powered money) that generation $t - 1$ starts with at time t

$p_t =$ the time t price of a unit of the monetary base in units of the time t consumption good

($1/p_t =$ the time t price level)

$B_t =$ the nominal face value, in terms of the monetary base, of the maturing government bonds owned by members of generation $t - 1$ at t

$P_t =$ the price at t, in terms of the monetary base, of a bond which pays one unit of the monetary base at $t + 1$

($1/P_t = 1$ plus the nominal interest rate at t).

This version of the cash flow constraint assumes for simplicity that all of the government's borrowing and lending takes the form of one-period nominal discount bonds, each bond when issued being a title to one unit of the monetary base at the next date. For a given path of the real deficit net of interest, a given sequence $G_1, G_2, \ldots, G_t$, for all $t \geq 1$, I will study how the economy is affected by alternative sequences for H_{t+1} and B_{t+1} (choices for the paths of base money and bonds, or for open market operations) which satisfy equation (1). I label the choices of the H_{t+1} and B_{t+1} sequences *monetary policy*.

Fixing the deficit sequence G_t means that the government does not vary either its expenditures or explicit taxes in response to different choices for the sequences of H_{t+1} and B_{t+1}. This means that government expenditures and explicit taxes are assumed to be indexed, or expressed in real terms. It also means that any decrease in government interest payments that accompanies an open market purchase of government bonds—such as occurs in the United States when the Federal Reserve returns the interest payments it receives to the Treasury—is used neither to finance additional government expenditures nor to reduce other taxes.

Discussing monetary policy in the sense of open market operations would be pointless if the model were not consistent with (a) both the monetary base and bonds being held and being worth something in terms of the consumption good and (b) bonds selling at a discount, $P_t < 1$, so that they bear interest in a way that makes them genuinely different from the monetary base. As the model stands, it is consistent with (a), but not with (b).

Elsewhere I have argued that legal restrictions on private financial intermediaries are generally necessary for nominally denominated default-free securities to bear nominal interest rates that are significantly positive and for monetary policy to have a role [Chapter 4]. Put very briefly, the argument is that, without any such legal restrictions, substantial nominal interest rates present a profit opportunity which private financial intermediaries exploit by buying interest-bearing bonds and selling liabilities (for example, bearer bank notes) that compete with base money. If such *arbitrage* does not make the monetary base worthless, then it drives nominal interest rates down to a level which just covers its costs (of printing bearer notes, for example). Moreover, if these costs are the same for everyone—private intermediaries and the government—then different open market policies are innocuous.

To prevent such arbitrage from rendering monetary policy meaningless in my model, I assume that a reserve requirement is imposed directly on each private lender. This means that each lender must hold in the form of base money a fraction, λ, of any savings (bonds or loans). This requirement implies that the gross real return lenders face is not simply the return on the bonds or loans the lender buys or makes, but is rather a weighted average (denoted r_t^a): the quantity λ times the gross real return on base money (r_t^m) plus the quantity $(1 - \lambda)$ times the gross real return on bonds or loans (r_t^l). Borrowers (dissavers), in contrast, face the same interest rate on their loans as does the government on its bonds (r_t^l). As we will see, the reserve requirement can produce a significantly positive nominal interest rate and an important role for monetary policy.

This kind of reserve requirement is intended to capture in a simple way the role that legal restrictions on private financial intermediaries play in actual economies. It accurately describes an economy in which all private lending or saving takes the form of bank or financial intermediary accounts which have a uniform reserve requirement. If these institutions operate competitively and costlessly, then the rate they pay on their liabilities, their deposits, is a weighted average of the rate they earn on reserves and the rate they earn on loans, the same weighted average described above as that facing private lenders in my model.

Equilibrium

I will be describing how this model economy evolves from $t = 1$ on into the indefinite future under the assumption that it evolves as a perfect foresight competitive equilibrium. *Competitive* means that people in the economy treat prices as beyond their control when they choose quantities, behavior assumed above in deriving the $S(r)$ and $D(r)$ curves. *Perfect foresight* in the model means that anticipated rates of return on assets equal actual or realized rates of return or, equivalently, that at each date t, $t \geq 1$, the young correctly anticipate the price level at the next date. *Equilibrium* means that all markets clear at each date t.

Market clearing in the model should be thought of as a sequence of trades of money and bonds for goods, trades which at each date simultaneously satisfy the supplies and demands of people and the government. At $t = 1$, the members of generation 0 (the old at $t = 1$) own $H_1 + B_1$, H_1 being the monetary base they carried over from the last period and B_1 being the face value of the government bonds they purchased when they were young. They cash in those bonds and offer the sum $H_1 + B_1$ in exchange for time 1 goods. At the same time, the government offers new bonds, B_2, and new base money, $H_2 - H_1$. In addition, the borrowers of generation 1 offer their own securities, private IOUs. All of these are purchased by the lenders of generation 1 in an equilibrium. At the next date, $t = 2$, the borrowers of generation 1 and the government repay their loans and a new set of transactions occurs similar to those at $t = 1$ but, of course, involving different people. This process is repeated date after date.

The conditions for such market clearing can be expressed succinctly.

DEFINITION.   Given λ, $H_1 + B_1 > 0$, and sequences for G_t and H_{t+1}, an equilibrium consists of sequences for p_t, P_t, r_t^m, r_t^l, r_t^a, and B_{t+1} that for all $t \geq 1$ satisfy equations (1) and

$$S(r_t^a) - D(r_t^l) = p_t(H_{t+1} + P_t B_{t+1}) \tag{2}$$

$$r_t^a \equiv \lambda r_t^m + (1 - \lambda)r_t^l \tag{3}$$

$$r_t^m = p_{t+1}/p_t \tag{4}$$

$$r_t^l = p_{t+1}/p_t P_t \tag{5}$$

$$r_t^l \geq r_t^m \tag{6}$$

$$p_t H_{t+1} \geq \lambda S(r_t^a) \tag{7}$$

with at least (6) or (7) at equality.

Equation (2) says that saving evaluated at the weighted average of the returns on base money and loans minus dissaving, or private borrowing, evaluated at the return on loans must equal the value of government liabilities. Equations (3), (4), and (5) define the return facing savers and contain our perfect foresight assumptions, namely, that the returns that determine choices at t match the actual returns. Inequalities (6) and (7) and the accompanying proviso are related to the reserve requirement. Inequality (6) says that the return on loans is at least as great as that on base money. If it were not, then unlimited gains could be made by borrowing and using the proceeds to acquire base money, activities which would not violate the reserve requirement. That being so, no equilibrium can violate (6). Inequality (7) expresses the reserve requirement: the value of base money must be at least as great as the established fraction times (gross) saving (or the value of the saving that lenders must hold as base money). The proviso arises in this way. If $r_t^l > r_t^m$, then wealth maximization implies that lenders hold no more than the minimum required amount of base money, which is to say that (7) holds at equality. Alternatively, if the value of base money exceeds the amount required to be held $[p_t H_{t+1} > \lambda S(r_t^a)]$, then wealth maximization implies that the return on base money is as great as the return on securities, which is (6) at equality.

Instead of trying to study all equilibria possible in this economy, I will assume that the real deficit net of interest, G_t, is a nonnegative constant, G, and focus on a small subset of equilibria, those for which real variables are constant through time. I will call these equilibria, which are relatively easy to describe, *stationary equilibria*. Stationary equilibria can also be distinguished according to whether or not (6) holds at strict inequality. Denoting constant values of r_t^m and r_t^l, respectively, r^m and r^l, I call an equilibrium in which $r^l > r^m$ a *binding equilibrium* and one in which $r^l = r^m$ a *nonbinding equilibrium*, where the words *binding* and *nonbinding* refer to whether or not the reserve requirement is actually constraining the choices of lenders.

The study of stationary equilibria is simplified by noting that in this economy attention can be limited to paths of fiat money and bonds, H_{t+1} and B_{t+1}, for which the ratio B_{t+1}/H_{t+1} is a constant, which I denote β. In a binding stationary equilibrium, the ratio B_{t+1}/H_{t+1} is necessarily a constant for all $t \geq 1$.[3] In a nonbinding stationary equilibrium, B_{t+1}/H_{t+1} need not be constant, but there is no harm in assuming that it is. As long as the paths of H_{t+1} and B_{t+1} are consistent with a nonbinding stationary equilibrium, there are paths with $B_{t+1}/H_{t+1} = \beta$, for some β, which are also consistent with the same stationary equilibrium. I will limit this monetary policy parameter, β, to be greater than -1.[4]

With the paths of H_{t+1} and B_{t+1} limited in this way, I can define a stationary equilibrium as follows.

DEFINITION.   Given λ, $H_1 + B_1 > 0$, G, and β, a stationary equilibrium consists of scalars (numbers) r^m, r^l, r^a, h, b, and p that satisfy

$$G = (1 - r^m)h + (1 - r^l)b \tag{8}$$

$$S(r^a) - D(r^l) = h + b \tag{9}$$

$$r^a = \lambda r^m + (1 - \lambda)r^l \tag{10}$$

$$r^l \geq r^m \tag{11}$$

$$h \geq \lambda S(r^a) \tag{12}$$

$$G = S(r^a) - D(r^l) - p_1(H_1 + B_1) \tag{13}$$

where either (11) *or* (12) *must hold at equality and where h denotes a constant real value of the monetary base*, $p_t H_{t+1}$, *and b denotes a constant real value of government bonds*, $p_t P_t B_{t+1}$.

Note that (8) is a stationary version of the government's cash flow constraint, equation (1), and that (13) comes from that constraint for the first date, $t = 1$. For constant real sequences, this definition and the earlier one are equivalent.[5]

Although I am mainly interested in binding stationary equilibria, understanding of the model will be enhanced by a brief study of nonbinding equilibria.

Nonbinding Stationary Equilibrium

Here, by definition, the returns on fiat money and bonds are equal, so in determining an equilibrium I seek a common value of r^m and r^l, which I will call simply r. According to equations (8) and (9), this r must satisfy

$$G = (1 - r)[S(r) - D(r)] \tag{14}$$

which is one equation in the unknown r. From equation (13), this r and p_1 must satisfy

$$G = [S(r) - D(r)] - p_1(H_1 + B_1) \tag{15}$$

where, recall, $H_1 + B_1$ is positive and is a given initial condition—the nominal wealth of the members of generation 0, the old at the first date. Finally, any r and positive p_1 satisfying equations (14) and (15) must also satisfy equation (12), the reserve requirement.[6] Note that equation (9) and the definitions of β, h, and b imply that $S(r) - D(r) = h(\beta + 1)$, or $h = [S(r) - D(r)]/(\beta + 1)$. Hence, equation (12) is satisfied if and only if

$$[S(r) - D(r)]/(\beta + 1) \geqslant \lambda S(r). \tag{16}$$

Since $S(r) - D(r) > 0$, a sufficiently small β, one near enough to -1, will imply that (16) is satisfied, while a sufficiently large β will rule that out.

To summarize, a nonbinding stationary equilibrium exists if, given G, there exist an r and a positive p_1 that satisfy equations (14) and (15) and if, given β, condition (16) is satisfied. There are, then, two separate reasons why such an equilibrium may not exist. One is that, given G, $S(r) - D(r)$ may not be large enough at r's that do not exceed 1 to satisfy equations (14) and (15). The other is that β may be too large to satisfy condition (16). In either case, I would look for a binding stationary equilibrium.

Binding Stationary Equilibrium

I begin the study of binding equilibria by finding two equations in the two rates of return, r^m and r^l, that must hold. Since $r^l > r^m$ in a binding equilibrium, inequality (12) must hold at equality. Substituting from it at equality and equation (9) into equation (8), I get the first equation, namely,

$$G = (1 - r^m)\lambda S(r^a) + (1 - r^l)[(1 - \lambda)S(r^a) - D(r^l)]. \tag{17}$$

The second equation, which is obtained by dividing equation (9) by (12) at equality, is

$$[S(r^a) - D(r^l)]/\lambda S(r^a) = 1 + (\beta r^m/r^l). \tag{18}$$

Since $r^a = \lambda r^m + (1 - \lambda)r^l$, equations (17) and (18) are two equations in two unknowns, r^m and r^l. If I can find a pair (r^m, r^l) satisfying equations (17) and (18) and $r^l \geqslant r^m$, then using that pair I would find p_1 from equation (13).

A Simple Special Case: Fixed Saving

Because equations (17) and (18) are complicated for general functions $S(r)$ and $D(r)$, I will examine in detail only a special case—one in which the saving of lenders is a constant level, S^*, that does not depend on the rate of return lenders face.[7] This assumption lets me solve equation (17) or r^m to get

$$r^m = [(\lambda S^* - G)/\lambda S^*] + \{(1 - r^l)[(1 - \lambda)S^* - D(r^l)]/\lambda S^*\} \tag{19}$$

and to solve equation (18) for βr^m to get

$$\beta r^m = r^l[(1 - \lambda)S^* - D(r^l)]/\lambda S^*. \tag{20}$$

Even though I have now made some very special simplifying assumptions, there remains a range of cases that potentially could be studied using equations (19) and (20). To narrow my focus further, I make three more assumptions. One involves the size of the deficit. For an equilibrium to exist, the real net-of-interest deficit, G, must not be so big that it cannot be financed through some combination of an inflation tax, the term $(1 - r^m)h$ in equation (8), and the earnings on government bonds, the term $(1 - r^l)b$ in equation (8). The assumption of constant saving implies a simple (sufficient) condition, which I adopt, that assures that G is not too big: the deficit is less than the monetary base in a binding equilibrium, or $G < \lambda S^*$. This assumption assures that the deficit could be financed by issues of base money only, with $b = 0$. Another, less critical assumption concerns the rate of return r^l that would clear the private credit market in the absence of government borrowing or lending, that is, with $\beta = 0$. This is the value of

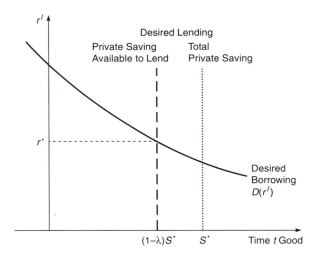

Figure 5.5
Market Supply of and Demand for the Time t Good When Saving Is Fixed

r^l which satisfies $(1 - \lambda)S^* = D(r^l)$. I denote this r^l value r^* and assume that $r^* > 1$ (see Figure 5.5). Finally, I assume that all the pairs (r^m, r^l) that satisfy equation (19) are such that $r^l > r^m$. This is to assume that, no matter what β is, there is no nonbinding equilibrium. These assumptions and $G > 0$ imply that the locus of pairs (r^m, r^l) that satisfy equation (19) is as sketched in Figure 5.6.

I can study the role of monetary policy in this special economy by adding to Figure 5.6's sketch of equation (19) sketches of several loci of pairs (r^m, r^l) that satisfy equation (20)—one for $\beta < 0$, one for $\beta = 0$, and one for $\beta > 0$. On Figure 5.6, the corresponding equilibrium values of r^m and r^l are labeled as the points E^-, E^0, and E^+. Note that the locus implied by equation (20) passes through the horizontal axis at $r^l = r^*$ and that it swings further to the right as β increases. This means that the larger is β, the larger is r^l. Moreover, r^l and p_1 are similarly related: the higher is r^l, the higher is p_1, or the lower is the price level at $t = 1$. This follows directly from equation (13) upon setting $S(r^a) = S^*$.

This special economy thus displays some of the difficult welfare choices policymakers face: the tighter is monetary policy (in the form of a larger β), the worse off are borrowers and the better off are the initial holders of nominal assets, the members of generation 0. Since there is a substantial range where r^m and r^l move in opposite directions in response to a larger

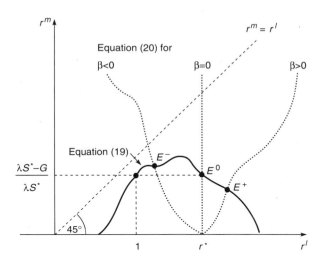

Figure 5.6
Alternative Equilibria When Saving Is Fixed

β, I cannot determine in general how a larger β affects their weighted average, r^a, the return facing lenders.

In several respects, Figure 5.6—in particular, a position like E^+ in Figure 5.6—seems quite close to the situation facing the Federal Reserve today. There is a net-of-interest deficit, $G > 0$; the government is a net debtor, $\beta > 0$; and real interest rates are significantly positive, $r^l > 1$.[8] According to the model, an easing of monetary policy from such a position, a decline in β, would lower the real interest rate, r^l, and lower the (steady-state) inflation rate. According to the model, the main price to be paid for this would be a one-time rise in the price level. Considering the different ways different types of people would be affected by such changes, the Fed's choices today do, indeed, seem difficult.

Concluding Remarks

Although the simple model economy I have described differs in innumerable ways from the actual economy, it does not do so in a way that exaggerates the difficulty of the choices facing those who determine monetary policy. The specification cannot easily be changed in a plausible way so as to produce a monetary policy that will benefit everybody. One way to get closer to such unanimity is to drop borrowers from the model by assuming that everyone in each generation is a lender. But such a specification seems most implausible. In such a model, there is nothing that corresponds to active private credit markets—to mortgage lending, for example. My model is more realistic than that, though it is admittedly simple. It has only three types of people, for example, and abstracts entirely from business cycles, from the international debt crisis, and from the fact that there are many countries whose monetary policies affect one another. Despite the minimal diversity of self-interest in the model, however, it clearly says that different monetary policies affect different people differently. Rather than exaggerating the difficulty of the choices facing policymakers, therefore, my model almost certainly understates it.[9]

Notes

1. I earlier used this model, a version of Samuelson 1958, to analyze the effects of credit controls (Wallace 1980). Here, as in that paper, the analysis may be fairly demanding for some readers. It requires familiarity with the material presented in an intermediate level (relative) price theory course.

2. These somewhat unusual results are not unprecedented. See Sargent and Wallace's paper [Chapter 6].

3. To prove this, divide equation (2) by equation (7) at equality to get $[S(r^a) - D(r^l)] \div \lambda S(r^a) = 1 + (P_t B_{t+1}/H_{t+1})$. From equation (3), $P_t = r_t^m/r_t^l = r^m/r^l$, a constant; thus, $B_{t+1} \div H_{t+1}$ is necessarily a constant.

4. A negative β for the United States would correspond to a situation in which little or no government debt was held outside the Federal Reserve and in which the Fed was a creditor to the private sector by way of loans to banks and others.

Note that the reserve requirement, λ, and β are genuinely different policy instruments in that the set of (r^m, r^l) outcomes achievable by varying both λ and β cannot be obtained by fixing β arbitrarily and varying only λ. [For example, if β in equation (20) is set at zero, then equations (19) and (20) generate a one-dimensional set of outcomes in the (r^m, r^l) plane as λ is varied. By varying both β and λ, a two-dimensional set of outcomes is achievable.] This implies that if alternative stationary equilibria for different settings of β and λ are interpreted as generating a three-dimensional utility possibility frontier—utilities of the current old, of lenders, and of borrowers—then some points achievable by varying both β and λ are not achievable by fixing β arbitrarily and varying only λ.

5. Equivalence means that, for given scalars satisfying equations (8)–(13), there are corresponding sequences satisfying (1)–(7) and that, for given constant real sequences satisfying (1)–(7), there are corresponding scalars satisfying (8)–(13).

6. Note that any such r does not exceed 1 and is such that $S(r) - D(r) > G \geqslant 0$.

7. One pair of assumptions that would make $S(r)$ a constant is that lenders have no endowment when they are old and that their indifference curves are those implied by a utility function of the Cobb-Douglas form.

8. In a growing economy, the relevant comparison is between r^l and 1 plus the average growth rate.

9. The model can be used to analyze questions other than those I addressed here. It can be used to study, for example, the effect of varying the magnitude of the reserve requirement or the effect of paying interest on required reserves or the effect of giving a special status to government bonds, say, by allowing holdings of them to qualify as reserves or by levying a lower reserve requirement against holdings of them than against holdings of private securities.

Although the model can also be used to study fiscal policy, doing so requires additional assumptions. Different levels of explicit taxes, besides implying different levels of G in the obvious way, imply different $S(r)$ and $D(r)$ curves. Different levels of real government purchases also imply different $S(r)$ and $D(r)$ curves unless these purchases are assumed to provide services the quantities of which do not affect the way individuals rank alternative bundles of private consumption.

6

Some Unpleasant
Monetarist Arithmetic

Thomas J. Sargent and
Neil Wallace

In his presidential address to the American Economic Association (AEA), Milton Friedman (1968b) warned not to expect too much from monetary policy. In particular, Friedman argued that monetary policy could not permanently influence the levels of real output, unemployment, or real rates of return on securities. However, Friedman did assert that a monetary authority could exert substantial control over the inflation rate, especially in the long run. The purpose of this paper is to argue that, even in an economy that satisfies monetarist assumptions, if monetary policy is interpreted as open market operations, then Friedman's list of the things that monetary policy cannot permanently control may have to be expanded to include inflation.

In the context of this paper, an economy that satisfies monetarist assumptions (or, a *monetarist economy*) has two characteristics: the monetary base is closely connected to the price level, and the monetary authority can raise *seignorage*, by which we mean revenue from money creation. We will show that, under certain circumstances, the monetary authority's control over inflation in a monetarist economy is very limited even though the monetary base and the price level remain closely connected. In particular, we will demonstrate that this is true when monetary and fiscal policies are coordinated in a certain way and the public's demand for interest-bearing government debt has a certain form.[1]

The public's demand for interest-bearing government debt constrains the government of a monetarist economy in at least two ways. (For simplicity, we will refer to publicly held interest-bearing government debt as *government bonds*.) One way the public's demand for bonds constrains the government is by setting an upper limit on the real stock of government bonds relative to the size of the economy. Another way is by affecting the

Reprinted from the *Federal Reserve Bank of Minneapolis Quarterly Review*, Fall 1981.

interest rate the government must pay on bonds. The extent to which these constraints bind the monetary authority and thus possibly limit its ability to control inflation permanently partly depends on the way fiscal and monetary policies are coordinated. To see this, consider two polar forms of coordination.

On the one hand, imagine that monetary policy dominates fiscal policy. Under this coordination scheme, the monetary authority independently sets monetary policy by, for example, announcing growth rates for base money for the current period and all future periods. By doing this, the monetary authority determines the amount of revenue it will supply the fiscal authority through seignorage. The fiscal authority then faces the constraints imposed by the demand for bonds, since it must set its budgets so that any deficits can be financed by a combination of the seignorage chosen by the monetary authority and bond sales to the public. Under this coordination scheme, the monetary authority can permanently control inflation in a monetarist economy, because it is completely free to choose any path for base money.

On the other hand, imagine that fiscal policy dominates monetary policy. The fiscal authority independently sets its budgets, announcing all current and future deficits and surpluses and thus determining the amount of revenue that must be raised through bond sales and seignorage. Under this second coordination scheme, the monetary authority faces the constraints imposed by the demand for government bonds, for it must try to finance with seignorage any discrepancy between the revenue demanded by the fiscal authority and the amount of bonds that can be sold to the public. Although such a monetary authority might still be able to control inflation permanently, it is less powerful than a monetary authority under the first coordination scheme. If the fiscal authority's deficits cannot be financed solely by new bond sales, then the monetary authority is forced to create money and tolerate additional inflation.

Under the second coordination scheme, where the monetary authority faces the constraints imposed by the demand for government bonds, the form of this demand is important in determining whether or not the monetary authority can control inflation permanently. In particular, suppose that the demand for government bonds implies an interest rate on bonds greater than the economy's rate of growth. Then, if the fiscal authority runs deficits, the monetary authority is unable to control either the growth rate of the monetary base or inflation forever.

The monetary authority's inability to control inflation permanently under these circumstances follows from the arithmetic of the constraints it faces. Being limited simply to dividing government debt between bonds and base money and getting no help from budget surpluses, a monetary authority trying to fight current inflation can only do so by holding down the growth of base money and letting the real stock of bonds held by the public grow. If the principal and interest due on these additional bonds are raised by selling still more bonds, so as to continue to hold down the growth in base money, then, because the interest rate on bonds is greater than the economy's growth rate, the real stock of bonds will grow faster than the size of the economy. This cannot go on forever, since the demand for bonds places an upper limit on the stock of bonds relative to the size of the economy. Once that limit is reached, the principal and interest due on the bonds already sold to fight inflation must be financed, at least in part, by seignorage, requiring the creation of additional base money. Sooner or later, in a monetarist economy, the result is additional inflation.

The first section of the paper establishes a version of this result in a model that is extremely monetarist. By imposing a simple quantity theory demand for base money, the model allows the government to raise seignorage and goes as far as anyone would go in assigning monetary policy influence over the price level. It is also monetarist in giving monetary policy influence over almost no real variables. Yet the model implies that, although fighting current inflation with tight monetary policy works temporarily, it eventually leads to higher inflation.

In the second section, we amend the model of the first section to include a more realistic demand for base money, one that depends on the expected rate of inflation. In a particular example of this second monetarist model, tighter money today leads to higher inflation not only eventually but starting today; tighter money today lacks even a temporary ability to fight inflation. While this example is extreme and may overstate the actual limits on tight money, it has the virtue of isolating a restrictive force on monetary policy that is omitted in the first section and that probably exists in the real world.

Tighter Money Now Can Mean Higher Inflation Eventually

We describe a simple model that embodies unadulterated monetarism. The model has the following features:

a. A common constant growth rate of n for real income and population.

b. A constant real return on government securities that exceeds n.

c. A quantity theory demand schedule for base or high-powered money, one that exhibits constant income velocity.[2]

A model with these features has the limitations on monetary policy stressed by Milton Friedman in his AEA presidential address: a natural, or equilibrium, growth rate of real income that monetary policy is powerless to affect and a real rate of interest on government bonds beyond the influence of monetary policy. We choose this model, one that embraces as unqualified a set of monetarist assumptions as we can imagine, to show that our argument about the limitations of monetary policy is not based on abandoning any of the key assumptions made by monetarists who stress the potency of monetary policy for controlling inflation. Instead, the argument hinges entirely on taking into account the future budgetary consequences of alternative current monetary policies when the real rate of return on government bonds exceeds n, the growth rate of the economy.

We describe fiscal policy by a time path or sequence $D(1), D(2), \ldots, D(t),$ $\ldots$, where $D(t)$ is measured in real terms (time t goods) and is defined as real expenditures on everything except interest on government debt minus real tax collections. From now on we will refer to $D(t)$ as the *deficit*, but keep in mind that $D(t)$ equals the real deficit as ordinarily measured less real interest payments. For convenience, we label the current date $t = 1$. We describe monetary policy by a time path $H(1), H(2), \ldots, H(t), \ldots$, where $H(t)$ is the stock of base or high-powered money at time t. If, for simplicity, we assume that the entire government debt consists of one-period debt, then we can write the consolidated government budget constraint (consolidating the Treasury and the Federal Reserve System) as[3]

$$D(t) = \{[H(t) - H(t-1)]/p(t)\} + \{B(t) - B(t-1)[1 + R(t-1)]\} \qquad (1)$$

for $t = 1, 2, \ldots$. We are letting $p(t)$ be the price level at time t, while $R(t-1)$ is the real rate of interest on one-period government bonds between time $t - 1$ and time t; $B(t-1)[1 + R(t-1)]$ is the real par value of one-period privately held government bonds that were issued at time $t - 1$ and fall due in period t, where $B(t-1)$ is measured in units of time $t - 1$ goods and $[1 + R(t-1)]$ is measured in time t goods per unit of time $t - 1$ goods. In equation (1), $B(t)$ is government borrowing from the private sector between periods t and $t + 1$, measured in units of time t goods. Equation (1) states that the deficit must be financed by issuing some combination of currency and interest-bearing debt. Finally, we let $N(t)$ be the population at time t. We assume that $N(t)$ grows at the constant rate n, or that

$$N(t + 1) = (1 + n)N(t) \qquad (2)$$

for $t = 0, 1, 2, \ldots$, with $N(0) > 0$ being given and n being a constant exceeding -1.

Dividing both sides of (1) by $N(t)$ and rearranging gives the following per capita form of the government's budget constraint:

$$B(t)/N(t) = \{[1 + R(t - 1)]/(1 + n)\} \times [B(t - 1)/N(t - 1)]$$

$$+ [D(t)/N(t)] - \{[H(t) - H(t - 1)]/[N(t)p(t)]\}. \qquad (3)$$

We shall now use equation (3) and our monetarist model—assumptions a, b, and c—to illustrate a version of the following proposition: if fiscal policy in the form of the $D(t)$ sequence is taken as given, then tighter current monetary policy implies higher future inflation.

We specify alternative time paths for monetary policy in the following way. We take $H(1)$ as predetermined and let alternative monetary policies be alternative constant growth rates θ of $H(t)$ for $t = 2, 3, \ldots, T$, where T is some date greater than or equal to 2. For $t > T$, we assume that the path of $H(t)$ is determined by the condition that the stock of interest-bearing real government debt per capita be held constant at whatever level it attains at $t = T$. The restriction on monetary policy from time T onward is consistent with there being a limit on the real debt per capita. Thus, with $H(1)$ taken as given, we assume that

$$H(t) = (1 + \theta)H(t - 1) \qquad (4)$$

for $t = 2, 3, \ldots, T$ and examine the consequences of various choices of θ and T.[4] We will say that one monetary policy is tighter than another if it is characterized by a smaller θ.

Notice that we have written equation (1) in terms of real debt and real rates of return. If we want to analyze a setting in which government bonds are not indexed, which is the situation in the United States today, then we must insure that anticipated inflation is the same as actual inflation. We impose that condition, in part, by supposing that both the path of fiscal policy, the $D(t)$ sequence, and the path of monetary policy, θ and T, are announced at $t = 1$ and known by private agents. Once we assume that, it does not matter whether nominal or indexed debt is issued from $t = 1$ onward.[5]

Now note that assumptions a and c imply that the price level at any time t is proportional to the time t stock of base money per capita, $H(t)/N(t)$, namely, that

$$p(t) = (1/h)[H(t)/N(t)] \qquad (5)$$

for some positive constant h.

From equation (5) it follows that, for $t = 2, \ldots, T$, one plus the inflation rate is given by $p(t)/p(t - 1) = (1 + \theta)/(1 + n)$. Thus, when we specify monetary policy, a θ and a T, we are simultaneously choosing the inflation rate for periods $t = 2, 3, \ldots, T$. We are interested in determining how the inflation rate for the periods after T depends on the inflation rate chosen for the periods before T.

We do this in two simple steps. We first determine how the inflation rate after T depends on the stock of interest-bearing real government debt per capita attained at T and to be held constant thereafter, denoting that per capita stock by $b_\theta(T)$. We then show how $b_\theta(T)$ depends on θ.

To find the dependence of the inflation rate for $t > T$ on $b_\theta(T)$, we use equation (3) for any date $t > T$, substituting into it $B(t)/N(t) = B(t - 1) \div N(t - 1) = b_\theta(T)$ and $H(t) = hN(t)p(t)$ as implied by (5). The result can be written as

$$1 - [1/(1 + n)][p(t - 1)/p(t)]$$
$$= ([D(t)/N(t)] + \{[R(t - 1) - n]/(1 + n)\}b_\theta(T))/h. \qquad (6)$$

Note that equation (6) makes sense only if the right-hand side is less than unity, a condition which itself places an upper bound on $b_\theta(T)$ if $[R(t - 1) - n]$ is positive, as we are assuming. If that condition holds and $[R(t - 1) - n]$ is a positive constant, as stated by assumption b, then the right-hand side of (6) is higher the higher $b_\theta(T)$ is. This in turn implies that the inflation rate is higher the higher $b_\theta(T)$ is, a conclusion that holds for all $t > T$.

To complete the argument that a tighter monetary policy now implies higher inflation later, we must show that the smaller θ is, the higher $b_\theta(T)$ is. To find $b_\theta(T)$ and its dependence on θ, we first find $B(1)/N(1) \equiv b(1)$ and then show how to find the entire path $b(1), b_\theta(2), b_\theta(3), \ldots, b_\theta(T)$.

We solve for $b(1)$ from the $t = 1$ version of equation (3), namely,

$$b(1) = \{\bar{B}(0)/[N(1)p(1)]\} + [D(1)/N(1)] - \{[H(1) - H(0)]/[N(1)p(1)]\}. \qquad (7)$$

Here, in place of $B(0)[1 + R(0)]$, we have inserted $\bar{B}(0) \div p(1)$, $\bar{B}(0)$ being the nominal par value of the debt issued at $t = 0$. By making this substitution, we avoid assuming anything about the relationship between actual and expected inflation from time $t = 0$ to time $t = 1$. In conjunction with equation (5), equation (7) lets us solve for $b(1)$ in terms of $D(1)$, $N(1)$, $H(1)$, $H(0)$, and $\bar{B}(0)$. Note that $b(1)$ does not depend on θ.

We now proceed to find $b_\theta(2), b_\theta(3), \ldots, b_\theta(T)$. Using equations (4) and (5) and the definition $b(t) = B(t)/N(t)$, we can write equation (3) as

$$b(t) = \{[1 + R(t-1)]/(1+n)\}b(t-1) + [D(t)/N(t)] - [h\theta/(1+\theta)] \quad (8)$$

for $t = 2, 3, \ldots, T$. By repeated substitution, it follows for any $t > 2$ and $t \leqslant T$ that

$$b_\theta(t) = \phi(t,1)b(1) + \left(\sum_{s=2}^{t} \phi(t,s)[D(s)/N(s)]\right) - \left([h\theta/(1+\theta)]\sum_{s=2}^{t}\phi(t,s)\right)$$

$$(9)$$

where $\phi(t,t) = 1$ and, for $t > s$,

$$\phi(t,s) = \left(\prod_{j=s}^{t-1}[1 + R(j)]\right)/(1+n)^{t-s}.$$

It follows from (9) that $b_\theta(T)$ is larger the smaller θ is.[6]

This completes our demonstration of a version of the proposition that less inflation now achieved through monetary policy on its own implies more inflation in the future. It is crucial for such a result that the real rate of return on government securities exceed n from T onward [see equation (6)] and that the path of fiscal policy given by $D(1), D(2), \ldots, D(t), \ldots$ not depend on θ.

Tighter Money Now Can Mean Higher Inflation Now

In the last section, we described circumstances in which tighter monetary policy lowers inflation in the present, but at the cost of increasing inflation in the future. Our having assumed a money demand schedule of the simplest quantity theory form [equation (5)] not only much simplified the analysis but also had the substantive aspect of ignoring any dependence of the demand for base money on the expected rate of inflation. This dependence is widely believed to be important; Bresciani-Turroni (1937) and Cagan (1956) found substantial evidence that it exists by studying countries that had undergone rapid inflation. This dependence complicates the dynamics of the influence of monetary policy on the price level. If the demand for money depends on the expected rate of inflation, then it turns out (see Sargent and Wallace 1973) that the current price level depends on the current level and all anticipated future levels of the money supply. This sets up a force whereby high rates of money creation anticipated in the future tend to raise the current rate of inflation. As we shall show, this force can limit the power of tighter monetary policy to deliver even a temporarily lower inflation rate.

We maintain all of the features of the last section except one: we replace equation (5) by[7]

$$H(t)/[N(t)p(t)] = (\gamma_1/2) - [(\gamma_2/2)p(t + 1)/p(t)] \qquad (10)$$

for $t \geqslant 1$, with $\gamma_1 > \gamma_2 > 0$. Equation (10) is a version of the demand schedule for money that Cagan (1956) used in studying hyperinflations. The equation is shown in our Appendix B to imply the following equation for the price level at t:

$$p(t) = (2/\gamma_1) \sum_{j=0}^{\infty} (\gamma_2/\gamma_1)^j [H(t + j)/N(t + j)].$$

This equation expresses the current price level in terms of the current value and all future values of the per capita supply of base money. So the current price level and inflation rate depend not only on how tight money is today, but also on how tight it is for all tomorrows. If the situation is, as in the last section, that tighter money now causes looser money later, then this equation for $p(t)$ suggests the possibility that tighter money today might fail to bring about a lower inflation rate and price level even today. We shall now provide an example in which this possibility is in fact realized.

As in the last section, policy consists of a deficit sequence $D(t)$, a date T after which monetary policy is determined by the condition that the real interest-bearing government debt per capita be held constant, and θ, the growth rate of the monetary base for periods before T. In the model of this section, the path of the price level before T depends on all of these aspects of policy and not just on θ, as was true in the model of the last section.

Appendix B describes a way of solving for the paths of the endogenous variables. Here we simply present an example in which a tighter monetary policy in the form of a lower θ implies a uniformly higher price level and inflation rate.

The economy of this example is characterized by $\gamma_1 = 3.0$, $\gamma_2 = 2.5$, $R = 0.05$, and $n = 0.02$. The common features of policy are a per capita deficit sequence $d(t)$ with $d(t) = 0.05$ for $t = 1, 2, \ldots, 10$ and $d(t) = 0$ for $t > 10$; $T = 10$; and $[H(0) + \tilde{B}(0)]/H(1) = 200/164.65$. Two different base money growth rates are studied: $\theta = 0.106$ and $\theta = 0.120$. Table 6.1 compares the inflation rates, per capita bond holdings, and per capita real money balances for the economy under the two policies. It turns out that the price level at $t = 1$ is 1.04 percent higher under the smaller θ, that is, the tighter policy.

This example is spectacular in that the easier, or looser, monetary policy is uniformly better than the tighter policy. (In terms of the model of Appendix A, the equilibrium for the looser monetary policy is Pareto

Table 6.1
A spectacular example of the potential effects of tight and loose monetary policy
Tight money: $\theta = 0.106$ Loose money: $\theta = 0.120$

Date (t)	Inflation rate $[p(t + 1)/p(t)]$		Per capita bond holdings $[B(t)/N(t)]$		Per capita real money balances $\{H(t)/[N(t)p(t)]\}$	
	Tight	Loose	Tight	Loose	Tight	Loose
1	1.0842	1.0825	.0811	.0815	.1202	.1469
2	1.0841	1.0808	.1196	.1180	.1448	.1490
3	1.0841	1.0789	.1592	.1552	.1449	.1514
4	1.0841	1.0768	.2000	.1933	.1449	.1540
5	1.0841	1.0743	.2420	.2321	.1449	.1571
6	1.0840	1.0716	.2853	.2718	.1450	.1606
7	1.0840	1.0684	.3297	.3121	.1450	.1641
8	1.0840	1.0647	.3755	.3532	.1450	.1691
9	1.0839	1.0605	.4227	.3949	.1451	.1744
$\geqslant 10$	1.0839	1.0556	.4712	.4372	.1451	.1805

Parameters

$\gamma_1 = 3.0$ $R = 0.05$ $d(t) = \begin{cases} 0.05 \text{ for } t = 1, 2, \ldots, 10. \\ 0 \text{ for } t > 10. \end{cases}$ $[H(0) + \bar{B}(0)]/H(1) = 200/164.65$
$\gamma_2 = 2.5$ $n = 0.02$

superior to that for the tighter monetary policy.) In this example, the tighter current monetary policy fails to even temporarily reduce inflation below the level it would be under the looser policy.[8]

Concluding Remarks

We have made two crucial assumptions to obtain our results.

One is that the real rate of interest exceeds the growth rate of the economy. We have made that assumption because it seems to be maintained by many of those who argue for a low rate of growth of money no matter how big the current deficit is. If we were to replace that assumption, we would instead assume that the public's demand for government bonds is an increasing function of the real rate of return on bonds, with an initial range over which that demand is positive at rates of return that are negative or less than the growth rate of the economy. We would still assume that the quantity of bonds demanded per capita has an upper bound. A demand function for government bonds like this would imply that monetary policy helps determine the real rate of interest on government bonds and that, for some monetary policies entailing low enough bond supplies, seignorage can be earned on bonds as well as on base money. However, an analysis that included such a demand schedule for bonds would share with ours the implication that a sufficiently tight current monetary policy can imply growth in government interest-bearing indebtedness so rapid that inflation in the future is higher than it would have been with an easier current monetary policy.

The other crucial assumption that we have made is that the path of fiscal policy $D(t)$ is given and does not depend on current or future monetary policies. This assumption is not about the preferences, opportunities, or behavior of private agents, as is our first crucial assumption, but is, rather, about the behavior of the monetary and fiscal authorities and the game that they are playing. Since the monetary authority affects the extent to which seignorage is exploited as a revenue source, monetary and fiscal policies simply have to be coordinated. The question is, Which authority moves first, the monetary authority or the fiscal authority? In other words, Who imposes discipline on whom? The assumption made in this paper is that the fiscal authority moves first, its move consisting of an entire $D(t)$ sequence. Given that $D(t)$ sequence, monetary policy must be determined in a way consistent with it, if that is possible. [As we have seen, it may not be possible if the $D(t)$ sequence is too big for too long.] Given this assumption about the game played by the authorities, and given our first crucial assumption, the monetary authority can make money tighter now only by making it looser later.

One can interpret proposals for monetary restraint differently than we have in this paper, in particular, as calls to let the monetary authority move first and thereby impose discipline on the fiscal authority. In this interpretation, the monetary authority moves first by announcing a fixed θ rule like (4) not just for $t = 2, 3, \ldots, T$, but for all $t \geqslant 1$. By doing this in a binding way, the monetary authority forces the fiscal authority to choose a $D(t)$ sequence consistent with the announced monetary policy. This form of permanent monetary restraint is a mechanism that effectively imposes fiscal discipline. Alternative monetary mechanisms that do impose fiscal discipline have been suggested, for example, fixed exchange rates or a commodity money standard such as the gold standard. Nothing in our analysis denies the possibility that monetary policy can permanently affect the inflation rate under a monetary regime that effectively disciplines the fiscal authority.

Appendix A: An Overlapping Generations Model That Generates Our Assumptions

This appendix describes a simple formal model that implies the assumptions used in the preceding paper. The model is a version of Samuelson's (1958) model of overlapping generations.

We describe the evolution of the economy from time $t = 1$ onward. The economy is populated by agents who each live two periods. In each period, only one type of good exists. At each time $t \geq 1$, there are born $N_1(t)$ identical poor people who are endowed after taxes with α_1 units of the good when young and α_2 units when old. At each date $t \geq 1$ there are also born $N_2(t)$ identical rich people who are endowed after taxes with β units of the good when young and zero units when old. We assume that $N_1(t) = (1 + n)N_1(t - 1)$ and $N_2(t) = (1 + n)N_2(t - 1)$ for $t \geq 1$, with $N_1(0)$ and $N_2(0)$ given and positive and $n > -1$. The total population is $N(t) = N_1(t) + N_2(t)$.

There is available in this economy a physical technology for converting the time t good into the time $t + 1$ good. In particular, if $k(t) \geq \underline{k}$ goods are stored at time $t \geq 1$, then $(1 + R)k(t)$ goods become available at time $t + 1$. This is a constant returns-to-scale technology with a constant real rate of return on investment of $R > 0$. We assume that there is a minimum scale of $\underline{k}$ at which this investment can be undertaken and that this minimum scale and the endowments satisfy $\beta/2 > \underline{k} > \alpha_1$. We also assume that a legal restriction on intermediation prevents two or more of the poor from sharing investments, thereby preventing the poor from holding the real investment.

The government issues both currency, which doesn't bear interest, and bonds, which do. The currency is held by the poor because government bonds are issued in such large minimum denominations that the poor cannot afford them. (Again, a legal restriction on intermediation is relied on to prevent two or more people from sharing a government bond.) There is no uncertainty in the model, so that the rich will hold government bonds only if the real interest rate on bonds at least equals that on private investment, which must be at least as large as the yield on currency.

As in our paper, the government finances a real deficit $D(t)$ by some combination of currency creation and bond creation. The government's budget constraint is

$$D(t) = \{[H(t) - H(t - 1)]/p(t)\} + [B(t) - B(t - 1)(1 + R)] \qquad (A1)$$

for $t \geqslant 1$, where $H(t)$ is the stock of base or high-powered money (currency) measured in dollars, $p(t)$ is the price level in dollars per time t goods, and $B(t)$ is government borrowing (from the private sector) in time t goods. The government's real deficit $D(t)$ is, then, measured in time t goods.

In addition, at time $t = 1$ there are $N_1(0)$ and $N_2(0)$ old poor and rich people, respectively, who hold $H(0)$ units of currency and maturing bonds of par nominal value $\bar{B}(0)$. The old alive at time $t = 1$ simply offer all of their currency inelastically in exchange for goods to those young at that time.

The young of each generation $t \geqslant 1$ are assumed to maximize the utility function $c_t^h(t)c_t^h(t + 1)$, where $c_t^h(s)$ is consumption of the s-period good by an agent of type h born at time t. Letting $w_t^h(s)$ be the endowment of the s-period good of an agent of type h born at t, and assuming that each agent faces a single rate of return R^h, a young agent h at generation t chooses a lifetime consumption bundle to maximize utility subject to the present-value constraint,

$$c_t^h(t) + [c_t^h(t + 1)/(1 + R^h)] = w_t^h(t) + [w_t^h(t + 1)/(1 + R^h)].$$

The solution to this problem is the saving function:

$$w_t^h(t) - c_t^h(t) = \{w_t^h(t) - [w_t^h(t + 1)/(1 + R^h)]\}/2. \tag{A2}$$

Since all saving of poor people is in the form of currency, if h is poor, $1 + R^h = p(t)/p(t + 1)$. Moreover, in the range where $p(t)/p(t + 1) < 1 + R$, only the poor hold currency. Thus, in this range, the money market equilibrium condition is that $H(t)/p(t)$ equals the total real saving of the poor, which by (A2) is $N_1(t)\{\alpha_1 - [\alpha_2 p(t + 1)/p(t)]\}/2$. Dividing by $N(t)$, we can write this condition as

$$H(t)/[N(t)p(t)] = \{\alpha_1 - [\alpha_2 p(t + 1)/p(t)]\} \times N_1(t)/2N(t). \tag{A3}$$

This is equation (10) if we let $\gamma_1/2 = \alpha_1 N_1(t)/2N(t)$ and $\gamma_2/2 = \alpha_2 N_1(t) \div 2N(t)$. [Recall that $N_1(t)/N(t)$ is constant.] We get equation (5) if $\alpha_2 = 0$.

According to (A2), each rich person saves a constant amount $\beta/2$ per period. As long as government bonds bear the real rate of return R, each rich person is indifferent between holding government bonds or holding private capital. However, in the aggregate, the rich only wish to save $N_2(t)\beta/2$ per period. The number $\beta/2$ determines an upper bound on per capita holdings of interest-bearing government debt, the sort of bound alluded to in the paper. We let $K(t)$ denote the total amount of real investment (storage), measured in goods, undertaken by the young members of generation t, all of them rich. We then have

$$K(t) + B(t) = N_2(t)\beta/2 = \bar{B}(t) \tag{A4}$$

where $B(t)$ is the amount of loans to the government. Equation (A4) expresses the result that additional government borrowing merely crowds out private investment on a one-for-one basis.

The national income identity can be written like this:

$$N_1(t)c_t^1(t) + N_1(t-1)c_{t-1}^1(t) + N_2(t)c_t^2(t) + N_2(t-1)c_{t-1}^2(t) + K(t) + G(t)$$

$$= N_1(t)\alpha_1 + N_1(t-1)\alpha_2 + N_2(t)\beta + T(t) + (1+R)K(t-1). \tag{A5}$$

Here $G(t)$ denotes government purchases and $T(t)$ denotes total direct taxes. The government deficit as defined in our paper is related to $G(t)$ and $T(t)$ by $D(t) = G(t) - T(t)$.

Thus, as long as solutions satisfy $p(t)/p(t+1) < 1 + R$ and the total real bond supply is less than $\bar{B}(t)$, the model just described implies all the assumptions made in the paper. This particular model also implies how different agents fare under different policies. The present-value budget constraint set out above indicates that each poor person is better off the lower the inflation rate, that each rich person is unaffected by the inflation rate, and that those who at $t = 1$ are in the second period of their lives and are holding currency or maturing bonds are better off the lower the initial price level, $p(1)$. These observations are what lie behind our claim in the paper that, for the example in the second section, the tight money policy is Pareto inferior to the loose money policy.[9]

Appendix B: A Model in Which Tighter Money Now Can Cause Higher Inflation Now

In this appendix, we analyze the model in the second section of the paper which generalizes the model of the first section by assuming that the demand schedule for base money depends on the expected rate of inflation. The particular demand schedule that we use resembles Cagan's (1956) famous demand schedule and can be deduced formally from the model in Appendix A by assuming that the poor of each generation are endowed with $\gamma_1 N(0)/N_1(0) > 0$ units of the consumption good when they are young and $\gamma_2 N(0)/N_1(0) > 0$ units when they are old. (The model in the first section of the paper emerges when we set $\gamma_2 = 0$.) Except for this generalization, all other features of the model remain as they were in the first section of the paper.

As before, we assume a demand schedule for base money of the form

$$H(t)/[N(t)p(t)] = (\gamma_1/2) - [(\gamma_2/2)p(t+1)/p(t)] \tag{B1}$$

for $t \geq 1$, where $\gamma_1 > \gamma_2 > 0$. [This is equation (10) in the second section of the paper.] Except for replacing equation (5) with this equation, we retain the features of the model in the paper's first section, including the budget restraint (1) and the law of motion of total population (2). We describe experiments similar to the one in that section: we hold the per capita real government debt $b(t)$ constant for $t > T$ and examine the choice of alternative rates of growth of base money θ for $t = 2, \ldots, T$. The step of replacing (5) with (B1) substantially complicates the dynamics of the system, as we shall see.

We begin by examining the behavior of the system for $t > T$. For $t > T + 1$ we specify as before that monetary policy is determined so that $b(t) = b(t - 1) = b(T)$. Using the budget constraint (1) together with this condition implies

$$[H(t) - H(t - 1)]/[N(t)p(t)] = \{[R(t - 1) - n]/(1 + n)\}b(T) + [D(t)/N(t)]$$
(B2)

for $t \geq T + 1$. We now assume that

$$D(t)/N(t) = d$$

for $t \geq T$, where d is a constant. This is a computationally convenient assumption, although the general flavor of our results does not depend on making it.

We now define per capita real balances as $m(t) \equiv H(t)/[N(t)p(t)]$ and the one-period gross inflation rate as $\pi(t) = p(t)/p(t - 1)$. In terms of these variables, equations (B1) and (B2) become

$$m(t) = (\gamma_1/2) - (\gamma_2/2)\pi(t + 1)$$
(B3)

for $t \geq 1$ and

$$m(t) - \{m(t - 1)/[\pi(t)(1 + n)]\} = \xi$$
(B4)

for $t \geq T + 1$, where

$$\xi = [(R - n)/(1 + n)]b(T) + d.$$

The variable ξ has the interpretation of the per capita deficit that must be financed by seignorage from time $T + 1$ onward. Eliminating $m(t)$ and $m(t - 1)$ from these equations by substituting (B3) into (B4) leads to the following nonlinear difference equation in $\pi(t)$ for $t \geq T + 1$:

$$\pi(t + 1) = \lambda - (\gamma_1/\gamma_2)[1/(1 + n)][1/\pi(t)]$$
(B5)

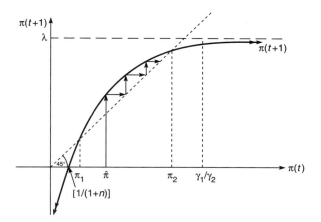

Figure 6.1
Equation (B5): $\pi(t + 1) = \lambda - (\gamma_1/\gamma_2)[1/(1 + n)][1/\pi(t)]$

where

$\lambda \equiv (\gamma_1/\gamma_2) + [1/(1 + n)] - (2\xi/\gamma_2).$

Equation (B5) is graphed in Figure 6.1. It is readily verified that if

$$\lambda^2 - \{4\gamma_1/[\gamma_2(1 + n)]\} > 0 \tag{B6}$$

then (B5) has two stationary points, their values being given by

$$\pi_1 = (1/2)[\lambda - (\lambda^2 - \{4\gamma_1/[\gamma_2(1 + n)]\})^{1/2}]$$
$$\pi_2 = (1/2)[\lambda + (\lambda^2 - \{4\gamma_1/[\gamma_2(1 + n)]\})^{1/2}]. \tag{B7}$$

We let $\bar{\xi}$ be the value of ξ for which the left-hand side of (B6) equals zero. Evidently, $\bar{\xi}$ is a function of γ_1, γ_2, and n and represents the maximum stationary per capita deficit that can be financed by seignorage. From (B7), it follows that, if $\xi = 0$, then $\pi_1 = 1/(1 + n)$, $\pi_2 = \gamma_1/\gamma_2$. From the graph of (B5), it immediately follows that, for $\bar{\xi} > \xi > 0$, $\pi_1 > 1/(1 + n)$, $\pi_2 < \gamma_1/\gamma_2$, and raising ξ causes π_1 to rise and π_2 to fall.

Inequality (B6) is a necessary and sufficient condition for it to be possible to finance the per capita deficit ξ by seignorage. Assuming (B6) is satisfied, there exists a multiplicity of inflation–real balance paths that finance the deficit. Any setting on $\pi(T)$ satisfying $\pi_1 < \pi(T) < \gamma_1/\gamma_2$, with $\pi(t)$ for $t > T + 1$ being given by (B5), results in the deficit being financed. (Later we shall describe the money supply paths needed to accomplish these paths for inflation.) The graph of (B5) shows that, for any $\pi_1 < \pi(T) < \gamma_1/\gamma_2$, $\pi(t) \to \pi_2$ as $t \to \infty$. Thus, there are three classes of inflation paths which finance the deficit:

1. The stationary path with $\pi(t) = \pi_1$ for $t > T$.
2. The stationary path with $\pi(t) = \pi_2$ for $t > T$.
3. Nonstationary paths with $\gamma_1/\gamma_2 > \pi(T) > \pi_1$ and $\lim_{t\to\infty} \pi(t) = \pi_2$.

We assume that the government selects the money supply path so that $\pi(T) = \pi_1$, that is, so that the deficit is financed by the uniformly lowest inflation rate path and, therefore, in view of (B3), the lowest price level path. This assumption is reasonable, since this selection leaves the government with the same resources as any other selection, while leaving holders of money better off.

Having determined the inflation rate $p(t)/p(t-1) = \pi_1$ for $t > T + 1$ from (B6), we can determine the time T real balances and price level by setting $t = T$ in (B3):

$$H(T)/[N(T)p(T)] = (\gamma_1/2) - (\gamma_2/2)\pi_1$$

or

$$p(T) = (2/\gamma_1)\{1/[1 - (\gamma_2/\gamma_1)\pi_1]\}[H(T)/N(T)]. \tag{B8}$$

Since $H(T)$ and $N(T)$ are given at T, this equation determines $p(T)$ as a function of π_1. Also, since $\pi(t)$ is constant for $t > T + 1$, we have from (B3) and the definition of $m(t) \equiv H(t)/[N(t)p(t)]$ that

$$H(t)/N(t) = \pi_1[H(t-1)/N(t-1)]$$

for $t \geq T + 1$, so that per capita nominal balances grow at the constant gross rate π_1, which is the rate of inflation for $t > T + 1$.

It is instructive to describe briefly the following alternative way to solve the system for $t > T + 1$ by obtaining a pair of linear difference equations. Define $h(t) \equiv H(t)/N(t)$, and write the budget constraint (B2) as

$$h(t) = [1/(1 + n)]h(t-1) + \xi p(t)$$

for $t \geq T + 1$ and the demand function for base money (B1) as

$$p(t) = (\gamma_2/\gamma_1)p(t + 1) + (2/\gamma_1)h(t)$$

for $t \geq 1$. Using the lag operator L, we write these two equations as

$$\{1 - [1/(1 + n)]L\}h(t) = \xi p(t) \tag{B9}$$

for $t \geqslant T + 1$ and

$$[1 - (\gamma_2/\gamma_1)L^{-1}]p(t) = (2/\gamma_1)h(t)$$

for $t \geqslant 1$. Solving the second equation in terms of $h(t)$ gives

$$p(t) = (2/\gamma_1)[1 - (\gamma_2/\gamma_1)L^{-1}]^{-1}h(t) + c(\gamma_1/\gamma_2)^t \tag{B10}$$

or

$$p(t) = (2/\gamma_1) \sum_{j=0}^{\infty} (\gamma_2/\gamma_1)^j h(t + j) + c(\gamma_1/\gamma_2)^t \tag{B11}$$

for $t \geqslant 1$, where c is any nonnegative constant. Substituting (B10) into (B9) and operating on both sides of the result with $[1 - (\gamma_2/\gamma_1)L^{-1}]$ gives the following homogenous difference equation in $h(t)$:

$$L^{-1}\{-1 + \lambda L - [1/(1 + n)](\gamma_1/\gamma_2)L^2\}h(t) = 0. \tag{B12}$$

The characteristic polynomial in L can be factored in the usual way so that

$$L^{-1}[(1 - \pi_1 L)(1 - \pi_2 L)]h(t) = 0 \tag{B13}$$

where π_1 and π_2 are the same roots given in (B7).

Since for $\xi > 0$ we have $\pi_1 < \pi_2 < \gamma_1/\gamma_2$, it follows that the geometric sum in current and future $h(t)$ that appears in (B11) converges for any $h(t)$ paths that satisfy (B13), or equivalently,

$$h(t) = (\pi_1 + \pi_2)h(t - 1) - \pi_1\pi_2 h(t - 2) \tag{B14}$$

for $t \geqslant T + 1$, with $h(T)$ given and $h(T + 1)$ free. To insure that the deficit is financed each period, we have to add two side conditions to those listed under (B14): we must set $c = 0$ in (B10) and set $h(T + 1)$ so that (B10) implies that $\pi(T + 1) < \gamma_1/\gamma_2$. All of the price level paths with $c > 0$ have $\lim_{t \to \infty} \pi(t) = \gamma_1/\gamma_2$, which in view of equations (B3) and (B4) implies that $\lim_{t \to \infty} m(t) = 0$ and that a positive deficit cannot be financed. Any path with $\pi(T) > \gamma_1/\gamma_2$ implies nonpositive real balances at T. Since we are assuming that the government selects $h(t) = \pi_1 h(t - 1)$, for $t > T + 1$, and $h(T)$ is given, equation (B11) with $t = T$ becomes equivalent to equation (B8). We note that the admissible paths given by (B14) with $h(T + 1) \neq \pi_1 h(T)$ have $\lim_{t \to \infty}[h(t)/h(t - 1)] = \pi_2$ and so constitute the per capita nominal money supply paths that correspond to the inflation paths with $\pi(T) > \pi_1$ in the graph of (B5).

In summary, we have that for $t \geq T$ the price level and the stock of base money per capita evolve according to

$$p(t) = (2/\gamma_1)\{1/[1 - (\gamma_2/\gamma_1)\pi_1]\}h(t) \tag{B15}$$

$$h(t + 1) = \pi_1 h(t) \tag{B16}$$

subject to $h(T)$ given, where π_1 is given by (B7).

We now describe the behavior of the price level, the supply of base money, and the stock of real government debt per capita for $t < T$. As in the first section of the paper, we assume a constant growth rate of base money [see equation (4) in the paper, which we repeat here as (B17)]:

$$H(t) = (1 + \theta)H(t - 1) \tag{B17}$$

for $t = 2, 3, \ldots, T$. Equation (B10) with $c = 0$ implies that for all $t \geq 1$

$$p(t) = (2/\gamma_1) \sum_{j=0}^{\infty} (\gamma_2/\gamma_1)^j h(t + j). \tag{B18}$$

Further, we know from (B17) and (B16) that for $t = 1, 2, \ldots, T - 1$

$$h(t + 1) = \mu h(t) \tag{B19}$$

where

$$\mu = (1 + \theta)/(1 + n) \tag{B20}$$

and for $t = T, T + 1, \ldots$

$$h(t + 1) = \pi_1 h(t). \tag{B16}$$

Let us define the parameter ϕ by

$$\phi = \gamma_2/\gamma_1 \tag{B21}$$

and write (B18) for $t \leq T$ as

$$p(t) = (2/\gamma_1) \sum_{j=0}^{T-t} \phi^j h(t + j) + (2/\gamma_1) \sum_{j=T-t+1}^{\infty} \phi^j h(t + j). \tag{B22}$$

Substituting (B19) and (B16) into (B22) and using some algebra implies

$$p(t) = (2/\gamma_1)\{[1 - \phi\pi_1 + (\pi_1 - \mu)\phi^{T-t+1}\mu^{T-t}]$$
$$\div [(1 - \phi\pi_1)(1 - \phi\mu)]\}h(t) \tag{B23}$$

for $t \leq T$.

Next, we define $s(t)$ as per capita seignorage:

$$s(t) \equiv [H(t) - H(t-1)]/[N(t)p(t)].$$

For $t \leqslant T$, we have that

$$s(t) = [h(t-1)/p(t)][\theta/(1+n)]$$

or

$$s(t) = [\theta/(1+\theta)][h(t)/p(t)].$$

Using (B23) in the above equation gives

$$s(t) = [\theta/(1+\theta)](\gamma_1/2)\{(1-\phi\mu)(1-\phi\pi_1)$$
$$\div [1 - \phi\pi_1 + (\pi_1 - \mu)\phi^{T-t+1}\mu^{T-t}]\} \qquad (B24)$$

for $t \geqslant 2$. Using (1) from the paper, the definition of $s(t)$, and the definition $d(t) = D(t)/N(t)$, we have the law of motion for per capita real interest-bearing government debt:

$$b(t) = [(1+R)/(1+n)]b(t-1) + d(t) - s(t) \qquad (B25)$$

for $T \geqslant t \geqslant 2$. Finally, we repeat equation (7) as equation (B26), which is the special version of (B25) for $t = 1$:

$$b(1) = \{\tilde{B}(0)/[N(1)p(1)]\} + d(1) - \{[H(1) - H(0)]/[N(1)p(1)]\} \qquad (B26)$$

where $\tilde{B}(0)$ is the nominal par value of the one-period interest-bearing debt that was issued at time $t = 0$.

In Table 6.2 we have collected the equations describing the equilibrium before and after T. Starting at $t = 1$, the system works as follows. We take as exogenous a time path of the per capita deficit net of interest payments, $\{d(t); t \geqslant 1\}$, with $d(t) = d$ for $t \geqslant T$. We further take as exogenous $\tilde{B}(0)$ and $H(0)$, which give the nominal par value of government debt inherited from the past. The date T is also taken as exogenous. The monetary authority chooses settings for $H(1)$ and θ. Then equations (B19), (B20), and (B23)–(B26) simultaneously determine $p(t)$ and $b(t)$ for $t = 1, \ldots, T$, while equation (B15) determines $p(t)$ for $t > T$.

The equations of the model are linear in the endogenous variables, given a value for π_1. However, from (B7) and the fact that $\xi = [(R-n) \div (1+n)]b(T) + d$, we see that π_1 is itself a function of $b(T)$, which in turn depends on the value of π_1 through its effect on the behavior of $p(t)$ and $s(t)$ for $1 \leqslant t < T$, via equation (B23). Thus, determining the equilibrium of the system involves solving a nonlinear system of equations.

Table 6.2
Equations describing the behavior of the system before and after T, the date interest-bearing government debt per capita is stabilized

Path of	Before $T (1 \leqslant t \leqslant T)$	After $T (t \geqslant T)$
Base money per capita	(B19) $h(t+1) = \mu h(t)$ (B20) $\mu = (1+\theta)/(1+n)$	(B16) $h(t+1) = \pi_1 h(t)$
Price level	(B23) $p(t) = (2/\gamma_1)\{[1 - \phi\pi_1 + (\pi_1 - \mu)\phi^{T-t+1}\mu^{T-t}]$ $\div [(1-\phi\pi_1)(1-\phi\mu)]\}h(t)$	(B15) $p(t) = (2/\gamma_1)\{1/[1 - (\gamma_2/\gamma_1)\pi_1]\}h(t)$
Real interest-bearing government debt per capita	(B25) $b(t) = [(1+R)/(1+n)]b(t-1) + d(t) - s(t)$ for $2 \leqslant t \leqslant T$ (B26) $b(1) = \{\tilde{B}(0)/[N(1)p(1)]\} + d(1)$ $\qquad - \{[H(1) - H(0)]/[N(1)p(1)]\}$	$b(t) = b(T)$
Seignorage per capita	(B24) $s(t) = [\theta/(1+\theta)][\gamma_1/2]\{(1 - \phi\mu)(1 - \phi\pi_1)$ $\div [1 - \phi\pi_1 + (\pi_1 - \mu)\phi^{T-t+1}\mu^{T-t}]\}$ for $2 \leqslant t \leqslant T$	$s(t) = (\gamma_1/2)(1 - \{1/[\pi_1(1 + n)]\})$ $\qquad \times [1 - (\gamma_2/\gamma_1)\pi_1]$
Real government deficit net of interest payments per capita	$d(t) = D(t)/N(t)$	$d(t) = d$

Parameters and definitions

$h(t) \equiv H(t)/N(t)$ $\qquad \phi = \gamma_2/\gamma_1$ $\qquad \pi_1 = (1/2)[\lambda - (\lambda^2 - \{4\gamma_1/[\gamma_2(1 + n)]\})^{1/2}]$

$N(t) = (1 + n)N(t - 1)$ $\qquad \xi \equiv [(R - n)/(1 + n)]b(T) + d$ $\qquad \lambda \equiv (\gamma_1/\gamma_2) + [1/(1 + n)] - (2\xi/\gamma_2)$

$\mu = (1 + \theta)/(1 + n)$

While the system can be solved in a variety of ways, we have found it convenient to use the following procedure based on backwards recursions. We begin by taking θ, but not $H(1)$, as given. We choose a value for $b(T)$ and solve (B7) for π_1. Then we recursively solve (B24) and (B25) backwards for values of $\{b(t), s(t + 1); t = T - 1, T - 2, \ldots, 1\}$. Also, from (B23) we can determine per capita real balances $h(t)/p(t)$ for $t = 1, \ldots, T$. Finally, given the values of $b(1)$ and $h(1)/p(1)$ thus determined, we solve equation (B26) for the value of $H(1)$ [or, equivalently, of $p(1)$]. This procedure produces a choice of $H(1)$ and θ and associated sequences for $b(t), p(t), h(t),$ and $s(t)$ that solve the system.

By employing iterations on this procedure, the model can be solved taking $b(1)$ as given. The method is simply to search over solutions of the type described in the previous paragraph, varying $b(T)$ until the specified initial value of $b(1)$ is found. In this way, a set of equilibria with different θ's can be calculated, each one of which starts from the same value of $b(1)$. In a similar fashion, equilibria can be generated with different θ's, each one of which starts from the same value of $H(1)$. [Of course, $b(1)$ will then differ across the different θ's.] This last procedure was the one used to generate the examples in the paper, each of which started with $H(1) = 164.65$.

We now describe the results of using this solution procedure to compute the equilibria of an economy with the parameters $\{\gamma_1, \gamma_2, N(0), d(t), \bar{B}(0), H(0), T, b(1)\}$ under different monetary policies, that is, different values of θ. Since the values of θ are different, the values of the economy's endogenous variables $\{p(t); t \geqslant 1\}$ and $\{b(t); t \geqslant 2\}$ will, in general, be different.

Table 6.3 compares two very different monetary policies in a particular economy. Under both policies, the economy has $\gamma_1 = 3.0$, $\gamma_2 = 2.5$, $N(0) = 1,000$, $n = 0.02$, $d(t) = 0.05$ for $1 \leqslant t \leqslant T$, $d(t) = d = 0$ for $t > T$, $\bar{B}(0) = 100$, $H(0) = 100$, $T = 10$, $b(1) = 0.08109$, and $R = 0.05$. The tight money policy is $\theta = 0.106$, while the loose money policy is $\theta = 0.120$. As can be seen from the table, for all $t \geqslant 1$, the tight money policy produces a uniformly higher inflation rate than the loose money policy. Note that, as expected, the loose money policy is associated with a slower rate of bond creation from $t = 1$ to $t = 10$ and that therefore that policy ends up permitting slower growth in base money from T on than does the tight money policy. Thus, tighter money now implies looser money later, as in the economy described in the first section of the paper.

In the present example, however, the effect of expected future rates of money creation on the current rate of inflation is sufficiently strong that tighter money initially produces higher inflation in both the present and the future. This happens because, via equation (B18), the higher eventual

Table 6.3
Another spectacular example of the potential effects of tight and loose monetary policy
Tight money: $\theta = 0.106$ Loose money: $\theta = 0.120$

Date (t)	Inflation rate $[p(t+1)/p(t)]$		Per capita bond holdings $[B(t)/N(t)]$		Per capita real money balances $\{H(t)/[N(t)p(t)]\}$	
	Tight	Loose	Tight	Loose	Tight	Loose
1	1.0842	1.0824	.0811	.0811	.1448	.1470
2	1.0841	1.0807	.1196	.1175	.1448	.1491
3	1.0841	1.0788	.1592	.1547	.1449	.1515
4	1.0841	1.0766	.2000	.1927	.1449	.1542
5	1.0841	1.0742	.2420	.2316	.1449	.1573
6	1.0840	1.0714	.2852	.2711	.1450	.1608
7	1.0840	1.0682	.3297	.3115	.1450	.1648
8	1.0840	1.0645	.3755	.3525	.1450	.1694
9	1.0839	1.0602	.4227	.3941	.1451	.1748
$\geqslant 10$	1.0839	1.0552	.4712	.4363	.1451	.1810

Parameters

$\gamma_1 = 3.0$ $R = 0.05$ $d(t) = \begin{cases} 0.05 \text{ for } t = 1, 2, \ldots, 10. \\ 0 \text{ for } t > 10. \end{cases}$ $H(0) = 100$ $N(0) = 1,000$
$\gamma_2 = 2.5$ $n = 0.02$ $\tilde{B}(0) = 100$ $b(1) = 0.08109$

rate of money creation associated with the lower path more than offsets the downward effects on the initial inflation rates that are directly associated with the lower initial rate of money creation. Like the closely related example in the paper, this comparison provides a spectacular example in which tighter money now fails to buy even a temporarily lower inflation rate than does looser money now.

Table 6.4 compares different θ's in an economy that provides an intermediate example, one between the paper's first section economy and the later spectacular examples. This economy maintains the parameters $\gamma_1 = 2.0$, $\gamma_2 = 1.5$, $N(0) = 1,000$, $n = 0.02$, $d(t) = 0.05$ for $1 \leqslant t \leqslant T$, $d(t) = d = 0$ for $t > T$, $\tilde{B}(0) = 100$, $H(0) = 100$, $T = 10$, $b(1) = 1.4999$, and $R = 0.05$. Here the tight money policy is $\theta = 0.01$, while the loose money policy is $\theta = 0.03$. Under tight money, the economy experiences a lower inflation rate for $1 \leqslant t \leqslant 5$, but a higher rate for $t \geqslant 5$. [Here the gross inflation rate at t is defined as the right-hand rate $p(t+1)/p(t)$.] In this case, the effect of the higher eventual rate of money creation that is associated with the initially tighter policy causes inflation to be higher even before T, when money actually becomes looser. But this effect is not strong enough to eliminate completely the temporary benefits of tight money

Table 6.4
An intermediate example of the potential effects of tight and loose monetary policy
Tight money: $\theta = 0.01$ Loose money: $\theta = 0.03$

Date (t)	Inflation rate $[p(t+1)/p(t)]$		Per capita bond holdings $[B(t)/N(t)]$		Per capita real money balances $\{H(t)/[N(t)p(t)]\}$	
	Tight	Loose	Tight	Loose	Tight	Loose
1	1.0043	1.0192	.1500	.1500	.2468	.2356
2	1.0089	1.0221	.2020	.1976	.2433	.2335
3	1.0150	1.0258	.2556	.2467	.2388	.2307
4	1.0227	1.0306	.3108	.2973	.2330	.2249
5	1.0326	1.0367	.3677	.3496	.2256	.2225
6	1.0449	1.0444	.4264	.4036	.2163	.2167
7	1.0601	1.0539	.4869	.4594	.2030	.2096
8	1.0781	1.0656	.5493	.5170	.1915	.2008
9	1.0989	1.0796	.6137	.5767	.1759	.1903
$\geqslant 10$	1.1221	1.0960	.6802	.6385	.1585	.1780

Parameters

$\gamma_1 = 2.0$ $R = 0.05$ $d(t) = \begin{cases} 0.05 \text{ for } t = 1, 2, \ldots, 10. \\ 0 \text{ for } t > 10. \end{cases}$ $H(0) = 100$ $N(0) = 1{,}000$
$\gamma_2 = 1.5$ $n = 0.02$ $\tilde{B}(0) = 100$ $b(1) = 1.4999$

on the current inflation. Still, notice that, compared to the paper's first section example, the effect of the initial tight money on the initial inflation rate is considerably weakened. With all other parameters the same, but $\gamma_2 = 0$ (the first section case), we would have had $p(t + 1)/p(t) = (1 + \theta)/(1 + n) = 0.9902$ for $1 \leqslant t \leqslant T$.

Appendix C: Sufficient Conditions for Tighter Money Now to Cause Higher Inflation Now

This appendix[10] establishes sufficient conditions for the case where a tighter monetary policy (lower θ) leads to a uniformly higher price level and inflation rate for all $t \geqslant 1$. The method is by construction: a pair of inequalities will be reduced to a single relation by the correct choice of certain parameter values. We satisfy the inequalities by making the implicit discount rate $[1 - (\gamma_2/\gamma_1)]$ sufficiently low, while maintaining convergence of the relevant infinite sum.

Let θ_h and θ_l denote a higher and a lower monetary growth policy, respectively; that is, $\theta_h > \theta_l$. Then we want both[11]

$$p_t(\theta_l) > p_t(\theta_h) \tag{C1}$$

and

$$p_{t+1}(\theta_l)/p_t(\theta_l) > p_{t+1}(\theta_h)/p_t(\theta_h) \tag{C2}$$

for all t. By (B15) and (B16) in Table 6.2, for $t \geq T$, $p_{t+1}(\theta)/p_t(\theta) = \pi_1(\theta)$. For policy experiments that fix b_1, it is clear that (over the relevant range) a lower θ leads to a higher b_T and hence to a higher ξ. This is exactly the statement that a tighter monetary policy now implies a higher deficit to be financed by seignorage from time $T+1$ on. From the graph of (B5) in Appendix B, it is clear that an increase in ξ increases the value of the root π_1. Therefore, $\pi_1(\theta_l) > \pi_1(\theta_h)$. Hence, condition (C2) is satisfied for $t \geq T$. Condition (C1) follows, at most, T' periods after T (where T' is finite), given (C2) for $t \geq T$.

Hence, we restrict attention to $t < T$. It is clear that, if (C2) holds for $t < T$, then $p_1(\theta_l) > p_1(\theta_h)$ implies (C1) for $t < T$ and therefore for all t. From (B26),

$$p_1(\theta) = [(\tilde{B}_0 + H_0)/N_1]/(b_1 - d_1 + \{H_1(\theta)/[N_1 p_1(\theta)]\}).$$

But by (B23),

$$H_1(\theta)/[N_1 p_1(\theta)] = h_1(\theta)/p_1(\theta)$$

$$= (\gamma_1/2)([1 - \phi\pi_1(\theta)][1 - \phi\mu(\theta)]/\{1 - \phi\pi_1(\theta)$$

$$+ [\pi_1(\theta) - \mu(\theta)]\phi^T\mu(\theta)^{T-1}\}).$$

Calling this $m_1(\theta)$, $p_1(\theta) = k_1/[k_2 + m_1(\theta)]$, where $k_1 \equiv (\tilde{B}_0 + H_0)/N_1$ and $k_2 \equiv b_1 - d_1$. Clearly, $k_1 > 0$. Then $k_2 + m_1(\theta) > 0$ for positive $p_1(\theta)$. Then $p_1(\theta_l) > p_1(\theta_h)$ if and only if $m_1(\theta_h) > m_1(\theta_l)$.

Define the function

$$\Gamma(\phi, \theta, t) = 1 - \phi\pi_1(\theta) + [\pi_1(\theta) - \mu(\theta)]\phi^{T-t+1}\mu(\theta)^{T-t}.$$

Then, using (B19), (B20), and (B23) to write out explicitly $p_{t+1}(\theta)/p_t(\theta)$ and the above characterization of the price level condition, (C1) and (C2) for $t < T$ are equivalent to

$$[1 - \phi\pi_1(\theta_h)][1 - \phi\mu(\theta_h)]/\Gamma(\phi, \theta_h, 1)$$

$$> [1 - \phi\pi_1(\theta_l)][1 - \phi\mu(\theta_l)]/\Gamma(\phi, \theta_l, 1) \tag{C3}$$

and

$$(1 + \theta_l)[\Gamma(\phi, \theta_l, t+1)/\Gamma(\phi, \theta_l, t)] > (1 + \theta_h)[\Gamma(\phi, \theta_h, t+1)/\Gamma(\phi, \theta_h, t)] \tag{C4}$$

for $t > T$. We need to choose $\phi = (\gamma_2/\gamma_1)$, θ_l, θ_h that satisfy (C3) and (C4) and support positive values for nominal balances, prices, and bond holdings and real values for π_1 and π_2.

Recall that, given b_1, b_T can be found if π_1 is known. But π_1 is a function of b_T. The only case where π_1 is determined independently of b_T is $\pi_1 = \pi_2 = [\phi(1 + n)]^{-1/2}$, as is easily seen by comparing (B12) and (B13). This occurs at the maximum value of ξ that yields real roots for the characteristic polynomial in (B13). Using this, we pick a θ_l to simplify (C3) and (C4). Conditions on parameter values that satisfy these two inequalities will then become transparent.

Let θ_l solve $\mu(\theta_l) = \pi_1(\theta_l) = [\phi(1 + n)]^{-1/2}$. Since $\mu(\theta_l) = (1 + \theta_l) \div (1 + n)$, this gives $\theta_l = (1 + n)^{1/2}\phi^{-1/2}$. Choosing $\pi_1 = \pi_2 = [\phi(1 + n)]^{-1/2}$ implies a value for ξ (and hence for b_T) by comparing (B12) and (B13). Then fixing θ_l determines b_1 by recursively solving (B24) and (B25) backwards. This value of b_1 is kept constant across policy experiments (different θ settings).

Choosing $\mu(\theta_l) = \pi_1(\theta_l)$ simplifies (C3) and (C4) to

$$[1 - \phi\pi_1(\theta_h)][1 - \phi\mu(\theta_h)]/\Gamma(\phi, \theta_h, 1) > 1 - \phi\mu(\theta_l) \tag{C5}$$

and

$$1 + \theta_l > (1 + \theta_h)[\Gamma(\phi, \theta_h, t + 1)/\Gamma(\phi, \theta_h, t)] \tag{C6}$$

for $t \leqslant T - 1$. It will be shown below that we want to set $\phi \cong [\pi_1(\theta_h)]^{-1}$. Then $\Gamma(\phi, \theta_h, t + 1)/\Gamma(\phi, \theta_h, t) \cong [\phi\mu(\theta_h)]^{-1}$, so that the right-hand side of (C6) is approximately t-independent. Therefore, consider (C6) for $t = 1$, and rewrite (C5):

$$[1 - \phi\mu(\theta_l)]^{-1} > \Gamma(\phi, \theta_h, 1)/\{[1 - \phi\pi_1(\theta_h)][1 - \phi\mu(\theta_h)]\} \tag{C7}$$

$$1 + \theta_l > (1 + \theta_h)[\Gamma(\phi, \theta_h, 2)/\Gamma(\phi, \theta_h, 1)]. \tag{C8}$$

Maintain $[1 - \phi\mu(\theta_h)]$ and $[1 - \phi\pi_1(\theta_h)]$ positive; multiply the left- and right-hand sides of (C7) by the corresponding sides of (C8) to get, after some manipulation,[12]

$$[(1 + \theta_l)/(1 + \theta_h)]\{[1 - \phi\mu(\theta_h)]/[1 - \phi\mu(\theta_l)]\} > \Gamma(\phi, \theta_h, 2)/[1 - \phi\pi_1(\theta_h)]. \tag{C9}$$

The left-hand side of (C9) is the product of two terms, each of which is easily seen to be slightly less than unity for small $(\theta_h - \theta_l) > 0$. Therefore, the left-hand side of (C9) is $(1 - \varepsilon)$ for small $\varepsilon > 0$.

Write the right-hand side of (C9) as

$$1 + \{[\pi_1(\theta_h) - \mu(\theta_h)]\phi^{T-t+1}\mu(\theta_h)^{T-t}\}/[1 - \phi\pi_1(\theta_h)] = 1 + \delta.$$

By the choice of θ_l, $\pi_1(\theta_l) = \mu(\theta_l)$. Therefore, $\theta_h > \theta_l$ implies $\pi_1(\theta_h) < \mu(\theta_h)$. Hence, $\delta < 0$ and can be made arbitrarily large in magnitude when ϕ approaches arbitrarily close to $\pi_1(\theta_h)^{-1}$ from below. This will satisfy condition (C9).

The condition for real and positive π_1 given b_T (for $d = 0$) is

$$b_T < (\gamma_2/2)[(1 + n)/(R - n)]((1/\phi) + [1/(1 + n)] - \{2/[\phi(1 + n)]^{1/2}\}).$$

Values for b_T that are too low will imply negative b_1. To guarantee strictly positive b_1, set b_T as high as desired by increasing both γ_2 and γ_1, keeping $\phi = \gamma_2/\gamma_1$ at the chosen value.

In recapitulation, the method involves carrying out the steps above in reverse order. Choose γ_2/γ_1 sufficiently close to 1; set γ_2 so that maximum b_T appears high enough. Calculate θ_l and work backwards from b_T to b_1. Then, using this value of b_1, set θ_h so that $(\theta_h - \theta_l)$ is small and positive.

Notes

Partly written during Sargent's visit at the National Bureau of Economic Research in Cambridge, Massachusetts. Danny Quah wrote Appendix C, performed all the computations, and gave very helpful criticisms and suggestions.

1. We will not exhaust the possible circumstances under which the monetary authority's control over inflation is very limited in monetarist economies. We will not even touch on the variety of nonmonetarist economies in which this is true. For examples of such nonmonetarist economies and a more general discussion of the ideas that underlie this paper, see Bryant and Wallace 1980. The messages of our paper are very similar to those of Miller 1981 and Lucas 1981a, b. Other related papers are McCallum 1978, 1981, and Scarth 1980.

2. In Appendix A, we analyze a simple general equilibrium model that implies all our assumptions. The model of that appendix has the virtue that, since individual agents are identified, policies can be compared in terms of the welfare of the individuals in the model.

3. Although the government collects income taxes on the interest payments on government debt, the pre-tax yield is what belongs in equation (1), as long as private securities and government securities are taxed at a common rate and as long as any change in $B(t - 1)$ is offset by an equal change in $K(t - 1)$ in the opposite direction, where $K(t - 1)$ is private investment measured in time $t - 1$ goods. To see this, define $g(t)$ as government expenditures (not including interest payments) minus all taxes except taxes on private and government securities, and let τ be the tax rate on interest earnings. Then the government cash flow constraint can be written

$$g(t) - \tau RK(t - 1) - \tau RB(t - 1) = \{[H(t) - H(t - 1)]/p(t)\} + \{B(t) - B(t - 1)(1 + R)\}.$$

Our Appendix A model implies complete crowding out, which can be expressed as $B(t - 1) + K(t - 1) = \bar{B}$, a constant. Substituting $\bar{B}$ into the last equation gives

$$g(t) - \tau R\bar{B} = \{[H(t) - H(t - 1)]/p(t)\} + \{B(t) - B(t - 1)(1 + R)\}$$

which is equivalent to (1) above, with $D(t) = g(t) - \tau R\bar{B}$.

4. The reader may have noted that the argument presented above does not depend on the magnitude of the $D(t)$ sequence. For the same economy, another way to specify policy is to have (4) hold until some given bound on per capita real debt is reached and have monetary policy be determined thereafter by the condition that the per capita real debt be held constant at that bound. Under assumptions a, b, and c, the following proposition is true for rules of this kind: If an $H(t)$ growth rate θ and a $D(t)$ sequence are such that the debt bound is reached at time T_θ and if $\hat{\theta} < \theta$, then, under the $H(t)$ growth rate $\hat{\theta}$, the given debt bound is reached at $T_{\hat{\theta}} < T_\theta$ and the inflation rate during the period from $T_{\hat{\theta}}$ to T_θ is higher under the $\hat{\theta}$ policy than under the θ policy.

5. This assumes a *rational expectations equilibrium*, which is equivalent to perfect foresight here because the model has no randomness. Thus, our statements involve comparing alternative paths for monetary and fiscal variables which are known in advance. The authorities are assumed to stick with the plans that they announce and not to default, in real terms, on the interest-bearing debt issued from time 1 onward, so that it is as if all interest-bearing debt were indexed. Such an assumption is appropriate for analyzing the alternative time sequences or strategies for monetary policy variables, despite the fact that governments have historically defaulted on substantial fractions of their interest-bearing debt by inflating it away. Such a default option is not available as a policy to which a government can plan to resort persistently.

6. Equation (9) can be used to determine the $D(t)$ sequences and the values of θ that satisfy the "if" clause of the proposition given in footnote 4.

7. Note that equation (5) is a special case of equation (10) with $h = \gamma_1/2$ and $\gamma_2 = 0$. See Appendix A for an underlying model that implies (10) and all of our other assumptions.

8. See Appendix C for a discussion of how to find parameter values which imply this seemingly paradoxical price level behavior.

9. By pursuing the example in the second section of the paper and other examples comparing the welfare of agents across stationary states, the model can be used to support Milton Friedman's 1948 prescription that the entire government deficit be financed by creating base money.

10. This appendix was written by Danny Quah, a graduate student at Harvard University.

11. For simplicity with the θ_h and θ_l notation, time is indicated by a subscript in this appendix, rather than parenthetically, as in the paper and other appendixes.

12. This procedure almost always obtains the desired example. I say "almost" because, strictly speaking, (C7) and (C8) imply (C9), but the converse is not true.

7

Some Pleasant
Monetarist Arithmetic

Michael R. Darby

Sargent and Wallace [in Chapter 6] are widely regarded to have demonstrated that monetary policy cannot be manipulated independently (exogenously) when the growth path of government expenditures and the tax structure are both fixed. More succinctly, Sargent and Wallace maintain that the only choice available to the central bank is not whether to monetize a government deficit but when—now or later. This result can be viewed as a generalization of the Blinder (1974), Blinder and Solow (1973), Tobin and Buiter (1976), and Steindl (1974) analyses of the stationary state when it is assumed that the monetary base is increased while government spending and the tax rate are fixed, so that government borrowing is adjusted passively via open market operations.[1] Although Sargent and Wallace's argument appears persuasive to such authors as King and Plosser (1985), I believe it is seriously wrong as a guide to understanding monetary policy in the United States. To prove my point, this paper first demonstrates that whether or not the government can independently manipulate money, spending, and taxes is not a theoretical question. Then I present evidence that, at least in the United States, the government can indeed independently manipulate all three instruments, with government debt adjusting in a passive but stable manner.

Pleasant Arithmetic Reverses a Key Sargent-Wallace Assumption

Miller (1983) has derived a version of the government budget constraint which is useful for studying the long-run growth equilibrium of the economy. Simplifying the notation of Miller's equation (6), we can rewrite this constraint as

$$G - T = \mu M + (\delta - r)D \qquad (1)$$

Reprinted from the *Federal Reserve Bank of Minneapolis Quarterly Review*, Spring 1984.

where the following are expressed as ratios to net national product (NNP),

G = government expenditures
     (excluding interest payments and taxes thereon)
T = government tax receipts
M = the monetary base
D = the stock of government debt

and where the following are rates per unit of time,

μ = the growth of the monetary base
δ = the growth of real government debt
r = the real after-tax interest rate.[2]

The constraint states that the excess of spending over taxes must be financed either by base money creation or by borrowing in excess of the amount needed to pay the real after-tax interest on the government debt.[3]

The question raised by Sargent and Wallace's article is whether only one value of money-creation revenue μM exists for which debt will be a stable fraction of NNP.[4] This question can be formalized by asking whether a steady-state equilibrium exists and is stable for alternative values of μM. The steady-state equilibrium debt-to-NNP ratio $\bar{D}$ is found from equation (1) to be

$$\bar{D} = (G - T - \mu M)/(\gamma - r) \tag{2}$$

where

γ = the growth rate of real NNP

and

$\gamma = \delta$ if the debt-to-NNP ratio D is constant.

Equation (2) says that if the government is spending more than it collects in explicit taxes and the inflation tax, there can still be a constant debt-to-NNP ratio if the real NNP growth rate γ exceeds the real after-tax interest rate r. However, if r exceeds γ, then any positive excess of G over $T + \mu M$ would indeed cause D to grow without limit. Sargent and Wallace simply assume that r exceeds γ, and hence they inevitably conclude that the government cannot independently choose μ, G, and T.

In contrast, my analysis proceeds here on the assumption that γ is greater than r. (I shall argue later in this paper that empirical evidence supports this assumption.) My basic reasoning is that the government will borrow more than enough to make interest payments on its debt if the debt-to-NNP ratio D is constant, and that this net borrowing $(\gamma - r)D$ increases with D.[5] As a result, higher deficits $G - T - \mu M$ will be associated with higher debt-to-NNP ratios, but these deficits can be financed indefinitely as a matter of arithmetic unless the real interest rate were equal to or greater than the growth rate of real income.

To check that the economy will in fact move toward the equilibrium debt-to-income ratio, suppose that the actual value of D differed from its steady-state value $\bar{D}$. The growth rate of D is $\delta - \gamma$, which is the difference in the growth rates of D's numerator and denominator. Straightforward manipulations and the assumption of either perfect foresight or indexed government bonds imply the growth rate relation[6]

$$\delta - \gamma = (\gamma - r)[(\bar{D} - D)/D]. \tag{3}$$

That is, the growth rate of the debt-to-income ratio will be positive if the actual D is less than its steady-state value $\bar{D}$, and negative if D exceeds $\bar{D}$. So D will gradually converge to $\bar{D}$ even if the economy were to start from another position, such as that which might result from cyclical deficits, wars, short-run monetary or fiscal policy, or changes in the underlying trend values of G, T, or μ which define the steady-state equilibrium.

An Example

To illustrate that alternative monetary policies are consistent with a given fiscal policy, consider the following simple example where

$G \; = 0.22$

$T \; = 0.18$

$\mu \; = 0.10/\text{year}$

$M = 0.10 \text{ year}$

$\gamma \; = 0.04/\text{year}$

$r \; = 0.02/\text{year}.$

By substituting these values into equation (2), we can determine the steady-state debt-to-income ratio as follows:

$$\bar{D} = [0.22 - 0.18 - (0.10/\text{year})(0.10 \text{ year})]$$

$$\div [(0.04/\text{year}) - (0.02/\text{year})]$$

$$= 0.03/(0.02/\text{year})$$

$$= 1.5 \text{ year.}$$

Suppose that the Fed decided to increase money growth to $\mu' = 0.20/\text{year}$ and that this induced M to fall to $M' = 0.09$ year. Then the new equilibrium debt-to-income ratio is

$$\bar{D}' = [0.22 - 0.18 - (0.20/\text{year})(0.09 \text{ year})]$$

$$\div [(0.04/\text{year}) - (0.02/\text{year})]$$

$$= 0.022/(0.02/\text{year})$$

$$= 1.1 \text{ year.}$$

When this policy is initiated, the growth rate of the debt-to-income ratio, using equation (3), would be

$$\delta - \gamma = [(0.04/\text{year}) - (0.02/\text{year})] \times [(1.1 \text{ year} - 1.5 \text{ year})/1.5 \text{ year}]$$

$$= -0.0053/\text{year.}$$

That is, over the first year of the new policy, the debt-to-income ratio would fall by approximately -0.0080 year [by calculating (1 year) $\times$ (-0.0053/year) $\times$ (1.5 year)] to the new level of 1.492 year. The rate of decline would decrease as D asymptotically approached $\bar{D}' = 1.1$ year.[7]

Thus, the government budget constraint does not pose any problems for the existence or stability of the steady-state equilibrium as money growth is varied exogenously with fiscal policy fixed. Similarly, either government spending or tax rates can be varied exogenously when the other fiscal variable and monetary policy are held unchanged. In this way, the standard macroeconomic practice of varying fiscal or monetary instruments while allowing government borrowing to adjust passively is shown to be consistent with a stable steady-state equilibrium.

Empirical Evidence Favors the Pleasant Arithmetic

Like Sargent and Wallace's, my discussion thus far has been basically an arithmetic exercise. In this section, however, I argue that the empirical evidence favors the relevance of my assumptions for the U.S. economy. I base my argument upon two substantial differences between the respective arithmetic exercises: (1) Sargent and Wallace use *before-tax* real yields instead of *after-tax* real yields, and (2) they assume that the relevant real yield exceeds the growth rate of real income.

Differences About the Relevant Real Yield

The differences over which real yield should be compared to real income growth are partly semantic and partly substantive. The semantic difference depends on how an exogenous fiscal policy is defined. Sargent and Wallace define an exogenous fiscal policy as a fixed path for the difference between government spending and taxes (exclusive of money or debt creation and interest payments) measured in terms of real goods. I instead hold the levels of each of these variables (and hence their difference) constant as a fraction of real income. Thus, if decreased money growth reduces real income, it would also reduce the level of the future real deficit, based on my assumption of constant deficits as a fraction of income.

This difference in the way exogenous fiscal policy is defined is relevant only if lower money growth (and hence a higher debt-to-income ratio) reduces real output, as supposed by Sargent and Wallace. They argue that crowding out will occur because, in their life-cycle framework, more government debt means that less wealth will be held in the form of capital. Thus, tax receipts on capital returns go down as tax receipts on government debt go up.[8]

Suppose instead that individuals are fully rational and care about their children as themselves. In that kind of world, government accounts are consolidated into those of the individuals whom it represents, so that whether the government finances by taxes or bonds is irrelevant to individual choices about consumption and the accumulation of physical capital. Measured saving will equal the unaffected capital accumulation plus however many new government bonds are issued instead of tax receipts. But individuals will not be concerned about how many IOUs they are writing to themselves.[9] It should be noted that, given this latter view of saving behavior, the real interest rate is unaffected by the level of the debt-to-income ratio.[10]

Thus, there are good reasons to suppose that the difference in the ways we define exogenous fiscal policy is not a substantive one after all. The fall in private capital, which Sargent and Wallace associate with higher levels of the debt-to-income ratio, need not occur. Nonetheless, it will be shown below that even the before-tax real yield on government securities has been generally well below the growth rate of real income. In that case, even in the Sargent and Wallace world, exogenous variations in the deficit need not be monetized by the central bank.

Real Yields Versus Real Growth

As anyone who has ever looked at before-tax real yields on government securities is aware, it is a simple matter to show that long-term before-tax real yields have not approached corresponding growth rates of real output. It follows directly that after-tax real yields must be even less. This is not to suggest that the real return to capital in the economy is less than the growth rate of real output; but the real rate of return on government bonds and bills is clearly far below this average social return. Presumably, the difference between government and private returns reflects both nonpecuniary services and a very low correlation with the market return, but that really is not at issue in understanding the implications of the government budget constraint.

Ibbotson and Sinquefield (1982) have compiled before-tax real rates of return for U.S. government bonds and Treasury bills from 1926 to 1981. The arithmetic means of the yields for long-term government bonds and Treasury bills are 0.3 and 0.1 (geometric means: −0.1 and 0.0) percent per annum, respectively.[11] So even if all holdings were tax exempt, the experience of the last 55 years suggests that the after-tax real yield on government securities has been nowhere near the 3.0 percent per annum average growth rate of real income over the same years.[12]

It would be possible to increase the estimated real yield somewhat, but I have been unable to find any study that indicates an average real yield on government securities as high as 3 percent, even without any allowance for income taxes. Taking account of income taxes would lower these estimates; so there seems to be no doubt empirically that for the United States, the growth rate of real income exceeds the after-tax real yield on government securities.

A Possible Reconciliation

The point of this paper is a technical one: In the United States, dynamic inconsistencies do not result from treating government expenditures, taxes, and money growth as simultaneously exogenous. A current deficit is therefore not per se inflationary in the sense of requiring future increased money growth, as claimed by Sargent and Wallace.

This conclusion would not hold for all economies, nor need it always hold for the United States. Suppose, for example, that as the ratio of government debt to income—and hence to physical capital—rises, the yield on government debt rises toward that of physical capital instead of remaining constant, as assumed above and by Sargent and Wallace. Then, if the equilibrium debt-to-income ratio were to increase to the point that the after-tax real yield on government securities equalled or exceeded the growth rate of real income, the economy would cross over to the explosive character analyzed by Sargent and Wallace. While this may have occurred for other countries in the past, the United States does not yet seem near that point.

To see this, first consider the fiscal 1983 deficit, estimated at $208 billion by the U.S. Council of Economic Advisers (1983, p. 26). If we allow for a cyclical component based on moving from the assumed 10.7 to 6.0 percent unemployment rate, the structural deficit would be about $117.5 billion less—that is, about $90 billion. This amount is only $5 billion more than actual fiscal 1982 interest payments. So even without taking account of the large offsetting state government surpluses, there is no evidence of substantial differences between long-term government spending (exclusive of interest) and net taxes. Furthermore, current ratios of government debt to income are far below the 1946 value of 1.1.[13]

Conclusion

Sargent and Wallace's propositions should not be generally applied in analyses of the U.S. economy or similar economies. Where the propositions are applied, they should be justified by evidence that the after-tax real yield on government bonds really does exceed the growth rate of real income or would do so under the circumstances being considered. It is hardly surprising that arithmetic alone cannot give a real answer to a substantive economic question.

Notes

The author acknowledges helpful conversations with John Haltiwanger and Tom Sargent. The research reported here was supported in part by the National Science Foundation (NSF Grant SES-8207336) and by the National Bureau of Economic Research's (NBER's) Project on Productivity and Industrial Change in the World Economy, and is part of the NBER's research program in International Studies. The opinions expressed here are those of the author, not those of the NSF or NBER; nor is this a report of the NBER.

1. This paper does not attempt to comment on the relevance of the balanced-budget condition within the stationary state. See, however, Fischer 1976 and Auerbach and Rutner 1977 on this point.

2. See Darby 1975. Further discussion of the use of the after-tax real yield appears later in this paper.

3. The standard national income accounting definition of the deficit counts as government borrowing and private saving that portion of after-tax nominal interest which represents an adjustment for decline in the real value of the nominal debt. In those terms, we would include in equation (1) the growth rate of the nominal debt $\delta + \pi$ and the nominal after-tax interest rate $r + \pi$, where the inflation rate π cancels. See Jump 1980 and Darby and Lothian 1983. Miller's equation (6) substitutes the steady-state condition that the growth rates of real NNP and real debt are equal, but we leave the equation in this form to analyze behavior out of full steady-state equilibrium.

4. The fraction of NNP which people desire to hold as money is a decreasing function of the nominal interest rate and hence μ. In the relevant range, μM increases with increases in μ, but not proportionately so.

5. An alternative term for net borrowing $(\gamma - r)D$ would be *negative debt service*.

6. These manipulations begin with the identity

$$\delta - \gamma \equiv [(r + \pi)D + G - T - \mu M - (\gamma + \pi)D]/D$$

which was obtained by taking the time derivative of the natural logarithm of D where the perfect foresight or indexing assumption allows us to express the nominal after-tax interest rate as the sum of the corresponding real interest rate and the actual, rather than expected, rate of inflation. (In the steady state, there is no need to distinguish actual from expected inflation.) Then, we have

$$\delta - \gamma = [(\gamma - r)/D] \times [(G - T - \mu M)/(\gamma - r)]$$

from which equation (3) follows by substitution of equation (2).

7. Note, however, that in the absence of perfect foresight or a prior refunding into indexed bonds of long-term bonds (see Darby and Lothian 1983), this adjustment will be much faster as the real value of the existing bonds and debt service drops.

8. Tobin (1965a) proposed a different mechanism by which inflation might reduce the private capital stock. In either case, as firms devote less inputs to conserving cash balances, improvements in the aggregate production function would tend to offset, eliminate, or dominate this capital stock effect, so that the effect of money growth on real output is theoretically ambiguous. I have assumed elsewhere (in Darby 1979a) that the production function effect dominates, so that lower inflation rates increase real output.

9. White (1978), Darby (1979b), and Kotlikoff and Summers (1981) all report evidence that bequest assets dominate life-cycle assets in total U.S. wealth, and this finding supports the assumption of concern about the welfare of one's children. Barro (1974, 1978a), Kochin (1974), and David and Scadding (1974) all present evidence in support of the ultrarational or Ricardian view. Note that if the government finances a tax cut with increased borrowing, saving increases not in anticipation of future increased taxes but in anticipation that, otherwise, total NNP would fall.

10. Plosser (1982), for example, finds that asset prices are unaffected by the extent to which a given level of government expenditures is financed by borrowing instead of taxes.

11. The corresponding nominal yields were 3.1 and 3.1 (arithmetic) and 3.0 and 3.0 (geometric).

12. Computed from real GNP data in Darby 1984 (Table A-20) and in FR Board 1983 (p. A52).

13. High ex post real interest rates experienced during 1981–82 appear to be a result of a slowing of inflation (compare 1929–33) and not a matter of a regime change to unprecedentedly high deficits.

8   A Reply to Darby

Preston J. Miller and
Thomas J. Sargent

A key result of Sargent and Wallace's "Some Unpleasant Monetarist Arithmetic" [Chapter 6] is that a permanently higher government deficit must eventually be accommodated by increases in the monetary base. In "Some Pleasant Monetarist Arithmetic" [Chapter 7], Darby argues that this result does not currently apply to the U.S. economy because it depends on an assumption which is not supported by the data. In this reply to Darby we explain why we find his argument unconvincing and why we remain concerned about the longer-term monetary implications of high prospective federal budget deficits.

Background

Sargent and Wallace describe an economic model in which the real growth rate γ and the real interest rate r are assumed to be constants for all time. It is also assumed that monetary and budget policies initially imply a steady-state equilibrium where the real interest rate exceeds the real growth rate $(r > \gamma)$. Given these assumptions, Sargent and Wallace show that any attempt to run a permanently higher deficit net-of-interest is simply not feasible unless the supply of base money is eventually increased. Without an eventual increase in the base-money supply, a permanent increase in the deficit would cause the ratio of interest-bearing government bonds to national income to diverge to infinity (see Figure 8.1), so at some point that ratio would outstrip the ratio of total wealth to income. That is, the government would eventually be unable to command the resources needed to pay its debt.

Darby's model retains Sargent and Wallace's assumptions that the real interest rate and real growth rate are constants, but it departs from their

Reprinted from the *Federal Reserve Bank of Minneapolis Quarterly Review*, Spring 1984.

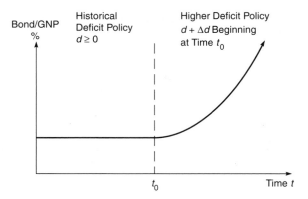

Figure 8.1 With Sargent-Wallace Assumption ($r > \gamma$)

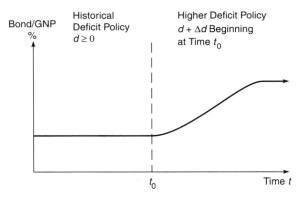

Figure 8.2 With Darby Assumption ($\gamma > r$)

Figures 8.1 and 8.2
Financing a Higher Deficit without Increasing the Supply of Base Money: Effect on Federal Bonds Held by the Public (as a percentage of GNP)

model by assuming that the real growth rate is greater than the real interest rate ($\gamma > r$). As a result, the consequences of a permanent increase in the deficit are very different from those claimed by Sargent and Wallace. Under Darby's assumption that $\gamma > r$, a permanent increase in the deficit is feasible even with no change in the supply of base money from its initial path. Such a policy change simply leads to a higher eventual level for the ratio of interest-bearing government bonds to national income (see Figure 8.2). Although the level of the bond-to-income ratio may be higher, the government can always command the resources needed to pay its debt.

Darby's Evidence

Darby examines U.S. data to determine whether Sargent and Wallace's or his own model is more appropriate as a description of the current situation facing the United States. His evidence, simple and direct, rests on taking the formal Sargent-Wallace model and his own version of their model quite literally. Since both models assume a constant real interest rate and real growth rate, the sign of the difference between these constant rates is the critical distinction between the two models. Darby's procedure is simply to compute the historical average of the difference between the real growth rate and the real interest rate. He interprets the sign of this difference as settling the matter: if $\gamma > r$ so that $\gamma - r$ is positive, Darby's model applies; if $r > \gamma$ so that $\gamma - r$ is negative, Sargent-Wallace's applies. As long as the formal models explicitly analyzed by Sargent-Wallace and Darby are taken literally, Darby's test is the natural one to perform.

Is Darby's Evidence Sufficient?

Our own interpretation of Darby's evidence, however, is conditioned by our preference not to take literally Sargent and Wallace's assumption that the real interest rate is constant and, therefore, independent of budget policy. Instead, Sargent and Wallace can be regarded as using their model to approximate a more complicated one in which the real interest rate is itself a function of the budget and monetary policies in place.[1] Their intent was to point out the choices facing monetary policymakers whenever budget policies cause the real interest rate to exceed the real growth rate. Such was the situation when Sargent and Wallace wrote their paper in the first half of 1981, a time when the real interest rate exceeded the real growth rate and when monetary and budget policymakers were announcing moves that seemed to imply that the real interest rate would continue to exceed the real growth rate for a sustained period.

In models more general than the one analyzed by Sargent and Wallace, the real interest rate on government bonds is not a constant but is partly determined as a rising function of the ratio of interest-bearing government bonds to base money. In such models, the difference between the real growth rate and real interest rate depends on the monetary and budget policies in place. From the perspective of these more general models, Darby's empirical evidence does not resolve the matter of the relevance of Sargent and Wallace's argument for the choices currently facing U.S. policymakers.

Viewed through such models, evidence that the real interest rate has averaged less than the real growth rate over some historical period may be interpreted as partly reflecting the monetary and budget policies in place during that historical period. The average difference between the real growth rate and the real interest rate would not be expected to remain the same after a change in monetary and budget policies, such as a switch to a regime with higher average deficits.[2] Moreover, in the context of more general models in which the real interest rate depends on monetary and budget policies, much more is involved than simply comparing a real growth rate with a real interest rate to determine the feasibility of financing a permanent increase in the deficit without resorting to printing more base money.

More Is Involved

In order to show that more is involved, we make use of a simple form of the steady-state budget constraint:[3]

$$d = (\pi + \gamma)m(r, \pi) + (\gamma - r)b(r, \pi) \qquad (1)$$

where the following are ratios to gross national product (GNP),

d = deficit net-of-interest

m = demand for base money

b = demand for government bonds

and where the following are rates per unit of time,

π = inflation

γ = real growth

r = real interest.

We assume the markets for money and bonds clear (that is, the supply of money and bonds equals the demand), so that

$$m(r, \pi) = M_t/Y_t \text{ and } b(r, \pi) = B_t/Y_t \tag{2}$$

where

M = stock of base money
B = stock of government bonds
Y = nominal GNP

and t subscripts denote a given time period. The steady-state budget constraint states that the deficit net-of-interest d must be financed by seignorage on money $(\pi + \gamma)m(r, \pi)$ and by seignorage on bonds $(\gamma - r)b(r, \pi)$. (*Seignorage* is the revenue the government earns from issuing money and bonds.) A deficit policy is feasible only when the government can earn enough seignorage on its money and bond issue to finance its deficit net-of-interest.

The steady-state budget constraint helps to make precise our analysis of the insufficiency of Darby's empirical evidence and to suggest what empirical evidence is sufficient in the context of more general models. Suppose the economy is initially in equilibrium such that, given a deficit net-of-interest d and a path of money M over time, the money-to-GNP and bond-to-GNP ratios (M_t/Y_t and B_t/Y_t) and the inflation rate, real growth rate, and real interest rate (π, γ, and r) are all constant over time. The issue is whether it is possible to raise the deficit net-of-interest for all time to a new level $d + \Delta d$ while keeping the path of money fixed at $\{M_t\}$ and have the economy converge to a new equilibrium where the ratios M_t/Y_t' and B_t'/Y_t' and the rates π', γ', and r' once again are all constant over time. From the steady-state budget constraint this is possible only if

$$d + \Delta d = (\pi' + \gamma')m(r', \pi') + (\gamma' - r')b(r', \pi'). \tag{3}$$

Equation (3) says that the deficit net-of-interest can be permanently raised to a higher level only if the total seignorage from money and bonds calculated at the new equilibrium rates (r', γ', and π', consistent with a fixed path of money) is enough to cover the higher deficit.

In general, to determine empirically if it is possible to finance a higher deficit net-of-interest $d + \Delta d$ by bond issue alone, we would require estimates of the elasticities of money demand and bond demand (in order to determine how these demands change when the rates of real interest and inflation change to r' and π'). We would also need an estimate of how the economy's real growth rate varies with the rates of real interest and inflation. It would then be possible to determine quantitatively how the seignorage represented on the right side of the steady-state budget constraint changes when the deficit net-of-interest on the left side changes.

Since the equilibrium rates depend on the policies in place, it is not sufficient to examine the average difference between the rates of real growth
and real interest ($\bar{y} - \bar{r}$) over some extended historical period, as Darby
does. If historically the government has been running a deficit d, then $\bar{y}$ and
$\bar{r}$ will reflect the rates corresponding to that policy—the rates y and r in
equation (1). In order to determine the feasibility of financing a higher
deficit $d + \Delta d$ by bond issue alone, however, estimates of y' and r' are
required—as shown in equation (3). Given a fixed path for the monetary
base, a proposed policy of running a persistently higher deficit net-of-
interest than has been observed historically would be expected to raise the
real interest rate relative to the real growth rate, thereby shifting their
relationship toward that supposed by Sargent and Wallace.

Another reason that simply looking at the difference between $\bar{y}$ and $\bar{r}$
does not suffice is because the change in seignorage caused by a change in
deficit policy depends on other factors—such as how the inflation rate
changes and how the new rates of interest and inflation affect the demands
for money and bonds [see equation (3)]. For example, an increase in the real
interest rate could generally be expected to cause people to shift their asset
holdings from money to bonds, thereby lowering the demand for money
while raising the demand for bonds.

A Model That Shows Darby's Evidence Isn't Sufficient

In order to illustrate that Darby's evidence is not sufficient, we consider a
simple monetarist model, which is taken from our more general class where
the real interest rate rises with the ratio of bonds to money. This model (see
Miller 1982) has the following features:

a. The real growth rate y is fixed.

b. The inflation rate π is determined by the growth in the stock of base
money.[4]

c. The real interest rate r is inversely related to the stock of private capital.

From the steady-state budget constraint, the change in seignorage as the
deficit d is increased to the new level $d + \Delta d$ while the path of money is
held constant is given by

$$\Delta \text{ seignorage} \cong t_B \Delta b + \Delta t_B b \tag{4}$$

where

$t_B = y - r$, the rate of seignorage on bonds

$\Delta t_B = r - r'$, the change in the rate of seignorage on bonds
$\Delta b = b(r', \pi) - b(r, \pi)$, the change in the demand for bonds.

Such a change in policy is feasible only if the seignorage increases by the same amount as the deficit.

In this model such a change in deficit policy has both a quantity and a price effect on bond seignorage ($t_B \Delta b$ and $\Delta t_B b$, respectively). When $\gamma > r$, the quantity effect is positive as the real demand for bonds increases at a positive seignorage rate ($\gamma - r$). The price effect, however, is negative as additional government debt drives out private capital and raises the real interest rate at which the government must borrow. In this model there is a maximum amount of bond seignorage that can be generated. For the additional deficit to be financed by bond issue alone, it is necessary that the seignorage from bonds initially be less than that maximum. Because the quantity and price effects are of opposite sign, seignorage is maximized at some real interest rate $r^* < \gamma$, as shown in Figures 8.3 and 8.4.

Two Cases

This simple model indicates two cases where we could observe historically that $\bar{\gamma} > \bar{r}$ and where it still would not be possible to finance a permanent increase in the deficit net-of-interest by bond issue alone. The first case is when the real interest rate is greater than or equal to the real interest rate at which seignorage from bonds is maximized: $\bar{r} \geqslant r^*$. In this case, any further increase in bond issue will cause the seignorage from bonds to decrease (see Figure 8.3). So even though $\bar{\gamma} > \bar{r}$, it would not be possible to finance any increase in deficits by bond issue alone. The second case is when the real interest rate is less than the rate at which seignorage from bonds is maximized, $\bar{r} < r^*$, but the increase in the deficit is too large. Since there is a finite maximum to bond seignorage, it is always possible that the increase in the deficit will exceed the maximum increase in bond seignorage (see Figure 8.4).

Which Arithmetic Best Applies Currently?

Current observations of the relationship between the real interest rate and real growth rate seem consistent with the implications of our simple model and the more general models of which ours is an example. It appears that since 1980, the real interest rate has tended to rise relative to the real growth rate as it became increasingly evident that the government had embarked on a historically unprecedented policy of large and persistent

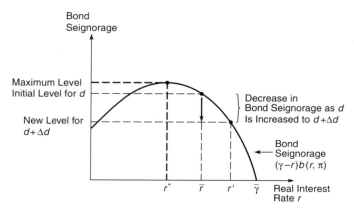

Figure 8.3 Case One: $\bar{r} \geqslant r^*$

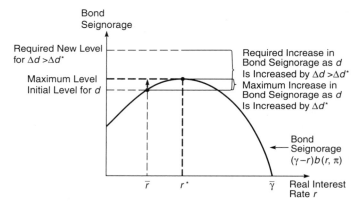

Figure 8.4 Case Two: $\bar{r} < r^*$

Figures 8.3 and 8.4
Two Cases Where Darby's Evidence Is Insufficient When r Rises with the Ratio of Bonds to Money

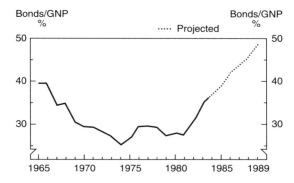

Figure 8.5
CBO Projections of the Bond-to-Income Ratio: Federal Bonds Held by the Public (as a percentage of GNP). Plotted for the end of fiscal years. Source: CBO (U.S. Congress 1984, p. 10).

deficits net-of-interest. With nominal interest rates currently far above the inflation rates predicted for and realized in 1984, the real interest rate seems to be high and the difference between the real growth rate and real interest rate $(\gamma - r)$ seems to be *negative*. These observations favor Sargent and Wallace's position.

Perhaps more direct evidence favoring Sargent and Wallace's position is contained in recent Congressional Budget Office (CBO) projections of a steady rise in the government's bond-to-GNP ratio (see Figure 8.5 and compare with Figures 8.1 and 8.2). The CBO projects this ratio assuming that the budget policies in place at the beginning of 1984 are maintained and that monetary policy does not accommodate the deficits (U.S. Congress 1984). Even under its assumption of modestly declining real interest rates (which already seems overly optimistic), the CBO's projected bond-to-GNP ratio rises steadily.

Because of the apparent error in the CBO's assumption for the real interest rate, the bond-to-GNP ratio would still be expected to rise for real growth rates higher than the roughly 3.5 percent assumed by the CBO (U.S. Congress 1984, p. 12). Thus, even under more optimistic assumptions about real growth, current deficit policy would still not be sustainable without future monetary accommodation.

Notes

1. In their concluding remarks, Sargent and Wallace indicate that they had in mind a model where the real interest rate depends on policy. They state that their assumption of a

constant real interest rate was made "because it seems to be maintained by many of those who argue for a low rate of growth of money no matter how big the current deficit is. If we were to replace that assumption, we would instead assume that the public's demand for government bonds is an increasing function of the real rate of return on bonds ..." (p. 6).

2. That the distribution of the sequence of equilibrium real interest rates depends on budget and monetary policies is an application of the principles underlying the Lucas critique to the problem at hand. See Lucas 1976.

3. The constraint is derived in Miller 1983, pp. 12–13. Its notation has been altered slightly here to conform with Darby's.

4. We assume a simple quantity demand function for money so that $m_1 = 0$.

9 Intergenerational Linkages and Government Budget Policies

S. Rao Aiyagari

Social security programs and deficit policies shift the burden of taxation across generations. In a social security program the working population is taxed with the proceeds being paid as benefits to the older and retired group. When the government runs a deficit it is choosing to borrow instead of taxing the current population. The debt may be rolled over for many years and eventually paid off by levying taxes on future generations.

An important issue in macroeconomics is whether and how such policies affect the private sector's saving behavior and hence the overall rate of capital accumulation and economic growth. Insight into this issue was provided by Barro (1974) who showed how these effects depend on the nature of *intergenerational linkages*, the financial connections between generations that can arise from altruistic motives. He considered the possibility that members of one generation may care about the welfare of another generation; parents may care for their children and choose to leave them bequests, or children may care for their parents by supporting them in retirement. He showed that if these links are sufficiently strong then a startling conclusion obtains: government budget policies may have no effects whatsoever on investment, growth, or the intergenerational distribution of wealth; that is, government policies may be *neutral*. Private saving behavior changes in such a way as to completely offset the intended effects of such policies. In the case of a social security program, children may simply reduce their support for parents dollar for dollar with the level of government support; in the case of a deficit, current generations may simply increase their saving and pass it on as bequests to future generations so they can afford to pay the higher taxes without suffering a loss in consumption.[1]

Reprinted from the *Federal Reserve Bank of Minneapolis Quarterly Review*, Spring 1987.

In this paper we will try to understand the economics of such offsetting private behavior. I first develop a simple model and analyze the effects of government policies in the absence of intergenerational linkages. Next I introduce such linkages and show how neutrality of government policies can obtain. Then I consider the relationship between neutrality and economic efficiency and show that there is no necessary connection between the two. That is, government policies may be neutral even when the economy is operating inefficiently, and they may not be neutral even when the economy is operating efficiently. After discussing some qualifications and extensions of the analysis, I conclude that considerations involving intergenerational linkages can serve to limit the potency of government policies but cannot eliminate the effects entirely.

A Model without Intergenerational Linkages

We will begin by constructing a simple model so that we can carefully analyze the above issues. The most natural model to study is clearly an overlapping generations model—one in which generations come and go but the economy (and the government!) goes on forever. The simplest such model is one in which there are equal numbers of only two generations alive at any date, the working young (y) and the retired old (o).[2] Assume that they are endowed with w_y and w_o units respectively of a single good which may be consumed or invested and that if k units are invested at date t then $f(k)$ units will become available for consumption at date $t + 1$. The function $f(k)$ represents the investment technology and is assumed to be strictly increasing with diminishing marginal product. Further, $f(0) = 0$; that is, returns are zero if there is no investment. The investment technology is represented by the curve labeled $f(k)$ in Figure 9.1. The marginal product of investment is the additional output obtained due to an additional unit of investment and corresponds to the slope of the $f(k)$ curve. As drawn, this slope is diminishing with the level of investment.

Let $c_y(t)$ and $c_o(t)$ be consumptions of the young and the old, respectively, at date t and let $U(c_y(t), c_o(t + 1))$ be the utility function representing preferences over lifetime consumption for the young at t. Note that the above specification implies that we are considering a case where each generation is completely selfish and cares only about its own lifetime consumption and does not care about the welfare of any other generation.

Government policies are described as follows. A social security tax of γ_s is imposed every period on each young and the proceeds are distributed every period equally to each old. In addition, the government has out-

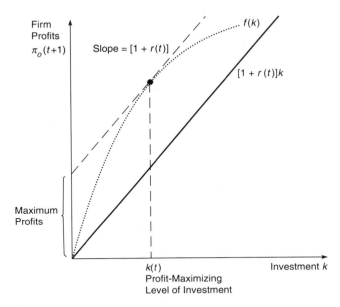

Figure 9.1
The Investment Technology and the Maximization of Firm Profits

standing debt obligations of face value d (measured in units of the good and per young person) which is constant over time. It follows that in every period additional taxes of $r(t)d/[1 + r(t)]$ per young person [where $r(t)$ is the real interest rate from t to $t + 1$] would have to be raised in order to make the interest payments on the debt.[3] We assume that a fraction θ of the needed taxes are levied on the young and the rest on the old. We denote by $\gamma_y(t)$ and $\gamma_o(t)$ the total taxes (less transfers) levied on the young and the old respectively, so that

$$\gamma_y(t) = \theta r(t)d/[1 + r(t)] + \gamma_s \tag{1}$$

$$\gamma_o(t) = (1 - \theta)r(t)d/[1 + r(t)] - \gamma_s. \tag{2}$$

It is now possible to explain the working of the model as follows. Investment is undertaken at each date by firms which are jointly owned by the young at that date. The firms choose the level of investment to maximize profits which are then paid back next period to the (then old) owners. Suppose that the firms invest $k(t)$ (per young person) at date t which is financed by issuing bonds. In order to be competitive these bonds must pay the same interest rate $r(t)$ as government debt. It follows that each firm's profits at $t + 1$, denoted $\pi_o(t + 1)$, are given by

$$\pi_o(t + 1) = f(k(t)) - [1 + r(t)]k(t). \tag{3}$$

As shown in Figure 9.1, the profit-maximizing level of investment is that at which the marginal product of investment [which is the slope of the curve labeled $f(k)$] equals $[1 + r(t)]$. It can also be seen that the level of investment, as well as maximum profits, decreases as the interest rate goes up. This makes sense since the higher interest rate increases the cost to firms of financing investment. The profits, $\pi_o(t + 1)$, are paid to the old at $t + 1$, who are the owners of the firms.

Consumption and saving decisions are made by the young at each date t so as to maximize their utility $U(\cdot, \cdot)$ subject to the budget constraints

$$c_y(t) + s(t) = w_y - \gamma_y(t) \tag{4}$$

$$c_o(t + 1) = w_o + [1 + r(t)]s(t) - \gamma_o(t + 1) + \pi_o(t + 1) \tag{5}$$

where $s(t)$ is saving by the young. The young use their saving to acquire government debt and bonds issued by firms. They are indifferent between the two since both bear the same interest rate. The old in the initial period (that is, at date 1) simply consume whatever they have, which is

$$c_o(1) = w_o + [1 + r(0)]s(0) - \gamma_o(1) + \pi_o(1). \tag{6}$$

The budget constraints (4) and (5) can be combined into a single wealth constraint by dividing (5) by $[1 + r(t)]$ and adding to (4). This yields

$$c_y(t) + c_o(t + 1)/[1 + r(t)] = [w_y - \gamma_y(t)]$$
$$+ [w_o - \gamma_o(t + 1) + \pi_o(t + 1)]/[1 + r(t)]. \tag{7}$$

The right-hand side of this equation is the present discounted value of a young person's lifetime disposable income, or *wealth*. The individual chooses consumption in each period of life given the interest rate and wealth. The choice of consumptions is depicted in Figure 9.2 as resulting from utility maximization subject to the above budget constraint. Saving may then be found from (4).

We will assume that a rise in the interest rate reduces current consumption; or equivalently, increases saving. We also assume that an increase in wealth increases current consumption but by a smaller amount than the increase in wealth. This is captured by letting α denote the marginal propensity to consume out of wealth [that is, the change in $c_y(t)$ due to a dollar's change in wealth] and assuming that α is positive but less than one. It follows from this that the effect of an increase in wealth on saving

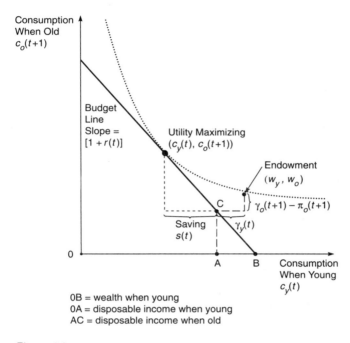

Figure 9.2
A Person's Lifetime Consumption Choices

depends on whether the increase in wealth is due to an increase in *current* disposable income or due to an increase in *future* disposable income. If it is entirely due to the former, saving must rise; whereas if it is entirely due to the latter, saving must fall.

The model specification is completed by imposing the equilibrium condition that

$$s(t) = d/[1 + r(t)] + k(t). \tag{8}$$

This condition simply states that total saving by the young must equal the sum of government debt and the bonds that firms issue to finance their investment.[4]

From equation (8) and Figure 9.2 we can now see why the response of private saving behavior to government policies is so important. If a change in the social security program (which changes the relative disposable incomes between the young and the old) affects private saving then it will also affect investment and hence the interest rate and the consumption allocation between the young and the old. Similarly, if an increase in government debt is not offset by a corresponding increase in private saving, then again investment, interest rates, and consumption allocations would be affected. Thus the response of private saving is the crux of the whole matter.

Using the budget constraints (4) and (5), the equation for firm profits (3), and the equilibrium condition (8), we can develop the national income identity for this simple model economy as follows:

$$c_y(t) + c_o(t) = w_y + w_o - [\gamma_y(t) + \gamma_o(t)] - s(t)$$

$$+ [1 + r(t-1)]s(t-1) + \pi_o(t)$$

$$= w_y + w_o - r(t)d/[1 + r(t)]$$

$$- \{k(t) + d/[1 + r(t)]\} + [1 + r(t-1)]$$

$$\times \{k(t-1) + d/[1 + r(t-1)]\} + f(k(t-1))$$

$$- [1 + r(t-1)]k(t-1)$$

$$= w_y + w_o - k(t) + f(k(t-1)). \tag{9}$$

Therefore, we have

$$c_y(t) + c_o(t) + k(t) = w_y + w_o + f(k(t-1)) \tag{10}$$

which states that total consumption plus investment equals total output, consisting of total endowment plus the returns on past investment. Alternatively, we can interpret (10) as the equilibrium condition in the goods market: total demand consisting of consumption demand and investment demand must equal the total supply of goods consisting of total endowment and current production. If we impose (10) and work backwards using (3)–(5), we can derive (8) as an implication. Thus, conditions (8) and (10) are equivalent.

Policy Effects

We can now describe the effects of the two types of government policies we are considering.

An Increase in Social Security
We interpret an increase in the social security program to mean an increase in social security taxes γ_s on the young with a matching increase in payments to the old. At date 1 it is clear that the old will consume all of the increase in the payments they receive. From the national income identity

(10) either the young will have to reduce their consumption or firms will have to reduce investment, or both. From the point of view of the young this program represents a reduction in current disposable income and an increase in future disposable income of the same magnitude. Assuming a positive interest rate, wealth will fall but by less than the fall in current disposable income. Therefore, current consumption will fall by less than the reduction in wealth and hence by less than the reduction in current disposable income; consequently saving will fall, too.[5] It follows from (8) that investment will fall. From Figure 9.1 it can be seen that the interest rate will have to rise in order to induce firms to reduce investment. There is a reduction in wealth for all future generations; the increase in current taxes is larger (in present-value terms) than the equal increase in future social security benefits. Of course, the initial old are the beneficiaries of the increase in the program.

An Increase in Government Debt

We interpret an increase in government debt in the following way. Assume that at date 1 the government increases the level of debt from d to d' and then maintains it at the new higher level forever. The increased borrowing at the initial date makes it possible to reduce taxes at that date. Assume that all of the reduction is passed on to the old at date 1. This corresponds to an increase in the deficit at date 1 financed by additional borrowing. Again it is clear that the initial old will consume all of the resulting increase in their disposable income. Therefore, from the national income identity (10), either investment or consumption by the young (or both) will have to fall. For the young at date 1, we can see that there is no change in current taxes (since the entire tax reduction is given to the old) but that there is an increase in future taxes. Hence current disposable income is the same but future disposable income is reduced. Consequently, their wealth falls, which reduces their current consumption and hence increases saving. The crucial question is whether current consumption by the young falls dollar for dollar with the increase in debt, or equivalently, whether saving rises dollar for dollar with the rise in debt. As can be seen from the national income identity (10) or the equilibrium condition for saving (8), in such a case there will be no effect on investment and hence interest rates. Since this is an important point we will consider it in some detail.

Suppose that at date 1 the market value of debt issued by the government goes up by one dollar. If interest rates do not change, then the face value of the debt must go up by $[1 + r(1)]$ dollars. Therefore, future taxes on the current young will go up by $(1 - \theta)r(1)(d' - d)/[1 + r(1)]$, which equals $(1 - \theta)r(1)$ dollars. Hence lifetime wealth of the young is reduced by $(1 - \theta)r(1)/[1 + r(1)]$ dollars, and consequently current consumption will be reduced by $\alpha(1 - \theta)r(1)/[1 + r(1)]$ dollars. It follows that the reduction in current consumption will be less than one dollar, or equivalently, saving will go up by less than one dollar. Therefore, the interest rate must rise in order to induce the young to increase their saving and cut their consumption by one dollar to match the corresponding increase in consumption by the old. It follows that investment must fall.[6]

As for future generations, assuming that the interest rate is positive, the increase in the level of debt implies an increase in their taxes (in both periods of life) and hence a reduction in wealth and consumption possibilities. It is not too difficult to argue that the interest rates faced by future generations must also be higher than before. If the interest rates remain the same, then it can be seen from (8) that saving must go up by $(d' - d) \div [1 + r(t)]$. The maximum increase in saving occurs when θ is zero. In that case, future disposable income decreases the most, causing saving to go up. The reduction in future disposable income is $r(t)(d' - d)/[1 + r(t)]$, which reduces wealth by $r(t)(d' - d)/[1 + r(t)]^2$ and hence reduces current consumption by $\alpha r(t)(d' - d)/[1 + r(t)]^2$. It follows that saving goes up by the same amount as the reduction in current consumption. This increase in saving, however, is still short of the required increase of $(d' - d)/[1 + r(t)]$ because $\alpha r(t)/[1 + r(t)]$ is less than one. In terms of (8), even in the most favorable case, saving will fall short of the increase in debt. Therefore, interest rates must rise to induce the young to save more on the one hand while inducing firms to invest less so that the equilibrium condition (8) can be met. The higher interest rate reduces investment permanently and thereby reduces the total availability of goods in the future.

Adding Intergenerational Linkages

Here we will consider how the conclusions of the previous section are affected by the introduction of intergenerational linkages. These linkages may take several forms: parents caring for the welfare of their children, children caring for their parents' welfare, or possibly both simultaneously. In addition, such caring may be *paternalistic* or *nonpaternalistic*. In the former, one generation cares not just about another generation's welfare but also about the levels of consumption of various goods. For example, parents may disapprove of their child's preference for beer instead of milk, or a child may disapprove of a parent's smoking or playing bingo. In nonpaternalistic caring, one generation cares only about the welfare of another and evaluates it the same way as the other does. In addition, there is no utility attached to the act of giving in and of itself separate from its effects on the recipient; there is no glow from being generous. We will mostly be concerned with nonpaternalistic caring though we will make some comments on what is likely to happen with other forms of caring. We will also restrict attention to the simple case where each member of a generation cares only about one other person in the next generation (descendant) or the previous one (single parent). The situation could get more complicated if we considered marriage between unrelated adults or grandparents caring directly about grandchildren (in addition to the indirect caring through their children).

The simplest way to specify utility when a parent cares about a child is as follows. Let $V(t)$ be the welfare of a member of generation t and let β be the discount factor, between zero and one. Then write

$$V(t) = U(c_y(t), c_o(t+1)) + \beta V(t+1) \qquad t = 0, 1, 2, \ldots . \tag{11}$$

Note that by repeatedly substituting for $V(t+1)$, $V(t+2)$, $\ldots$, and so forth, we can rewrite (11) as

$$V(t) = U(c_y(t), c_o(t+1)) + \beta U(c_y(t+1), c_o(t+2)) + \cdots . \tag{12}$$

The case where a child cares about the welfare of the parent may be specified as

$$V(t) = U(c_y(t), c_o(t+1)) + \beta V(t-1) \qquad t = 1, 2, 3, \ldots \tag{13}$$

$$V(0) = U(c_y(0), c_o(1)). \tag{14}$$

Again it follows that by repeated substitution we can write the welfare of a member of generation t as

$$V(t) = U(c_y(t), c_o(t+1)) + \beta U(c_y(t-1), c_o(t)) + \cdots . \tag{15}$$

It is, of course, possible to have both of these types of linkages occurring simultaneously. We will, however, analyze them one at a time. The discount factor indicates that (since it is less than one) even though one generation may care about another's welfare, it attaches a smaller weight to the other's welfare than to its own. In this sense generations are still somewhat selfish.[7]

Parent to Child

How do members of one generation express their concern for the welfare of another? In the case where parents care about children we assume that they may leave a bequest which the children can either consume or save. Let $b(t)$ denote the bequest received by a generation t person from its $t - 1$ parent. The budget constraints of such a person would have to be modified to reflect bequests as follows:

$$c_y(t) + s(t) = w_y + b(t) - \gamma_y(t) \tag{16}$$

$$c_o(t + 1) = w_o + [1 + r(t)]s(t) - \gamma_o(t + 1) + \pi_o(t + 1) - b(t + 1). \tag{17}$$

We assume that the generation t person takes $b(t)$ as given (since it is chosen by the parent) and chooses $b(t + 1)$ in addition to consumption and saving. We also require that bequests be nonnegative; that is, a parent may give to but not take away from the next generation. It is now easy to describe the choice of bequests. A generation t person would find it optimal to make an additional dollar's worth of bequest so long as the loss in its own utility (due to the reduction in own second-period consumption) is outweighed by the gain in the next generation's utility (due to the increase in wealth) discounted by β. This leads to the condition

$$MU_2(c_y(t), c_o(t + 1)) \geqslant \beta MU_1(c_y(t + 1), c_o(t + 2))$$

$$\text{with equality if } b(t + 1) > 0. \tag{18}$$

In (18), MU_2 and MU_1 stand for the marginal utility of consumption in the second and the first period of life, respectively.[8] The left-hand side of (18) measures the loss in utility to the old at $t + 1$ due to an additional dollar's bequest made to the young at $t + 1$ since this (potentially) reduces the old's consumption by a dollar. The right side of (18) is the discounted gain in utility to the young due to the corresponding increase in their consumption. From (12) we see that so long as the loss in utility to the old is less than the discounted gain in utility to the young, the old will benefit by increasing their bequest. On the other hand, if the loss in utility to the parent exceeds the discounted gain to the child, then the parent would not be willing to make any bequest; that is, the bequest will be zero. This corresponds to having a strict inequality in (18). However, if the bequest is positive, then it must be that the loss and the gain must offset each other exactly at the margin. This corresponds to having an equality in (18). When there is strict inequality in (18), the bequest motive is termed *nonoperative*; otherwise it is termed *operative*.

We will first analyze the effects of government policies under the provisional assumption that bequests are operative in every period. Next we will consider what happens when bequests are never operative. Finally we will explore the conditions under which bequests might or might not be operative.

Consider what happens when the government increases the level of social security taxes and benefits by, say, a dollar. This raises the utility of the parent but lowers the marginal utility. Correspondingly, it lowers the child's utility but raises its marginal utility. Therefore, from every parent's perspective, the loss in utility from making a bequest has been reduced and the gain in utility to the child has been increased. It follows that it would be advantageous to increase the level of the bequest. By how much? Exactly one dollar because that restores the balance between the parent's and the child's marginal utilities that prevailed before the increase in social security levels. We thus come to the startling conclusion that consumption levels, saving, and hence investment and interest rates are all completely unaffected: the increase in social security benefits to the old is totally offset by a matching increase in bequests from the old to the young.

What about an increase in the level of government debt by one dollar? (Recall that the government's additional borrowing results in a tax cut for the initial old.) As one can guess, the old at date 1 will pass on their tax reduction of one dollar to the generation 1 young. The young will save the entire amount, earning $[1 + r(1)]$ in their second period. They will use a part $(1 - \theta)r(2)[1 + r(1)]/[1 + r(2)]$ to pay the higher taxes in their second period and pass on the rest $[1 + r(1)][1 + \theta r(2)]/[1 + r(2)]$ as bequests to their children. They, in turn, will use a part $\theta r(2)[1 + r(1)] \div [1 + r(2)]$ to pay the higher taxes on them in their first period and save the remaining $[1 + r(1)]/[1 + r(2)]$ dollars, earning $[1 + r(1)]$ in their second period (that is, at date 3). From here on the story just repeats. It follows that the saving by the young in each generation will have gone up by exactly the increase in the market value of government debt and hence that investment and therefore interest rates will have remained the same. Similarly, everyone's consumption pattern remains the same. Private saving goes up dollar for dollar with reductions in government saving (increases in the deficit) so that economy-wide saving (which equals investment) is unaffected. We thus come to the conclusion that deficits (due to tax cuts) financed by borrowing have no effects on the economy so long as every generation is linked to the next one by operative bequests.

What happens if the bequest motive is not operative? For simplicity, assume that it is never operative. Then the initial old will not pass on their extra wealth (whether due to an increase in social security benefits or due to a tax cut financed by more borrowing) to the young and neither will the initial young make any bequest to their young the period after, and so on. It is as if every generation behaves in a strictly selfish fashion, and the effects are the same as if there were no intergenerational linkages. If the bequest motive were operative for some generations but not all, then the effects would be somewhat less than when no linkages exist, but policies would still not be neutral.

It is interesting and useful to understand when the bequest motive might or might not be operative. As condition (18) states, the bequest motive will not be operative if the marginal utility of consumption for the old exceeds the discounted marginal utility of consumption for the young. In view of diminishing marginal utility it follows that this will happen when consumption of the old is much smaller than consumption of the young. This is likely to be the case when the endowment of the old is much smaller than that of the young and when the investment technology is not too productive. This makes sense because then the old do not have much wealth to pass on and further, they value their low second-period consumption much more highly than the relatively larger consumption of the young. This consideration suggests the following. Suppose that initially the bequest motive is not operative. As the size of the social security transfers to the old or their debt-financed tax cuts increase, their wealth and second-period endowment increase, thereby making it more and more likely that the bequest motive will become operative. At that point any further increases in these policies will be neutral.

Child to Parent

We now consider what happens if the linkage runs from children to parents. We denote by $g(t)$ the gift given by a generation t young to its parent. The budget constraints of a generation t person become

$$c_y(t) + s(t) = w_y - g(t) - \gamma_y(t) \tag{19}$$

$$c_o(t + 1) = w_o + [1 + r(t)]s(t) + g(t + 1) - \gamma_o(t + 1) + \pi_o(t + 1). \tag{20}$$

This individual takes $g(t + 1)$ as given (since that is chosen by the next generation) and chooses $g(t)$ in addition to consumption and saving. As is natural we restrict $g(t)$ to be nonnegative; a child may give to but not take from its parent. Analogous to (18) the condition for gifts to be made is

$$MU_1(c_y(t), c_o(t + 1)) \geqslant \beta MU_2(c_y(t - 1), c_o(t))$$

$$\text{with equality if } g(t) > 0. \tag{21}$$

The interpretation of this condition is also similar to (18). If the loss in utility to generation t (which is MU_1) from making an additional unit of gift to the parent exceeds the discounted gain in utility (βMU_2) to the parent, then a gift would not be made. If a gift is being made, then at the margin the loss and the gain must exactly offset each other. As with the bequest motive, the gift motive is said to be operative if there is an equality of marginal utilities in (21); otherwise it is termed nonoperative.

It is also easy to see the mechanism by which government policies might be neutralized under this type of linkage. Suppose that the gift motive is operative in every period. Then an increase in the level of social security payments to the old will lead to a reduction by the same amount of the gifts being passed on from child to parent—assuming that the increase in payments is not larger than the initial level of gifts so that the gift motive remains operative. Similarly, a tax cut given to the old and financed by additional borrowing will cause a matching reduction in gifts from young to old with the reduction being saved to make up for the difference in future taxes. Thus, private saving rises dollar for dollar with the deficit so that investment, interest rates, and consumption allocations remain unaffected. The same proviso about the bequest motive remaining operative applies to the gift motive as well. If the gift motive is never operative, then the effects are the same as if there were no such intergenerational linkage. If the motive is operative at some dates but not all, then the effects will be somewhat moderated.

It is also easy to understand when the gift motive is likely to be operative. As condition (21) indicates, if the consumption of the young is relatively small compared to the old, then MU_1 is likely to be larger than MU_2 so that gifts will not be made. This is likely to happen when the young are relatively poorly endowed compared to the old. Debt-financed tax cuts to the old and increases in social security, both of which transfer wealth toward the old, obviously make it less likely that the gift motive will operate.

Other Considerations

So far, we have considered a model in which all the individuals in any generation were identical with regard to their lifetime endowments and utility functions. It would be more realistic to allow for some heterogeneity among members of each generation. This will lead to the possibility that bequests or gifts may be operative across some members of the old and young generations while for others, neither is operative. So long as there are some people in some generations who are not linked via operative bequests (gifts) to the next (previous) generation, government policies will not be neutral. However, the larger the fraction of each generation that is linked via operative bequests or gifts, the smaller will be the impact of government policies.

Another point that should be kept in mind is that even if initially the bequest or the gift motive is operative, a sufficiently large change in government policy may lead to the motive becoming nonoperative and hence the policy change will be nonneutral. If initially the gift motive is operative, a sufficiently large increase in the social security program can make it nonoperative. Similarly, if the bequest motive is operative initially, a tax increase on the initial old with a corresponding reduction in the deficit and government debt may make it nonoperative. The neutrality result that we have demonstrated is true only for those changes in government policy such that the bequest (or the gift) motive is operative before as well as after the policy change.

Neutrality and Economic Efficiency

If government policies are neutral, then is the economy operating as efficiently as possible? Conversely, if the economy is operating efficiently will government policies be neutral? The concept of *efficiency* we will use is the following: the economy is operating efficiently if it is not possible to increase total consumption at some date without reducing total consumption at some other date.

That the answer to the first question is negative can be seen from a more detailed analysis of the gift motive. Suppose that the economy is in a steady state so that consumption allocations, investment, interest rates, and gifts (assumed operative) are constant over time. Individuals will choose consumptions over the two periods of their life such that

$$MU_1(c_y, c_o)/MU_2(c_y, c_o) = 1 + r. \tag{22}$$

This can be seen from Figure 9.2. The left side of (22) is the marginal rate of substitution between first- and second-period consumption (the slope of the indifference curve) and the right side of (22) is the slope of the budget line. From condition (21) we then have that

$$1 + r = \beta < 1 \tag{23}$$

so that the interest rate must be negative so long as the gift motive is operative. The steady-state version of the national income identity (10) yields

$$c_y + c_o = w_y + w_o + rk \tag{24}$$

which indicates that the total availability of goods can be *increased in every period by permanently reducing investment.* Consequently, so long as the gift motive is operative and investment is positive, the economy is operating inefficiently. It is not difficult to construct examples that exhibit these features.

However, if the interest rate is positive then it would not be possible to increase the supply of goods in every period. If investment at date 1 is increased then the supply of goods in that period must be less, whereas if investment is permanently decreased then the supply of goods in the future must be less. Thus an investment program will be efficient if the interest rate is positive.[9] It does not follow, however, that if the economy is operating efficiently then government policies will be ineffective! For example, we can construct situations such that the interest rate satisfies

$$1 < 1 + r < 1/\beta. \tag{25}$$

In such a case the bequest motive cannot be operative [see conditions (18) and (22)] and neither can the gift motive. Therefore, policies will not be neutral and yet the economy is efficient since the interest rate is positive. This discussion also reveals that when the bequest motive is operative (in every period) so that $1 + r$ equals $1/\beta$, we have a situation in which the economy is efficient and policies are neutral.

Some Qualifications and Extensions

Here we will discuss some qualifications for the bequest or the gift motive to be operative and for government policies to be neutral. We have already seen that the bequest or the gift motive has to be operative in order for government policies of the type considered to be neutral. We have also discussed the conditions on endowment patterns that lead to one or the other motive being operative. It should also be emphasized that the *same* motive has to be operative both before and after the policy change for it to be neutral. This should be clear from the previous discussion on neutrality and efficiency. When the bequest motive is operative $1 + r$ equals $1/\beta$ (in the steady state), whereas when the gift motive is operative $1 + r$ equals β. It follows that the interest rate cannot be the same if different motives are operative before and after the policy change and hence neither can investment be the same.

Another qualification is that there be no impediments to the smooth operation of credit markets (Drazen 1978). An easy way to see why this is important is to consider a model with three generations alive at each date (old, middle aged, and young). Suppose that people receive endowments only in the middle period. Young individuals will then borrow to provide for consumption. In the next period they will receive a bequest from the old and use the bequest plus the endowment to repay the previous loan and make additional loans to the new generation of young. In their last period, the receipts from loans made previously will be used partly for consumption with the rest being passed on as bequests to the middle aged. The role of credit markets can be seen to be crucial because without them the old cannot acquire assets (by lending in the previous period) in order to finance consumption and bequests. If credit markets are perfect and bequests are operative, then a social security program that taxes the middle aged with the proceeds going to the old may be neutralized by bequests in the reverse direction. On the other hand, if there are no credit markets, then such a policy cannot be neutralized because the bequest motive will not be operative initially.

Another qualification concerns the nature of taxes imposed. The previous analysis assumed that all taxes were lump sum, that is, unrelated to the economic decisions being made by agents. On the other hand, if the government were to levy taxes on consumption or on income (defined to include interest income), then the consumption/saving decisions of agents (as well as their labor/leisure decisions, if the labor supply were elastic) may get distorted in spite of there being operative bequests or gifts. This conclusion, however, depends on the assumption that bequests (or gifts) continue to be made in a lump-sum fashion. There is no reason why this should be so when taxes are distortionary. Bequests and gifts may themselves be conditioned on behavior in a way that neutralizes "distortionary" taxes (Bernheim and Bagwell 1986).

It was mentioned previously that intergenerational linkages may exhibit either paternalistic or nonpaternalistic caring. The neutrality results depend crucially on the linkage being nonpaternalistic. If, for instance, people derive pleasure from the act of giving per se, which is unrelated to the effects of the bequest or the gift on the receiver, then changes in government policies will not be neutralized by compensating changes in private bequests or gifts.

A final qualification that we have omitted throughout our discussion is that of uncertain lifetimes and imperfect annuities markets (Eckstein, Eichenbaum, and Peled 1985). These can result in involuntary bequests and a beneficial role for compulsory social security programs. The latter can arise because in the absence of government intervention, individuals dealing in imperfect or nonexistent annuities markets may be unable to properly share the risks of inopportune death.

An extension of the setup in this paper would be to modify the implicit assumption that the family tree originating from one initial old does not overlap with that of any other initial old. This is clearly unrealistic considering the predominance of reproduction by marriage among previously unrelated persons. The nature of linkages within the same generation and across members of different generations can get quite complex under this system with overlapping family trees. This leads to a situation in which different members of the older generation may care about the same members of the younger generation or indirectly about the same members of the next-to-next generation and so on.[10] This results in horizontal linkages among members of the same generation and in bequest externalities in which one set of parents may reduce their bequest given that the child is also receiving a bequest from another set of parents.

Under this extended setup, the proliferation of linkages *widens* the scope for neutrality of government policies. As an example, government transfers from one set of parents-in-law to the other set can be neutralized by the first reducing their bequest to their son (or daughter) and the second increasing their bequest to their daughter (or son). Thus, not only intergenerational transfers but within-generation transfers may also turn out to be neutral. This, together with the neutrality of "distortionary" taxes discussed previously, suggests that the scope of neutrality results is uncomfortably wider than that of the Ricardian doctrine (Bernheim and Bagwell 1986).[11] While a significant number of economists may be willing to accept the latter, very few would go along with the much wider neutrality results. This suggests that some important considerations are being overlooked in the present framework of intergenerational linkages. Alternatively, one could argue that the framework of linkages is not a good approximation to reality and that the Ricardian doctrine is (approximately) valid for reasons entirely different from the effects of intergenerational linkages.

Conclusion

It seems clear that the presence of intergenerational linkages limits the potency of government budget policies. Whether or not this limitation is strong enough so that policies of realistic magnitudes are best approximated as being neutral can only be judged by detailed empirical investigation. If government policies are judged to be approximately neutral, then we need not worry about the effects on private saving, investment, or the intergenerational distribution of wealth. If they are not, then there are legitimate grounds for being concerned about the burden of taxation that is being passed on to future generations and the crowding out effects of government debt on capital accumulation.

Notes

1. The idea that government deficit policies may be neutral, first formulated by the English economist David Ricardo (1772–1823), is known as the *Ricardian doctrine*.

2. While this simplification makes it easier to understand the issues, it is not very useful for empirical applications because it requires that each period in the model be thought of as corresponding roughly to 35 years.

3. This follows because the government budget constraint in each period is

Face Value of Debt Outstanding = Taxes + Market Value of New Debt.

Since the face value of debt outstanding is constant at d, the market value of new debt at date t must be $d/[1 + r(t)]$.

4. Since firms finance all of their investment by issuing bonds, the value of bonds issued equals their investment.

5. Note that this conclusion follows even if the interest rate is negative. In this case, wealth and current consumption rise and hence saving falls.

6. In macroeconomics this is known as *crowding out*, or the displacement of private investment by increased government borrowing. Rising interest rates are what accomplish this: higher rates induce private savers to channel their saving toward government bonds instead of real capital.

7. Our specifications of intergenerational linkages follow those of J. Carmichael (1982).

8. *Marginal utility of consumption* is the extra utility obtained by increasing consumption by one unit. The *law of diminishing marginal utility* states that marginal utility decreases as consumption levels increase. In contrast, *total utility*, measured by $U(\cdot, \cdot)$, always increases when consumption levels increase.

9. The interest rate condition takes this form because we are assuming a *stationary economy*, one with no growth. In a growing economy the corresponding condition for efficiency is that the interest rate must exceed the growth rate.

10. Suppose we interpret each person to be a couple. Then a male child of one couple and a female child of another couple form a person in the next generation. Clearly, this person may receive bequests from both sets of parents. Two persons in the older generation may also be linked by marriage in the next-to-next generation, and so on.

11. As discussed before, this need not imply that the resulting allocations are efficient.

10

Playing by the Rules: A Proposal for Federal Budget Reform

V. V. Chari and Preston J. Miller

The federal budget mess just won't go away. Despite the discipline of Gramm-Rudman-Hollings (GRH), the government is running ever larger budget deficits, making poor decisions and spending an inordinate amount of time on the process. In 1990 the budget deficit reached $220 billion. This year, after the torturous passage of a package of expenditure cuts and tax increases, it's projected to exceed $300 billion. Yet the original GRH deficit target for fiscal 1991 was zero. Voters are concerned; Congress is concerned; the administration is concerned. Although there is widespread agreement that something is seriously wrong with the budget process, there is less agreement about what should be done about it. In response to this concern, many proposals for reform have been suggested. Yet they miss the mark: they fail to address the problems inherent in the budget process and are not based on sound economic principles.

We provide a conceptual framework for budget policy. Based on this framework, we propose that the federal government change accounting practices, institute rules on debt issue, and impose enforcement mechanisms. Our proposal will produce budgets that are balanced over time in an appropriate rather than an arbitrary sense. Our proposal also will help inform the decision makers and the public about their policy options and the financial consequences of those options. Of course, our proposal will not cure all the ills in the budget process. Hard choices will still have to be made.

But first a bit of history. Since the late 1960s, the federal government has consistently run large deficits (Figure 10.1). These large deficits have led to a dramatic increase in the federal debt as a percentage of GNP in the 1980s (Figure 10.2). Interest payments to service this debt have absorbed an increasing proportion of our national product (Figure 10.3).

Reprinted from the *Federal Reserve Bank of Minneapolis 1990 Annual Report*.

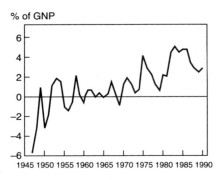

Figure 10.1 Net Deficit

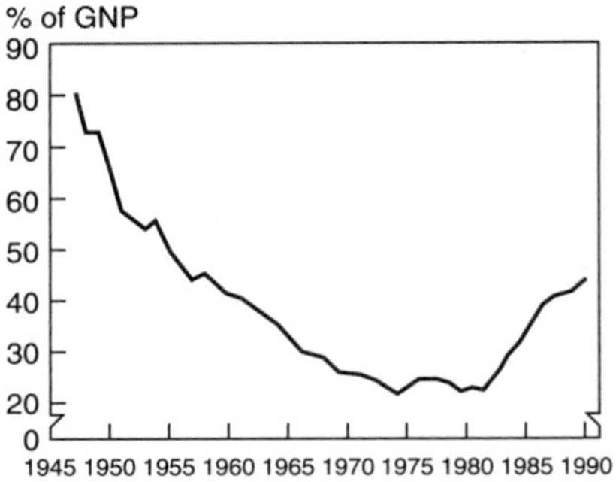

Figure 10.2 Net Financial Liabilities

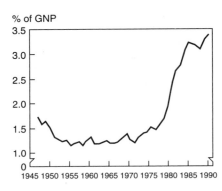

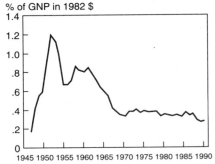

Figure 10.3 Net Interest Payments

Figure 10.4 Construction Expenditures

Figures 10.1–10.4
Components of the Federal Budget. Sources: U.S. Department of Commerce and Department of the Treasury.

The debilitating consequences of a growing federal debt are well known. Large interest payments leave us with less to pay for education, highways, national defense, and a variety of useful causes. A growing federal debt tends to raise interest rates and to increase pressure on the Federal Reserve System to follow inflationary policies. This litany of ills may be familiar; nonetheless, it is alarming.

To make things worse, even though total nondefense expenditures have been allowed to grow at double-digit rates, too little money has been allocated for capital projects, such as highways, airports, and sewer systems. Federal capital spending in fiscal 1991 is projected to be roughly 2.2 percent of GNP, down from 4.4 percent of GNP in the early 1960s. Construction expenditures, which are an important component of capital spending, have declined over the postwar period (Figure 10.4). Surely we can do better than to leave our children decayed highways, crumbled bridges, and antiquated sewer systems, with little or no ability to repair or replace any of them because of the enormous tax bills coming due for services consumed before they were even born.

We are not the first to offer solutions: The Gramm-Rudman-Hollings Act (GRH) and the reforms of last fall were attempts to respond to these problems. While these attempts to reach a balanced budget are laudable, we think our proposal is better. Specifically, we propose that the federal government adopt the following:

• Record transactions on an accrual basis and maintain separate operating and capital budgets,

• Require that the combined operating budget in the current and subsequent fiscal years be balanced, and establish overall limits on capital spending,

• Institute enforcement mechanisms based on performance to ensure that the rules are being followed,

• Set up rainy day funds to meet contingencies.

We would, of course, not be averse to an escape clause suspending the rules in the event of a war or national emergency. But we think that such suspension should require a supermajority of votes in Congress and the assent of the president.

Why do we need these or any rules at all? Why not rely on policymakers to make good decisions? The problem is that the policymaking process is fundamentally biased against the future. Without rules to constrain policy decisions, we will continue to have bad outcomes. So the question is not whether to have rules, it is which rules to have. The current rules do not address the bias, nor are they based on sound economic principles. In the rest of the essay, we explain the bias in policymaking, show that the current set of rules is inadequate, and argue that our rules will yield good outcomes.

The Need for Policy Rules

Our political system encourages elected officials to adopt policies that are biased against the future. They are biased, because they are not what voters ideally would like. Voters tend to have a long-term view on policy issues.

They care about the outcomes of policy decisions not only over their own lifetimes but over the lifetimes of their descendants. Elected officials, however, tend to adopt a short-term view on policy issues.

But why should this be so? If voters could keep themselves fully informed, closely monitor decisions, and understand the effects of alternative policies, surely they would force their elected officials to act in the public's interest. Voters would boot out officials who acted badly or develop institutional arrangements that set up proper incentives. But voters have neither the ability nor the incentive to get the information necessary to do these things.

It is especially difficult for voters to decide whether policymakers are making wise choices on decisions that will yield benefits or costs several years into the future. So even though voters care about the future, they weight current results heavily. They rationally reward policymakers who make decisions yielding large current benefits even if some of those decisions impose future costs. In order to get reelected, policymakers have incentives to make decisions that are systematically biased against the future. Thus, it is not especially helpful to argue that if incumbent policymakers were replaced, wiser policies would be chosen. The problem is that the system encourages policymakers to adopt the short-term view.

This bias results in decisions weighted toward current rather than future consumption. In particular, these decisions mean too much deficit financing, too little capital investment, and a proclivity to put off until tomorrow projects which should be undertaken today. The immediate benefit to elected officials is easily seen. Deficit financing shifts the tax burden for current consumption into the future. This allows more consumption now but less in the future as the taxes are paid. Less capital investment frees up resources and allows more consumption now, but since fewer resources have been invested, there is a smaller supply of goods available for future consumption. Elected officials can also make more resources available for current consumption by putting off projects such as maintenance of the infrastructure or closure of insolvent thrifts. But the problem is that such actions leave fewer resources available in the future as the real costs of the necessary, but delayed, expenditures escalate.

This policymaking bias against the future is not unique to the government, however. Corporate stockholders face many of the same problems as voters in deciding whether corporate managers are acting wisely. Corporate managers act on behalf of stockholders, yet they have different interests. Stockholders have incomplete knowledge about the managers' decisions and the consequences of the managers' actions. These are features of the so-called *agency problem*.

Furthermore, no single stockholder has much incentive to monitor management's actions. Stockholdings are typically dispersed among many individuals. Each stockholder has an incentive to let other stockholders monitor the firm. As a result, typically there is less monitoring of firms' actions than would occur if the stockholders could act jointly. This is known as the *free rider problem*.

Voters also face the agency and free rider problems. It is difficult to know the consequences of policymakers' actions, and each voter has an incentive to free ride on other voters. The agency and free rider problems can be mitigated but not entirely solved. If stockholders cannot entirely solve these problems, certainly voters cannot be expected to solve them completely either, since compared to corporate decisions, government policy decisions are aimed at more diverse objectives, and the responsibility for them is more diffuse.

How stockholders attempt to manage the agency and free rider problems suggests ways voters might deal with them, though. Publicly traded corporations, for example, are required to adopt standard accounting practices (known as Generally Accepted Accounting Principles) to inhibit inaccurate presentation of information. Corporate charters also limit management's discretion. We think these ideas can and should be used to design better policy procedures for the federal government. Corporations also adopt a variety of other practices to align managers' and stockholders' interests, including incentive contracts for managers, hostile takeovers, and so on. It is not apparent how, or even whether, these other practices can be transferred to the government, so here we will stick to practices that seem readily transferable.

The agency and free rider problems point to a need for rules to limit policymakers' discretion. To understand why we are proposing new rules, it is important to understand what's wrong with the old ones.

The Problems with the Old Rules

The Gramm-Rudman-Hollings Process

Prior to the fall 1990 reforms, the budget process was designed to work roughly as follows: Early in January the president would submit to Congress a budget for the fiscal year beginning October 1. By the time Congress would adjourn in the summer it would pass bills and a budget resolution specifying amounts to be appropriated to discretionary spending programs and changes to be made to rules for entitlement programs and taxes. In mid-August the Office of Management and Budget (OMB) would determine whether the projected deficit for the upcoming fiscal year exceeded the GRH target by more than $10 billion. If it did, automatic spending cuts would be made according to a statutory formula to ensure that the projected deficit met the target. Then at some point Congress would raise the debt ceiling so that there was authority to issue additional debt to finance the projected deficit.

The GRH procedure was supposed to lead to balanced budgets and to eliminate the government's deficit financing bias by the use of rules. The procedure did not come close to achieving its goal and the original GRH targets had to be revised several times (Table 10.1). In addition, the process led to other problems.

Rather than curbing the government's bias to excessively discount the future, the GRH process fed it. By focusing on the projected budget deficit in the approaching fiscal year, the process encouraged deficit financing, discouraged capital spending, and made it more attractive to delay necessary expenditures.

Paradoxically, the GRH process made deficit financing easier by encouraging the substitution of gimmicks for real actions. The gimmicks included the exchanging of assets, time-shifting of payments, movement of expenditures off the budget, and use of unrealistic economic and technical assumptions. Selling government assets, such as loans, for cash resulted in budget savings, even though all that occurred was the exchange of one asset for another one of comparable value. Time-shifting created one-time fictitious savings by taking payments scheduled for the approaching fiscal year and moving them into the current fiscal year where they were simply spilt milk, or into the following fiscal year where they were not yet subject to a sequester. For example, the government achieved savings in an approaching fiscal year by taking payments such as employees' pay and farm subsidies due out in late September and delaying them until early October of the following fiscal year. Then without retribution, the government was able to switch the payments back once the new fiscal year was entered. Movement of expenditures off-budget, such as was done for the U.S. Postal Service and the Resolution Trust Corporation (RTC), produced budget savings by a stroke of the pen without doing anything real. Finally, projected deficits were reduced by use of optimistic economic and technical assumptions that overestimated tax revenue, underestimated interest expense, and understated the costs of existing programs.

Just how extensively were these gimmicks used? Robert Reischauer, director of the Congressional Budget Office (CBO), notes that the amount

Table 10.1
Gramm-Rudman: Receding targets (by fiscal year; in billions of dollars)

	1986	1987	1988	1989	1990	1991	1992	1993	1994	1995
Actual deficit	$221.2	$149.7	$155.1	$153.4	$220.4					
Gramm-Rudman I (1985)	171.9	144.0	108.0	72.0	36.0	0				
Gramm-Rudman II (1987)		144.0	136.0	100.0	64.0	28.0	0			
Gramm-Rudman III (1990)						327.0	349.8	285.2	157.5	117.3

Note: Due to bookkeeping changes, the Gramm-Rudman III deficit targets are not directly comparable to those of the first two versions of the antideficit law. New accounting rules exclude the surplus in the Social Security trust funds from the deficit calculations; that has the effect of increasing the deficit by at least $60 billion a year. These latest targets are larger than those in the original 1990 budget deal because of pre-planned adjustments in the president's 1992 budget.

Source: *Congressional Quarterly Weekly Report*, February 9, 1991, Vol. 49, No. 6, page 337.

of permanent deficit reduction enacted in the GRH period averaged a bit less than in the pre-GRH period of same duration: "What is different about the two periods is the reliance on one-time savings that became a feature of the GRH period.... In the pre-GRH period, these gimmicks occurred so infrequently that CBO did not keep systematic track of them. In the GRH era, fully half of the apparent deficit reduction has been achieved by such devices" (Reischauer 1990). Reischauer also notes that under GRH the amount of budget savings in the president's budget attributable to overly optimistic economic and technical assumptions more than tripled.

The GRH process, combined with existing accounting practices, also made capital spending highly susceptible to the knife. Existing accounting practices treat spending on capital projects, such as bridges, no differently than spending on current consumption, such as legal counseling. Yet the two are fundamentally different. A capital project provides services in the current year as well as in the future, while current consumption provides services only in the year in which they were purchased. As a result of this difference, spending on a capital project can be preferable to spending on current consumption yet can return less in benefits in the current year since it also provides benefits in future years. When GRH forced budget cuts in an approaching year, the existing accounting practice led government officials to believe that a dollar cut from capital spending would cause less immediate loss in benefits than would a dollar cut from current consumption. To understand better why this is so, consider the following example.

Suppose the government has decided to build a bridge at a cost of $30 million which is expected to provide services over 30 years worth $6.4 million per year. Suppose the interest rate is 10 percent so that the present value of these services is $60 million. With the present value of the benefits at double the cost, the bridge obviously should be built. But under the government's accounting system, dropping the project saves $30 million in costs and sacrifices only $6.4 million in benefits. In contrast, a $30 million cut in spending on a less attractive current consumption item, for which benefits only matched costs, would sacrifice $30 million in benefits. Given the short-term focus of GRH, accounting exercises such as these might well explain why capital spending was so susceptible to the knife.

In addition to capital spending, GRH made it unattractive to spend money on other projects having short-term costs and long-term benefits. For example, the government avoided proper maintenance of nuclear armaments plants to save money in the short term. Because of that neglect, the cost of keeping these plants operating has escalated and the additional cost is now estimated by the CBO to be roughly $160 billion spread over the next 40 years. Another painful example is the savings and loan crisis. If the government had dealt with the problem when it surfaced in 1986, it would have meant closing some insolvent thrifts at an estimated cost of $10 billion to $15 billion. But the government balked, at least in part because it didn't want to put more pressure on itself to abide by the GRH targets. So spending to remedy the problem was delayed, the problem mushroomed, and the cost to the government as estimated by the CBO and the General Accounting Office rose to over $150 billion in present-value terms.

The GRH process not only generated poor results, it also contributed to delays and confusion. Without a conceptual framework, policymakers were forced to debate each minor budget variation as if it were a new theme.

The Fall 1990 Reforms

The government was well aware that the budget process was in need of repair and direction. The administration suggested numerous reforms, including instituting a line-item veto and changing the accounting procedures for loans and guarantees. The budget committees in both chambers of Congress held hearings on reform, several bills proposing reforms were introduced, and the budget package that finally was passed last fall contains important reforms of the process.

It's too early to judge whether the fall reforms will lead to improvements in the process, but it's not too early to argue they don't go far enough. These reforms still fail to provide government officials with a conceptual framework for making decisions, and the definition of budget deficits and the targets for them remain arbitrary.

The reforms make it more difficult to exceed the deficit targets, but they also make it easier to raise the targets (see box for details on the reforms). Under the new process, there are constraints placed not only on the size of the total budget deficit as before, but also separately on entitlements, revenues, and three types of discretionary spending. In addition, a series of three sequesters can be prompted by spending overruns in the prior fiscal year. These reforms give Congress less maneuvering room to exceed budget deficit targets. But at the same time, the reforms allow the deficit targets to be raised for economic and technical reasons, emergencies, and increased spending on deposit insurance activities. Since the targets are arbitrary, the government is highly likely to use these loopholes to continue its deficit spending ways.

The reforms also fail to resolve problems associated with the current accounting system. Under the fall reforms it is still possible to achieve budget "savings" by shifting payments forward into future fiscal years,

---

Main Features of the Fall 1990 Budget Process Reforms

- *Five-Year Budgeting.* Budget resolutions and necessary reconciliation bills must project spending, revenues, and deficits for five years.
- *Discretionary Spending Caps.* Appropriations bills must stay within separate caps for defense, foreign aid, and domestic discretionary spending for fiscal 1991–93; for fiscal 1994–95, the law sets overall discretionary spending caps.
- *Enforcement.* A complicated set of sequesters ensures that spending stays within the caps in the bill. Essentially, these sequesters apply if the Office of Management and Budget determines that spending will exceed the caps. The sequesters also "look back" to offset spending increases or revenue cuts in the prior fiscal year.
- *Pay-As-You-Go Entitlements and Revenues.* Bills containing increases in entitlement or other mandatory spending or reducing revenues must be offset by entitlement cuts or revenue increases.
- *Social Security and Deposit Insurance.* Social Security receipts and expenditures will no longer be included in budget calculations. Increased spending for deposit insurance activities—chiefly the savings and loan salvage operation—will not be allowed to trigger sequesters.
- *Emergencies.* If requested to do so by the president, Congress could enact emergency appropriations, entitlement increases, or revenue cuts without triggering sequesters.
- *War and Recession.* A declaration of war would still cancel the sequester process. Congress could still vote to cancel the sequester process in the event of a projected recession or measured economic growth below 1 percent for two consecutive quarters.

---

although the reforms remove much of the incentive to shift them back to the current fiscal year. That's because past spending overruns could prompt a sequester and thus are no longer treated as spilt milk. However, the reforms do nothing to address the bias against capital spending. Capital expenditures are still treated no differently from current expenditures.

We have argued that rules are needed to address the policy bias problem, but we have seen that bad rules can create further problems. While the fall 1990 reforms improve the original GRH rules, a lot more should be done. That is why we offer our proposal.

The fall reforms of the budget process provide a transition to a more balanced federal budget. But even if they take us to that destination, problems will remain. Without a logical basis for their targets, policymakers will find ways to violate them. Without a sound accounting system, they will continue to bias their decisions. And without a conceptual framework, they will continue to debate every budget nuance as if it were a new problem.

The Case for Our Rules

Basic Principles

Our budget proposal is a set of reforms intended to reduce both the policymaking bias and the confusion associated with current procedures, and it's guided by four basic economic principles.

First, the budget should be balanced in a present-value sense without use of the inflation tax. This principle is based on an accounting identity and on a stated goal of macroeconomic policy. The identity says that what goes out from the government must come in, and it implies that the present value of government expenditures cannot exceed the present value of government receipts. Since it would be inefficient for the government to take in more than was needed, it follows that the present value of government expenditures should equal the present value of government receipts. In this equality receipts can include proceeds from the inflation tax, that is, the depreciation caused by inflation in the value of government nominal liabilities. However, based on statements in Humphrey-Hawkins legislation and congressional testimony of high officials in the Federal Reserve, we take price stability to be a goal of policy. With zero inflation as a goal, the first principle follows.

Second, benefits should outweigh costs. This follows from the theory of economic policymaking which requires that government officials weigh alternative programs in terms of their economic benefits and costs to society. Since the services of programs occur over time, the government must measure benefits and costs in expected, present-value terms. Those benefits and costs are dated to occur when resources are transferred in and out of the private sector. Thus, when the government hires workers, the economic cost occurs when the workers enter the public sector and not when the government gets around to mailing their checks.

The third economic principle is that users pay. That beneficiaries of government programs should pay is partly a fairness argument. It also has the virtue of making it more likely that the benefits of public programs exceed their costs, since those costs cannot be pushed off on noninvolved parties. This principle suggests that borrowing to finance current consumption is unacceptable because that method of financing pushes the costs off to future generations who do not benefit from the consumption. In contrast, it also suggests that borrowing to finance capital spending is acceptable since future generations will benefit from the services of that capital. Obviously this principle cannot be applied across the board. By definition, income redistribution programs, such as welfare, cannot be financed by recipients. But some other programs, such as the national parks and the highway system, would fall squarely under the user-pays principle. And most other programs would fall under this principle in a general way. Current services should be paid for by the current generation. And transfers to the poor of one generation, which are designed to even the income distribution, should be paid for by the wealthy of the same generation.

Our fourth economic principle, tax smoothing, is an implication of studies of the tax structure. The implication follows as long as the *deadweight loss*, the distortions caused by the tax and the resources burned up in collecting it, rises disproportionately with the tax rate. That is, the deadweight loss more than doubles when the tax rate doubles. Tax smoothing means that when the government has commitments to spend in the future, it should begin taxing for them today. This is true whether those commitments are contractual, such as underfunded pensions, or noncontractual but fairly certain to occur, such as wars or natural disasters. What this means in practice is that it's more efficient to raise taxes a little bit now and keep them there than it is to wait and raise them a lot when the spending takes place.

We believe that these four simple principles suggest reforms of the budget process which help deal with the policy bias problem. We also believe they can provide guidance on many current budgetary issues.

Our Reforms in More Detail

Our proposal for reform is hardly radical. It is composed of modest changes in accounting procedures, rules on debt issue, and enforcement mechanisms. Most of the changes are either incorporated into budget practices of corporations and state and local governments or included in other proposals for federal budget reform.

The accounting changes we propose are that expenditures and receipts be recorded on an accrual basis and that separate accounts be maintained for operating and capital items. These accounting changes follow directly from our cost-benefit timing and user-pays principles. Our cost-benefit timing principle requires that expenditures and receipts be recorded when the activity giving rise to them occurs; that is, they should be recorded on an accrual basis. Our user-pays principle suggests that it is not appropriate to borrow for operating expenses but it may be appropriate to borrow for capital. Therefore, it follows that separate accounts should be maintained for operating and capital items.

These accounting changes allow the financial effects of alternative policy actions to be more accurately represented. This facilitates official decision making and also makes it easier for voters to monitor officials' actions. Our proposals for accounting changes are not original. They have been proposed by the General Accounting Office (GAO) and they have been included in a bill introduced by Sen. Herbert Kohl of Wisconsin. Most firms and state governments, as well as the Federal Reserve, maintain separate operating and capital accounts. The federal budget is reported on an accrual basis in the National Income Accounts, and the budget, calculated as the GAO and we recommend, is produced by the OMB in a timely manner. Thus, all that is new here is that we are proposing using this existing budget information as the basis for policy deliberations and rules.

The rule changes we propose limit the amount of debt the government can issue on its operating and capital accounts. The rules follow from our principles and from our attempts to reduce the policy bias. Although they involve only minor changes to existing rules, they provide explicit policy targets.

We propose to limit the debt that can be issued on the operating budget by requiring that the combined estimated and projected budget balance be zero in the current and subsequent fiscal years. Since the accounts would be maintained on an accrual basis, the proposal allows operating debt to be issued temporarily when there is a mistiming of payments and receipts. It also could be issued temporarily when unforeseen spending increases or revenue losses occur. However, by including the current year's deficit in the calculation, the government would have to implement policies to eliminate debt caused by mistakes in budget projections. This proposal is similar to current GRH procedures and suggested balance-the-budget amendments. What is new in our proposal is that the budget being balanced is the operating budget and that adherence to the rule leads straightforwardly to present-value balance of the entire budget, without inflation, as our first principle requires.

But why a two-year rule rather than a five-year rule or a month-by-month rule? Given the nature of the policy bias against the future, a rule requiring a balanced budget over a fairly short time frame is desirable. Otherwise, policymakers can continue to run deficits while claiming they will be offset by surpluses at some distant time. However, neither spending nor tax revenues can be forecasted very accurately, and unforeseen events do occur. Thus, if the time frame is too short, policymakers will continually be forced to make changes to expenditure programs or tax rates. In our view, a two-year rule is a reasonable compromise.

We propose to limit the debt that can be issued on the capital budget by requiring Congress to pass a bill annually authorizing debt issue up to a specified ceiling. While this is much like current procedures, our ceiling applies only to debt issued to finance capital spending. This means that the ceiling would be an independent control on capital spending. It would not be redundant, required as it is now, to accommodate the operating deficits Congress has planned. Since all capital spending would be financed by debt issue, setting a ceiling on debt would be equivalent to setting a ceiling on federal capital spending. This would let policymakers better decide on a desirable mix of private and public capital. More capital spending would be desirable as long as the benefits of a project were at least as large as its costs. We view a ceiling on total capital spending as desirable so that Congress as a whole can effectively force constituencies for capital spending to compete with each other. This reduces the incentives to spend excessively on capital equipment.

We propose to enforce the rules using approaches similar to current practices. The rule on operating debt would be enforced with a sequester. The sequester could be applied in a disaggregated way, as it is under current procedures. The sequester would be triggered whenever the combined operating deficit in the current and succeeding year exceeded some small amount—say $10 billion to match the trigger amount under GRH. The sequester would require cuts in spending or increases in revenue to achieve combined budget balance. Thus, if there were an unforeseen deficit of $20 billion in the current fiscal year, the government would have to adopt policies leading to a $20 billion surplus in the succeeding year. We would limit the amount of deficit reduction in a sequester to 0.5 percent of GNP, which is roughly the amount of reduction that experts testified could be implemented without causing major economic disruptions.

The rule on capital debt would be self-enforcing. The Treasury simply would not be authorized to issue debt above the legislated ceilings.

Our proposals so far are derived from our economic principles of present-value balance, cost-benefit comparison, and user-pays, but seem in conflict with our tax-smoothing principle. The reason is that government spending and revenues fluctuate due to causes that cannot be perfectly anticipated. Wars and recessions are as likely to occur in the future as they have in the past, but it's hard to know when. Therefore, meeting the two-year balanced budget rule would require sharp changes in tax rates when these contingencies occur. To avoid these kinds of changes in tax rates, we propose that rainy day funds be set up to meet contingencies. These rainy day funds would be set apart from the operating budget. Inflows of cash into these funds would be counted as outlays for the operating budget, and outflows from these funds would be counted as receipts. By drawing down the funds in bad times and building them up in good times, tax rates would not have to be adjusted in conflict with our tax-smoothing principle. Since we recognize the temptation to raid these funds in good times, we suggest that a supermajority in Congress be required to use these funds.

What Our Reforms Will Accomplish

Our reforms are intended to lessen the government's bias to overly discount the future and to remove some of the confusion that surrounds current budgetary practices. We argue that they lessen the bias by making deficit financing more difficult, capital spending more attractive, and procrastinating more costly. We argue that they reduce the confusion by providing a framework based on economic principles.

How do we make deficit spending more difficult? Reporting the accounts on an accrual basis takes away the budget "savings" options of selling off assets for cash and delaying payments to government employees or program beneficiaries. Accrual accounting records when activities take place and not when exchanges or payments are made. Including an explicit makeup for past errors in the enforcement mechanism reduces the incentive to use overly optimistic economic and technical assumptions. Mistakes require painful adjustments in the upcoming year. And, as we argue later, requiring present-value balance makes the movement of items to off-budget status less advantageous. However, the most important contribution the proposal makes to controlling deficits is that it provides a definition of budget deficit and specifications of targets which are guided by economic principles and, thus, have some logical basis.

One problem with the GRH targets is that they were designed to lead to budget balance for an arbitrary definition of the budget. There is no economic principle that suggests the deficit should be zero when capital transactions are included in the definition of balance. Moreover, under the GRH deficit definition there are different targets depending on whether Social Security or the RTC are included.

Our definition and targets are not as arbitrary as those of GRH, and that should make it harder to raise or disregard the deficit targets. They are guided by the present-value principle. The definition makes clear that capital transactions are excluded from the zero deficit target. Having a clearer idea of the reason for the targets should make it easier to stay the course.

Our proposal also makes capital spending more attractive by putting it on a more equal footing with current spending. A dollar cut from capital spending would have a comparable effect in the current fiscal year to a dollar cut from current spending. That is because in our proposal the operating cost of a capital asset is spread out over the life of the asset. While the purchase price of the asset is reported in the capital budget, only the annual depreciation and interest financing expense are reported on the operating budget. Thus, a dollar cut from capital spending cuts current spending by the amount of depreciation and interest. Our method spreads the cost of capital equipment over the years it provides services, while the current method charges it all to the current year. Our yearly charge is essentially what it would cost the government if it rented the capital from a private party.

The main difference between our method and current practices is how it treats dollars saved on capital spending in the current year. If the government decided not to purchase capital equipment, our method would show that the savings in current expenses would be only depreciation and interest. According to current practices the savings would be the cost of the capital purchase, which is much larger. As a result, current practices make cuts in capital spending look more attractive to policymakers than they really are.

As is usual under standard accounting principles, we would require that the government's assets be carried on its books at the lesser of cost or market value. If the government did not maintain such assets appropriately, their market value would fall, resulting in a larger depreciation charge and adversely affecting the government's operating budget. When the assets do not have an apparent market value, such as a nuclear armaments plant, they would be carried at cost. However, if they were not properly maintained, they would cease being useful prematurely, and the government then would be forced to write off the asset as depreciation on the operating budget.

Our method also requires quick action to balance the budget when circumstances change. In this sense, under our proposal the federal government would be forced to act like state and local governments now do. Under our proposal, difficult choices could not be simply passed on to future Congresses and administrations.

To illustrate how our proposal and the economic principles on which it is based could work to reduce the confusion surrounding current budgetary issues, we examine the treatment of trust funds, the RTC, loans and guarantees, and future commitments.

The controversy over trust funds, such as Social Security, is whether they should be on-budget or off-budget. If on-budget, their balances would be included in deficit calculations and targets. If off-budget, they would not.

Our present-value balance principle gives some guidance on this issue. To move a program off-budget means that the program should have an independent budget. It should neither rely on revenue from the general budget nor should its earmarked revenue be accessible to other programs in the budget. If it's not independent, then it's not truly a trust fund and it's not truly off-budget. The question of whether Social Security should be off-budget is then a question of whether its budget should be independent of the general budget. If the answer is yes, then by the present-value principle the Social Security budget and the general budget should be balanced independently in a present-value sense. If the answer is no, then just the sum of the two budgets should be balanced in present value. Within this framework, policymakers must first decide whether they want Social Security to have an independent budget, and if they do, they will find their choices to be quite limited on the financing of committed Social Security benefits. For instance, experts believe that given current benefit schedules and tax rates the Social Security system is balanced in present-value terms. Thus, by the present-value and tax-smoothing principles, policymakers would not be allowed to lower Social Security tax rates unless they also lowered the benefits.

We should also point out that our analysis of the policy bias problem suggests that trust fund accounting can be a useful disciplinary device. Because voters lack the information required to monitor the actions of policymakers, it's hard to monitor whether policymakers are following the cost-benefit principle. This monitoring difficulty is particularly acute when expenditures are financed out of general tax revenues. Beneficiaries have every reason to argue that the benefits accruing to them are large, whether they value the services a lot or a little. Dedicated programs with independent revenue sources that have strong safeguards against raiding the treasury can be useful in solving the monitoring problem. From this perspective, trust funds are not merely an accounting device; rather, they serve an important economic function.

We also recognize that trust funds can be abused. Given the bias in policymaking, policymakers have an incentive to postpone costs and accelerate benefits. For example, policymakers have an incentive to run a deficit or a smaller surplus than is desirable on the Social Security system. The result is that future benefits must be reduced or future taxes raised if the system is to be independently balanced. One crude way to limit abuses of this kind is to require that trust funds not run a deficit.

The issue on RTC spending is how to split it up into on-budget and off-budget. The RTC handles the assets and liabilities of failed thrifts. Since RTC spending relies on general revenues, our reasoning on trust funds suggests all of it belongs on-budget. The drive to move some of it off-budget was mainly a result of the current procedure's failure to distinguish capital spending from operating expenses. What typically occurs is that the RTC takes over a failed thrift with assets valued at, say, $700 million and insured deposits of, say, $1 billion. The $1 billion must be paid off immediately, while the $700 million in assets is sold gradually over a number of years. By current methods the $1 billion is treated as a current expenditure. Then, when the assets are sold over time, the sale receipts are treated as revenue. The payoff to depositors is funded by debt issue and the debt is in effect reduced when the assets are sold. The interest is also treated as an expenditure. The current procedure clearly overstates the deficit in the current year, since it assigns no value to the assets the government acquires. The drive to move RTC spending off-budget was a clumsy attempt to correct this problem.

Using our procedures, only the capital loss and interest expense would show up on the operating budget. That budget would not be affected by the timing of asset sales. When the RTC initially takes over the failed thrift, it would be considered a capital purchase of $1 billion financed by debt. However, since the assets were worth only $700 million, there would be an immediate write-off of $300 million charged to depreciation. As with other capital purchases, there also would be an associated interest expense. Future asset sales would affect the operating budget only to the extent that actual sale values differed from the capital budget's assumed market values. Thus, using our procedures, RTC spending would be treated no differently from other capital spending.

Capital budgeting also would clarify the treatment of government loans and guarantees. These items involve subsidies that are realized when private parties fail to maintain payments on loans. Past budget practices have treated the government loss of loan revenue or payment on a loan guarantee as a budget deficit increase at the time they occur. Thus, it appears to policymakers as a good way to give out subsidies now and pay for them much later. Under our proposal, loans and guarantees would be included in the capital budget as assets and liabilities, respectively. The subsidies on loans and guarantees would show up on the operating budget at the time the loans and guarantees were granted. Under our proposal policymakers would be confronted immediately with the costs of the subsidies. We should point out that the way loans and guarantees affect the operating budget under our proposal is similar to how they will affect the GRH budget following last year's reforms.

Finally, our tax-smoothing principle suggests that revenue should be collected today for future commitments. Currently the money is not collected until after the event occurs. Some of the commitments are contractual or explicit, such as pensions, and for these the government might make advance payments into something like an escrow account. Other commitments are not explicit but are fairly certain to occur in the future, such as wars and natural disasters. For these we have proposed that the government make advance payments into a rainy day account. The purpose of the escrow and rainy day accounts is to provide present-value budget balance without having to change tax rates. Assuming that the government's capital expenditures rise at the same rate as national income, the effect of the accounts is to lower the government's debt-to-income ratio over time until the commitments are realized and then to allow them to rise at that time. Over long periods of time, the debt-to-income ratio would remain constant.

The purpose of using our procedures to examine these issues is to show their practical value. We believe they can considerably reduce the confusion surrounding current budget practices.

Objections to Our Reforms

Since aspects of our proposal have been tossed around for some time, we can anticipate two important objections to it. One objection is that it does not accommodate countercyclical policy, and the other is that our proposal would encourage policymakers to move everything over to the capital budget. Although these objections have some validity, we believe they are not decisive. We believe the constraint on countercyclical policy is not very costly, and we believe safeguards can be put in place to limit misclassification of expenditures.

Consider first the loss in flexibility to conduct fiscal policy. Our proposal allows some limited countercyclical policy, but it does not allow the government to suspend the rules in case of a recession. The availability of a rainy day fund would, in any case, allow for some countercyclical fiscal policy. But when an unforeseen shortfall does occur, it could be accommodated in the current year, provided it is made up for in the succeeding year.

The government would also be able to increase capital spending in a recession when interest rates were low, because such spending then would generate less interest expense.

Nonetheless, our proposal is more rigid on countercyclical policymaking than current procedures. We do not think this rigidity is very costly because we are unaware of any evidence that discretionary countercyclical budget policy works. Most studies show that lags in responding to recessions cause any stimulative effects of fiscal policy to occur too late, well into the ensuing recovery. Furthermore, the rigidity could be beneficial. If the decline in the growth rate of real output goes on for a long period, perhaps there is a secular as well as a cyclical element. To the extent that an output decline signals a long-term reduction in output growth, the government should reduce spending.

Consider next the objection that policymakers will want to move everything to the capital budget. To a great extent that's true, but we argue that now everything, in effect, is treated as a capital expense. The government can borrow to finance any expenditure. So by strictly defining what is a capital expenditure, as states have done and as the GAO proposes for the federal government, many expenditures can be kept off the capital budget.

Even with strict definitions, though, there will be problems with misclassifications or understating of depreciation on capital items. Some expenditures that provide benefits in future years would be classified as current. In fact, we would favor including most human resource programs, such as those for education, crime control, and health, on the operating budget. We do not deny that a better educated, better protected, and healthier population will make people better off in the future. We also do not deny that requiring these expenditures to be paid in full in the current year could lead to underfunding. It is just our judgment that the underfunding bias would be no greater than the policymakers' bias to overspend on current consumption. Thus, we judge that by strictly limiting the capital budget to long-lived physical and nominal assets, a small cost in terms of underfunding of some expenditures would be more than offset: there would be a smaller bias toward overspending on current consumption, which now is facilitated by abuse of the debt-issue option.

The government would also try to understate depreciation, as states and corporations have been known to do. It could classify some current consumption items as capital items and assign them value, even though, in a sense, they are fully depreciated in the current year and have no value. Or it could just overstate the value of some of its physical or nominal assets. This is where watchdogs such as the CBO and GAO would have to be on the alert. The logic of our proposal requires that depreciation be accurately recorded on the operating budget. If it were not, the budget situation could be seriously misrepresented. Understatement of asset depreciation led to the unrecognized deterioration in the financial condition of many state and local governments and various financial institutions.

Transition

How do we get from the current system to our proposed system? Some of our reforms—accrual accounting and separating the capital and operating budgets—could and should be adopted for fiscal 1992. All that is required is that policymakers look at a different set of books. However, an immediate move to a balanced budget would require enormous and disruptive increases in taxes or reductions in spending. We believe the government should move to a balanced operating budget over a three- to five-year period. Over this period, the goal of monetary policy should be to reduce the inflation rate gradually to zero.

Such transition periods have been abused in the past, but we think our enforcement mechanism provides a way to limit future abuses. Specifically, we propose imposing annual limits on the operating budget deficit during the transition period. These limits would be enforced with a sequester. If the limits are exceeded within a given year, then the sequester would require cuts in spending or increases in revenues in the following year. These proposals, combined with the fall 1990 reforms enacted by Congress, would go a long way to reducing the deficit to zero over roughly a five-year span.

It's also possible to frontload the pain of spending reductions and tax increases to a greater extent than is now mandated under the fall 1990 reforms. One major problem with the GRH process was that large deficit reductions were supposed to occur toward the end of the targets, and this problem persists though to a lesser extent with the fall 1990 reforms. When the real pain of deficit reduction is postponed, however, the temptation to revise the targets often becomes irresistible. The only credible way around this problem is to ensure that substantial deficit reduction occurs in the early years of the transition period.

Our Rules Are No Panacea

We would like to conclude by claiming it would be all smooth sailing if only our proposal were accepted. But of course we know that's not true.

No change in the process can make the difficult choices confronting policy-makers easy. They still would have to decide whose ox to gore by cutting spending or increasing taxes. But we think policymakers would make better decisions if they understood what they were up against and what the consequences of their actions would be. No change in budget process is going to solve the policy bias problem or keep the government out of financial difficulty. Better budget processes than the federal government now employs have not stopped these problems with corporations or state governments. We nevertheless strongly believe our proposal can lessen the magnitude of the problems.

Will our proposal work, or is a more drastic measure such as a constitu-tional amendment necessary? We believe that the situation is not yet so dire as to warrant such an extreme action. Concern over the budget is widespread enough in the nation and among policymakers that we feel the problems described here can be addressed legislatively.

The budget mess will not be completely cleaned up even if all our reforms are adopted. Hard choices will still have to be made. But we will no longer have the choice of inflicting costs upon future generations for programs that benefit us.

Suggested Readings

On Political Economy

A classic in the field is ...
Downs, Anthony. 1957. *Economic theory of democracy.* New York: Harper Press.

Other excellent readings are ...
Buchanan, James, and Tullock, Gordon. 1962. *The calculus of consent.* Ann Arbor: University of Michigan Press.

Olson, Mancur. 1971. *The logic of collective action.* Cambridge, Mass.: Harvard University Press.

On Agency Theories of the Firm

Alchian, Armen A., and Demsetz, Harold. 1972. Production, information costs, and eco-nomic organization. *American Economic Review* 62 (December): 777–95.

Jensen, Michael C., and Meckling, William H. 1976. Theory of the firm: Managerial behavior, agency costs and ownership structure. *Journal of Financial Economics* 3 (October): 305–60.

On Recent Budget Policy

Miller, Preston. 1989. Gramm-Rudman-Hollings' hold on budget policy: Losing its grip? *Federal Reserve Bank of Minneapolis Quarterly Review* 13 (Winter): 11–21.

Reischauer, Robert. 1990. Taxes and spending under Gramm-Rudman-Hollings. *National Tax Journal* 43 (September): 223–32.

Schick, Allen. 1990. *The capacity to budget.* Washington, D.C.: Urban Institute Press.

On Last Fall's Reforms

Congressional Quarterly staff. 1990. Budget-reconciliation bill. *Congressional Quarterly*, December 1, pp. 4012–36.

On Proposed Reforms

Bowsher, Charles A. 1988. Budget reform for the federal government. Statement before the Committee on Governmental Affairs, U.S. Senate, June 7.

Budget reform proposals. 1989. Joint hearings before the Committee on Governmental Affairs and the Committee on the Budget, U.S. Senate, October 18, 26.

Acknowledgments

We wish to thank Rudolph Penner, Alice Rivlin, Mark Sniderman, Eugene Steuerle, and John Sturrock for useful comments on an earlier draft.

III

Monetary and Budget Policy Analysis in Open Economies

Consider a world with many countries in which each government issues its own money and bonds. Compared to a closed economy, there now must be an explanation not only for why individuals hold their country's money when their government's bonds are available, but also for why they hold it when the other governments' money and bonds are available. The explanations one provides have implications for the economic effects of a country's monetary and budget policies on it and other countries and also for the feasibility of alternative exchange rate regimes.

In the first chapter in this section (Chapter 11), Wallace considers what exchange rate regimes are feasible in a world with country-specific fiat monies. He argues that markets in fiat monies are different from markets in other goods. In particular, fiat monies have no intrinsic value and are valued as are other financial assets, solely in terms of their expected rates of return. Without any kinds of restrictions on use, different fiat monies would be perfect substitutes. In this case, any set of exchange rates would be consistent with an equilibrium: the market could not determine a unique equilibrium.

Wallace's point is easy to see if, as a thought experiment, we substitute for the fiat monies of two countries, a dollar bill and a newly introduced U.S. coin. If the United States doesn't identify the denomination of the coin, market forces in the private sector cannot determine a unique value either. Any value—1¢, 2¢, ..., 99¢, ...—once established, could remain forever and thus would be consistent with an equilibrium.

Wallace's analysis and this example suggest that an international floating exchange rate system is not feasible without financial restrictions, such as capital controls. Thus, only three exchange rate regimes are feasible in which all countries' fiat monies are held:

• Floating exchange rates with financial restrictions that make country-specific monies imperfect substitutes.

• Fixed exchange rates with no financial restrictions. In this regime, there is a single world money.

• Fixed exchange rates with financial restrictions. In this regime, the monetary and budget policies of all countries must be perfectly coordinated to generate the same expected rate of return on their monies, that is, the same expected inflation path.

In Chapter 12, Miller and Wallace study an international model that assumes the first of the three feasible regimes. Their assumption of floating exchange rates with country-specific monies seems to describe the period since the breakdown in 1971 of the Bretton Woods system of fixed exchange rates. The financial restrictions used in their model are country-specific reserve requirements on savings—the same legal restriction used in Wallace's model for closed economies, that was described in the previous section. In their chapter, Miller and Wallace also assume a world market in public and private bonds.

Many of the results of the Miller-Wallace model mirror those of the Wallace model, but some new ones emerge. Because of the frictions due to the reserve requirements, changes in a country's monetary policies affect real rates of return and affect the welfare of different groups of agents differently. One new result is that the effect on the real interest rate of a change in one country's monetary policy is likely to be less in an open-economy model than in a closed-economy model. For instance, in an open-economy model, an increased amount of debt in public hands that results from a tightening in a country's monetary policy, such as an open market sale, can be financed with world savings rather than just the country's savings. The interest rate effect is smaller because net savings worldwide are more interest-elastic than those in a single country. A second new result is that the real and welfare effects of a change in a country's monetary policy are transmitted abroad. Because of these external effects, Miller and Wallace show that in their model there is some scope for international monetary policy coordination.

The final chapter in this section (Chapter 13), by Rolnick and Weber, draws heavily on the analysis in Wallace's chapter. Based on estimates of the costs of running a floating exchange rate system compared to a fixed exchange rate system, the authors argue that a fixed exchange rate system is preferable.

Rolnick and Weber's argument for the advantages of a fixed exchange rate system is supported by the example of the U.S. monetary system. They point out that each Federal Reserve Bank issues its own identifiable notes and that the notes of the different Banks trade at a fixed one-for-one rate. This system has obviously facilitated trade across the country.

Subsequently, some have argued that the Rolnick-Weber example of a national fixed exchange rate system does not apply to the international monetary system. In the world economy there is neither the labor mobility nor the explicit agreement to share *seignorage* (the inflation tax payoff from creating money) that there is among Federal Reserve Districts.

Do these criticisms overturn the Rolnick-Weber policy conclusion? That is still an open question. What is not questionable is that the Rolnick-Weber example hones in on a key point: the relative success of a fixed exchange rate system depends on the participants' ability to enter into binding agreements to limit and share the seignorage.

11

Why Markets in Foreign Exchange Are Different from Other Markets

Neil Wallace

In the United States today, a substantial majority of economists agrees that some or all of the task of determining exchange rates should be left to private markets. The notion seems to be that basic or fundamental factors determine equilibrium relative prices of currencies—that is, exchange rates —in much the same way that tastes, technology, and endowments interact in markets to determine equilibrium relative prices for other things.

If there is any disagreement, it seems to be only about whether some government intervention is desirable in order to keep actual exchange rates close to the equilibrium exchange rates supposedly determined by fundamentals. Interventionists claim that speculation plays an important role in foreign exchange markets, one that at times prevents exchange rates from attaining even approximately their equilibrium values. Noninterventionists respond by turning my title into a challenging question. Why, they ask, are markets for foreign exchange different from other markets? Presumably, there is speculation whenever views about future prices affect current demands and supplies and, hence, current prices. Such speculation is pervasive. Can it be established that there is *more* speculation in foreign exchange markets than in other markets? And even if that could be established, could the desirability of government intervention depend on the *amount* of speculation? In the view of noninterventionists, such a conclusion runs counter to invisible-hand propositions. These depend for their validity only on general qualitative assumptions. They do not depend on whether there is little or much speculation.

Thus, there seems to be a certain consistency in the view of noninterventionists. If currencies are very much like other things, then why, indeed, not let private markets determine their relative prices? But today's currencies are not like other things. Because of this, the noninterventionist view

Reprinted from the *Federal Reserve Bank of Minneapolis Quarterly Review*, Fall 1979.

is fallacious—and more seriously flawed than even interventionists have suggested.

The objects traded in today's foreign exchange markets are *fiat currencies*. In particular, currencies now are not tied to different weights of gold or other metals. Economists have long known and agreed that fiat currencies are very special objects, not at all like other things. What they seem not to have recognized is that this specialness tells us why markets in foreign exchange are different, qualitatively, from other markets.

For fiat currencies, there are no inherent fundamentals that determine equilibrium exchange rates. Without binding legal restrictions on asset holdings that prevent one currency from being substituted for another either directly or indirectly via international borrowing and lending, demands for different currencies are determined not in part by speculation, but entirely by speculation. One consequence is an indeterminacy proposition: *Without government intervention in foreign exchange markets and without binding restrictions on currency holdings, exchange rates, price levels, and in general all prices are indeterminate.* A closely related consequence is that the fixed rate–floating rate dichotomy is inadequate both for descriptive analysis and for policy analysis. When exchange rates are not fixed, a crucial role is played either by legal restrictions on asset holdings or by anticipated government intervention. These are the only forces that determine exchange rates when rates are not explicitly fixed, and these are not comparable to the fundamentals that determine prices in other markets. A so-called laissez-faire floating rate monetary system does not give rise to a determinate equilibrium, let alone to one to which invisible-hand conclusions apply.

These assertions follow from postulates about fiat currencies. As we will see, these postulates and their implications make clear why one goes badly astray by reasoning about the international monetary system from an analogy between fiat currencies and other objects like apples, oranges, and shares in General Motors.

Postulates: The Nature of Fiat Currencies

I will take as postulates three generally accepted properties of any fiat currency:

1. It is intrinsically useless.
2. It is unbacked.
3. It is costless to produce.

The first postulate says that a fiat currency is never wanted for its own sake. One person gives up goods—leisure or other objects that are wanted per se—for some amount of the fiat currency only because the person expects to be able subsequently to exchange the currency for goods. Put somewhat differently, this postulate says that there is only an indirect or derived demand for fiat currency; it is wanted only to the extent that it makes possible future consumption.

The second postulate says that the issuer of a fiat currency does not promise to exchange it for any other object. From the point of view of the issuer, a unit of fiat currency is a claim on no more than a fresh piece of the same thing. As has always been recognized, it is this postulate that distinguishes fiat money from commodity money and from other assets like shares in General Motors; the issuer of a fiat currency does not promise to pay the bearer now or in the future an amount of gold or a dividend or anything else.

The third postulate is simply a convenient way to express the idea that a fiat currency is an object whose value in exchange exceeds the marginal cost of producing another unit of it.

These postulates cast doubt on the analogy that advocates of floating rates use to support their view: Since private markets can price apples in terms of oranges, they can price one currency in terms of another. Neither apples nor oranges nor shares in General Motors satisfy the above postulates.

Supplies of Fiat Currencies

The second and third postulates—that fiat currency is unbacked and is costless to produce—have well-known and almost unanimously accepted implications for the provision or supply of fiat currencies: Their provision cannot be left to the market. More precisely, one cannot allow for free entry into the provision of fiat currency. Indeed, leading advocates of floating exchange rates, such as Milton Friedman, have long espoused this view:

Some external limit must be placed on the volume of a fiduciary [that is, fiat] currency in order to maintain its value. Competition does not provide an effective limit, since the value of the promise to pay, if the currency is to remain fiduciary, must be kept higher than the cost of producing additional units. The production of a fiduciary currency is, as it were, a technical monopoly, and hence, there is no such presumption in favor of the private market as there is when competition is feasible.[1]

This widely accepted implication for the supplies of fiat currencies makes clear that the analogy between fiat currencies and other things is far from complete. For most objects, supplies *and* demands can be determined in a free market, one in which neither supply nor demand is regulated. For fiat currencies, most economists agree that supplies must be regulated and that, at most, demands can be left unregulated.

Demands for Fiat Currencies

The United States has recently issued a new coin: the Susan B. Anthony dollar. The sense in which free-market or unregulated demands for fiat currencies are determined entirely by speculation can be seen by considering how the market would price Anthonys in terms, say, of Lincolns ($5 bills) in different circumstances.

Suppose that an Anthony had no numeral on it, just a picture. If the government says that now and in the future it stands ready to exchange five Anthonys for one Lincoln and vice versa, then the Anthony becomes a "one," even though there is no numeral on it. Suppose, instead, that there are fixed stocks of Anthonys and Lincolns outstanding today and that the government says that starting in June 1980 and thereafter it will exchange five Anthonys for one Lincoln and vice versa. Will five Anthonys still exchange for one Lincoln? Our postulates dictate an affirmative answer. If not, then the rates of return from now until June 1980 on Lincolns and Anthonys would have to differ, and that would violate the first fiat currency postulate—that currency is intrinsically useless. In other words, the announced future exchange ratio is today's market exchange ratio. And, so long as the announcement is believed, it does not matter whether the date at which exchanges are offered is June 1980, June 1982, or June 1988.

This is not true for apples and oranges, or for shares in GM and shares in Chrysler. While the government could readily make effective any exchange ratio between Anthonys and Lincolns, it would have some trouble doing that for apples and oranges or for shares in GM and shares in Chrysler. Even if that difficulty is ignored, the future exchange ratio is only one of the influences on the current relative price of the fruits or the shares. For apples and oranges, the influence of the future exchange rate is limited by the fact that apples and oranges are wanted per se, for eating and so forth. For shares in GM and shares in Chrysler, its influence is limited by the fact that there are dividend streams. For Anthonys and Lincolns, there are no such fundamentals to help determine the current relative price.

The most startling difference between Anthonys and Lincolns, on the one hand, and the fruits or the shares, on the other hand, is what happens when no future exchange ratio is announced. In the case of apples and oranges or of shares in GM and shares in Chrysler, a current exchange ratio is determined without any government help. But what about Anthonys and Lincolns? For simplicity, suppose that there are fixed and unchanging quantities of the two. Even in this simple case, it is absurd to suppose that fundamental factors could guide the market to find an equilibrium exchange rate. Is it less absurd to suppose that an unfettered market could find an exchange rate between German marks and Lincolns?

That it is no less absurd is the content of the indeterminacy proposition to which we now turn. That proposition explains why a floating rate system with unregulated demands for fiat currencies is, to put it mildly, unworkable.

Indeterminacy Under Laissez-Faire Floating Rates

For simplicity, let there be two countries and two currencies, the supplies of which at time t are given and denoted by $M_1(t)$ and $M_2(t)$. (As the reader will see, the generalization to any number of countries and currencies is trivial.) I will argue that in the absence of government intervention in exchange markets and in the absence of legal restrictions on asset holdings—for example, restrictions on who may hold and use what currency—there is indeterminacy. I will do this by arguing that if there is an equilibrium for any positive and unchanging exchange rate, then there is an equilibrium for any other positive and unchanging exchange rate.

Given the paths of the individual currencies, we may define a world currency supply, denoted $M(t)$, by $M(t) = M_1(t) + RM_2(t)$, where R is some positive and unchanging exchange rate. Clearly, then, different values of R imply different paths of the world currency supply, $M(t)$. The argument that any of these paths generates an equilibrium if any one of them does has two ingredients. First, any unchanging exchange rate, R, and our second postulate imply that the rate of return on one currency is equal to the rate of return on the other in every period. Second, although different values of R imply different paths of the world currency supply, these paths are similar in one crucial respect. For a wide class of supply paths for the individual currencies, the limiting growth rate of the world currency supply, $M(t)$, does not depend on R. While this similarity is enough to yield the indeterminacy result in many complete models, the essential ideas are brought out by considering the simple case where the individual currency supplies are constant over time.

If the supplies of the individual currencies are constant over time, then different values of R imply different unchanging world currency supplies. In this case, the indeterminacy proposition is simply that if there is an equilibrium for one currency supply, then there is also an equilibrium for any other currency supply. Again, we may quote Friedman:

[The provision of fiat currency] is a monopoly that so far as I know has a unique property — the total value to the community of the stock of the monopoly product is entirely independent of the number of units in the stock. For any other item entering into economic exchange that I can think of, be it shoes or hats or tables or houses or even honorific titles, the aggregate value of the stock in terms of other goods depends on the number of units in it, at least outside some limits. For money, it does not. If there are five million pieces of paper, or five thousand, or five hundred million, as long as the number is relatively stable, the aggregate value is the same; the only effect is that each unit separately has a smaller or larger value as the case may be; that is, prices expressed in terms of the money are higher or lower.[2]

But this argument may not seem sufficient. Although different exchange rates imply different world currency supplies, they also imply different compositions of it. The larger is R, the greater is the fraction of the world currency supply that takes the form of currency issued by country two. If the indeterminacy proposition is correct, then that fraction can be anything. In particular, for large enough R, everyone in the world—both residents of country one and residents of country two—use the currency of country two almost exclusively, while for small enough R, the reverse is true. Can this really be?

Why not? First, recall that the rates of return on the two currencies are the same. Second, by hypothesis, no legal restrictions prevent residents of one country from using the currency of another. In these circumstances, why would residents of country one prefer their own national currency and residents of country two prefer theirs? Could it be because residents of a particular country prefer the color of or the pictorial design on the currency of their own country? Such preferences violate the postulate that currency is intrinsically useless and, moreover, seem silly.

Without legal restrictions, there is no reason why national borders should determine currency usage. Canadian dollars have long circulated in areas of the United States that border Canada. That being so, one can imagine a much larger use of Canadian currency in the United States. For another example, the Bank of America recently wanted to offer deposits denominated in Japanese currency but was officially discouraged. Suppose that this quasi-legal restriction had not been imposed. One could then well imagine that Japanese currency would circulate in California. And, if in California, why not in Nevada and Arizona? Or, to take another example, without legal restrictions, can't one imagine United States dollars circulating widely in Mexico? If questions like these are answered affirmatively, as I think they must be, then the fraction of the world money supply in a particular form can be anything. This implies that the exchange rate is indeterminate. Moreover, if the exchange rate is indeterminate, then so is the distribution of wealth and, hence, in general all prices.[3]

But what should we make of this indeterminacy proposition? How do we reconcile it with observations on historical episodes in which exchange rates have floated? And how do we account for the observation that national borders do, in large measure, determine currency usage? Moreover, if we accept the indeterminacy proposition, what are its policy implications? There is, I think, a single route to answers to these questions. The indeterminacy proposition is based on hypotheses that specify an absence of government intervention in exchange markets and/or specify an absence of legal restrictions on asset holdings. At least some of these hypotheses must be abandoned.

Non–Laissez-Faire Floating Rate Systems

Economists have, by and large, approached the positive analysis of international monetary arrangements in terms of a dichotomy: fixed exchange rates or floating exchange rates. The indeterminacy proposition, however, says that the floating rate regime is not well-defined without legal restrictions on asset holdings or government intervention. It suggests the following approach. When analyzing any situation in which exchange rates are not fixed explicitly, try to identify the less obvious forms of intervention in exchange markets and/or the restrictions on asset holdings that could produce a determinate equilibrium.

One less obvious form of intervention in foreign exchange markets was hinted at above. Anticipated intervention can play much the same role as actual intervention.

Two widely cited episodes of so-called floating exchange rates are the post–Civil War period in the United States when "greenbacks" were not officially tied to gold, and the post–World War I period when the British pound was not officially tied to gold. One common feature of both episodes is that gold convertibility was subsequently restored. That being so, it seems farfetched to analyze those episodes as if people thought at the time that gold convertibility would never be restored. Therefore, for these episodes, probable future restoration of gold convertibility is a form of government intervention that constitutes a departure from the hypotheses that produce indeterminacy.[4]

For today's currencies, restoration of convertibility into a commodity seems farfetched. But it is not unreasonable to say that post–World War II floating rate episodes have been accompanied by anticipated intervention if exchange rates wandered too far—too far, perhaps, from those that would have prevailed under pervasive controls on asset holdings. The intervention may be exchange market intervention by countries acting cooperatively or may involve the imposition of restrictions on asset holdings which makes feasible intervention by a country acting alone. Thus, for example, from this point of view, it is reasonable to explain the behavior of the U.S. dollar in exchange markets over the period August 1971 to November 1978 in terms of the U.S. government, with the implicit agreement of other countries, "talking down" the value of the dollar. It is also understandable that some market participants expressed doubts about how much had been accomplished in November 1978 because the U.S. did not impose restrictions on asset holdings.

In fact, today the most obvious and important departures from the hypotheses yielding indeterminacy are actual or threatened restrictions on capital-account transactions. Such restrictions tend to prevent one currency from being substituted for another, both directly and indirectly by way of international borrowing and lending. To the extent that this is accomplished, the indeterminacy disappears.

There are many instances of actual restrictions on asset holdings. (In the case of Israel, both the controls on asset holdings and their partial removal in 1977 have been widely commented on, if not completely understood.) Instances of threatened restrictions are harder to identify, but can play much the same role as actual restrictions. Thus, suppose that the equilibrium exchange rate between M_1 and M_2 would be $\bar{R}$ in the presence of pervasive capital controls, and suppose that it is anticipated that any sizable departure of the actual exchange rate from $\bar{R}$ will trigger the imposition of pervasive controls. Then, it can be shown that the exchange rate stays close to $\bar{R}$.[5]

There is, moreover, a close relationship between the role of controls on asset holdings in producing determinate exchange rates and the notion that equilibrium exchange rates are determined by the condition that trade be balanced. In order to understand this relationship, it is helpful to begin with what economists call the *barter theory of trade*, that part of trade theory which analyzes economic connections among countries in models that do not contain currencies or, therefore, exchange rates.

It is, by now, well known that trade can be out of balance, even permanently, in such barter or nonmonetary models. Essentially, imbalance of trade is accompanied by residents of one country being net creditors or debtors to residents of other countries, or, what amounts to the same thing, by residents of one country owning on net more or less than all the assets located in their own country.[6] In these nonmonetary models, one way to insure trade balance is to rule out by law any capital-account transactions, any net borrowing between residents of one country and residents of other countries, and any ownership of assets not located in the country of residence. As a matter of accounting, such a prohibition implies trade balance.

Now consider a model in which there is a role for currency, a model in which there is a demand for currency. Again, as a matter of accounting, the imposition of laws that preclude capital-account transactions—and, hence, the ownership by residents of one country of currency issued by other countries—implies trade balance. It also, as suggested above, implies a well-defined demand for the currency issued by the home country and, hence, a determinate exchange rate. But the result that pervasive capital controls implies both trade balance and a determinate exchange rate is quite different from the fallacious notion that trade balance is a natural state of affairs and that an equilibrium exchange rate is determined by the condition that trade be balanced.

Many readers, I suspect, will argue that this discussion overemphasizes restrictions on asset holdings like capital controls at the expense of more subtle restrictions like those implied by legal-tender laws. While these readers may concede that only legal, non–laissez-faire restrictions create well-behaved demands for individual currencies, they might assert, first, that restrictions like legal-tender laws do produce such demands, and second, that such restrictions are in effect in all countries at all times. That being so, they might claim, one is justified in simply assuming that there are well-behaved demands for individual currencies, whether or not more explicit restrictions like capital controls are in effect. I am doubtful.

First, the pervasiveness of legal-tender laws has not seemed to prevent the occurrence of hyperinflations during which the fraction of wealth held in the form of a particular currency has approached zero. Second, an explicit analysis of legal-tender laws—which, by the way, would have to recognize that they amount to explicit restrictions like a requirement that real tax liabilities be paid in the form of a particular currency—would suggest that such laws at best imply lower bounds on the amount of wealth held in the form of a particular currency. So long as the total demand for currency in each country exceeds the lower bound implied by the country's legal-tender laws, the absence of other asset restrictions or intervention implies a range of indeterminacy. That the indeterminacy range is large is suggested by the fact that most countries have at times found it necessary to resort to more explicit restrictions on asset holdings. A large indeterminacy range is also consistent with the behavior of exchange rates and money supplies in many countries during the last few years. That behavior cannot be easily interpreted in terms of well-behaved demand functions for individual currencies.

Policy Options in a World of Many Fiat Currencies

Noninterventionist advocates of floating rates have painted a rosy picture of floating exchange rates. Milton Friedman, for instance, asserts that a floating rate system can be as free of capital-account and trade restrictions as a single currency system:

The basic fact is that a unified currency and a system of freely floating exchange rates are members of the same species even though superficially they appear very different. Both are free market mechanisms for interregional or international payments. Both permit exchange rates to move freely. Both exclude any administrative or political intermediary in payments between residents of different areas. Either is consistent with free trade between areas, or with a lessening of trade restrictions.[7]

Unfortunately, the picture is a mirage. Friedman's claims about freely floating exchange rates rest on the notion that without legal restrictions of various kinds the demands for individual currencies are well behaved. That view, in turn, rests on no more than an analogy between currencies and other objects, an analogy that we have seen to be faulty. Since freely floating exchange rates imply indeterminacy, such an international monetary system is not an option. The alternatives to fixed exchange rates are various kinds of implicit intervention schemes and implicit or explicit restrictions on asset holdings.

That these are the options follows from the properties of fiat currency described above, in particular, that fiat currency is intrinsically useless and unbacked. The formation of the European Monetary Union is consistent with these properties. The predominant view in the United States about feasible international monetary systems is not.

Unfortunately, none of the feasible options is without drawbacks. As is widely understood, a system of cooperatively fixed exchange rates requires that national control over currency issue be surrendered. In essence, it requires that countries coordinate the degree to which they tax by inflation or, in other words, the degree to which they finance current expenditures with permanent additions to indebtedness. The alternatives, though, are also unpleasant. They involve the imposition of controls on the kinds of assets individuals can hold.

It is becoming widely recognized that the value of the U.S. dollar in terms of goods and its value in terms of other currencies are closely related. It is also widely recognized that domestic policies in the United States— essentially, the degree to which we resort to taxation by permanent increases in indebtedness—must be brought into line with that of other countries if the U.S. dollar is to have a stable value in terms of other currencies. What is not widely recognized is that coordination of budget policies in this sense is only one of the conditions needed to stabilize both the goods value and the foreign currency value of the U.S. dollar. Without intervention in exchange markets or restrictions on asset holdings, indeterminacy prevails. That being so, we should at least consider pursuing an explicit policy directed toward cooperative and permanent exchange market intervention or toward controls on asset holdings. The alternative is to leave market participants guessing or speculating about future actions of these kinds.

Notes

This is a revised version of a talk presented at a seminar at the University of Minnesota. I am indebted to colleagues at the University and at the Federal Reserve Bank of Minneapolis, especially Arthur Rolnick, for helpful comments. The ideas expressed were developed jointly by John Kareken and me (1978a, b). [Author names and years refer to the works listed at the end of this volume.]

1. Friedman 1960, p. 7.

2. Friedman 1960, p. 7.

3. For a formal argument and one that establishes the existence of equilibria of this sort for constant and nonconstant paths of the individual currency supplies, see Kareken and Wallace 1978a. By the way, it is not evident that only constant exchange rate paths can be equilibria. I suspect, but have not yet shown, that any member of a wide class of random exchange rate paths also qualifies as an equilibrium.

4. Alternatively, one may say that "greenbacks" and post–World War I British pounds were not fiat currencies: they violate the second postulate. They should be treated as discount bonds that were in (partial) default: holders were uncertain both about the date at which each would pay off in terms of gold and about the amount of the payoff.

5. For explicit analyses of policy schemes that specify contingent and possibly random future intervention and asset-holding restrictions, see Kareken and Wallace 1978a and Nickelsburg 1980.

6. See Gale 1971, 1974 and Kareken and Wallace 1977.

7. Friedman 1968a, p. 7.

12 International Coordination of Macroeconomic Policies: A Welfare Analysis

Preston J. Miller and Neil Wallace

Coordination among countries of their monetary and budget policies has been proposed recently as a way to improve the current system of floating exchange rates. This proposal has been prompted by the apparent failure of the floating rate system to eliminate *policy interdependence*, the effects of one country's policies on other countries' economies. Although the floating rate system has seemed to allow countries greater freedom in their choice of monetary and budget policies, in the last few years many countries have complained about being hurt by other countries' policies—especially those of the United States. Our study suggests that, because of policy inter-dependence, some form of international coordination of macroeconomic policies would, indeed, improve the floating exchange rate system.

This conclusion—that countries would in some sense be better off if they choose macro policies jointly than if they choose those policies independently—is implied by a simple model of a world economy. The ingredients of the model that are crucial for the conclusion are its assumptions about currency and debt markets and about a country's well-being:

• Currencies of different countries are not direct substitutes; each country's currency ends up being held only by its own residents.

• The interest-bearing debt of any one government trades in an integrated world credit market where it competes with debt issued by other governments and by private residents of all countries.

• Government borrowing affects the world interest rate. (Residents of a country don't match changes in their government's borrowing with offsetting changes in their own borrowing, partly because they don't expect the government's outstanding debt to be retired in their lifetime.)

Reprinted from the *Federal Reserve Bank of Minneapolis Quarterly Review*, Spring 1985.

• A country's well-being depends on both the world real interest rate and its own price level because some of its residents borrow at the world rate and some hold wealth in the form of the country's currency.

We think these assumptions are good approximations of conditions in the actual world economy. Moreover, they are present, at least implicitly, in many models. This study is the first, however, to systematically analyze the implications of these assumptions for the issue of international coordination of macroeconomic policies.[1]

A Preview of the Study

Before presenting the formal description and analysis of our model, we describe briefly and informally the model, its defense, and its implications for policy coordination.

The Model

The model is designed to make qualitative predictions about the economic outcomes across countries of alternative national monetary and budget policies. The outcomes are equilibrium sequences of price levels, interest rates, and lifetime consumption patterns for the residents of different countries. The demands and supplies that appear explicitly in the model are those for bonds, or securities—all of which are traded in one world market —and for base monies, or currencies, one for each country. The *equilibrium* sequences are those which equate demands and supplies of bonds and base monies at each date.

The model has only one good per date and, aside from consumption of that good, only one economic activity: borrowing and lending. We assume that each of several countries is populated by an infinite sequence of identical overlapping generations whose members live two periods. Each generation in each country consists of two groups on opposite sides of the credit market: borrowers and savers. The private supplies and demands for bonds and monies are derived from the behavior of these groups. The borrowers supply private bonds. The savers, besides demanding bonds, demand the base money of their country because they have to; a reserve requirement forces them to hold some fraction of their savings as domestic currency. This restriction ensures that each country's base money is held even when other currencies and securities bear higher returns; it also produces the model's separate currency markets. At the first date of the model, the people in each country who are in the second period of their lives own the initial outstanding stock of their country's monetary base.

The private demands and supplies depend on agents' price expectations, which are assumed to be *rational*. The model has no uncertainty, so this means the expected prices coincide with those that actually prevail.

Each government determines additions to the supply of its bonds and money by its choice of budget and monetary policies. Budget policy is made by choosing the path over time of the real *deficit net-of-interest*: the real value of the government's budget deficit, excluding from government expenditures any interest payments or receipts. (Throughout, we hold real taxes constant, so that a change in budget policy corresponds to a change in real government consumption.) Monetary policy is made by choosing the division of government debt over time between bonds and money. Governments do not buy and sell each other's currencies; in this sense, exchange rates float.

Primarily in order to keep the analysis simple, we consider only budget policies for which the deficit net-of-interest is constant over time and only monetary policies for which the ratio of bonds to base money is constant over time. For these policies, there is an equilibrium which takes a simple form. It has a constant world real interest rate and constant country-specific inflation rates. These imply that the situation of different generations in each country is constant over time.

A Defense of the Model

We defend our model in two ways: by showing that it is internally consistent and by showing that its implications are broadly consistent with recent events.

We show that the model is internally consistent by building it from a theory of individual behavior and proving that under reasonable conditions an equilibrium exists for given policies. The equilibrium assures us that the actions of individual agents are mutually consistent and lead to the aggregate outcomes our model implies.

We show that the model's implications are broadly consistent with recent events by comparing actual economic experience to the model's predictions for the qualitative effects of a change in monetary and budget policies like that implemented recently by the United States and other countries.

For this purpose, we describe the model's implications for the adoption in one country of a permanently easier budget policy together with a nonaccommodating monetary policy, with other countries remaining passive. Specifically, we assume that one country permanently increases its government's real budget deficit net-of-interest and accompanies that with an increase in the ratio of government bonds to base money which keeps unaffected the quantity of base money at the date of the policy change. Passiveness by other countries means that they do not respond with changes in their budget policies (their real government purchases and taxes) or their monetary policies (their ratios of government bonds to base money).

When we compare the model's predictions for this set of policies with actual events, we identify the active country with the United States, the period of the model with four years, and the first period with the four years beginning in 1981. Our representation of policy, at least for the active country, seems to be a reasonable description of what has actually occurred in the United States beginning in 1981. In the four years since then, the U.S. net-of-interest budget deficit rose from its previous average of nearly zero to an average of 2 percent of gross national product, and the ratio of U.S. government bonds to base money rose, roughly, from 4 to 6.

The model's predictions for the direction that various economic variables change in response to such policy changes are shown in Table 12.1. These predictions roughly match recent experience. Since 1981, we have seen higher real interest rates, an enhanced value of the U.S. dollar relative to the currencies of debtor governments, and a higher U.S. current account deficit. (The higher inflation rate prediction for the United States is a prediction of the future course of the price level which assumes no subsequent change in the real deficit net-of-interest or in the ratio of bonds to money.)

Implications for Policy Coordination

For some purposes, policymakers might want more than qualitative predictions or descriptions of the effects of given policies. They might want to know what policies other countries would adopt in various circumstances. A country contemplating a change in policy surely would want to know if and how other countries would respond. It could also want to know whether it could end up in a better position if it joined with other countries to choose monetary and budget policies than if they all proceeded, in some sense, independently. A standard mathematical theory, called *game theory*, deals with such questions. We apply that theory to the choice of monetary policy in our model.

Table 12.1
The international effects of easing a country's budget policy without monetary accommodation

Variable	Active country [United States]	Passive countries Debtor government	Creditor government
Real interest rate	+	+	+
Inflation rate	+	+	−
Nominal interest rate	+	+	+
Initial price level	0	+	−
Initial value of currency relative to active country's	n.a.	−	+
Initial current account deficit	+	−	+ or −

+ = increases   0 = no change
− = decreases   n.a. = not applicable

To apply it, we need to add to the model assumptions about the objectives or goals pursued by countries. We assume that countries try to do the best they can for their residents. In our model, this is complicated by the fact that each country is populated by groups of people whose interests do not coincide.

In an equilibrium with a constant real interest rate and constant inflation rates, each country is populated by three well-defined groups. There is a group of people who, at the date of the policy choice, own assets denominated in domestic currency and are thus better off the lower the starting price level. There is another group, the current and future savers, whose savings earn a return which is a weighted average (determined by the reserve requirement) of the real return on the country's monetary base and that on securities. These people are better off the higher is this average real return. Finally, there is the group of current and future borrowers who borrow at the real return on securities and who, therefore, are better off the lower is that real return. This correspondence between predicted paths for price levels and the interest rate and the well-being of these different groups implies conflicts of interest—for example, between a country's borrowers, who prefer an easier monetary policy, and the initial owners of its monetary base, who prefer a tighter monetary policy.

An objective for a country must weight these competing interests. The objective we adopt, maximization of a social welfare function, assumes this is done. The social welfare function of a country describes how the government trades off the well-being of its three different groups as it makes policy decisions.

Using a social welfare function for each country, we compare what happens if each country chooses a monetary policy that maximizes that function taking as given the choices of the monetary policies of other countries—our way of describing noncooperation—with what happens if countries choose their monetary policies jointly, or cooperatively. We find, for the special case of identical countries, that every country can do better if all countries cooperate than if they do not. This doing better, of course, is in terms of the country's social welfare function. Every person in each country is not better off under cooperation. Rather, given the way social welfare functions (the governments) weight the different groups in each country, cooperation results in a higher value of each social welfare function, but at the expense of at least one group in each country.

Although we demonstrate a gain from cooperation only in a very special model, the result is likely to hold in any model which shares these crucial features of ours: separate country-by-country markets in currencies and an integrated world credit market in which government borrowing affects the world interest rate. These features produce policy interdependence: one country's policy affects others through the effects of its borrowing on the world real interest rate. The features also produce a kind of asymmetry: a country's choice of monetary policy affects its borrowers and borrowers in other countries in the same way, but affects the initial owners of currency and savers in its country differently than those in other countries. This asymmetry is what produces the gain from cooperation.

The Model

Our model is a multi-country version of the single-country model used by Wallace [in Chapter 5]. Here we describe the model and study the equilibrium for a special case in which the saving behavior of individuals in each country takes a particularly simple form.[2]

A Typical Country

Each country in our model has a private sector and a public sector.

Private Demands and Supplies
Each country k (for $k = 1, 2, \ldots, K$) is populated by overlapping generations, the members of which live two periods. At each date t (where t is an

integer) a new generation, generation t, appears. Its members are present in the economy at t (when they are young) and at $t + 1$ (when they are old). We assume that people do not move between countries, a standard assumption in models of international trade.

The model contains one good at each date, the time t good, that is common to all countries.[3] This good can be costlessly and instantly transported from one country to another. There is, however, no production; the time t good cannot be produced or used to produce any other good (that is, any good available at any other time than t).

Each member of generation t has preferences over private consumption of the time t and time $t + 1$ goods, preferences that are representable by a utility function or an indifference curve map of the usual sort. These preferences are unaffected by government consumption. Each such member also has an income stream or endowment consisting of some amount of the time t good and some amount of the time $t + 1$ good.

We assume that different generations are identical and that within each country each generation has a special kind of diversity. Each generation consists of two groups of people. Members of one group, called *lenders* (or savers), are identical and have preferences and endowments that lead them to want to lend (or save) at most rates of return. Members of the other group, called *borrowers* (or dissavers), are also identical and have preferences and endowments that lead them to want to borrow (or dissave) at most rates of return.

These assumptions imply that the competitive desired trades by the members of each group in country k can be described as functions of the terms of trade between the time t good and the time $t + 1$ good faced by the members of each group. We let $S^k(\cdot)$ denote the aggregate supply function or curve of the time t good (or desired lending or saving) of the lender group of generation t in country k and let $D^k(\cdot)$ denote the aggregate demand curve for the time t good (or desired borrowing or dissaving) of the borrower group for generation t in country k. In each case, the argument of the function is the intertemporal terms of trade which we express by the price of the time t good in units of the time $t + 1$ good (the gross real rate of return) faced by the members of the respective group. In general, as we will see, lenders, who are subject to a reserve requirement, face a different and lower rate of return than borrowers. We assume that $D^k(\cdot)$ is decreasing where it is positive.[4]

Since we will be describing how this economy evolves over time from the initial (or current) date, which we label $t = 1$, we need to add to the above description of the competitive behavior of the young of each generation in country k a description of the behavior of the country's people who are in the second period of their lives at $t = 1$, the initial (or current) old. We assume that their preferences are such that they try to consume as much of the time 1 good as they can and that they are endowed, or start, with some of the time 1 good and some nominally denominated assets (assets valued in terms of the current price level). Their implied competitive behavior is very simple: they supply all their assets at any positive price in terms of the time 1 good.

These assumptions imply some simple relationships between prices, including rates of return, and the well-being of individuals in country k: the initial old are better off the more valuable are their nominally denominated assets at time 1; lenders, or savers, in any generation t (for $t \geq 1$) are better off the higher the rate of return they earn on savings; borrowers in any generation t (for $t \geq 1$) are better off the lower the rate of return at which they can borrow. It is in terms of these relationships that we will describe how one country's policy affects other countries and how cooperation can or cannot improve welfare.

Government Policy
Each country in the model has a budget policy and a monetary policy. Budget policy is a sequence of the real net-of-interest deficit (the difference between real government consumption and real taxes, the latter of which we hold fixed throughout). Monetary policy is sequences of the monetary base and the interest-bearing government debt which finance the deficit. Consistent with this, we write the cash flow constraint of country k's combined budget and monetary authority as

$$G_t^k = p_t^k(H_{t+1}^k - H_t^k) + p_t^k(P_t^k B_{t+1}^k - B_t^k) \tag{1}$$

which must hold for all dates $t \geq 1$. Here G_t^k, measured in units of the time t good, is government k's real deficit net-of-interest. The first term on the right side of equation (1) is the value in terms of the time t good of government k's addition to its outstanding monetary base, and the second term is the value of its addition to its outstanding debt, which consists of one-period, zero coupon (pure discount) bonds. Specifically, the variables on the right side of equation (1) are defined this way:

H_t^k = The country k monetary base that generation $t - 1$ starts with at time t.

$p_t^k =$ The time t price of a unit of the country k monetary base in units of the time t consumption good ($1/p_t^k =$ the country k price level at time t).

$B_t^k =$ The nominal face value, in terms of the country k monetary base, of the maturing country k government bonds owned by members of generation $t - 1$ at time t.

$P_t^k =$ The price at time t, in terms of the country k monetary base, of a bond that pays one unit of the country k monetary base at time $t + 1$. [The country k nominal interest rate at t is $(1/P_t^k) - 1$.]

To insure that the monetary base of country k has value in equilibrium and that its bonds can bear nominal interest in equilibrium ($P_t^k < 1$), we assume that country k imposes (and is able to costlessly enforce) a reserve requirement on its residents' saving. Any resident of country k that saves a positive amount must hold a fraction λ^k of that amount in the form of country k base money. This requirement implies that the gross real rate of return faced by country k lenders at time t is the following weighted average: $\bar{r}_t^k = \lambda^k R_t^k + (1 - \lambda^k)r_t$, where R_t^k is the gross real rate of return on the country k monetary base, namely, p_{t+1}^k/p_t^k, and r_t is the gross real rate of return on loans, the single real return on loans in all countries.

As discussed more fully by Wallace [in Chapter 5], this reserve requirement is intended to capture in a simple way the role played by legal restrictions on private borrowing and lending in actual economies. Taken literally, it is an accurate description of an economy in which all individual lending, or saving, by residents of a country must take the form of accounts at banks or financial intermediaries, and these institutions must hold some fraction of the amount in those accounts in the form of the country's base money, but can otherwise hold assets in any form they want. If these institutions operate competitively and costlessly, then the rate they pay on their liabilities (their deposits) is a weighted average of the rate they earn on reserves and the rate they earn on loans, the weighted average described above as that facing private lenders.

World Equilibrium

Before formally describing the conditions for equilibrium in our world of K countries, we must describe some conditions on prices and interest rates, *arbitrage* conditions, that are implicit in the above description of individual trading opportunities. The first involves arbitrage between goods and monies, and the second involves arbitrage among securities.

As noted above, we are assuming that the single good in our world economy can be costlessly transported between countries. The first arbitrage condition—commonly known as *purchasing power parity*—is that the prices of the monies of any two countries in terms of the good and the exchange rate between the two monies are such that no gains can be made from the following set of transactions: selling the good in country k, using the resulting country k money to buy country k' money, and using the country k' money to buy the good in country k'. As the reader can verify, the condition that no gain be possible from such transactions is that the exchange rate $e_t^{k,k'}$, the price of country k money in units of country k' money at date t, be equal to the ratio of prices of monies:

$$e_t^{k,k'} = p_t^k / p_t^{k'}. \tag{2}$$

The second arbitrage condition is that interest rates facing borrowers in the K countries of our world economy are such that they imply the same terms of trade at any date t between the time t good and the time $t + 1$ good. This condition is implied by the assumption that anyone in any country can borrow and lend in any other country subject only to the reserve requirement on positive saving. Under this assumption, we cannot have an equilibrium in which the real return on loans in one country exceeds that in another country because in such a situation no saver would want to hold securities bearing the lower return (a demand consistent with reserve requirements) and every borrower would want to borrow at the lower rate. Together, these imply an excess supply of the securities bearing the lower return and an excess demand for those bearing the higher return, which, of course, cannot be an equilibrium. Thus, the assumption that individuals and governments can borrow and lend anywhere subject only to the reserve requirement implies that our world economy has only one real rate of return on loans. In the notation introduced above, it implies a single real rate of return on loans, r_t.

For prices, including interest rates and exchange rates, that satisfy these two arbitrage conditions, the real trading opportunities facing individuals are those we have described—essentially, trading present consumption for future consumption or, equivalently, trading present consumption for assets which are promises of future consumption.

Now we can describe what we mean by a competitive, perfect foresight equilibrium for this world economy. *Competitive* means that people treat prices as beyond their control when they choose quantities. *Perfect foresight* here means that anticipated rates of return on assets equal actual or realized rates of return or, more particularly, that at each date t the young correctly anticipate the price of the monies of the different countries in terms of goods at the next date. *Equilibrium* means that all markets clear at each date. From now on, we will refer to a competitive, perfect foresight equilibrium as simply an *equilibrium*.

The formal definition of equilibrium that we give below is valid only for values of r_t for which the borrowers of each country actually borrow or, more precisely, only for values of r_t for which $D^k(r_t) \geq 0$ for every k. The following notation allows us to state this condition concisely. Let $\bar{r}^k$ be such that $D^k(\bar{r}^k) = 0$, and let $\bar{r}$ be the smallest of the $\bar{r}^k$ for $k = 1, 2, \ldots, K$. Then $D^k(r) \geq 0$ for all k if $r \leq \bar{r}$. This condition appears as part of the following definition of an equilibrium:

DEFINITION. *Given each country's reserve requirement λ^k, its initial nominal indebtedness including its base money $H_1^k + B_1^k$ (a total which is assumed positive), sequences for its real net-of-interest deficit G_t^k, and a sequence for its base money H_{t+1}^k, an equilibrium consists of a sequence for r_t satisfying $r_t \leq \bar{r}$ and sequences for each country for p_t^k, P_t^k, R_t^k, $\bar{r}_t^k$, and B_{t+1}^k that for all $t \geq 1$ satisfy equation (1), the cash flow constraint for each country, and*

$$\sum_k [S^k(\bar{r}_t^k) - D^k(r_t)] = \sum_k [p_t^k(H_{t+1}^k + P_t^k B_{t+1}^k)] \tag{3}$$

$$\bar{r}_t^k = \lambda^k R_t^k + (1 - \lambda^k) r_t \tag{4}$$

$$R_t^k = p_{t+1}^k / p_t^k \tag{5}$$

$$r_t = p_{t+1}^k / p_t^k P_t^k \tag{6}$$

$$r_t \geq R_t^k \tag{7}$$

$$p_t^k H_{t+1}^k \geq \lambda^k S^k(\bar{r}_t^k) \tag{8}$$

where for each country k (4)–(8) must hold and either (7) or (8) must hold at equality.

Equation (3) says that world net private saving—the sum over countries of each country's saving supplied at the weighted average of the return on its base money and the return on securities less each country's private borrowing—must equal the total world value of government liabilities. Equations (4), (5), and (6) define the returns facing savers and borrowers in each country and contain our perfect foresight assumption—namely, that the returns that determine choices at t match the actual returns. Note that (6) implies that the ratio of a country's gross inflation rate, p_t^k / p_{t+1}^k, to its gross nominal interest rate, $1/P_t^k$, is the same for all countries. Inequalities (7) and (8) and the accompanying proviso are related to the reserve requirement. Inequality (7) says that the return on loans is at least as great as that on the base money of each country. If it were not, then unlimited gains could be made by borrowing and using the proceeds to acquire base money, activities which would not violate the reserve requirement. That being so, no equilibrium can violate (7). Inequality (8) expresses the reserve requirement: the value of country k base money must be at least as great as the required fraction λ^k times gross saving of the residents of country k. The proviso arises in this way. If $r_t > R_t^k$, then wealth maximization implies that country k residents and everyone else hold no more of country k base money than the minimum required, which is to say that (8) holds at equality. Alternatively, if the value of country k's base money exceeds the minimum required to be held $[p_t^k H_{t+1}^k > \lambda^k S^k(\bar{r}_t^k)]$, then wealth maximization implies that the return on country k base money is as great as the return on securities, which is (7) at equality.[5]

Instead of trying to study all possible equilibria for this economy for arbitrary sequences of government policies, we study a limited class of policies and potential equilibria under those policies. We study only policies for which each country's real net-of-interest deficit is a constant, $G_t^k = G^k$, and each country's ratio of government bonds to base money is a constant, $B_{t+1}^k / H_{t+1}^k = \beta^k$. For such policies, we attempt to describe only those equilibria for which all real variables are constant over time, equilibria we call *stationary* equilibria. For such policies, we formally define a stationary equilibrium as follows:

DEFINITION.   *Given* λ^k, $H_1^k + B_1^k > 0$, G^k, *and* β^k *for each* k, *a stationary equilibrium consists of a scalar* $r \leq \bar{r}$ *and of scalars* R^k, $\bar{r}^k$, h^k, b^k, *and* p_1^k *for each* k, *where* h^k *denotes a constant real value of the country* k *monetary base,* $p_t^k H_{t+1}^k$, *and* b^k *denotes a constant real value of the government bonds of country* k, $p_t^k P_t^k B_{t+1}^k$, *that satisfy*

$$G^k = (1 - R^k)h^k + (1 - r)b^k \tag{9}$$

$$\sum_k [S^k(\bar{r}^k) - D^k(r)] = \sum_k (h^k + b^k) \tag{10}$$

$$\bar{r}^k = \lambda^k R^k + (1 - \lambda^k)r \tag{11}$$

$$r \geq R^k \tag{12}$$

$$h^k \geq \lambda^k S(\bar{r}^k) \tag{13}$$

$$G^k = h^k + b^k - p_1^k(H_1^k + B_1^k) \tag{14}$$

where either (12) *or* (13) *must hold at equality.*

Note that equation (9) is the stationary version of the country k cash flow constraint, equation (1), and that (14) comes from that constraint for the first date, $t = 1$. For constant real sequences, this definition of an equilibrium and the earlier one are equivalent.

Below we make assumptions that imply that stationary equilibria are necessarily *binding*, equilibria for which (13) holds at equality. We focus on binding stationary equilibria because we suspect that they are the relevant ones for the current world economy.[6] Our approach to studying binding stationary equilibria is to solve equations (9)–(11) and equation (13) at equality for the h^k, b^k, and rates of return and then to verify that the implied solution satisfies (12). If it does and if it implies a positive p_1^k using equation (14), then it is a valid solution.

If equilibria are binding, we can reduce equations (9)–(11) and (13) at equality, $3K + 1$ equations, to $K + 1$ equations in $K + 1$ unknowns, r and the R^k. From the definitions of h^k and b^k, we have

$$b^k/h^k = \beta^k P_t^k. \tag{15}$$

Since, by (5) and (6), $P_t^k = R_t^k/r_t$, a constant in a stationary equilibrium, we can rewrite (15) as

$$b^k = h^k \beta^k R^k/r. \tag{16}$$

Then, upon substituting the right sides of (16) and (13) at equality into (9) and (10) we have, respectively,

$$G^k = \lambda^k S^k(\bar{r}^k)[(1 - R^k) + (1 - r)\beta^k R^k/r] \tag{17}$$

$$\sum_k [S^k(\bar{r}^k) - D^k(r)] = \sum_k [\lambda^k S^k(\bar{r}^k)(1 + \beta^k R^k/r)]. \tag{18}$$

If we use (11) to replace $\bar{r}^k$ by the weighted average of R^k and r, then the resulting versions of equations (17) and (18) are the $K + 1$ equations in the $K + 1$ unknowns, r and R^k for each k, that we referred to above. Moreover, as noted above, if the solution for these $K + 1$ equations satisfies (12) and is such that (14) can be solved for a positive p_1^k for each k, then the solution is a valid binding equilibrium.

A Special Case

Since (17) and (18) are complicated equations for general functions $S^k(\cdot)$ and $D^k(\cdot)$, we will study in detail only a special case of the model, one in which each $S^k(\cdot)$ function is a constant, denoted S^k, which does not depend on the return, $\bar{r}^k$.[7] This case is easy to study because for it, as we now show, equations (17) and (18) can be rewritten as a set of completely *recursive* equations, equations which can be solved one at a time.

We begin by solving equation (17) for R^k/r, obtaining

$$R^k/r = (1 - G^k/\lambda^k S^k)/[r(1 + \beta^k) - \beta^k]. \tag{19}$$

Solving (17) in this way is valid if $r(1 + \beta^k) - \beta^k \neq 0$. Below we present conditions that insure that the implied solution for r is such that this holds. Then, if we substitute the right side of (19) into the right side of (18) and at the same time impose the constant saving assumption, we can write the result as

$$E(r) = F(r; \beta, G) \tag{20}$$

where

$$E(r) \equiv \sum_k [(1 - \lambda^k)S^k - D^k(r)]$$

$$F(r; \beta, G) \equiv \sum_k \{(\lambda^k S^k - G^k)\beta^k/[r(1 + \beta^k) - \beta^k]\}$$

and where $\beta = (\beta^1, \beta^2, \ldots, \beta^K)$ and $G = (G^1, G^2, \ldots, G^K)$. Note that $E(r)$, an increasing function of r, is the world private excess demand for securities if the reserve requirement is binding in every country. The function $F(r; \beta, G)$ can be interpreted as the supply of securities by all the governments, a supply implied by the stationary versions of their cash flow constraints, bindingness of all the reserve requirements, and the choices of government portfolios, the β^k. If equation (20), which contains only one unknown, r, can be solved, then its solution can be used in equation (19) to find R^k. It can also be used to find p_1^k, the country k initial value of base money, from the following equation:

$$p_1^k = (\lambda^k S^k - G^k)r(1 + \beta^k)/[r(1 + \beta^k) - \beta^k]. \tag{21}$$

Equation (21) is obtained from (14)—with $H_1^k + B_1^k = 1$—by substituting for h^k and b^k from (13) and (16) at equality and for R^k/r from (19).[8]

The propositions we want to establish, mainly about solutions to equations (19)–(21), are implied by the following assumptions:

ASSUMPTION 1. $\lambda^k S^k > G^k \geqslant 0$ and $\beta^k > -1$ for all k.

ASSUMPTION 2. $\sum_k [S^k - D^k(1)] < 0$.

ASSUMPTION 3. $\bar{r} > 1$ and $E(\bar{r}) > \left[\sum_k (\lambda^k S^k - G^k)\right]/(\bar{r} - 1)$.

ASSUMPTION 4. $rD'(r)/D(r) < -1$,   where $D(r) \equiv \sum_k D^k(r)$.

The first part of Assumption 1 places bounds on the net-of-interest deficit; the upper bound is such that the deficit can be financed with $\beta^k = 0$; the lower bound says that, net of interest, the budget is not in surplus. The second part of Assumption 1 limits ratios of government debt to base money to those that keep the sum of the monetary base and the face value of government debt positive. Assumption 2 says that net private saving is negative at $r \leqslant 1$, that is, at negative and zero real interest rates. Together, these two assumptions have the following consequence:

PROPOSITION 1.   *Under Assumptions 1 and 2, any stationary equilibrium has* $r > 1$ *and is a binding equilibrium.*

(Proofs of Propositions 1–3 appear in Appendix A.)

Assumption 3 assures that we get a binding equilibrium with $r < \bar{r}$. It assures that no matter how large are the β^k—that is, no matter how tight monetary policies are—there is an equilibrium with $r < \bar{r}$.[9] Note that if countries are identical, so that, among other things, $D^k(\bar{r}) = 0$ for all k, then Assumption 3 is implied by the simple condition $1 - \lambda > \lambda/(\bar{r} - 1)$.

PROPOSITION 2.   *Under Assumptions 1–3, a binding equilibrium with* $r < \bar{r}$ *exists.*

Proposition 2 leaves open the possibility that there are several solutions to equation (20) and, hence, several binding equilibria with $r < \bar{r}$. The next proposition shows that the elasticity condition, Assumption 4, rules out this possibility.

PROPOSITION 3.   *Under Assumptions 1–3 and either Assumption 4 or the existence of an equilibrium with* $F(r; \beta, G) \geqslant 0$, *equation (20) has a unique solution with* $r < \bar{r}$.

The arguments in the proofs of Propositions 2 and 3 (in Appendix A) imply that the functions $E(r)$ and $F(r; \beta, G)$ are essentially as shown in Figures 12.1 and 12.2. That is, $F(r; \beta, G)$ crosses $E(r)$ only once and from above on the left. Thus, under the assumptions of Proposition 3, we can define the unique value of $r < \bar{r}$ that satisfies (20) as a function of β and G, say,

$$r = \phi(\beta, G). \tag{22}$$

By direct substitutions into (19) and (21), we get the corresponding unique solutions for R^k and p_1^k. Then, given the solutions for p_1^k, we use (2) to solve for $e_1^{k,k'}$.

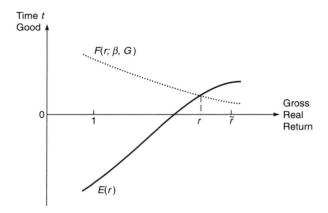

Figure 12.1 If All β's Positive

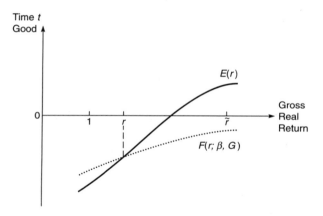

Figure 12.2 If All β's Negative

Figures 12.1 and 12.2
Possible Real Interest Rate Solutions to Equation (20)

The Effects of a Policy Change: The Model's Predictions vs. Recent Events

Existence of equilibria under given policies in our model indicates a kind of internal consistency. Now we want to describe a kind of external consistency as well—to show, that is, that the model's predictions for policies like those adopted in the world in the last few years roughly agree with what has in fact occurred. We adopt the assumptions of Proposition 3 and generate the model's qualitative predictions by determining how the unique world equilibrium changes when one nation's budget and monetary policies change.

We characterize the policies actually adopted in recent years as the adoption of a more expansionary budget policy in the face of a nonaccommodating monetary policy in the United States coupled with a passive policy response in the rest of the world. Labeling the United States *country 1*, we represent the adoption of a more expansionary budget policy as a permanent increase in the U.S. budget deficit net-of-interest G^1. Given this change in budget policy, we represent a nonaccommodating U.S. monetary policy as a permanent change in β^1 which keeps the monetary base in the period of the policy change, H_2^1, at what it otherwise would have been.[10] We represent the passive policy response in the rest of the world as no change in the rest of the model's G's and β's.

In order to make the qualitative predictions of our combined budget and monetary policy experiment better understood, we first describe the model's predictions for each policy change alone. This exercise also shows that our model cannot explain recent events by a change in just U.S. budget policy, but instead gives monetary policy a prominent role.

The structure of the model and the solutions indicate that all effects on other countries of a change in country 1's budget and monetary policies result from a change in the real interest rate.[11] Because of this, we solve once for the effects of a change in the real interest rate on the inflation rate, the nominal interest rate, the price level, and the current account deficit of a passive country—one whose G and β are fixed. Then, to determine the effects of a change in country 1's policies on other countries, we need only use equation (20) to determine how that change affects the real interest rate.

The analysis continues with an examination of own-country effects of policy changes. These effects are generally different from the cross-country effects because of some direct effects on the government's budget in addition to the interest rate change. Then, given the own-country and cross-country effects, we calculate the change in the own-country's exchange rate—the value of its currency relative to other countries'—and the change in its balance on current account.

In our calculation of a country's current account balance, we assume that all foreign debt contracted at time $t - 1$ by individuals of generation $t - 1$ is paid off at time t at the gross real interest rate r_{t-1}. Thus, at time t, the real value of total foreign claims on country k, K_t^k, is the excess of total domestic borrowing at time t—by individual residents and the government, $D^k(r_t)$ and $p_t^k(H_{t+1}^k + P_t^k B_{t+1}^k)$, respectively—over total domestic saving, S^k:

$$K_t^k = D^k(r_t) + p_t^k(H_{t+1}^k + P_t^k B_{t+1}^k) - S^k. \tag{23}$$

The current account deficit, C_t^k, measures the increase over time in real foreign claims on country k, which can be written using (1) as

$$C_t^k \equiv K_t^k - K_{t-1}^k = D^k(r_t) + G^k + p_t^k(H_t^k + B_t^k) - S^k - K_{t-1}^k. \tag{24}$$

Two points can be made from (24) about a country's real current account deficit. First, in a stationary equilibrium, K_t^k must be constant for $t \geqslant 1$, so that the current account deficit must be zero for $t \geqslant 2$. However, since K_1^k can be different from K_0^k, C_1^k can be different from zero. Second, by substituting for terms on the right side of (24), we see that the current account deficit measures the excess of consumption in country k—by the old, the young borrowers, the young lenders, and the government—over total endowments (the country k trade deficit) plus net interest payments on foreign debt $(r_{t-1} - 1)K_{t-1}^k$. We assume in our policy experiments that $(r_0 - 1)K_0^k$ is unaffected by the choice of policy at time 1.

The effects of a change in the real interest rate on a passive country's inflation rate, nominal interest rate, price level, and current account deficit are calculated by differentiating equations (19), (21), and (24) holding its policies G and β fixed. In these calculations we assume Assumptions 1–4 hold. (The derivatives are displayed in Appendix B, and the effects of an increase in the real interest rate are displayed in Table 12.2.)

The results in Table 12.2 are best understood in terms of the impact of a higher real interest rate on a passive government's budget. If the government is a debtor, then a higher real interest rate raises its interest payments and forces it to increase the rate at which it is issuing both money and debt. If it is a creditor, then the reverse occurs.

The model's qualitative predictions for the effects of a policy change in country 1 are determined in two steps. First we obtain general expressions for the changes in the real interest rate and the own-country inflation rate,

Table 12.2
The effects of a higher real interest rate r on a passive country k

Variable	Debtor government $(\beta^k > 0)$	Creditor government $(\beta^k < 0)$
Inflation rate $(1/R^k - 1)$	+	−
Nominal interest rate $(r/R^k - 1)$	+	+
Price level $(1/p_1^k)$	+	−
Current account deficit (C_1^k)	−	+ or −

+ = increases   − = decreases

nominal interest rate, price level, current account deficit, and exchange rates by differentiating equations (20), (19), (21), (24), and (2). (These derivatives are also displayed in Appendix B.) In the second step, we identify country 1 as the United States and, in addition to Assumptions 1–4, we make two assumptions. We assume, quite realistically, that the U.S. government is a debtor, so that $\beta^1 > 0$, and that the governments of all other countries collectively are debtors in the sense that

$$\sum_{k=2}^{K} \chi^k \beta^k (1 + \beta^k) \geqslant 0$$

where

$$\chi^k \equiv (\lambda^k S^k - G^k)/[r(1 + \beta^k) - \beta^k]^2 > 0$$

by Assumption 1. The discussion that follows invokes these additional assumptions.

Tighter U.S. Monetary Policy

The first policy we evaluate is a tighter monetary policy in country 1, which we have identified as the United States. We increase β^1, the ratio of government bonds to money in the United States, holding all other β's and all G's constant. The predictions from our model are combined with the results from Table 12.2, and all are displayed in Table 12.3.

The results in Table 12.3 have an intuitive explanation. An increase in β^1 decreases the amount of money and increases the amount of government bonds outstanding in the United States. The drop in money produces a lower price level and thus a higher real value of government bonds. The increase in the supply of real debt in the world capital market causes the real interest rate to rise and generates the cross-country effects discussed

Table 12.3
The effects of a tighter U.S. monetary policy

		Other countries	
Variable	United States $(\beta^1 > 0)$	Debtor government $(\beta^k > 0)$	Creditor government $(\beta^k < 0)$
Real interest rate (r)	+	+	+
Inflation rate $(1/R^k - 1)$	+	+	−
Nominal interest rate $(r/R^k - 1)$	+	+	+
Price level $(1/p_1^k)$	−	+	−
Value of currency relative to dollar $(1/e_1^{1,k})$	n.a.	−	−
Current account deficit (C_1^k)	+	−	+ or −

$+$ = increases $-$ = decreases   n.a. = not applicable

earlier. Some of the additional real debt is purchased by foreign residents, causing the U.S. current account deficit to rise. With more bonds outstanding at a higher real interest rate, the real interest expense on government debt rises and forces the U.S. government to make greater use of the inflation tax.

Easier U.S. Budget Policy with Monetary Accommodation . . .

Now we evaluate an easier budget policy in the United States. We increase G^1, the U.S. real budget deficit net-of-interest, which corresponds to an increase in real government consumption, holding constant all β's and all other G's. The predictions from our model are combined with the results from Table 12.2, and all are displayed in Table 12.4.

The effects in the United States of an easing in its budget policy seem counterintuitive. They are explained by the monetary accommodation implied by a fixed β^1 in the face of a higher G^1. At the initial real interest rate, an increase in G^1 leaves the demand for government bonds, $E(r)$, unaffected. The increase in G^1 affects the supply, however, in a way that depends on β^1. When $\beta^1 > 0$, the higher deficit with a fixed β^1 implies sufficient monetary expansion to reduce the real value of government debt. The excess demand for bonds causes the real interest rate to fall, and that generates the cross-country effects discussed earlier. The monetary accommodation results in a higher U.S. price level, and the decline in U.S. borrowing causes the U.S. current account deficit to shrink. Although the interest expense on U.S. government debt falls due to both a lower real

Table 12.4
The effects of an easier U.S. budget policy with monetary accommodation

	United States ($\beta^1 > 0$)	Other countries Debtor government ($\beta^1 > 0$)	Creditor government ($\beta^k < 0$)
Variable			
Real interest rate (r)	−	−	−
Inflation rate ($1/R^k - 1$)	+	−	+
Nominal interest rate ($r/R^k - 1$)	+	−	−
Price level ($1/p_1^k$)	+	−	+
Value of currency relative to dollar ($1/e_1^{1 \cdot k}$)	n.a.	+	+
Current account deficit (C_1^k)	−	+	+ or −

+ = increases   − = decreases   n.a. = not applicable

stock of bonds and a lower real interest rate, the fall does not offset the increase in the budget deficit net-of-interest. With a higher deficit inclusive of interest, the U.S. government must make greater use of the inflation tax.

... And without Monetary Accommodation

Finally, we evaluate an easier budget policy with a nonaccommodating monetary policy in the United States—what seems to represent actual U.S. policies in the past four years. It is a combination of the previous two experiments, involving an increase in β^1 and an increase in G^1. Since the effects of such increases are often of opposite signs, the effects of the combined policy experiment cannot simply be deduced from the previous experiments.

In this experiment we increase G^1 and let the model determine the increase in β^1 required to keep the initial money stock H_2^1 unchanged from what it otherwise would have been. All other β's and G's are held constant. To do this experiment, we use equation (1) for the first date to solve for β^1 as a function of G^1 and H_2^1, namely,

$$\beta^1 = (r/R^1)(G^1/\lambda^1 S^1 + \psi)$$

where

$$\psi \equiv (H_1^1 + B_1^1 - H_2^1)/H_2^1.$$

We next substitute this expression for β^1 into (19), (20), and (21) to get, respectively,

$$R^1/r = (1 + \psi)/r - (\lambda^1 S^1 \psi + G^1)/\lambda^1 S^1 \tag{25}$$

$$E(r) = \sum_{k=2}^{K} (\lambda^k S^k - G^k)\{\beta^k/[r(1 + \beta^k) - \beta^k]\} + \lambda^1 S^1(1 + \psi) + G^1 \tag{26}$$

$$p_1^1 = \lambda^1 S^1(1 + \psi)/(H_1^1 + B_1^1). \tag{27}$$

Our policy experiment then translates into determining the effects in this new system of an increase in G^1 holding ψ (and hence H_2^1) constant.

By combining these results with the cross-country effects in Table 12.2, we get the Table 12.1 results that we described in the preview to the paper. As we discussed there, these predictions seem generally consistent with actual experience.

These results highlight how the effects of a budget policy change depend on the accompanying monetary policy. When we hold constant H_2^1 —rather than β^1 as in the previous experiment—the effects of an increase in G^1 seem more in accord with intuition. When H_2^1 is held constant, the initial price level is unaffected by the increase in G^1. That increase must then increase the supply of real debt in the world capital market, and this causes a rise in the real interest rate, which in turn leads to the cross-country effects in Table 12.1. Some of the real debt is bought by foreign residents, so that the U.S. current account deficit increases. With a higher deficit net-of-interest and higher interest expense, the United States must make greater use of the inflation tax.

Choosing Monetary Policies: Cooperation vs. Noncooperation

Countries obviously interact in our model, in the sense that one country's policy choices affect residents of other countries. Here we take all budget policies as given and consider whether cooperation among countries in choosing monetary policies, the β^k, would be desirable for the world. We address this question by comparing what happens if countries cooperate in choosing monetary policies with what happens if they do not.

We make the comparison using the following definitions of *not cooperating* and *cooperating*. *Not cooperating* will mean that each country k chooses its own monetary policy, β^k, to maximize its social welfare function taking as given the monetary policies of all the other countries, β^j for all $j \neq k$.[12] The outcome of noncooperation will be described by a vector $\hat{\beta} = (\hat{\beta}^1, \hat{\beta}^2, \ldots, \hat{\beta}^K)$ that simultaneously satisfies these conditions for all countries. In the terminology of game theory, such an outcome is called a *Nash equilibrium*. *Cooperating* will mean that all the β^k are chosen to maximize a weighted average of the social welfare functions of the individual countries. We will show that these definitions and our model imply that cooperation is desirable in the sense that it can produce a higher value of every country's social welfare function than does not cooperating.

Our first task, then, is to describe the social welfare function of a country. Since we are considering only stationary equilibria, the country k social welfare function can be expressed as a function of three arguments: the welfare of a country k initial old person, that of a country k saver in any generation, and that of a country k borrower in any generation. Moreover, since current old persons are better off the higher is p_1^k, since savers are better off the higher is $\bar{r}^k = \lambda^k R^k + (1 - \lambda^k)r$, and since borrowers are better off the higher is $1/r$, we can express country k's welfare as a function of those three variables, namely, as a function $u^k(p_1^k, \bar{r}^k, 1/r)$ where u^k is increasing in each of its arguments and is in other respects like an ordinary utility function.[13]

The next step is to express social welfare for country k in terms of the monetary policy parameters, the vector $\beta = (\beta^1, \beta^2, \ldots, \beta^K)$. This is done by substituting the solutions for p_1^k, $\bar{r}^k$, and r that we found earlier into the expression for u^k. To do this, we use (22) with the argument G suppressed —$r = \phi(\beta)$—and express the solutions for R^k and p_1^k, as implied by (19) and (21), as

$$R^k = \phi_2^k(\beta) \equiv \phi(\beta)(1 - G^k/\lambda^k S^k) \div [\phi(\beta)(1 + \beta^k) - \beta^k] \tag{28}$$

$$p_1^k = \phi_3^k(\beta) \equiv \phi(\beta)(\lambda^k S^k - G^k)(1 + \beta^k) \div [\phi(\beta)(1 + \beta^k) - \beta^k]. \tag{29}$$

Then, recalling that $\bar{r}^k = \lambda^k R^k + (1 - \lambda^k)r$, we let

$$V^k(\beta^k, \beta^{)k(}) \equiv u^k\{\phi_3^k(\beta), \lambda^k \phi_2^k(\beta) + (1 - \lambda^k)\phi(\beta), 1/\phi(\beta)\} \tag{30}$$

where $\beta^{)k(} = (\beta^1, \beta^2, \ldots, \beta^{k-1}, \beta^{k+1}, \ldots, \beta^K)$, the vector β with β^k excluded.

As noted above, we are assuming that what happens under *noncooperation* is described by a Nash equilibrium with each country k choosing β^k, taking $\beta^{)k(}$ as given. Formally, then, the noncooperative solution is a vector $(\hat{\beta}^1, \hat{\beta}^2, \ldots, \hat{\beta}^K)$ such that, for each k, $\beta^k = \hat{\beta}^k$ maximizes $V^k(\beta^k, \beta^{)k(})$. We can view *cooperation* as leading to the choice of any feasible vector β, in particular, one that maximizes $\sum w^k V^k(\beta^k, \beta^{)k(})$, where w^k is the weight given to the country k social welfare function and the summation is over the K countries.

We appraise the noncooperative solution under the assumptions that the world economy consists of identical countries and that the noncooperative solution for such a world is one with a common value of β^k, what is called a *symmetric* Nash equilibrium.[14] The assumption of identical countries simplifies the presentation and does not prejudice the results toward cooperation.[15] Very generally, if cooperation is desirable in a world of identical countries, then it is desirable in a world of dissimilar countries. We then have the following proposition:

PROPOSITION 4. *If countries are identical and Assumptions 1–4 hold, then monetary policies generally exist that imply a higher value of the common social welfare function u than is implied by any noncooperative solution with a common value of β^k for all k (any symmetric Nash equilibrium).*

The proof of this proposition in Appendix C shows that a small common departure of all the β^k from their common Nash equilibrium value will in general raise the value of the common function V, as defined in equation (30), from its value at the Nash equilibrium.

The proof shows, however, that there is no general presumption about whether the higher value of social welfare is achieved at lower or higher values of the β^k (with an easier or tighter monetary policy). It implies that if the social welfare function does not attach any weight to savers (to $\bar{r}^k$), then better cooperative outcomes are achieved at lower values of the β^k. If, alternatively, the welfare function does not attach any weight to the initial owners of currency (to p_1^k), then better cooperative outcomes are achieved at higher values of the β^k. These results also follow from an examination of the trade-offs among triplets ($p_1^k, \bar{r}^k, 1/r$) faced, on the one hand, by a country acting noncooperatively (taking other countries' policies as given) and those faced, on the other hand, by all countries acting jointly (and varying all the β^k in unison). As also shown in Appendix C, a given increase in $1/r$ (a benefit to borrowers) is achieved at the expense of a larger decrease in p_1^k (a cost to the initial old) when a country acts noncooperatively than when all countries act jointly. And a given increase in $1/r$ is achieved at the expense of a smaller decrease in $\bar{r}^k$ (a cost to savers) when a country acts noncooperatively than when all countries act jointly. Obviously, then, if the social welfare function attaches weight to the well-being of all three groups, then the better cooperative outcomes can occur at either lower or higher common values of the β^k. The following two examples illustrate these possibilities.

The examples are of a world economy with three identical countries. In each country, each generation consists of one saver endowed with 1 unit of the consumption good when young and nothing when old and one borrower endowed with nothing when young and 1.05 units of the consumption good when old. Each person has a utility function equal to the sum of the logarithms of first- and second-period consumption. These assumptions imply $S^k = 0.5$ and $D^k(r) = 1.05/2r$ for all k. We also assume that $\lambda^k = 0.1$ and $G^k = 0.005$ for all k. Finally, we let $u^k(p_1^k, \bar{r}^k, 1/r) = (0.01)\ln(p_1^k) + \alpha \ln(\bar{r}^k) + \ln(1/r)$, where α is a parameter.[16] If $\alpha = 1$, then the symmetric Nash equilibrium values are

$$(\beta^k, p_1^k, \bar{r}^k, 1/r) = (-0.267, 0.0341, 1.118, 1/1.139)$$

and, as can easily be verified, better outcomes are achieved at (slightly) lower values of the β^k. If $\alpha = 2$, then the symmetric Nash equilibrium values are

$$(\beta^k, p_1^k, \bar{r}^k, 1/r) = (0.558, 0.0638, 1.178, 1/1.217)$$

and better outcomes are achieved at higher values of the β^k.[17]

Perusal of Appendix C will verify that cooperation is desirable in this model because of the asymmetry discussed in the preview. One country's policy affects its borrowers and those of other countries in the same way, but affects its initial old and its savers in a quite different way than it affects the initial old and savers of other countries because each country's money is held only by its residents.[18] Since the asymmetry is more important the smaller is each country relative to the world economy, the desirability of cooperation in our model does not depend on countries being, in any sense, large relative to the world economy.

Conclusion

We have shown that in a particular model some form of coordination would improve the workings of a floating exchange rate system. We have identified crucial features of our model as separate country-by-country markets in currencies and an integrated world market in securities in which government borrowing affects interest rates. We have also suggested that our conclusion is likely to hold in most models that share these features. However, even if these features are accepted as approximating conditions in the actual world economy, our conclusion cannot be taken as recommending a particular policy.

Within the confines of our particular model, we have seen that no general conclusion emerges concerning whether better cooperative outcomes are achieved at tighter or easier monetary policies. How cooperation changes policies depends on the objective trade-offs as well as on the weights each country assigns the utilities of different groups of people.

Since features within our model affect the form that desirable cooperation takes, we expect that departures from our model would also affect it.
We can imagine reasonable departures in several directions:

• Different *economic environments*—for example, environments with more
general asset demands, uncertainty, and nontraded goods.

• Different *policy choices*—for example, nonconstant sequences of policies
and policies parameterized in different ways.

• Different *noncooperative equilibrium concepts*—for example, ones that do
not treat the countries symmetrically and ones that have countries take into
account the policy responses of other countries.

• Different *cooperative equilibrium concepts*—for example, ones that take
account of enforcement problems arising from uncertainty.

We do not know how these departures would change the form that desirable cooperation would take.

Thus, although we have identified one set of general conditions about
the world's markets in currencies and securities that imply some role for
cooperation, our analysis does not imply a particular way of achieving
desirable cooperation. It does suggest that there is a plausible rationale for
the proposal that countries coordinate their macroeconomic policies under
floating exchange rates. However, it leaves quite open what precise form
that coordination should take.

Appendix A: Proofs of Propositions 1–3

PROPOSITION 1.   *Under Assumptions 1 and 2, any stationary equilibrium has*
$r > 1$ *and is a binding equilibrium.*

Proof.   By (13) and $\beta^k > -1$, $h^k + b^k > 0$. But then, by (10) and Assumption 2, $r > 1$. To see that a nonbinding stationary equilibrium cannot exist,
note that $R^k = r > 1$ and $h^k + b^k > 0$ imply that the right side of (9) is
negative, which contradicts Assumption 1.

PROPOSITION 2.   *Under Assumptions 1–3, a binding equilibrium with $r < \bar{r}$*
exists.

Proof.   We will show that equation (20) has a solution with $r \, \varepsilon \, (1, \bar{r})$. That
and Assumption 1 will imply immediately that the right side of (19) is
positive and less than unity ($0 < R^k < r$) and that the right side of (21) is
positive ($p_1^k > 0$).

Since $E(r)$ and $F(r; \beta, G)$ are continuous functions of r (for fixed β and G), to show that (20) has a solution with $r \, \varepsilon \, (1, \bar{r})$ we need only show that $E(1) < F(1; \beta, G)$ and that $E(\bar{r}) > F(\bar{r}; \beta, G)$.

We have $E(1) = \sum[S^k - D^k(1)] - \sum \lambda^k S^k < -\sum \lambda^k S^k$, the inequality being a consequence of Assumption 2. We also have $F(1; \beta, G) = \sum(\lambda^k S^k - G^k)\beta^k > -\sum(\lambda^k S^k - G^k) \geqslant -\sum \lambda^k S^k$, both inequalities being consequences of Assumption 1. Thus, $E(1) < F(1; \beta, G)$.

Since $F(r; \beta, G)$ is increasing in β^k for each k, $F(\bar{r}; \beta, G)$ is less than the limit of $F(\bar{r}; \beta, G)$ as $\beta^k \to \infty$ for every k. This limit is $[\sum_k (\lambda^k S^k - G^k)] \div (\bar{r} - 1)$. Therefore, Assumption 3 implies that $E(\bar{r}) > F(\bar{r}; \beta, G)$.

PROPOSITION 3. *Under Assumptions 1–3 and either Assumption 4 or the existence of an equilibrium with $F(r; \beta, G) \geqslant 0$, equation (20) has a unique solution with $r < \bar{r}$.*

Proof. Since Proposition 3 is obviously true if $\beta^k = 0$ for all k, we proceed under the assumption that $\beta^k \neq 0$ for at least some k. Letting $f(r) \equiv F(r; \beta, G)$, we first establish that

$$f'(r) < -(1/r) f(r). \tag{A1}$$

Note that $f'(r) = -\sum x_k(r) y_k(r)$, where $x_k(r) = (\lambda^k S^k - G^k)\beta^k \div [r(1 + \beta^k) - \beta^k]$ and $y_k(r) = 1/[r - \beta^k/(1 + \beta^k)]$. We also have that if $\beta^k > 0$, then $x_k(r) > 0$ and $y_k(r) > 1/r$, while if $\beta^k < 0$, then $x_k(r) < 0$ and $y_k(r) < 1/r$. Therefore, $-f'(r) = \sum x_k(r) y_k(r) > (1/r)\sum x_k(r) = (1/r) f(r)$. Thus, we have (A1).

Inequality (A1) says that $f(r)$ [which is identical to $F(r; \beta, G)$] is downward-sloping wherever F is not negative. Thus, if (20) has a solution where $f \geqslant 0$—say, at r_+—then it is the only solution. There cannot be a solution at $r > r_+$ because $E(r)$ is increasing and f can never get to a higher value than $f(r_+)$ without violating (A1). There cannot be a solution with $r < r_+$ because then f could never get to a value as great as $f(r_+)$ without violating (A1). [Note that we get an equilibrium where $F \geqslant 0$ if enough of the β^k are positive. Thus, if $\beta^k \geqslant 0$ for all k, then we have a unique solution to (20) without appeal to Assumption 4.]

When there is no solution with $F \geqslant 0$, we need Assumption 4. Since $E(1) < F(1; \beta, G) \equiv f(1)$, uniqueness is implied if $f'(r) < E'(r)$ at any solution.

At any solution, we have the following string:

$$f'(r) < -(1/r) f(r) = -(1/r) E(r) = -(1/r)\sum(1 - \lambda^k)S^k + (1/r)D(r)$$
$$\leqslant -(1/r)\sum(1 - \lambda^k)S^k - D'(r) < -D'(r) = E'(r). \tag{A2}$$

The first inequality is (A1); the second (an equality) uses the assumption that we are at a solution; the third (an equality) uses the definition of $E(r)$; the fourth uses Assumption 4 and the fact that $D(r) > 0$ at any $r < \bar{r}$.

Appendix B: Expressions for the Effects of One Country's Policy Changes

Here we display expressions for the derivatives of key variables with respect to the real interest rate in a passive country and with respect to policy variables in the own-country.

Effects of a Change in the Real Interest Rate on Passive Country k

Derivative with respect to r of		From
(B1)	R^k: $-(\chi^k \beta^k / \lambda^k S^k)$	(19)
(B2)	R^k/r: $-[\chi^k(1 + \beta^k)/\lambda^k S^k]$	(19)
(B3)	p_1^k: $-\chi^k \beta^k (1 + \beta^k)$	(21)
(B4)	C_1^k: $D^{k'}(r) - \chi^k \beta^k (1 + \beta^k)$	(20), (24)

Effects of a Change in Country 1's Monetary Policy

Derivative with respect to β^1 of		From
(B5)	r: $\chi^1 r / a_0 *$	(20)
(B6)	R^1: $-(\chi^1 r / \lambda^1 S^1)[(\chi^1 \beta^1 / a_0) + (r - 1)]$	(19), (20)
(B7)	R^1/r: $-(\chi^1 / \lambda^1 S^1)\{[\chi^1 r(1 + \beta^1)/a_0] + (r - 1)\}$	(19), (20)
(B8)	p_1^1: $\chi^1 r\{1 - [\chi^1 \beta^1 (1 + \beta^1)/a_0]\}$	(20), (21)
(B9)	$e_1^{1,k}$: $(e_1^{1,k}/a_0)(\{\sum_{j=2}^{K} [\chi^j \beta^j (1 + \beta^j) - D'(r)]$	(21), (B3), (B8)
	$\div (1 + \beta^1)[r(1 + \beta^1) - \beta^1]\}$	
	$+ \chi^1 \beta^1 / [r(1 + \beta^k) - \beta^k])$	
(B10)	C_1^1: $\chi^1 r\{\sum_{k=2}^{K} [\chi^k \beta^k (1 + \beta^k) - D^{k'}(r)]$	
	$\div \sum_{k=1}^{K} [\chi^k \beta^k (1 + \beta^k) - D^{k'}(r)]\}$	(20), (24)

$*a_0 \equiv \sum_{k=1}^{K} \chi^k \beta^k (1 + \beta^k) - D'(r) > 0$ by Assumptions 1–4.

Effects of a Change in Country 1's Budget Policy with Monetary Accommodation

Derivative with respect to G^1 (with fixed β^1) of		From
(B11)	r: $\quad (-1/a_0)\{\beta^1/[r(1+\beta^1)-\beta^1]\}$	(20)
(B12)	R^1: $\quad a_1[-ra_0 + \chi^1(\beta^1)^2]^*$	(19), (20)
(B13)	R^1/r: $\quad a_1[-a_0 + \chi^1\beta^1(1+\beta^1)]$	(19), (20)
(B14)	p_1^1: $\quad a_2[-ra_0 + \chi^1(\beta^1)^2]^*$	(20), (21)
(B15)	$e_1^{1,k}$: $\quad -(e_1^{1,k}/a_0)(\{\beta^1(1+\beta^k)$	
	$\qquad \div [r(1+\beta^1)-\beta^1][r(1+\beta^k)-\beta^k]\}$	
	$\qquad + \{[\sum_{j=2}^{K} \chi^j\beta^j(1+\beta^j) - D'(r)]$	
	$\qquad \div (\lambda^1 S^1 - G^1)\})$	(21), (B3), (B14)
(B16)	C_1^1: $\quad -\{\beta^1/[r(1+\beta^1)-\beta^1]\}$	
	$\qquad \times \{\sum_{k=2}^{K} [\chi^k\beta^k(1+\beta^k) - D^{k'}(r)]$	
	$\qquad \div \sum_{k=1}^{K} [\chi^k\beta^k(1+\beta^k) - D^{k'}(r)]\}$	(20), (24)

Effects of a Change in Country 1's Budget Policy without Monetary Accommodation

Derivative with respect to G^1 (with fixed H_2^1) of		From
(B17)	r: $\quad 1/[a_0 - \chi^1\beta^1(1+\beta^1)]$	(26)
(B18)	R^1: $\quad (-1/\lambda^1 S^1)(\{(\lambda^1 S^1\psi + G^1)$	
	$\qquad \div [a_0 - \chi^1\beta^1(1+\beta^1)]\} + r)$	(25)
(B19)	R^1/r: $\quad -[(1+\psi)/r^2]/[a_0 - \chi^1\beta^1(1+\beta^1)]$	(25)
(B20)	p_1^1: $\quad 0$	(27)
(B21)	$e_1^{1,k}$: $\quad (e_1^{1,k}/p_1^1)[\chi^k\beta^k(1+\beta^k)]$	
	$\qquad \div [a_0 - \chi^1\beta^1(1+\beta^1)]$	(21), (B3), (B20)
(B22)	C_1^1: $\quad \{\sum_{k=2}^{K} [\chi^k\beta^k(1+\beta^k) - D^{k'}(r)]\}$	
	$\qquad \div \{\sum_{k=1}^{K} [\chi^k\beta^k(1+\beta^k) - D^{k'}(r)] - D^{1'}(r)\}$	(24), (26)

$^*a_1 \equiv \{\lambda^1 S^1[r(1+\beta^1)-\beta^1]a_0\}^{-1} > 0.\ a_2 \equiv [(1+\beta^1)\lambda^1 S^1]a_1 > 0.$

Appendix C: Proof of Proposition 4 and Derivation of the Model's Trade-offs

Proof of Proposition 4

PROPOSITION 4.   *If countries are identical and Assumptions 1–4 hold, then monetary policies generally exist that imply a higher value of the common social welfare function u than is implied by any noncooperative solution with a common value of β^k for all k (any symmetric Nash equilibrium).*

Proof.   Let 1_{K-1} denote a $K-1$ element vector of 1's, and let $V_1(\cdot, \cdot)$ denote the partial derivative of V with respect to its first argument. We show that the derivative of $V[\beta, \beta(1_{K-1})]$ with respect to β is generally different from zero when it is evaluated at a symmetric Nash equilibrium, $\hat{\beta}$, which satisfies the first-order condition $V_1[\hat{\beta}, \hat{\beta}(1_{K-1})] = 0$.

Since $dV[\beta, \beta(1_{K-1})]/d\beta = V_1[\beta, \beta(1_{K-1})] + \{(K - 1) \times V_\chi[\beta, \beta(1_{K-1})]\}$, where V_χ denotes the partial derivative of V with respect to any argument other than the first, and since $V_1[\hat{\beta}, \hat{\beta}(1_{K-1})] = 0$, our task is to derive an expression for $V_\chi[\beta, \beta(1_{K-1})]$ and evaluate it at $\beta = \hat{\beta}$.

From (30),

$$V_\chi[\beta, \beta(1_{K-1})] = u_1(\partial\phi_3^k/\partial\beta^j) + u_2\lambda(\partial\phi_2^k/\partial\beta^j)$$

$$+ [(1 - \lambda)u_2 - (u_3/r^2)](\partial\phi/\partial\beta^j) \tag{C1}$$

$$V_1[\beta, \beta(1_{K-1})] = u_1(\partial\phi_3^k/\partial\beta^k) + u_2\lambda(\partial\phi_2^k/\partial\beta^k)$$

$$+ [(1 - \lambda)u_2 - (u_3/r^2)](\partial\phi/\partial\beta^k) \tag{C2}$$

where u_i stands for the partial derivative of u with respect to its ith argument and where the partial derivatives of ϕ, ϕ_2^k, and ϕ_3^k—see equations (22), (28), and (29)—are computed as in Appendix B.

At a symmetric Nash equilibrium, the right side of (C2) is zero and $\partial\phi/\partial\beta^k = \partial\phi/\partial\beta^j$. These imply, by substitution from (C2) into (C1), that

$$V_\chi[\hat{\beta}, \hat{\beta}(1_{K-1})] = u_1[(\partial\phi_3^k/\partial\beta^j) - (\partial\phi_3^k/\partial\beta^k)] + u_2\lambda[(\partial\phi_2^k/\partial\beta^j) - (\partial\phi_2^k/\partial\beta^k)].$$
$$\tag{C3}$$

Since, by (28) and (29),

$$(\partial\phi_3^k/\partial\beta^j) - (\partial\phi_3^k/\partial\beta^k) = -\lambda SR/[r(1 + \beta) - \beta] \tag{C4}$$

$$(\partial\phi_2^k/\partial\beta^j) - (\partial\phi_2^k/\partial\beta^k) = R(r - 1)/[r(1 + \beta) - \beta] \tag{C5}$$

we have

$$V_\gamma[\hat{\beta}, \hat{\beta}(1_{K-1})] = -\{\lambda\hat{R}/[\hat{r}(1+\hat{\beta}) - \hat{\beta}]\} \times [u_1 S - u_2(\hat{r} - 1)]. \tag{C6}$$

Although the terms in the second factor on the right side of (C6)—that involving u_1 and u_2—have opposite signs, they are generally not of equal magnitudes. Thus, $V_\gamma[\hat{\beta}, \hat{\beta}(1_{K-1})]$ is generally not zero.

Cooperative and Noncooperative Trade-offs

Write (19) as $R^k = g(\beta^k, r)$ and (21) as $p_1^k = h(\beta^k, r)$. Also, let $dr/d\beta^k = \partial\phi(\beta)/\partial\beta^k$ and $dr/d\beta = \sum_k \partial\phi(\beta)/\partial\beta^k$. If these derivatives are evaluated at $\beta^k = \beta$ for all k, then $dr/d\beta = K dr/d\beta^k$, which is used below.

We begin by finding the trade-offs between R^k and r. We have

$$dR^k/d\beta^k = g_1 + g_2(dr/d\beta^k) \tag{C7}$$

where g_i is the partial derivative of g with respect to its ith argument. Therefore,

$$(dR^k/dr)_N = (dR^k/d\beta^k)/(dr/d\beta^k)$$

$$= g_1/(dr/d\beta^k) + g_2 \tag{C8}$$

where N denotes *noncooperative* (holding $\beta^j = \hat{\beta}$ for $j \neq k$). Also,

$$dR^k/d\beta = g_1 + g_2 dr/d\beta \tag{C9}$$

and, therefore,

$$(dR^k/dr)_C = (dR^k/d\beta)/(dr/d\beta)$$

$$= g_1/(dr/d\beta) + g_2 \tag{C10}$$

where C denotes *cooperative* (varying all the β^k together). Therefore,

$$(dR^k/dr)_C - (dR^k/dr)_N = -(K-1)g_1/(dr/d\beta) > 0 \tag{C11}$$

since $dr/d\beta^k > 0$ and, from (19), $g_1 = -(1 - G/\lambda S)(r - 1) \div [r(1 + \beta^k) - \beta^k]^2 < 0$.

Then, since $\bar{r}^k = \lambda R^k + (1 - \lambda)r$, we know immediately that $(d\bar{r}^k/dr)_C - (d\bar{r}^k/dr)_N$ is λ times the right side of (C11).

Finally, in exactly the same way as we got (C11), we get

$$(dp_1^k/dr)_C - (dp_1^k/dr)_N = -(K-1)h_1/(dr/d\beta) < 0. \tag{C12}$$

The inequality in (C12) is a consequence of $h_1 = (\lambda S - G)r \div [r(1 + \beta^k) - \beta^k]^2 > 0$ [see (21)].

To get the corresponding trade-offs between $\bar{r}^k$ and $1/r$ and that between p_1^k and $1/r$, simply multiply (C11) and (C12) by $-r^2$.

Notes

1. Coordination of macroeconomic policies has been studied before, but using models with very different basic ingredients. See Cooper 1985 for a survey of previous research.

2. The special case should make our presentation accessible to undergraduate students of economics—at least those whose background includes intermediate microeconomic theory and some calculus.

3. Under well-known conditions, the single time t good can be interpreted as a composite good. See, for example, Kareken and Wallace 1981, p. 210.

4. If the arguments of borrowers' utility functions are normal goods, then $D^k(\cdot)$ is decreasing where it is positive. For a more detailed description of the derivation of the $S^k(\cdot)$ and $D^k(\cdot)$ functions, see the Wallace paper [Chapter 5] or the section on the derivation of demand in any intermediate price theory text.

5. Two conditions in this definition depend on the restriction $r_t \leqslant \bar{r}$. Without it, the argument of $D^k(\cdot)$ in (3) is not necessarily r_t and the right side of (8) would have to be $\lambda^k S^k(\bar{r}_t^k) + \lambda^k \max[0, -D^k(\bar{r}_t^k)]$.

6. One significant feature of nonbinding equilibria is perfect substitution among the monetary bases of the different countries. See Kareken and Wallace 1981 for a discussion of the consequences of such substitution.

7. If lenders have a utility function of the Cobb-Douglas form and if their endowment is entirely in the form of income when they are young, then $S^k(\cdot)$ is a constant fraction of that income (and does not depend on any rate of return).

8. Setting $H_1^k + B_1^k = 1$ for all k saves space and is innocuous. It amounts to no more than choosing monetary units of the different countries in a particular way.

9. Examples of economies with $\bar{r}$ as large as we want are easy to produce. For example, if every borrower in every country has a Cobb-Douglas utility function which weights consumption when young and when old equally and has the same lifetime income pattern, say, w_1^b when young and w_2^b when old, then $\bar{r} = w_2^b/w_1^b$.

10. Note that the United States cannot adhere to the original path of H^1 for all time. This is not a stationary policy, because it requires in each period an increase in β^1 and, hence, an increase in r. In a finite number of periods such a policy would cause the interest payments on the debt to exceed potential tax revenue.

11. In terms of Figures 12.1 and 12.2, we determine how changes in β and G shift the curve $F(r; \beta, G)$ and, hence, move the intersection of $E(r)$ and $F(r; \beta, G)$.

12. If the world has many similar countries, so that each is a small part of the world economy, then taking other countries' monetary policies as given is approximately the same as taking the world interest rate r as given, as unaffected by the choice of β^k.

13. In particular, we assume that the upper contour sets of u^k are strictly convex.

14. We do not prove existence of a symmetric Nash equilibrium. It is easy to make assumptions about V which guarantee such existence—namely, that for each possible common

value for monetary policy chosen by other countries, country k has a unique best policy which is neither indefinitely easy (in the direction of -1) nor indefinitely tight (in the direction of ∞) and which depends in a continuous way on the policy chosen by other countries. However, it is hard to make appealing assumptions about the structure and the social welfare function u^k that imply these conditions.

15. The assumption of identical countries in our model does have one special consequence. It implies that a symmetric cooperative optimum is achieved if each country both imposes capital controls which rule out any international borrowing and lending and chooses its monetary policy, its β, to maximize its social welfare function.

16. Note that this particular u^k is actually a weighted sum of indirect utilities, since (aside from additive constants) the indirect utility function of the initial old person who holds the initial nominal debt of country k is $\ln(p_1^k)$, that of the country k saver in each generation is $\ln(r^k)$, and that of any borrower is $\ln(1/r)$.

17. For the above form of $D^k(r)$, equation (20) is quadratic in r at a common value of β. This permits us to find an explicit form for the function V and for its partial derivative with respect to its first argument. For each example, the symmetric Nash equilibrium was found by numerically solving for the common value of the β^k for which that partial derivative is zero.

18. The asymmetry and, we strongly suspect, the desirability of cooperation would not be present if all the initial old and all the savers held all the different currencies in the same proportion. The kind of asymmetry we find is implied as long as the currency of country k is held predominantly by its residents.

13

A Case for Fixing Exchange Rates

Arthur J. Rolnick and Warren E. Weber

Economic historians will look back on the 1980s as the decade in which the experiment with floating currencies failed.

—*The Economist*, January 6, 1990

Ever since Adam Smith first explained how the free market, like an invisible hand, guides self-interested individuals to produce what is efficient and best for society, most economists have supported a laissez-faire approach to most economic problems. The information and technical requirements needed to allocate scarce economic resources efficiently and desirably are considerable. As a result, economic planners are unlikely to do a better job than individuals responding to market-determined prices. Indeed, experience suggests that economic planners almost always do much worse. And even when the market fails to allocate resources efficiently, finding a better, nonmarket solution is often difficult.

When it comes to exchange rates, though, the laissez-faire approach has not lived up to its billings. The free market system of floating exchange rates established in the early 1970s was supposed to provide a mechanism for correcting trade imbalances and stabilizing economic activity. It was also supposed to allow exchange rates to better reflect underlying economic fundamentals—such as incomes, money supplies, and interest rates. Ultimately, the link between rates and fundamentals was to lead to more predictable exchange rates than under the fixed rate system of Bretton Woods (1944–1970). Contrary to these expectations, the post–Bretton Woods era has witnessed trade imbalances generally larger and more persistent, economic fluctuations generally as wide and as frequent, and exchange rates much more volatile and unpredictable.

Reprinted from the *Federal Reserve Bank of Minneapolis 1989 Annual Report*.

Are fixed exchange rates a viable alternative? Many say no. They argue that fixed rates are economically and politically infeasible and that trying to impose them will only create instability, not avoid it. As evidence, the proponents of floating rates cite the collapse of Bretton Woods. Nevertheless, we maintain there is a convincing case that a fixed exchange rate system is feasible and should be established. Theory shows it feasible, and overlooked empirical evidence shows it possible. Such a system requires international monetary policy coordination, which entails more than just agreeing on the world's money growth. But this coordination is a small price to pay for the benefits of eliminating the costly uncertainty of floating exchange rates.

What's Wrong with Floating Exchange Rates?

By 1974, the major industrialized countries had ended the fixed exchange rate system agreed on thirty years earlier at Bretton Woods, New Hampshire. Many economists hailed the end of the Bretton Woods system as a triumph for free markets: No longer would exchange rates be set by governments and subject to the vagaries of political developments. No longer could speculators get rich by anticipating and, at times, even precipitating exchange rate adjustments. And no longer could fiscally irresponsible economies export their inflationary policies to the rest of the world.

Expectations for the post–Bretton Woods era were high: Market-driven exchange rates would more efficiently correct trade imbalances and help stabilize aggregate demand across countries. Floating rates would also leave countries completely free to pursue independent monetary policies. And exchange rates would be determined by underlying economic fundamentals, just like the prices of other goods and services. So, even though rates might fluctuate more than under Bretton Woods, these fluctuations would become fairly predictable.

Sixteen years have passed, but most of these benefits are yet to be realized or, if realized, the gains from them appear to be small.

Initially Appealing . . .

Advocates of floating exchange rates base their case on the proposition that free markets tend to allocate resources efficiently. More specifically, they claim that a floating rate system has two main benefits: economic stability and policy independence.

The first benefit—economic stability—would be achieved because a floating system helps make prices for internationally traded goods and services more flexible. As a result, floating rates would help balance international trade and stabilize aggregate demand across countries.

Floating exchange rates would help balance trade in the following way. When a country runs a trade *deficit* (imports more goods and services than it exports), some other country (or countries) runs a trade *surplus* (exports more goods and services than it imports). To bring trade into balance, the prices of goods and services produced in the deficit country must fall and those in the surplus country must rise. If the prices of goods and services are slow to adjust (as is often argued, at least for downward price adjustments), then the trade imbalance will persist. With floating exchange rates, the trade imbalance causes the value of a deficit country's currency to fall relative to the surplus country's currency because relatively fewer goods and services are being purchased from the deficit country. The decline in the exchange rate implies that the *terms of trade* (the price of the goods and services of the deficit country in terms of the goods and services of the surplus country) will decline, even if price levels do not change. Therefore, the demand for goods and services of the deficit country increases while the demand for those of the surplus country falls.

By making the prices of internationally traded goods and services more flexible, floating exchange rates would also supposedly help stabilize aggregate demand and employment across countries—adjustments that proponents say would be much slower and more economically painful if exchange rates were fixed. Consider, for example, a country in an economic downturn. Its domestic investment and production decline, unemployment rises, and income and consumption falter. The weak economy drives the price of the country's currency down. This decline, in turn, lowers the price of its exports, stimulating foreign demand and helping offset the decline in domestic demand. In this way, floating rates tend to act automatically as economic stabilizers.

The second benefit of a floating exchange rate system, backers claim, is that it would give each country autonomy over its monetary policy. Under a floating rate system, monetary policies in each country can freely respond to domestic economic problems while international currency markets determine the appropriate level of exchange rates. Policy independence would also let each country choose the average rate of money supply growth to help meet its government's need for revenue.

Although proponents of floating exchange rates recognize that the benefits of stability and policy independence are not costless, they nevertheless argue that the costs are relatively small and manageable. An obvious cost is that currency prices can vary. People who buy and sell goods and services internationally must face the risk that the currency they accept in trade may change in value. The greater the volatility of exchange rates, the greater the potential risk. Even so, proponents of floating rates argue that this risk is unlikely to be so large. Since they believe that exchange rates are tied to economic fundamentals and since these fundamentals tend to change slowly, they expect exchange rate fluctuations to be modest—or at least fairly predictable. Moreover, they argue that financial markets will quickly provide ways to hedge unpredictable movements in rates.

... Eventually Disappointing

Sixteen years under a floating exchange rate system have not yielded the expected benefits, nor have the system's costs been as small as anticipated. Judged against its proponents' initial expectations, the floating rate system has proved disappointing.

One expected benefit of floating exchange rates was that they would contribute to economic stability by helping correct trade imbalances. But since 1974, trade imbalances generally have been larger and more persistent. We can see this by looking at net exports (a common measure of trade imbalances) for four major industrialized countries: West Germany, Great Britain, the United States, and Japan. (See Figures 13.1–13.4.) Germany's trade balance fluctuated between deficit and surplus from 1961 until 1981; since then, it has been running a persistent trade surplus. In Great Britain and the United States, the absolute levels of trade imbalances have been larger and more persistent after Bretton Woods. Japan is an exception; its persistent trade deficit during Bretton Woods has been corrected since rates began to float.

Floating exchange rates seem to have performed somewhat better as automatic economic stabilizers, but the effect has not been general. A comparison of the same four countries' cyclical fluctuations in real output during and after Bretton Woods shows that only in Japan were fluctuations smaller in the floating rate period. In Germany, fluctuations were about the same during and after Bretton Woods. In Great Britain and the United States, fluctuations in real output have been larger after Bretton Woods.

The second benefit of floating exchange rates, allowing countries to pursue their own independent monetary policies, has been realized; but the advantages from this autonomy seem small. With an independent monetary policy, a country can use such policy to influence the course of its economy. Though academics continue to debate how effectively monetary policy can influence economic activity, among policymakers there is a growing consensus that stable and predictable policy rules coordinated across countries are best. For example, the Group of Seven (G-7) nations (the United States, West Germany, Japan, Great Britain, France, Canada, and Italy) have met several times in the last five years to develop a framework for discussing economic issues. This effort has gradually led to a greater degree of policy coordination and to joint attempts to reduce exchange rate volatility. And the European Community, which has agreed to eliminate most trade barriers among members by 1992, is seriously considering a European Monetary Union with coordinated monetary policies, fixed exchange rates, and ultimately a single currency.

Another advantage of an independent monetary policy is the control it gives a country over *seigniorage*, the revenue obtained from money creation. But for most countries, seigniorage is a relatively minor share of total revenues. In the United States, for example, seigniorage accounts for less than 2 percent of federal revenues. Further, relinquishing control of money growth by coordinating monetary policies with other countries does not mean a country loses seigniorage; it only means losing control of the amount received.

Meanwhile, the costs of floating exchange rates have been far greater than many expected. Exchange rate volatility has been large, and much of it seems largely unpredictable. Unpredictable fluctuations are a risk (or cost) borne by people who buy and sell goods and services internationally. Although the market has provided means of hedging this risk, the cost of unpredictable exchange rate fluctuations still has not been eliminated.

The greater volatility of exchange rates in the post–Bretton Woods period is clearly seen in Figure 13.5. But exchange rate volatility is risky only if it is unpredictable. The advocates of floating rates contend that economic fundamentals are a driving force behind exchange rate fluctuations. So even though rates could be volatile, exchange rate fluctuations would be largely predictable, based on knowledge of current and past fundamentals. As a result, they argue, exchange rate risk would be small.

Recent economic research, however, shows that for the most part, exchange rate fluctuations under floating rates have not been predictable.[1] The research tried to gauge how helpful economic fundamentals are in predicting exchange rate fluctuations. This was done by evaluating the forecasting accuracy of two competing types of models for predicting exchange rates. The first type, *structural* models, relies on the relative differences in past and current economic fundamentals to forecast exchange

Billions of 1982 Marks

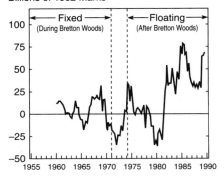

Figure 13.1 West Germany

Billions of 1982 Pounds

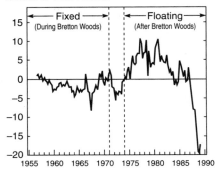

Figure 13.2 Great Britain

rates. The second type, a *naive* model, simply says that the best forecast of future exchange rates is the current rate. Because changes in fundamentals have no predictive power in the naive model, it implies that fluctuations in exchange rates are unpredictable. Comparisons of the models' forecasting accuracy revealed that, in most cases, the naive model outperformed the structural models. Even when it did not, exchange rate fluctuations were still difficult to predict. These results support the view that exchange rate volatility has been largely unpredictable under floating rates.

In what sense is exchange rate uncertainty a cost? Consider a German company buying electronic equipment from a U.S. manufacturer. On delivery of the goods, say in six months, the German company is willing to pay for them in dollars at the agreed price. To the extent that the exchange rate

Billions of 1982 Dollars

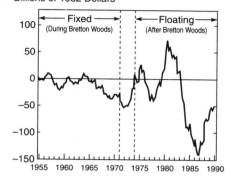

Figure 13.3 United States

Trillions of 1982 Yen

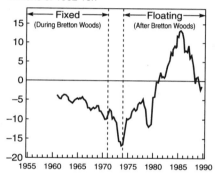

Figure 13.4 Japan

Figures 13.1–13.4
The Trade Imbalances of Four Nations under Fixed and Floating Exchange Rates. Quarterly Net Exports for Selected Years (Seasonally Adjusted Annual Rates). Source: Board of Governors of the Federal Reserve System.

Index, 1982 = 100

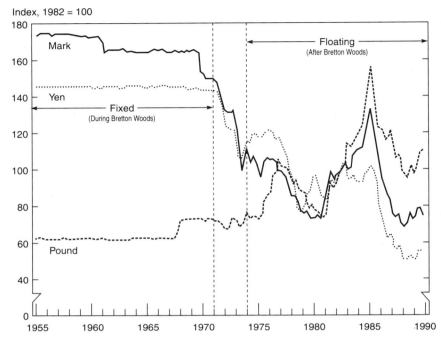

Figure 13.5
Exchange Rate Volatility under Fixed and Floating Rates: Price of the U.S. Dollar in Terms of West German, British, and Japanese Currencies. Source: Board of Governors of the Federal Reserve System.

in six months cannot be predicted, the buyer is exposed to exchange rate risk. The risk doesn't vanish if the U.S. manufacturer agrees to accept German marks on delivery; in that case, it just falls on the seller. Generally, we expect to find some form of risk sharing between buyer and seller. In practice, a hedge is usually purchased. Estimates of the cost of such hedges range from 0.5 to 3 percent of total foreign sales. In the United States, for example, total trade in goods and services was $1.3 trillion in 1989, so the estimated cost of hedging ranges from $6.5 billion to $39 billion. That cost puts a heavy burden on the United States and its trading partners.

These estimates, however, may understate the cost of exchange rate risk. Many businesses, finding the price of an exchange rate hedge too high, may choose not to trade internationally. In other words, the cost of exchange rate risk applies to potential as well as actual international transactions.

Are Fixed Exchange Rates Better?

That the floating exchange rate system adopted in the early 1970s has not worked as anticipated does not necessarily imply that a better system is available to replace it. The conventional argument rules out fixed rates as an option by claiming that such systems are unsustainable. Some evidence—notably the Bretton Woods collapse—seems to bear this out.

We maintain, however, that the conventional argument is flawed: It does not take seriously a distinctive trait of today's currencies. When that trait is seriously considered, theory suggests there is a demonstrably better system. If countries are willing to coordinate their monetary policies, they can fix exchange rates and eliminate the burden of exchange rate risk on international trade.

In Theory Yes ...

Those who argue that fixed exchange rates cannot work assume, at least implicitly, that currency is essentially no different from other goods. Since exchange rates are the relative prices of currencies and since standard price theory demonstrates that it is impossible to fix the relative prices of goods in the long run, skeptics argue that a fixed exchange rate system is not feasible.

The conventional argument against the feasibility of fixing prices goes like this: The relative price of two goods can be fixed only if buffer stocks of the goods exist to absorb excess demand. Eventually, however, the demand for a good relative to its supply must become so large that it depletes any buffer stocks held. Once these stocks are depleted, price fixing is impossible.

But the conventional argument does not apply to exchange rates because today's currencies are *fiat*: they are intrinsically worthless pieces of paper that are virtually costless to produce. This means that a government can always avoid depleting the buffer stock of its currency simply by printing more. Therefore, fixing exchange rates is feasible, and any rate will work.[2]

That fixed exchange rates are theoretically feasible, however, does not mean they are politically acceptable. Under fixed rates, the country with the fastest growing money supply gets the most seigniorage (revenue) from money creation. More important, some of this seigniorage is collected from residents of other countries because, with fixed exchange rates, the inflation caused by one country's money growth is experienced by residents of all countries. This outcome is bound to be politically unacceptable to other countries. A country can prevent another from exporting inflation by letting its own exchange rate appreciate. As a result, countries will not adhere to fixed rates unless they are willing to coordinate their monetary policies.

The policy coordination necessary for fixed exchange rates, however, is not that all countries agree to have their money supplies grow at roughly the same rate. Even if these money growth rates were the same and other economic fundamentals unchanged, recent research shows that exchange rates can fluctuate simply because people think they will.[3] (This result may explain why exchange rates have continued to be volatile even though the G-7 countries have been moving to coordinate long-term monetary policies over the past decade.)

The policy coordination required to fix exchange rates has two components:

• Each country must agree to swap its currency for another's at the fixed rate in any amount and at any time.

• Countries must agree on the total growth of money and how the resulting seigniorage will be distributed among them.

Central banks would have no problem meeting the first component. If a central bank temporarily ran out of a foreign currency, it could always swap its own currency for the other with the appropriate foreign central bank. This arrangement prevents exchange rates from fluctuating because of speculation, since it guarantees that any amount of a currency demanded will always be supplied at the fixed price. And if countries meet the second component, they will have no incentive to overissue their monies.[4]

... And Yes in Practice

Our case for fixing exchange rates is based on more than just theoretical speculation. Despite the collapse of Bretton Woods, there is a well-functioning yet often-overlooked system of fixed exchange rates in place today. Its existence demonstrates the feasibility and advantages of a fixed rate system.

The Bretton Woods system is usually cited as evidence of the fragility of fixed exchange rate systems. If the fixed rates do not reflect underlying economic fundamentals, so the argument goes, the rates are not sustainable. Even if rates are initially set correctly, fundamentals can quickly change and cause currencies to become under- or overvalued.

But Bretton Woods is not really a test of whether a fixed exchange rate system will work. A fixed rate system requires that policy coordination include an agreement among countries about the amount of seigniorage and its distribution. This component of policy coordination was missing from the Bretton Woods system, which attempted to fix exchange rates while still allowing each country some control over its own seigniorage.

A proper test of whether fixed exchange rates are feasible needs evidence from a system with the two required components of policy coordination in place. There is such a system, and it is running smoothly—the monetary system of the United States today.

To many, the notion that the United States has a fixed exchange rate system may come as a surprise. The notes issued by the Federal Reserve System look like and are used as a single currency. Each note is printed in black and green ink, each has "The United States of America" inscribed on front and back, and each says it is a "Federal Reserve Note" and "legal tender for all debts, public and private." Furthermore, the notes exchange at par: a twenty-dollar bill swaps one-for-one with any other twenty-dollar bill, one-for-two with any ten-dollar bills, and so forth.

In what sense, then, does the United States have something other than a single currency? A closer look reveals that, in fact, each of the twelve district banks in the Federal Reserve System issues its own notes. (See Figure 13.6.) Each note is identified by its Federal Reserve district bank in four ways: First, on the front left is a circle with the district bank's name written around the inside. Second, in the middle of that circle is a bold, black letter representing the Federal Reserve district of origin—**A** for the first district, **B** for the second, and so forth. Third, the letter symbol is the first character of the serial number, which is printed twice on the front of each bill. Fourth, the district's number is printed on the front four times.

Granted, these differences among Federal Reserve notes are much less distinct than those between, say, U.S. and Italian currencies. Nevertheless, in a physical sense, U.S. currency is not strictly uniform. The importance of these physical differences is that they represent the possibility that the United States could choose to have a floating exchange rate system among the currencies of the twelve Federal Reserve districts. Instead, the United States has chosen a system of fixed exchange rates.

That the United States has had no trouble maintaining its fixed exchange rate system demonstrates that such a system is feasible. Despite changes in economic fundamentals among Federal Reserve districts, the United States has not been forced to adjust the exchange rates between district curren-

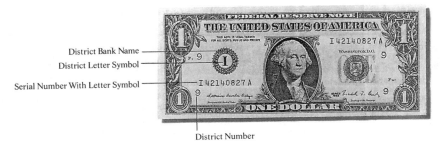

District Bank Name

District Letter Symbol

Serial Number With Letter Symbol

District Number

Figure 13.6
A Close Look at a Federal Reserve Note

cies. This is not what the skeptics of fixed rates claim would happen. What if the Ninth District economy were declining while the other district economies were expanding? Or what if the Ninth District were running a trade deficit with the rest of the country? Then, skeptics claim, there should be some downward pressure on Ninth District currency. This, of course, has never happened, nor is it likely.

The reason the U.S. system of fixed exchange rates works is that it has the two required components of monetary policy coordination: First, the district Federal Reserve banks have an agreement to swap their currencies for any other district's at the fixed rate in any amount and at any time. Because of this agreement, we doubt that many people have ever lost sleep over the exchange value of their district's notes relative to another's. (Have you ever checked to see which district Fed issued the notes you were being handed?)

Second, district Fed banks also have an agreement on how to set the rate of money growth and how to distribute the resulting seigniorage. Each district bank participates in the policy process (at Federal Open Market Committee meetings), and a unified policy action is carried out for all twelve districts. No individual district bank can pursue its own monetary policy.[5] Furthermore, all seigniorage is pooled and disbursed by the U.S. Treasury. That is, by design, no district bank can gain by issuing more of its notes than another. Even if all notes were issued by, say, the Ninth District, the revenue would still be pooled and disbursed by the centralized authority (the Treasury).

This example of the U.S. monetary system shows that when the two required components of policy coordination are met, a fixed exchange rate system is feasible.

What Should Be Done?

Policymakers have been led to believe that a floating exchange rate system is best. They were told that allowing rates to float would help balance international trade, reduce economic instability across countries, and allow governments to pursue independent monetary policies. They were also told that the cost of exchange rate risk would be small.

They were misled. Floating rates have brought neither balance to trade accounts nor stability to economic activity. Instead, they have added a significant cost to international trade in the form of greater uncertainty about exchange rates than most expected.

Policymakers were also led to believe that in the long run, floating exchange rates are the only feasible system. They were told that fixed exchange rates are not feasible and that exchange rates must ultimately reflect changing economic conditions.

Again, they were misled. Exchange rates can be fixed by governments if monetary policies are coordinated. Coordination requires that countries agree to swap currencies at the fixed rates and agree on a monetary policy and how to distribute the resulting seigniorage.

The question, then, is not whether countries can fix exchange rates but whether they should. Should they coordinate their monetary policies and eliminate unpredictable changes in exchange rates? Or should they opt for policy independence and accept the cost of exchange rate risk?

We think there is a convincing case for fixing exchange rates. Experience suggests that the costs of coordinating monetary policies are small compared with the benefits from eliminating unnecessary exchange rate uncertainty.

Notes

We owe a deep intellectual debt to Neil Wallace, professor of economics at the University of Minnesota and adviser to the Federal Reserve Bank of Minneapolis. His work on the theory of money and exchange rates has motivated the ideas presented here. Several of his important writings are listed in the suggested readings at the end of this essay.

1. For details of this research, see the articles by Meese and Rogoff (1983), Schinasi and Swamy (1989), and Meese (1990).

2. The choice of a particular exchange rate will, of course, affect the distribution of wealth. For example, in the proposed monetary reunification of Germany, the issue in choosing the exchange rate between East and West German marks is not one of feasibility but one of wealth redistribution.

3. This point, made by King, Wallace, and Weber (1992), is supported by the evidence that exchange rate fluctuations are unpredictable.

4. A gold standard is another way to achieve fixed exchange rates. Under a gold standard, not only does each country give up control of its monetary policy but monetary policy also becomes *exogenous*. That is, for countries on a gold standard, the rate of increase of their money supply is determined not by policy coordination on their part but by the rate of gold production—a factor outside their control. This loss of control may be an unacceptable cost.

5. While Federal Reserve districts must coordinate monetary policies, they do not have to coordinate fiscal policies. Each district (more correctly, each state within a district) can freely pursue its own fiscal policy, but none can finance its budget shortfalls by printing money. Similarly, countries that agree to fix exchange rates would still maintain autonomy over their fiscal policies.

Suggested Readings

Committee for the Study of Economic and Monetary Union. 1989. Report on Economic and Monetary Union in the European Community. April 12.

The Economist. 1990. A Brief History of Funny Money. January 6, pp. 21–24.

The Economist. 1990. Time to Tether Currencies. January 6, pp. 15–16.

Friedman, Milton. 1953. The Case for Flexible Exchange Rates. In *Essays in Positive Economics*, pp. 157–203. Chicago: University of Chicago Press.

Hakkio, Craig S. 1989. Exchange Rates in the 1980s. Research Division Working Paper 89-04. Federal Reserve Bank of Kansas City.

Johnson, Harry G. 1969. The Case for Flexible Exchange Rates, 1969. *Review* 51 (June): 12–24. Federal Reserve Bank of St. Louis.

Kareken, John, and Wallace, Neil. 1981. On the Indeterminacy of Equilibrium Exchange Rates. *Quarterly Journal of Economics* 96 (May): 207–22.

King, Robert G.; Wallace, Neil; and Weber, Warren E. 1992. Nonfundamental Uncertainty and Exchange Rates. *Journal of International Economics* 32 (February): 83–108.

McKinnon, Ronald I. 1988. Monetary and Exchange Rate Policies for International Financial Stability: A Proposal. *Journal of Economic Perspectives* 2 (Winter): 83–103.

Meese, Richard. 1990. Currency Fluctuations in the Post–Bretton Woods Era. *Journal of Economic Perspectives* 4 (Winter): 117–34.

Meese, Richard A., and Rogoff, Kenneth. 1983. Empirical Exchange Rate Models of the Seventies: Do They Fit Out of Sample? *Journal of International Economics* 14 (February): 3–24.

Melamed, Leo, ed. 1988. Foreword to *The Merits of Flexible Exchange Rates*, pp. ix–xvii. Fairfax, Va.: George Mason University Press.

Schinasi, Garry J., and Swamy, P. A. V. B. 1989. The Out-of-Sample Forecasting Performance of Exchange Rate Models When Coefficients Are Allowed to Change. *Journal of International Money and Finance* 8 (September): 375–90.

Solomon, Robert. 1977. *The International Monetary System, 1945–1976: An Insider's View*. New York: Harper & Row.

Townsend, Robert M. 1977. The Eventual Failure of Price Fixing Schemes. *Journal of Economic Theory* 14 (February): 190–99.

Wallace, Neil. 1979. Why Markets in Foreign Exchange Are Different From Other Markets. *Federal Reserve Bank of Minneapolis Quarterly Review* 3 (Fall): 1–7. Reprinted in *Federal Reserve Bank of Minneapolis Quarterly Review* 14 (Winter 1990): 12–18 [and as Chapter 11 in this volume].

Wallace, Neil. 1988. A Suggestion for Oversimplifying the Theory of Money. *Economic Journal* 98 (No. 390): 25–36. Reprinted in *Federal Reserve Bank of Minneapolis Quarterly Review* 14 (Winter 1990): 19–26.

IV   Business Cycle Analysis

What began as a modest exercise became a major area of research in empirical macroeconomics. The exercise, initially conducted by Kydland and Prescott, was to determine how much of business cycle fluctuations could be attributed to real factors, in particular, shocks to technology. Their surprising finding that so much could be attributed to technology shocks led these researchers and others to extend and refine their model and methods in order to sharpen and broaden their results—a process that continues today.

Kydland and Prescott's method was to compare the observed variation and comovements of variables, such as output, employment, consumption, and investment, with those generated by a neoclassical growth model. The model initially used contains only real variables; that is, it has no money or other financial assets, and thus it has relative prices but no price levels. It also assumes competitive market-clearing in which the aggregate demand and supply functions are explicitly derived from the optimal decision rules of price-taking economic agents. The fluctuations in the model are generated by subjecting the model to *technology shocks*, defined as the differences between actual output in a period and that predicted by a Cobb-Douglas production function conditional on actual capital and labor inputs. Parameter values are either chosen based on independent microeconomic studies or chosen to generate observed long-term averages. For instance, parameters of utility functions are chosen based on findings of a number of studies of individual behavior, and the coefficients of the production function are chosen to generate the observed average shares of capital and labor income. This method of quantifying parameters is called *calibration*.

Based on their calibrated model, Kydland and Prescott found that a surprisingly large portion of business cycle fluctuations—on the order of 70 percent—could be attributed to technology shocks. This finding and the methodology used to produce it had several important implications:

• Business cycles occur as natural outcomes in general equilibrium models. They occur although individuals are assumed to act rationally and markets are assumed to clear. Thus, the occurrence of recessions is not by itself grounds for the kinds of government policy intervention that traditional Keynesian economists advocated.

• In the postwar period, technology shocks have been more important than monetary and budget policy changes in driving the business cycle. In contrast, traditional Keynesian analysis ignored technology shocks as causes of business cycles.

• Plausible quantitative models can be built for policy analysis that are not subject to the Lucas critique. Although government spending and tax policies were not explicitly included in the Kydland-Prescott model, they clearly could be. And since the decision-making problems of individual agents were explicitly considered, it also is clear that when policies change, new decision rules can be derived and a solution to the model can be found that is consistent with the new policies.

• A useful way of characterizing business cycle data is in terms of deviation from a time-varying trend. Kydland and Prescott characterized the data that way partly because that is what their theory suggests. In their model it is roughly true that the deterministic elements generate steady-state growth paths that correspond to the trends, while the shocks to the model generate the deviations about the steady states. Thus, it is natural to equate business cycle fluctuations with movements about a trend. They also characterized data this way because doing so yields a consistent way to relate movements in different data series.

• Calibration can be a useful alternative to formal systemwide estimation as an approach to empirically quantifying general equilibrium models. Two advantages of calibration are that it is relatively easy to implement, and, by drawing on micro studies and long-term observations, it makes the values of parameters consistent with broad findings in the literature. However, its main advantage, Kydland and Prescott claim, is that it does not cause parameters to take on crazy values when the model is known to be based on false assumptions. For instance, Kydland and Prescott assume in their model that technology shocks are the sole source of business cycle fluctuations when their analysis suggests it can explain only 70 percent. If they were to use systemwide estimation, estimates of coefficients would be thrown off, because the estimates would be attempting to correct for the 30 percent source of fluctuations which was deliberately excluded from the model.[1]

This discussion might give readers the impression that real business cycle models are the unchallenged front-runner in the field of empirical macroeconometrics. That would be a false impression: they are being challenged and criticized by economists on both sides of the revolution. The chapters in this section discuss and illustrate some of the pros and cons of real business cycle models, some of the challenges to Kydland and Prescott's early work, and some of the responses real business cycle researchers have made to those challenges.

The first three chapters in this section frame a debate between Prescott and Summers. Chapter 14, "Theory Ahead of Business Cycle Measurement" by Prescott, serves several functions: It illustrates how real business cycle models are constructed and calibrated, it describes the then-current (in 1986) state of knowledge in real business cycle research, and it is the focus of the next two chapters. The Prescott paper was originally presented at a Carnegie-Rochester Conference on Public Policy and was published in a volume of the conference proceedings.

In the second chapter of the debate (Chapter 15), Summers argues that Prescott's real business cycle model is not relevant to the business cycles actually observed. He has four main criticisms of the model:

• Parameter values are not tightly tied down by growth and micro observations, as Prescott contends.

• Prescott's technology shocks really are an amalgam of many forces, including labor hoarding.

• Money and other financial assets, which are excluded from Prescott's model, are important in explaining business cycles.

• Market failure, which plays no part in Prescott's model, plays a central role in business fluctuations.

Summers's criticisms are addressed in the final chapter of the debate (Chapter 16). Prescott defends the modeling methodology of real business cycle researchers and their estimates of some key parameters. He argues that real business cycle models are consistent with the data.

While defenders of real business cycle models did not necessarily agree with Summers's indictments of that approach, they nevertheless took his criticisms seriously. The remaining chapters in this section address some of Summers's concerns.

In Chapter 17, Kydland and Prescott defend their basic methodology. They argue that the proper approach is to report key business cycle facts first and then develop general equilibrium theories to explain them. They define such facts as deviations from trend and then describe some of the key observations about these facts.

One of these observations can be viewed as a response to Summers's comments that their initial model excluded money and, hence, had no price level. Summers argues that analysis of comovements of output and the price level would help determine the importance of alternative sources of economic disturbances. Monetary and budget policy shocks generally would be expected to shift demand more than supply, so that output and the price level would tend to move together. Technology shocks, in contrast, would be expected to shift supply more than demand, so that output and the price level would tend to move in opposite directions. Kydland and Prescott observe that since the early 1950s, U.S. output and the price level have tended to move in opposite directions, which is consistent with their analysis stressing the importance of technology shocks in driving postwar business cycles.

In Chapter 18, Hansen and Wright consider ways to patch up the standard real business cycle model to bring its predictions more in accord with labor market observations, such as those pointed out by Summers. In particular, the standard model does not match two labor market facts: that the number of hours worked varies much more than productivity (real wages) and that the correlation between these two time series is close to zero.

Hansen and Wright examine, within a unified setting, four adjustments to the standard real business cycle model that have been proposed to improve the model's labor market predictions. None of the adjustments involves changing the assumptions that agents optimize and markets clear. The authors conclude that each of the adjustments can improve the model's labor market predictions somewhat without upsetting its predictions for the rest of the economy.

Chapter 19, by Aiyagari, can be viewed as an attempt to formalize in the context of general equilibrium models some of Summers's major concerns. Those concerns in a general way were that real business cycle models do not capture or explain many of the phenomena associated with business cycles such as swings in optimism and pessimism of the public, markets that are powerless to pull the economy out of a low output-low employment state, and the volatility of financial markets beyond what can be explained by shocks to economic fundamentals.

Aiyagari concludes that these phenomena can indeed be formalized in general equilibrium models—although in ones quite different from those considered by Prescott. Important in Aiyagari's models is that agents face an uncertain future and have to form expectations. The equilibrium outcomes that obtain depend on agents' expectations: When agents are optimistic, an equilibrium consistent with those expectations exists; when they are pessimistic, a different equilibrium, consistent with those expectations, exists.

The chapters by Hansen and Wright and Aiyagari contain a similar message: the initial real business cycle models do not have all the answers. If those models are construed as attempts to construct general equilibrium models of the business cycle, however, then it does seem possible to answer criticisms, such as those of Summers, without abandoning the general equilibrium approach.

Real business cycle modeling is still an ongoing research effort. Despite the criticisms which have been raised, the major implications of the effort, which were listed earlier, still seem valid.

Note

1. Despite these advantages, calibration, as practiced by Kydland and Prescott, has some disadvantages. One is that it gives no indication of the uncertainty about the coefficient values. Thus, there is no way to judge whether some key implications of a calibrated model are significant. A second disadvantage is that no loss function is specified, so that different calibrations cannot be ranked in terms of goodness of fit.

14

Theory Ahead
of Business
Cycle Measurement

Edward C. Prescott

Economists have long been puzzled by the observations that during peace-time industrial market economies display recurrent, large fluctuations in output and employment over relatively short time periods. Not uncommon are changes as large as 10 percent within only a couple of years. These observations are considered puzzling because the associated movements in labor's marginal product are small.

These observations should not be puzzling, for they are what standard economic theory predicts. For the United States, in fact, given people's ability and willingness to intertemporally and intratemporally substitute consumption and leisure and given the nature of the changing production possibility set, it would be puzzling if the economy did not display these large fluctuations in output and employment with little associated fluctuations in the marginal product of labor. Moreover, standard theory also correctly predicts the amplitude of these fluctuations, their serial correlation properties, and the fact that the investment component of output is about six times as volatile as the consumption component.

This perhaps surprising conclusion is the principal finding of a research program initiated by Kydland and me (1982) and extended by Kydland and me (1984), Hansen (1985a), and Bain (1985). We have computed the competitive equilibrium stochastic process for variants of the constant elasticity, stochastic growth model. The elasticities of substitution and the share parameters of the production and utility functions are restricted to those

Reprinted from the *Federal Reserve Bank of Minneapolis Quarterly Review*, Fall 1986. This is an edited version of a paper that was presented at a Carnegie-Rochester Conference on Public Policy and appeared in a volume of the conference proceedings: *Real Business Cycles, Real Exchange Rates and Actual Policies*, ed. Karl Brunner and Allan H. Meltzer, Carnegie-Rochester Conference Series on Public Policy, vol. 25, Autumn 1986, pp. 11–24. The paper appears here with the permission of Elsevier Science Publishers, B.V. (North-Holland). ©

that generate the growth observations. The process governing the technology parameter is selected to be consistent with the measured technology changes for the American economy since the Korean War. We ask whether these artificial economies display fluctuations with statistical properties similar to those which the American economy has displayed in that period. They do.[1]

I view the growth model as a paradigm for macro analysis—analogous to the supply and demand construct of price theory. The elasticities of substitution and the share parameters of the growth model are analogous to the price and income elasticities of price theory. Whether or not this paradigm dominates, as I expect it will, is still an open question. But the early results indicate its power to organize our knowledge. The finding that when uncertainty in the rate of technological change is incorporated into the growth model it displays the business cycle phenomena was both dramatic and unanticipated. I was sure that the model could not do this without some features of the payment and credit technologies.

The models constructed within this theoretical framework are necessarily highly abstract. Consequently, they are necessarily false, and statistical hypothesis testing will reject them. This does not imply, however, that nothing can be learned from such quantitative theoretical exercises. I think much has already been learned and confidently predict that much more will be learned as other features of the environment are introduced. Prime candidates for study are the effects of public finance elements, a foreign sector, and, of course, monetary factors. The research I review here is best viewed as a very promising beginning of a much larger research program.

The Business Cycle Phenomena

The use of the expression *business cycle* is unfortunate for two reasons. One is that it leads people to think in terms of a time series' business cycle component which is to be explained independently of a growth component; our research has, instead, one unifying theory of both of these. The other reason I do not like to use the expression is that it is not accurate; some systems of low-order linear stochastic difference equations with a nonoscillatory deterministic part, and therefore no cycle, display key business cycle features. (See Slutzky [1927] 1937). I thus do not refer to business cycles, but rather to business cycle *phenomena*, which are nothing more nor less than a certain set of statistical properties of a certain set of important aggregate time series. The question I and others have considered is, Do the stochastic difference equations that are the equilibrium laws of motion for the stochastic growth display the business cycle phenomena?

More specifically, we follow Lucas (1977, p. 9) in defining the business cycle phenomena as the recurrent fluctuations of output about trend and the comovements among other aggregate time series. Fluctuations are by definition deviations from some slowly varying path. Since this slowly varying path increases monotonically over time, we adopt the common practice of labeling it *trend*. This trend is neither a measure nor an estimate of the unconditional mean of some stochastic process. It is, rather, defined by the computational procedure used to fit the smooth curve through the data.

If the business cycle facts were sensitive to the detrending procedure employed, there would be a problem. But the key facts are not sensitive to the procedure if the trend curve is smooth. Our curve-fitting method is to take the logarithms of variables and then select the trend path $\{\tau_t\}$ which minimizes the sum of the squared deviations from a given series $\{Y_t\}$ subject to the constraint that the sum of the squared second differences not be too large. This is

$$\min_{\{\tau_t\}_{t=1}^T} \sum_{t=1}^T (Y_t - \tau_t)^2$$

subject to

$$\sum_{t=2}^{T-1} [(\tau_{t+1} - \tau_t) - (\tau_t - \tau_{t-1})]^2 \leqslant \mu.$$

The smaller is μ, the smoother is the trend path. If $\mu = 0$, the least squares linear time trend results. For all series, μ is picked so that the Lagrange multiplier of the constraint is 1600. This produces the right degree of smoothness in the fitted trend when the observation period is a quarter of a year. Thus, the sequence $\{\tau_t\}$ minimizes

$$\sum_{t=1}^T (Y_t - \tau_t)^2 + 1600 \sum_{t=2}^{T-1} [(\tau_{t+1} - \tau_t) - (\tau_t - \tau_{t-1})]^2.$$

The first-order conditions of this minimization problem are linear in Y_t and τ_t, so for every series, $\tau = AY$, where A is the same $T \times T$ matrix. The deviations from trend, also by definition, are

$$Y_t^d = Y_t - \tau_t \quad \text{for} \quad t = 1, \ldots, T.$$

Unless otherwise stated, these are the variables used in the computation of the statistics reported here for both the United States and the growth economies.

An alternative interpretation of the procedure is that it is a high pass linear filter. The facts reported here are essentially the same if, rather than

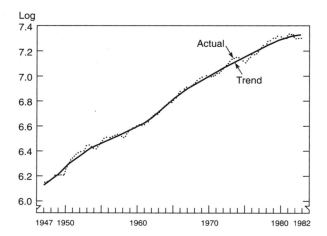

Figure 14.1
Actual and Trend Logs of U.S. Gross National Product: Quarterly, 1947−82. Source of basic data: Citicorp's Citibase data bank.

defining the deviations by $Y^d = (I - A)Y$, we filtered the Y using a high pass band filter, eliminating all frequencies of 32 quarters or greater. An advantage of our procedure is that it deals better with the ends of the sample problem and does not require a stationary time series.

To compare the behaviors of a stochastic growth economy and an actual economy, only identical statistics for the two economies are used. By definition, a *statistic* is a real valued function of the raw time series. Consequently, if a comparison is made, say, between the standard deviations of the deviations, the date t deviation for the growth economy must be the same function of the data generated by that model as the date t deviation for the American economy is of that economy's data. Our definitions of the deviations satisfy this criterion.

Figure 14.1 plots the logs of actual and trend output for the U.S. economy during 1947−82, and Figure 14.2 the corresponding percentage deviations from trend of output and hours of market employment. Output and hours clearly move up and down together with nearly the same amplitudes.

Table 14.1 contains the standard deviations and cross serial correlations of output and other aggregate time series for the American economy during 1954−82. Consumption appears less variable and investment more variable than output. Further, the average product of labor is procyclical but does not vary as much as output or hours.

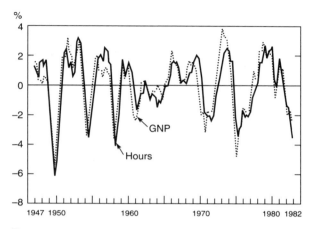

Figure 14.2
Deviations from Trend of Gross National Product and Nonfarm Employee Hours in the
United States: Quarterly, 1947–82. Source of basic data: Citicorp's Citibase data bank.

Table 14.1
Cyclical behavior of the U.S. economy (deviations from trend of key variables, 1954:1–
1982:4)

Variable x	Standard deviation	Cross correlation of GNP with		
		$x(t-1)$	$x(t)$	$x(t+1)$
Gross national product	1.8%	.82	1.00	.82
Personal consumption expenditures				
Services	.6	.66	.72	.61
Nondurable goods	1.2	.71	.76	.59
Fixed investment expenditures	5.3	.78	.89	.78
Nonresidential investment	5.2	.54	.79	.86
Structures	4.6	.42	.62	.70
Equipment	6.0	.56	.82	.87
Capital stocks				
Total nonfarm inventories	1.7	.15	.48	.68
Nonresidential structures	.4	−.20	−.03	.16
Nonresidential equipment	1.0	.03	.23	.41
Labor input				
Nonfarm hours	1.7	.57	.85	.89
Average weekly hours in mfg.	1.0	.76	.85	.61
Productivity (GNP/hours)	1.0	.51	.34	−.04

Source of basic data: Citicorp's Citibase data bank.

The Growth Model

This theory and its variants build on the neoclassical growth economy of Solow (1956) and Swan (1956). In the language of Lucas (1980a, p. 696), the model is a "fully articulated, artificial economic system" that can be used to generate economic time series of a set of important economic aggregates. The model assumes an aggregate production function with constant returns to scale, inputs labor n and capital k, and an output which can be allocated either to current consumption c or to investment x. If t denotes the date, $f: R^2 \to R$ the production function, and z_t a technology parameter, then the production constraint is

$$x_t + c_t \leqslant z_t f(k_t, n_t)$$

where $x_t, c_t, k_t, n_t \geqslant 0$. The model further assumes that the services provided by a unit of capital decrease geometrically at a rate $0 < \delta < 1$:

$$k_{t+1} = (1 - \delta)k_t + x_t.$$

Solow completes the specification of his economy by hypothesizing that some fraction $0 < \sigma < 1$ of output is invested and the remaining fraction $1 - \sigma$ consumed and that n_t is a constant—say, $\bar{n}$—for all t. For this economy, the law of motion of capital condition on z_t is

$$k_{t+1} = (1 - \delta)k_t + \sigma z_t f(k_t, \bar{n}).$$

Once the $\{z_t\}$ stochastic process is specified, the stochastic process governing capital and the other economic aggregates are determined and realizations of the stochastic process can be generated by a computer.

This structure is far from adequate for the study of the business cycle because in it neither employment nor the savings rate varies, when in fact they do. Being explicit about the economy, however, naturally leads to the question of what determines these variables, which are central to the cycle.

That leads to the introduction of a stand-in household with some explicit preferences. If we abstract from the labor supply decision and uncertainty (that is, $z_t = \bar{z}$ and $n_t = \bar{n}$), the standard form of the utility function is

$$\sum_{t=0}^{\infty} \beta^t u(c_t) \quad \text{for} \quad 0 < \beta < 1$$

where β is the subjective time discount factor. The function $u: R_+ \to R$ is twice differentiable and concave. The commodity space for the deterministic version of this model is l_∞, infinite sequences of uniformly bounded consumptions $\{c_t\}_{t=0}^{\infty}$.

The theorems of Bewley (1972) could be applied to establish existence of a competitive equilibrium for this l_∞ commodity-space economy. That existence argument, however, does not provide an algorithm for computing the equilibria. An alternative approach is to use the competitive welfare theorems of Debreu (1954). Given local nonsaturation and no externalities, competitive equilibria are Pareto optima and, with some additional conditions that are satisfied for this economy, any Pareto optimum can be supported as a competitive equilibrium. Given a single agent and the convexity, there is a unique optimum and that optimum is the unique competitive equilibrium allocation. The advantage of this approach is that algorithms for computing solutions to concave programming problems can be used to find the competitive equilibrium allocation for this economy.

Even with the savings decision endogenous, this economy has no fluctuations. As shown by Cass (1965) and Koopmans (1965), the competitive equilibrium path converges monotonically to a unique rest point or, if z_t is growing exponentially, to a balanced growth path. There are multisector variants of this model in which the equilibrium path oscillates. (See Benhabib and Nishimura 1985 and Marimon 1984.) But I know of no multisector model which has been restricted to match observed factor shares by sector, which has a value for β consistent with observed interest rates, and which displays oscillations.

When uncertainty is introduced, the household's objective is its expected discounted utility:

$$E\left\{\sum_{t=0}^{\infty} \beta^t u(c_t)\right\}.$$

The commodity vector is now indexed by the history of shocks; that is, $\{c_t(z_1, \ldots, z_t)\}_{t=0}^{\infty}$ is the commodity point. As Brock and Mirman (1972) show, if the $\{z_t\}$ are identically distributed random variables, an optimum to the social planner's problem exists and the optimum is a stationary stochastic process with $k_{t+1} = g(k_t, z_t)$ and $c_t = c(k_t, z_t)$. As Lucas and Prescott (1971) show, for a class of economies that include this one, the social optimum is the unique competitive equilibrium allocation. They also show that for these homogeneous agent economies, the social optimum is also the unique sequence-of-markets equilibrium allocation. Consequently, there are equilibrium time-invariant functions for the wage $w_t = w(k_t, z_t)$ and the rental price of capital $r_t = r(k_t, z_t)$, where these prices are relative to the date t consumption good. Given these prices, the firm's period t problem is

$$\max_{k_t, n_t \geqslant 0} \{y_t - r_t k_t - w_t n_t\}$$

subject to the output constraint

$$y_t \leqslant z_t f(k_t, n_t).$$

The household's problem is more complicated, for it must form expectations of future prices. If a_t is its capital stock, its problem is

$$\max E \sum_{t=0}^{\infty} \beta^t u(c_t)$$

subject to

$$c_t + x_t \leqslant w_t \bar{n} + r_t a_t$$

$$a_{t+1} \leqslant (1 - \delta)a_t + x_t$$

and given $a_0 - k_0$. In forming expectations, a household knows the relation between the economy's state (k_t, z_t) and prices, $w_t = w(k_t, z_t)$ and $r_t = r(k_t, z_t)$. Further, it knows the process governing the evolution of the per capita capital stock, a variable which, like prices, is taken as given.

The elements needed to define a *sequence-of-markets equilibrium* are the firm's policy functions $y(k_t, z_t)$, $n(k_t, z_t)$, and $k(k_t, z_t)$; the household's policy functions $x(a_t, k_t, z_t)$ and $c(a_t, k_t, z_t)$; a law of motion of per capita capital $k_{t+1} = g(k_t, z_t)$; and pricing functions $w(k_t, z_t)$ and $r(k_t, z_t)$. For equilibrium, then,

- The firm's policy functions must be optimal given the pricing functions.

- The household's policy functions must be optimal given the pricing functions and the law of motion of per capita capital.

- Spot markets clear; that is, for all k_t and z_t

$$\bar{n} = n(k_t, z_t)$$

$$k_t = k(k_t, z_t)$$

$$x(k_t, k_t, z_t) + c(k_t, k_t, z_t) = y(k_t, z_t).$$

(Note that the goods market must clear only when the representative household is truly representative, that is, when $a_t = k_t$.)

- Expectations are rational; that is,

$$g(k_t, z_t) = (1 - \delta)k_t + x(k_t, k_t, z_t).$$

This definition still holds if the household values productive time that is allocated to nonmarket activities. Such time will be called *leisure* and denoted l_t. The productive time endowment is normalized to 1, and the household faces the constraints

$$n_t + l_t \leqslant 1$$

for all t. In addition, leisure is introduced as an argument of the utility function, so the household's objective becomes the maximization of

$$E \sum_{t=0}^{\infty} \beta^t u(c_t, l_t).$$

Now leisure—and therefore employment—varies in equilibrium.

The model needs one more modification: a relaxation of the assumption that the technology shocks z_t are identically and independently distributed random variables. As will be documented, they are not so distributed. Rather, they display considerable serial correlation, with their first differences nearly serially uncorrelated. To introduce high persistence, we assume

$$z_{t+1} = \rho z_t + \varepsilon_{t+1}$$

where the $\{\varepsilon_{t+1}\}$ are identically and independently distributed and ρ is near 1. With this modification, the recursive sequence-of-markets equilibrium definition continues to apply.

Using Data to Restrict the Growth Model

Without additional restrictions on preferences and technology, a wide variety of equilibrium processes are consistent with the growth model. The beauty of this model is that both growth and micro observations can be used to determine its production and utility functions. When they are so used, there are not many free parameters that are specific to explaining the business cycle phenomena and that cannot be measured independently of those phenomena. The key parameters of the growth model are the intertemporal and intratemporal elasticities of substitution. As Lucas (1980a, p. 712) emphasizes, "On these parameters, we have a wealth of inexpensively available data from census cohort information, from panel data describing the reactions of individual households to a variety of changing market conditions, and so forth." To this list we add the secular growth observations which have the advantage of being experiments run by nature with large changes in relative prices and quantities and with idiosyncratic factors averaged out.[2] A fundamental thesis of this line of inquiry is that the measures obtained from aggregate series and those from individual panel data must be consistent. After all, the former are just the aggregates of the latter.

Secularly in the United States, capital and labor shares of output have been approximately constant, as has r, the rental price of capital. However, the nation's real wage has increased greatly—more than 100 percent since the Korean War. For these results to hold, the model's production function must be approximately Cobb-Douglas:

$$z_t f(k_t, n_t) = z_t k_t^{1-\theta} n_t^{\theta}.$$

The share parameter θ is equal to labor's share, which has been about 64 percent in the postwar period, so $\theta = 0.64$. This number is smaller than that usually obtained because we include services of consumer durables as part of output. This alternative accounting both reduces labor's share and makes it more nearly constant over the postwar period.

The artificial economy has but one type of capital, and it depreciates at rate δ. In fact, different types of capital depreciate at different rates, and the pattern of depreciation over the life of any physical asset is not constant. Kydland and I (1982, 1984) simply pick $\delta = 0.10$. With this value and an annual real interest rate of 4 percent, the steady-state capital–annual output ratio is about 2.6. That matches the ratio for the U.S. economy and also implies a steady-state investment share of output near the historically observed average. Except for parameters determining the process on the technology shock, this completely specifies the technology of the simple growth model.

A key growth observation which restricts the utility function is that leisure per capita l_t has shown virtually no secular trend while, again, the real wage has increased steadily. This implies an elasticity of substitution between consumption c_t and leisure l_t near 1. Thus, the utility function restricted to display both constant intertemporal and unit intratemporal elasticities of substitution is

$$u(c_t, l_t) = ([c_t^{1-\phi} l_t^{\phi}]^{1-\gamma} - 1)/(1 - \gamma)$$

where $1/\gamma > 0$ is the elasticity of substituting between different date composite commodities $c_t^{1-\phi} l_t^{\phi}$. This leaves γ and the subjective time discount factor β [or, equivalently, the subjective time discount rate $(1/\beta) - 1$] to be determined.

The steady-state interest rate is

$$i = (1/\beta) - 1 + \gamma(\dot{c}/c).$$

As stated previously, the average annual real interest rate is about 4 percent, and the growth rate of per capita consumption $\dot{c}/c$ has averaged nearly 2 percent. The following studies help restrict γ. Tobin and Dolde (1971) find that a γ near 1.5 is needed to match the life-cycle consumption patterns of individuals. Using individual portfolio observations, Friend and Blume (1975) estimate γ to be near 2. Using aggregate stock market and consumption data, L. Hansen and Singleton (1983) estimate γ to be near 1. Using international data, Kehoe (1984) also finds a modest curvature parameter γ. All these observations make a strong case that γ is not too far from 1. Since the nature of fluctuations of the artificial economy is not very sensitive to γ, we simply set γ equal to 1. Taking the limit as $\gamma \to 1$ yields

$$u(c_t, l_t) = (1 - \phi)\log c_t + \phi \log l_t.$$

This leaves β and ϕ still to be determined.

Hansen (1985b) has found that growing economies—that is, those with z_t having a multiplicative, geometrically growing factor $(1 + \lambda)^t$ with $\lambda > 0$ —fluctuate in essentially the same way as economies for which $\lambda = 0$. This justifies considering only the case $\lambda = 0$. If $\lambda = 0$, then the average interest rate approximately equals the subjective time discount rate.[3] Therefore, we set β equal to 0.96 per year or 0.99 per quarter.

The parameter ϕ is the leisure share parameter. Ghez and Becker (1975) find that the household allocates approximately one-third of its productive time to market activities and two-thirds to nonmarket activities. To be consistent with that, the model's parameter ϕ must be near two-thirds. This is the value assumed in our business cycle studies.

Eichenbaum, Hansen, and Singleton (1988) use aggregate data to estimate this share parameter ϕ, and they obtain a value near five-sixths. The difference between two-thirds and five-sixths is large in the business cycle context. With $\phi = 2/3$, the elasticity of labor supply with respect to a temporary change in the real wage is 2, while if $\phi = 5/6$, it is 5. This is because a 1 percent change in leisure implies a $\phi/(\phi - 1)$ percent change in hours of employment.

We do not follow the Eichenbaum-Hansen-Singleton approach and treat ϕ as a free parameter because it would violate the principle that parameters cannot be specific to the phenomena being studied. What sort of science would economics be if micro studies used one share parameter and aggregate studies another?

The Nature of the Technological Change

One method of measuring technological change is to follow Solow (1957) and define it as the changes in output less the sum of the changes in labor's input times labor share and the changes in capital's input times capital share. Measuring variables in logs, this is the percentage change in the technology parameter of the Cobb-Douglas production function. For the U.S. economy between the third quarter of 1955 and the first quarter of 1984, the standard deviation of this change is 1.2 percent.[4] The serial autocorrelations of these changes are $\rho_1 = -0.21$, $\rho_2 = -0.06$, $\rho_3 = 0.04$, $\rho_4 = 0.01$, and $\rho_5 = -0.05$. To a first approximation, the process on the percentage change in the technology process is a random walk with drift plus some serially uncorrelated measurement error. This error produces the negative first-order serial correlation of the differences.

Further evidence that the random walk model is not a bad approximation is based on yearly changes. For the quarterly random walk model, the standard deviation of this change is 6.63 times the standard deviation of the quarterly change. For the U.S. data, the annual change is only 5.64 times as large as the quarterly change. This, along with the negative first-order serial correlation, suggests that the standard deviation of the persistent part of the quarterly change is closer to $5.64/6.63 = 0.85$ than to 1.2 percent. Some further evidence is the change over four-quarter periods—that is, the change from a given quarter of one year to the same quarter of the next year. For the random walk model, the standard deviation of these changes is 2 times the standard deviation of the quarterly change. A reason that the standard deviation of change might be better measured this way is that the measurement noise introduced by seasonal factors is minimized. The estimate obtained in this way is 0.95 percent. To summarize, Solow growth accounting finds that the process on the technology parameter is highly persistent, with the standard deviation of change being about 0.90.[5]

The Solow estimate of the standard deviation of technological change is surely an overstatement of the variability of that parameter. There undoubtedly are non-negligible errors in measuring the inputs. Since the capital input varies slowly and its share is small, the most serious measurement problem is with the labor input. Fortunately there are two independent measures of the aggregate labor input, one constructed from a survey of employers and the other from a survey of households. Under the assumption of orthogonality of their measurement errors, a reasonable estimate of the variance of the change in hours is the covariance between the changes in the two series. Since the household survey is not used to estimate aggregate output, I use the covariance between the changes in household hours and output as an estimate of the covariance between aggregate hours and output. Still using a share parameter of $\theta = 0.75$, my estimate of the standard deviation of the percentage change in z_t is the square root of $\text{var}(\Delta \hat{y}) - 2\theta \text{cov}(\Delta \hat{h}_1, \Delta \hat{y}) + \theta^2 \text{cov}(\Delta \hat{h}_1, \Delta \hat{h}_2)$, where the caret (^) denotes a measured value. For the sample period my estimate is 0.763 percent. This is probably a better estimate than the one which ignores measurement error.

Still, my estimate might under- or overstate the variance of technological change. For example, the measurement of output might include significant errors. Perhaps measurement procedures result in some smoothing of the series. This would reduce the variability of the change in output and might reduce the covariance between measured hours and output.

Another possibility is that changes in hours are associated with corresponding changes in capital's utilization rate. If so, the Solow approach is inappropriate for measuring the technology shocks. To check whether this is a problem, I varied θ and found that $\theta = 0.85$ yields the smallest estimate, 0.759, as opposed to 0.763 for $\theta = 0.75$. This suggests that my estimate is not at all sensitive to variations in capital utilization rates.

To summarize, there is overwhelming evidence that technological shocks are highly persistent. But tying down the standard deviation of the technology change shocks is difficult. I estimate it as 0.763. It could very well be larger or smaller, though, given the accuracy of the measurements.

The Statistical Behavior of the Growth Models

Theory provides an equilibrium stochastic process for the growth economy studied. Our approach has been to document the similarities and differences between the statistical properties of data generated by this stochastic process and the statistical properties of American time series data. An alternative approach is to compare the paths of the growth model if the technological parameters $\{z_t\}$ were those experienced by the U.S. economy. We did not attempt this because theory's predictions of paths, unlike its predictions of the statistical properties, are sensitive to what Leamer (1983, p. 43) calls "whimsical" modeling assumptions. Another nontrivial problem is that the errors in measuring the innovations in the z_t process are as large as the innovations themselves.

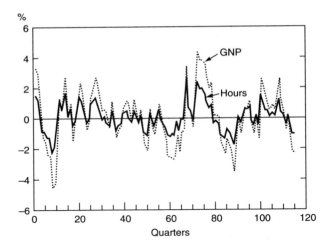

Figure 14.3
Deviations from Trend of GNP and Hours Worked in the Basic Growth Economy

The Basic Growth Model

With the standard deviation of the technology shock equal to 0.763, theory implies that the standard deviation of output will be 1.48 percent. In fact, it is 1.76 percent for the post–Korean War American economy. For the output of the artificial economy to be as variable as that, the variance of the shock must be 1.0, significantly larger than the estimate. The most important deviation from theory is the relative volatility of hours and output. Figure 14.3 plots a realization of the output and employment deviations from trend for the basic growth economy. A comparison of Figures 14.2 and 14.3 demonstrates clearly that, for the American economy, hours in fact vary much more than the basic growth model predicts. For the artificial economy, hours fluctuate 52 percent as much as output, whereas for the American economy, the ratio is 0.95. This difference appears too large to be a result of errors in measuring aggregate hours and output.

The Kydland-Prescott Economy

Kydland and I (1982, 1984) have modified the growth model in two important respects. First, we assume that a distributed lag of leisure and the market-produced good combine to produce the composite commodity good valued by the household. In particular,

Table 14.2
Cyclical behavior of the Kydland-Prescott economy

Variable x	Standard deviation	Cross correlation of GNP with		
		$x(t-1)$	$x(t)$	$x(t+1)$
Gross national product	1.79%	.60	1.00	.60
	(.13)	(.07)	(—)	(.07)
Consumption	.45	.47	.85	.71
	(.05)	(.05)	(.02)	(.04)
Investment	5.49	.52	.88	.78
	(.41)	(.09)	(.03)	(.03)
Inventory stock	2.20	.14	.60	.52
	(.37)	(.14)	(.08)	(.05)
Capital stock	.47	−.05	.02	.25
	(.07)	(.07)	(.06)	(.07)
Hours	1.23	.52	.95	.55
	(.09)	(.09)	(.01)	(.06)
Productivity (GNP/hours)	.71	.62	.86	.56
	(.06)	(.05)	(.02)	(.10)
Real interest rate (annual)	.22	.65	.60	.36
	(.03)	(.07)	(.20)	(.15)

Note: These are the means of 20 simulations, each of which was 116 periods long. The numbers in parentheses are standard errors.
Source: Kydland and Prescott 1984.

$$u\left(c_t, \sum_{i=0}^{\infty} \alpha_i l_{t-i}\right) = (1/3)\log c_t + (2/3)\log \sum_{i=0}^{\infty} \alpha_i l_{t-i}$$

where $\alpha_{i+1}/\alpha_i = 1 - \eta$ for $i = 1, 2, \ldots$ and $\sum_{i=0}^{\infty} \alpha_i = 1$. Kydland (1983) provides justification for this preference ordering based on an unmeasured, household-specific capital stock that, like c_t and l_t, is an input in the production of the composite commodity. The economy studied has $\alpha_0 = 0.5$ and $\eta = 0.1$. This increases the variability of hours.

The second modification is to permit the workweek of capital to vary proportionally to the workweek of the household. For this economy, increases in hours do not reduce the marginal product of labor as much, so hours fluctuate more in response to technology shocks of a given size.

The statistical properties of the fluctuations for this economy are reported in Table 14.2. As is clear there, hours are now about 70 percent as variable as output. This eliminates much of the discrepancy between theory and measurement. If the standard deviation of the technology shock is 0.72 percent, then fluctuations in the output of this artificial economy are as large as those experienced in the U.S. economy.

A comparison of Tables 14.1 and 14.2 shows that the Kydland-Prescott economy displays the business cycle phenomena. It does not quite demonstrate, however, that there would be a puzzle if the economy did not display the business cycle phenomena. That is because the parameters α_0 and η have not been well tied down by micro observations.[6] Better measures of these parameters could either increase or decrease significantly the amount of the fluctuations accounted for by the uncertainty in the technological change.

The Hansen Indivisible Labor Economy

Labor economists have estimated labor supply elasticities and found them to be small for full-time prime-age males. (See, for example, Ashenfelter 1984.) Heckman (1984), however, finds that when movements between employment and nonemployment are considered and secondary workers are included, elasticities of labor supply are much larger. He also finds that most of the variation in aggregate hours arises from variation in the number employed rather than in the hours worked per employed person.

These are the observations that led Hansen (1985a) to explore the implication of introducing labor indivisibilities into the growth model. As shown by Rogerson (1988), if the household's consumption possibility set has nonconvexities associated with the mapping from hours of market production activities to units of labor services, there will be variations in the number employed rather than in the hours of work per employed person. In addition, the aggregate elasticity of labor supply will be much larger than the elasticity of those whose behavior is being aggregated. In this case aggregation matters, and matters greatly.

There certainly are important nonconvexities in the mapping from hours of market activities to units of labor services provided. Probably the most important nonconvexity arises from the considerable amount of time required for commuting. Other features of the environment that would make full-time workers more than twice as productive as otherwise similar half-time workers are not hard to imagine. The fact that part-time workers typically are paid less per hour than full-time workers with similar human capital endowments is consistent with the existence of important nonconvexities.

Hansen (1985a) restricts each identical household to either work $\bar{h}$ hours or be unemployed. His relation is as depicted by the horizontal lines in Figure 14.4. This assumption is not as extreme as it appears. If the relation were as depicted by the curved line, the behavior of the economy would

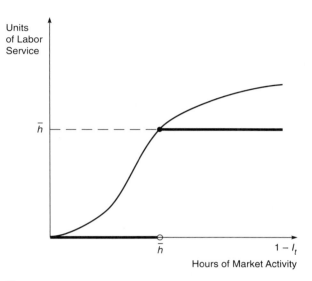

Figure 14.4
Relation between Time Allocated to Market Activity and Labor Service

be the same. The key property is an initial convex region followed by a concave region in the mapping from hours of market activity to units of labor service.

With this modification, lotteries that specify the probability of employment are traded along with market-produced goods and capital services. As before, the utility function of each individual is

$$u(c, l) = (1/3)\log c + (2/3)\log l.$$

If an individual works, $l = 1 - \bar{h}$; otherwise, $l = 1$. Consequently, if π is the probability of employment, an individual's expected utility is

$$E\{u(c, l)\} = (1/3)\log c + (2/3)\pi\log(1 - \bar{h}).$$

Given that per capita consumption is $\bar{c}$ and per capita hours of employment $\bar{n}$, average utility over the population is maximized by setting $c = \bar{c}$ for all individuals. If $\bar{l}$, which equals $1 - \pi\bar{h}$, denotes per capita leisure, then maximum per capita utility is

$$U(\bar{c}, \bar{l}) = (1/3)\log \bar{c} + (2/3)[(1 - \bar{l})/\bar{h}]\log(1 - \bar{h}).$$

This is the utility function which rationalizes the per capita consumption and leisure choices if each person's leisure is constrained to be either $1 - \bar{h}$

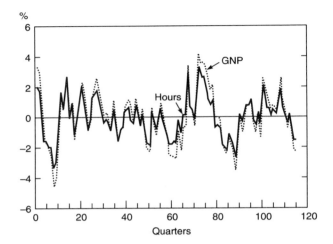

Figure 14.5
Deviations from Trend of GNP and Hours Worked in Hansen's Indivisible Labor Economy
Source: Gary D. Hansen, Department of Economics, University of California, Santa Barbara.

or 1. The aggregate intertemporal elasticity of substitution between different date leisures is infinity independent of the value of the elasticity for the individual (in the range where not all are employed).

Hansen (1985a) finds that if the technology shock standard deviation is 0.71, then fluctuations in output for his economy are as large as those for the American economy. Further, variability in hours is 77 percent as large as variability in output. Figure 14.5 shows that aggregate hours and output for his economy fluctuate together with nearly the same amplitude. These theoretical findings are the basis for my statement in the introduction that there would be a puzzle if the economy did not display the business cycle phenomena.

Empirical Labor Elasticity

One important empirical implication of a shock-to-technology theory of fluctuations is that the empirical labor elasticity of output is significantly larger than the true elasticity, which for the Cobb-Douglas production function is the labor share parameter. To see why, note that the capital stock varies little cyclically and is nearly uncorrelated with output. Consequently, the deviations almost satisfy

$$y_t = \theta h_t + z_t$$

where y_t is output, h_t hours, and z_t the technology shock. The empirical elasticity is

$$\eta = \operatorname{cov}(h_t, y_t)/\operatorname{var}(h_t)$$

which, because of the positive correlation between h_t and z_t, is considerably larger than the model's θ, which is 0.64. For the basic, Kydland-Prescott, and Hansen growth economies, the values of η are 1.9, 1.4, and 1.3, respectively.

Because of measurement errors, the empirical elasticity for the American economy is not well-estimated by simply computing the ratio of the covariance between hours and output and dividing by the variance of hours. The procedure I use is based on the following probability model:

$$\hat{y}_t = y_t + \varepsilon_{1t}$$

$$\hat{h}_{1t} = h_t + \varepsilon_{2t}$$

$$\hat{h}_{2t} = h_t + \varepsilon_{3t}$$

where the caret (^) denotes a measured value. The ε_{it} are measurement errors. Here the $\hat{h}_{1t}$ measure of hours uses the employer survey data while the $\hat{h}_{2t}$ measure uses the household survey data. Since these are independent measures, a maintained hypothesis is that ε_{2t} and ε_{3t} are orthogonal. With this assumption, a reasonable estimate of $\operatorname{var}(h_t)$ is the sample covariance between $\hat{h}_{1t}$ and $\hat{h}_{2t}$. Insofar as the measurement of output has small variance or ε_{1t} is uncorrelated with the hours measurement errors or both, the covariance between measured output and either measured hours series is a reasonable estimate of the covariance between output and hours. These two covariances are 2.231×10^{-4} and 2.244×10^{-4} for the sample period, and I take the average as my estimate of $\operatorname{cov}(h_t, y_t)$ for the American economy. My estimate of the empirical labor elasticity of output is

$$\hat{\eta} = [\operatorname{cov}(\hat{h}_{1t}, \hat{y}_t) + \operatorname{cov}(\hat{h}_{2t}, \hat{y}_t)]/2\operatorname{cov}(\hat{h}_{1t}, \hat{h}_{2t}) = 1.1.$$

This number is considerably greater than labor's share, which is about 0.70 when services of consumer durables are not included as part of output. This number strongly supports the importance of technological shocks in accounting for business cycle fluctuations. Nevertheless, the number is smaller than those for the Kydland-Prescott and Hansen growth economies.

One possible reason for the difference between the U.S. economy and the growth model empirical labor elasticities of output is cyclical measurement errors in output. A sizable part of the investment component of output is hard to measure and therefore not included in the U.S. National

Product Accounts measure of output, the gross national product (GNP). In particular, a firm's major maintenance expenditures, research and development expenditures, and investments in human capital are not included in GNP. In good times—namely, when output is above trend—firms may be more likely to undertake major repairs of a not fully depreciated asset, such as replacing the roof of a 30-year-old building which has a tax life of 35 years. Such an expenditure is counted as maintenance and therefore not included in GNP even though the new roof will provide productive services for many years. The incentive for firms to do this is tax savings: by expensing an investment rather than capitalizing it, current tax liabilities are reduced. Before 1984, when a railroad replaced its 90-pound rails, the expenditure was treated as a maintenance expense rather than an investment expenditure. If these and other types of unmeasured investment fluctuate in percentage terms more than output, as do all the measured investment components, the volatility of GNP is larger than measured. We do know that investment in rails was highly procyclical and volatile in the postwar period. A careful study is needed to determine whether the correction for currently unmeasured investment is small or large.

Another reason to expect the American economy's labor elasticity to be less than the model's is that the model shocks are perfectly neutral with respect to the consumption and investment good transformation. Persistent shocks which alter the product transformation frontier between these goods would cause variation in output and employment but not in the productivity parameters. For fluctuations so induced, the empirical labor elasticity of output would be the true elasticity. Similarly, relatively permanent changes in the taxing of capital—such as altering depreciation rates, the corporate income tax rate, or the investment tax credit rate—would all result in fluctuations in output and employment but not in the productivity parameters.

A final reason for actual labor elasticity to be less than the model's is the way imports are measured. An increase in the price of imported oil, that is, an increase in the quantity of output that must be sacrificed for a given unit of that input, has no effect on measured productivity. From the point of view of the growth model, however, an oil price increase is a negative technology shock because it results in less output, net of the exports used to pay for the imported oil, available for domestic consumption and investment. Theory predicts that such shocks will induce variations in employment and output, even though they have no effect on the aggregate production function. Therefore, insofar as they are important, they reduce the empirical labor elasticity of output.

Extensions

The growth model has been extended to provide a better representation of the technology. Kydland and I (1982) have introduced a technology with more than one construction period for new production capacity.[7] We have also introduced inventory as a factor of production. This improves the match between the model's serial correlation properties and the U.S. postwar data, but has little effect on the other statistics.

Kydland (1984) has introduced heterogeneity of labor and found that if there are transfers from high human capital people to low human capital people, theory implies that hours of the low fluctuate more than hours of the high. It also implies a lower empirical labor elasticity of output than the homogeneous household model.

Bain (1985) has studied an economy that is richer in sectoral detail. His model has manufacturing, retailing, and service-producing sectors. A key feature of the technology is that production and distribution occur sequentially. Thus there are two types of inventories—those of manufacturers' finished goods and those of final goods available for sale. With this richer detail, theory implies that different components of aggregate inventories behave in different ways, as seen in the data. It also implies that production is more volatile than final sales, an observation considered anomalous since inventories can be used to smooth production. (See, for example, Blinder 1986.)

Much has been done. But much more remains to be explored. For example, public finance considerations could be introduced and theory used to predict their implications. As mentioned above, factors which affect the rental price of capital affect employment and output, and the nature of the tax system affects the rental price of capital. Theory could be used to predict the effect of temporary increases in government expenditures such as those in the early 1950s when defense expenditures increased from less than 5 to more than 13 percent of GNP. Theory of this type could also be used to predict the effect of terms-of-trade shocks. An implication of such an exercise most likely will be that economies with persistent terms-of-trade shocks fluctuate differently than economies with transitory shocks. If so, this prediction can be tested against the observations.

Another interesting extension would be to explicitly model household production. This production often involves two people, with one specializing in market production and the other specializing in household production while having intermittent or part-time market employment. The fact that, cyclically, the employment of secondary wage earners is much more volatile than that of primary wage earners might be explained.

A final example of an interesting and not yet answered question is, How would the behavior of the Hansen indivisible labor economy change if agents did not have access to a technology to insure against random unemployment and instead had to self-insure against unemployment by holding liquid assets? In such an economy, unlike Hansen's, people would not be happy when unemployed. Their gain of more leisure would be more than offset by their loss as an insurer. Answering this question is not straightforward, because new tools for computing equilibria are needed.

Summary and Policy Implications

Economic theory implies that, given the nature of the shocks to technology and people's willingness and ability to intertemporally and intratemporally substitute, the economy will display fluctuations like those the U.S. economy displays. Theory predicts fluctuations in output of 5 percent and more from trend, with most of the fluctuation accounted for by variations in employment and virtually all the rest by the stochastic technology parameter. Theory predicts investment will be three or more times as volatile as output and consumption half as volatile. Theory predicts that deviations will display high serial correlation. In other words, theory predicts what is observed. Indeed, if the economy did not display the business cycle phenomena, there would be a puzzle.

The match between theory and observation is excellent, but far from perfect. The key deviation is that the empirical labor elasticity of output is less than predicted by theory. An important part of this deviation could very well disappear if the economic variables were measured more in conformity with theory. That is why I argue that theory is now ahead of business cycle measurement and theory should be used to obtain better measures of the key economic time series. Even with better measurement, there will likely be significant deviations from theory which can direct subsequent theoretical research. This feedback between theory and measurement is the way mature, quantitative sciences advance.

The policy implication of this research is that costly efforts at stabilization are likely to be counterproductive. Economic fluctuations are optimal responses to uncertainty in the rate of technological change. However, this does not imply that the amount of technological change is optimal or invariant to policy. The average rate of technological change varies much both over time within a country and across national economies. What is needed is an understanding of the factors that determine the average rate at which technology advances. Such a theory surely will depend on the institutional arrangements societies adopt. If policies adopted to stabilize the economy reduce the average rate of technological change, then stabilization policy is costly. To summarize, attention should be focused not on fluctuations in output but rather on determinants of the average rate of technological advance.

Notes

This paper was presented at a Carnegie-Rochester Conference on Public Policy and appears in a volume of the conference proceedings. It appears here with the kind permission of Allan H. Meltzer, editor of that volume. The author thanks Finn E. Kydland for helpful discussions of the issues reviewed here, Gary D. Hansen for data series and some additional results for his growth economy, Lars G. M. Ljungqvist for expert research assistance, Bruce D. Smith and Allan H. Meltzer for comments on a preliminary draft, and the National Science Foundation and the Minneapolis Federal Reserve Bank for financial support. The views expressed herein are those of the author alone.

1. Others [Barro (1981) and Long and Plosser (1983), for example] have argued that these fluctuations are not inconsistent with competitive theory that abstracts from monetary factors. Our finding is much stronger: standard theory predicts that the economy will display the business cycle phenomena.

2. See Solow 1970 for a nice summary of the growth observations.

3. Actually, the average interest rate is slightly lower because of risk premia. Given the value of γ and the amount of uncertainty, the average premium is only a fraction of a percent. See Mehra and Prescott 1985 for further details.

4. I use Hansen's (1984) human capital—weighted, household hour series. The capital stock and GNP series are from Citicorp's Citibase data bank.

5. The process $z_{t+1} = 0.9z_t + \varepsilon_{t+1}$ is, like the random walk process, highly persistent. Kydland and I find that it and the random walk result in essentially the same fluctuations.

6. Hotz, Kydland, and Sedlacek (1988) use annual panel data to estimate α_0 and η and obtain estimates near the Kydland-Prescott assumed values.

7. Altug (1983) has introduced two types of capital with different gestation periods. Using formal econometric methods, she finds evidence that the model's fit is improved if plant and equipment investment are not aggregated.

15

Some Skeptical Observations on Real Business Cycle Theory

Lawrence H. Summers

The increasing ascendancy of real business cycle theories of various stripes, with their common view that the economy is best modeled as a floating Walrasian equilibrium, buffeted by productivity shocks, is indicative of the depths of the divisions separating academic macroeconomists. These theories deny propositions thought self-evident by many academic macroeconomists and all of those involved in forecasting and controlling the economy on a day-to-day basis. They assert that monetary policies have no effect on real activity, that fiscal policies influence the economy only through their incentive effects, and that economic fluctuations are caused entirely by supply rather than demand shocks.

If these theories are correct, they imply that the macroeconomics developed in the wake of the Keynesian Revolution is well confined to the ashbin of history. And they suggest that most of the work of contemporary macroeconomists is worth little more than that of those pursuing astrological science. According to the views espoused by enthusiastic proponents of real business cycle theories, astrology and Keynesian economics are in many ways similar: both lack scientific support, both are premised on the relevance of variables that are in fact irrelevant, both are built on a superstructure of nonoperational and ill-defined concepts, and both are harmless only when they are ineffectual.

The appearance of Ed Prescott's stimulating paper, "Theory Ahead of Business Cycle Measurement" [Chapter 14 in this volume], affords an opportunity to assess the current state of real business cycle theory and to consider its prospects as a foundation for macroeconomic analysis. Prescott's paper is brilliant in highlighting the appeal of real business cycle theories and making clear the assumptions they require. But he does not make much effort at caution in judging the potential of the real business

Reprinted from the *Federal Reserve Bank of Minneapolis Quarterly Review*, Fall 1986.

cycle paradigm. He writes that "if the economy did not display the business cycle phenomena, there would be a puzzle," characterizes without qualification economic fluctuations as "optimal responses to uncertainty in the rate of technological change," and offers the policy advice that "costly efforts at stabilization are likely to be counterproductive."

Prescott's interpretation of his title is revealing of his commitment to his theory. He does not interpret the phrase *theory ahead of measurement* to mean that we lack the data or measurements necessary to test his theory. Rather, he means that measurement techniques have not yet progressed to the point where they fully corroborate his theory. Thus, Prescott speaks of the key deviation of observation from theory as follows: "An important part of this deviation could very well disappear if the economic variables were measured more in conformity with theory. That is why I argue that theory is now ahead of business cycle measurement. . . ."

The claims of real business cycle theorists deserve serious assessment, especially given their source and their increasing influence within the economics profession. Let me follow Prescott in being blunt. My view is that real business cycle models of the type urged on us by Prescott have nothing to do with the business cycle phenomena observed in the United States or other capitalist economies. Nothing in Prescott's papers or those he references is convincing evidence to the contrary.

Before turning to the argument Prescott presents, let me offer one lesson from the history of science. Extremely bad theories can predict remarkably well. Ptolemaic astronomy guided ships and scheduled harvests for two centuries. It provided extremely accurate predictions regarding a host of celestial phenomena. And to those who developed it, the idea that the earth was at the center seemed an absolutely natural starting place for a theory. So, too, Lamarckian biology, with its emphasis on the inheritance of acquired characteristics, successfully predicted much of what was observed in studies of animals and plants. Many theories can approximately mimic any given set of facts; that one theory can does not mean that it is even close to right.

Prescott's argument takes the form of the construction of an artificial economy which mimics many of the properties of actual economies. The close coincidence of his model economy and the actual economy leads him to conclude that the model economy is a reasonable if abstract representation of the actual economy. This claim is bolstered by the argument that the model economy is not constructed to fit cyclical facts but is parameterized on the basis of microeconomic information and the economy's long-run properties. Prescott's argument is unpersuasive at four levels.

Are the Parameters Right?

First, Prescott's claim to have parameterized the model on the basis of well-established microeconomic and long-run information is not sustainable. As one example, consider a parameter which Prescott identifies as being important in determining the properties of the model, the share of household time devoted to market activities. He claims that is one-third. Data on its average value over the last century indicate, as Martin Eichenbaum, Lars Hansen, and Kenneth Singleton (1988) have noted, an average value of one-sixth over the past 30 years. This seems right—a little more than half the adult population works, and those who work work about a quarter of the time. I am unable to find evidence supporting Prescott's one-third figure in the cited book by Gilbert Ghez and Gary Becker (1975). To take another example, Prescott takes the average real interest rate to be 4 percent. Over the 30-year period he studies, it in fact averaged only about 1 percent. This list of model parameters chosen somewhat arbitrarily could be easily extended.

A more fundamental problem lies in Prescott's assumption about the intertemporal elasticity of substitution in labor supply. He cites no direct microeconomic evidence on this parameter, which is central to his model of cyclical fluctuations. Nor does he refer to any aggregate evidence on it. Rather, he relies on a rather selective reading of the evidence on the intertemporal elasticity of substitution in consumption in evaluating the labor supply elasticity. My own reading is that essentially all the available evidence suggests only a minimal response of labor to transitory wage changes. Many studies (including Altonji 1982; Mankiw, Rotemberg, and Summers 1985; and Eichenbaum, Hansen, and Singleton 1988) suggest that the intertemporal substitution model cannot account at either the micro or the macro level for fluctuations in labor supply.

Prescott is fond of parameterizing models based on long-run information. Japan has for 30 years enjoyed real wage growth at a rate four times the U.S. rate, close to 8 percent. His utility function would predict that such rapid real wage growth would lead to a much lower level of labor supply by the representative consumer. I am not aware that this pattern is observed in the data. Nor am I aware of data suggesting that age/hours profiles are steeper in professions like medicine or law, where salaries rise rapidly with age.

Prescott's growth model is not an inconceivable representation of reality. But to claim that its parameters are securely tied down by growth and micro observations seems to me a gross overstatement. The image of a big loose tent flapping in the wind comes to mind.

Where Are the Shocks?

My second fundamental objection to Prescott's model is the absence of any independent corroborating evidence for the existence of what he calls *technological shocks*. This point is obviously crucial since Prescott treats technological shocks as the only driving force behind cyclical fluctuations. Prescott interprets all movements in measured total factor productivity as being the result of technology shocks or to a small extent measurement error. He provides no discussion of the source or nature of these shocks, nor does he cite any microeconomic evidence for their importance. I suspect that the vast majority of what Prescott labels technology shocks are in fact the observable concomitants of labor hoarding and other behavior which Prescott does not allow in his model.

Two observations support this judgment. First, it's hard to find direct evidence of the existence of large technological shocks. Consider the oil shocks, certainly the most widely noted and commented on shocks of the postwar period. How much might they have been expected to reduce total factor productivity? In one of the most careful studies of this issue, Ernst Berndt (1980, p. 85) concludes that "energy price or quantity variations since 1973 do not appear to have had a significant direct role in the slowdown of aggregate labor productivity in U.S. manufacturing, 1973–77." This is not to deny that energy shocks have important effects. But they have not accounted for large movements in measured total factor productivity.

Prescott assumes that technological changes are irregular, but is unable to suggest any specific technological shocks which presage the downturns that have actually taken place. A reasonable challenge to his model is to ask how it accounts for the 1982 recession, the most serious downturn of the postwar period. More generally, it seems to me that the finding that measured productivity frequently declines is difficult to account for technologically. What are the sources of technical regress? Between 1973 and 1977, for example, both mining and construction displayed negative rates of productivity growth. For smaller sectors of the economy, negative productivity growth is commonly observed.

A second observation casting doubt on Prescott's assumed driving force is that while technological shocks leading to changes in total factor productivity are hard to find, other explanations are easy to support. Jon Fay and James Medoff (1985) surveyed some 170 firms on their response to downturns in the demand for their output. The questions asked were phrased to make clear that it was exogenous downturns in their output that were being inquired about. Fay and Medoff (1985, p. 653) summarize their results by stating that "the evidence indicates that a sizeable portion of the swings in productivity over the business cycle is, in fact, the result of firms' decisions to hold labor in excess of regular production requirements and to hoard labor." According to their data, the typical plant in the U.S. manufacturing sector paid for 8 percent more blue-collar hours than were needed for regular production work during the trough quarter of its most recent downturn. After taking account of the amount of other worthwhile work that was completed by blue-collar employees during the trough quarter, 4 percent of the blue-collar hours paid for were hoarded. Similar conclusions have been reached in every other examination of microeconomic data on productivity that I am aware of.

In Prescott's model, the central driving force behind cyclical fluctuations is technological shocks. The propagation mechanism is intertemporal substitution in employment. As I have argued so far, there is no independent evidence from any source for either of these phenomena.

What About Prices? ...

My third fundamental objection to Prescott's argument is that he does price-free economic analysis. Imagine an analyst confronting the market for ketchup. Suppose she or he decided to ignore data on the price of ketchup. This would considerably increase the analyst's freedom in accounting for fluctuations in the quantity of ketchup purchased. Indeed, without looking at the price of ketchup, it would be impossible to distinguish supply shocks from demand shocks. It is difficult to believe that any explanation of fluctuations in ketchup sales that did not confront price data would be taken seriously, at least by hard-headed economists.

Yet Prescott offers us an exercise in price-free economics. While real wages, interest rates, and returns to capital are central variables in his model, he never looks at any data on them except for his misconstrual of the average real interest rate over the postwar period. Others have confronted models like Prescott's to data on prices with what I think can fairly be labeled dismal results. There is simply no evidence to support any of the price effects predicted by the model. Prescott's work does not resolve— or even mention—the empirical reality emphasized by Robert Barro and Robert King (1984) that consumption and leisure move in opposite directions over the business cycle with no apparent procyclicality of real wages. It is finessed by ignoring wage data. Prescott's own work with Rajnish Mehra (1985) indicates that the asset pricing implications of models like the

one he considers here are decisively rejected by nearly 100 years of historical experience. I simply do not understand how an economic model can be
said to have been tested without price data.

I believe that the preceding arguments demonstrate that real business
cycle models of the type surveyed by Prescott do not provide a convincing
account of cyclical fluctuations. Even if this strong proposition is not
accepted, they suggest that there is room for factors other than productivity shocks as causal elements in cyclical fluctuations.

... And Exchange Failures?

A fourth fundamental objection to Prescott's work is that it ignores the fact
that partial breakdowns in the exchange mechanism are almost surely dominant factors in cyclical fluctuations. Consider two examples. Between 1929
and 1933, the gross national product in the United States declined 50
percent, as employment fell sharply. In Europe today, employment has not
risen since 1970 and unemployment has risen more than fivefold in many
countries. I submit that it defies credulity to account for movements on this
scale by pointing to intertemporal substitution and productivity shocks. All
the more given that total factor productivity has increased more than twice
as rapidly in Europe as in the United States.

If some other force is responsible for the largest fluctuations that we
observe, it seems quixotic methodologically to assume that it plays no role
at all in other smaller fluctuations. Whatever mechanisms may have had
something to do with the depression of the 1930s in the United States or
the depression today in Europe presumably have at least some role in
recent American cyclical fluctuations.

What are those mechanisms? We do not yet know. But it seems clear
that a central aspect of depressions, and probably economic fluctuations
more generally, is a breakdown of the exchange mechanism. Read any
account of life during the Great Depression in the United States. Firms had
output they wanted to sell. Workers wanted to exchange their labor for it.
But the exchanges did not take place. To say the situation was constrained
Pareto optimal given the technological decline that took place between
1929 and 1933 is simply absurd, even though total factor productivity
did fall. What happened was a failure of the exchange mechanism. This
is something that no model, no matter how elaborate, of a long-lived
Robinson Crusoe dealing with his changing world is going to confront.
A model that embodies exchange is a minimum prerequisite for a serious
theory of economic downturns.

The traditional Keynesian approach is to postulate that the exchange mechanism fails because prices are in some sense rigid, so they do not attain market-clearing levels and thereby frustrate exchange. This is far from being a satisfactory story. Most plausible reasons why prices might not change also imply that agents should not continue to act along static demand and supply curves. But it hardly follows that ignoring exchange failures because we do not yet fully understand them is a plausible strategy.

Where should one look for failures of the exchange process? Convincing evidence of the types of mechanisms that can lead to breakdowns of the exchange mechanism comes from analyses of breakdowns in credit markets. These seem to have played a crucial role in each of the postwar recessions. Indeed, while it is hard to account for postwar business cycle history by pointing to technological shocks, the account offered by, for example, Otto Eckstein and Allen Sinai (1986) of how each of the major recessions was caused by a credit crunch in an effort to control inflation seems compelling to me.

Conclusion

Even at this late date, economists are much better at analyzing the optimal response of a single economic agent to changing conditions than they are at analyzing the equilibria that will result when diverse agents interact. This unfortunate truth helps to explain why macroeconomics has found the task of controlling, predicting, or even explaining economic fluctuations so difficult. Improvement in the track record of macroeconomics will require the development of theories that can explain why exchange sometimes works well and other times breaks down. Nothing could be more counterproductive in this regard than a lengthy professional detour into the analysis of stochastic Robinson Crusoes.

Note

An earlier version of these remarks was presented at the July 25, 1986, meeting of the National Bureau of Economic Research Economic Fluctuations Group.

16

Response to a Skeptic

Edward C. Prescott

New findings in science are always subject to skepticism and challenge. This is an important part of the scientific process. Only if new results successfully withstand the attacks do they become part of accepted scientific wisdom. Summers [in Chapter 15 in this volume] is within this tradition when he attacks the finding I describe [in Chapter 14] that business cycles are precisely what economic theory predicts given the best measures of people's willingness and ability to substitute consumption and leisure, both between and within time periods. I welcome this opportunity to respond to Summers' challenges to the parameter values and the business cycle facts that I and other real business cycle analysts have used. In challenging the existing quality of measurement and not providing measurement inconsistent with existing theory, Summers has conceded the point that theory is ahead of business cycle measurement.

Miscellaneous Misfires

Before responding to Summers' challenges to the measurements used in real business cycle analyses, I will respond briefly to his other attacks and, in the process, try to clarify some methodological issues in business cycle theory as well as in aggregate economic theory more generally.

Prices

Summers asks, Where are the prices? This question is puzzling. The mechanism real business cycle analysts use is the one he and other leading people in the field of aggregate public finance use: competitive equilibrium. Competitive equilibria have relative prices. As stated in the introduction of

Reprinted from the *Federal Reserve Bank of Minneapolis Quarterly Review*, Fall 1986.

"Theory Ahead of Business Cycle Measurement" [Chapter 14 in this volume], the business cycle puzzle is, Why are there large movements in the time allocated to market activities and little associated movements in the real wage, the price of people's time? Along with that price, Kydland and I (1982, 1984) examine the rental price of capital. An infinity of other relative prices can be studied, but these are the ones needed to construct national income and product accounts. The behavior of these prices in our models conforms with that observed.

In competitive theory, an economic environment is needed. For that, real business cycle analysts have used the neoclassical growth model. It is the preeminent model in aggregate economics. It was developed to account for the growth facts and has been widely used for predicting the aggregate effects of alternative tax schemes as well. With the labor/leisure decision endogenized, it is the appropriate model to study the aggregate implications of technology change uncertainty. Indeed, in 1977 Lucas, the person responsible for making business cycles again a central focus in economics, defined them (p. 23) as deviations from the neoclassical growth model— that is, fluctuations in hours allocated to market activity that are too large to be accounted for by changing marginal productivities of labor as reflected in real wages. Lucas, like me and virtually everyone else, assumed that, once characterized, the competitive equilibrium of the calibrated neoclassical growth economy would display much smaller fluctuations than do the actual U.S. data. Exploiting advances in theory and computational methods, Kydland and I (1982, 1984) and Hansen (1985a) computed and studied the competitive equilibrium process for this model economy. We were surprised to find the predicted fluctuations roughly as large as those experienced by the U.S. economy since the Korean War.

Some economists have been reluctant to use the competitive equilibrium mechanism to study business cycle fluctuations because they think it is contradicted by a real-world observation: some individuals who are not employed would gladly switch places with similarly skilled individuals who are. Solow (1986, p. S34), for example, predicted that "any interesting and useful solution to that riddle will almost certainly involve an equilibrium concept broader, or at least different from, price-mediated market-clearing." Rogerson (1984) proved him wrong. If the world had no nonconvexities or moral hazard problems, Solow would be correct. But the mapping between time allocated to market activities and units of labor service produced does have nonconvexities. Time spent commuting is not producing labor services, yet it is time allocated to market activity. With nonconvexities, competitive equilibrium theory implies that the commodities traded or priced are complicated contracted arrangements which can include employment lotteries with both winners and losers. As shown by Hansen (1985a), competitive theory accounts well for the observation that the principal margin of adjustment in aggregate hours is the number of people employed rather than the number of hours worked per person—as well as for the observation of so-called involuntary unemployment.

Technology Shocks

Another Summers question is, Where are the technology shocks? Apparently, he wants some identifiable shock to account for each of the half dozen postwar recessions. But our finding is not that infrequent large shocks produce fluctuations; it is, rather, that small shocks do, every period. At least since Slutzky ([1927] 1937), some stable low-order linear stochastic difference equations have been known to generate cycles. They do not have a few large shocks; they have small shocks, one every period. The equilibrium allocation for the calibrated neoclassical growth model with persistent shocks to technology turns out to be just such a process.

My Claims

Summers has perhaps misread some of my review of real business cycle research [in this volume]. There I do not argue that the Great American Depression was the equilibrium response to technology shocks as predicted by the neoclassical growth model. I do not argue that disruptions in the payment and credit system would not disrupt the economy. That theory predicts one factor has a particular nature and magnitude does not imply that theory predicts all other factors are zero. I only claim that technology shocks account for more than half the fluctuations in the postwar period, with a best point estimate near 75 percent. This does not imply that public finance disturbances, random changes in the terms of trade, and shocks to the technology of exchange had no effect in that period.

Neither do I claim that theory is ahead of macroeconomic measurement in all respects. As Summers points out, Mehra and I (1985) have used the representative agent construct to predict the magnitude of the average risk premium of an equity claim over a real bill. Our predicted quantity is small compared to the historically observed average difference between the yields of the stock market and U.S. Treasury bills. But this is not a failure of the representative agent construct; it is a success. We used theory to predict the magnitude of the average risk premium. That the representative agent model is poorly designed to predict differences in borrowing and lending rates—to explain, for example, why the government can borrow at a rate at least a few percentage points less than the one at which most of us can borrow—does not imply that this model is not well designed for other purposes—for predicting the consequences of technology shocks for fluctuations at the business cycle frequencies, for example.

Measurement Issues

Summers challenges the values real business cycle analysts have selected for three model parameters. By arguing that historically the real U.S. interest rate is closer to 1 percent than to the model economy's approximately 4 percent, he is questioning the value selected for the subjective time discount factor. He explicitly questions our value for the leisure share parameter. And Summers' challenge to the observation that labor productivity is procyclical is implicitly a challenge to my measure of the technology shock variance parameter.

Real Interest Rate

Summers points out that the real return on U.S. Treasury bills over the last 30 years has been about 1 percent, which is far from the average real interest rate of the economies that Kydland and I have studied. But for the neoclassical growth model, the relevant return is not the return on T-bills. It is the return on tangible capital, such things as houses, factories, machines, inventories, automobiles, and roads. The return on capital in the U.S. business sector is easily calculated from the U.S. National Income and Product Accounts, so we use it as a proxy for the return on U.S. capital more generally. This number is obtained by dividing the income of capital net of the adjusted capital consumption allowance by the capital stock in the business sector. For the postwar years, the result is approximately 4 percent, about the average real return for the model economies.

Preferences

Summers also questions the value of the leisure share parameter and argues that it is not well tied down by micro observation at the household level, as we claim. This is a potentially important parameter. If it is large, the response of labor supply to temporary changes in the real wage is large. Only if that response is large will large movements in employment be associated with small comovements in the real wage.

Kydland and I conclude that the leisure share parameter is not large based on findings reported by Ghez and Becker (1975). They report (p. 95) that the annual productive time endowment of U.S. males is 5,096 hours. They also say (p. 95) that U.S. females allocate about 75 hours per week to personal care, leaving 93 hours of production time per week. This multiplied by 52 is 4,836 hours, the annual productive time endowment of females. Ghez and Becker also report the average annual hours of employment for noninstitutionalized, working-age males as about 2,000 hours (pp. 85–91). If females allocate half as many hours to market employment as do males, the average fraction of time the U.S. working-age population spends in employment is about 0.30. Adding to this the time spent commuting yields a number close to those for our models. (They are all between 0.30 and 0.31 in Kydland and Prescott 1982 and 1984.)

Initially Kydland and I used time additive preferences, and the predictions of theory for productivity movements were as large in percentage terms as aggregate hour movements. This is inconsistent with observations, so I did not take seriously the prediction of theory that a little over half the aggregate output fluctuations in the postwar period were responses to technology shocks. At that time, measurement was still ahead of theory. Then, the prediction of theory would have been consistent with the relative movement of productivity and aggregate hours, and technology shocks would have accounted for the business cycle phenomena, if the leisure share parameter were five-sixths. With the discipline we used, however, this share parameter had to be consistent with observations on household time allocation. That we are now debating about a theory of aggregate phenomena by focusing on household time allocation is evidence that economic theory has advanced. Now, like physical scientists, when economists model aggregate phenomena, the parameters used can be measured independently of those phenomena.

In our 1982 paper, Kydland and I did claim that fluctuations of the magnitude observed could plausibly be accounted for by the randomness in the technological change process. There we explored the implications of a distributed lag of leisure being an argument of the period utility function rather than just the current level of leisure. Like increasing the leisure share parameter, this broadening results in larger fluctuations in hours in response to technology shocks. Kydland (1983) then showed that an unmeasured household-specific capital stock could rationalize this distributed lag. In addition, the lag was not inconsistent with good micro measurement, and these parameters could be measured independently of the business cycle phenomena. The distributed lag was a long shot, though, so we did not claim that theory had caught up to measurement.

Since then, however, two panel studies found evidence for a distributed lag of the type we considered (Hotz, Kydland, and Sedlacek 1988; Eckstein and Wolpin 1989). With this development, theory and measurement of the business cycle became roughly equal.

Subsequently, an important advance in aggregate theory has made moot the issue of whether Kydland's and my assumed preferences for leisure are supported by micro measurement. Given an important nonconvexity in the mapping between time allocated to market activities and units of labor service produced, Rogerson (1984) showed that the aggregate elasticity of labor supply to temporary changes in the real wage is large independent of individuals' willingness to intertemporally substitute leisure. This nicely rationalized the disparate micro and macro labor findings for this elasticity—the microeconomists' that it is small (for example, Ashenfelter 1984) and the macroeconomists' that it is large (for example, Eichenbaum, Hansen, and Singleton 1988). Hansen (1985a) introduced this non-convexity into the neoclassical growth model. He found that with this feature theory predicts that the economy will display the business cycle phenomena even if individuals' elasticity of labor supply to temporary changes in the real wage is small. Further, with this feature he found theory correctly predicts that most of the variation in aggregate hours of employment is accounted for by variation in the number of people employed rather than in the number of hours worked per person.

Technology

Uncertainty

In our 1982 paper, Kydland and I searched over processes for the techno-logical change process. We did sensitivity analysis with the other param-eters, but found the conclusions relatively insensitive to their assumed values (except for the distributed lag of leisure parameters just discussed). The parameters of the technological change process did affect our predic-tions of the aggregate implications of uncertainty in the technology parameter. In fact, Lucas (1987) criticized us for searching for the best fit. In "Theory Ahead of Business Cycle Measurement," I directly examined the statistical properties of the technology coefficient process. I found that the process is an approximate random walk with standard deviation of change in the logs approximately 0.00763 per quarter. When this number is used in the Hansen model, fluctuations predicted are even larger than those observed. In Kydland's and my model (1984), they are essentially equal to those observed.

Some, on the basis of theory, think that the factors producing technological change are small, many, and roughly uncorrelated. If so, by the law of large numbers, these factors should average out and the technological change process should be very smooth. I found [in Chapter 14] empirical evidence to the contrary. Others have too. Summers and Heston (1984) report the annual gross national products for virtually every country in the postwar period. They show huge variation across countries in the rate of growth of per capita income over periods sufficiently long that business cycle variations are a minor consideration. Even individual countries have large variation in the decade growth rates of per capita output. Given Solow's (1957) finding that more than 75 percent of the changes in per capita output are accounted for by changes in the technology parameter, the evidence for variation in the rate of technological advance is strong.

Obviously, economists do not have a good theory of the determinants of technological change. In this regard, measurement is ahead of theory. The determinants of the rate of technological change must depend greatly on the institutions and arrangements that societies adopt. Why else should technology advance more rapidly in one country than in another or, within a country, more rapidly in one period than in another? But a theory of technological change is not needed to predict responses to technological change.

The key parameter is the variance of the technology shock. This is where better measurement could alter the prediction of theory. Is measuring this variance with Solow's (1957) method (as I did) reasonable? I showed that measures of the technology shock variance are insensitive to cyclical variations in the capital utilization rate. Even if that rate varies proportionately to hours of employment and the proportionality constant is selected so as to minimize the measured standard deviation of the technology shock, that measured deviation is reduced only from 0.00763 to 0.00759. Further, when the capital utilization rate varies in this way for the model, the equilibrium responses are significantly larger. Variation in the capital utilization rate does not appear to greatly bias my estimate of the importance of technological change variance for aggregate fluctuations.

Perhaps better measurement will find that the technological change process varies less than I estimated. If so, a prediction of theory is that the amount of fluctuation accounted for by uncertainty in that process is smaller. If this were to happen, I would be surprised. I can think of no plausible source of measurement error that would produce a random walk–like process for technological change.

Labor Hoarding

Summers seems to argue that measured productivity is procyclical because measurement errors are cyclical. To support his argument, he cites a survey by Fay and Medoff (1985), which actually has little if anything to say about cyclical movements. Fay and Medoff surveyed more than 1,000 plant managers and received 168 usable responses. One of the questions asked was, How many extra blue-collar workers did you have in your recent downturn? They did not ask, How many extra workers did you have at the trough quarter and at the peak quarter of the most recent business cycle? Answers to those questions are needed to conclude how the number of extra blue-collar workers reported by managers varies over the cycle. Even if these questions had been asked, though, the response to them would not be a good measure of the number of redundant workers. Such questions are simply too ambiguous for most respondents to interpret them the same way.

The argument that labor hoarding is cyclical is not supported by theory either. The fact that labor is a quasi-fixed factor of production in the sense of Oi (1962) does not imply that more workers will be hoarded in recessions than in expansions. In bad times a firm with low output may be less reluctant to lay off workers than in good times because the worker is less likely to be hired by another firm. This argument suggests that labor hoarding associated with firm-specific output variations should be procyclical. Leisure consumed on the job also may be less in bad times than in good because work discipline may be greater. That is, an entrepreneur might be less reluctant to fire a worker in bad times because the worker can more easily be replaced. One might reasonably think, therefore, that labor's quasi-fixed nature makes measured productivity less, not more, cyclically volatile than productivity really is.

There is another, better reason to think that. In the standard measures of aggregate hours of employment, the hours of an experienced MBA from one of the best business schools are treated the same as those of a high school dropout. Yet these hours do not on average command the same price in the market, which is evidence that they are not the same commodity. In the neoclassical growth model, the appropriate way to aggregate hours is in terms of effective units of labor. That is, if the MBA's productivity is five times that of the high school dropout, then each hour of the MBA's time is effectively equivalent to five hours of the high school dropout's time. The work of Kydland (1984) suggests this correction is an important one. The more educated and on average more highly paid have much less variability in annual hours of employment than do the less educated. Kydland (1984, p. 179) reports average hours and average wages as well as sensitivity of hours to the aggregate unemployment rate for adult males categorized by years of schooling. His figures imply that a 1 percentage point change in the aggregate unemployment rate for adult males is associated with a 1.24 percent change in equally weighted hours. When those hours are measured as effective units of labor, the latter change is only 0.65 percent. This is strong evidence that if the labor input were measured correctly, the measure of productivity would vary more.

To summarize, measurement of the labor input needs to be improved. By questioning the standard measures, Summers is agreeing that theory is ahead of business cycle measurement. More quantitative theoretic work is also needed, to determine whether abstracting from the fact that labor is a partially fixed factor affects any of the real business cycle models' findings. Of course, introducing this feature—or others—into these models may significantly alter their predictions of the aggregate implications of technology uncertainty. But respectable economic intuition must be based on models that have been rigorously analyzed.

To Conclude

Summers cannot be attacking the use of competitive theory and the neoclassical growth environment in general. He uses this standard model to predict the effects of alternative tax policies on aggregate economic behavior. He does not provide criteria for deciding when implications of this model should be taken seriously and when they should not be. My guess is that the reason for skepticism is not the methods used, but rather the unexpected nature of the findings. We agree that labor input is not that precisely measured, so neither is technological uncertainty. In other words, we agree that theory is ahead of business cycle measurement.

17 Business Cycles: Real Facts and a Monetary Myth

Finn E. Kydland and
Edward C. Prescott

Ever since Koopmans (1947) criticized Burns and Mitchell's (1946) book on *Measuring Business Cycles* as being "measurement without theory," the reporting of business cycle facts has been taboo in economics. In his essay, Koopmans presents two basic criticisms of Burns and Mitchell's study. The first is that it provides no systematic discussion of the theoretical reasons for including particular variables over others in their empirical investigation. Before variables can be selected, Koopmans argues, some notion is needed of the theory that generates the economic fluctuations. With this first criticism we completely agree: Theory is crucial in selecting which facts to report.

Koopmans' second criticism is that Burns and Mitchell's study lacks explicit assumptions about the probability distribution of the variables. That is, their study lacks "assumptions expressing and specifying how random disturbances operate on the economy through the economic relationships between the variables" (Koopmans 1947, p. 172). What Koopmans has in mind as such relationships is clear when he concludes an overview of Burns and Mitchell's so-called measures with this sentence: "Not a single demand or supply schedule or other equation expressing the behavior of men [that is, people] or the technical laws of production is employed explicitly in the book, and the cases of implicit use are few and far between" (p. 163). Koopmans repeatedly stresses this need for using a structural system of equations as an organizing principle (pp. 169–70). Economists, he argues, should first hypothesize that the aggregate time series under consideration are generated by some probability model, which the economists must then estimate and test. Koopmans convinced the economics profession that to do otherwise is unscientific. On this point we strongly disagree with Koopmans: We think he did economics a grave

Reprinted from the *Federal Reserve Bank of Minneapolis Quarterly Review*, Spring 1990.

disservice, because the reporting of facts—without assuming the data are generated by some probability model—is an important scientific activity. We see no reason for economics to be an exception.

As a spectacular example of facts influencing the development of economic theory, we refer to the growth facts that came out of the empirical work of Kuznets and others. According to Solow (1970, p. 2), these facts were instrumental in the development of his own neoclassical growth model, which has since become the most important organizing structure in macroeconomics, whether the issue is one of growth or fluctuations or public finance. Loosely paraphrased, the key growth facts that Solow lists (on pp. 2–3) are

• Real output per worker (or per worker-hour) grows at a roughly constant rate over extended time periods.

• The stock of real capital, crudely measured, grows at a roughly constant rate which exceeds the growth rate of labor input.

• The growth rates of real output and the stock of capital goods tend to be similar, so the capital-to-output ratio shows no systematic trend.

• The rate of profit on capital has a horizontal trend.

These facts are neither estimates nor measures of anything; they are obtained without first hypothesizing that the time series are generated by a probability model belonging to some class. From this example, no one can deny that the reporting of growth facts has scientific value: Why else would Kuznets have received a Nobel Prize for this work? Or Solow, as well, for developing a parsimonious theory that rationalizes these facts— namely, his neoclassical growth model?

The growth facts are not the only interesting features of these aggregate time series. Also of interest are the more volatile changes that occur in these and other aggregates—that is, the cyclical behavior of the time series. These observations are interesting because they apparently conflict with basic competitive theory, in which outcomes reflect people's ability and willingness to substitute between consumption and leisure at a given point in time and between consumption at different points in time.

The purpose of this article is to present the business cycle facts in light of established neoclassical growth theory, which we use as the organizing framework for our presentation of business cycle facts. We emphasize that the statistics reported here are not measures of anything; rather, they are statistics that display interesting patterns, given the established neoclassical growth theory. In discussions of business cycle models, a natural question is, Do the corresponding statistics for the model economy display these patterns? We find these features interesting because the patterns they seem to display are inconsistent with the theory.

The study of business cycles flourished from the 1920s through the 1940s. But in the 1950s and 1960s, with the development of the structural system-of-equations approach that Koopmans advocated, business cycles ceased to be an active area of economic research. Now, once again, the study of business cycles, in the form of recurrent fluctuations, is alive. At the leading research centers, economists are again concerned with the question of why, in market economies, aggregate output and employment undergo repeated fluctuations about trend.[1]

Instrumental in bringing business cycles back into the mainstream of economic research is the important paper by Lucas (1977), "Understanding Business Cycles." We follow Lucas in defining *business cycles* as the deviations of aggregate real output from trend. We complete his definition by providing an explicit procedure for calculating a time series trend that successfully mimics the smooth curves most business cycle researchers would draw through plots of the data. We also follow Lucas in viewing the business cycle facts as the statistical properties of the comovements of deviations from trend of various economic aggregates with those of real output.

Lucas' definition differs importantly from that of Mitchell (1913, 1927), whose definition had guided students of business cycles up until World War II. Mitchell represents business cycles as sequences of expansions and contractions, particularly emphasizing turning points and phases of the cycle. We think the developments in economic theory that followed Mitchell's work dictate Lucas' representation of cycles.

Equipped with our operational definition of cyclical deviations, we present what we see as the key business cycle facts for the United States economy in the post–Korean War period (1954–1989). Some of these facts are fairly well known; others, however, are likely to come as a surprise because they are counter to beliefs often stated in the literature.

An important example of one of these commonly held beliefs is that the price level always has been procyclical and that, in this regard, the postwar period is no exception. Even Lucas (1977, p. 9) lists procyclical price levels among business cycle regularities. This perceived fact strongly influenced business cycle research in the 1970s. A more recent example of this misbelief is when Bernanke (1986, p. 76) discusses a study by King and Plosser (1984): "Although some points of their analysis could be criticized (for example, there is no tight explanation of the relation between transaction services and the level of demand deposits, and the model does not yield a strong prediction of price procyclicality), the overall framework is not implausible." Even more recently, Mankiw (1989, p. 88), in discussing the same paper, points out that "while the story of King and Plosser can explain the procyclical behavior of money, it cannot explain the procyclical behavior of prices." We shall see that, in fact, these criticisms are based on what is a myth. We show that during the 35 years since the Korean War, the price level has displayed a clear *countercyclical* pattern.

Other misperceptions we expose are the beliefs that the real wage is either countercyclical or essentially uncorrelated with the cycle and that the money stock, whether measured by the monetary base or by M1, leads the cycle.

The real facts documented in this paper are that major output components tend to move together over the cycle, with investment in consumer and producer durables having several times larger percentage deviations than does spending on nondurable consumption.

Alternative Views of Business Cycles

To many, when we talk about cycles, the picture that comes to mind is a sine wave with its regular and recurrent pattern. In economics and other sciences, however, the term *cycle* refers to a more general concept. One of the best-known examples of cycles is the sunspot cycle, which varies in length from under 10 years to nearly 20 years. The significant fact about cycles is the recurrent nature of the events.

In 1922, at a Conference on Cycles, representatives from several sciences discussed the cyclical phenomena in their fields. The participants agreed on the following definition (quoted in Mitchell 1927, p. 377) as being reasonable for all the sciences: "In general scientific use ... the word (cycle) denotes a recurrence of different phases of plus and minus departures, which are often susceptible of exact measurement." Our definition of business cycles is consistent with this general definition, but we refer to departures as *deviations*.

Mitchell's Four Phases

In 1913, Wesley C. Mitchell published a major work on business cycles, in it reviewing the research that had preceded his own. The book presents his largely descriptive approach, which consists of decomposing a large number of time series into sequences of cycles and then dividing each cycle into four distinct phases. This work was continued by Mitchell (1927) and by Burns and Mitchell (1946), who defined business cycles as

... a type of fluctuation found in the aggregate economic activity of nations that organize their work mainly in business enterprises: a cycle consists of expansions occurring at about the same time in many economic activities, followed by similarly general recessions, contractions, and revivals which merge into the expansion phase of the next cycle; this sequence of changes is recurrent but not periodic; in duration business cycles vary from more than one year to ten or twelve years; they are not divisible into shorter cycles of similar character with amplitudes approximating their own (p. 3).

From the discussion in their books, it is clear the authors view business cycles as consisting of four phases that inevitably evolve from one into another: prosperity, crisis, depression, and revival. This view is expressed perhaps most clearly by Mitchell ([1923] 1951, p. 46), who writes: "Then in order will come a discussion of how prosperity produces conditions which lead to crises, how crises run into depressions, and finally how depressions after a time produce conditions which lead to new revivals." Mitchell clearly had in mind a theoretical framework consistent with that view. In defending the use of the framework of four distinct cyclical phases, Mitchell later wrote that "most current theories explain crises by what happens in prosperity and revivals by what happens in depression" (Mitchell 1927, p. 472). (For an extensive overview of these theories and their relationship to Mitchell's descriptive work, see Haberler 1937.)

We now know how to construct model economies whose equilibria display business cycles like those envisioned by Mitchell. For example, a line of research that gained attention in the 1980s demonstrates that cyclical patterns of this form result as equilibrium behavior for economic environments with appropriate preferences and technologies. (See, for example, Benhabib and Nishimura 1985 and Boldrin 1989.) Burns and Mitchell would have been much more influential if business cycle theory had evolved in this way. Koopmans (1957, pp. 215–16) makes this point in his largely unnoticed "second thought" on Burns and Mitchell's work on business cycles.

In retrospect, it is now clear that the field of business cycles has moved in a completely different direction from the one Mitchell envisioned. Theories with deterministic cyclical laws of motion may a priori have had considerable potential for accounting for business cycles; but in fact, they have failed to do so. They have failed because cyclical laws of motion do not arise as equilibrium behavior for economies with empirically reasonable preferences and technologies—that is, for economies with reasonable statements of people's ability and willingness to substitute.

Frisch's Pendulum

As early as the 1930s, some economists were developing business cycle models that gave rise to difference equations with random shocks. An important example appears in a paper by Ragnar Frisch ([1933] 1965). Frisch was careful to distinguish between impulses in the form of random shocks, on the one hand, and their propagation over time, on the other. In contrast with proponents of modern business cycle theory, he emphasized damped oscillatory behavior. The concept of equilibrium was interpreted as a system at rest (as it is, for instance, in the science of mechanics).

The analogy of a pendulum is sometimes used to describe this view of cycles. Shocks are needed to provide "energy in maintaining oscillations" in damped cyclical systems. Frisch reports that he was influenced by Knut Wicksell, to whom he attributes the following: "If you hit a wooden rocking horse with a club, the movement of the horse will be very different to that of the club" (quoted in Frisch [1933] 1965, p. 178). The use of the rocking horse and pendulum analogies underscores their emphasis on cycles in the form of damped oscillations.

The research of Frisch and Wicksell received considerable attention in the 1930s, but no one built on their work. Construction stopped primarily because the neoclassical growth model and the necessary conceptual tools (particularly the Arrow-Debreu general equilibrium theory) had not yet been developed. Since the tools to do quantitative dynamic general equilibrium analysis weren't available, whereas statistical time series techniques were advancing rapidly, it's not surprising that quantitative system-of-equation models—especially the Keynesian income-expenditure models—received virtually all the attention.

Slutzky's Random Shocks

An entirely different way of generating cycles is suggested by the statistical work of Eugen Slutzky ([1927] 1937). Slutzky shows that cycles resembling business fluctuations can be generated as the sum of random causes —that is, by a stable, low-order, stochastic difference equation with large positive real roots.

The following exercise illustrates how Slutzky's method can generate cycles. Let the random variable e_t take the value 0.5 if a coin flip shows heads and -0.5 if tails. Assume that

$$y_{t+1} = 0.95y_t + e_{t+1}. \tag{1}$$

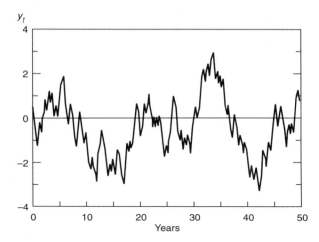

Figure 17.1
Cycles Generated by Slutzky's Mechanism

By repeated substitution, y_t is related to current and past shocks in the following way:

$$y_t = e_t + 0.95e_{t-1} + 0.95^2 e_{t-2} + \cdots + 0.95^{t-1} e_1 + 0.95^t y_0. \tag{2}$$

The y_t are geometrically declining sums of past shocks. Given an initial value y_0 and a fair coin, this stochastic difference equation can be used to generate a random path for the variable y.

Figure 17.1 plots a time series generated in this way. The time series displays patterns that Burns and Mitchell (1946) would characterize as business cycles.[2] The amplitudes and duration of cycles are variable, with the duration varying from 1 to 12 years and averaging about $3\frac{1}{2}$ years. The time series seems to display cycles in Mitchell's sense of expansions containing the seed for recessions and vice versa. But, by construction, recessions do not contain the seed of subsequent expansions. At each point in time, the expected future path is monotonic and converges to the zero mean, with 5 percent of the distance being closed in each quarterly time period.

Another demonstration of the role that random shocks can play appears in a paper by Adelman and Adelman (1959). Using the Klein-Goldberger model, they show that by adding random shocks to the model, it produces aggregate time series that look remarkably like those of the post–World War II economy of the United States. The deterministic version of this model converges almost monotonically to a point. This exercise forcefully demonstrates that a stochastic process can generate recurrent cycles while its deterministic version can converge monotonically.

Advancing to Lucas' Deviations

In the 1940s and the 1950s, while macroeconometric system-of-equations models were being developed, important theoretical advances were being made along entirely different fronts. By the early 1960s, economists' understanding of the way economic environments work in general equilibrium had advanced by leaps and bounds. The application of general equilibrium theory in dynamic environments led to theoretical insights on the growth of economies; it also led to important measurements of the parameters of the aggregate production function that formed the foundation for neoclassical growth theory. Thus, by the late 1960s, there were two established theories competing for dominance in aggregate economics. One was the behavioral-empirical approach reflected in the Keynesian system-of-equations models. The other was the neoclassical approach, which modeled environments with rational, maximizing individuals and firms. The neoclassical approach dominated public finance, growth theory, and international trade. As neoclassical theory progressed, an unresolvable conflict developed between the two approaches. The impasse developed because dynamic maximizing behavior is inconsistent with the assumption of invariant behavioral equations, an assumption that underlies the system-of-equations approach.

Not until the 1970s did business cycles again receive attention, spurred on by Lucas' (1977) article, "Understanding Business Cycles." There, Lucas viewed business cycle regularities as "comovements of the deviations from trend in different aggregative time series." He defined the business cycle itself as the "movements about trend in gross national product." Two types of considerations led Lucas to this definition: the previously discussed findings of Slutzky and the Adelmans, and the important advances in economic theory, especially neoclassical growth theory. We interpret Lucas as viewing business cycle fluctuations as being of interest because they are at variance with established neoclassical growth theory.

Another important theoretical advance of the 1960s and 1970s was the development of recursive competitive equilibrium theory. This theory made it possible to study abstractions of the aggregate economy in which optimizing economic behavior produces behavioral relations in the form of low-order stochastic difference equations. The role these advances played for Lucas' thinking is clear, as evident from one of his later articles discussing methods and problems in business cycle theory (see Lucas 1980a).

In contrast with Mitchell's view of business cycles, Lucas does not think in terms of sequences of cycles as inevitable waves in economic activity, nor does he see a need to distinguish among different phases of the cycle. To Lucas, the comovements over time of the cyclical components of economic aggregates are of primary interest, and he gives several examples of what he views as the business cycle regularities. We make explicit and operational what we mean by these terms and present a systematic account of the regularities. When that step is implemented quantitatively, some regularities emerge that, in the 1970s, would have come as a surprise— even to Lucas.

Modern Business Cycle Theory

In the 1980s and now in the early 1990s, business cycles (in the sense of recurrent fluctuations) increasingly have become a focus of study in aggregate economics. Such studies are generally guided by perceived business cycle regularities. But if these perceptions are not in fact the regularities, then certain lines of research are misguided.

For example, the myth that the price level is procyclical largely accounts for the prevalence in the 1970s of studies that use equilibrium models with monetary policy or price surprises as the main source of fluctuations. At the time, monetary disturbances appeared to be the only plausible source of fluctuations that could not be ruled out as being too small, so they were the leading candidate. The work of Friedman and Schwartz (1963) also contributed to the view that monetary disturbances are the main source of business cycle fluctuations. Their work marshaled extensive empirical evidence to support the position that monetary policy is an important factor in determining aggregate output, employment, and other key aggregates.

Since the early studies of Burns and Mitchell, the emphasis in business cycle theory has shifted from essentially pure theoretical work to quantitative theoretical analysis. This quantitative research has had difficulty finding an important role for monetary changes as a source of fluctuations in real aggregates. As a result, attention has shifted to the role of other factors—technological changes, tax changes, and terms-of-trade shocks. This research has been strongly guided by business cycle facts and regularities such as those to be presented here.

Along with the shift in focus to investigating the sources and nature of business cycles, aggregate analysis underwent a methodological revolution. Previously, empirical knowledge had been organized in the form of equations, as was also the case for the early rational expectations models. Muth (1960), in his pioneering work on rational expectations, did not break with this system-of-equations tradition. For that reason, his econometric program did not come to dominate. Instead, the program which has prevailed is the one that organizes empirical knowledge around preferences, technology, information structure, and policy rules or arrangements. Sargent (1981) has led the development of tools for inferring values of parameters characterizing these elements, given the behavior of the aggregate time series. As a result, aggregate economics is no longer a separate and entirely different field from the rest of economics; it now uses the same tools and empirical knowledge as other branches of economics, such as finance, growth theory, public finance, and international economics. With this development, measurements and quantitative findings in those other fields can be used to restrict models of business cycles and make our knowledge about the quantitative importance of cyclical disturbances more precise.

Business Cycle Deviations Redefined

Because economic activity in industrial market economies is characterized by sustained growth, Lucas defines business cycles as deviations of real gross national product (GNP) from trend rather than from some constant or average value. But Lucas does not define *trend*, so his definition of business cycle deviations is incomplete. What guides our, and we think his, concept of trend is steady-state growth theory. With this theory there is exogenous labor-augmenting technological change that occurs at a constant rate; that is, the effectiveness of labor grows at some constant rate. Steady-state growth is characterized by per capita output, consumption, investment, capital stock, and the real wage all growing at the same rate as does technology. The part of productive time allocated to market activity and the real return on capital remain constant.

If the rate of technological change were constant, then the trend of the logarithm of real GNP would be a linear function of time. But the rate of technological change varies both over time and across countries. (*Why* it varies is the central problem in economic development or maybe in all of economics.) The rate of change clearly is related to the arrangements and institutions that a society uses and, more important, to the arrangements and institutions that people expect will be used in the future. Even in a relatively stable society like the United States since the Second World War, there have been significant changes in institutions. And when a society's institutions change, there are changes in the productivity growth of that society's labor and capital. In the United States, the rate of technological change in the 1950s and 1960s was significantly above the U.S. historical average rate over the past 100 years. In the 1970s, the rate was significantly below average. In the 1980s, the rate was near the historical average. Because the underlying rate of technological change has not been constant in the period we examine (1954–1989), detrending using a linear function of time is inappropriate. The scheme used must let the average rate of technological change vary over time, but not too rapidly.

Any definition of the trend and cycle components, and for that matter the seasonal component, is necessarily statistical. A *decomposition* is a representation of the data. A representation is useful if, in light of theory, it reveals some interesting patterns in the data. We think our representation is successful in this regard. Our selection of a trend definition was guided by the following criteria:

• The trend component for real GNP should be approximately the curve that students of business cycles and growth would draw through a time plot of this time series.

• The trend of a given time series should be a linear transformation of that time series, and this transformation should be the same for all series[3]

• Lengthening the sample period should not significantly alter the value of the deviations at a given date, except possibly near the end of the original sample.

• The scheme should be well defined, judgment free, and cheaply reproducible.

These criteria led us to the following scheme. Let y_t, for $t = 1, 2, \ldots, T$, denote a time series. We deal with logarithms of a variable, unless the variable is a share, because the percentage deviations are what display the interesting patterns. Moreover, when an exponentially growing time series is so transformed, it becomes linear in time. Our trend component, denoted τ_t, for $t = 1, 2, \ldots, T$, is the one that minimizes

$$\sum_{t=1}^{T} (y_t - \tau_t)^2 + \lambda \sum_{t=2}^{T-1} [(\tau_{t+1} - \tau_t) - (\tau_t - \tau_{t-1})]^2 \tag{3}$$

for an appropriately chosen positive λ. (The value of λ will be specified momentarily.) The first term is the sum of the squared deviations $d_t =$

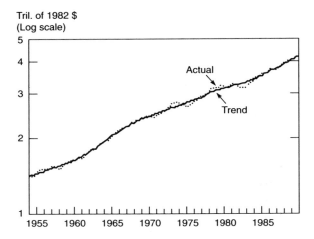

Figure 17.2
Actual and Trend of U.S. Real Gross National Product: Quarterly, 1954–1989. Source of basic data: Citicorp's Citibase data bank.

$y_t - \tau_t$. The second term is multiple λ of the sum of the squares of the trend component's second differences. This second term penalizes variations in the growth rate of the trend component, with the penalty being correspondingly larger if λ is larger.

The first-order conditions for this convex minimization problem are linear and can be solved for the τ_t.[4] We found that if the time series are quarterly, a value of $\lambda = 1600$ is reasonable. With this value, the implied trend path for the logarithm of real GNP is close to the one that students of business cycles and growth would draw through a time plot of this series, as shown in Figure 17.2. The remaining criteria guiding our selection of a detrending procedure are satisfied as well.

We have learned that this procedure for constructing a smooth curve through the data has a long history in both the actuarial and the natural sciences. Stigler (1978) reports that actuarial scientists used this method in the 1920s. He also notes that John von Neumann, who undoubtedly reinvented it, used it in the ballistics literature in the early 1940s. That others facing similar problems developed this simple scheme attests to its reasonableness. What is surprising is that economists took so long to exploit this scheme and that so many of them were so hostile to the idea when it was finally introduced into economics.[5]

Business Cycle Facts and Regularities

We emphasize that our selection of the facts to report is guided by neoclassical growth theory. This theory, currently the established one in aggregate economics, is being used not only to study growth and development but also to address public finance issues and, more recently, to study business cycles. The facts we present here are the values of well-defined statistics for the U.S. economy since the Korean War (1954–1989). We refer to consistent patterns in these numbers as business cycle *regularities*.

The statistics presented in Tables 17.1–17.4 provide information on three basic aspects of the cyclical behavior of aggregates:

- The amplitude of fluctuations
- The degree of comovement with real GNP (our measure of pro- or countercyclicality)
- The phase shift of a variable relative to the overall business cycle, as defined by the behavior of cyclical real GNP.

We emphasize that, except for the share variables shown in Table 17.2, these statistics are percentage, not absolute, deviations. For instance, the percentage deviation of investment expenditures is more than three times that of total real GNP. Since this component averages less than one-fifth of real GNP, its absolute volatility is somewhat less than that of total output.

In the tables, the degree of contemporaneous comovement with real GNP is indicated in the $x(t)$ column. The statistics in that column are the correlation coefficients of the cyclical deviations of each series with the cyclical deviations of real GNP. A number close to one indicates that a series is highly *procyclical*; a number close to one but of the opposite sign indicates that a series is *countercyclical*. A number close to zero means that a series does not vary contemporaneously with the cycle in any systematic way, in which case we say the series is *uncorrelated* with the cycle.

The remaining columns of the tables also display correlation coefficients, except the series have been shifted forward or backward, relative to real GNP, by from one to five quarters. To some extent these numbers indicate the degree of comovement with GNP. Their main purpose, however, is to indicate whether, typically, there is a phase shift in the movement of a time series relative to real GNP. For example, if for some series the numbers in the middle of each table are positive but largest in column $x(t - i)$, where $i > 0$, then the numbers indicate that the series is procyclical but tends to peak about i quarters before real GNP. In this case we say the series *leads*

Table 17.1
Cyclical behavior of U.S. production inputs (deviations from trend of input variables, quarterly, 1954–1989)

Variable x	Volatility (% std. dev.)	Cross correlation of real GNP with										
		$x(t-5)$	$x(t-4)$	$x(t-3)$	$x(t-2)$	$x(t-1)$	$x(t)$	$x(t+1)$	$x(t+2)$	$x(t+3)$	$x(t+4)$	$x(t+5)$
Real gross national product	1.71	−.03	.15	.38	.63	.85	1.00	.85	.63	.38	.15	−.03
Labor input												
Hours (household survey)	1.47	−.10	.05	.23	.44	.69	.86	.86	.75	.59	.38	.18
Employment	1.06	−.18	−.04	.14	.36	.61	.82	.89	.82	.67	.47	.25
Hours per worker	.54	.08	.21	.35	.49	.66	.71	.59	.43	.29	.11	−.02
Hours (establishment survey)	1.65	−.23	−.07	.14	.39	.66	.88	.92	.81	.64	.42	.21
GNP/hours (household survey)	.88	.11	.21	.34	.48	.50	.51	.21	−.02	−.25	−.34	−.36
GNP/hours (establishment survey)	.83	.40	.46	.49	.53	.43	.31	−.07	−.31	−.49	−.52	−.50
Average hourly real compensation (business sector)	.91	.30	.37	.40	.42	.40	.35	.26	.17	.05	−.08	−.20
Capital input												
Nonresidential capital stock*	.62	−.58	−.61	−.51	−.48	−.31	−.08	.16	.39	.56	.66	.70
Structures	.37	−.45	−.51	−.55	−.53	−.44	−.29	−.10	.09	.25	.38	.45
Producers' durable equipment	.99	−.57	−.58	−.53	−.41	−.22	.02	.26	.47	.62	.70	.71
Inventory stock (nonfarm)	1.65	−.37	−.33	−.23	−.05	.19	.50	.72	.83	.81	.71	.53

*Based on quarterly data, 1954:1–1984:2.
Source of basic data: Citicorp's Citibase data bank.

Table 17.2
Cyclical behavior of U.S. output and income components (deviations from trend of product and income variables, quarterly, 1954–1989)

Variable x	Volatility (% std. dev.)	Cross correlation of real GNP with										
		$x(t-5)$	$x(t-4)$	$x(t-3)$	$x(t-2)$	$x(t-1)$	$x(t)$	$x(t+1)$	$x(t+2)$	$x(t+3)$	$x(t+4)$	$x(t+5)$
Real gross national product	1.71	−.03	.15	.38	.63	.85	1.00	.85	.63	.38	.15	−.03
Consumption expenditures	1.25	.25	.41	.56	.71	.81	.82	.66	.45	.21	−.02	−.21
Nondurables and services	.84	.20	.38	.53	.67	.77	.76	.63	.46	.27	.06	−.12
Nondurables	1.23	.29	.42	.52	.62	.69	.69	.57	.38	.16	−.05	−.22
Services	.63	.03	.25	.46	.63	.73	.71	.60	.49	.39	.23	.07
Durables	4.99	.25	.38	.50	.64	.74	.77	.60	.37	.10	−.14	−.32
Investment expenditures	8.30	.04	.19	.39	.60	.79	.91	.75	.50	.21	−.05	−.26
Fixed investment	5.38	.09	.25	.44	.64	.83	.90	.81	.60	.35	.08	−.14
Nonresidential	5.18	−.26	−.13	.05	.31	.57	.80	.88	.83	.68	.46	.23
Structures	4.75	−.40	−.31	−.17	.03	.29	.52	.65	.69	.63	.50	.34
Equipment	6.21	−.18	−.04	.14	.39	.65	.85	.90	.81	.62	.38	.15
Residential	10.89	.42	.56	.66	.73	.73	.62	.37	.10	−.15	−.34	−.45
Government purchases	2.07	.00	−.03	−.03	−.01	−.01	.05	.09	.12	.17	.27	.34
Federal	3.68	.00	−.05	−.08	−.09	−.09	−.02	.03	.06	.10	.19	.24
State and local	1.19	.06	.10	.17	.25	.26	.25	.20	.16	.19	.27	.36
Exports	5.53	−.50	−.46	−.34	−.14	.11	.34	.48	.53	.53	.53	.45
Imports	4.92	.11	.18	.30	.45	.61	.71	.71	.51	.28	.03	−.19
Real net national income												
Labor income*	1.58	−.18	−.02	.18	.42	.68	.88	.90	.80	.62	.40	.19
Capital income**	2.93	.10	.24	.44	.63	.79	.84	.60	.30	.02	−.19	−.29
Proprietors' income and misc.†	2.70	.11	.24	.38	.55	.62	.68	.46	.29	.11	.02	−.10

*Employee compensation is deflated by the implicit GNP price deflator.
**This variable includes corporate profits with inventory valuation and capital consumption adjustments, plus rental income of persons with capital consumption adjustment, plus net interest, plus capital consumption allowances with capital consumption adjustment, all deflated by the implicit GNP price deflator.
†Proprietors' income with inventory valuation and capital consumption adjustments, plus indirect business tax and nontax liability, plus business transfer payments, plus current surplus of government enterprises, less subsidies, plus statistical discrepancy.
Source of basic data: Citicorp's Citibase data bank.

Table 17.3
Cyclical behavior of U.S. output and income component shares (deviations from trend of product and income variables, quarterly, 1954–1989)

Variable x	Mean % of GNP	Volatility (% std. dev.)	Cross correlation of real GNP with										
			$x(t-5)$	$x(t-4)$	$x(t-3)$	$x(t-2)$	$x(t-1)$	$x(t)$	$x(t+1)$	$x(t+2)$	$x(t+3)$	$x(t+4)$	$x(t+5)$
Gross national product													
Consumption expenditures	63.55	.58	.29	.15	-.06	-.32	-.56	-.78	-.68	-.52	-.33	-.17	-.03
Nondurables and services	54.79	.70	.06	-.08	-.27	-.51	-.72	-.89	-.73	-.50	-.23	.01	.18
Durables	8.76	.33	.36	.43	.48	.54	.56	.53	.36	.15	-.10	-.31	-.44
Investment expenditures	15.85	1.07	.03	.18	.36	.56	.75	.87	.71	.47	.18	-.09	-.30
Fixed investment	15.16	.56	.11	.25	.40	.57	.74	.81	.77	.61	.40	.14	-.08
Change in business inventories	.69	.69	.04	.07	.24	.40	.56	.69	.48	.22	-.05	-.25	-.40
Government purchases	20.13	.57	.04	-.09	-.25	-.40	-.55	-.61	-.52	-.36	-.15	.09	.28
Net exports	.47	.45	-.51	-.51	-.48	-.43	-.37	-.28	-.17	.00	.17	.30	.38
Net national income*													
Labor income	58.57	.47	-.29	-.36	-.45	-.52	-.47	-.39	-.03	.23	.42	.48	.46
Capital income	24.38	.42	.19	.25	.36	.43	.48	.43	.17	-.13	-.35	-.48	-.46
Proprietors' income and misc.	17.04	.34	.18	.19	.17	.17	.06	.00	-.16	-.19	-.20	-.11	-.11

* For explanations of the national income components, see notes to Table 17.2.
Source of basic data: Citicorp's Citibase data bank.

Table 17.4
Cyclical behavior of U.S. monetary aggregates and the price level (deviations from trend of money stock, velocity, and price level, quarterly, 1954–1989)

Variable x	Volatility (% std. dev.)	Cross correlation of real GNP with										
		$x(t-5)$	$x(t-4)$	$x(t-3)$	$x(t-2)$	$x(t-1)$	$x(t)$	$x(t+1)$	$x(t+2)$	$x(t+3)$	$x(t+4)$	$x(t+5)$
Nominal money stock*												
Monetary base	.88	−.12	.02	.14	.25	.36	.41	.40	.37	.32	.28	.26
M1	1.68	.01	.12	.23	.33	.35	.31	.22	.15	.09	.07	.07
M2	1.51	.48	.60	.67	.68	.61	.46	.26	.05	−.15	−.33	−.46
M2 − M1	1.91	.53	.63	.67	.65	.56	.40	.20	−.01	−.21	−.39	−.53
Velocity*												
Monetary base	1.33	−.26	−.15	.00	.22	.40	.59	.50	.37	.22	.08	−.08
M1	2.02	−.24	−.19	−.12	−.01	.14	.31	.32	.27	.20	.10	.00
M2	1.84	−.63	−.59	−.48	−.29	−.05	.24	.34	.40	.43	.44	.43
Price level												
Implicit GNP deflator	.89	−.50	−.61	−.68	−.69	−.64	−.55	−.43	−.31	−.17	−.04	.09
Consumer price index	1.41	−.52	−.63	−.70	−.72	−.68	−.57	−.41	−.24	−.05	.14	.30

* Based on quarterly data, 1959:1–1989:4.
Source of basic data: Citicorp's Citibase data bank.

the cycle. Correspondingly, a series that *lags* the cycle by $j > 0$ quarters would have the largest correlation coefficient in the column headed by $x(t + j)$. For example, productivity is a series that leads the cycle, whereas the stock of inventories is one that lags the cycle.

We let the neoclassical growth model dictate which facts to examine and how to organize them. The aggregate economy can be divided broadly into three sectors: businesses, households, and government. In the business sector, the model emphasizes production inputs as well as output components. Households allocate income earned in the business sector to consumption and saving. In the aggregate, there is an accounting relation between household saving and business investment. Households allocate a fraction of their discretionary time to income-earning activities in the business sector. The remaining fraction goes to nonmarket activities, usually referred to as leisure but sometimes (perhaps more appropriately) as input to household production. This time-allocation decision has received little attention in growth theory, but it is crucial to business cycle theory. The government sector, which is at the heart of public finance theory, also could play a significant role for business cycles.

The standard version of the neoclassical growth model abstracts from money and therefore provides little guidance about which of the nominal variables to examine. Given the prominence that monetary shocks have held for many years as the main candidate for the impulse to business cycles, it seems appropriate that we also examine the cyclical behavior of monetary aggregates and nominal prices.

Real Facts

Production Inputs
We first examine real (nonmonetary) series related to the inputs in aggregate production. The cyclical facts are summarized in Table 17.1. Since it is not unreasonable to think of the inventory stock as providing productive services, we include this series with the labor and capital inputs.

The two most common measures of the labor input are aggregate hours-worked according to the household survey and, alternatively, the payroll or establishment survey. We see in Table 17.1 that total hours with either measure is strongly procyclical and has cyclical variation which, in percentage terms, is almost as large as that of real GNP. (For a visual representation of this behavior, see Figure 17.3). The capital stock, in contrast, varies smoothly over the cycle and is essentially uncorrelated with contemporaneous real GNP. The correlation is large, however, if the capital stock is

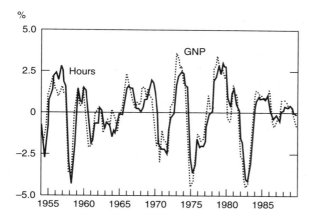

Figure 17.3
Deviations from Trend of U.S. Real Gross National Product and Hours Worked: Quarterly,
1954–1989. The estimate of hours worked uses the establishment survey. Source of basic
data: Citicorp's Citibase data bank.

shifted back by about a year. In other words, business capital lags the cycle
by at least a year. The inventory stock also lags the cycle, but only by
about half a year. In percentage terms, the inventory stock is nearly as
volatile as quarterly real GNP.

The hours-worked series from the household survey can be decomposed
into employment fluctuations on the one hand and variations in hours per
worker on the other. Employment lags the cycle, while hours per worker is
nearly contemporaneous with it, with only a slight lead. Much more of the
volatility in total hours worked is caused by employment volatility than
by changes in hours per worker. If these two subseries were perfectly
correlated, their standard deviations would add up to the standard deviation of total hours. Although not perfectly correlated, their correlation is
quite high, at 0.86. Therefore, employment accounts for roughly two-thirds
of the standard deviation in total hours while hours per worker accounts
for about one-third.

As a measure of the aggregate labor input, aggregate hours has a problem: it does not account for differences across workers in their relative
contributions to aggregate output. That is, the hours of a brain surgeon are
given the same weight as those of an orderly. This disparity would not be
problematic if the cyclical volatility of highly skilled workers resembled
that of the workers who are less skilled. But it doesn't. The hours of the
less-skilled group are much more variable, as established in one of our

recent studies (Kydland and Prescott 1989). Using data for nearly 5,000 people from all major demographic groups over the period 1969–82, we found that, cyclically, aggregate hours is a poor measure of the labor input. When people were weighted by their relative human capital, the labor input for this sample and period varied only about two-thirds as much as did aggregate hours. We therefore recommend that the cyclical behavior of labor productivity (as reported by GNP/hours in Table 17.1) be interpreted with caution.

Since the human-capital-weighted cyclical measure of labor input fluctuates less than does aggregate hours, the implicit real wage (the ratio of total real labor compensation to labor input) is even more procyclical than average hourly real compensation. (For the latter series, see Table 17.1.) This finding that the real wage behaves in a reasonably strong procyclical manner is counter to a widely held belief in the literature. (For a fairly recent expression of this belief, see the article by Lawrence Summers [Chapter 15], which states that there is "no apparent procyclicality of real wages.")

Output Components

Real GNP is displayed in Figure 17.4, along with its three major components: consumption, investment, and government purchases. These three components do not quite add up to real GNP, the difference being accounted for by net exports and change in business inventories. Because household investment in consumer durables behaves similarly to fixed investment in the business sector, we have added those two series. By far the largest component (nearly two-thirds) of total output is consumption of nondurable goods and services. This component, moreover, has relatively little volatility. The chart shows that the bulk of the volatility in aggregate output is due to investment expenditures.

The cyclical components (relative to cyclical real GNP) of consumer nondurables and services, consumer durable investment, fixed investment, and government purchases are reported in Table 17.2 and plotted in Figures 17.5–17.8. From the table and figures, can see that all but government purchases are highly procyclical. Household and business investments in durables have similar amplitudes of percentage fluctuations. Expenditures for consumer durables leads slightly while nonresidential fixed investment lags the cycle, especially investment in structures. Consumer nondurables and services is a relatively smooth series.

Some of the interesting features of the other components are that government purchases has no consistent pro- or countercyclical pattern, that

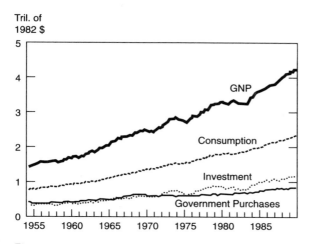

Figure 17.4
U.S. Real Gross National Product and Its Components: Quarterly, 1954–1989. Consumption includes nondurable goods and services. Investment is the sum of consumer durable investment and business fixed investment. Components do not add to total because net exports and the change in business inventories are excluded. Source of basic data: Citicorp's Citibase data bank.

imports is procyclical with no phase shift, and that exports is procyclical but lags the cycle by from six months to a year.

The cyclical behavior of the major output components, measured as shares of real GNP, is reported in Table 17.3. Using fractions rather than the logarithms of the series permits us to include some series that could not be used in Table 17.2 because they are negative during some quarters. We see that the change in business inventories is procyclical. Net exports is a countercyclical variable, with the association being strongest for exports shifted back by about a year.

Factor Incomes
Tables 17.2 and 17.3 also provide information about factor incomes, which are the components of national income. The cyclical behavior of factor incomes is described in terms of their levels (Table 17.2) and their shares of GNP (Table 17.3). Since proprietors' income includes labor and capital income, we treat this component (plus some small miscellaneous components) separately. We find that proprietors' income, as a share of national income, is uncorrelated with the cycle.

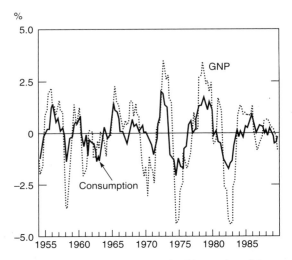

Figure 17.5 Consumption of Nondurable Goods and Services

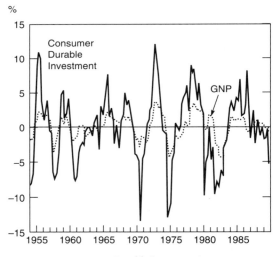

Figure 17.6 Consumer Durable Investment

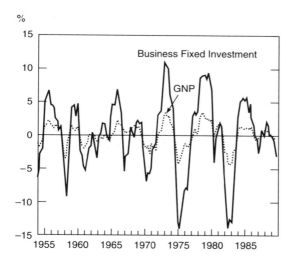

Figure 17.7 Business Fixed Investment

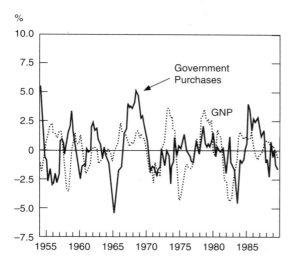

Figure 17.8 Government Purchases

Figures 17.5–17.8
Deviations from Trend of U.S. Real Gross National Product and Its Components: Quarterly,
1954–1989. Source of basic data: Citicorp's Citibase data bank.

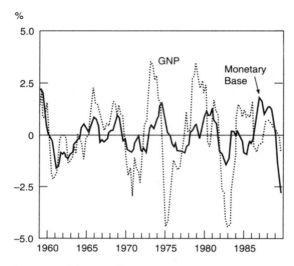

Figure 17.9 Monetary Base

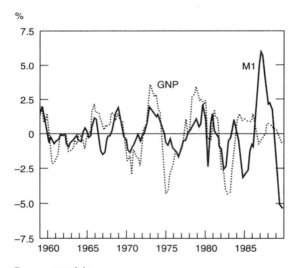

Figure 17.10 M1

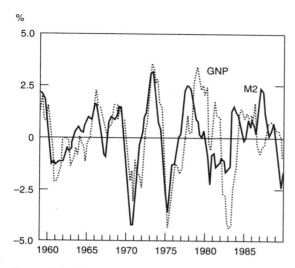

Figure 17.11 M2

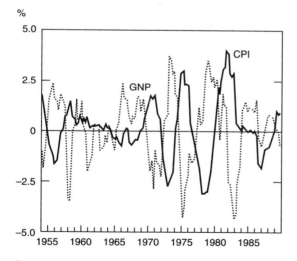

Figure 17.12 Price Level (Consumer Price Index)

Figures 17.9–17.12
Deviations from Trend of U.S. Real Gross National Product and Selected Nominal Aggregates: Quarterly, 1959–1989; for the price level, 1954–1989. Source of basic data: Citicorp's Citibase data bank.

Table 17.2 shows that both labor income and capital income are strongly procyclical and that capital income is highly volatile. Table 17.3 shows that, measured as shares of total income, labor income is countercyclical while capital income is procyclical.

Nominal Facts

The statistical properties of the cyclical components of various nominal aggregates are summarized in Table 17.4, and four of these series along with cyclical real GNP are plotted on Figures 17.9–17.12.

Monetary Aggregates
There is no evidence that either the monetary base or M1 leads the cycle, although some economists still believe this monetary myth. Both the monetary base and M1 series are generally procyclical and, if anything, the monetary base lags the cycle slightly.

An exception to this rule occurred during the expansion of the 1980s. This expansion, so long and steady, has even led some economists and journalists to speculate that the business cycle is dead (Zarnowitz 1989 and *The Economist* 1989). During the expansion, M1 was uncommonly volatile, and M2, the more comprehensive measure of the money stock, showed some evidence that it leads the cycle by a couple quarters.

The difference in the behavior of M1 and M2 suggests that the difference of these aggregates (M2 minus M1) should be considered. This component mainly consists of interest-bearing time deposits, including certificates of deposit under $100,000. It is approximately one-half of annual GNP, whereas M1 is about one-sixth. The difference of M2 − M1 leads the cycle by even more than M2, with the lead being about three quarters.

From Table 17.4 it is also apparent that money velocities are procyclical and quite volatile.

Price Level
Earlier in this paper, we documented the view that the price level is always procyclical. This myth originated from the fact that, during the period between the world wars, the price level *was* procyclical. But because of the Koopmans taboo against reporting business cycle facts, no one bothered to ascertain the cyclical behavior of the price level since World War II. Instead, economists just carried on, trying to develop business cycle theories in which the price level plays a central role and behaves procyclically. The fact is, however, that whether measured by the implicit GNP deflator

or by the consumer price index, the U.S. price level clearly has been countercyclical in the post–Korean War period.

Concluding Remarks

Let us reemphasize that, unlike Burns and Mitchell, we are not claiming to measure business cycles. We also think it inadvisable to start our economics from some statistical definition of trend and deviation from trend, with growth theory being concerned with trend and business cycle theory with deviations. Growth theory deals with both trend and deviations.

The statistics we report are of interest, given neoclassical growth theory, because they are—or maybe were—in apparent conflict with that theory. Documenting real or apparent systematic deviations from theory is a legitimate activity in the natural sciences and should be so in economics as well.

We hope that the facts reported here will help guide the selection of model economies to study. We caution that any theory in which pro-cyclical prices figure crucially in accounting for postwar business cycle fluctuations is doomed to failure. The facts we report indicate that the price level since the Korean War moves countercyclically.

The fact that the transaction component of real cash balances (M1) moves contemporaneously with the cycle while the much larger nontransaction component (M2) leads the cycle suggests that credit arrangements could play a significant role in future business cycle theory. Introducing money and credit into growth theory in a way that accounts for the cyclical behavior of monetary as well as real aggregates is an important open problem in economics.[6]

Notes

The authors thank the National Science Foundation for financial support.

1. The view of Hayek (1933, p. 33) in the 1930s and Lucas (1977, p. 7) in the 1970s is that answering this question is one of the outstanding challenges to economic research.

2. King and Plosser (1989) describe a well-defined, judgment-free scheme that successfully mimics the Burns and Mitchell procedure. The description of the cycles in the time series plotted in Figure 17.1 is based on this procedure.

3. The reason for linearity is that the first two moments of the transformed data are functions of the first two moments, and not the higher moments, of the original data. The principal rationale for the same transformation being applied to all time series is that it makes little sense to carry out the analog of growth accounting with the inputs to the production function subject to one transformation and the outputs subject to another.

4. A short FORTRAN subroutine that efficiently computes the trend and deviations components is available on request to the Research Department, Federal Reserve Bank of Minneapolis. The computation time required by this algorithm increases linearly with the length of the sample period, as do storage requirements.

5. This approach was introduced in an unpublished paper by Hodrick and Prescott (1980).

6. Two interesting attempts to introduce money into growth theory are the work of Cooley and Hansen (1989) and Hodrick, Kocherlakota, and D. Lucas (1991). Their approach focuses on the transaction role of money.

18

The Labor Market in Real Business Cycle Theory

Gary D. Hansen and Randall Wright

The basic objective of the real business cycle research program is to use the neoclassical growth model to interpret observed patterns of fluctuations in overall economic activity. If we take a simple version of the model, calibrate it to be consistent with long-run growth facts, and subject it to random technology shocks calibrated to observed Solow residuals, the model displays short-run cyclical behavior that is qualitatively and quantitatively similar to that displayed by actual economies along many important dimensions. For example, the model predicts that consumption will be less than half as volatile as output, that investment will be about three times as volatile as output, and that consumption, investment, and employment will be strongly positively correlated with output, just as in the postwar U.S. time series.[1] In this sense, the real business cycle approach can be thought of as providing a benchmark for the study of aggregate fluctuations.

In this article, we analyze the implications of real business cycle theory for the labor market. In particular, we focus on two facts about U.S. time series: the fact that hours worked fluctuate considerably more than productivity and the fact that the correlation between hours worked and productivity is close to zero.[2] These facts and the failure of simple real business cycle models to account for them have received considerable attention in the literature. [See, for example, the extended discussion by Christiano and Eichenbaum (1992) and the references they provide.] Here we first document the facts. We then present a baseline real business cycle model (essentially, the divisible labor model in Hansen 1985a) and compare its predictions with the facts. We then consider four extensions of the baseline model that are meant to capture features of the world from which this model abstracts. Each of these extensions has been discussed in the litera-

Reprinted from the *Federal Reserve Bank of Minneapolis Quarterly Review*, Spring 1992.

ture. However, we analyze them in a unified framework with common functional forms, parameter values, and so on, so that they can be more easily compared and evaluated in terms of how they affect the model's ability to explain the facts.

The standard real business cycle model relies exclusively on a single technology shock to generate fluctuations, so the fact that hours worked vary more than productivity implies that the short-run labor supply elasticity must be large. The first extension of the model we consider is to recognize that utility may depend not only on leisure today but also on past leisure; this possibility leads us to introduce *nonseparable preferences*, as in Kydland and Prescott 1982.[3] This extension of the baseline model has the effect of increasing the relevant elasticity, by making households more willing to substitute leisure in one period for leisure in another period in response to short-run productivity changes. At the same time, with these preferences, households do not increase their work hours in response to permanent productivity growth. Thus, the nonseparable leisure model generates an increased standard deviation of hours worked relative to productivity without violating the long-run growth fact that hours worked per capita have not increased over long periods despite large increases in productivity.

The second extension of the baseline real business cycle model we consider is to assume that labor is *indivisible*, so that workers can work either a fixed number of hours or not at all, as in Hansen 1985a. In this version of the model, all variation in the labor input must come about by changes in the number of employed workers, which is the opposite of the standard model, where all variation comes about by changes in hours per worker. Although the data display variation along both margins, the indivisible labor model is perhaps a better abstraction, since the majority of the variance in the labor input in the United States can be attributed to changes in the number of employed workers. In the equilibrium of the indivisible labor model, individual workers are allocated to jobs randomly, and this turns out to imply that the aggregate economy displays a large labor supply elasticity even though individual hours do not respond at all to productivity or wage changes for continuously employed workers. The large aggregate labor supply elasticity leads to an increased standard deviation of hours relative to productivity, as compared to the baseline model.

Neither nonseparable utility nor indivisible labor changes the result that the real business cycle model implies a large positive correlation between hours and productivity while the data display a near-zero correlation. This result arises because the model is driven by a single shock to the aggregate production function, which can be interpreted as shifting the labor demand curve along a stable labor supply curve and inducing a very tight positive relationship between hours and productivity. Hence, the next extension we consider is to introduce *government spending* shocks, as in Christiano and Eichenbaum 1992. If public consumption is an imperfect substitute for private consumption, then an increase in government spending has a negative wealth effect on individuals, which induces them to work more if leisure is a normal good. Therefore, government spending shocks can be interpreted as shifting the labor supply curve along the labor demand curve. Depending on the size of and the response to the two shocks, with this extension the model can generate a pattern of hours versus productivity closer to that found in the data.

The final extension we consider is to introduce *household production* as in Benhabib, Rogerson, and Wright 1991. The basic idea is to recognize that agents derive utility from home-produced as well as market-produced consumption goods and derive disutility from working in the home as well as in the market. In this version of the model, individuals, by working less at home, can increase hours of market work without reducing leisure as much. Therefore, the addition of household production increases the short-run labor supply elasticity and the standard deviation of hours relative to productivity. Furthermore, to the extent that shocks to household production are less than perfectly correlated with shocks to market production, individuals will have an incentive to substitute between home and market activity at a point in time. This is in addition to the standard incentive to substitute between market activity at different dates. Therefore, home production shocks, like government spending shocks, shift the labor supply curve and can generate a pattern of hours versus productivity closer to that found in the data.

Our basic finding is that each of these four extensions to the baseline real business cycle model improves its performance quantitatively, even though the extensions work through very different economic channels. As will be seen, some of the resulting models seem to do better than others along certain dimensions, and some depend more sensitively than others on parameter values. Our goal here is not to suggest that one of these models is best for all purposes; which is best for any particular application will depend on the context. Rather, we simply want to illustrate here how incorporating certain natural features into the standard real business cycle model affects its ability to capture some key aspects of labor market behavior.

Table 18.1
Cyclical properties of U.S. time series, 1955:3–1988:2

Data series*	Variable j	% S.D. σ_j	Variable vs. output σ_j/σ_y	cor(j, y)	Hours vs. productivity σ_h/σ_w	cor(h, w)
Output	y	1.74	1.00	1.00	—	—
Consumption	c	.84	.48	.75	—	—
Investment	i	5.48	3.16	.90	—	—
Labor market:						
1. Household survey (all industries)						
Hours worked	h	1.42	.82	.87	1.64	.10
Productivity	w	.87	.50	.58		
2. Establishment survey (nonag. industries)						
Hours worked	h	1.63	.94	.88	1.95	−.13
Productivity	w	.84	.48	.36		
3. Nonag. industries (from household survey)						
Hours worked	h	1.75	1.01	.76	1.44	−.35
Productivity	w	1.21	.70	.34		
4. Efficiency units (from Hansen 1991)						
Hours worked	h	1.66	.96	.74	1.37	−.30
Productivity	w	1.22	.70	.41		

* All series are quarterly, are in 1982 dollars, and have been logged and detrended with the Hodrick-Prescott filter. The output series, y, is the gross national product; c is consumption of nondurables and services; and i is fixed investment. Productivity is $w = y/h$.
Sources: Citicorp's Citibase data bank and Hansen 1991.

The Facts

In this section, we document the relevant business cycle facts. We consider several measures of hours worked and productivity and two sample periods (since some of the measures are available only for a shorter period). As Prescott did [in Chapter 14], we define the *business cycle* as fluctuations around some slowly moving trend. For any given data series, we first take logarithms and then use the Hodrick-Prescott filter (as described by Prescott [in Chapter 14]) to remove the trend

Table 18.1 contains some summary statistics for quarterly U.S. data that are computed from deviations constructed in this manner. The sample period is from 1955:3 to 1988:2. The variables are y = output, c = consumption (nondurables plus services), i = fixed investment, h = hours worked, and w = average productivity (output divided by hours worked).[4]

Table 18.2
Cyclical properties of U.S. time series, 1947:1–1991:3

Data series*	Variable j	% S.D. σ_j	Variable vs. output		Hours vs. productivity	
			σ_j/σ_y	$cor(j, y)$	σ_h/σ_w	$cor(h, w)$
Output	y	1.92	1.00	1.00	—	—
Consumption	c	.86	.45	.71	—	—
Investment	i	5.33	2.78	.73	—	—
Labor market:						
1. Household survey (all industries)						
Hours worked	h	1.50	.78	.82	1.37	.07
Productivity	w	1.10	.57	.63		
2. Establishment survey (nonag. industries)						
Hours worked	h	1.84	.96	.90	2.15	−.14
Productivity	w	.86	.45	.31		

* All series are quarterly, are in 1982 dollars, and have been logged and detrended with the Hodrick-Prescott filter. The output series, y, is the gross national product; c is consumption of nondurables and services; and i is fixed investment. Productivity is $w = y/h$.
Sources: Citicorp's Citibase data bank and Hansen 1991.

For each variable j, we report the following statistics: the (percent) standard deviation σ_j, the standard deviation relative to that of output σ_j/σ_y, and the correlation with output $cor(j, y)$. We also report the relative standard deviation of hours to that of productivity σ_h/σ_w and the correlation between hours and productivity $cor(h, w)$.

We present statistics for four measures of h and w. Hours series 1 is total hours worked as recorded in the household survey and covers all industries. Hours series 2 is total hours worked as recorded in the establishment survey and covers only nonagricultural industries. These two hours series could differ for two reasons: they are from different sources, and they cover different industries.[5] To facilitate comparison, we also report, in hours series 3, hours worked as recorded in the household survey but only for nonagricultural industries. Finally, hours series 4 is a measure of hours worked in efficiency units.[6]

The reason for the choice of 1955:3–1988:2 as the sample period is that hours series 3 and 4 are only available for this period. However, the other series are available for 1947:1–1991:3, and Table 18.2 reports statistics from this longer period for the available variables.

Both Table 18.1 and Table 18.2 display the standard business cycle facts. All variables are positively correlated with output. Output is more variable than consumption and less variable than investment. Hours are slightly less variable than or about as variable as output, with σ_h/σ_y ranging between 0.78 and 1.01, depending on the hours series and the period. Overall, all variables are more volatile in the longer period, but the relative volatilities of the variables are about the same in the two periods. (An exception is investment, which looks somewhat less volatile relative to output in the longer period.)

We want to emphasize two things. First, hours fluctuate more than productivity, with the magnitude of σ_h/σ_w ranging between 1.37 and 2.15, depending on the series and the period. Second, the correlation between hours and productivity is near zero or slightly negative, with cor(h, w) ranging between -0.35 and 0.10, depending on the series and the period. Figure 18.1 shows the scatter plot of h versus w from hours series 1 for the longer sample period. (Plots from the other hours series look similar.)

The Standard Model

In this section, we present a standard real business cycle model and investigate its implications for the facts just described.

The model has a large number of homogeneous households. The representative household has preferences defined over stochastic sequences of consumption c_t and leisure l_t, described by the utility function

$$U = E \sum_{t=0}^{\infty} \beta^t u(c_t, l_t) \tag{1}$$

where E denotes the expectation and β the discount factor, with $\beta \in (0, 1)$. The household has one unit of time each period to divide between leisure and hours of work:

$$l_t + h_t = 1. \tag{2}$$

The model has a representative firm with a constant returns-to-scale Cobb-Douglas production function that uses capital k_t and labor hours h_t to produce output y_t:

$$y_t = f(\tilde{z}_t, k_t, h_t) = \exp(\tilde{z}_t)k_t^\theta h_t^{1-\theta} \tag{3}$$

where θ is the capital share parameter and $\tilde{z}_t$ is a stochastic term representing random technological progress. In general, we would assume that $\tilde{z}_t = z_t + \bar{z}t$, where $\bar{z}$ is a constant yielding exogenous deterministic growth and z_t evolves according to the process

$$z_{t+1} = \rho z_t + \varepsilon_t \tag{4}$$

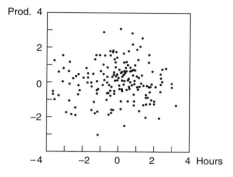

Figure 18.1 The U.S. Data, 1947:1–1991:3 Based on the Household Survey

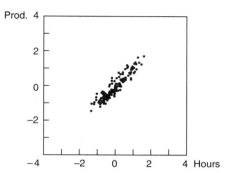

Figure 18.2 The Standard Model

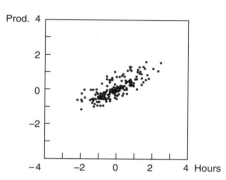

Figure 18.3 The Nonseparable Leisure Model

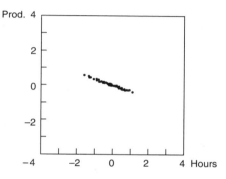

Figure 18.4 The Government Spending Model without Technology Shocks ...

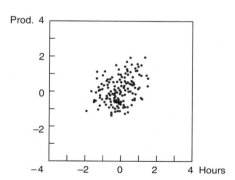

Figure 18.5 ... And with Technology Shocks

Figures 18.1–18.5
Hours Worked vs. Productivity in the Data and the Models: Percentage Deviations from Trend. Source of basic data: Citicorp's Citibase data bank.

where $\rho \in (0, 1)$ and ε_t is independent and normally distributed with mean zero and standard deviation σ_ε. However, in this paper, we abstract from exogenous growth by setting $\bar{z} = 0$.[7] Capital evolves according to the law of motion

$$k_{t+1} = (1 - \delta)k_t + i_t \tag{5}$$

where δ is the depreciation rate and i_t investment. Finally, the economy must satisfy the resource constraint

$$c_t + i_t = y_t. \tag{6}$$

We are interested in the competitive equilibrium of this economy. Since externalities or other distortions are not part of this model (or the other models that we consider), the competitive equilibrium is efficient. Hence, we can determine the equilibrium allocation by solving the social planner's problem of maximizing the representative agent's expected utility subject to feasibility constraints. That problem in this case is to maximize U subject to equations (2)–(6) and some initial conditions (k_0, z_0). The solution can be represented as a pair of stationary decision rules for hours and investment, $h_t = h^*(k_t, z_t)$ and $i_t = i^*(k_t, z_t)$, that determine these two variables as functions of the current capital stock and technology shock. The other variables, such as consumption and output, can be determined from the decision rules using the constraints, while prices can be determined from the relevant marginal conditions.

Standard numerical techniques are used to analyze the model. We choose functional forms and parameter values and substitute the constraint $c_t + i_t = f(z_t, k_t, h_t)$ into the instantaneous return function u to reduce the problem to one of maximizing an objective function subject to linear constraints. Then we approximate the return function with a quadratic return function by taking a Taylor's series expansion around the deterministic steady state. The resulting linear-quadratic problem can be easily solved for optimal linear decision rules, $h_t = h(k_t, z_t)$ and $i_t = i(k_t, z_t)$; see Hansen and Prescott 1991 for details. Using these decision rules, we simulate the model, take logarithms of the artificially generated data, apply the Hodrick-Prescott filter, and compute statistics on the deviations (exactly as we did to the actual time series). We run 100 simulations of 179 periods (the number of quarters in our longer data set) and report the means of the statistics across these simulations.

Preferences are specified so that the model is able to capture the long-run growth fact that per capita hours worked display no trend despite large increases in productivity and real wages. When preferences are time separable, capturing this fact requires that the instantaneous utility function satisfy

$$u(c, l) = \log(c) + v(l) \tag{7}$$

or

$$u(c, l) = c^\sigma v(l)/\sigma \tag{8}$$

where σ is a nonzero parameter and $v(l)$ is an increasing and concave function. (See King, Plosser, and Rebelo 1987, for example.) Intuitively, the growth facts imply that the wealth and substitution effects of long-run changes in productivity cancel, so the net effect is that hours worked do not change.[8] We consider only preferences that satisfy (7) or (8); in fact, for convenience, we assume that

$$u(c, l) = \log(c) + A\log(l). \tag{9}$$

Parameter values are calibrated as follows. The discount factor is set to $\beta = 0.99$ so as to imply a reasonable steady-state real interest rate of 1 percent per period (where a period is one quarter). The capital share parameter is set to $\theta = 0.36$ to match the average fraction of total income going to capital in the U.S. economy. The depreciation rate is set to $\delta = 0.025$, which (given the above-mentioned values for β and θ) implies a realistic steady-state ratio of capital to output of about 10 and a ratio of investment to output of 0.26. The parameter A in the utility function (9) is chosen so that the steady-state level of hours worked is exactly $h = 1/3$, which matches the fraction of discretionary time spent in market work found in time-use studies (for example, Juster and Stafford 1991). Finally, the parameter ρ in (4) is set to $\rho = 0.95$, and the standard deviation of ε is set to $\sigma_\varepsilon = 0.007$, which are approximately the values settled on by Prescott (Chapter 14).

We focus on the following statistics generated by our artificial economy: the standard deviation of output; the standard deviations of consumption, investment, and hours relative to the standard deviation of output; the ratio of the standard deviation of hours to the standard deviation of productivity; and the correlation between hours and productivity. The results are shown in Table 18.3, along with the values for the same statistics from our longer sample from the U.S. economy (from Table 18.2). We emphasize the following discrepancies between the simulated and actual data. First, the model has a predicted standard deviation of output which is considerably less than the same statistic for the U.S. economy in either period. Second,

Table 18.3
Cyclical properties of U.S. and model-generated time series

| Type of data or model | % s.d. of output σ_y | Variable vs. output | | | | Hours vs. productivity | |
		Consumption σ_c/σ_y	Investment σ_i/σ_y	Hours σ_h/σ_y	Productivity σ_w/σ_y	σ_h/σ_w	cor(h, w)
U.S. time series*							
Output	1.92	.45	2.78	—	—	—	—
Hours worked:							
1. Household survey (all industries)	—	—	—	.78	.57	1.37	.07
2. Establishment survey (nonag. industries)	—	—	—	.96	.45	2.15	−.14
Models**							
Standard	1.30	.31	3.15	.49	.53	.94	.93
Nonseparable leisure	1.51	.29	3.23	.65	.40	1.63	.80
Indivisible labor	1.73	.29	3.25	.76	.29	2.63	.76
Government spending	1.24	.54	3.08	.55	.61	.90	.49
Home production	1.71	.51	2.73	.75	.39	1.92	.49

*U.S. data here are the same as those in Table 18.2; they are for the longer time period: 1947:1–1991:3.
**The standard deviations and correlations computed from the models' artificial data are the sample means of statistics computed for each of 100 simulations. Each simulation has 179 periods, the number of quarters in the U.S. data.
Source: Citicorp's Citibase data bank.

the model predicts that σ_h/σ_w is less than one, while it is greater than one in the data. Third, the correlation between hours and productivity in the model is far too high.

The result that output is not as volatile in the model economy as in the actual economy is not too surprising, since the model relies exclusively on a single technology shock, while the actual economy is likely to be subject to other sources of uncertainty as well. The result that in the model hours worked do not fluctuate enough relative to productivity reflects the fact that agents in the model are simply not sufficiently willing to substitute leisure in one period for leisure in other periods. Finally, the result that hours and productivity are too highly correlated in the model reflects the fact that the only impulse driving the system is the aggregate technology shock.

Figure 18.2 depicts the scatter plot between h and w generated by the model. Heuristically, Figure 18.2 displays a stable labor supply curve traced out by a labor demand curve shifting over time in response to technology shocks. This picture obviously differs from that in Figure 18.1.

Nonseparable Leisure

Following Kydland and Prescott (1982), we now attempt to incorporate the idea that instantaneous utility might depend not just on current leisure, but rather on a weighted average of current and past leisure. Hotz, Kydland, and Sedlacek (1988) find evidence in the panel data that this idea is empirically plausible. One interpretation they discuss concerns the fact that individuals need to spend time doing household chores, making repairs, and so on, but after doing so they can neglect these things for a while and spend more time working in the market until the results of their home work depreciate. The important impact of a nonseparable utility specification for our purposes is that, if leisure in one period is a relatively good substitute for leisure in nearby periods, then agents will be more willing to substitute intertemporally, and this increases the short-run labor supply elasticity.

Assume that the instantaneous utility function is $u(c_t, L_t) = \log(c_t) + A\log(L_t)$, where L_t is given by

$$L_t = \sum_{i=0}^{\infty} a_i l_{t-i} \tag{10}$$

and impose the restriction that the coefficients a_i sum to one. If we also impose the restriction that

$$a_{i+1} = (1 - \eta)a_i \tag{11}$$

for $i = 1, 2, \ldots$, so that the contribution of past leisure to L_t decays geometrically at rate η, then the two parameters a_0 and η determine all of the coefficients in (10). Since L_t, and not simply l_t, now provides utility, individuals are more willing to intertemporally substitute by working more in some periods and less in others. (At the same time, in a deterministic steady state or along a deterministic balanced growth path, this model delivers the correct prediction concerning the effect of productivity growth on hours worked.)

The equilibrium can again be found as the solution to a social planner's problem, which in this case maximizes U subject to (2)–(6), (10)–(11), and initial conditions.[9] The parameter values we use for the preference structure are $a_0 = 0.35$ and $\eta = 0.10$, which are the values implied by the estimates in Hotz, Kydland, and Sedlacek 1988; other parameter values are the same as in the preceding section.

The results are in Table 18.3. Notice that output is more volatile here than in the standard model, with σ_y increasing from 1.30 to 1.51. Also, the standard deviation of hours worked relative to that of productivity has increased considerably, to $\sigma_h/\sigma_w = 1.63$, and the correlation between hours and productivity has decreased somewhat to 0.80. Figure 18.3 depicts the scatter plot of h versus w generated by this model. Although these points trace out a labor supply curve that is flatter than the one in Figure 18.2, the model still does not generate the cloud in Figure 18.1. We conclude that introducing nonseparable leisure improves things in terms of σ_h/σ_w, but does little for $\text{cor}(h, w)$.

Indivisible Labor

We now take up the indivisible labor model of Hansen (1985a), in which individuals are constrained to work either zero or $\hat{h}$ hours in each period, where $0 < \hat{h} < 1$. Adding this constraint is meant to capture the idea that the production process has important nonconvexities or fixed costs that may make varying the number of employed workers more efficient than varying hours per worker. As originally shown by Rogerson (1984, 1988), in the equilibrium of this model, individuals will be randomly assigned to employment or unemployment each period, with consumption insurance against the possibility of unemployment. Thus, this model generates fluctuations in the number of employed workers over the cycle. As we shall see, it also has the feature that the elasticity of total hours worked increases relative to the standard model.

Let π_t be the probability that a given agent is employed in period t, so that $H_t = \pi_t \hat{h}$ is per capita hours worked if we assume a large number of ex ante identical agents. Also, let c_{0t} denote the consumption of an unemployed agent and c_{1t} the consumption of an employed agent. As part of the dynamic social planning problem, π_t, c_{0t}, and c_{1t} are chosen to maximize

$$Eu(c_t, l_t) = \pi_t u(c_{1t}, 1 - \hat{h}) + (1 - \pi_t)u(c_{0t}, 1) \tag{12}$$

in each period, subject to the following constraint:

$$\pi_t c_{1t} + (1 - \pi_t)c_{0t} = c_t \tag{13}$$

where c_t is total per capita consumption. When $u(c, l) = \log(c) + A\log(l)$, the solution can be shown to imply that $c_{1t} = c_{0t} = c_t$.[10]

Therefore, in the case under consideration, expected utility can be written

$$Eu(c_t, l_t) = \log(c_t) + \pi_t A\log(1 - \hat{h}) = \log(c_t) - BH_t \tag{14}$$

where $B \equiv -A\log(1 - \hat{h})/\hat{h} > 0$ and, as defined above, H_t is hours worked per capita. Therefore, the indivisible labor model is equivalent to a divisible labor model with preferences described by

$$\tilde{U} = E \sum_{t=0}^{\infty} \beta^t \tilde{u}(c_t, H_t) \tag{15}$$

where $\tilde{u}(c_t, H_t) = \log(c_t) - BH_t$. Based on this equivalence, we can solve the indivisible labor model as if it were a divisible labor model with a different instantaneous utility function, by maximizing $\tilde{U}$ subject to (2)–(6) and initial conditions.[11]

Two features of the indivisible labor economy bear mention. First, as discussed earlier, fluctuations in the labor input come about by fluctuations in employment rather than fluctuations in hours per employed worker. This is the opposite of the standard model and is perhaps preferable, since the majority of the variance in total hours worked in the U.S. data is accounted for by variance in the number of workers.[12] Second, the indivisible labor model generates a large intertemporal substitution effect for the representative agent because instantaneous utility, $\tilde{u}(c, H)$, is linear in H, and therefore the indifference curves between leisure in any two periods are linear. This is true despite the fact that hours worked are constant for a continuously employed worker.

Return to Table 18.3 for the results of our simulations of this model.[13] The indivisible labor model is considerably more volatile than the standard model, with σ_y increasing from 1.30 to 1.73. Also, σ_h/σ_w has increased from 0.94 to 2.63, actually somewhat high when compared to the U.S. data. Of course, this model is extreme in the sense that all fluctuations in the labor input result from changes in the number of employed workers, and models in which both the number of employed workers and the number of hours per worker vary fall somewhere between the standard divisible labor model and the indivisible labor model with respect to this statistic. (See Kydland and Prescott 1991 or Cho and Cooley 1989, for example.) Finally, the model implies that $\text{cor}(h, w) = 0.76$, slightly lower than the models discussed above but still too high. For the sake of brevity, the scatter plot between h and w is omitted; for the record, it looks similar to the one in Figure 18.3, although the indivisible labor model displays a little more variation in hours worked.

Government Spending

We now introduce stochastic government spending, as in Christiano and Eichenbaum 1992. (That paper also provides motivation and references to related work.)

Assume that government spending, g_t, is governed by

$$\log(g_{t+1}) = (1 - \lambda)\log(\bar{g}) + \lambda\log(g_t) + \mu_t \qquad (16)$$

where $\lambda \in (0, 1)$ and μ_t is independent and normally distributed with mean zero and standard deviation σ_μ. Furthermore, as in Christiano and Eichenbaum 1992, assume that μ_t is independent of the technology shock. Also assume that government spending is financed by lump-sum taxation and that it enters neither the utility function nor the production function.[14] Then the equilibrium allocation for the model can be found by solving the planner's problem of maximizing U subject to (16), (2)–(5), and, instead of (6), the new resource constraint

$$c_t + i_t + g_t = y_t. \qquad (17)$$

An increase in g_t is a pure drain on output here. Since leisure is a normal good, the negative wealth effect of an increase in g_t induces households to work more. Intuitively, shocks to g_t shift the labor supply curve along the demand curve at the same time that technology shocks shift the labor demand curve along the supply curve. This first effect produces a negative relationship between hours and productivity, while the second effect produces a positive relationship. The net effect on the correlation between hours and productivity in the model depends on the size of the g_t shocks and on the implied wealth effect, which depends, among other things, on the parameter λ in the law of motion for g_t (because temporary shocks have a smaller wealth effect than permanent shocks). Hence, the calibration of this law of motion is critical. An ordinary least squares regression based on equation (16) yields estimates for λ and σ_μ of 0.96 and 0.021, respectively. (In addition, the average of g_t/y_t in our sample, which is 0.22, is used to calibrate $\bar{g}$.)

For the results, turn again to Table 18.3. The government spending model actually behaves very much like the standard model, except that the correlation between hours and productivity decreases to $\text{cor}(h, w) = 0.49$, which is better than the previous models although still somewhat larger than the U.S. data. Figure 18.4 displays the scatter plot generated by the model with only government spending shocks (that is, with the variance in the technology shock set to $\sigma_\varepsilon = 0$), and Figure 18.5 displays the scatter plot for the model with both shocks. These charts illustrate the intuition behind the results: technology shocks shift labor demand and trace out the labor supply curve, government shocks shift labor supply and trace out the labor demand curve, and both shocks together generate a combination of these two effects. The net results will be somewhat sensitive to the size of and the response to the two shocks; however, for the estimated parameter values, this model generates a scatter plot that is closer to the data than does the standard model.[15]

Home Production

We now consider the household production model analyzed in Benhabib, Rogerson, and Wright 1991. (That paper also provides motivation and references to related work.)

Instantaneous utility is still written $u(c, l) = \log(c) + A\log(l)$, but now consumption and leisure have a different interpretation. We assume that

$$c_t = [ac_{Mt}^e + (1 - a)c_{Ht}^e]^{1/e} \tag{18}$$

$$l_t = 1 - h_{Mt} - h_{Ht} \tag{19}$$

where c_{Mt} is consumption of a market-produced good, c_{Ht} is consumption of a home-produced good, h_{Mt} is hours worked in the market sector, and h_{Ht} is hours worked in the home, all in period t. Notice that the two types of work are assumed to be perfect substitutes, while the two consumption goods are combined by an aggregator that implies a constant elasticity of substitution equal to $1/(1 - e)$.

This model has two technologies, one for market production and one for home production:

$$f(z_{Mt}, k_{Mt}, h_{Mt}) = \exp(z_{Mt})k_{Mt}^\theta h_{Mt}^{1-\theta} \tag{20}$$

$$g(z_{Ht}, k_{Ht}, h_{Ht}) = \exp(z_{Ht})k_{Ht}^{\eta}h_{Ht}^{1-\eta} \tag{21}$$

where θ and η are the capital share parameters. The two technology shocks follow the processes

$$z_{Mt+1} = \rho z_{Mt} + \varepsilon_{Mt} \tag{22}$$

$$z_{Ht+1} = \rho z_{Ht} + \varepsilon_{Ht} \tag{23}$$

where the two innovations are normally distributed with standard deviations σ_M and σ_H, have a contemporaneous correlation $\gamma = \text{cor}(\varepsilon_{Mt}, \varepsilon_{Ht})$, and are independent over time. In each period, a capital constraint holds: $k_{Mt} + k_{Ht} = k_t$, where total capital evolves according to $k_{t+1} = (1 - \delta)k_t + i_t$. Finally, the constraints

$$c_{Mt} + i_t = f(z_{Mt}, k_{Mt}, h_{Mt}) \tag{24}$$

$$c_{Ht} = g(z_{Ht}, k_{Ht}, h_{Ht}) \tag{25}$$

imply that all new capital is produced in the market sector.

The parameters β, θ, δ, and ρ are set to the values used in the previous sections. The two utility parameters A and a are set to deliver steady-state values of $h_M = 0.33$ and $h_H = 0.28$, as found in the time-use studies (Juster and Stafford 1991), and the capital share parameter in the household sector is set to $\eta = 0.08$, implying a steady-state ratio of c_H/c_M of approximately $1/4$.[16] The variances of the two shocks are assumed to be the same: $\sigma_H = \sigma_M = 0.007$. The parameter e, which determines the elasticity of substitution between c_M and c_H, and γ, which is the correlation between ε_M and ε_H, are set to the benchmark values used in Benhabib, Rogerson, and Wright 1991: $e = 0.8$ and $\gamma = 2/3$.

The results are at the bottom of Table 18.3. In the home production model, output is more volatile than in the standard model and about as volatile as in the indivisible labor model. The standard deviation of hours relative to productivity has increased considerably compared to the standard model, to $\sigma_h/\sigma_w = 1.92$. And $\text{cor}(h, w)$ has decreased to 0.49, the same as in the model with government spending.[17]

The intuition behind these results is that agents substitute in and out of market activity more in the home production model than in the standard model because they can use nonmarket activity as a buffer. The degree to which agents do this depends on their willingness to substitute c_M for c_H, as measured by e, and on their incentive to move production between the two sectors, as measured by γ. (Lower values of γ entail more frequent divergence between z_M and z_H and, hence, more frequent opportunities to specialize over time.) Note that some aspects of the results do not actually depend on home production being stochastic.[18] However, the correlation between productivity and market hours does depend critically on the size of the home technology shock, exactly as it depends on the size of the second shock in the government spending model. We omit the home production model's scatter plot between h and w, but it looks similar to that of the model with government shocks.

Conclusion

We have presented several extensions to the standard real business cycle model and analyzed the extent to which they help account for the U.S. business cycle facts, especially those facts concerning hours and productivity. Introducing nonseparable leisure, indivisible labor, or home production increases the elasticity of hours worked with respect to short-run productivity changes. Introducing a second shock, either to government spending or to the home production function, reduces the correlation between hours worked and productivity.[19]

Note that our goal has not been to convince you that any of these models is unequivocally to be preferred. Our goal has been simply to explain some commonly used real business cycle models and compare their implications for the basic labor market facts.

Notes

This paper is also available in Spanish in *Cuadernos Economicos de ICE*, a quarterly publication of the Ministerio de Economía y Hacienda. The paper appears here with the permission of that publication's editor, Manuel Santos.

1. These properties are also observed in other countries and time periods. See Kydland and Prescott's paper [Chapter 17 in this volume] for an extended discussion of the postwar U.S. data, and see Blackburn and Ravn 1991 or Backus and Kehoe 1992 for descriptions of other countries and time periods.

2. Although we concentrate mainly on these cyclical facts, we also mention an important long-run growth fact that is relevant for much of our discussion: total hours worked per capita do not display trend growth despite large secular increases in average productivity and real wages.

3. Note that these preferences are nonseparable between leisure in different periods: they may or may not be separable between leisure and consumption in a given period.

4. We use the letter w because average productivity is proportional to marginal productivity (given our functional forms), which equals the real *wage* rate in our models.

5. The establishment series is derived from payroll data and measures hours paid for, while the household series is taken from a survey of workers that attempts to measure hours

actually worked. These two measures could differ, for example, because some workers may be on sick leave or vacation but still get paid. The household series is a better measure of the labor input, in principle, but because it is based on a survey of workers rather than payroll records, it is probably less accurate.

6. Efficiency units are constructed from hours series 3 by disaggregating individuals into age and sex groups and weighting the hours of each group by its relative hourly earnings; see Hansen 1991 for details.

7. Adding exogenous growth does not affect any of the statistics we report (as long as the parameters are recalibrated appropriately) given the way we filter the data; therefore, we set $\bar{z} = 0$ in order to simplify the presentation. See Hansen 1989.

8. Other specifications can generate a greater short-run response of hours worked to productivity shocks; but while this is desirable from the point of view of explaining cyclical observations, it is inconsistent with the growth facts. For example, the utility function used in Greenwood, Hercowitz, and Huffman 1988, $u(c, l) = v(c + Al)$, has a zero wealth effect and hence a large labor supply elasticity, but implies that hours worked increase over time with productivity growth. This specification is consistent with balanced growth if we assume the parameter A grows at the same average rate as technology. Although such an assumption may seem contrived, it can be justified as the reduced form of a model with home production in which the home and market technologies advance at the same rate on average, as shown in Greenwood, Rogerson, and Wright, forthcoming.

9. For the solution techniques that we use, this problem is expressed as a dynamic program. The stock of accumulated past leisure is defined to be X_t, and we write

$$L_t = a_0 l_t + \eta(1 - a_0)X_t$$

$$X_{t+1} = (1 - \eta)X_t + l_t.$$

These equations replace (10) and (11) in the recursive formulation.

10. This implication follows from the fact that u is separable in c and l and does not hold for general utility functions; see Rogerson and Wright 1988.

11. Since the solution to the planner's problem in the indivisible labor model involves random employment, we need to use some type of lottery or sunspot equilibrium concept to support it as a decentralized equilibrium; see Shell and Wright 1993.

12. See Hansen 1985a for the U.S. data. Note, however, that European data display greater variance in hours per worker than in the number of workers; see Wright 1991, p. 17.

13. The new parameter B is calibrated so that steady-state hours are again equal to $1/3$; the other parameters are the same as in the standard model.

14. A generalization is to assume that instantaneous utility can be written $u(C, l)$, where $C = C(c, g)$ depends on private consumption and government spending. The special case where $C = c$ is the one we consider here, while the case where $C = c + g$ can be interpreted as the standard model, since then increases in g can be exactly offset by reductions in c and the other variables will not change. Therefore, the model with $C = c + g$ generates exactly the same values of all variables, except that $c + g$ replaces c. The assumption that c and g are perfect substitutes implies that they are perfectly negatively correlated, however. A potentially interesting generalization would be to assume that

$$C(c, g) = [\alpha c^\varphi + (1 - \alpha)g^\varphi]^{1/\varphi}$$

where $1/(1 - \varphi)$ is the elasticity of substitution.

15. The size of the wealth effect depends on the extent to which public consumption and private consumption are substitutes. For example, if they were perfect substitutes, then a unit increase in g would simply crowd out a unit of c with no effect on hours worked or any of the other endogenous variables. We follow Christiano and Eichenbaum 1992 in considering the extreme case where g does not enter utility at all. Also, the results depend on the (counterfactual) assumption that the shocks to government spending and technology are statistically independent. Finally, the results depend on the estimates of the parameters in the law of motion (16). The estimates in the text are from the period 1947:1–1991:3 and are close to the values used in Christiano and Eichenbaum 1992. Estimates from our shorter sample period, 1955:3–1988:2, imply a higher λ of 0.98 and a lower σ_μ of 0.012, which in simulations yield $\mathrm{cor}(h, w) = 0.65$.

16. The two parameters θ and η can be calibrated to match the observed average levels of market capital (producer durables and nonresidential structures) and home capital (consumer durables and residential structures) in the U.S. economy. This requires a lower value for θ and a higher value for η than used here, as discussed in Greenwood, Rogerson, and Wright, forthcoming.

17. The exact results are somewhat sensitive to changes in the parameters e and γ, for reasons discussed in the next paragraph.

18. Even if the variance of the shock to the home technology is set to zero, shocks to the market technology will still induce relative productivity differentials across sectors. And even if the two shocks are perfectly correlated and of the same magnitude, agents will still have an incentive to switch between sectors over time because capital is produced exclusively in the market. It is these effects that are behind the increase in the labor supply elasticity.

19. Other models can be constructed by combining the extensions considered here. Other extensions not considered here can also affect the implications of the model for the labor market facts, including distorting taxation as in Braun 1990 or McGrattan 1991 and nominal contracting as in Cho and Cooley 1990.

19

Economic Fluctuations without Shocks to Fundamentals; Or, Does the Stock Market Dance to Its Own Music?

S. Rao Aiyagari

I can calculate the motions of the heavenly bodies, but not the madness of people.
—Sir Isaac Newton

Last October's dramatic 23 percent decline in the U.S. stock market sent shock waves through the economy, policymakers, and economists. Non-economists and economists alike scurried to find some previously unforeseen new development that might explain the crash. Could the crash have been caused by the sudden appearance of a comet, by a supernova explosion in a distant galaxy, or by a startling change in sunspot activity? Or perhaps it was caused by psychological factors? Until recently, most economists would have pooh-poohed such ideas as crazy.

To an economist (and also to market analysts on Wall Street) it seems natural to look for changes in consumer tastes or technological factors as possible explanations. After all, one would expect that a sudden shift in consumer tastes toward eating out would drive up the stocks of fast-food chains and restaurants or that a new technological development in the computer industry would drive up the stocks of computer firms. (This surely explains why a considerable amount of market research on Wall Street consists of keeping track of technological developments and shifts in consumer trends.) It is not easy, however, to see why there should be any relationship between extraterrestrial happenings and new developments in consumer tastes or technology.

Thus it is that most of the currently popular models of economic fluctuations are based on recurring random shocks to economic *fundamentals*. These fundamentals consist, of course, of consumer tastes and the techno-

Reprinted from the *Federal Reserve Bank of Minneapolis Quarterly Review*, Winter 1988.

logical possibilities available to firms. Shocks to consumer tastes affect the demands for various goods, whereas shocks to technology—by affecting costs of production—affect the supplies of various goods. In this way, these shocks give rise to fluctuations in prices and quantities. In the absence of such continued random influences on tastes or technology, the currently popular models would predict that the economy would (in a reasonable amount of time) settle down into a steady state, with no fluctuations whatsoever.[1]

The stock market crash has revived interest in the possibility of explaining fluctuations without such shocks to fundamentals. One clear reason for this renewed interest has been the inability of economists or market analysts to find any new developments in tastes or technology which could explain a crash of that magnitude. The appeal to psychological factors or, in general, random factors unrelated to fundamentals is, however, not new. In 1936, toward the end of the Great Depression, John Maynard Keynes published his classic *General Theory of Employment, Interest, and Money*, in which he attributed business fluctuations not to random shocks to tastes or technology, but to the *animal spirits* of investors. That is, investors may be seized by moods of optimistic or pessimistic expectations which bear no necessary relation to any changes in tastes or technology. Keynes also asserted that such expectations on the part of investors need not necessarily be irrational. The moods of optimism or pessimism can cause investors to either expand or contract investment spending; this, in turn, can lead to either an overall economic expansion or a contraction, thereby justifying the optimistic or pessimistic expectations. Thus, these animal spirits can become self-fulfilling and hence be *rational*.[2] This alternative view of business fluctuations may be described as *nonfundamental, intrinsic,* or *endogenous.*

In this article I explain how economic fluctuations can occur without shocks to fundamentals. This is not to say that taste or technology shocks do not exist or that they are totally unimportant. Instead, the purpose here is to try and understand whether there exist forces intrinsic to an economic system that tend toward instability; whether such instability is bad from the point of view of economic welfare; and, if so, what sorts of policies or institutions may be set in place to avoid such instability and put the economy on a steady course.[3]

To explain these issues, I describe two models that illustrate intrinsic fluctuations and the role of animal spirits. Both models are simplified versions of existing ones that are part of the burgeoning literature on intrinsic fluctuations. Throughout the paper, the emphasis is on explaining how

such fluctuations can arise in an environment in which the economic fundamentals consisting of tastes and technology are unchanging over time.
Further, in both models, expectations are assumed to be rational. Without
this assumption, one can explain anything, given a sufficiently perverse or
irrational view of the world. Requiring beliefs to be rational imposes a
notion of consistency between beliefs and reality and rules out explanations based on a pathological view of the world.

The first model described is a simple model of stock price determination
in which consumers may hold many possible sets of beliefs that may be
self-fulfilling and hence rational. Some of these beliefs may even be based
on random factors totally unrelated to the objective factors of tastes and
technology.[4] Furthermore, some of these beliefs lead the economy to a
steady course while many others set the economy on a wildly fluctuating
path.[5]

The second model described is a model of frictional unemployment in
which production and exchange take place in a decentralized fashion.[6] I
show that there may be several stable paths for the economy along which
beliefs are self-fulfilling. Among these, some involve high employment and
output whereas others involve low employment and output, depending on
whether expectations are optimistic or pessimistic. In addition, there are
many fluctuating paths corresponding to changing moods of optimism and
pessimism. I argue that the low employment and output situation has
some resemblance to the widespread lack of confidence and consequent
breakdown of market interactions that seem to characterize deep economic
depressions.

Can such models explain the qualitative and quantitative properties of
economic fluctuations in real economies? Perhaps. But I attempt no such
explanations here, since the models described are chosen for their exposi-
tional simplicity rather than their ability to explain observed business fluctuations. I believe it is much too early to judge the empirical applicability
of these models, for only recently have economists started analyzing such
models. Further development and elaboration of such models may prove to
be empirically useful, in addition to being theoretically insightful.

Are there any policy implications that emerge from the study of these
models? Yes, although these implications are subject to some important
qualifications. I show that for each model there exist very simple policies
which can eliminate all fluctuations and set the economy on a unique stable
course. In addition, for the frictional unemployment model I show that such
a policy can move the economy from a state of low employment and
output to one of high employment and output in which many people are
better off and none is worse off.

A Stock Price Model

In this section I describe and analyze a simple model of stock price determination and then discuss an appropriate stabilization policy.

Consider an environment that is completely stationary and in which there is one unit of a perfectly divisible asset (a *stock*, if you like) which pays a constant and known stream of dividends forever. Consumers can purchase shares in this stock with a view to obtaining dividends and capital gains when the shares are sold. The current stock price depends on the current demand, which in turn depends on the capital gains (or losses) that consumers expect. This, in turn, depends on the price at which the stock can be sold, which again depends on the demand for the stock on the part of future buyers. I show by means of examples how, even in a completely stationary environment, the stock price can be subject to wild gyrations. My exposition is based on the models of Grandmont (1985) and Azariadis (1981).[7]

People, Preferences, and Prices

Suppose that at each date t, numbered 1, 2, 3, ..., a representative consumer who lives for two periods is born. A consumer born at date t is *young* at t and *old* at $t + 1$. Assume that at date 1, in addition to the young consumer, there is also an old consumer who was born in the previous period. In each period of life, the consumer is endowed with one unit of total time, which may be divided between leisure time and working time. When the consumer is young, each unit of working time results in w_1 units of the consumption good and when old, each unit of working time results in w_2 units of the consumption good. The consumption good is nonstorable and may be either consumed or traded. The old consumer at date 1 is endowed with one unit of a stock which yields a constant dividend stream of d (in units of consumption) each period. The old consumer will, of course, collect the current dividend and then trade the stock for consumption from the young at date 1. The young consumer, in turn, will hold the shares till period 2, then collect the dividend and sell the shares to the new young at date 2. This process then goes on forever.

Let $c_1(t)$ and $c_2(t)$ be the consumptions at date t of the young and the old consumers, respectively, and let $l_1(t)$ and $l_2(t)$ be the amounts of leisure time enjoyed by the young and the old. The young consumer at each date t maximizes lifetime utility, denoted by u and given by

$$u = U(c_1(t)), l_1(t)) + V(c_2(t + 1), l_2(t + 1)). \tag{1}$$

In equation (1), the functions $U(\cdot)$ and $V(\cdot)$ represent utility derived in the first and second periods of life. Utility in each period of life depends on consumption and the amount of leisure time enjoyed in that period.

The budget constraints faced by the consumer are

$$c_1(t) = w_1[1 - l_1(t)] - p(t)s(t) \tag{2}$$

$$c_2(t + 1) = w_2[1 - l_2(t + 1)] + [p^e(t + 1) + d]s(t). \tag{3}$$

In equations (2) and (3), $p(t)$ is the stock price at t, $p^e(t + 1)$ is the consumer's expectation (held with certainty) of the stock price at $t + 1$, and $s(t)$ is the quantity of shares purchased by the young at t. Equation (2) states that consumption by the young equals the total output produced when young minus the value of shares purchased. Note that $[1 - l_1(t)]$ is the amount of time spent working when young, and hence $w_1[1 - l_1(t)]$ is the output produced when young. Equation (3) states that consumption by the old equals the total output produced when old plus the dividends on shares held and the proceeds from the sale of shares. The consumer chooses lifetime consumptions, leisure times, and the demand for shares $s(t)$ in order to maximize lifetime utility given by (1).

The determination of the stock price is shown in Figure 19.1. It is easy to show that the demand for shares depends on $p(t)$ and $p^e(t + 1)$ and that demand is downward sloping in the current price $p(t)$. (See the Appendix for a derivation.) Figure 19.1 depicts a demand curve such that the demand for shares is decreasing in $p(t)$. The position of the demand curve in Figure 19.1 depends on the expected future price $p^e(t + 1)$. The supply of shares is perfectly inelastic at one unit since there is a fixed amount of one unit of the stock available, all of which is supplied by the old inelastically. Thus. the equilibrium condition for shares is given by

$$s(t) = 1. \tag{4}$$

That is, the equilibrium price $p(t)$ must be such that the demand for shares equals the supply.

Since the position of the demand curve for shares in Figure 19.1 depends on the consumer's expectation of next period's price, it follows that the current equilibrium price of shares also depends on the price expected to prevail next period. Now assume that the expectations of consumers are *rational*; that is, the price that consumers at t expect will prevail at $t + 1$ is in fact the actual price at $t + 1$. Therefore, we have

$$p^e(t + 1) = p(t + 1). \tag{5}$$

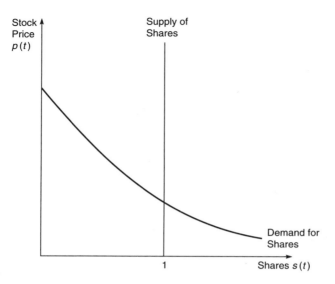

Figure 19.1
How the Stock Price Is Determined in the Model. The position of the demand curve
depends on the expected future price $p^e(t + 1)$.

It follows that the current equilibrium price $p(t)$ depends on next period's
price $p(t + 1)$. This relationship is illustrated in Figure 19.2 for a particular
choice of the utility functions $U(\cdot)$ and $V(\cdot)$. These functions have been
chosen in such a way as to generate a hump-shaped curve in which the
hump occurs to the left of the 45-degree line.

It is important to understand the reason for the particular hump-shaped
curve (with the hump occurring to the left of the 45-degree line) shown in
Figure 19.2, since this shape is the source of fluctuations to be described.
This shape arises due to the conflict between the *substitution effect* and the
wealth effect of a change in $p(t + 1)$ on the demand for shares. These effects
may be explained as follows. An increase in $p(t + 1)$ increases the rate of
return on the stock, thereby making saving for future consumption more
attractive. This induces the consumer to reduce current consumption and
increase saving, and therefore increases the demand for shares. This is the
substitution effect. However, an increase in $p(t + 1)$ also increases the
value of savings in the form of shares and therefore increases wealth. This
perceived increase in wealth causes the consumer to increase current (as
well as future) consumption. The increase in current consumption reduces
the demand for shares. This is the wealth effect. Consequently, the substitu-

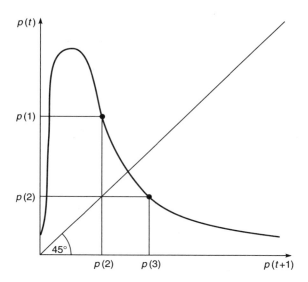

Figure 19.2
The Relationship between Today's and Tomorrow's Stock Price

tion effect and the wealth effect of an increase in $p(t + 1)$ have opposite effects on the demand curve for shares. At low values of $p(t + 1)$ the substitution effect dominates the wealth effect; as a result, an increase in $p(t + 1)$ increases the demand for shares. Thus, the demand curve in Figure 19.1 shifts to the right, thereby increasing the current equilibrium price $p(t)$. At high values of $p(t + 1)$ the wealth effect dominates the substitution effect; as a result, an increase in $p(t + 1)$ reduces the demand for shares. Therefore, the demand curve in Figure 19.1 shifts to the left, thereby lowering the current equilibrium price $p(t)$. This conflict between the two effects is the reason for the hump-shaped relationship between $p(t)$ and $p(t + 1)$ depicted in Figure 19.2—a relationship which yields a variety of possibilities for fluctuations.

Since Figure 19.2 gives a relationship between the stock price today and the stock price tomorrow, it is possible to calculate some equilibrium time paths for the stock price for various parameter values. The way to do this is also illustrated in Figure 19.2. Start with some price $p(1)$ at date 1. Then find a price $p(2)$ such that the point $(p(1), p(2))$ is on the hump-shaped curve. Then use the 45-degree line to transpose $p(2)$ to the vertical axis and find a price $p(3)$ such that the point $(p(2), p(3))$ is on the curve. By proceeding this way, we can construct a time path for the stock price. This time path constitutes a perfect foresight equilibrium path because each pair of prices $(p(t), p(t + 1))$ has the property (by construction) that $p(t)$ is the equilibrium price at t, given that consumers expect the price at $t + 1$ to be $p(t + 1)$.

Once we have an equilibrium time path for the stock price, we can also calculate time paths for the real interest rate and total output by making use of the following relationships. The real interest rate $r(t)$ from t to $t + 1$ is given by

$$r(t) = [p(t + 1) - p(t) + d]/p(t). \tag{6}$$

There is a simple linear relationship between total output $y(t)$ and the stock price $p(t)$ for the chosen utility functions $U(\cdot)$ and $V(\cdot)$; that is,

$$y(t) = a + bp(t). \tag{7}$$

Equation (7) is derived in the Appendix.

Illustrations of Intrinsic Fluctuations

In what follows, I illustrate the variety of fluctuations that can be generated by the model. Each illustration corresponds to a different choice of utility functions.

At this point it is worth emphasizing that each economy illustrated is completely stationary in terms of its characteristics over time. Each generation looks exactly the same as any other in terms of its tastes, endowments, and productivities. That is, the fundamentals of each economy are constant over time. In spite of this constancy in the fundamentals, we will see that it is possible for the stock price, real interest rate, and output to exhibit pretty wild behavior.

Periodic and Bizarre Paths
The model can generate a variety of periodic time paths. In Figures 19.3 and 19.4 we see that there is indeed a constant time path that can be generated for the stock price. This price, denoted p^*, corresponds to the intersection in Figure 19.3 of the 45-degree line and the hump-shaped curve between $p(t)$ and $p(t + 1)$. If all consumers expect that the price next period will be p^*, then it will be p^* today and hence forever. From equations (6) and (7), it follows that the interest rate and output will also be constant over time in this example. However, Figures 19.3 and 19.4 also show how another time path for the stock price can be generated, along which it

follows an up-and-down cyclical path that repeats every two periods. Therefore, equations (6) and (7) imply that along this alternative path, the interest rate and output will also exhibit a similar pattern. In Figures 19.5 and 19.6 we see the generation of a four-period cycle in stock prices (and hence also in the interest rate and output). Figures 19.7 and 19.8 show how a three-period cycle can be generated.

The model can also generate some bizarre time paths. Figure 19.9 depicts a pretty bizarre time path for the stock price in which it is hard to discern any strictly periodic pattern. Figure 19.10 shows a pattern that is hard to distinguish from a time path that might be generated due to the presence of random shocks, even though such shocks have been explicitly ruled out in constructing these illustrations.

Although we have shown only one or two of the possible time paths of the stock price for each example, there are in fact many possible time paths for each set of parameter values. For instance, the example that gives rise to the four-period cycle of Figure 19.6 can also give rise to a two-period cycle. The example that produces the bizarre path of Figure 19.9 can also give rise to cycles of two, four, and eight periods as well as periods of some higher powers of two. And the parameter values used to generate Figure 19.8 can also give rise to cycles of *every integer* period in addition to the bizarre sorts of time paths, as in Figures 19.9 and 19.10, which seem to lack any periodic pattern.[8] Furthermore, in every example there is an equilibrium path along which the stock price is constant over time. This is because in all of these examples, the nature of the relationship between $p(t)$ and $p(t + 1)$ is similar to the hump-shaped curve shown in Figure 19.2. This constant time path is indicated by the line marked p^* on the figures.

Animal Spirits and Hemlines
We now turn to an illustration of the kind of time path that can be generated when consumers are driven by animal spirits. Suppose consumers believe the following maxim:

When hemlines are up, stocks will be up;
when hemlines are down, stocks will be down.

Suppose further that the fashion industry decides randomly when hemlines will be up and when they will be down, perhaps by consulting a different astrologer each period. Even though such randomness has no connection with the tastes, endowments, or productivities of consumers in the model, it turns out that stock prices (and hence interest rates and output) respond to such extraneous randomness.

Relationships between Today's and Tomorrow's Stock Price

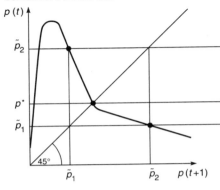

Figure 19.3 When $\mu = 4.0$

Equilibrium Time Paths for the Stock Price

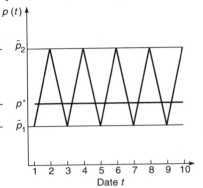

Figure 19.4 A Two-Period Cycle

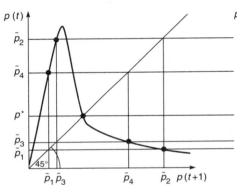

Figure 19.5 When $\mu = 6.0$

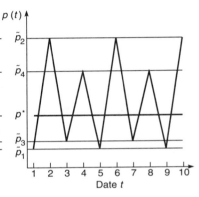

Figure 19.6 A Four-Period Cycle

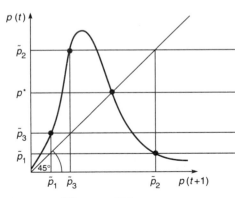

Figure 19.7 When $\mu = 11.0$

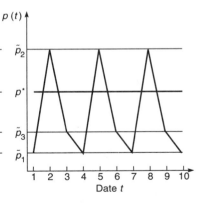

Figure 19.8 A Three-Period Cycle

Figures 19.3–19.8
Some Periodic Cycles Generated by the Stock Price Model. These figures are based on computer simulations. For details of the parameter values and simulation method used, see the Appendix.

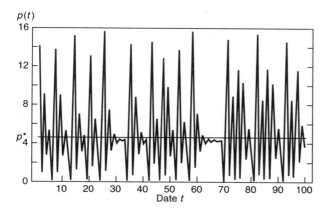

Figure 19.9 When $\mu = 7.5$

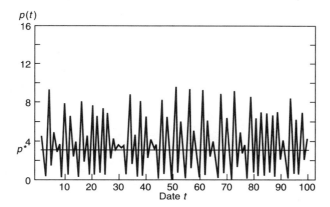

Figure 19.10 When $d = 0.001$, $\bar{p} = 10.0$, and $\mu = 15.0$

Figures 19.9 and 19.10
Some Bizarre Time Paths for the Stock Price. These figures are reproduced from actual computer simulations. For details of the parameter values and simulation method used, see the Appendix.

I now explain how such beliefs, which have no relation to economic fundamentals, can be self-fulfilling. Let the indexes i and j indicate the state of hemlines at dates t and $t + 1$, respectively, and suppose that each index takes the value of 1 or 2, depending on whether hemlines are high or low. In state i, let p_i be the stock price, s_i the demand for shares, $c_1(i)$ and $c_2(i)$ the consumptions of the young and the old, and $l_1(i)$ and $l_2(i)$ the leisure times of the young and the old. Let π_{ij} be the probability that the hemline state at $t + 1$ is j, given that the hemline state at t is i. The young consumer at t maximizes expected utility given the state i at t. This is denoted by $E(u|i)$. Using (1), the expression for expected utility can be written as

$$E(u|i) = U(c_1(i), l_1(i)) + \sum_j \pi_{ij} V(c_2(j), l_2(j)). \tag{8}$$

In equation (8), we are simply adding up the utilities in each possible state in the second period of life, weighted by the respective probabilities.

The consumer's budget constraints can be written, by analogy with (2) and (3), as

$$c_1(i) = w_1[1 - l_1(i)] - p_i s_i \tag{9}$$

$$c_2(j) = w_2[1 - l_2(j)] + (p_j + d)s_i. \tag{10}$$

The interpretation of the constraints (9) and (10) is similar to that for (2) and (3).

It is now possible to solve for the consumer's demand for shares. We can then impose the equilibrium condition (4) and solve for the prices p_1 and p_2. (Details are provided in the Appendix.) These prices together with the probabilities π_{ij} determine the possible time paths for the stock price. Such an equilibrium is self-fulfilling, or rational, because the distribution of future prices on the basis of which the consumer determines the demand for shares is in fact the actual distribution of prices that lead to equilibrium between the demand for and supply of shares. Thus, the consumer's beliefs are consistent with the actual behavior of equilibrium prices.

Figure 19.11 shows an example in which the stock price fluctuates randomly between two values, marked p_1 and p_2, with probabilities as noted. The reason for such behavior is the following. If the current state i of hemlines were to be different (say, 2 instead of 1), then the probabilities π_{ij} for the future state j of hemlines will be different. Given the belief held by consumers about the relationship between hemlines and stock prices, the probabilities π_{ij} affect the consumer's expectation of tomorrow's stock price. This influences the consumer's current demand for the stock and hence its current price.

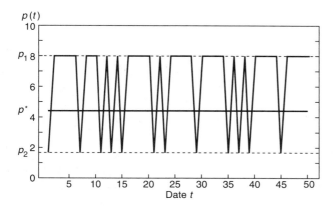

Probability Matrix:

$$\begin{bmatrix} \pi_{11} & \pi_{12} \\ \pi_{21} & \pi_{22} \end{bmatrix} = \begin{bmatrix} .49 & .51 \\ .95 & .05 \end{bmatrix}$$

π_{ij} = probability that the stock price is p_j tomorrow, given that it is p_i today, for i =1,2.

Figure 19.11
The Hemline Example: An Equilibrium Time Path Generated When Consumers Believe That Movements in Stock Prices and Hemlines Correspond ($\mu = 8.0$). This figure is reproduced from an actual computer simulation. For details of parameter values and simulation method used, see the Appendix.

For this result, it is indeed important that the probabilities π_{ij} vary as i varies. That is, the probability distribution of future hemline states must differ if the current hemline state is different. Otherwise, the consumer's expectation of tomorrow's stock price will be independent of the current state and hence so will be the consumer's demand for shares. Consequently, the current equilibrium price will be the same no matter what the current state is. Rational expectations then imply that the stock price must be constant forever.

Summary
So far we have seen many examples in which even though there is always a path along which stock prices and other variables are constant, there are also many other equilibrium paths along which stock prices and other macroeconomic variables can exhibit somewhat unusual fluctuations. Therefore, it follows that the economy can exhibit instability even when there is a stable path that is attainable if only consumers would believe in it.

Policy Implications

What implications does this simple stock price model have for consumer welfare and government policy? It turns out that every one of the equilibrium paths we have studied has the property of being *Pareto optimal*; that is, it is not possible to make some consumer better off without hurting some other consumer.[9] Therefore, there is no government policy that will improve everyone's lot. However, this conclusion depends on how seriously we take the assumption of *perfect foresight*. Remember that every one of the equilibrium paths was constructed on the assumption that it was perfectly foreseen by all consumers. If consumers make occasional mistakes in expectations, then the welfare properties of the paths discussed may no longer be true. Consequently, there may exist government policies that enhance the welfare of all consumers.

The perfect foresight assumption may not seem unreasonable if the economy has been moving along a constant path or perhaps along a path with an easily discernible cyclical pattern. Then we may reasonably expect that consumers, by looking at the past behavior of stock prices, will be able to form accurate forecasts of their future behavior, somewhat like the chartists on Wall Street. However, some of the paths we have seen (for instance, those in Figures 19.9 and 19.10) are so complex that it is hard to imagine how anyone could form an accurate forecast of the future behavior of stock prices based on past observations.[10] When such forecasting seems difficult, the assumption of rational expectations may be somewhat questionable. At the very least, however, one can argue that the government *ought* to pursue policies that put the economy on a stable path, thereby making it easier for consumers to form accurate forecasts of the future and thus keeping the economy moving along a stable path. The justification for this argument is simply that mistaken expectations are much more likely when the economy is following a highly unstable path.

Do there exist government policies that can eliminate all the highly fluctuating paths we have seen are possible and push the economy inexorably onto a constant path with no fluctuations whatsoever? In the context of the stock price model, there is in fact a fairly simple policy that can achieve this objective: Let the government announce a benchmark stock price p', which is less than w_1, and also levy a tax (or subsidy, if negative) at the proportional rate $[1 - p'/p(t)]$ on the value of shares held by the old at each date t (including the initial old). The proceeds of this tax are handed over to the young at t as a lump-sum rebate (or tax, if negative), denoted $\tau(t)$. This policy will alter the budget constraints (2) and (3) as follows:

$$c_1(t) = w_1[1 - l_1(t)] - p(t)s(t) + \tau(t) \tag{11}$$

$$c_2(t + 1) = w_2[1 - l_2(t + 1)] + [p(t + 1) + d]s(t)$$

$$- [1 - p'/p(t + 1)]p(t + 1)s(t)$$

$$= w_2[1 - l_2(t + 1)] + (p' + d)s(t). \tag{12}$$

Along an equilibrium path, the rebate $\tau(t)$ must satisfy the following relationship:

$$\tau(t) = p(t) - p'. \tag{13}$$

Equation (13) follows because in equilibrium the quantity of shares sold is unity, and hence the value of shares sold is $p(t)$. Therefore, taxes paid must be $p(t)[1 - p'/p(t)]$, which equals $[p(t) - p']$.

It is possible to show that under such a policy, the only possible equilibrium path for the stock price (and hence for the interest rate and output) is a constant one. (See the Appendix for details.) The reason for this is as follows. Since the government taxes away any excess of $p(t + 1)$ above the benchmark price p' [or subsidizes the difference if $p(t + 1)$ falls short of p'], the consumer is, in effect, faced with a future price that is always equal to p'. Consequently, the consumer's current demand for shares depends on p' but not on $p(t + 1)$. Therefore, the current equilibrium price $p(t)$ also depends on p' only and is hence constant over time. This simple policy, therefore, eliminates the possibility of all fluctuations and leads the economy onto a stable path. In addition, it is possible to choose the benchmark price p' in order to ensure that the equilibrium path is Pareto optimal.

The policy just described should be viewed with caution, however. Even though it works for the simple stock price model, it may not work for a more complex model with more assets, uncertainty, and capital accumulation. In practice, the policy is likely to be very difficult to define and implement and may also have undesirable side effects on risk taking and investment. To judge the overall desirability of such a policy, these potential ill effects would have to be weighed against the possible benefits from a stabilized economy and improved forecasting.

A Model of Frictional Unemployment

We now turn to the second model chosen to illustrate intrinsic fluctuations and the role of animal spirits—a model of frictional unemployment.

The concept of *frictional unemployment* plays an important role in policy discussions in government and the media. Frictional unemployment represents unemployment resulting from the imperfect matching of workers and employment opportunities. The *natural* rate of unemployment represents the normal level of frictional unemployment and is taken as the benchmark for full employment. It is often said that in the 1960s, full employment corresponded roughly to a natural rate of unemployment between 3 and 4 percent, while in the 1970s the natural rate of unemployment increased to around 6 percent. This is considered relevant for aggregate demand policies because it is thought that any attempt to keep the unemployment rate below the natural rate will only result in spiraling inflation. In spite of this, most models of business fluctuations eschew any attempt to explain the determination of frictional unemployment and instead focus on explaining the characteristics of fluctuations around the natural rate of unemployment. In contrast, I show here that an explicit attempt to model frictional unemployment leads to some very surprising results and some important policy implications.

The model discussed consists of a large number of producer-traders who can only trade bilaterally, if at all. I show that because of this decentralization, there may be several stationary equilibria in some of which employment and output are higher and many people are better off (and none is worse off) than in others. Which of these equilibria obtains depends on whether the expectations of the producer-traders are optimistic or pessimistic. In addition, there may be fluctuations in employment and output due to changing moods of optimism and pessimism. The model is a simplified version of Diamond's (1984).[11]

An Island Economy

Consider a hypothetical economy in which there are a large number of individuals scattered all over a large number of islands, one person per island. Each individual has the opportunity to produce one unit of a specialized good which is of no use to the producer but is desired by all the other persons. Therefore, each person would like to be able to exchange the good produced (if that person chooses to produce) for the product of another person. This setup is designed to capture the notion that in large, modern industrial economies, people develop specialized skills which are, for the most part, of no use to themselves. Instead, these skills (or goods produced with them) are sold to others and the proceeds are used to purchase goods produced by others.

Assume that the cost of production, measured in units of foregone utility u, is different for different people and varies between u_1 and u_2, where

$0 < u_1 < u_2 < \infty$. Let the distribution function $G(u)$ denote the fraction of people whose costs of production are no higher than u. If an individual chooses to produce, then that person must engage in a search for other producers (across the many islands) in order to trade. Assume that each person can visit only one other island and that the probability of running into a producer (as opposed to a nonproducer) is π. Also assume that each unit of the good yields a utility of u^* when traded. Therefore, if a producer is successful in meeting a trading partner, then each of them receives utility u^*. If a producer is unsuccessful in meeting a trading partner, then the producer receives zero utility, since the product is useless to its maker.[12]

It is now easy to describe an individual's decision regarding whether or not to engage in production. Intuitively, if the probability of meeting another producer π is sufficiently large relative to the cost of production u, then it pays to produce. More formally, the following condition describes the production decision:

If $\pi u^* \geq u$, then produce;

if $\pi u^* < u$, then do not produce.

(14)

In (14), πu^* is the expected benefit (utility) from producing and u is the cost. It follows that the fraction of producers (and also the per capita output) y is given by

$$y = G(\pi u^*). \tag{15}$$

Assume also that $u_2 < u^*$. This assumption has the following implication. If producers could costlessly communicate and trade with each other, then the best situation is one in which everyone produces and trades. Such a situation might arise if all trade took place in a centralized market with everyone present. In this case it pays for even the producer with the highest production costs to produce, and therefore per capita output will be at its maximum possible level of one. In this model the lack of communication and hence coordination among the many producer-traders is the *friction* which prevents a costless centralized market from arising. We will see that because of this friction, it will not be possible to attain the maximum possible per capita output. In fact, the situation could be considerably worse.

Next I need to describe how the probability of a successful match between producers is related to the decisions of all the people. It is intuitively clear that if either all persons or all but one person decide not to produce and seek out trading partners, then the probability π is zero. If everyone decides to produce and seek out trading partners, then the probability of a successful match will be high.[13] Therefore, in general, there is an increasing relationship between the fraction of people who decide to produce and the probability of a match. This is described by the increasing function $f(y)$ as follows:

$$\pi = f(y). \tag{16}$$

Equilibria

It is now easy to describe the determination of the equilibrium values of π and y. Figure 19.12 graphs the two relationships between π and y as given by equations (15) and (16). Equation (15) is marked by G, while (16) is marked by f. By virtue of my assumptions, both functions are increasing.[14] Any intersection of the two curves gives an equilibrium pair (π, y). This pair has the property that given the probability of a match π, a fraction y of people find it profitable to produce; and given the fraction of producers, each person's expectation of the probability of a successful match is accurate. We see that in Figure 19.12 there are three possible equilibrium pairs (π, y), marked low, middle, and high.

There are two remarkable features of this simple model of production and trading. The first is that there may be several equilibria which are distinguished by varying levels of output and trade, depending on the expectations of producers regarding trading opportunities. If expectations are optimistic, so that people think the probability of successfully consummating trade is high, then many people will be induced to produce and seek out partners. This in turn leads to a high probability of success, thereby justifying the optimistic beliefs. This corresponds to the high equilibrium in Figure 19.12, indicating a high level of output and trade. If people have pessimistic expectations of being able to trade, then few will be induced to produce and look for trades. This in turn leads to a low probability of a successful match, thereby justifying the pessimism. In Figure 19.12 this is indicated by the low equilibrium, for low (in this case, zero!) output and trade.

Also shown in Figure 19.12 is a middle equilibrium outcome which, however, is unstable. This is because if some nonproducers become slightly more optimistic than at the middle outcome, then they will choose to produce, which increases the probability of a match for everyone sufficiently that even more nonproducers will choose to produce, and so on, until the high equilibrium is reached. Conversely, if some producers be-

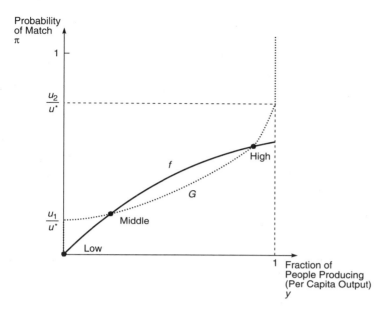

Figure 19.12
Three Equilibria for the Frictional Unemployment Model

come slightly more pessimistic than at the middle outcome, then they will choose not to produce, which decreases the probability of a match sufficiently for the remaining producers so that more producers will stop production, and so on, until the low equilibrium is reached and the economy shuts down. The situation of the low equilibrium economy resembles that of a depression economy.

In fact, the three equilibria marked in Figure 19.12 are not the only equilibria for this economy. There also exist many other equilibria characterized by fluctuations in which output and employment are forever shifting between the high and low equilibria. For instance, suppose people believe that when sunspot activity is high the economy will be in the good (high equilibrium) state and when sunspot activity is low the economy will be in the bad (low equilibrium) state. That is, people become optimistic or pessimistic depending on whether sunspot activity is high or low. Then indeed it will be the case that the state of the economy will fluctuate between the high and the low equilibria precisely in tune with sunspot activity! These fluctuations will be just like the ones for the stock price model's economy, as depicted in the hemline example of Figure 19.11, in which people were driven by animal spirits bearing no relation to economic fundamentals.[15]

A second remarkable feature of this hypothetical economy is that some people are unambiguously better off and no one is worse off (in terms of expected utility) at the high equilibrium than at the low one, yet there is no market mechanism that can move the economy out of the low equilibrium and toward the high. Specifically, all those who are producing at the high equilibrium are better off than they were at the low one (or they would not be producing), and those who are not producing at the high equilibrium are no worse off than at the low.[16]

Policy Implications

Is there a government policy that can get the economy out of the doldrums at the low equilibrium and move it permanently to the better equilibrium with high employment and output? In fact, it is possible to suggest such a policy in the context of the island economy.

Consider a production subsidy equal to u'/u^* units of the good, where u' is just slightly larger than u_1. Suppose that this subsidy is financed by a sales tax of σ levied on successful trades. This policy changes condition (14) to

If $(1 - \sigma)\pi u^* + u' \geq u$, then produce;

if $(1 - \sigma)\pi u^* + u' < u$, then do not produce.

(17)

Equation (15) describing the fraction of people who choose to produce (and also the per capita output) gets modified to

$$y = G((1 - \sigma)\pi u^* + u').$$ (18)

Equation (16) continues to describe the probability of a successful match as a function of the fraction of producers.

In Figure 19.13 the relation between π and y described by equation (18) has been superimposed on the previous relations described by equations (15) and (16) and shown in Figure 19.12. The new curve, indicated by $\hat{G}$, has a positive intercept on the horizontal axis, unlike G of Figure 19.12. This is because even if the probability of a successful match is zero, a positive fraction of producers (those with production costs between u_1 and u') will find it profitable to produce in order to collect the subsidy. However, the new curve $\hat{G}$ must pass through the same high equilibrium point. This is because in equilibrium the sales taxes collected must be just suffi-

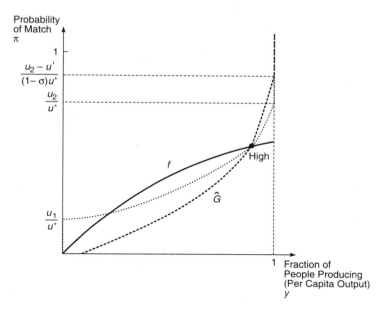

Figure 19.13
A Policy That Produces Only a High Equilibrium

cient to pay for the production subsidies. This requires that the following relationship hold:

$$\sigma \pi y = u'y/u^*. \tag{19}$$

When we substitute equation (19) in (18), we see that it reduces to equation (15) at equilibrium, which shows that the new equilibrium, according to equations (17), (18), and (19), is the same as the high one. However, we see that whereas in Figure 19.12 there are three possible equilibria, in Figure 19.13 the high equilibrium is the only one. The low depression equilibrium in Figure 19.12 is no longer a possible equilibrium in Figure 19.13. This is because even under the most pessimistic assumptions regarding trading opportunities, a positive fraction of people will produce and look for trading partners. Therefore, such grossly pessimistic expectations are incompatible with equilibrium, and the only equilibrium is the one corresponding to optimistic expectations. Thus, such a production subsidy financed by a sales tax can move the economy to a better and higher level of output.

It should also be noted that because the equilibrium under such a policy is unique, there cannot be any fluctuations in output and employment resulting from changing moods of optimism and pessimism. Therefore, such a policy, in addition to making it possible to achieve a better and higher level of output, also eliminates fluctuations and leads the economy onto a stable path.

This policy conclusion needs to be qualified because of the friction in the model. The policy conclusion depends very critically on there being some external entity (say, a *government*) which is outside the economic system of producer-traders and which is able to impose taxes and distribute subsidies. Indirectly, the government is performing a coordinating role by moving goods across people and islands costlessly via taxes and subsidies—a role which the islanders are, by assumption, unable to perform for themselves. In the absence of such an external entity, it is not at all clear whether such policies are even feasible and whether there exist any feasible policies that can improve matters. Therefore, the fact that an economy is in a bad equilibrium state may not necessarily imply that anything can be done about it.

Conclusion

I now summarize what I think economists are learning by studying the sorts of models I have described in this paper. I should emphasize that this is a tentative report on a relatively new and ongoing research program rather than a definitive judgment of a ripe old one. The important points seem to be the following.

Most business cycle models explain fluctuations in economic variables as resulting from the effects of taste and technology shocks continually impinging on the economy. While some of these models are able to explain some of the qualitative and quantitative features of observed business fluctuations, there are many phenomena that they have difficulty explaining or for which explanations based on taste or technology shocks strain credibility. Some of these phenomena include the high degree of volatility of the financial markets, the great sensitivity of these markets to apparently unrelated events, and deep depressions like the one in 1929.[17]

These considerations suggest that perhaps even in the absence of any taste or technology shocks hitting the economy and even when the environment is completely stationary, the economy might be unstable and exhibit fluctuations. As Keynes argued, the economy might be driven by investors' animal spirits, which need bear no relation to economic fundamentals. Further, the economy might simply become stuck in a situation of low employment and output, with market forces being powerless to move the economy to a better situation of higher employment and output.

I have shown by means of two examples that it is not at all difficult to construct simple model economies that exhibit the above properties. The stock price model generates a variety of periodic and aperiodic paths for the stock price as well as paths driven by purely extraneous shocks having no relation to fundamentals. The frictional unemployment model seems to capture to some extent the cycle of pessimism followed by the breakdown of market interactions followed by more pessimism—a cycle that may be an integral part of severe depressions. I have also shown that in each of these models there exist appropriate government policies that, although subject to some important qualifications, are capable of eliminating fluctuations. Additionally, in the frictional unemployment model such policies can lift the economy out of a state of low output and move it to a better state with higher output.

I therefore conclude that there are important advances in understanding to be gained by further study of models of intrinsic fluctuations.

Appendix: More About the Models

This Appendix provides the details of solving the stock price model and explains the simulation method used to generate time paths for the stock price. I also explain how my exposition of the stock price model and the frictional unemployment model differs from the models on which they are based.

The Stock Price Model

I assume the following form for the utility function in equation (1) of the text:

$$u = c_1(t)^{\alpha_1} l_1(t)^{1-\alpha_1} + \{\beta[c_2(t+1)^{\alpha_2} l_2(t+1)^{1-\alpha_2}]^{1-\mu}/(1-\mu)\}. \tag{A1}$$

I assume that $0 < \alpha_1 < 1$, $0 < \alpha_2 < 1$, $\beta > 0$, and $\mu > 0$, but that $\mu \neq 1$. If $\mu = 1$, the second term in (A1) should be replaced by

$$\beta[\alpha_2 \ln c_2(t+1) + (1 - \alpha_2) \ln l_2(t+1)].$$

Here I note some of the differences between my model and the ones of Grandmont (1985) and Azariadis (1981). The main difference is that the asset in their models pays a zero dividend forever, rather than a positive dividend. One may think of their asset as corresponding to cash. In addition, my specification of the utility function is a special case of that of Grandmont (1985). If I set α_1 to zero and α_2 to unity (so that people consume only leisure when young and only the consumption good when old), then my specification of the utility function becomes a special case of that of Azariadis (1981). Grandmont (1985) analyzes only deterministic fluctuations, like the ones generated in Figures 19.3–19.10, where there is no uncertainty about the time path of prices. Azariadis (1981) analyzes fluctuations, like the hemline example in Figure 19.11, which are generated by extraneous uncertain events that have no connection to tastes or technology.

Consumer Choices and Equilibrium

I now analyze the consumer's choices of lifetime consumptions, leisure times, and the quantity of shares to buy, given the current stock price and the expected future price.

First, the consumer will equate the marginal rate of substitution between leisure time and consumption in each period of life to the corresponding opportunity cost of leisure time. The opportunity cost of leisure time is w_1 when the consumer is young and w_2 when old. This leads to the following relationships:

$$(1 - \alpha_1)c_1(t)/\alpha_1 l_1(t) = w_1 \tag{A2}$$

$$(1 - \alpha_2)c_2(t + 1)/\alpha_2 l_2(t + 1) = w_2. \tag{A3}$$

Second, the consumer will equate the marginal rate of substitution between consumption at t and consumption at $t + 1$ to the gross expected rate of return on the stock. This yields

$$(\alpha_1/\beta\alpha_2)[l_1(t)/c_1(t)]^{1-\alpha_1}[c_2(t + 1)^{\alpha_2}l_2(t + 1)^{1-\alpha_2}]^{\mu}$$

$$\times [c_2(t + 1)/l_2(t + 1)]^{1-\alpha_2}$$

$$= [p^e(t + 1) + d]/p(t). \tag{A4}$$

We may now substitute for $l_1(t)$ and $l_2(t + 1)$ from (A2) and (A3) into equations (2) and (3) of the text to obtain the following simplified expressions for the consumer's budget constraints:

$$c_1(t) = \alpha_1[w_1 - p(t)s(t)] \tag{A5}$$

$$c_2(t + 1) = \alpha_2\{w_2 + [p^e(t + 1) + d]s(t)\}. \tag{A6}$$

Next we may substitute for $l_1(t)$ and $l_2(t + 1)$ from (A2) and (A3), and $c_2(t + 1)$ from (A6) into (A4) to obtain

$$\{w_2 + [p^e(t + 1) + d]s(t)\}^\mu = A[p^e(t + 1) + d]/p(t). \tag{A7}$$

Equation (A7) determines the demand for shares in terms of $p(t)$ and $p^e(t + 1)$. The coefficient A in (A7) is given by

$$A = \beta[\alpha_1 w_1/(1 - \alpha_1)]^{1-\alpha_1}[\alpha_2 w_2/(1 - \alpha_2)]^{(1-\alpha_2)(\mu-1)} \div \alpha_1 \alpha_2^{\mu-1}. \tag{A8}$$

It may be verified from equation (A7) that the demand for shares is decreasing in the current price $p(t)$. Now substitute equations (4) and (5) in (A7) to get the following relationship between $p(t)$ and $p(t + 1)$:

$$p(t) = f(p(t + 1)) \equiv A[p(t + 1) + d]/[p(t + 1) + d + w_2]^\mu. \tag{A9}$$

The graph of $p(t)$ against $p(t + 1)$ will be hump shaped (as in Figure 19.2) provided $\mu > 1$ and $w_2 > (\mu - 1)d$. Any time path for $p(t)$ that satisfies (A9) for all t constitutes a perfect foresight or rational expectations equilibrium.

Output and the Stock Price
A simple relationship between total output and the stock price can be obtained as follows. From equations (2)–(5) we have

$$c_1(t) + c_2(t) = w_1[1 - l_1(t)] + w_2[1 - l_2(t)] + d$$

$$= y(t). \tag{A10}$$

Substituting from equations (A5), (A6), (4), and (5) into equation (A10), we obtain the following linear relationship between $y(t)$ and $p(t)$:

$$y(t) = \alpha_1 w_1 + \alpha_2(w_2 + d) + (\alpha_2 - \alpha_1)p(t). \tag{A11}$$

Parameter Values and Simulation Method
I now describe the choice of parameter values and the method of simulation used to produce the intrinsic fluctuations shown in Figures 19.3–19.11. Except for Figure 19.10, I chose these values: $\alpha_1 = \frac{1}{4}$, $\alpha_2 = \frac{1}{2}$, $w_1 = 50$, and $d = 0.01$. The parameter μ was varied from 2 to 20 in steps of one-half. The parameters w_2 and β were chosen indirectly as follows: Let $\bar{p}$ be the maximum value of $f(p)$ and let p_m be the value of p at which $f(\cdot)$ attains its maximum. These values are illustrated in Figure 19.14. The value of p_m may be found by setting the derivative of $f(\cdot)$ equal to zero and solving for p. This yields

$$p_m = [w_2/(\mu - 1)] - d \tag{A12}$$

$$\bar{p} = A/[\mu^\mu(p_m + d)^{\mu-1}]. \tag{A13}$$

We may now substitute for w_2 and A from (A12) and (A13) into (A9) and express the function $f(\cdot)$ in terms of the parameters p_m, $\bar{p}$, μ, and d. I chose $p_m = 1$ and $\bar{p} = 2\mu + 1$. The implied values of w_2 and β may now be found using (A12), (A13), and (A8). Figure 19.10 was generated using the same parameter values as above, with the following exceptions: $d = 0.001$, $\mu = 15.0$, and $\bar{p} = 10.0$. Note that the values of $\bar{p}$ and p_m are chosen such that $\bar{p} > p_m$. That is, the hump occurs to the left of the 45-degree line. Equivalently, the curve cuts the 45-degree line at p^* with a negative slope. This is crucial in order to be able to generate fluctuations.

Figures 19.3–19.9 were generated by iterating backward using the relationship between $p(t)$ and $p(t + 1)$ given by equation (A9). That is, I started with a terminal value of the stock price and worked backward to find the values of the stock price at earlier dates. Figure 19.10, however, was generated by iterating forward. This procedure has to be used with care. As Figure 19.14 shows, there are two possible values of $p(t + 1)$ for some values of $p(t)$. Which value of $p(t + 1)$ to choose may depend on whether there exists some value of $p(t + 2)$ that can follow $p(t + 1)$ and whether there is some value of $p(t + 3)$ that can follow $p(t + 2)$, and so on. For instance, if $p(t)$ is too small, then for whichever value of $p(t + 1)$ we pick, there will be no value of $p(t + 2)$ that can follow it. If $p(t)$ is somewhat larger, then only the larger of the two values of $p(t + 1)$ can be chosen. However, if $p(t)$ is sufficiently large, then either of the two values of $p(t + 1)$ is a legitimate choice. In generating Figure 19.10, this type of situation was resolved by selecting randomly between the two values.

Note that the backward iteration time path in Figure 19.9 can be extended indefinitely into the future by starting with the terminal price and using the forward iteration procedure that generated Figure 19.10. As noted in the previous paragraph, to do this it is, of course, necessary that the terminal price be not too low. Therefore, the time path in Figure 19.9 does indeed constitute a legitimate equilibrium time path that satisfies (A9) for all t.

Solving the Hemline Example
I now show how to solve the hemline example presented in the text (and depicted there in Figure 19.11). Substitute from equations (1) and (A1) into equation (8) to get the following expression for expected utility:

$$E(u|i) = c_1(i)^{\alpha_1} l_1(i)^{1-\alpha_1} + \left\{ \beta \sum_{j=1}^{2} \pi_{ij}[c_2(j)^{\alpha_2} l_2(j)^{1-\alpha_2}]^{1-\mu}/(1 - \mu) \right\}. \qquad (A14)$$

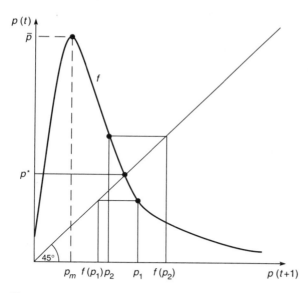

Figure 19.14
Illustrating the Choices for Parameter Values and for Prices in the Hemline Example

In deriving (A14), it is implicitly assumed that the young consumer at date t is born *after* the current state i is realized. In the contrary case, equation (A14) would have to be modified by also adding up the utilities in each state when young, weighted by the respective probabilities. In addition, we would have to recognize the possibilities for risk sharing between the young and the old, which will alter the budget constraints (9) and (10). By assuming that the young consumer is born after the current state is realized, we rule out such risk-sharing arrangements. This assumption leads to (A14) and the budget constraints (9) and (10). The assumption is indeed very crucial because in the contrary case it can be shown that it is *impossible* for stock prices to fluctuate in response to extraneous events like hemlines or sunspots. For a demonstration of this statement, see Azariadis 1981.

I now analyze in several steps the consumer's choice problem. As before, the consumer equates the marginal rate of substitution between leisure and consumption in each period and in each state to the corresponding opportunity cost. This yields the following conditions, analogous to (A2) and (A3):

$$(1 - \alpha_1)c_1(i)/\alpha_1 l_1(i) = w_1 \tag{A15}$$

$$(1 - \alpha_2)c_2(j)/\alpha_2 l_2(j) = w_2. \tag{A16}$$

Now substitute equations (A15) and (A16) into equations (A14), (9), and (10) to simplify them as follows:

$$E(u|i) = [(1 - \alpha_1)/\alpha_1 w_1]^{1-\alpha_1} c_1(i) + \{\beta[(1 - \alpha_2)/\alpha_2 w_2]^{(1-\alpha_2)(1-\mu)}$$

$$\times \sum_{j=1}^{2} \pi_{ij} c_2(j)^{1-\mu}/(1 - \mu)\} \qquad (A17)$$

$$c_1(i) = \alpha_1(w_1 - p_i s_i) \qquad (A18)$$

$$c_2(j) = \alpha_2[w_2 + (p_j + d)s_i]. \qquad (A19)$$

We can now substitute (A18) and (A19) in (A17) and maximize expected utility by choice of s_i. This leads to the following condition:

$$p_i = A \sum_{j=1}^{2} [\pi_{ij}(p_j + d)]/[w_2 + (p_j + d)s_i]^\mu. \qquad (A20)$$

We may now substitute the equilibrium condition (4) in (A20) to obtain

$$p_i = A \sum_{j=1}^{2} [\pi_{ij}(p_j + d)]/(w_2 + p_j + d)^\mu$$

$$= \sum_j \pi_{ij} f(p_j) \qquad (A21)$$

for $i = 1, 2$, where $f(\cdot)$ is the same function as in (A9).

We thus have two equations in the two unknowns, p_1 and p_2. Note that there is always a solution in which p_1 and p_2 both equal p^*. When p_1 equals p_2, the two equations in (A21) collapse to a single equation because the sum of probabilities $(\pi_{i1} + \pi_{i2})$ must be unity for each i. The resulting equation is the same as equation (A9) with $p(t)$ equal to $p(t + 1)$, and the solution is p^*. This solution corresponds to the case where the stock price is unaffected by people's belief about hemlines and the stock market. If we can find probabilities π_{ij} such that there is a solution in which p_1 and p_2 are different, then we have an example where the stock price responds to "rational" animal spirits.

Such an example can be constructed as follows. First, substitute $\pi_{12} = 1 - \pi_{11}$ and $\pi_{21} = 1 - \pi_{22}$ in equation (A21) and solve for π_{11} and π_{22} to obtain

$$\pi_{11} = [f(p_2) - p_1]/[f(p_2) - f(p_1)] \qquad (A22)$$

$$\pi_{22} = [p_2 - f(p_1)]/[f(p_2) - f(p_1)]. \qquad (A23)$$

I look for a solution such that $p_1 > p^* > p_2$ and such that the points $(p_1, f(p_1))$ and $(p_2, f(p_2))$ lie on the downward-sloping branch of the curve $f(\cdot)$. It follows that we must have $f(p_2) > f(p_1)$. (See Figure 19.14 for an illustration.) Since the probabilities π_{11} and π_{22} must each be between zero and one, we require that p_1 and p_2 satisfy the following conditions:

$$f(p_1) < p_1 < f(p_2) \tag{A24}$$

$$f(p_1) < p_2 < f(p_2). \tag{A25}$$

Figure 19.14 shows two values, p_1 and p_2, that satisfy the two inequalities. The associated probabilities π_{ij} can be calculated from (A22) and (A23).

For the examples presented here, it is important that the slope of the curve at p^*, shown in Figure 19.14, be negative and greater than one in absolute value in order to generate periodic cycles other than the constant time path corresponding to p^*. This slope condition is also crucial for generating the hemline example of Figure 19.11. Otherwise, the inequalities (A24) and (A25) cannot be met. In fact, it turns out that for the type of model presented here, such a hemline equilibrium will exist *if and only if* there exists a two-period cycle such as the one generated in Figures 19.3 and 19.4 (see Azariadis and Guesnerie 1986). A heuristic argument for the *if* part of this statement can be made as follows. A two-period cycle corresponds to having π_{11} and π_{22} each equal to zero. Therefore, it will generally be possible to find differing values for p_1 and p_2 if π_{11} and π_{22} are both positive but small. The *only if* part is not generally true. For example, if the $f(\cdot)$ function has a slope that is positive and greater than one at p^* (this can never happen in the present model), then there cannot be a two-period cycle. However, it is possible to find differing values for p_1 and p_2 and values for the probabilities π_{11} and π_{22} that satisfy equations (A22) and (A23).

As noted in the text, it is also important that the probabilities π_{ij} depend on i. Otherwise, the only solution to (A21) is $p_1 = p_2 = p^*$. This follows because the right-hand side of (A21) is then independent of i.

The Tax/Subsidy Policy

I now analyze the tax/subsidy policy described in the text. The consumer's choices lead to the same conditions as before, namely, equations (A2), (A3), and (A4), except that $p^e(t + 1)$ is replaced by p'. This is because the after-tax gross rate of return on the stock is given by $(p' + d)/p(t)$. As before, we may substitute for $l_1(t)$ and $l_2(t + 1)$ from (A2) and (A3), $s(t)$ from (4), and $\tau(t)$ from (13) into equations (11) and (12) to obtain

$$c_1(t) = \alpha_1(w_1 - p') \tag{A26}$$

$$c_2(t + 1) = \alpha_2(w_2 + p' + d). \tag{A27}$$

Next, we may substitute for $l_1(t)$ and $l_2(t + 1)$ from (A2) and (A3), and $c_2(t + 1)$ from (A27) into equation (A4) and replace $p^e(t + 1)$ by p' to get the following version of equation (A9):

$$p(t) = A(p' + d)/(p' + d + w_2)^\mu. \tag{A28}$$

This proves that the equilibrium stock price will be constant over time. The equilibrium price under such a policy need not equal the benchmark price p'. This will happen only when p' is the same as p^*, where p^* is the price depicted in Figure 19.14. This follows from equations (A9) and (A28) and the figure. Further, if the government announces p^* as the benchmark price, then it can be seen from equation (13) that along the equilibrium path there will be no taxes or rebates.

The Frictional Unemployment Model

Here I explain in some detail the difference between Diamond's (1984) model and my simplified version of it. As stated in note 11, Diamond's model is dynamic since he allows the good to be stored. However, no more than one unit of the good may be stored; therefore, production cannot be resumed until the current inventory is sold. Thus, at any given time, the economy consists of some people who hold a unit in inventories and cannot produce any more until they have sold it and of others who have zero inventories and can produce. Further, over time a given individual may receive a variety of production opportunities which may differ in cost. The individual may, therefore, choose either to take advantage of the current production opportunity or to wait for a better (less costly) one. This makes the decision to produce a more complicated dynamic problem, and thereby makes the derivation of the G curve in Figure 19.12 more difficult.

Notes

1. For a recent example of one such model, see Prescott's paper [Chapter 14 in this volume]. The fluctuations in Prescott's model are driven by shocks to technology.

2. Expectations are said to be *rational* if beliefs regarding possible future events are (probabilistically) correct, that is, verified by the actual future course of events. In a world without uncertainty, this amounts to having perfect foresight regarding future developments.

3. It should be clear that allowing for taste or technology shocks would only magnify the fluctuations.

4. This may be viewed as capturing Keynes' notion of animal spirits. Fluctuations resulting from such beliefs are often referred to as *sunspot* fluctuations (see Cass and Shell 1983).

5. Models exhibiting these features have been studied extensively by many people, among whom the following are prominent: Costas Azariadis (1981), David Cass and Karl Shell (1983), and Jean-Michel Grandmont (1985).

6. Models of this type were pioneered and studied by Peter Diamond (1984).

7. The mathematical details of solving the model are given in the Appendix, where I also note the (very minor) differences between my exposition and the models of Grandmont (1985) and Azariadis (1981).

8. The variety of different periodic cycles that can exist simultaneously was discovered by the Russian mathematician A. N. Sarkovskii and systematized in a beautiful mathematical theorem. See Grandmont 1985 (pp. 1019–20) for a more detailed explanation.

9. This property is named after the Italian economist and sociologist Vilfredo Pareto (1848–1923). The converse of this property, that it is possible to improve someone's welfare without hurting anyone else, is known as *Pareto nonoptimality*. In this case it would generally be possible to find government policies that would make everyone better off.

10. This is only partially true in the present model because of its very simple structure. For instance, one can use past data on stock prices to plot the current price against the future price, as in Figure 19.2. In a more complex model such simple procedures will no longer be useful.

11. The main difference between Diamond's model and my simplified version is that his is dynamic, since he allows production to be stored as inventories, whereas I assume that production is nonstorable; hence, my version is static. See the Appendix for a fuller discussion of the differences.

12. I also assume that production must occur prior to trade and that no production is possible once trade starts. This assumption rules out the possibility that someone who initially chose not to produce might wish to produce after encountering another producer. This corresponds to the real-world feature that most production is not for immediate sale but for inventory, with sales occurring subsequently out of inventory.

13. The probability of a successful match need not be one even in this case when everyone decides to produce. Imagine that there are two producers on two islands. If each producer decides with equal chance either to stay home or to go to the other island, then there is only a 50-50 chance that the two will meet.

14. Intuitively, the curve marked G must be increasing because as π goes up the expected utility of producing and trading goes up. This increase in expected utility induces more people to undertake production, thereby increasing output.

15. Here is another illustration of Keynes' idea of self-fulfilling animal spirits.

16. This feature is in sharp contrast to the traditional economic model of perfect competition as described by, say, Debreu (1959b). All of the equilibria in the Debreu model are Pareto optimal. Therefore, in that model it is impossible for one equilibrium to dominate another, in the sense that some consumers are better off and none is worse off.

17. For instance, Keynesians like Franco Modigliani have ridiculed neoclassical economists by saying that the only way to explain the Great Depression on the basis of neoclassical theories is to attribute it to a "severe attack of contagious laziness!" (Modigliani 1977, p. 6).

V   Empirical Macroeconomics

Readers might feel shortchanged, since this section contains only two chapters—and both by Christiano. So to get their fair allotment, readers may want to read these chapters twice.

The chapters describe directions taken in empirical macroeconomics following the Lucas critique. They can be read once as how-to manuals. Each chapter describes exercises in modern empirical macroeconomics. In each, real business cycle models are constructed, empirically quantified, and tested. In the second chapter, the model is revised to lessen discrepancies between the model's implications and actual observations. The methodology that is described reveals a constant interplay between theory and observations.

The chapters can be read a second time as original pieces of research. Each lays out a recent economic puzzle and proposes to solve it using a specially constructed, empirical macroeconomic model.

The puzzle that is the focus of Chapter 20 concerns aggregate consumption behavior. For many years economists have used Milton Friedman's *permanent income hypothesis* to explain why U.S. data series show aggregate consumption to be smoother than aggregate income. According to this hypothesis, people's consumption today depends on their expected lifetime income. Since consumers were thought by economists to view some part of any unexpected current income change as transitory, the permanent income hypothesis was thought to suggest that consumers will not change their spending one-for-one with changes in their current income. Hence, consumption will be observed to be smoother than income.

Recently, Angus Deaton described an empirical puzzle relating to that explanation. (See Chapter 20.) Using a model of income that he judged to best fit the data, Deaton found that a change in current income actually leads to a more than one-for-one change in expected lifetime income. Thus, the permanent income hypothesis together with Deaton's model of income implies paradoxically that consumption should be more volatile than income.

After recounting the formal steps in Deaton's argument, Christiano suggests separate empirical and theoretical considerations that could solve Deaton's puzzle. He first shows that the income process cannot be empirically estimated with enough precision to determine whether expected lifetime income responds more or less than one-for-one to changes in current income. That is, models of income that are statistically indistinguishable from Deaton's imply there is no puzzle.

Christiano then presents a theoretical argument, which holds that underlying economic shocks leading to changes in income will in general also lead to changes in interest rates. Thus, even though consumption could respond to income as Deaton says, the change in interest rates can dampen that effect. Once again, consumption would be found to be less volatile than income. Christiano concludes this chapter by reporting some results from an empirical business cycle model he constructed that support his theoretical argument.

In Chapter 21, Christiano addresses a monetary theory puzzle. He notes the common wisdom that an immediate effect of an unexpected, expansionary move in monetary policy is a reduction in the nominal interest rate. The puzzle is why the early monetary versions of real business cycle models produce the opposite effect.

Christiano considers an expansionary move in monetary policy a helicopter drop and notes that it can have two opposite effects. One is to lower interest rates by putting more liquidity into the system. The other is to raise interest rates by raising inflationary expectations. For the common-wisdom relationship to hold, the liquidity effect must be quantitatively more important than the anticipated inflation effect.

The reverse had to be true in the early monetary versions of real business cycle models. These models were constructed in response to criticisms, such as Summers', which emphasized the importance of monetary factors in business cycle movements. In these models, money is introduced using a *cash-in-advance constraint*: Economic agents in these models must use previously accumulated cash to make purchases. Christiano points out that these models miss entirely the liquidity effect of a monetary policy change.

Christiano attempts to solve the puzzle by changing the information structure of these monetary models. He examines variations of these models which differ in the amount of information economic agents are assumed to have before they make decisions. Although Christiano finally is able to produce a model consistent with the common-wisdom relationship, that model is not successful in confronting some other regularities in the data. Thus, Christiano's work provides clues to the puzzle's solution, but it does not completely solve the puzzle.

20

Why Is Consumption Less Volatile Than Income?

Lawrence J. Christiano

Many of today's public policy issues—such as the potential economic impacts of the federal budget deficit and proposed changes in taxes—require an understanding of how households make consumption spending decisions. Indeed, some issues hinge on it. For example, recently in the *Quarterly Review*, Aiyagari [in Chapter 9 in this volume] described two views about how consumption decisions are made which have strikingly different implications for large government deficits. One says such deficits have no effect on interest rates, investment, or saving; the other, that they drive up interest rates, reduce investment, and impoverish the next generation.

Despite the substantial policy issues at stake, economists are still struggling to understand consumption decision making at even the most basic level. In fact, recently their uncertainty has seemed to increase.

For a long time, economists thought they at least had generally agreed on an explanation for what is perhaps the most basic fact about these decisions, the fact that over time the total amount people spend changes much less than the total amount they earn—or as an economist would say, aggregate consumption is much less volatile than aggregate income. The traditional explanation (due to Milton Friedman) is known as the *permanent income hypothesis*. It assumes, roughly, that people make their spending decisions based on what they expect their income to be in the long run, not just the short run. Their spending doesn't necessarily change, therefore, whenever their income changes. Many of those income changes are expected and so already built into people's spending plans. The rest are surprise income changes, but many of them may not change spending, either, if people don't think they are going to last. Spending should be considerably affected by surprise income changes that seem *permanent*, that

Reprinted from the *Federal Reserve Bank of Minneapolis Quarterly Review*, Fall 1987.

is, but only minimally by those that seem *temporary*. The traditional assumption has been, moreover, that most surprise income changes are temporary; hence, consumption should be less volatile than income, which it is.

Recently, though, some economists have lost confidence in this explanation for the basic consumption/income relationship. Based on their analysis of aggregate income data, they have concluded that the traditional view, according to which surprise changes in income are temporary, is implausible. Instead, they are convinced that it is more plausible for households to respond to a surprise increase in income of, say, $1 by raising their outlook for income forever. Specifically, the long-run income outlook should be raised about $1.60, according to Deaton (1986). Deaton pointed out the dramatic implications of these developments for economists' traditional way of thinking about consumption. He showed that when the permanent income hypothesis is combined with this new view about the nature of surprise income changes, then the implications of the traditional argument are stood on their head. The prediction now is that consumption ought to be more volatile than income, not less. Deaton's paradox (as it has come to be called) suggests to many that something is seriously wrong with the traditional explanation for a basic economic fact.

The situation is actually not so grave. Despite Deaton's challenge, the traditional explanation for the consumption/income relationship might still be right. Several researchers have argued that estimates of the long-run impact of a surprise change in income based on aggregate postwar U.S. income data are too imprecise to support any conclusion, including Deaton's. This should not be surprising, since—as I show here—the relevant long run for this issue is from 10 to 15 years and U.S. postwar data offer only three or four nonoverlapping intervals of this length. Efforts are currently under way to increase the precision of estimates of the impact of surprise income changes by, for example, bringing income data from many countries into the analysis. Still, controversy on the magnitude of the impact continues, and in the end, Deaton's estimate may prove to be the best. However, even if that were true, the traditional explanation for the consumption/income relationship may not be too wrong. Results in Christiano 1987c—summarized here—suggest that even if Deaton's view of the impact of a surprise change in income is accepted, a small change in another of the permanent income model's assumptions is enough to pull the theory's implications back into line with the basic economic fact.

Essentially, the model adjustment involves changing the assumed source of the surprise income changes. The permanent income model, by assuming that the return to investing in capital is fixed, implicitly posits that the return is unrelated to the factors that produce output movements. The adjusted model I describe embodies the *real business cycle* perspective (associated with Kydland and Prescott 1982, Long and Plosser 1983, and Prescott [Chapter 14]).[1] In that type of model, income changes stem from productivity shocks that simultaneously change the reward to investing. Therefore, the response of consumption to an unexpected, permanent jump in income is relatively restrained, as households simultaneously increase saving in order to take advantage of the increased return to investing. Evidently, the key ingredient of this proposed way to resolve the Deaton paradox is a presumed positive correlation between income and the anticipated return to investing in capital. Determining whether this proposal actually resolves the paradox, then, requires determining whether the required correlation is empirically plausible. This is the subject of ongoing research.

Thus, there are at least two possible ways to resolve the Deaton paradox. One is to revert to the traditional view that the effect of a surprise change in income is temporary. The other is to modify the permanent income model's assumed source of income fluctuation. Neither of these two proposed ways to resolve the paradox does so decisively yet; each requires further research to establish its plausibility. That is why the title of this paper is a question.

My objective here is to describe the Deaton paradox and the proposals to resolve it, at a fairly basic level. I thus describe the basic building blocks: the permanent income model, the real business cycle model, and several mathematical models about the persistence of surprise changes in income. Since the second proposed resolution to the paradox requires comparing the permanent income and real business cycle models, they need to be placed on a comparable basis. This is done by showing that they both belong to a general family of models called the *equilibrium growth* (or simply *growth*) model, which is increasingly becoming the standard framework for analysis in macroeconomics.[2] (The observation that the permanent income model is a special case of the growth model—something not generally known—is due to Sargent 1986 and L. Hansen 1985.)

The Equilibrium Growth Model

Here I lay the groundwork for describing the permanent income and real business cycle models by describing the simplest equilibrium growth model which includes them as special cases. First I describe the growth model in general, informal terms. This description follows recent developments which show that the growth model can be thought of as an economy populated by numerous heterogeneous, mortal people. I also describe an alternative interpretation of that model economy according to which it is populated by just one fictitious agent who lives forever. Because of this agent's resemblance to Defoe's fictional character, I call the agent *Robinson Crusoe*. This interpretation of the growth model is conventional and very convenient for my formal discussion of the growth model.

An Informal Look at the Multiagent Economy

The growth model is an abstract economy populated by a large number of households and firms. As time evolves in the growth economy, some people are born into households and others die. During their lifetimes, people choose how much of the economy's good to consume and how to divide their time between *labor*, defined as work in the marketplace, and other activities, which are conventionally (and perhaps inappropriately) called *leisure*. If their income exceeds current consumption, they lend (or save) the difference; otherwise, they borrow (save a negative amount). People are purposeful in that their choices reflect their *preferences*, their attitudes about consumption today versus consumption tomorrow and about work versus leisure. The mathematical representation of preferences is the *utility function*.

Different people in the growth model have different preferences and labor productivities, reflecting in part their different ages. Therefore, a given person's saving might be positive at some times and negative at others. Moreover, at any given time, some people's saving is positive and others' is negative. Total saving, if positive, results in the accumulation of capital—things like factories, office buildings, and airplanes. If total saving is negative, the capital stock wears out. The fact that capital can accumulate means that production in this economy can increase over time; this is why it is called a *growth* model.

Firms possess the economy's *technology*, the knowledge about how to convert capital and labor effort into output. The mathematical representation of technology is the *production function*.

The growth model economy is simpler than an actual economy in several respects. In an actual economy, output is composed of many different goods (for example, cars, houses, food, health services, transportation). The growth model abstracts from this diversity by consolidating everything into one homogeneous good. Similarly, it abstracts from the many different actual types of capital by assuming that the capital stock is homogeneous and reflects past accumulation of the single produced good. The relationship of capital and output in the growth model is much like that of clay and putty: one is a hardened, congealed version of the other.

The multitude of people and firms in the growth model interact anonymously in markets.[3] These are *competitive* markets in the sense that prices are not set by any individual households or firms. Given the prices of labor and goods, people determine how much labor they want to supply and how many goods they want to buy. In addition, through their saving behavior, households acquire ownership of the stock of capital, which earns a competitive return (a rental rate) from firms. Given market prices, firms demand labor and the services of capital and they supply goods. In a competitive equilibrium, then, market prices are such that labor, goods, and capital markets clear; that is, they are *in equilibrium*. This is why the growth model is called an *equilibrium* model.

I must emphasize, however, that markets being in equilibrium in this model does not imply that everything in it is fixed over time. Quite the contrary: the equilibrium values of all variables in the growth model economy can change constantly over time in ways that are only imperfectly predictable. This reflects the constant, difficult to predict changes in the factors that determine the productivity of capital and labor (including weather, strikes, inventions, managerial skills, and the educational level and technical skills of workers). These factors, called *fundamentals* or *technology shocks*, account in part for the unpredictability inherent in actual economies.

A Formal Look at the Robinson Crusoe Economy

A *solution* to the growth model is a detailed specification of everyone's consumption, hours worked, and saving activity, along with prices such as wages and interest rates on loans. Here, though, I am only concerned with economywide averages of variables, particularly average consumption and income. And I only need some prices, such as the wage rate and the rate of interest. Fortunately, economywide average values of a growth model's equilibrium variables can be computed without first calculating each person's consumption, hours worked, and saving. These average values can instead be viewed as reflecting the choices of a single, fictitious agent who lives forever—who represents an average across the multitude of diverse, finite-lived people living in the growth economy. This representative Robinson Crusoe—like agent has preferences over economywide average consumption and work and chooses these variables subject to the available technology for converting capital and work into output, so as to maximize utility over an infinite-horizon lifetime.[4]

Technology

In deciding what to do with output in the growth economy, Robinson Crusoe faces a *resource constraint*: uses of final output cannot exceed the amount available. The growth model assumes that gross output, which I call y_t, is allocated to only two uses: consumption, c_t, and gross capital investment, dk_t. (For a discussion of the empirical measures of these and other variables used later, see the Appendix.) This, then, is the resource constraint:

$$c_t + dk_t = y_t. \tag{1}$$

The production function specifies how output is related to the factors of production. The permanent income and real business cycle models assume only three factors of production: capital, hours worked, and a term representing the fundamentals. These are here denoted by k_t, h_t, and z_t, respectively. An abstract representation of the production function, which includes those assumed by the permanent income and real business cycle models as special cases, is

$$y_t = f(k_t, z_t h_t). \tag{2}$$

The production function, f, indicates that the greater the value of the fundamentals, z_t, the more productive is an average hour's work.

Gross capital investment, dk_t, and the stock of capital, k_t, are linked in this way:

$$k_{t+1} = (1 - \delta)k_t + dk_t. \tag{3}$$

Here δ is the quarterly rate of depreciation of the stock of capital.[5] Thus, if the stock of capital is k_t at the beginning of quarter t, then the undepreciated part of that stock which remains at the end of the quarter is $(1 - \delta)k_t$. The stock of capital available at the beginning of next quarter, k_{t+1}, is composed of this plus the part of y_t devoted to investment, dk_t.

Taken together, equations (1)–(3) describe the basic trade-offs faced by Robinson Crusoe. In particular, the more leisure, l, is taken now (that is, the lower is h_t), the less current output is available for consumption and investment. High current consumption reduces the rate of capital accumulation, which reduces the future stock of capital. So high current consumption comes at the expense of reduced future output. In principle, even the determination of the fundamentals, z_t, involves trade-offs. For example, time devoted to education must be taken from time in the home or at work. The permanent income and real business cycle models abstract from the factors that determine z_t by simply assuming it evolves exogenously, or outside the model. (See Lucas 1988a and Romer 1986 for models in which the economic decisions that determine z_t are modeled explicitly.)

Preferences

How Robinson Crusoe resolves the basic trade-offs is determined by this agent's preferences. As of date t, Crusoe is assumed to value alternative uncertain paths of consumption and leisure, $\{c_{t+j}, l_{t+j}; j = 0, 1, 2, \ldots\}$, according to the following expected, discounted utility function:

$$E_t\{u(c_t, l_t) + \beta u(c_{t+1}, l_{t+1}) + \beta^2 u(c_{t+2}, l_{t+2}) + \cdots\} = E_t \sum_{j=0}^{\infty} \beta^j u(c_{t+j}, l_{t+j})$$

(4)

where $0 < \beta < 1$. Here leisure and hours worked are linked by the restriction $l_t + h_t = T$, the total number of hours available in a quarter; u is the period utility function; and $E_t x$ is the expected value of x, conditional on information available at the beginning of quarter t.

According to (4), Crusoe cares not only about current consumption and leisure, but also about their future values. Therefore, at date t all of y_t is not necessarily consumed; some of it is saved (that is, $dk_t > 0$) for future consumption.

Model Solution

A solution to this model is a mathematical equation relating Robinson Crusoe's decisions at a given date to information available to Crusoe at that date. Such an equation is called a *contingency plan*. In particular, at date t Crusoe chooses contingency plans for setting c_{t+j}, h_{t+j}, and k_{t+1+j} for $j = 0, 1, 2, \ldots$ as a function of information available contemporaneously, $\Omega_{t+j} = \{z_{t+j-s}, c_{t+j-1-s}, h_{t+j-1-s}, k_{t+j-s}; s = 0, 1, 2, 3, \ldots\}$ to maximize (4) subject to (1)–(3) and a specification of the statistical properties of z_t.[6] These contingency plans are functions c, h, and k:

$$c_{t+j} = c(\Omega_{t+j}), \quad h_{t+j} = h(\Omega_{t+j}), \quad k_{t+1+j} = k(\Omega_{t+j}).$$

(5)

Crusoe's contingency plans for dk_{t+j} and l_{t+j} can be derived from k and h using (3) and the fact that $l_t = T - h_t$.

The Robinson Crusoe perspective on the growth model not only makes solving the model for equilibrium quantities easier, but also can be used to compute equilibrium prices. I will use this representative agent approach to get formulas for the prices I will need later. One is the market-clearing *wage rate*, w_t, which is the marginal product of labor: $\partial f(k_t, z_t h_t)/\partial h_t$. Therefore, income attributable to labor effort, y_{ht}, is $w_t h_t$ or

$$y_{ht} = [\partial f(k_t, z_t h_t)/\partial h_t] h_t. \tag{6}$$

Note that w_t and y_{ht} can be computed using the equilibrium values of k_t and h_t. Another market price I need is the *risk-free rate of interest*, r_t. This is the yield on a bond which, at a cost of one unit of the time t consumption good, entitles the holder to $1 + r_t$ units of the consumption good in period $t + 1$ with certainty. From the Robinson Crusoe perspective, $1 + r_t$ is the number of date $t + 1$ goods Crusoe requires to be compensated for giving up one unit of the good in period t. In utility terms, Crusoe's cost of giving up that unit is approximately $u'(c_t) \equiv \partial u(c_t)/\partial c_t$. From the perspective of date t, Crusoe's benefit of $1 + r_t$ goods in period $t + 1$ is $\beta E_t(1 + r_t)u'(c_{t+1}) = \beta(1 + r_t)E_t u'(c_{t+1})$. The risk-free rate of interest is the value of r_t that equates benefits and costs:

$$1 + r_t = u'(c_t)/[\beta E_t u'(c_{t+1})]. \tag{7}$$

The consumption contingency plan, c, can be used to express r_t as a function of Ω_t. According to (7), the risk-free rate is low if the marginal utility of consumption next period is expected to be high. This reflects the fact that if Crusoe values consumption next period highly, then Crusoe requires few goods next period to be compensated for giving up a relatively low-valued date t good. What this corresponds to in the multiagent market economy that Crusoe stands in for is this: When people value consumption next period highly, then the current supply of loans is large and a low interest rate is sufficient to clear the loan market.

The risk-free rate of interest, r_t, must be distinguished from the *return on investment in capital*, which is $1 + R_t = [\partial f(k_{t+1}, z_{t+1}h_{t+1})/\partial k_{t+1}] + (1 - \delta)$. The bracketed part of this sum is the direct increment to period $t + 1$ output due to a one-unit increment in the capital stock, k_{t+1}. The other term $(1 - \delta)$ is the amount of extra capital, per unit of capital invested, left over at the end of $t + 1$. Unlike the value of r_t, the value of R_t is uncertain at date t since it will be determined in part by z_{t+1}, which is unknown at date t. (Recall that k_{t+1} is chosen at date t, so it is known then.) A particular difference between r_t and R_t, then, is that the former is not and the latter is a random variable as of date t. In general, it is not even true that $E_t R_t = r_t$.

The difference between $E_t R_t$ and r_t is called the *risk premium*. A formula for it can be obtained by studying the costs and benefits Robinson Crusoe weighs when contemplating investment in an extra unit of capital. In particular, to increase k_{t+1} by one unit, Crusoe has to reduce c_t by one unit, with utility cost $u'(c_t)$. The payoff at date $t + 1$ of this investment is $1 + R_t$, and the utility of this from the perspective of date t is $\beta E_t u'(c_{t+1})(1 + R_t)$.[7] Now, Crusoe invests up to the point where benefits equal costs, so that $u'(c_t) = \beta E_t u'(c_{t+1})(1 + R_t)$. Any two random variables x and y are related as $\text{cov}(x, y) = Exy - ExEy$, where $\text{cov}(x, y)$ denotes the covariance between x and y. Thus, $u'(c_t)/\beta = \{\text{cov}_t[u'(c_{t+1}), 1 + R_t] + E_t u'(c_{t+1})E_t(1 + R_t)\}$. Dividing by $E_t u'(c_{t+1})$, using (7), and rearranging yields

$$E_t R_t - r_t = -\text{cov}_t[u'(c_{t+1}), 1 + R_t]/E_t u'(c_{t+1}). \tag{8}$$

Since $E_t u'(c_{t+1}) \geqslant 0$, the risk premium is negatively related to the indicated conditional covariance term. So if the payoff on investing in capital $(1 + R_t)$ is negatively correlated with marginal utility, then the expected return on capital, $E_t R_t$, exceeds the risk-free return.[8] This is because investments in capital are relatively unattractive—they yield the highest return when returns are least valued—so that a high yield is needed to induce people to invest. Note that if f is linear in k_t—so that R_t is a constant— then the risk premium is zero and $r_t = R_t = r$, a constant. This is not surprising, since investment in capital is then risk free. (In the permanent income model, f is linear.)

The Permanent Income Model

Here I follow Sargent 1986 and L. Hansen 1985 in deriving the permanent income hypothesis from a growth model with a particular specification of preferences and technology. I call this model the *permanent income model*. I derive a formula for the ratio of the volatilities of consumption and labor income that it implies and show how the size of this ratio is determined by the properties of labor income over time (its *dynamic* properties). I present the result not well known before Deaton 1986: that when labor income takes a particular form, this model can imply that consumption is more volatile than labor income.

The Model and an Approximate Solution

The permanent income version of the growth model has the following restrictions:

$$u(c_t, l_t) = -(c_t - b)^2/2, \quad f(k_t, z_t h_t) = qk_t + z_t h_t, \quad \beta(q + 1 - \delta) = 1 \tag{9}$$

where $0 < \beta < 1$ and $b > 0$. Note that the utility function u does not include l_t explicitly. Instead, to avoid complications of no concern here, I abstract from the determination of h_t (and, hence, l_t) by assuming it evolves exogenously over time.[9] This and the fact that the production function f is linear in $z_t h_t$ implies that labor income is exogenous, with $y_{ht} = z_t h_t$. The fact that f is linear in k_t implies that the risk-free rate of interest in the economy is a constant r, equal to $R = q - \delta$. That is,

$$r = q - \delta. \tag{10}$$

This and the assumption on preferences imply, approximately, that households set consumption c_t at the highest possible level they think they can sustain indefinitely, given their expectations for labor income. This highest sustainable level of consumption is called *permanent income*, which accounts for the model's name.[10]

   To compute permanent income, substitute for y_t and dk_t in (1) from (2), (3), and (9). Then use (10) and the fact that $z_t h_t = y_{ht}$ to get

$$k_{t+1} = (1 + r)k_t + y_{ht} - c_t. \tag{11}$$

Now consider a consumption decision made at date t, when k_t and y_{ht} are known to the household. Let c_t be the maximum consumption level households expect to be able to sustain indefinitely. It must satisfy not only (11), but also future versions of (11):

$$k_{t+1+i} = (1 + r)k_{t+i} + E_t y_{ht+i} - c_t \tag{12}$$

for all $i = 1, 2, 3, \dots$. It can be shown that the maximum value of c_t that satisfies (11), (12), and $k_t \geqslant 0$ is

$$c_t = rW_t \tag{13}$$

where

$$W_t = k_t + \left[(1 + r)^{-1} \sum_{i=0}^{\infty} (1 + r)^{-i} E_t y_{ht+i} \right]. \tag{14}$$

Equations (13) and (14) define the permanent income hypothesis. There, rW_t and W_t are per capita *permanent income* and *wealth*, respectively. Note that wealth has two parts: k_t, which is called *nonhuman wealth*, and the other, bracketed piece, *human wealth*. Nonhuman wealth is just the existing stock of capital. The term for human wealth is the present discounted value of expected future labor income. It is the value that the work force of the society would have if there were a stock market in workers.

Equation (13) expresses c_t as a function of information available at date t and so is a solution to the permanent income model. This can be seen by noting that (13) [with (14)] is in the same form as (5), expressing c_t as a function of date t information: k_t and the information in the date t conditional expectation. Equation (13) is not an explicit solution for c_t until the statistical properties of y_{ht} are specified, so the conditional expectation can be evaluated. As we will see, those statistical properties can make a great difference in the model's implications for the relative volatility of consumption and labor income.

A Formula for the Consumption/Income Relationship

The key implication of the permanent income model here is its implication for the relative volatility of consumption and income. To get a formula for this, I first need an expression for the change in consumption $c_t - c_{t-1}$.

Recall the permanent income model's implication that c_t is set at a level that households believe is sustainable indefinitely. This implies that c_t differs from c_{t-1} only when something happens to income at the start of quarter t that was not anticipated in quarter $t - 1$, when c_{t-1} was set. Since the interest rate in the permanent income model is fixed by the linearity assumption on f, the only component of earnings in t that is uncertain as of $t - 1$ is labor income. Thus, c_t differs from c_{t-1} in this model only if period t labor income differs from what was expected in quarter t.

But the magnitude of the difference, $c_t - c_{t-1}$, depends only in part on the exact magnitude of the unexpected component of period t labor income. It also depends on how much the unexpected part of y_{ht} induces households to revise their expectations about period $t + s$ labor income, for $s = 1, 2, 3, \ldots$. The permanent income model implies that $c_t - c_{t-1}$ is the *annuity value* of the revision to expectations about period $t + s$ labor income for $s = 0, 1, 2, 3, \ldots$.[11] This can be derived formally by subtracting (8) lagged one period from itself and using (11) and (14) to arrive at

$$c_t - c_{t-1} = r\left[(1 + r)^{-1} \sum_{i=0}^{\infty} (1 + r)^{-i}(E_t y_{ht+i} - E_{t-1} y_{ht+i}) \right]. \tag{15}$$

The expression $E_t y_{ht+i} - E_{t-1} y_{ht+i}$ is the revision in households' expectation about future labor income y_{ht+i} due to the new information available in period t, but not in period $t - 1$. One of these terms, $E_t y_{ht} - E_{t-1} y_{ht} = y_{ht} - E_{t-1} y_{ht}$, is called the *innovation* (or surprise change) in y_{ht} and is the difference between y_{ht} and what people expected it to be as of date $t - 1$. Note that if all of these revised expectation terms are zero, then $c_t = c_{t-1}$:

consumption does not change. The right side of (15) is the annuity value of the revisions to the outlook for current and future income. So a compact way to characterize (15) is this: according to the permanent income model, the change in consumption is the annuity value of revisions to the outlook for current and future income. Equation (15) is what I call the *fundamental equation* of the permanent income model.[12]

I make a proportionality assumption so that (15) can be substantially simplified:

$$E_t y_{ht+i} - E_{t-1} y_{ht+i} = \psi_i (y_{ht} - E_{t-1} y_{ht}) \tag{16}$$

for $i = 1, 2, 3, \ldots$. Also, let $\psi_0 \equiv 1$. The parameter ψ_i is a multiplier which says how much the forecast of y_{ht+i} for $i > 1$ is revised as a result of an innovation in y_{ht}.[13]

The simplification of the fundamental equation, (15), is obtained by substituting (16) into it:

$$c_t - c_{t-1} = \Psi (y_{ht} - E_{t-1} y_{ht}) \tag{17}$$

where

$$\Psi = r(1 + r)^{-1} \sum_{i=0}^{\infty} (1 + r)^{-i} \psi_i. \tag{18}$$

For obvious reasons, we can call Ψ the *annuity value of a $1 innovation in labor income*. It can also be thought of, though, as the ratio of the volatilities (or the *relative volatility*) of consumption and labor income. This interpretation derives from the fact that one measure of the volatility of a variable is the standard deviation of its innovation. The innovation in consumption, according to the permanent income model, is $\Psi (y_{ht} - E_{t-1} y_{ht})$. This has standard deviation $\Psi \sigma$, where σ is the standard deviation of the innovation in y_{ht}.

The Importance of the Dynamic Properties of Labor Income

Now I can show how the value of Ψ depends on the dynamic properties of y_{ht}, particularly on how long an innovation lasts.

Some Simple Examples
Recall that, according to the fundamental equation of the permanent income model, the only thing that prompts households in this economy to change consumption is something that induces a revision in the outlook for current or future labor income. Only $y_{ht} - E_{t-1} y_{ht} \neq 0$ can trigger a revi-

sion in the outlook for income at dates $t + j$ for $j > 0$. There are two extreme possibilities. On the one hand, an innovation in y_{ht} could trigger a revision of the same size in the outlook for income at all future dates ($\psi_i = 1, i \geq 0$); then the innovation in y_{ht} is said to be *permanent*. On the other hand, an innovation in y_{ht} may trigger no revision in future income ($\psi_i = 0, i > 0$); then the innovation is said to be *temporary*. According to (15), the *persistence* of the income innovation (its degree of permanence) makes a great deal of difference in terms of the impact on consumption. Two simple examples show this.

EXAMPLE 1.   *A Permanent Innovation*. Suppose the innovation in labor income today is $100, and households are induced to also raise their estimate of future income $100. That is, $E_t y_{ht+j} - E_{t-1} y_{ht+j} = \$100$ for $j = 0, 1, 2,$ .... Then, according to (15), households adjust consumption by the annuity value of this innovation. For any interest rate, r, the annuity value is

$$r[(1 + r)^{-1}(\$100) + (1 + r)^{-2}(\$100) + (1 + r)^{-3}(\$100) + \cdots]$$

$$= r(\$100/r) = \$100.$$

Thus, when the innovation in income is permanent, households increase consumption by the full amount of the innovation. Under these circumstances, that is the maximum increase in consumption they can sustain into the indefinite future.

EXAMPLE 2.   *A Temporary Innovation*. Now suppose that a $100 innovation in labor income is thought by households to be temporary, so it has no effect on their outlook for income in subsequent periods. That is, $E_t y_{ht} - E_{t-1} y_{ht} = \$100$ and $E_t y_{ht+j} - E_{t-1} y_{ht+j} = 0$ for $j > 0$. If the quarterly interest rate $r = 1$ percent, the annuity value of this innovation is

$$0.01[(1.01)^{-1}(\$100) + 0 + \cdots] \cong 0.01(\$100) = \$1.$$

Thus, when a $100 innovation is viewed as temporary, (15) implies that households increase consumption only $1 and invest the remaining $99. With the rate of interest 1 percent and a $100 temporary increase in income, $1 is the maximum increase in consumption that can be sustained indefinitely.

The dependence of consumption's response on the persistence of an innovation is further illustrated by Example 3. This is more realistic than the first two because it explicitly models the uncertainty in y_{ht}. Doing so clarifies the nature of an innovation and makes precise the link between it and revisions to future forecasts. In addition, the form that the labor income process takes in Example 3 is a simple version of the one used later with actual U.S. data. Finally, Example 3 shows that there are many other possibilities in addition to the extreme ones in which an innovation is either permanent or temporary.

EXAMPLE 3.   *Innovations with Explicit Uncertainty.* Suppose this is the labor income process:

$$y_{ht} = \mu + \phi y_{ht-1} + \varepsilon_t.$$

This is called a *first-order autoregressive* [AR(1)] model for y_{ht} (*autoregressive* because y_{ht} depends on its own previous values, or *lags; first-order* because here there is just one lag). Here, ε_t is an unpredictable random variable with zero mean, and μ and ϕ are constants. Also, $E_{t-1} y_{ht} = \mu + \phi y_{ht-1}$, so that ε_t is the innovation in y_{ht}. It is easy to confirm that here $E_t y_{ht+j} - E_{t-1} y_{ht+j} = \phi^j \varepsilon_t$ for $j = 0, 1, 2, \ldots$ (that is, $\psi_i = \phi^i, i \geqslant 0$).[14]

For concreteness, suppose that $\phi = 0.5$. Then this model of labor income says that when there is a \$100 innovation in y_{ht} (when $\varepsilon_t = 100$), households are induced to raise their forecast of next period's income by \$50, the following period's by \$25, and so on. The revision to the outlook of income far into the future is close to zero since $\phi^j \varepsilon_t$ gets smaller as j increases, as long as ϕ is less than one in absolute value. Evidently, for $0 < \phi < 1$, the situation is intermediate to those in Examples 1 and 2; when $\phi = 1$, it is exactly Example 1; and when $\phi = 0$, it is Example 2.

For this model, the annuity value of an innovation to income is, from equation (18),

$$\Psi = r(1 + r)^{-1} \sum_{i=0}^{\infty} [\phi(1 + r)^{-1}]^i = r(1 + r - \phi)^{-1}.$$

The dependence of Ψ on r and ϕ shows that the annuity value of an innovation (or the relative volatility of consumption and labor income) depends on the interest rate and the persistence properties of labor income which, in this example, are governed by ϕ. The more persistent the innovation—that is, the greater ϕ—the higher is Ψ. When $\phi = 1$, the change in consumption is, as in Example 1, the whole of the innovation in income [$\Psi(1, r) = 1$]. When $\phi = 0$, the change in consumption, as in Example 2, is a tiny fraction, approximately r, of the innovation in income [$\Psi(0, r) = r/(1 + r)$].

A notable feature of Ψ here, which will play a role later, is that it is very sensitive to changes in ϕ when ϕ is near 1. If, for example, $r = 1$ percent and ϕ moves only slightly, from 0.900 to 0.980 to 0.990 to 0.999, Ψ leaps at the same time from 0.090 to 0.330 to 0.500 to 0.909. This is not surprising. The fact that ψ_i is a function of the ith power of ϕ implies that a very small change in the value of ϕ has a growing effect on the ψ_i's as the time horizon increases (for larger values of i). Moreover, for values of ϕ near 1, the effect is already appreciable after only two years (for $i \geqslant 7$). For example, $(0.9)^7 = 0.48$, but $(0.999)^7 = 0.99$. The relative weight of ψ_7 in Ψ is substantial, being equal to $(1 + r)^{-7} = 0.93$ for $r = 1$ percent. [See equation (18).]

A possibility that will arise with the actual U.S. data is that the annuity value of the innovation in income could exceed the innovation itself ($\Psi > 1$). This would happen when the innovation induced households to raise their forecast of future income by an amount sufficiently larger than the innovation. The following example is designed to illustrate this possibility in the simplest setting. The example also illustrates a way to analyze the effects on consumption of an income innovation by decomposing the innovation into parts. This method is useful to study the effects of the type of innovations in y_{ht} that are in the actual U.S. data.

EXAMPLE 4.　*A More-Than-Permanent Innovation.* Suppose that the current period's innovation in labor income is $100 and that this induces households to raise their expectations about future income by more than $100— say, by $150 ($\psi_i = 1.5, i > 0$). If the interest rate is 1 percent, the annuity value of this innovation is

$$0.01[(1.01)^{-1}(\$100) + (1.01)^{-2}(\$150) + (1.01)^{-3}(\$150) + \cdots] = \$149.50.$$

This example can be thought of as a combination of Examples 1 and 2. Specifically, it is equivalent to the household receiving a permanent positive innovation in income of $150 (which causes consumption to jump $150) coupled with a temporary negative income innovation of $50 (which causes consumption to drop $0.50).

The Real World
The AR(1) model for y_{ht} in Example 3 is too simple to represent the actual U.S. labor income data. Those data suggest a more complicated model:

$$y_{ht} = \mu + \alpha t + \rho_1 y_{ht-1} + \rho_2 y_{ht-2} + \varepsilon_t \tag{19}$$

where μ, α, ρ_1, and ρ_2 are constants and, again, ε_t is a random variable with zero mean. This is a second-order autoregressive [AR(2)] model with trend for y_{ht}. It will be convenient to write (19) in terms of ϕ_1 and ϕ_2, defined as the values of ϕ which solve $\phi^2 - \rho_1 \phi - \rho_2 = 0$. These are called the *AR roots* of y_{ht}. Since $\phi_1 + \phi_2 = \rho_1$ and $\phi_1\phi_2 = -\rho_2$, (19) can be rewritten as

$$y_{ht} = \mu + \alpha t + (\phi_1 + \phi_2)y_{ht-1} - \phi_1\phi_2 y_{ht-2} + \varepsilon_t. \tag{20}$$

Note that (20) can be rewritten as

$$y_{ht} - \phi_1 y_{ht-1} = \mu + \alpha t + \phi_2(y_{ht-1} - \phi_1 y_{ht-2}) + \varepsilon_t. \tag{21}$$

Now we can see that the representation of labor income can take at least two very different forms. When $\phi_1 = 1$, $|\phi_2| < 1$, and $\alpha = 0$, equation (19) is an AR(1) model in first differences of y_{ht}: $y_{ht} - y_{ht-1}$. This type of model is usually written in the form of equation (21). [The AR(1) model in first differences is Deaton's preferred model.] It is known as a *difference stationary* representation because in this form y_{ht} is not covariance stationary (its variance is not defined), but its first difference is. This means, roughly, that the changes in y_{ht} fluctuate with constant amplitude about a constant mean over time, while the levels of y_{ht} follow no particular trend. When ϕ_1 and ϕ_2 are both less than one in absolute value and α is possibly nonzero, equation (19) is a *trend stationary* representation for y_{ht}. In this form, the levels of y_{ht} fluctuate with constant amplitude about a linear trend in time. Evidently, these two forms are special cases of the AR(2) model with trend.

It is obvious from (19) [or (20), (21)] that the random variable $\varepsilon_t = y_{ht} - E_{t-1}y_{ht}$, the surprise change in labor income. In addition, it can easily be verified that

$$E_t y_{ht+j} - E_{t-1}y_{ht+j} = [\phi_1/(\phi_1 - \phi_2)]\phi_1^j \varepsilon_t - [\phi_2/(\phi_1 - \phi_2)]\phi_2^j \varepsilon_t \tag{22}$$

so that

$$\psi_j = [\phi_1/(\phi_1 - \phi_2)]\phi_1^j - [\phi_2/(\phi_1 - \phi_2)]\phi_2^j \tag{23}$$

for $j = 0, 1, 2, \ldots$. Note that when either ϕ_1 or ϕ_2 are zero, this model reduces to the one in Example 3. Note also that when ϕ_1 and ϕ_2 are both nonzero, the effect on the forecast revision of ε_t looks like the sum of the effects of two innovations like those in Example 3. The first is $[\phi_1/(\phi_1 - \phi_2)]\varepsilon_t$ with persistence parameter ϕ_1, and the second is $[-\phi_2/(\phi_1 - \phi_2)]\varepsilon_t$ with persistence parameter ϕ_2. (This sort of possibility was suggested by Example 4.) Not surprisingly, the annuity value of ε_t is just the sum of the annuity values of these two innovations:

$$\Psi(\phi_1, \phi_2, r) = [r/(1 + r - \phi_1)][\phi_1/(\phi_1 - \phi_2)]$$

$$+ [r/(1 + r - \phi_2)][-\phi_2/(\phi_1 - \phi_2)]. \tag{24}$$

Two things are worth noting about Ψ. First, when one of the ϕ's is 1 and the other is positive, then (20) is an AR(1) in first differences form and Ψ exceeds 1. Thus, consumption is more volatile than income. This may be seen by noting that when, say, $\phi_1 = 1$, (24) becomes $(1 + r)/[1 + r - \phi_2]$, which always exceeds 1 if $\phi_2 > 0$. For example, $\Psi(1.0, 0.5, 0.01) = 1.98$. This case is similar to the one in Example 4 in that an innovation in income is more than permanent. To see this, substitute $\phi_1 = 1$, $\phi_2 = 0.5$, $r = 0.01$, and $\varepsilon_t = \$100$ into (23) to find that given a \$100 innovation in labor income the household revises its forecast of this income j periods in the future by $(2 - 0.5^j) \times \$100$. For $j = 0$, 1, 2, and 3, this is \$100, \$150, \$175, and \$187.50. The decomposition method in Example 4 can also help understand this more-than-permanent feature. When one of the roots (say, ϕ_1) of y_{ht} equals 1 and the other is between 0 and 1, then an innovation has a permanent part, $[1/(1 - \phi_2)]\varepsilon_t$, and a temporary negative part, $-[\phi_2 \div (1 - \phi_2)]\varepsilon_t$. Because the temporary part is negative, the revision in the outlook for income several periods in the future exceeds the innovation in income. (See Example 4.)

A second notable feature of Ψ is that it is very sensitive to changes in one of the roots of y_{ht} (the ϕ's) when that root is near 1. The relative volatility of consumption and income, that is, depends a lot on how long the income innovation is expected to last. As in Example 3, this is not surprising once one notes from (23) that ψ_i is a function of the ith power of each of the roots of y_{ht}. A consequence of this is that very small changes in a root when its value is close to 1 produce large changes in ψ_i's starting as soon as two years out ($i \geqslant 7$). Since those ψ's have substantial weight in Ψ, it follows that their sensitivity to the roots of y_{ht} translates into a sensitivity for Ψ. For example, if $r = 1$ percent, $\phi_2 = 0.5$, and ϕ_1 starts at 0.9, then small changes in ϕ_1—from 0.900 to 0.980 to 0.990 to 0.999— produce large increases in Ψ—from 0.18 to 0.66 to 0.99 to 1.80. To put this more concretely, if $r = 1$ percent, $\phi_1 = 0.9$, and $\phi_2 = 0.5$, then this permanent income model predicts that households spend just \$18 of a \$100 innovation in income and invest the rest. But if $\phi_1 = 0.999$ and nothing else is different, then the model has a dramatically different prediction: households respond to the \$100 income innovation by increasing consumption \$180—\$80 more than the income increase, which they get by reducing investment.

The Deaton Paradox . . . ?

It is well known that changes in income from one quarter to the next are positively correlated. So when Deaton estimated the AR(1) first difference representation using labor income data, the coefficient on the change in y_{ht-1} came out positive, implying that $\Psi > 1$. More precisely, his estimate of Ψ is close to 1.6. Thus, the permanent income model together with the AR(1) model in first differences of labor income implies that consumption ought to be roughly one and a half times as volatile as labor income. This conflicts sharply with the empirical fact that consumption is only about half as volatile as labor income. This conflict is ironical—and paradoxical—because many economists have believed that the observed relative smoothness of consumption is the principal reason for taking the permanent income model seriously.

Despite Deaton's finding based on the AR(1) difference model, there continues to be debate on whether there really is a paradox. In part, this is due to the fact that other models of income, which appear to fit the labor income data equally well, do not yield the counterfactual implication Deaton got. The continued controversy also reflects the suspicion that any measure of the long-run effect of an innovation in income based on postwar U.S. data must be extremely imprecise and unreliable. According to the permanent income model, the 10–15-year effects of an income innovation have a significant influence on the consumption decision, yet the postwar data include only three or four nonoverlapping intervals of this length. The continuing controversy over the existence of a paradox indicates the possibility that, in the end, the traditional assumption that income innovations are temporary may be vindicated.

Deaton's Results

Here I reproduce Deaton's empirical results using a slightly different measure of labor income than he used. My measure is 0.66 times gross output (y_t). The reason for the factor 0.66 is that it is roughly the fraction of gross output due to labor in the postwar U.S. data. I estimated a trend stationary model and an AR(1) difference model by the method of ordinary least squares, using the 111 quarterly observations on these data between the third quarter of 1956 and the first of 1984. The results:

Trend Model

$$y_{ht} = 172.29 + 0.78t + 1.35y_{ht-1} - 0.39y_{ht-2} + \hat{\varepsilon}_t; \qquad \hat{\sigma}_\varepsilon = 49.3 \qquad (25)$$
$$\phantom{y_{ht} = }\; (2.2) \quad\;\; (1.8) \quad\;\; (14.7) \quad\quad (-4.3)$$

AR(1) Difference Model

$$\Delta y_{ht} = 11.55 + 0.37\Delta y_{ht-1} + \hat{\varepsilon}_t; \qquad \hat{\sigma}_\varepsilon = 49.8. \qquad (26)$$
$$\phantom{\Delta y_{ht} = }\; (2.3) \quad\;\; (4.1)$$

In (26), $\Delta y_{ht} \equiv y_{ht} - y_{ht-1}$. The numbers in parentheses beneath the equations' parameter estimates are t-statistics, and $\hat{\sigma}_\varepsilon$ is the standard deviation of the fitted regression disturbances, $\hat{\varepsilon}_t$. Note that the two models have approximately the same implication for the volatility of labor income, σ_ε: that it is roughly \$50 per quarter. This is consistent with Deaton's finding that both models fit the data equally well.

To determine the models' implications for the volatility of consumption, the permanent income model requires that Ψ be computed. This in turn requires the roots of y_{ht}. These are 0.92 and 0.43 in the trend model and 1.0 and 0.37 in the difference. The implied values of Ψ are, then,

Trend

$$\Psi(0.92, 0.43, 0.01) = 0.19$$

$$(27)$$

Difference

$$\Psi(1.0, 0.37, 0.01) = 1.58.$$

The implications of these two models for the response of consumption to an innovation in income are obviously very different. The trend model implies that households respond to a \$100 innovation in income by increasing spending only \$19 and investing the rest. The difference model implies instead that they increase spending \$158 and reduce investment \$58. The trend model's 0.19 is more realistic than the AR(1) difference model's 1.58 since 0.19 is considerably closer to the empirical amount of smoothness in consumption (roughly 0.5).

The different implications of the two models reflect their different maximal roots: 0.92 and 1.0. That is clear when the 0.92 root in the trend model is replaced by 1.0: its Ψ jumps from 0.19 to 1.74, just about the value of Ψ in the difference model. This sensitivity of Ψ to variations in the value of a root that is near 1 is striking. The reason for it is that such changes have a large effect on the trend or difference model's implication for the long-run effect of an innovation and the permanent income model assigns substantial weight to these long-run effects in the consumption decision. The effects of an income innovation on expectations of future income are measured by each model's ψ_i's. Figure 20.1 displays how the two estimated models measure these ψ_i's in the ten years after an innovation. Note how the two models' ψ_i's are similar in the first year (in the first few quarters), but then they diverge. Note also, in Figure 20.2, how slowly the consumption decision's weights on the ψ_i's die out. The weight on the ψ for the forecast revision ten years after the innovation is still about 70 percent of that for the initial quarter. [Recall from (18) that the relative weight on ψ_i is $(1 + r)^{-i}$.]

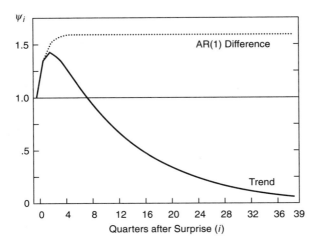

Figure 20.1 Revisions to the Income Outlook Induced by a $1 Surprise Income Increase in the Two Labor Income Models

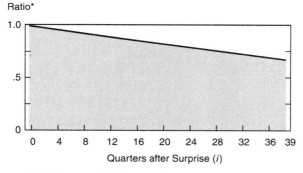

*Weight on ψ_i relative to weight on ψ_0

Figure 20.2 Weights on Revisions to the Income Outlook in the Consumption Decision of the Permanent Income Model

Figures 20.1 and 20.2
Explaining the Trend and Difference Models' Different Implications for the Consumption/Income Relationship

Evidently, according to the permanent income model, the relationship between consumption and income depends on very long-run properties of the labor income process. But the trend and AR(1) difference models differ substantially on what those properties are. Yet, according to Deaton, it is impossible to determine which model fits the income data better. Essentially, this is because, with only 30 years of data, a root of 0.92 is virtually indistinguishable statistically from 1.0 (Christiano and Ljungqvist 1988).

A Questionable Resolution

One potential resolution to the Deaton paradox is to replace Deaton's assumption that the long-run effect of an income innovation is strong with the traditional view that it is weak. The results above suggest that one way to do this is to replace Deaton's AR(1) difference representation of income by the trend model. Today we seem to have no statistical basis for ruling this out. Nevertheless, there are serious questions about the plausibility of the trend model which prevent it from supplying a convincing resolution to the paradox. The difference model is more plausible, and there are other difference models than Deaton's. Among them is at least one which implies the traditional assumption that an income innovation is relatively transient and, in particular, does not imply the paradox. Unfortunately, even this way to restore the traditional view of the income innovation is controversial.

The Implausible Trend Model
Despite its more realistic Ψ, the trend model cannot now be used to resolve Deaton's paradox. This is because there is empirical evidence that the trend model is implausible. This is clear in Figure 20.3, where you see quarterly levels of per capita labor income in the United States between the mid-1950s and the mid-1980s and a trend line computed from just the first 15 years of data and extended through the rest of the period. Evidently, a household that lived through the 1950s and 1960s, and believed the trend model of income, would have had serious doubts by the mid-1970s since its expectation for income to return to the old trend would have been repeatedly disappointed. The peak of the 1971–73 U.S. expansion just barely brought labor income back to the old trend line, and the 1975 recession seems to have driven it away permanently. Thus, the trend specification for income cannot be used without formally taking account of the possibility that households discarded their old trend specification and somehow settled on a new one.[15] That highly complex modeling problem is certainly beyond the scope of this paper.[16]

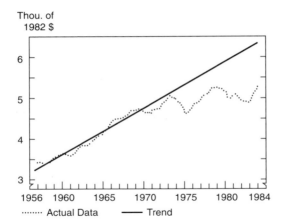

Figure 20.3 Levels with a Linear Trend

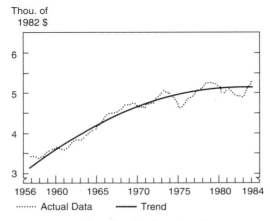

Figure 20.4 Levels with a Quadratic Trend

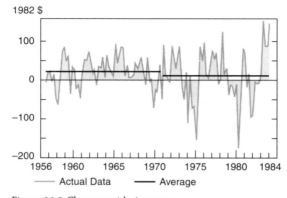

Figure 20.5 Changes with Averages

Figures 20.3–20.5
Three Views of Household Labor Income: 3rd Quarter 1956–1st Quarter 1984 in the
United States. Source of basic data: See Appendix.

An alternative resolution to that problem is to modify the trend specification in (25) by adding a term in t^2, that is, by making the equation's trend quadratic, so that it curves as the data appear to. Unfortunately, this has its own problems. I reestimated this quadratic trend model, and its implied trend appears in Figure 20.4.[17] Note the bow shape of the trend. The role of the bow is to capture the apparent deterioration in economic performance that occurred in the 1970s and early 1980s. Assuming households used this quadratic trend model to forecast income is equivalent to assuming that in the 1950s they confidently expected that 20 years later the economy would be weak. This seems implausible, to say the least. I think it is much more probable that in the 1950s households looking 20 years ahead found an upturn as likely as a downturn.

In sum, there are two problems with using the trend model to try to resolve Deaton's paradox. One is that the assumption underlying Deaton's own specification—that households used the same linear trend model to forecast income throughout the postwar era—seems implausible because it conflicts sharply with the properties of the income data themselves. The other problem is that a solution to the first problem—replacing the linear trend by a quadratic—is unattractive because it presumes an implausible amount of foresight by households.

The Unreliable Difference Model

The trend model is not the only alternative to Deaton's specification which rationalizes the traditional view about the effect of an income innovation. There are difference models other than Deaton's which also do this. Moreover, the problems encountered with the trend model do not occur if we instead assume that households think of labor income as a difference rather than a trend process. This can be seen in Figure 20.5, which plots the quarterly changes in the levels of y_{ht} since the mid-1950s. The two straight horizontal lines indicate the averages of the changes during two periods: from the third quarter of 1956 to the third of 1970 and from the fourth quarter of 1970 to the first of 1984. According to the difference model, when there is an unusually large or small change in income, all that can be expected is that the quarterly changes eventually return to some fixed underlying constant; the levels of y_{ht} do not necessarily return to any previous trend.

Under this view, the U.S. economy suffered several particularly bad shocks in 1975 and in the early 1980s, but after each one the quarterly changes returned to their underlying long-run average, which itself was fixed. This view is consistent with Figure 20.5's sawtooth pattern for the

1970s and 1980s. The contractions reflect the effects of bad shocks, and the expansions represent the resumption of the previous quarterly average change. Although the average change is slightly lower in the 1970s and 1980s than in the preceding two decades, it is not sufficiently smaller to shake the confidence of a believer in the difference specification.[18] Thus, we can plausibly assume that households used the same difference specification to forecast labor income throughout this period.

Therefore, the difference specification avoids the linear trend's problem in that the assumption that households used the same difference model to forecast income throughout the postwar period seems plausible. In addition, the difference model manages to capture the bow shape of postwar income data without assigning an implausible degree of foresight to households, as the quadratic trend model does. The difference model's account for the bow is that there were a couple of episodes of bad negative shocks which drove down the level of income, but did not alter its average change. According to the difference model, from the perspective of the 1950s, the economy 20 years later was just as likely to bow up as down, since a couple of episodes of good shocks are as likely as a couple of episodes of bad shocks.

Although a difference representation for y_{ht} appears more plausible than a trend representation, this does not mean that Deaton's AR(1) difference specification is necessarily the preferred one. An alternative is the unobserved components model studied by Clark (1987) and Watson (1986). The estimated version of that difference model implies that the long-run effect of a \$1 innovation to income is considerably less than \$1, so that with this representation of income the permanent income model implies an empirically plausible degree of consumption volatility. Obviously, either the AR(1) model or the unobserved components model (or both) must be giving a misleading estimate of the long-run impact of an income innovation. Further research is required to establish which one of these models yields the most plausible measure.

Cochrane (1988) argues that neither one is reliable for this measurement. Even though the reported standard errors for the long-run effect of an income innovation are small, he argues that the precision is spurious and reflects aspects of the models' structure, in which we can have little confidence. Cochrane proposes a procedure for measuring the long-run impact of an income innovation that does not depend on specifying a particular model of income. Application of this procedure to postwar U.S. data confirms that precisely estimating persistence with such a small data set is difficult (Campbell and Mankiw 1987). This has led some researchers to expand the U.S. data set by considering data from other countries as well (Campbell and Mankiw 1989, Kormendi and Meguire 1987).

In summary, we don't know yet which assumption is the most plausible: the traditional one, which is that income innovations are transient, or Deaton's, which is that they have a strong, permanent effect. Therefore, we cannot rule out the possibility that the paradox will ultimately be resolved by restoring the traditional view about the effect of an income innovation.

The Real Business Cycle Alternative

Again, one way to possibly resolve the Deaton paradox is to modify Deaton's AR(1) difference specification for labor income. Another way is to preserve that specification and consider the possibility that other parts of the permanent income model are misspecified. Here I do that by shifting to another equilibrium growth model, a close relative: a real business cycle model. I describe this model and show that, even though in it labor income is an AR(1) difference process, consumption is substantially less volatile than labor income.

The principal distinction between the permanent income and real business cycle models, which accounts for the latter's superior performance here, is that the permanent income model assumes the interest rate is fixed whereas the real business cycle model does not. Besides elaborating on this, I show here that there is a sense in which—aside from their family connection—these two are very similar models.

The Model

Like the permanent income model, the real business cycle model is a growth model with its own particular specification for preferences (the utility function u) and technology (the production function f):

$$u(c_t, l_t) = \ln c_t + \gamma l_t, \quad f(k_t, z_t h_t) = (z_t h_t)^{(1-\theta)} k_t^\theta \tag{28}$$

where γ and θ are parameters and, recall, c_t is consumption, l_t leisure, k_t the capital stock, h_t hours worked, and z_t the factors affecting productivity. Two features distinguish this model from the permanent income model. One is that here l_t appears in the u function. This implies that the hours decision is modeled explicitly; labor income, y_{ht}, is determined by the model (is endogenous). The other distinguishing feature is that f is not linear in k_t in the real business cycle model. This implies that in this model the risk-free interest rate fluctuates rather than remains constant and the risk premium is not zero.

I adopt the following specification for the real business cycle model's z_t:

$$z_t = z_{t-1} \exp(x_t), \quad x_t = \mu + \rho x_{t-1} + \varepsilon_t. \tag{29}$$

The random variable x_t is the growth rate of z_t with the indicated AR(1) representation. This is an AR(1) difference specification for $\log z_t$. To see this, note that (29) can be rewritten as $\log z_t = (1 + \rho) \log z_{t-1} - \rho \log z_{t-2} + \mu + \varepsilon_t$. Then

$$\log z_t - \log z_{t-1} = \mu + \rho(\log z_{t-1} - \log z_{t-2}) + \varepsilon_t. \tag{30}$$

The real business cycle model has considerably more parameters than the permanent income model. I assigned these values to them: $\rho = -0.077$, $\mu = 0.0035$, $\gamma = 0.0026$, $\beta = 0.99$, $\delta = 0.018$, $\theta = 0.39$, and $\sigma_\varepsilon = 0.019$. This value for δ is required if the gross investment series implied by $dk_t \equiv k_{t+1} - (1 - \delta)k_t$ is to resemble the gross investment series published by the U.S. Department of Commerce. Values for θ, γ, and $\mu/(1 - \rho)$ are chosen to roughly match the model's implications for the average values of h_t, c_t/y_t, and k_t/y_t with their empirical counterparts in U.S. data for the period from the second quarter of 1956 to the first of 1984. The implied averages (and empirical values) for these variables are 323.9 (320.4), 0.72 (0.72), and 11.32 (10.58), respectively. The values of ρ, μ, and σ_ε are based on regression analysis of the time series properties of z_t, which can be measured using data on y_t, k_t, and h_t given the value assigned to θ. (See Christiano 1988 for a careful discussion of this method of selecting parameter values.)

The method used to solve the model is described in Christiano 1987a,b, and the algebraic formulas for the decision rules are reported in Christiano 1987c (n. 4). All the data used are discussed in the Appendix.

Partial Success

I compute the real business cycle model's implication for the relative volatility of consumption and income by forming the ratio of an innovation in consumption to an innovation in labor income. This ratio is Ψ, according to (17).

To facilitate the interpretation of the outcome of this calculation, I first discuss part of the real business cycle model's innovation response functions. Figure 20.6 shows the first 30 quarters of the responses of c_t, h_t, dk_t, and y_t to a one standard deviation innovation in the growth rate of the technology shock z_t in period 2, assuming that the system is on a steady-state growth path in periods 0 and 1 (that is, $\varepsilon_2 = 0.019$ and $\varepsilon_t = 0$ for

%

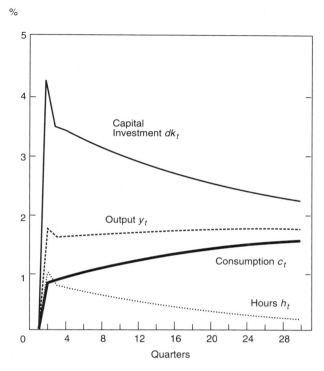

Figure 20.6
The Impact of a Technology Shock in the Real Business Cycle Model: Percent Deviation of Shocked Path from Steady-State, Unshocked Path. The shock is an unexpected 1.9% increase in z_t in quarter 2; steady-state growth is assumed in quarters 0 and 1.

$t = 0, 1, 3, 4, \ldots$). More precisely yet, the curves in Figure 20.6 are the quarterly percentage deviations in these variables from a baseline scenario in which $\varepsilon_t = 0$ for $t = 0, 1, 2, 3, \ldots$.

With the assumed structure of z_t, the innovation in ε_t drives z_t 1.9 percent above its baseline growth path in period 2, after which it declines to a path 1.76 percent above the baseline. After the shock, all the model's variables except h_t and the risk-free rate of interest, r_t, end up 1.76 percent above their baselines. The exceptions at first are increased by the shock, but eventually return to the value they had before it.

As Figure 20.6 shows, consumption rises only gradually to its higher growth path. One way to explain this is to recall Robinson Crusoe. In particular, Crusoe chooses not to adjust consumption immediately after an unexpected productivity increase because this agent also wants to increase saving and investment in order to take advantage of the temporarily higher rate of return on investment. That higher rate is reflected in capital investment's strong shock response. The incentive the shock creates to delay consumption by increasing saving is known as the *substitution effect*, whereas the incentive to increase consumption because the long-run ability to consume has increased is called the *income effect*.

Though the interest rate, r_t, does rise in response to the innovation in x_t, the rise is quite small. It is so small, in fact, that it is not shown in Figure 20.6. In the steady state, $r_t = 0.01667$; after the shock, it jumps to 0.01728, then declines monotonically back to 0.01667. Thus, the effect on the interest rate is a negligible six one-hundredths of a basis point.

In Figure 20.6, note the early spikes in the responses of dk_t, h_t, and y_t. This reflects the fact that 7.15 percent of the initial 1.9 percent jump in z_t is only temporary. The lack of a spike in c_t reflects the small response of consumption to a temporary disturbance, which, in turn, explains the pronounced spike in capital investment. (Here the income effect on consumption is very small, whereas the substitution effect on investment is not.) Hours also respond fairly strongly to the temporary component in the productivity shock (as explained in Hansen 1985a).

My goal here, remember, is to see how the model estimates the ratio of the jumps in consumption and labor income. The model's ratio of the jumps in consumption and total income in period 2 is 0.32; that is, consumption's innovation is about 32 percent of income's. In this model, $y_{ht} = (1 - \theta)y_t = 0.61y_t$. Thus, the relevant relative volatility implied by the model is 0.32/0.61 = 0.52. This real business cycle model seems to come close to matching the observed relative volatility of consumption and labor income, which is roughly one-half.

Unfortunately, though, I cannot claim to have entirely resolved the paradox raised by Deaton. That is because the model is clearly flawed: successive changes in income have correlation of about -0.119, reflecting the fact that the serial correlation properties of equilibrium output in the model closely mimic those of z_t. A naive application of the permanent income model's formula for Ψ thus yields $\Psi(1.0, -0.119, 0.01) = 0.89$, considerably less than the value of 1.58 implied by U.S. data. To get a version of the real business cycle model with a more reasonable autocorrelation structure for changes in y_t, I changed ρ to 0.2, but left all other parameter values, including $\rho/(1 - \mu)$, unchanged. With these parameter values, the model's first-order autocorrelation of labor income changes is about 0.35, and $\Psi(1.0, 0.35, 0.01) = 1.53$. Then the ratio of an innovation in consumption to an innovation in labor income is 0.84—higher than before, and than it should be, but about half as high as Deaton's paradoxical ratio. And unlike Deaton's ratio, the real business cycle model's is, like the actual ratio, less than 1; this model does, that is, correctly predict that consumption is less volatile than labor income.

The Essential Difference . . .

The reason for the real business cycle and permanent income models' sharply different implications seems to lie in the different nature of the shocks they assume. According to the real business cycle model, disturbances to output result from shocks that are expected to be permanent and which affect the rate of return on investment in capital. As we have seen, therefore, a rise in income signals not only that households' long-term ability to consume has risen, but also that the return on investment has. By itself, the increase in the long-run ability to consume motivates households to substantially increase consumption today. This income effect on consumption is partially offset, though, by the substitution effect as households take advantage of the increased return to saving.[19] In contrast, the permanent income model assumes that shocks affect the average product of capital, not the marginal product. Because of this and the linearity of f in k, the model implies a fixed interest rate, thus allowing only the income effect to operate on consumption. When shocks are partially permanent, the income effect is very strong, which accounts for the model's counterfactual implications when the difference specification is used.

. . . And a Surprising Similarity

Surprisingly, despite their very different implications for the volatility of consumption, the permanent income and real business cycle models have very similar implications for other dynamic characteristics of consumption. In particular, they both imply—at least roughly—that consumption follows a *random walk*. This means that consumption in the current period is the best predictor of consumption next period, so that any change in consumption is uncorrelated with information available in the current period or earlier.

The permanent income model implies that consumption is exactly a random walk. This can quickly be verified from equation (7) and the fact that $\beta(1 + r) = 1$ [from (9) and (10)]. To see this, note that here (7) implies that $E_t u'(c_{t+1}) = u'(c_t)$, or $E_t c_{t+1} = c_t$ under the model's specification of u in (9). (See note 12.)

In the real business cycle model, r_t is not a constant; but recall how little it moved. This suggests that consumption is approximately a random walk in this model as well. To demonstrate this property, I used the model to simulate 1,000 sets of 112 observations for c_t, dk_t, h_t, and r_t. This was done using the approximate decision rules in Christiano 1987c (n. 4), starting the initial capital stock on a steady-state growth path, and using ε_t's drawn independently from a normal random number generator with mean zero and standard error 0.019. I needed 112 artificial observations because this is the length of my U.S. data set. For each artificial data set, I computed the correlation between the change in the log of consumption and the lag-one change in the log of consumption, income, and capital investment. In addition, I computed the correlation between the change in the log of consumption and lag-one hours worked and the lag-one real rate of interest. (I work in logs because the real business cycle model implies that is necessary to induce covariance stationarity.)

Table 20.1 shows the means of the real business cycle model correlations across the 1,000 artificial data sets along with their associated standard deviations. The table also shows the correlations based on U.S. data. Note that all of the model correlations are small and have large standard deviations. In this sense, they are all close to zero, which is what they would be if consumption in the model were exactly a random walk. I computed (but

Table 20.1
A random walk in the real business cycle model

| | Correlations with consumption growth* | | |
| | Model simulations** | | |
First-lag variables correlated with consumption growth*	Standard deviation	Mean	U.S. estimates†
Consumption growth*	.108	.059	.271
Income growth*	.098	.045	.204
Hours worked	.129	.079	−.057
Investment growth*	.093	.038	.161
Interest rate	.130	.079	.104

*The growth of a variable x_t is defined as $\log x_t - \log x_{t-1}$.
**These are the results of 1,000 simulations, each 112 quarters long.
†The data period is from the 2nd quarter of 1956 to the 1st of 1984.
Source of U.S. data: See Appendix.

don't show) the correlations up to lag four; they are also small, with large standard errors.[20]

As is obvious in the table, the model's random walk implication does not square well with the actual U.S. data. In Christiano 1987b, I argue that much of the discrepancy can be accounted for by the fact that the data are time averaged. A similar argument in the context of the permanent income model is made in Christiano, Eichenbaum, and Marshall 1991.

Appendix: The U.S. Data Used in the Models

The U.S. data used in the models in the accompanying paper are primarily standard measures available from standard sources. (For a detailed discussion, see Christiano 1987d.)

The resource constraint, (1) in the paper, divides all output, y_t, into only two categories: consumption, c_t, and investment, dk_t. In view of this, I consolidate private and government spending. Thus, c_t and dk_t are private plus public consumption and investment, respectively. *Private consumption* here has three components: personal consumption expenditures on nondurables and on services and the service flow from the stock of durable goods held by households. My measure of the service flow is from the data base documented in Brayton and Mauskopf 1985. For the other two components of private consumption, I use the U.S. Department of Commerce National Income and Product Accounts (NIPA). *Public consumption* is measured as the NIPA government purchases of goods and services, but reduced by an update of the measure of government investment discussed in Musgrave 1980. *Investment* is the sum of that government investment, NIPA personal expenditures on durables, and NIPA private domestic investment. *Gross output* is the NIPA measure of gross national product plus the service flow from the stock of consumer durables minus net exports.

The *stock of capital*, k_t, is defined as the beginning-of-quarter stock of public and private equipment and structures plus the stock of consumer durables plus public and private residential capital. This definition conforms with the definition of investment. Given the U.S. data on dk_t and k_t, equation (3) in the accompanying paper can be used to measure the quarterly *rate of depreciation* in the capital stock, δ. I use Hansen's (1984) measure of *hours worked*, h_t.

Variables are converted to per capita terms by the working-age population, measured in a way that conforms with Hansen's (1984) measure of hours worked. All flow variables (c_t, dk_t, y_t, h_t) are measured at a quarterly rate.

A Feel for the Numbers

You may want an idea of the size of these measured variables. In the United States, between the second quarter of 1956 and the first quarter of 1984, the average values of h_t, c_t/y_t, and k_t/y_t are 320.4 hours, 0.72, and 10.58, respectively. In addition, the average value of the ratio of labor income to total income (y_{ht}/y_t) is roughly 0.66 and has been remarkably constant throughout the 20th century (Christiano 1988, n. 3). Although no value of the quarterly depreciation rate results in an exact fit of the paper's equation (3), the value $\delta = 0.018$ seems to do best. This implies an annual depreciation rate of 7.4 percent. Since in the data k_t is composed of many different kinds of capital, $\delta = 0.018$ should be thought of as a kind of average depreciation rate across different kinds of capital, each with a different rate of depreciation. Included, for example, are both toasters and houses, which presumably have very different depreciation rates.

Notes

1. In these models, only *real* things, like unexpected productivity changes (or *shocks*), cause recurring fluctuations in general activity. *Nominal* things, like money, play no role.

2. Since the permanent income and real business cycle models do not include money, neither does the growth model I describe here. For a growth model that incorporates money, see Marshall 1992.

3. For a detailed discussion of the competitive markets in which households and firms are assumed to interact, see Prescott's paper [Chapter 14 in this volume] and Hansen 1985a. They describe two different—though equivalent—market settings. Prescott considers a *sequence of markets* equilibrium in which households and firms meet and trade every quarter. Hansen describes a *date zero* market equilibrium in which households and firms meet just once, at the beginning of time, to sign contracts. Hansen's discussion takes place explicitly in the context of the permanent income model.

4. It is beyond the scope of this paper to formally present the growth model economy at the level of the finite-lived individual agents who are assumed to populate it. (For this, see Aiyagari 1987.) Instead, I start the formal part of my discussion at the level of the Robinson Crusoe interpretation. However, it is important to remember that this particular interpretation of the growth model has little economic interest in itself and is intended only to facilitate solving for the economywide average values of the model's variables. The economically interesting interpretation of the growth model is the one in which numerous heterogeneous agents with finite lives interact in competitive markets. In practice, once Robinson Crusoe's preferences and the technology available to this agent are specified, the degree of heterogeneity in the underlying multiagent economy is severely restricted.

5. Equation (3) implicitly abstracts from population growth. If the gross rate of population growth were a constant, n, then (3) would have to be written $k_{t+1} = [(1 - \delta)/n]k_t + dk_t$. Although I implicitly set $n = 1$ throughout this paper, in the computation of the solution to the real business cycle model, I set $n = 1.00325$, which corresponds to an annual popula-

tion growth rate of roughly 1.2 percent. For a formal treatment of that model which exhibits where and why n enters into the mathematical equations that describe the real business cycle model, see Christiano 1987c.

6. The maximization problem must also obey the nonnegativity constraints: k_t, h_t, c_t, y_t, $dk_t \geq 0$. According to the last one, capital investment is *irreversible*; once put in place it cannot be reduced at a rate faster than the depreciation rate. This is consistent with the putty/clay analogy mentioned above.

7. In general, $E_t u'(c_{t+1})(1 + R_t) \neq (1 + R_t)E_t u'(c_{t+1})$ since R_t is not known at date t. (As pointed out below, the permanent income model R_t is an exception: it is a constant.) This is to be contrasted with the risk-free rate, r_t, which is known at date t, so that $E_t u'(c_{t+1})(1 + r_t) = (1 + r_t)E_t u'(c_{t+1})$.

8. This illustrates an important result in the theory of finance, namely, that the risk premium on an asset reflects not its variance but the covariance of its payoff with consumption. For example, if the covariance term in (8) is positive, so that capital investment represents insurance against periods in which the marginal utility of consumption is high, then the risk premium is negative. In this case, the volatility of the payoff on capital investment makes it more desirable than the risk-free asset.

9. See Christiano, Eichenbaum, and Marshall 1991 for a version of the permanent income hypothesis which models the household hours decision explicitly. I avoid that approach here because it only complicates matters without altering the principal implications of concern here: those for the consumption/income relationship.

10. The exact solution to the permanent income model is not analytically tractable (Chamberlain and Wilson 1984). It is a contingency plan for c_t and k_t which maximizes (4) subject to (1), (9), and c_t, k_t, $dk_t \geq 0$. The contingency plan for c_t that I describe—in which c_t is equated with permanent income—is the exact, unique solution to a modified version of the permanent income model in which the restrictions c_t, k_t, $dk_t \geq 0$ are not imposed and $E_t \sum_{j=0}^{\infty} \beta^j k_{t+j}^2 < \infty$ is imposed. (See L. Hansen 1985 for a formal derivation of this solution.) I hope that this solution is a good approximation to the solution of the original model. Research to investigate this issue would be worthwhile.

11. The *annuity value* of a stream of possibly different payments—say, $x(1)$, $x(2)$, $x(3)$, ...—is the corresponding constant payment stream with equal present value. Suppose, for example, that the interest rate is $1 + r$. Then the present value PV of $x(s)$ for $s = 1, 2, 3, \ldots$ is $\sum_{s=1}^{\infty} (1 + r)^{-s} x(s)$. The corresponding annuity value is $r \times PV$. As expected, if $x(s) = x$, a constant for all s, then $r \times PV = x$.

12. An implication of a well-known property of conditional expectations is that $E_{t-1}[E_t y_{ht+i} - E_{t-1} y_{ht+i}] = 0$ for $i \geq 0$. Thus, according to equation (15), $E_{t-1} c_t = c_{t-1}$: consumption is a random walk. This implication of the permanent income model was pointed out in the famous paper by Hall (1978b), who also derived equation (15).

13. The proportionality assumption, (16), amounts to an assumption that only past y_{ht} is useful in forecasting future y_{ht}, that the addition of past c_t, for example, does not help (c_t does not Granger-cause y_{ht}). Also, this assumption implies that the regression of $c_t - c_{t-1}$ on current and past y_{ht} has a fitted disturbance identically equal to zero. This can be seen from (17) below, which has current and past y_{ht} on the right side of the equality and no error term. [Past y_{ht} appears only implicitly, in $E_{t-1} y_{ht}$, which is a function only of y_{ht} (because of the Granger-causality observation).] Christiano, Eichenbaum, and Marshall (1991) avoid this grossly counterfactual implication by working in an environment in which a proportionality

relation like (16) does not hold. To follow their lead here would complicate matters without altering my conclusions, according to Campbell and Deaton 1989 and West 1988.

14. To see this, simply note that y_{ht+j} can be expressed as $y_{ht+j} = \mu(1 + \phi + \phi^2 + \cdots + \phi^j) + \phi^{j+1}y_{ht-1} + \varepsilon_{t+j} + \phi\varepsilon_{t+j-1} + \phi^2\varepsilon_{t+j-2} + \cdots + \phi^j\varepsilon_t$. Then $E_t y_{ht+j} = \mu(1 + \phi + \phi^2 + \cdots + \phi^j) + \phi^{j+1}y_{ht-1} + \phi^j\varepsilon_t$ since $E_t\varepsilon_{t+s} = 0$ for $s > 0$. Also, $E_{t-1}y_{ht+j} = \mu(1 + \phi + \phi^2 + \cdots + \phi^j) + \phi^{j+1}y_{ht-1}$.

15. The trend in Figure 20.3 is $3{,}096.02 + 28.13t$ and was estimated by regressing y_{ht} on a constant and time trend over the period from the third quarter of 1956 to the third of 1970. Formal tests over the period from the third quarter of 1956 to the first of 1984 confirm the visual impression that there was a break in trend in the third quarter of 1970. This is based on the following regression:

$$y_{ht} = \underset{(3.3)}{398.90} + \underset{(2.1)}{131.41}d_t + \underset{(3.1)}{3.57}t - \underset{(-2.4)}{2.43}d_t t + \underset{(14.2)}{1.30}y_{ht-1} - \underset{(-4.7)}{0.42}y_{ht-2}$$

where d_t is a dummy variable that is zero before the fourth quarter of 1970 and one after the third quarter of 1970 and numbers beneath the point estimates are t-statistics. The t-statistic on $d_t t$ is large enough to reject the null hypothesis that the associated coefficient is zero, indicating a significant change in trend. I repeated this test with log y_{ht} instead of y_{ht} in the above regression and got the same result.

16. Perron (1989) argues that a trend model with an exogenous change in the coefficient on t fits postwar U.S. data better than a difference model.

17. The trend in Figure 20.4 is $2{,}936.51 + 37.93t - 0.16t^2$ and is the one implied by the following regression, estimated over the period from the third quarter of 1956 to the first of 1984:

$$y_{ht} = \underset{(3.1)}{336.81} + \underset{(2.6)}{3.94}t - \underset{(-2.1)}{0.02}t^2 + \underset{(14.2)}{1.31}y_{ht-1} - \underset{(-4.6)}{0.41}y_{ht-2}; \qquad \hat{\sigma}_\varepsilon = 48.5.$$

Numbers in parentheses are t-statistics. Note the statistical significance of the coefficient on t^2. I also tested the null hypothesis that the constant and coefficients on t and t^2 did not change in the third quarter of 1970. This joint null hypothesis fails to be rejected since the F-statistic has significance level 0.49. The quadratic trend model's Ψ is 0.09, about half the linear trend model's Ψ. This is not surprising because the deviations of the data from the quadratic trend are more temporary than the deviations from the linear trend. This is because the bow in the quadratic trend better mimics the apparent bow in the data.

18. To test this formally, I estimated this AR(1) difference model for y_{ht} over the period from the third quarter of 1956 to the first of 1984:

$$y_{ht} - y_{ht-1} = \underset{(2.1)}{14.19} - \underset{(-0.6)}{5.26}d_t + \underset{(4.0)}{0.37}(y_{ht-1} - y_{ht-2})$$

where d_t is the dummy variable described in note 15 and numbers in parentheses are t-statistics. The small size of the t-statistic on the coefficient of d_t indicates there is no evidence against the null hypothesis that the mean quarterly change of labor income has remained unchanged. Again, I repeated this test for logs of y_{ht}, with the same result.

19. Another model that illustrates this possibility is in Christiano, Eichenbaum, and Marshall 1991. The model there which is most relevant is called the *discrete time stochastic labor requirement model*, which has two technology shocks: one affects average productivity, and one affects the intertemporal rate of return on investment. Here, as in Deaton's version of the permanent income model, the average productivity shock is specified to be an AR(1) in

first differences. Econometric estimation of the model's parameters results in positive estimated correlation between the innovations in the average and marginal productivity shocks. This, in turn, results in the model having an empirically reasonable prediction for the relative volatility of consumption and income. The mechanism by which this is accomplished is identical to that in my real business cycle model.

20. The real business cycle model has many other implications as well. Some of these are explored in Christiano 1987c.

21

Modeling the Liquidity Effect of a Money Shock

Lawrence J. Christiano

To choose a monetary policy, officials at the Federal Reserve need to determine and compare the likely economic effects of all their alternatives. Obviously, they can't do that using the real world as their laboratory. Their only practical option is to experiment with artificial economies, or *models*. Often policymakers work out these experiments in their heads, using a simple, intuitive version of the model of a favored economic adviser or a former professor. Sometimes they complement this approach by computer experiments, using elaborate, mathematically explicit models. Either way, though, the wisdom of the policies that are ultimately selected depends critically on the quality of the models used to select them.

Economists are searching for a good model that can help monetary policymakers make wise choices. For a while, back in the 1960s, economists thought they had such a model—or, at least, they seemed likely to have one soon. Their hopes rested with the large 200-plus equation macro-econometric models of the time, which were based on the ideas of John Maynard Keynes. Beginning in the 1970s, however, those models were seriously challenged by economic theory and experience. This led academic economists to explore in other directions. Although the search has not yet led to a good model, I think one path looks particularly promising. In this paper, I describe and evaluate the work of some researchers now on that path and attempt to move a little further down it myself.

An important characteristic for a good model to have is the ability to reproduce the real world's response to simple monetary policy experi-

Reprinted from the *Federal Reserve Bank of Minneapolis Quarterly Review*, Winter 1991. This chapter includes revisions made to correct an error in the original article that was brought to the author's attention by Professors Don Schlagenhauf and Jeff Wrase of Arizona State University.

ments. Many economists agree, for instance, that the evidence supports the following view: when the Fed surprises financial markets by suddenly increasing the rate of growth of the money supply, the nominal interest rate falls, and employment and output rise, at least in the short run.[1] The presumption that this is what happens is a basic premise guiding the implementation of monetary policy: when the Fed wants to get the interest rate on federal funds down, reserves are injected into the financial system, not withdrawn from it.

The effect of such a surprise change in money growth (a positive *money shock*) is thought to be the result of two opposing forces. One is known among economists as the *liquidity effect*: The extra money in the economy pushes down interest rates, which stimulates economic activity. The other force, which pushes interest rates up and may depress economic activity, is known as the *anticipated inflation effect*. That occurs if, as seems plausible based on the data, a surprise increase in money growth leads people to expect more such increases in the future, and so more inflation. That leads borrowers and lenders to add an inflation premium to interest rates. This may lead to a reduction in employment and output if, for example, interest charges are an important component of firms' operating costs. The widespread view among economists is that the liquidity effect of a money shock is stronger than the anticipated inflation effect, at least in the short run.[2] Milton Friedman's 1967 presidential address to the American Economic Association contains the classic statement of this view (Friedman 1968b). He suggests that the liquidity effect dominates for one or two years after a money shock.

This view about the dominant liquidity effect is missing from one otherwise very promising class of models. They are monetary versions of the *real business cycle models* pioneered by Kydland and Prescott (1982) and Long and Plosser (1983). Real business cycle models have been surprisingly successful at accounting for several nonmonetary features of U.S. business cycles [Chapter 14 in this volume]. They have been less successful, however, once money is involved. Existing versions of these models that include a role for money imply that the immediate response to a positive money shock is a rise in interest rates and a fall in employment and output. This reflects that these models display only the anticipated inflation effect; they miss the liquidity effect altogether.

Why that is so I explain here. I do it by working with a prototype version of a monetary-real business cycle model, one that introduces money by requiring that transactions in the economy be financed with previously accumulated cash. This type of model is known as a *cash-in-advance model*.[3]

Then I go on to describe a modification to this type of model that was recently proposed by Lucas (1990) and analyzed further by Fuerst (1992) as a way to introduce the liquidity effect.[4] The modification is to assume that households cannot continuously revise their consumption and saving decisions. Thus, after a money shock, they cannot immediately adjust to the changed financial market circumstances. The *Fuerst-Lucas model* preserves the cash-in-advance model's assumption that the Fed conducts its open market operations directly with financial institutions. Those institutions are assumed to be in continuous contact with the firms which borrow from them in order to finance their operations. It is easy to see that the modification introduces a liquidity effect. With households out of the picture in the short run, firms have to absorb a disproportionately large share of a money injection, which creates a downward pressure on the nominal interest rate. By lowering firms' costs, a lower interest rate encourages them to borrow more and expand the scale of their operations, which creates an upward pressure on economic activity.

Of course, merely introducing a liquidity effect into the model may not be enough. The liquidity effect must be sufficiently strong to dominate the anticipated inflation effect. Whether or not that is true in this model depends on the precise relationship among its variables, or the values of its parameters. Fuerst (1992) shows that there exist feasible parameter values for which the liquidity effect dominates. However, I find that for plausible parameter values it doesn't.

I then investigate a natural modification to the Fuerst-Lucas model. I assume that firms' investment decisions, like households' consumption and saving decisions, are not revised continuously and so do not respond instantaneously to a money shock. In a plausibly parameterized version of the model (what I call the *sluggish capital model*), my change produces a liquidity effect stronger than the anticipated inflation effect. Unfortunately, though, the model then breaks down in another way: It no longer accounts very well for some nonmonetary features of U.S. business cycles.

Despite this mixed result, I see monetary versions of real business cycle models as potentially good models for the Fed to experiment with. My study shows where further work on this type of model is required and suggests what direction that work should take.

The Model Economies

Similarities and Differences

Cash Flow

All the model economies I work with here share the same pattern of cash flow among their three types of economic agents: *households*, goods-producing *firms*, and *financial intermediaries*. Before discussing the differences between the model economies, I will emphasize their similarities by discussing this cash-flow pattern.

In the models, time evolves in discrete units, called *periods* (which are specified to be one quarter long in the quantitative results reported later). At the beginning of a period, households are in possession of the economy's entire stock of money, which they have accumulated from labor, interest, and dividend earnings in the previous period. During the first part of a period, households circulate all their money to firms by consumption purchases and loans to the financial intermediaries, which then relend the money to firms. New money enters the economy by an injection from the monetary authority into the financial intermediaries, and this is also lent to firms. This flow of money from households and the monetary authority to firms is diagrammed in Figure 21.1.

The models' financial intermediaries are abstractions intended to capture the great variety of real-world institutions and markets that let households supply funds, directly or indirectly, to the ultimate users: firms that use physical capital and workers to produce the economy's output. The stock exchange is an example of a direct channel, since it lets households give funds directly to firms. Examples of indirect channels are banks and money market funds, since these institutions accept money from households and relend it to firms. Thus, the funds moving from households to financial intermediaries in the models include such things as money used to acquire stock, money deposited in banks to increase a household's saving account balance, and money sent to money market funds. They also represent the retained earnings of corporations, these being thought of as paid to households, which then channel the funds back to firms through financial intermediaries.

Money is circulated back to households at the end of the period by the channels diagrammed in Figure 21.2.

Two sources of cash to households are their paychecks, which they get directly from the firms, and firm dividend payments, which are funneled to them by the financial intermediaries. Firm dividend income is simply all the

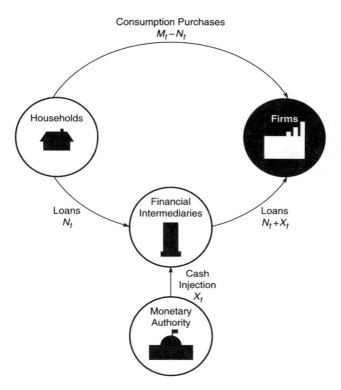

Figure 21.1 To Firms

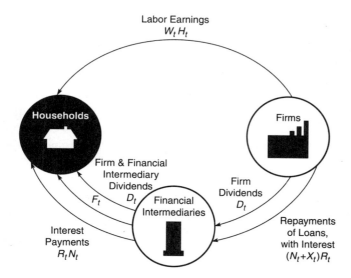

Figure 21.2 Back to Households

Figures 21.1 and 21.2
Cash Flow in the Model Economies

cash firms have on hand at the end of the period: their sales receipts net of expenses; households get this income because they own the firms.

Two other sources of cash to households originate with firms' repayment of loans received from the financial intermediaries. One component of these repayments reflects loans to firms of money the intermediaries borrowed from households at the beginning of the period. This is returned to households in the form of interest and principal payments. Another component reflects loans to firms of the cash injections received by the intermediaries from the monetary authority. Firms' repayments of these loans are transmitted to households in the form of financial intermediary dividend payments. Households get these dividend payments because they also own the financial intermediaries.

This cash-flow pattern is clearly a simplification of what happens in the real world. There, the pattern is not nearly as synchronized as it is in the models. For example, never in the real world is all the economy's cash concentrated in the hands of households. Also, unlike in the models, the decision intervals of real-world households are not fixed at one period. Rather, these intervals are unsynchronized, are of various lengths, and are chosen independently by each individual household.

Timing
The models are distinguished by the flexibility agents have in responding to surprise changes in the economy, or *shocks*. Agents in the models experience two types of shocks: a cash injection by the monetary authority, which I will call a *money growth shock* (or just a *money shock*), and a change in the state of technology of firms, which I will call a *technology shock*. The flexibility of an agent's response to either of these types of shocks is determined by the timing of the agent's decision in relation to the timing of the shock.

The *basic cash-in-advance model* assumes agents have perfect flexibility in responding to a shock: all decisions are made after—and therefore completely reflect—the current-period surprise change in money growth or technology. These decisions include those of households deciding how to split their money holdings between consumption and loans—their *portfolio* decisions—and how to split their time between labor and leisure. The decisions also include those of firms deciding how much labor to hire and how much to expand their plant and equipment, that is, to *invest*.

The other two versions of the model assume agents have less-than-perfect flexibility in responding to a shock. The *Fuerst-Lucas model* assumes households make their portfolio decisions before they know the current-period value of a surprise change. The rationale for this assumption is not modeled, but presumably it reflects costs that make continually altering the quantity of cash spent on consumption, with every new bit of information, less-than-optimal behavior. All other decisions in the Fuerst-Lucas model are assumed to be perfectly flexible and so to fully reflect the current-period value of a shock.

The third model, the *sluggish capital model*, assumes that both the household portfolio decisions and the firm investment decisions must be made before the current value of a shock is known. The assumption that investment cannot respond instantly to a shock is intended to capture the real-world fact that investment decisions require at least some advance planning. All other decisions in the sluggish capital model are assumed to respond perfectly flexibly to a shock.

A Closer Look

I now describe in more detail the circumstances faced by the agents in the models.

Households

Households supply labor and purchase the output of the firms, which in the models is limited to one type of good. Households also own the firms and the financial intermediaries.

At the beginning of each period t, the models assume households have the economy's entire money stock, M_t, at their disposal. They have two uses for these funds: N_t dollars are loaned to the financial intermediaries, while $M_t - N_t$ dollars are set aside to purchase the consumption good during the current period. In particular, if P_t is the period t price level for the one good and C_t the households' period t consumption of that good, then households face a *cash-in-advance constraint*:

$$P_t C_t = M_t - N_t. \tag{1}$$

The assumption captured here—that all consumption purchases must be paid for with previously accumulated cash—is obviously extreme; it ignores the real-world pervasiveness of credit.[5]

To better understand equation (1), compare it with the less extreme assumption that households simply find it convenient to use some cash in making purchases. This convenience may arise from a reduction in costs (*transaction costs*) that comes from using cash. For example, gasoline station owners offer a lower price to cash customers because doing business with them costs the owners less than doing business with credit card customers. These considerations suggest an alternative to equation (1) that captures its spirit without being so extreme. In particular, one could specify that households do not require cash for purchases, but that, for a given level of purchases, they suffer a loss of some kind that can be decreased by holding cash balances.[6] This alternative to the cash-in-advance approach to money demand that is implicit in (1) is referred to as the *transaction cost approach* to money demand.[7]

As noted earlier, in the models here, households have four sources of money at the beginning of each period. These are labor income in the previous period, $W_{t-1}L_{t-1}$; interest earnings on cash loaned to financial intermediaries in the previous period, $R_{t-1}N_{t-1}$; dividend payments from financial intermediaries, F_{t-1}; and dividend payments from firms, D_{t-1}. Here, W_{t-1} denotes the period $t-1$ wage rate, L_{t-1} denotes the hours of work supplied by households during period $t-1$, and R_{t-1} denotes the gross return at the end of period $t-1$ on one dollar loaned at the beginning of period $t-1$. Each household's *budget constraint* specifies that its uses and sources of money be equated:[8]

$$(M_t - N_t) + N_t = R_{t-1}N_{t-1} + F_{t-1} + D_{t-1} + W_{t-1}L_{t-1}. \tag{2}$$

One feature of equations (1) and (2) is worth stressing. As emphasized above, according to (1), households can only buy the consumption good with the cash balances that are available to them at the beginning of a period. An implication of this is that they cannot apply labor earnings from the current period to current-period consumption.

One way to visualize this aspect of the model is to think of each household as containing two members: a worker and a shopper. At the beginning of a period, the shopper is given the sum $M_t - N_t$ to purchase C_t. The worker goes to work and receives a paycheck for labor services just a bit too late to pass it on to the shopper in the current period; the soonest the worker can make the paycheck available for spending is the next period. The intent of this abstraction is to capture the fact that receipts and payments of real-world households are not fully synchronized. This fact— together with a desire to use at least some cash in transactions, captured rather bluntly by (1), and an unwillingness to spend a lot of effort juggling between cash and interest-bearing accounts, captured by the fixed planning interval assumption—may be a major reason real-world households do not hold smaller amounts of money.

The situation in which the households find themselves in period t depends on the version of the model under consideration.

Consider first the basic cash-in-advance model. In this model, in period t, each household takes M_t, R_t, P_t, W_t, F_t, and D_t as given. In addition, it knows what values these variables $\{R_{t+j}, P_{t+j}, W_{t+j}, F_{t+j}, D_{t+j};$ $j = 1, 2, 3, \ldots\}$ will take on, depending on the future (as yet unknown) realizations of the technology and money growth shocks. Taking as given these things and the fact that (1) and (2) must be satisfied in all periods, the household selects values for C_t, L_t, and N_t and contingency plans for its future decisions. These plans relate future decisions, C_{t+j}, L_{t+j}, and N_{t+j}, to the values taken on by the shocks in periods $t + j$ and earlier, for $j = 1, 2,$ $3, \ldots$. These objects are selected to maximize expected discounted utility:

$$E_t \sum_{j=0}^{\infty} (\beta^*)^j u(C_{t+j}, L_{t+j}). \tag{3}$$

In (3), E_t is the expectation operator, conditional on all information available in periods t and earlier; β^* is the discount rate; and u is the period utility function.

The following utility function (which nests as a special case standard ones used in the real business cycle literature) will be used in the quantitative analysis reported later:

$$u(C_t, L_t) = \begin{cases} [C_t^{(1-\gamma)}(1 - L_t)^{\gamma}]^{\psi}/\psi & \text{for} \quad \psi \neq 0 \\ (1 - \gamma)\log(C_t) + \gamma\log(1 - L_t) & \text{for} \quad \psi = 0. \end{cases} \tag{4}$$

Here, $1 - L_t$ denotes the quantity of leisure time, and the total time available for work—the time endowment—is set at 1. This fixes the units in which L_t is measured in terms of fractions of the time endowment. If, for example, one prefers to think instead in terms of hours worked per quarter, and the time endowment is 16 hours per day (hence, 1,460 hours per quarter), then $L_t = 0.5$ signifies 730 hours of work per quarter. When the curvature parameter, ψ, is set to zero, (4) is the utility function used in two real business cycle models: Hansen's (1985a) divisible labor model and the model in Long and Plosser 1983. When $\psi \neq 0$, this is the utility function used in the real business cycle model in Kydland and Prescott 1982.

Although the household's problem was just posed as having to choose values for three variables (C, L, and N), the fact that (1) must always hold implies that we can ignore one of those decisions. In particular, I think of the household's problem as having to choose a set of plans for only $\{L_{t+j}, N_{t+j}; j \geqslant 0\}$. Plans for these variables then automatically imply plans for C_{t+j} via (1) for $j \geqslant 0$.

Now consider a household's situation in the Fuerst-Lucas and sluggish capital models. Here, the funds households decide to lend to financial intermediaries, N_{t+j}, must be contingent on realizations of the shocks in periods $t + j - 1$ and earlier, for $j \geqslant 0$. This is because these models assume that the portfolio decision must be made before the current-period realization of the shocks. The other decision, how many hours to work, L_{t+j}, is contingent on the period $t + j$ realized values of the shocks for $j \geqslant 0$.

Firms
In all three models, firms possess the economy's capital stock, K_t, and its production technology. They use these and the hours of labor they hire, H_t, to produce output.

Output is related to the inputs through this production technology:

$$f^*(K_t, z_t H_t) \equiv K_t^\alpha (z_t H_t)^{(1-\alpha)} + (1 - \delta^*)K_t \tag{5}$$

where $0 < \alpha < 1$; z_t is the state of technological knowledge, which is determined outside the model; δ^* is the fixed rate of depreciation on a unit of capital; and $f^*(K_t, z_t H_t) - (1 - \delta^*)K_t$ is gross output, Y_t. The state of technology has two parts: a deterministic trend, $\exp(\mu t)$, and random deviations about that trend, $\exp(\theta_t)$. That is,

$$z_t = \exp(\mu t + \theta_t). \tag{6}$$

More about the law of motion of θ_t will be said later.

Each period, besides hiring labor, firms invest in capital. Before hiring workers or investing, though, firms must borrow cash from financial intermediaries. This is because they start the period with no cash: all cash accumulated in the previous period is assumed to have been distributed through dividends. In particular, firms must borrow an amount of cash equal to

$$W_t H_t + P_t I_t \tag{7}$$

where I_t denotes gross purchases of investment goods:

$$I_t \equiv K_{t+1} - (1 - \delta^*)K_t. \tag{8}$$

In (7), P_t is the price of a unit of investment goods. This is identical to the price of the consumption good since the economy's single output good can be transformed one-for-one into consumption or investment goods. The dividends a firm pays out at the end of period t, D_t, equal its total cash receipts, $P_t Y_t$, minus its total cash outlays:

$$D_t = P_t Y_t - R_t(W_t H_t + P_t I_t). \tag{9}$$

The expression after the minus sign in (9) represents the cash firms need to repay the financial intermediaries at the end of the period in return for borrowing $W_t H_t + P_t I_t$ at the beginning of the period.

Through firms' control over investment, they confront a trade-off between current and future dividends. For example, by setting I_t at a high level, a firm raises future dividends at the cost of lower current dividends. Because firms face this trade-off, something has to be assumed about how they weigh current and future dividends when they make employment and investment decisions. Since firms are owned by households, a natural assumption is that each firm behaves in the best interests of its shareholders. Thus, I assume a firm values a dividend dollar in a particular period t by the marginal utility to the households of a dollar at the end of period t. So the firm seeks to maximize

$$E_t \sum_{j=0}^{\infty} [(\beta^*)^{j+1} u_{c,t+j+1}/P_{t+j+1}] D_{t+j}. \tag{10}$$

Here the bracketed term is the marginal utility to a shareholder of a dollar received at the end of period $t + j$. The reason the subscript $t + j + 1$ appears here is that a dollar at the end of period $t + j$ cannot be spent until the following period. Firms take $u_{c,t+j}$, P_{t+j}, W_{t+j}, and R_{t+j} as given functions of the realizations of the shocks at and before period $t + j$, for $j \geqslant 0$.

In the basic cash-in-advance model and in the Fuerst-Lucas model, the firms seek to maximize (10) by choice of contingency plans which relate I_{t+j}, H_{t+j} to the period $t + j$ and earlier values of the shocks, for $j \geqslant 0$. In the sluggish capital model, I_{t+j} is a function of the shocks in period $t + j - 1$ and earlier, while H_{t+j} continues to be a function of the shocks in period $t + j$ and earlier.

Financial Intermediaries

In the models, financial intermediaries accept loans, N_t, from households, which are repaid at the end of the period at a gross rate of interest, R_t. Financial intermediaries loan this money to firms at the same rate of interest. Firms' loans must be repaid at the end of the period, in time for the financial intermediaries to use the proceeds to repay households.

Financial intermediaries also receive new cash injections, X_t, from the economy's monetary authority. This money is also loaned to firms, which repay $R_t X_t$ at the end of the period. This is distributed to households in the form of dividends F_t. Thus, financial intermediary dividend payments are

$$F_t = R_t X_t. \tag{11}$$

Finally, the financial intermediaries act as a conduit for sending firms' dividends, D_t, to households.

Shocks and Equilibrium

The shocks in the model economies are disturbances to the random part of technology, θ_t, and to the rate of growth of money, x_t. Here, $x_t \equiv X_t/M_t$, where X_t, again, is cash injections from the monetary authority to the financial intermediaries. I assume that the two shocks enter this way:

$$\theta_t = (1 - \rho_\theta)\theta + \rho_\theta\theta_{t-1} + \varepsilon_{\theta,t} \tag{12}$$

$$x_t = (1 - \rho_x)x + \rho_x x_{t-1} + \varepsilon_{x,t}. \tag{13}$$

The shocks to technology and money growth, $\varepsilon_{\theta,t}$ and $\varepsilon_{x,t}$, are mutually uncorrelated at all leads and lags and are uncorrelated with θ_{t-j}, x_{t-j}, $j > 0$. They are the part of θ_t and x_t that cannot be predicted based on past values of the variables in the model. For this reason, $\varepsilon_{\theta,t}$ and $\varepsilon_{x,t}$ are referred to as the *unexpected* components of θ_t and x_t. The parameters ρ_θ and ρ_x in equations (12)–(13) control the autocorrelation properties of θ_t and x_t. In particular, the correlation between θ_t and θ_{t-j} is just ρ_θ^j for $j > 0$. A similar interpretation for ρ_x also exists. Finally, θ and x are the unconditional means of θ_t and x_t, and I denote the standard deviation of $\varepsilon_{\theta,t}$ and $\varepsilon_{x,t}$ by $\sigma_{\varepsilon,\theta}$ and $\sigma_{\varepsilon,x}$.

In general equilibrium in these models, firms and financial intermediaries maximize the value of dividends, households maximize utility, and markets clear. Clearing in the loan market requires that the demand for cash loans, $W_t H_t + P_t I_t$, and the supply of cash loans, $N_t + X_t$, be equated:

$$W_t H_t + P_t I_t = N_t + X_t. \tag{14}$$

Similarly, clearing in the labor market requires that labor demand, H_t, and labor supply, L_t, be equated:

$$H_t = L_t. \tag{15}$$

Goods market-clearing requires that demand, $C_t + I_t$, equal supply, Y_t:

$$C_t + I_t = Y_t. \tag{16}$$

The cash-in-advance constraint and loan market-clearing imply that the demand for and the supply of money be equated. Period t demand for money is the sum of household demand, $P_t C_t$, and firm demand, $W_t H_t + P_t I_t$. Period t supply of money is M_{t+1}. The money market-clearing condition is, then,

$$P_t C_t + W_t H_t + P_t I_t = M_t + X_t = M_{t+1}. \tag{17}$$

The first equality follows from (1) and (14), and the second follows by definition of M_{t+1}.

Solving the Basic Cash-in-Advance Model

To quantify the impact of the shocks in the three models requires *solving* the models. That means determining, given an arbitrary pattern of realizations of the shocks, how much firms will invest and how much households will work, save, and consume in equilibrium. It also means determining the equilibrium rate of inflation and nominal rate of interest. Here I use a particular strategy to solve the basic cash-in-advance model.

My solution strategy focuses on several *efficiency conditions* that must be satisfied given that markets clear and agents optimize. In addition to enabling me to solve the models, these conditions play other important roles in the analysis. First, they are used to gain intuition about the dynamic impact (the impact over time) of money growth shocks on interest rates, employment, and output. This intuition is useful as a guide for interpreting the quantitative results. Second, the efficiency conditions are used to derive the models' implications for money demand regressions of the kind reported in the money demand literature. Third, the efficiency conditions are used to define econometric estimators for the models' parameters.

Employment Decisions

Households
To start solving the basic cash-in-advance model, I derive an efficiency condition associated with households' decision about how many hours to work, L_t. The condition is obtained by positing that households have set L_t optimally and then working out the implication of the fact that no change in that decision can increase expected discounted utility, (3).

Suppose, for example, that a household were to increase labor supply by one unit. The utility cost of this is $-u_{L,t}$, where $-u_{L,t} \equiv -\partial u(C_t, L_t)/\partial L_t$ evaluated at the optimal choices of C_t and L_t. The benefit is that the household earns a wage, W_t, which can be spent next period on W_t/P_{t+1} units of the economy's consumption good. The discounted value of this to the household is $\beta^* u_{c,t+1} W_t/P_{t+1}$, where $u_{c,t+1} \equiv \partial u(C_{t+1}, L_{t+1})/\partial C_{t+1}$. Here, the derivative is evaluated at the optimal plan for C_{t+1} and L_{t+1}. From the household's perspective in period t, this benefit is a random variable since, under its optimal plan, C_{t+1} and L_{t+1} are functions of θ_{t+1} and x_{t+1}, which are not known in period t. The household's concern is with expected utility, (3), so it evaluates the benefit as $E_t \beta^* u_{c,t+1} W_t / P_{t+1}$ or, equivalently, $(W_t / P_t) E_t \beta^* u_{c,t+1} (P_t / P_{t+1})$.

If the household's undisturbed plan were, indeed, optimal, as we suppose, then the costs and benefits of the above one-unit deviation from the optimal plan must exactly match. Thus,

$$-u_{L,t} = (W_t / P_t) E_t \beta^* u_{c,t+1} (P_t / P_{t+1}). \tag{18}$$

Some intuition about (18) may be obtained by graphing it in the standard, static real wage/labor effort diagram, as in Figure 21.3. There, $-u_{L,t} (E_t \beta^* u_{c,t+1} P_t / P_{t+1})^{-1}$ is graphed conditional on the specification of the utility function (4) and on fixed values of C_t and $\pi^e_{t+1} \equiv (E_t u_{c,t+1} P_t / P_{t+1})^{-1}$. From (4), it is easy to see that labor supply is independent of C_t when $\psi = 0$ and shifts left with a decrease in C_t when $\psi < 0$. This is because the marginal utility of leisure is not a function of C_t when $\psi = 0$, but increases with a decrease in C_t when $\psi < 0$. Similarly, when $\psi > 0$, labor supply shifts right with a decrease in C_t. Now consider the dependence of labor supply on π^e_{t+1}, which roughly is an increasing function of the expected gross change in the price level from one period to the next. Labor supply shifts left with an increase in this variable. This is because a given real wage, W_t / P_t, is worth less to a household the higher inflation is since the household cannot spend it until the next period.

Firms

Now consider the decisions of firms to hire hours of labor, H_t. Suppose a firm considers the following change from its optimal employment plan. It borrows one dollar in period t, at a cost of owing R_t at the end of the period. It uses the dollar to hire $1/W_t$ units of labor time, which increases the firm's revenue by $P_t f^*_{H,t} / W_t$, where $f^*_{H,t} = \partial f^*(K_t, z_t H_t) / \partial H_t$ evaluated at the optimal choices of K_t and H_t. In equilibrium, these costs and benefits must cancel:

$$W_t R_t / P_t = f^*_{H,t}. \tag{19}$$

Failure of (19) to hold would contradict the assumption in (10) that firms maximize the present value of dividends. For example, if the left side of (19) exceeded the right, then firms could increase dividends simply by decreasing the hours of labor employed.

Expression (19), labor demand, is also graphed in Figure 21.3. There, it is conditional on a given value of the capital stock, K_t, the state of technol-

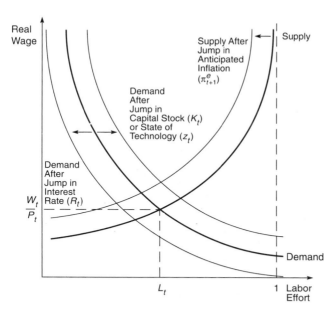

Figure 21.3
Labor Market Equilibrium

ogy, z_t, and the interest rate, R_t. An increase in R_t shifts labor demand left because this increases the cost of hiring labor, which can only be covered by raising labor's marginal productivity. For a given value of the capital stock and the state of technology, this requires reducing the amount of labor hired. Increases in the capital stock or technological knowledge shift labor demand right, since both increase labor productivity.

Saving/Investment Decisions

Households
I now derive an efficiency condition associated with households' decision on how much money, N_t, to lend to financial intermediaries, or their saving decision. This, too, is done by studying the costs and benefits associated with a particular deviation from a household's optimal decision.

In particular, suppose the household increases N_t by one dollar. On the cost side, this would decrease consumption spending by one dollar, which would decrease period t real consumption by $1/P_t$, which would decrease utility by $u_{c,t}/P_t$. On the benefit side, the extra dollar invested with the financial intermediaries would generate R_t dollars at the end of the period. These can be used to buy R_t/P_{t+1} units of the consumption good next period. The discounted expected value of those goods is $E_t R_t \beta^* u_{c,t+1}/P_{t+1}$. If the original plan is optimal, as we suppose, then these costs and benefits must be equal:

$$u_{c,t}/P_t = \beta^* R_t E_t(u_{c,t+1}/P_{t+1}). \tag{20}$$

Equation (20) can be used to gain insight into the model's implication for the link between interest rates and inflation and, hence, money growth. To do this, it is convenient to rewrite (20) in terms of R_t:

$$R_t = (u_{c,t}/P_t)/(\beta^* E_t u_{c,t+1}/P_{t+1}) = \{E_t[(\beta^* u_{c,t+1}/u_{c,t})(P_t/P_{t+1})]\}^{-1}. \tag{21}$$

In the expression to the right of the first equality, the numerator is the utility value of a dollar in period t and the denominator is the discounted expected value of the utility value of a dollar in period $t + 1$. According to (20)–(21), households select N_t so as to equate the relative utility value of a dollar in period t and period $t + 1$ to the one-period nominal rate of interest.

The relationship between the nominal rate of interest and other variables in (20)–(21) is closely related to the classic theory of interest determination outlined by Irving Fisher (1930). According to that theory, the interest rate is the sum of the real rate of interest and expected inflation. These are referred to as the nominal interest rate's *Fisherian fundamentals*, or just its *fundamentals*.

The real rate of interest, r_t, is the amount of consumption goods the household is willing to give up next period in exchange for receiving a unit of consumption in the current period. It is straightforward to show that

$$r_t = \{E_t(\beta^* u_{c,t+1}/u_{c,t})\}^{-1}. \tag{22}$$

Now rewrite (21) using the formula $E_t x_t y_t = E_t x_t E_t y_t + cov_t(x_t, y_t)$, where E_t and cov_t denote the expectations and covariance operators, conditional on information available at time t. Use this and (22) to get

$$R_t = \{r_t^{-1} E_t(1/\pi_{t+1}) + cov_t(\beta^* u_{c,t+1}/u_{c,t}, P_t/P_{t+1})\}^{-1} \tag{23}$$

where $\pi_{t+1} \equiv P_{t+1}/P_t$, the gross rate of inflation. According to (23), when there is no uncertainty, $R_t = r_t \pi_{t+1}$. This is approximately the sum of the real rate of interest and the rate of inflation.[9] In addition, if the covariance term in (23) is small enough to ignore, then $R_t = r_t[E_t(1/\pi_{t+1})]^{-1}$, which to a first approximation is also the sum of the real interest rate and the expected inflation rate.

This suggests that, in the basic cash-in-advance model, R_t is determined by its Fisherian fundamentals. This determination rests sensitively on households' willingness and ability to quickly adjust their lending, N_t, so as to ensure that (20)–(23) hold in each period. Interestingly, many studies have documented that (20) is not supported by the data (for example, L. Hansen and Singleton 1982). One interpretation of that fact is that household borrowing is not as flexible as the basic cash-in-advance model assumes.

Firms
Now consider the firms' decisions to invest.

Suppose a firm borrows P_t dollars to buy one unit of extra capital, so that $P_t R_t$ has to be repaid at the end of period t. The extra capital does not generate extra revenue until period $t + 1$. At the end of that period, the firm's investment generates $P_{t+1}[f_K^*(K_{t+1}, z_{t+1}H_{t+1}) + (1 - \delta^*)(R_{t+1} - 1)]$ dollars. These extra dollars are the sum of two parts. First is the addition to revenues, $P_{t+1}[f_K^*(K_{t+1}, z_{t+1}H_{t+1}) - (1 - \delta^*)]$, generated by the increment to period $t + 1$ output. Second is the reduced end-of-period $t + 1$ interest and principal payments, $(1 - \delta^*)P_{t+1}R_{t+1}$, that reflect that firms can cut back investment by $(1 - \delta^*)$ units next period. The firm must compare the cost of reducing dividend payments by $P_t R_t$ dollars at the end of period t to the benefit of increasing dividend payments by $P_{t+1}[f_K^*(K_{t+1}, z_{t+1}H_{t+1}) + (1 - \delta^*)(R_{t+1} - 1)]$ dollars at the end of period $t + 1$.

According to (10), it compares these alternatives by weighing them by shareholders' marginal value of a dollar. In particular, the period t utility cost to a shareholder of reducing dividends at the end of period t is the reduction in period $t + 1$ utility that results from having to reduce period $t + 1$ consumption by $1/P_{t+1}$: $\beta^* E_t u_{c,t+1}/P_{t+1}$. Similarly, the value to a shareholder of an extra dividend dollar at the end of period $t + 1$ is $(\beta^*)^2 E_t u_{c,t+2}/P_{t+2}$. Using these weights to value the costs and benefits of a change from the firm's optimal plan leads to this condition:

$$R_t P_t E_t(\beta^* u_{c,t+1}/P_{t+1}) = E_t P_{t+1}[f_K^*(K_{t+1}, z_{t+1}H_{t+1}) + (1 - \delta^*)(R_{t+1} - 1)]$$
$$\times [(\beta^*)^2 u_{c,t+2}/P_{t+2}]. \tag{24}$$

If (24) did not hold, then firms could increase (10) by changing investment. Thus, (24) must hold at their optimal investment level.

The assumption that firms and households optimize implies that the efficiency conditions—(18), (19), (20), and (24)—hold not just in period t, but also in all future periods. In the Appendix, I show how these conditions, together with the household cash-in-advance and budget constraints, (1) and (2), and the market-clearing conditions, (14)–(16), can be used to actually compute the equilibrium quantities and prices for the model, conditional on a set of values being assigned to the model parameters.

Money Demand

The basic cash-in-advance model implies that, in equilibrium, a relationship exists among real balances, the nominal interest rate, and output which resembles an empirical money demand equation.

To see this, first combine the money market-clearing condition, (17), and the goods market-clearing condition, (16), to derive a convenient expression for the income velocity of money, V_t:

$$V_t \equiv Y_t/(M_{t+1}/P_t)$$

$$= Y_t/[Y_t + (W_t/P_t)H_t]$$

$$= Y_t/[Y_t + (1 - \alpha) Y_t/R_t]$$

$$= 1/[1 + (1 - \alpha)/R_t]. \tag{25}$$

Here, the second equality makes use of firms' production function, (5), and firms' demand for labor, (19). Expression (25) shows that money velocity and the nominal interest rate are positively related.

Now linearly expand the log of the last expression in (25) about $R_t -1 = R - 1$, where R is the *nonstochastic steady-state* value of R_t. (By this I mean the constant value to which R_t eventually settles when the shocks, $\varepsilon_{\theta,t}$ and $\varepsilon_{x,t}$, are both held fixed at zero.) This expansion produces an expression that closely resembles the money demand equation in the literature:

$$\log(M_{t+1}/P_t) = a - b(R_t - 1) + c\log(Y_t) \tag{26}$$

where

$$a = \log(1 + [(1 - \alpha)/R]) + \{(1 - \alpha)(R - 1)/[R^2 + R(1 - \alpha)]\} \tag{27}$$

$$b = -(1 - \alpha)/[R^2 + (1 - \alpha)R] \tag{28}$$

$$c = 1. \tag{29}$$

To fix units, suppose the nominal interest rate changes one percentage point, expressed at an annual rate, and output, Y_t, is held fixed. According to (26), real money demand then falls $b/4$ percent. (Here, b is divided by 4 because the time period of the model is one quarter, while we consider the

impact of a change in the annualized rate of interest.) Since the only efficiency condition used to derive (26) is (19) and—as will become evident
later—that equation holds in all three models, it follows that (26) does too.
Because equation (26) resembles what is called a *money demand function* in
the empirical literature, it is natural to refer to b and c as *money demand
elasticities*.[10]

An important finding of the literature is that the lagged dependent
variable in an empirical money demand equation enters statistically very
significantly on the right side. For example, Goldfeld and Sichel (1990,
Table 8.1) report t-statistics for the coefficient on lagged real balances that
range from 12 to 67, depending on the data sample. It is readily verified
that a version of (26) augmented to include a lagged dependent variable
implies that the short- and long-run money demand elasticities differ. Since
the right side of (26) has no lagged real balances, models of this paper
cannot easily account for that feature of empirical money demand
equations.[11]

Looking for a Dominant Liquidity Effect: Qualitatively . . .

Here I do a qualitative analysis: I try to determine what the models imply
for the signs of the responses of the interest rate, employment, and output
to a money growth shock. I reach definite conclusions about this for the
basic cash-in-advance model, but not for the two modified models. It turns
out that they require a quantitative analysis, which I will do in the next
section.

In the Basic Model

To start the qualitative analysis, I use the efficiency and market-clearing
conditions to establish that the basic cash-in-advance model cannot rationalize the widespread view that the liquidity effect is dominant: a money
growth shock drives the nominal interest rate down and employment and
output up, at least in the short run. If the money shock is temporary in this
model, then it has no effect on these variables. If the shock is persistent, as
is empirically plausible, then the variables respond by moving in the opposite directions than they're supposed to: the nominal interest rate rises, and
employment and output fall.

A Temporary Money Shock
An unexpected change in the money growth rate, x_t, is temporary if it has
no impact on future money growth rates. In (13), such a shock to x_t is given

by $\varepsilon_{x,t}$, and it does not affect x_{t+j}, for $j > 0$, if $\rho_x = 0$. Of course, a temporary shock to the money growth rate corresponds to a permanent jump in the level of the money stock. This kind of monetary disturbance in the basic cash-in-advance model is known to be neutral (Greenwood and Huffman 1987, Sargent 1987b): it does not affect current or future consumption, investment, employment, and output; it results in an equiproportionate jump in current and future prices and wages, so that it does not affect the rate of inflation; and it does not affect the nominal and real rates of interest.

A key feature of the basic cash-in-advance model's neutrality property is that all agents increase their cash expenditures in equal proportion to the money shock. Thus, if $\varepsilon_{x,t} = 0.20$, so that the money stock jumps 20 percent, then households' consumption expenditures, $M_{t+j} - N_{t+j}$, and firms' employment and investment expenditures, $N_{t+j} + X_{t+j}$, also jump 20 percent, for $j \geq 0$. Obviously, if each agent's cash expenditures increase 20 percent and so do prices and wages, then agents can still afford the unshocked level of consumption, employment, and investment. In addition, it is easily confirmed (at least in the nonstochastic version of the model economy) that the efficiency conditions (18), (19), (20), and (24) continue to be satisfied with this response.

For later purposes I want to highlight the implications for N_{t+j}, for $j \geq 0$, of the result that all agents' cash expenditures increase in equal proportion to a temporary money growth shock. Suppose that without the shock, x_{t+j}, M_{t+j}, and N_{t+j} would have been 0, 100, and 50, respectively, for $j \geq 0$. With the shock, $x_t = 0.20$ and $x_{t+j} = 0$ for $j > 0$. Then an increase in all agents' cash expenditures of 20 percent in each of periods t, $t + 1$, $t + 2$, ... requires that $N_t = 40$ and $N_{t+j} = 60$ for $j > 0$. Thus, households reduce the amount of money they send to financial intermediaries in the period of the shock by 10 dollars. In this way, they increase their nominal consumption spending by 10 dollars, which is a 20 percent increase over the 50 dollars they would have spent otherwise.

The reduction in cash supplied by households to financial intermediaries in the period of the shock also assures that cash available to intermediaries, $N_t + X_t$, does not rise more than 20 percent. For example, if households for some reason did not reduce the cash they supplied, then the amount of cash at financial intermediaries would jump 40 percent to 70 dollars. As long as $R_t > 1$, financial intermediaries would lend the money to firms, which would spend it. With some agents (firms) having to absorb a disproportionate share of the increased stock of money, a basic condition for the neutrality result fails.

A Persistent Money Shock

Now suppose a disturbance to money growth, $\varepsilon_{x,t}$, increases not just x_t, but also x_{t+j}, for $j > 0$. This would be true if $\rho_x > 0$ in (13). Greenwood and Huffman (1987) and Sargent (1987b) have shown in models closely related to mine that this leads to a rise in R_t and a fall in L_t and, hence, in output.

The intuition for this result is straightforward. Think of the experiment as a combination of two. First is an unexpected temporary jump in x_t, like the one just considered. That has no impact on R_t, L_t, or P_{t+1}/P_t. Second is an unexpected upward revision in the forecast of x_{t+1}. That, not surprisingly, exerts upward pressure on P_{t+1}/P_t. Because the Fisher relation holds in this model and because there is very little impact on the real rate of return, a jump in R_t results. But, by inspecting Figure 21.3, we can see that the jump in anticipated inflation shifts labor supply left and the jump in R_t shifts labor demand left. Thus, employment and output fall. The higher anticipated inflation acts like a tax on both sides of the labor market. To labor suppliers, the extra inflation means that dollars earned while working will buy less. To labor demanders, the inflation premium in the nominal interest rate means that labor costs more.[12]

In the basic cash-in-advance model, a persistent increase in the rate of money growth also acts like a tax on investment and thus discourages it.[13] Perhaps the simplest way to see this is to consider the long-run impact of a permanent increase in money growth arising from an increase in the value of the average money growth rate, x. In the long run, with the shocks held at zero—that is, in nonstochastic steady state—R_t and r_t settle to constants—say, R and r. Similarly, inflation, $K_t/(z_t L_t)$, and L_t settle to constants, $K/(zL)$ and L. Thus, in nonstochastic steady state, (24) is just

$$Rr = f_K^*(K/(zL), 1) + (1 - \delta^*)(R - 1). \tag{30}$$

[Here I have exploited the fact that, when f^* is defined by (5), $f_K^*(K_t, z_t L_t) = f_K^*(K_t/(z_t L_t), 1)$.] According to (30), a higher value of R—induced by a jump in the money growth rate, x—leads firms to operate at a point where the marginal product of capital is higher, since r is independent of x and $r > 1 - \delta^*$. (Formulas for R and r are given in note 19.) The reason for this is that the nominal rate of interest is part of the cost of investing, since firms must raise the cash in advance. To cover this cost, the marginal product of capital must be higher, which requires lowering the ratio of capital to labor. But the analysis of the labor market indicated that L_t falls with a persistent jump in x_t. Thus, the fact that $K/(zL)$ falls implies that K itself falls.

To summarize, a persistent jump in money growth raises anticipated inflation and, by the Fisher effect, the nominal interest rate. Because higher inflation rates and nominal interest rates act like a tax on market activity, the amount of that activity—employment, investment, and output—falls.

In Two Modified Models

With Sluggish Household Saving

So, the basic cash-in-advance model cannot rationalize the widely held view that a positive money growth shock—temporary or persistent— drives the nominal rate of interest down and the level of employment and output up. Why not? A literature, associated with Grossman and Weiss (1983), Rotemberg (1984), and Lucas (1990), has suggested that the key to understanding the economic impact of a money shock is to recognize that it does not impact equally on all economic agents. The basic cash-in-advance model assumes that it does.

To see that it does, recall what happens in the basic cash-in-advance model when there is a permanent increase in the money stock. There, a money growth shock is neutral in that it has no impact on the nominal or real interest rates, the inflation rate, output, employment, investment, or consumption. A key requirement for this neutrality result is that cash expenditures by all agents—both households and firms—increase by the same proportion as the money injection in the period of the shock. In particular, for households this means reducing N_t, the money they lend to the financial intermediaries in the period of the shock. In the real world, this could be accomplished, for example, by reducing bank saving deposits or signaling firms during a shareholder meeting to increase dividend payments.

Recently, Fuerst (1992) and Lucas (1990) have argued that the ideas of Grossman and Weiss (1983) and Rotemberg (1984) could be captured in the basic cash-in-advance model by assuming that households have to set N_t before they know x_t and, hence, P_t, W_t, and R_t. Then, when a permanent jump in money occurs, N_t cannot be adjusted in the way that the neutrality result requires. The validity of this assumption rests in part on whether there is in fact some sluggishness in the way household portfolio, or saving, decisions are made in the real world.

As we will see below, there are values of the Fuerst-Lucas model parameters for which the nominal interest rate falls and employment and output expand in the period of a money growth shock. The intuition about why the model can produce such a result is straightforward.

Consider, for example, a temporary shock to the money growth rate. With N_t unable to fall in response, more of the extra cash (than in the basic cash-in-advance model) has to be absorbed by firms. What has to happen for this extra cash to be absorbed?

This question is easy to answer if only the nominal interest rate is assumed to change. With other variables fixed, equation (19) indicates that the only way to get firms to absorb more cash for employment and output purposes is to lower the rate of interest. (That is, for H_t to expand at a fixed W_t/P_t, R_t must fall.) Similarly, equation (24) indicates that the only way to get firms to invest more funds is also for R_t to fall.[14] This reasoning suggests that the Fuerst-Lucas model responds to a temporary injection of money by a fall in R_t.

The problem with this reasoning is that other variables do change. In particular, I will show that for plausible values of the model parameters, the nominal interest rate will rise and employment and output will fall in the period of a shock in the Fuerst-Lucas model. Thus, the signs of the responses to a money growth shock in the Fuerst-Lucas model are ambiguous. This result is consistent with the fact that a money growth shock also triggers an anticipated inflation effect in this model. The signs of the equilibrium interest rate, employment, and output responses depend on which is stronger: the anticipated inflation effect or the liquidity effect. This, in turn, depends on what values are assigned to the parameters.

That a money growth shock, especially a persistent one, could even in principle drive the nominal interest rate down in the Fuerst-Lucas model may be surprising in light of my discussion of the nominal interest rate in the basic cash-in-advance model. There I argued that the nominal interest rate is determined by its Fisherian fundamentals: anticipated inflation and the real interest rate. Focusing on the Fisher relation leads to two considerations which suggest that a money injection leads to, if anything, an increase in the nominal interest rate. First, a persistent rise in the money stock would, if anything, contribute to a rise in inflation. Second, in the Fuerst-Lucas model, such a money shock would drive down consumption if it caused the current price level to rise. Other things the same, this would tend to drive up the real interest rate as $u_{c,t}$ rose [as can be seen in (22)]. Both of these considerations suggest that the nominal interest rate ought to rise, not fall, with a positive money shock.

There is, however, no puzzle here. In the Fuerst-Lucas model, the connection of the nominal interest rate to Fisherian fundamentals is broken.

To see this, recall that the basic cash-in-advance model's implications for R_t were derived from (20), which only holds if households adjust N_t fully in the light of all period t information. But note: this condition is ruled out in the Fuerst-Lucas model. Here, households must make the N_t decision before they know x_t, θ_t, P_t, and R_t.

To derive the appropriate Fuerst-Lucas analog condition to (20), I retrace the reasoning that led to (20). Optimality of the households' choice of N_t implies that no feasible change generates an increase in utility. Consider a small positive disturbance in N_t. The cost of this is $E_{t-1}(u_{c,t}/P_t)$. The presence of the conditional expectation reflects that, at the time N_t is selected, households do not know what C_t, P_t, or L_t will be, since those values depend on the realization of θ_t and x_t. The benefit of the positive disturbance in N_t is $E_{t-1}R_t\beta^*(u_{c,t+1}/P_{t+1})$. Equality of costs and benefits requires that

$$E_{t-1}(u_{c,t}/P_t) = E_{t-1}R_t\beta^*(u_{c,t+1}/P_{t+1}). \tag{31}$$

This is the analog of (20) which holds in the Fuerst-Lucas model.

It is convenient to express this condition in a slightly different form. First, define $\Lambda_t = R_t E_t \beta^*(u_{c,t+1}/P_{t+1}) - (u_{c,t}/P_t)$, so that $E_{t-1}\Lambda_t = 0$.[15] Then solve this for R_t:

$$R_t = [\Lambda_t + (u_{c,t}/P_t)]/(\beta^* E_t u_{c,t+1}/P_{t+1}) \tag{32}$$

which is comparable to (21).

Fuerst (1992) calls the term Λ_t the *liquidity effect*. It measures the relative value of money in the loan market and in the consumption goods market. When $\Lambda_t < 0$, money is more valuable in the goods market since households would be willing to borrow at a higher rate than R_t if they had the opportunity to do so, while firms are willing to borrow at R_t exactly. For this reason, Fuerst says, when $\Lambda_t < 0$, the loan market is relatively liquid, whereas when $\Lambda_t > 0$, the goods market is. In the basic cash-in-advance model, where households and firms have equal access to financial intermediaries, $\Lambda_t = 0$ always. In the Fuerst-Lucas model, however, Λ_t is only zero on average because $E_{t-1}\Lambda_t = 0$ implies that $E\Lambda_t = 0$. Thus, in this model, the connection of R_t to Fisherian fundamentals holds only on average, not period by period. For example, if Λ_t is negative, then the nominal interest rate is low compared to what fundamentals dictate. In particular, if a money growth shock induces a sufficiently large fall in Λ_t, then R_t could jump even if anticipated inflation and the real rate of interest, $u_{c,t}/(\beta^* E_t u_{c,t+1})$, jump.

The efficiency conditions for the Fuerst-Lucas model are, then, (18), (19), (24), and (31). The Appendix shows how these conditions can be used to solve this model.

Also with Sluggish Firm Investment
Now let's modify the basic cash-in-advance model further, by adding one quite realistic assumption to the Fuerst-Lucas model: Firm investment deci-

sions must be made before firms know the current-period values of the technology and money growth shocks, $\varepsilon_{\theta,t}$ and $\varepsilon_{x,t}$. This assumption captures the real-world idea that investment plans must be made in advance, that they are costly and time-consuming to change.

Because this sluggish capital model closes off investment as a potential outlet for an unexpected money injection, it can make employment and output respond positively to a money shock more easily than the other models can. Of course, the sluggish capital model does not make an unambiguous prediction about the employment or output response since a money shock may simultaneously induce other changes that shift the labor supply curve left.

The efficiency conditions associated with the sluggish capital model are (18), (19) (since labor supply and demand decisions are still made after θ_t and x_t are observed), (31), and a suitably modified version of (24):

$$E_{t-1} R_t P_t (\beta^* u_{c,t+1}/P_{t+1})$$
$$= E_{t-1} P_{t+1} [f_K^*(K_{t+1}, z_{t+1} H_{t+1}) + (1 - \delta^*)(R_{t+1} - 1)][(\beta^*)^2 u_{c,t+2}/P_{t+2}].$$
$$(33)$$

... And Quantitatively

In this section, I investigate some quantitative properties of the three models described above. First I explain how I chose values for the models' parameters. Then I report what the models say are the interest rate, employment, and output effects of money growth shocks.[16]

Parameter Values

The period in the models is assumed to be one quarter. Each model has 12 free parameters: β^*, ψ, θ, α, γ, δ^*, μ, x, ρ_θ, ρ_x, $\sigma_{\varepsilon,\theta}$, and $\sigma_{\varepsilon,x}$.

Three of these are set without reference to actual U.S. data. I set the discount rate, β^*, at $1.03^{-0.25}$. In the baseline experiments, I set the curvature parameter, ψ, to 0. This is the value used by Long and Plosser (1983) and Hansen (1985a). However, results based on alternative values of ψ are reported too. The parameter θ, which is simply a scale variable, is arbitrarily set to 1.

The other parameters are set based on U.S. data for the inclusive period from the first quarter of 1959 to the first quarter of 1984. For Y_t, C_t, L_t, K_t, and I_t, I use the quarterly data used in Christiano 1988. For money, I use U.S. monetary base data, adjusted for reserve requirement changes, which are available from Citicorp's Citibase data bank.[17] The per capita consumption measure is the sum of private sector consumption of non-durables and services, the imputed rental value of the stock of consumer durables, and government consumption. The per capita hours-worked data are constructed from Hansen's (1984) hours-worked data, and the per capita capital stock data are the sum of the stock of consumer durables, producer structures and equipment, government and private residential capital, and government nonresidential capital. Data on per capita investment, I_t, are the flow data that match the capital stock concept. For further details on all these data, see Christiano 1987d, 1988.

The depreciation rate, δ^*, is estimated to be 0.0212, the sample average of the depreciation rates implied by (8) and the data on K_t and I_t.[18] The estimate of the average growth rate of the state of technology, μ, is 0.0041, ✓ the sample average of the growth rate of per capita output, Y_t. The average money growth rate, x, is set to 0.0119, the sample average of the growth rate of the monetary base.

I next consider the values of α and γ, the utility and technology parameters, and the remaining parameters of the shocks.

Utility and Technology
One way to select values for α and γ aligns the models' implications for the means of L_t and K_t/Y_t with the corresponding sample averages.

The models' mean implications for these variables correspond roughly to the values to which they converge when $\sigma_{\varepsilon,x} = \sigma_{\varepsilon,\theta} = 0$, or their steady-state values. The steady-state values of L_t and K_t/Y_t, denoted L and K/Y, are straightforward to compute given values for the models' parameters. The formulas for the computations are identical for the three models, since they are in fact the same model when there is no uncertainty.[19]

The formulas make it possible to compute α and γ given values for K/Y; the leisure-to-labor ratio, $(1 - L)/L$; and the values already assigned to the other parameters. According to Christiano 1988 (Table 1), the sample averages of K/Y and per capita hours worked are 10.59 and 320.5, respectively. If households can devote a maximum of 16 hours per day to market activity, then the quarterly time endowment is 1,460 hours. This indicates that the empirical ratio of market-to-nonmarket activity averages 0.28, so that $(1 - L)/L = 1/0.28$. Substituting these values into the steady-state formulas gives $\alpha = 0.35$ and $\gamma = 0.76$. [Because this procedure of assigning values to α and γ is based on matching sample averages (or first moments), I call it a *first-moment estimator*.] These estimates of α and γ, together with the already assigned parameter values, imply that $R = 1.0195$ (an 8 percent

Table 21.1
Estimated money growth models
$x_t = (M_{t+1} - M_t)/M_t$
$x_t = (1 - \rho_x)x + \rho_x x_{t-1} + \varepsilon_{x,t}$

Estimation period	Coefficients		Standard deviation of shock $\sigma_{\varepsilon,x}$
	$(1 - \rho_x)x$	ρ_x	
Full sample:			
1959:2−1984:1	.0025	.80	.0041
Subsamples:			
1959:2−1969:4	.0014	.81	.0037
1970:1−1984:1	.0110	.32	.0038

Note: In these models, M = U.S. base money. See note 17 for details.
Source of basic data: Citicorp's Citibase data bank.

annual nominal interest rate) and that $C/Y = 0.73$, virtually the same as the sample average of C_t/Y_t reported in Christiano 1988 (Table 1).

Shocks
Values for the parameters of the money growth process, ρ_x and $\sigma_{\varepsilon,x}$, are obtained from U.S. time series data on base money growth, $x_t = (M_{t+1} - M_t)/M_t$, for the inclusive period from the second quarter of 1959 to the first quarter of 1984; those data are plotted in Figure 21.4. Note how in the first half of the sample x_t seems to follow an upward trend, while in the second half it seems to fluctuate around a constant 1.5 percent quarterly growth rate. Not surprisingly, inference about the persistence of shocks to x_t is very sensitive to how this low-frequency behavior is accommodated.

One way to show this is to fit first-order autoregressive models [like (13)] to data on x_t using different subsamples. Results of doing that are reported in Table 21.1. When a first-order autoregressive model is fit to the entire sample, the coefficient ρ_x on lagged x_t is 0.80. This relatively high value reflects the autoregression's attempt to interpret the upward trend in the earlier part of the sample as a slow reversion to a stochastic mean of around 0.015. When the same calculation is done using data from the later part of the sample, the autoregressive coefficient, not surprisingly, is much smaller: 0.32. In light of these results, I use the persistence estimate obtained from the full sample as my benchmark, but I also consider the impact on my results of lower persistence.

An estimate of the state of technology, z_t, is obtained using data on Y_t, K_t, and H_t; equation (5); and $\alpha = 0.35$. The result is plotted in Figure 21.5. These data exhibit the same trend behavior as do the money growth data

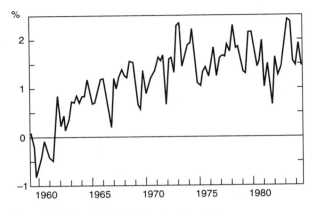

Figure 21.4 Growth in the Monetary Base (x_t)

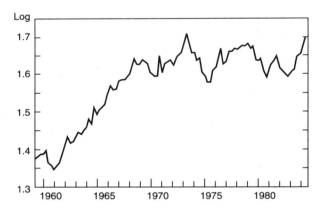

Figure 21.5 The State of Technology (log z_t)

Figures 21.4 and 21.5
U.S. Data Used to Parameterize the Shocks: Quarterly, 1959:2–1984:1. Sources: Citicorp's Citibase data bank and Christiano 1988.

in Figure 21.4. Not surprisingly, therefore, the same subsample instability appears when equations (6) and (12) are fit to those data.

A careful analysis along these lines is reported by Burnside, Eichenbaum, and Rebelo (1990). They fit a first-order autoregression to the linearly detrended logarithm of z_t over the same three subsamples reported in Table 21.1.[20] Using the whole sample, they find that $\rho_\theta = 0.9857$ and $\sigma_{\varepsilon,\theta} = 0.01369$. Over the first subsample, they get $\rho_\theta = 0.8624$ and $\sigma_{\varepsilon,\theta} = 0.00923$; over the second, $\rho_\theta = 0.8842$ and $\sigma_{\varepsilon,\theta} = 0.015538$. Clearly, if we insist on the simple autoregressive model with linear time trend for $\log z_t$ posited here (and used in the real business cycle literature), there is considerable uncertainty about what a plausible set of parameters for that model is. I will here take Burnside, Eichenbaum, and Rebelo's full sample results as the benchmark parameter values.

The Effects of a Money Shock

I now turn to an analysis of the dynamic properties of the models.[21] I begin by investigating the models' ability to account for a dominant liquidity effect on interest rates and employment and output. My results are consistent with the earlier analysis: The basic cash-in-advance model does not exhibit a dominant liquidity effect in equilibrium. Whether or not the Fuerst-Lucas model can do so depends on parameter values; for plausible values, it does not. In contrast with the others, the sluggish capital model easily rationalizes a dominant liquidity effect.

I start with the immediate, or contemporaneous, impact in the three models of a shock to the money growth rate, shown in Table 21.2 for various settings of ψ, ρ_x, and δ^*. The other parameters are set at their benchmark values. In the table, R_x is the percentage-point change in the nominal interest rate associated with a one-percentage-point unexpected increase in money growth; L_x is the percentage change in labor effort associated with that increase. (Unless otherwise stated, all rates are quarterly.)

Let's start with the results for the basic cash-in-advance model. Note that whenever $\rho_x = 0$ in this model, $R_x = L_x = 0$. This reflects that, when $\rho_x = 0$, an unexpected change in money growth is purely temporary and so is neutral. In particular, there is a permanent, one-time jump in the money stock which leads to a contemporaneous, equiproportionate jump in current and anticipated price levels, leaving the anticipated inflation rate unaffected. Also, the nominal interest rate remains unchanged, as do employment and investment. Contrast this with what happens when there is positive persistence in money growth shocks, or $\rho_x > 0$. Then anticipated

Table 21.2
The contemporaneous impact of a money growth shock in the three models:
Percentage-point change in the nominal interest rate (R_x) and percentage change in hours worked (L_x) in the period of a one-percentage-point surprise increase in money growth†

| | Parameters‡ | | | Models | | | | | |
| | | | | Basic cash-in-advance | | Fuerst-Lucas | | Sluggish capital | |
Rows	Utility ψ	Persist. ρ_x	Deprec. δ^*	R_x	L_x	R_x	L_x	R_x	L_x
(1)	0	0	1.00	0	0	-.910	.419	-4.35	2.010
(2)	0	0	.02	0	0	-.028	-.011	-3.11	1.500
(3)	0	.80	1.00	.699	-1.250	-.693	-.612	-2.97	.440
(4)	-4	0	1.00	0	0	-.899	-.166	-4.47	2.130
(5)	0	.80	.02	.290	-2.120	.200	-2.150	-2.26	-.944
(6)	0	.32	.02	.101	-.375	.064	-.390	-2.97	1.102
(7)	-4	.32	.02	.126	-.283	-.216	-.922	-2.93	1.129

† The derivatives, $L_x = d \log L/d\varepsilon_x$ and $R_x = dR/d\varepsilon_x$, are evaluated in nonstochastic steady state.
‡ The parameter ψ is a curvature parameter on the utility function, (4); ρ_x is the autocorrelation of money growth; and δ^* is the rate of depreciation on capital in equation (8). The other parameters are set at $\beta^* = 1.03^{-0.25}$, $\mu = 0.0041$, $x = 0.012$, $\rho_\theta = 0.9857$, $\alpha = 0.35$, and $\gamma = 0.76$.

inflation increases and raises the nominal interest rate. In addition, by acting as a tax on labor effort, the jump in anticipated inflation produces a fall
in labor supply and, thus, a fall in equilibrium employment.

Now turn to the Fuerst-Lucas model. The best case here for the dominant liquidity effect is when capital depreciates completely in one period
and money growth has no persistence, in row (1). Then a one-percentage-
point temporary increase in money growth produces a 91-basis-point fall
in the nominal interest rate. At the same time, employment jumps by
almost half a percent, as firms use the extra liquidity to expand employment and investment.

The remaining rows for the Fuerst-Lucas model show that moving away
from these parameter values, in the direction of greater empirical plausibility, overturns the results. For example, row (2) indicates that when the
depreciation rate is dropped to an empirically plausible level, the positive
impact on employment observed in row (1) turns negative. The reason
for this is that with less depreciation, the return on capital falls less rapidly
with an expansion in investment. As a result, after a monetary injection, relatively more funds are absorbed into investment and less into
employment.[22]

Row (3) in Table 21.2 indicates the marginal impact of increasing the
persistence of the money growth shock. That also has the effect of making
employment fall with a positive money shock. This reflects the effects of a
phenomenon already observed in the basic cash-in-advance model. The
persistent change in money growth pushes up the anticipated rate of inflation, producing a reduction in labor supply. In equilibrium, this reduction
overwhelms the positive impact of the increased liquidity on labor demand.

Row (4) displays the marginal impact of increasing the curvature on the
utility function. This also has the effect of making the employment response to a positive money growth shock negative. The reason for this is
that, by driving up the price level, the money shock forces consumption to
fall contemporaneously because of the cash constraint (1) and the fact that
N_t cannot respond to the shock by assumption. It is readily confirmed from
equation (4) that the fall in consumption drives up the marginal utility of
leisure when $\psi < 0$. As a result, labor supply falls and, in equilibrium, so
does employment.

Thus far, however, none of the changes from the row (1) parameterization have overturned the implication of the Fuerst-Lucas model that a
money growth shock produces a fall in the nominal interest rate. In all of
these cases, the liquidity effect on the interest rate dominates the anticipated inflation effect in equilibrium. When the changes are considered joint-

Detrended
Goods

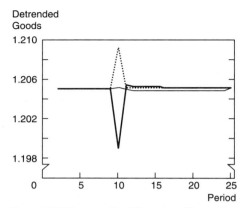

Figure 21.6 Consumption $[C_t \exp(-\mu t)]$

% of
Avail. Time

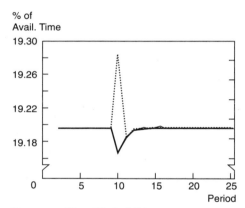

Figure 21.7 Time Worked (L_t)

Detrended
Goods

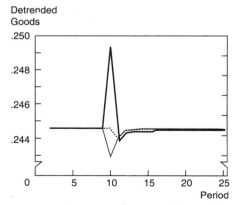

Figure 21.8 Investment $[l_t \exp(-\mu t)]$

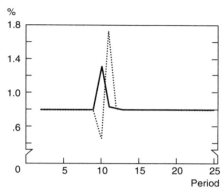

Figure 21.9 Inflation $\{[(P_t/P_{t-1})-1]100\}$

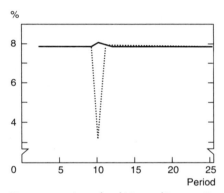

Figure 21.10 Annualized Nominal Interest Rate $[(R_t - 1)400]$

—————— Basic Cash-in-Advance Model
—————— Fuerst-Lucas Model
········ Sluggish Capital Model

Figures 21.6–21.10
The Dynamic Effects of a Money Growth Shock in the Three Models: Responses of Model
Variables to a One-Standard-Deviation Money Growth Shock in Period 10

ly, however, the liquidity effect is overwhelmed by the anticipated inflation effect.

This is the implication of the results in rows (5)–(7). Row (5) gives the values for R_x and L_x associated with the benchmark parameter values. Note that the anticipated inflation effect on the interest rate now swamps the liquidity effect. In addition, the reduction in labor supply from anticipated inflation dominates any positive demand effect from a money injection. In fact, here the equilibrium effects of the money growth shock are not much different from what they are in the basic cash-in-advance model. Interestingly, dropping persistence in x_t to the not-unreasonable value of 0.32 [as in row (6)] does not change the qualitative result, but it does reduce the negative employment impact of a money shock. Row (7) indicates that increasing the curvature of the utility function has little impact.

Next, consider what happens in the sluggish capital model, which is shown in the final pair of columns in Table 21.2. Recall that, in this model, the role of investment in absorbing an infusion of liquidity is limited by the fact that the real level of investment is temporarily inflexible. Other things the same, this should enhance the positive impact on labor demand of a money infusion. The results in Table 21.2 indicate that for most parameterizations, it does: the equilibrium effect on employment of a money infusion is, indeed, positive. Only when a money growth shock is very persistent [as in row (5)] does the negative impact on labor supply occasioned by the shock dominate the positive impact on labor demand. Note, however, how very large the interest rate impact of a money shock is in this model. In all cases, a one-percentage-point surprise jump in the money growth rate produces a drop in the nominal interest rate greater than two percentage points. At an annual rate, this translates roughly into a drop of eight percentage points.

Now let's look at the longer-term impact of a money growth shock. Figures 21.6–21.10 show the contemporaneous and lagged responses of the models' key variables to a one-standard-deviation disturbance, $\varepsilon_{x,t}$, in the money growth rate. In all cases, the economy is assumed to start in nonstochastic steady state in period 1 and to experience the shock in period 10. Each figure shows how the variable responds in the three models. The parameterization underlying the impulse response functions in these figures corresponds to that underlying row (6) in Table 21.2: $\beta^* = 1.03^{-0.25}$, $\mu = 0.0041$, $\theta = 1$, $x = 0.012$, $\rho_\theta = 0.9857$, $\alpha = 0.35$, $\gamma = 0.76$, $\psi = 0$, $\rho_x = 0.32$, and $\delta^* = 0.02$.

Five features in these figures are worth noting.

First, incorporating the Fuerst-Lucas assumptions into the basic cash-in-advance model has virtually no impact on the equilibrium employment and interest rate responses to a money growth shock (Figures 21.7 and 21.10).

Second, the liquidity effect in the sluggish capital model exists only in the period of the shock (Figures 21.7 and 21.10). In addition to being empirically implausible, this lack of persistence is a problem for another reason. In particular, the liquidity effect would likely disappear if the period length in the model were made shorter than the data sampling interval and the observed data were viewed as time-averaged. Such sensitivity is a significant shortcoming, since I have little confidence in the exact period length specification of my models.

Third, in all cases but one, the impulse responses starting the period after the shock virtually coincide across all models. The exceptional case is inflation (Figure 21.9), which is quite high in the sluggish capital model in the period after the shock, as prices catch up after the fall in price level that occurs in the period of the shock. This initial fall in the price level in this model reflects that the money growth shock has a relatively greater impact on the supply of output than on its demand.[23]

A fourth notable feature in the charts is the surge in investment that occurs in the period of the shock in the Fuerst-Lucas model (Figure 21.8). It is by suppressing this as an outlet for the money infusion that the sluggish capital model predicts a positive employment response to a money shock.

Fifth, note how the Fuerst-Lucas and sluggish capital models both imply that the consumption and price responses to a money growth shock are opposite in sign (Figures 21.6 and 21.9). This reflects the effect of the cash-in-advance constraint, equation (1). King (1990) presents evidence that suggests this is counterfactual.

To summarize, my results confirm that the basic cash-in-advance model cannot rationalize the widespread view that the liquidity effect overwhelms the anticipated inflation effect on the interest rate and on employment, at least in the short run. It also cannot rationalize a positive employment and output effect of a money infusion. Although in principle, the Fuerst-Lucas version of the model can rationalize this, in practice it fails to do so for plausible parameter values. For these values, the anticipated inflation effect associated with a money injection (which is emphasized by the basic cash-in-advance model) dominates in equilibrium.

A modification of the Fuerst-Lucas model which reduces the magnitude of the anticipated inflation effect on equilibrium employment would obviously help. One way to accomplish this may be to model the transaction motive for holding money in a way that gives agents more flexibility than does the cash-in-advance assumption. Another may be to allow certain purchases, like investment, to be made entirely on credit. It would be interesting to see whether the liquidity effect dominates in equilibrium in a version of the Fuerst-Lucas model modified in these ways.

Finally, the results in Table 21.2 suggest that—qualitatively, at least—the widespread view about the impact of a money infusion is rationalized by a plausibly parameterized version of the sluggish capital model. However, the dominant liquidity effect shows little persistence in that model, according to the evidence in Figures 21.6–21.10; it plays a quantitatively significant role only in the period of the shock itself.

Looking at Other Model Implications

The modifications of the basic cash-in-advance model intended to capture the dominant liquidity effect would be questionable if they simultaneously resulted in drastically reduced empirical performance on other dimensions. Here I investigate the ability of the modified models to account for various other properties of the data, in particular, how volatile variables are, on average, and how much their movements are correlated with those of output. The results, reported in Tables 21.3–21.5, are mixed: the modifications help on some dimensions and hurt on others.

Volatility

Table 21.3 contains measures of the volatility of relevant variables in the three models and in actual U.S. data. All statistics shown there have been computed using data that were first logged and then detrended by the Hodrick-Prescott filter (described by Prescott [in Chapter 14 of this volume]). Statistics in all rows except (2)–(4) are standard deviations. Statistics in rows (2)–(4) are standard deviations divided by the standard deviation of output.

Note that the U.S. data column in Table 21.3 includes results for several variables not yet mentioned. In particular, it includes two measures of the price level—the consumer price index (CPI) and the implicit price deflator of the gross national product—and the two measures of inflation corresponding to them. Also, three measures of the income velocity of money, V, are included. They correspond to the monetary base measure discussed above, as well as two of the Fed's broader monetary aggregates, M1 and M2. Finally, two short-term nominal interest rates are included: the yield on three-month Treasury bills (T-bills) and the effective yield on federal funds.

Table 21.3
Volatility in the U.S. data and in the three models

Rows	Variables		U.S. data 1959:1– 1984:1	Models* Basic cash-in- advance	Fuerst- Lucas	Sluggish capital
(1)	Real output, Y		.017	.013	.013	.015
(2)	Consumption, C		.490	.630	.880	.990
(3)	Employment, L		1.000	.290	.300	.520
(4)	Investment, I		2.590	2.990	3.130	2.660
(5)	Price level, P	CPI	.016	.015	.015	.018
(6)		Deflator	.010			
(7)	Inflation, P/P_{-1}	CPI	.005	.011	.011	.019
(8)		Deflator	.004			
(9)	Income velocity of money, V	MB	.0130	.0008	.0008	.0053
(10)		M1	.0130			
(11)		M2	.0190			
(12)	Nominal interest rate, R	T-bills	.0033	.0022	.0021	.0140
(13)		Fed. funds	.0046			

Note: Results in this table are based on standard deviations of data that have been first logged and then detrended using the Hodrick-Prescott filter. Actual standard deviations are reported in all but rows (2)–(4). Standard deviations in rows (2)–(4) have been divided by the standard deviation of output. Before logging and filtering, nominal interest rates were expressed at a gross quarterly rate.
*Model results are averages across 20 simulations of 101 observations each.
Sources of basic data: Rows (1)–(4): See Christiano 1988.
　　　　　　　　　Rows (5)–(13): Citicorp's data bank.

Consider first the real variables: Y, C, L, and I [in rows (1)–(4)].

One dramatic finding here is how much the rigidities in the modified models add to the relative volatility of consumption. In the basic cash-in-advance model, the relative volatility is already high compared to that in the data. Incorporating the rigidities of the Fuerst-Lucas and sluggish capital models adds substantially to that. This increased volatility in consumption reflects in part the effects of equation (1) and the assumption that households' portfolio decision, N_t, cannot respond contemporaneously to a shock. These two things imply that when the price level moves in response to an unexpected shock, consumption has to move in equal proportion, but in the opposite direction. These factors have the effect of exposing consumption to a considerable amount of extraneous variation. The models' households could feasibly control this variation by keeping extra cash balances on hand. However, that is unacceptably costly in these models, where the real return differential between money and bank loans averages eight percentage points, at an annual rate.

Offering households less costly ways to deal with price risk would probably reduce the models' counterfactually high implications for consumption volatility. A promising approach might be to model the transaction motive for holding money to give households more flexibility—say, by letting them get by with less cash than $P_t C_t$ at the cost of some leisure time or consumption. This sort of flexibility might also eliminate the Fuerst-Lucas and sluggish capital models' implication that the effects on consumption and the price level of an unexpected shock are opposite in sign.

Another dramatic implication of the models in Table 21.3—also counterfactual—concerns employment volatility [row (3)]. In the data, the volatility of labor effort is about the same as that of output. In the models, though, employment's volatility is considerably less than output's. Interestingly, the sluggish capital model actually does better on this dimension than the other models. However, it still substantially undershoots the observed relative volatility of hours worked.

The poor performance of a nonmonetary version of this model has already been documented (Hansen 1985a), and it is not surprising that a monetary version also underpredicts the volatility of work effort. Presumably, incorporating the assumption of indivisible labor, along the lines of Hansen 1985a and Rogerson 1988, would increase the models' volatility of labor.[24]

Finally, note that all the models account fairly well for the observed volatility of investment [row (4)].

Among the nominal variables, the most dramatic implication of the models lies with the nominal rate of interest, R [in rows (12)–(13)]. Interest rates simulated using the basic cash-in-advance and Fuerst-Lucas models are less volatile than their empirical counterparts. However, the reverse is true for interest rates simulated with the sluggish capital model: Rates from this model are far more volatile than those in the U.S. data. This is not surprising, in light of the model's very strong interest rate impact of a money growth shock reported in Table 21.2.

Another result that stands out in Table 21.3 is how smooth the income velocity of money, V, is in the models compared to the data [rows (9)–(11)]. This is reminiscent of a result for an endowment economy reported by Hodrick, Kocherlakota, and Lucas (1991). Interestingly, the sluggish capital model is closer to the data on this dimension, but its implied volatility of V is still less than half that in the data.

The results on the models' implications for money demand, equation (26), can be used to gain insight into why V is so smooth in the sluggish capital model despite the high volatility of interest rates. Substituting $R = 1.0195$, $\alpha = 0.35$ into the formula for b [equation (28)], we find that the interest elasticity of money demand, $b/4$, implied by the models is 0.1. This is much smaller than the estimates in the empirical literature. For example, Lucas (1988b, Table 4) and Stock and Watson (1991, Table 2) estimate this elasticity to be between 9 and 10.[25] If the sluggish capital model's interest elasticity had been empirically more plausible, then (other things unchanged) velocity would have been more volatile. This suggests that the model's empirical implications may be improved by incorporating a more flexible transaction model of money demand, since presumably this would increase the interest sensitivity of velocity.

Finally, note (in Table 21.3) that although the sluggish capital model captures reasonably well the volatility of the price level [rows (5)–(6)], it substantially overshoots the volatility of inflation [rows (7)–(8)]. Evidently, real-world prices are stickier than those anticipated by the model. Sims (1989) has made a similar observation in the context of a related model.

On net, it is hard to say whether the sluggish capital model is an improvement over the other models in terms of its implications for volatility. The sluggish capital modification hurts with consumption, but helps with employment. It hurts with inflation, but helps with velocity. Whether it helps or hurts with interest rates is not clear, since the sluggish capital model overshoots while the other models undershoot.

A question of independent interest is how much money growth shocks contribute to fluctuations in these models. One way to answer this question is to set $\sigma_{\varepsilon,x}$, the standard deviation of the unexpected part of money growth, to zero in the simulations. Doing so, I find that the basic cash-in-advance model, the Fuerst-Lucas model, and the sluggish capital model imply output standard deviations of 0.013, 0.013, and 0.014, respectively. These numbers are trivially less than those reported in Table 21.3 [row (1)]. Thus, in these models, money shocks contribute almost nothing to output fluctuations.

Correlations with Output

Tables 21.4 and 21.5 present measures of how movements in output are related to movements of other variables in the U.S. data and in the three models.

Table 21.4
Dynamic correlations between output and other variables in the U.S. data and in the three models: The real variables

| Variable, v_t | Data source | Correlation of real output with | | |
		v_{t-1}	v_t	v_{t+1}
Real output, Y	U.S. data	.81	1.00	.81
	Models:			
	Basic cash-in-advance	.67	1.00	.67
	Fuerst-Lucas	.67	1.00	.67
	Sluggish capital	.52	1.00	.52
Consumption, C	U.S. data	.63	.68	.55
	Models:			
	Basic cash-in-advance	.64	.98	.71
	Fuerst-Lucas	.57	.87	.37
	Sluggish capital	.44	.90	.15
Employment, L	U.S. data	.62	.75	.68
	Models:			
	Basic cash-in-advance	.65	.91	.54
	Fuerst-Lucas	.64	.92	.56
	Sluggish capital	.31	.82	.10
Investment, I	U.S. data	.85	.90	.72
	Models:			
	Basic cash-in-advance	.68	.98	.61
	Fuerst-Lucas	.49	.71	.78
	Sluggish capital	.37	.57	.93

Sources of basic data: See Table 21.3.

Table 21.4 reports these dynamic correlations for the real variables only.

Generally, the contemporaneous correlations in the models are somewhat higher than those in the U.S. data. The results for investment are a notable exception. The contemporaneous correlation between investment and output is substantially lower in both the Fuerst-Lucas and sluggish capital models than that in the data.

Even more interesting, these models imply that investment lags output by one quarter. This reflects the effects of the rigidities that inhibit households from financing an increase in investment in the period of a technology shock. In the Fuerst-Lucas model, some expansion in investment can nevertheless be financed in the period of a shock simply because a falling price level increases the value of the predetermined nominal loans made by households to the financial intermediaries. (The falling price level can be understood using standard textbook reasoning and the fact that the positive shock to technology generates an increase in output.) However, in the sluggish capital model, investment is assumed to be predetermined. As a

Table 21.5
Dynamic correlations between output and other variables in the U.S. data and in the three models: The nominal variables

Variable, v_t	Data source	Correlation of real output with		
		v_{t-1}	v_t	v_{t+1}
Price level, P	U.S. data: CPI	−.67	−.55	−.32
	Deflator	−.65	−.57	−.38
	Models:			
	Basic cash-in-advance	−.58	−.89	−.62
	Fuerst-Lucas	−.57	−.89	−.61
	Sluggish capital	−.47	−.91	−.34
Inflation, P/P_{-1}	U.S. data: CPI	.12	.38	.52
	Deflator	.04	.17	.26
	Models:			
	Basic cash-in-advance	−.31	−.39	.33
	Fuerst-Lucas	−.29	−.39	.34
	Sluggish capital	−.17	−.40	.51
Money, M	U.S. data: MB	.39	.49	.48
	M1	.66	.65	.48
	M2	.70	.56	.32
	Models:			
	Basic cash-in-advance	.05	.03	−.04
	Fuerst-Lucas	.06	.04	−.03
	Sluggish capital	−.04	−.08	.02
Income velocity of money, V	U.S. data: MB	.38	.65	.55
	M1	.09	.41	.44
	M2	−.16	.19	.31
	Models:			
	Basic cash-in-advance	.08	.11	.06
	Fuerst-Lucas	.08	.13	.01
	Sluggish capital	−.07	−.38	.24
Nominal interest rate, R	U.S. data: T-bills	.04	.30	.44
	Fed. funds	.01	.30	.49
	Models:			
	Basic cash-in-advance	.08	.11	.06
	Fuerst-Lucas	.08	.13	.01
	Sluggish capital	.07	−.38	.24

Sources of basic data: See Table 21.3.

result, there is no investment response to a technology shock until one period after the shock. Expanding investment then still makes sense since by assumption the shocks are highly persistent.

Table 21.5 reports dynamic correlations in the models and the data for the nominal variables.

Consider the detrended price level first. As pointed out by Kydland and Prescott [in Chapter 17 in this volume], the price level covaries negatively with output, whether measured by the CPI or by the gross national product deflator. The models have roughly the same implication. This is consistent with my earlier observation that technology shocks dominate in the models' dynamics.

Notice, however, how differently detrended inflation behaves. In the data, inflation is positively associated with output, both contemporaneously and at the one-quarter lag. In addition, inflation lags the cycle in the sense that it is most strongly correlated with detrended output one quarter earlier. By contrast, in all three models, inflation has a negative contemporaneous correlation with output. However, the models resemble the data in that detrended output is positively correlated with inflation one quarter later.

Next, consider the money data. The models imply that detrended money is roughly uncorrelated with output, while the data imply some correlation. Again, the very low correlation implied by the models is consistent with my earlier observation that money shocks play only a small role in the models' dynamics. Note that, in the data, the broader monetary aggregates lead the cycle; that is, detrended output is more highly correlated with their earlier values. This seems like an interesting fact that a richer version of these models should be able to confront.

The results for velocity are broadly similar to those for money.

Finally, consider the results for the nominal interest rate.

Note that in the data, both my measures of short-term rates lag the cycle. That is, detrended output is more highly correlated with future values of the interest rate than with contemporaneous values. In the models, by contrast, the nominal interest rate is more nearly coincident with the cycle. That is, the strongest cross-correlation is with the contemporaneous value of output.

In addition, although the nominal interest rate is positively correlated with the contemporaneous value of output in the basic cash-in-advance and Fuerst-Lucas models, it is negatively correlated with that value in the sluggish capital model. This reflects that, in the first two models, the impact of a positive technology shock on the nominal interest rate is positive, while in the sluggish capital model, it is negative. This negative impact presumably reflects that the sluggish capital model's assumption of a predetermined investment level in effect subtracts an important source of demand for funds from the loan market.

Overall, the dynamic correlations reported in Tables 21.4 and 21.5 seem to suggest that both the Fuerst-Lucas and sluggish capital models are a step backward from the basic cash-in-advance model. This conclusion is based principally on the models' implications for the cyclical properties of investment and interest rates. The rigidities appear to make investment lag the cycle, by inhibiting a quick increase in financing for investment in response to a technology shock.[26] This factor may also account for the sluggish capital model's counterfactual implication that output covaries negatively with the rate of interest. These considerations suggest considering a modified version of the sluggish capital model in which household portfolio decisions and firm investment decisions are made after the technology shock, but still before the money growth shock. That assumption may be plausible if agents have some advance notice about disturbances to technology.

Summary and Directions for Further Research

Monetary versions of real business cycle models have great potential as laboratories for evaluating monetary policies which have real-world effects we do not yet understand. Before these models can be used with confidence for this, however, we need to be sure that they can at least replicate the effects of simple monetary policy experiments we think we do understand. I have focused on one simple experiment: an unanticipated change in the money growth rate, or a money growth shock. Many economists believe that a positive money shock drives the interest rate down and output and employment up, at least in the short run. Put differently, they think the liquidity effect dominates the anticipated inflation effect.

Simple monetary versions of real business cycle models predict the opposite. For example, when money is introduced by a cash-in-advance constraint, interest rates jump and output and employment fall after a money shock in the empirically plausible case that the shock triggers expectations of increased future money growth.[27] I argued that this reflects the role of the anticipated inflation effect and the absence of a liquidity effect.

I have explored ways of introducing a liquidity effect into this type of model, with mixed results. First, I used a device proposed by Lucas (1990), a rigidity in the household's nominal saving decision. With this modification, the model (the Fuerst-Lucas model) does produce a liquidity effect, but one too small relative to the anticipated inflation effect. Next, I changed the model in another way and managed to increase the magnitude of the liquidity effect enough so that it dominates the anticipated inflation effect. However, the dominant liquidity effect in the resulting model (the sluggish capital model) displays no persistence; it exists only in the period of the shock. Also, the model has implications for money demand and for several features of the U.S. business cycle which contradict the facts.[28] Obviously, more work needs to be done on monetary versions of real business cycle models.

Martin Eichenbaum and I have begun that work. We are exploring model specifications which enhance the likelihood that the Lucas rigidity will produce a dominant, persistent liquidity effect. We seek models that also avoid some of the counterfactual money demand and business cycle implications of the models in this paper.

To reduce the anticipated inflation effect, we are taking steps in the direction of realism by giving agents more flexibility in the way they finance their transactions than they have had here. In the paper I explained how, besides reducing the strength of the anticipated inflation effect, such modifications should help correct several counterfactual implications of the Fuerst-Lucas and sluggish capital models: their overprediction of the response of average employment to average inflation, their overprediction of the volatility of consumption, their implication that the impacts of a money growth shock on consumption and the price level must have opposite signs (which is empirically implausible, according to King 1990), and their low interest elasticity of money demand and consequent excess smoothness of money velocity.

To increase the liquidity effect, we plan to modify the assumption implicit in the models of this paper that the production period of firms and the decision period of the Federal Reserve coincide. More plausible is the assumption that production decisions take an appreciable amount of time to implement, while the Fed's decisions do not; they are implemented virtually instantaneously. Thus, when the Fed drains money from the financial system, at least some firms are likely to have already committed themselves to a production plan which they cannot easily adjust without suffering significant costs. Managers of such firms will be willing to pay a substantial premium to borrow the funds needed to continue financing their inputs and avoid interrupting production.[29] Under these circumstances, a negative money shock could produce a substantial rise in the interest rate.

To introduce persistence into the liquidity effect, we are exploring ways of making utility and production functions depend on lagged variables. One way to do this is to make the marginal utility of consumption an increasing function of lagged consumption, as in the *habit persistence* utility function.[30] Such a modification may help overcome another counterfactual implication of the models in this paper: that the short- and long-run money demand elasticities with respect to the interest rate coincide. In empirical money demand functions, the long-term elasticity greatly exceeds the short-term elasticity.

Preliminary results of this further research are encouraging. Thus, there is reason to hope that we are making progress toward a model that can confidently be used to conduct monetary policy experiments.

Appendix: Finding Approximate Solutions to the Models

Here I describe the solution strategy underlying the results in the preceding paper. First I discuss the undetermined coefficient method used to obtain linearized decision rules. The basic idea behind this method is conveyed through a simple example. Then I show how to express the equations of the paper's models in a form suitable for applying the undetermined coefficient method. This involves, principally, handling complications that arise from the presence of sustained growth in the state of technology z_t, equation (6), and in the money supply M_t, equation (13).

An Undetermined Coefficient Method

Consider a one-sector neoclassical growth model in which there is only a saving/consumption decision to be made.

The competitive equilibrium solves the following planning problem: Maximize expected utility $E\sum_{t=0}^{\infty}\beta^t u(c_t)$ subject to the goods market-clearing condition $c_t + k_{t+1} - (1 - \delta)k_t = f(k_t, \theta_t)$, where β is the discount rate, c_t is consumption, k_t is the capital stock, δ is the depreciation rate on capital, f is the production function, and θ_t is a technology shock. I assume that

$$E[\theta_{t+1}|\theta_t, k_t] = \alpha_0 + \alpha_1 \theta_t \tag{A1}$$

where α_0 and α_1 are given constants.

The efficiency condition for capital investment requires that

$$E[u_c(c_t) - \beta u_c(c_{t+1})\{f_k(k_{t+1}, \theta_{t+1}) + 1 - \delta\}|\theta_t, k_t] = 0 \tag{A2}$$

for all $t \geq 0$, where f_k denotes the partial derivative of f with respect to its first argument and u_c denotes the marginal utility of consumption. After c_t is substituted out from the goods market-clearing condition,

$$E[v(k_t, k_{t+1}, k_{t+2}, \theta_t, \theta_{t+1})|\theta_t, k_t] = 0. \tag{A3}$$

Here

$$v(k_t, k_{t+1}, k_{t+2}, \theta_t, \theta_{t+1}) \equiv u_c[f(k_t, \theta_t) + (1 - \delta)k_t - k_{t+1}]$$

$$- \beta u_c[f(k_{t+1}, \theta_{t+1}) + (1 - \delta)k_{t+1} - k_{t+2}]$$

$$\times [f_k(k_{t+1}, \theta_{t+1}) + 1 - \delta]. \tag{A4}$$

The exact solution to the problem is a function, $k_{t+1} = g(k_t, \theta_t)$, that satisfies (A3); that is,

$$E[v(k_t, g(k_t, \theta), g[g(k_t, \theta), \theta_{t+1}], \theta_t, \theta_{t+1})|\theta_t, k_t] = 0 \tag{A5}$$

for all $k_t \geq 0$ and for all θ_t.

Determining g exactly can be computationally very costly. However, it may not be necessary. In several examples (Danthine, Donaldson, and Mehra 1989 and Christiano 1990a), Kydland and Prescott's (1982) suggestion that g be approximated by a linear function has been found to work well.

Following is a simple three-step procedure that delivers a linear approximation, G, to g:

1. Find the value of k that solves $v(k, k, k, \theta, \theta) = 0$, where $\theta \equiv E\theta_t$. The variable k is the value to which k_t tends in the nonstochastic version of the problem, where θ_t is held to its unconditional mean.

2. Compute V, the first-order Taylor series expansion of v about $k_t = k_{t+1} = k_{t+2} = k$ and $\theta_t = \theta_{t+1} = \theta$.

3. Define the following linear function:

$$k_{t+1} = G(k_t, \theta_t) \equiv G_0 + G_1 k_t + G_2 \theta_t \tag{A6}$$

where G_0, G_1, G_2 are (as yet) undetermined constants. Select values of G_0, G_1, G_2 so that the analog of (A5) is satisfied with v replaced by V:

$$E[V(k_t, G(k_t, \theta_t), G[G(k_t, \theta_t), \theta_{t+1}], \theta_t, \theta_{t+1})|\theta_t, k_t] = \tilde{G}_0 + \tilde{G}_1 k_t + \tilde{G}_2 \theta_t = 0 \tag{A7}$$

where $\tilde{G}_i$ are functions of G_0, G_1, G_2 for each $i = 1, 2, 3$. In (A7), the first equality follows by the linearity of V, G, and $E[\theta_{t+1}|\theta_t, k_t]$. The requirement that the last equality is satisfied for all $k_t \geq 0$ and all θ_t requires that

$$\tilde{G}_0 = \tilde{G}_1 = \tilde{G}_2 = 0. \tag{A8}$$

Equation (A8) represents three equations in the three unknowns, G_0, G_1, and G_2. These equations, in addition to a transversality-type condition, $|G_1| \leqslant \beta^{1/2}$, can be used to find unique values for G_0, G_1, and G_2.

To compute first- and second-moment implications like those analyzed in the paper, use the decision rule, G, and the time series model for θ_t to simulate artificial data on θ_t and k_t. The resource constraint can be used to compute the implied consumption data. Statistical analysis can then be performed on these data.

Three observations on the linearization procedure are in order.

First, a simple modification to the above procedure can be used to compute a log-linear decision rule: $\bar{k}_{t+1} = \overline{G}_0 + \overline{G}_1 \bar{k}_t + \overline{G}_2 \theta_t$, where $\bar{k}_t \equiv \log k_t$. Simply define

$$\bar{v}(\bar{k}_t, \bar{k}_{t+1}, \bar{k}_{t+2}, \theta_t, \theta_{t+1}) = v[\exp(\bar{k}_t), \exp(\bar{k}_{t+1}), \exp(\bar{k}_{t+2}), \theta_t, \theta_{t+1}]. \tag{A9}$$

Then replace $\bar{v}$ by $\overline{V}$, the linear expansion of $\bar{v}$ about $\bar{k}_t = \bar{k}_{t+1} = \bar{k}_{t+2} = \log k$ and $\theta_t = \theta_{t+1} = \theta$. Finally, find the values of $\overline{G}_0$, $\overline{G}_1$, $\overline{G}_2$ which solve the analog of (A5) with v replaced by $\overline{V}$, subject to the condition $|\overline{G}_1| \leqslant \beta^{1/2}$.

Second, the undetermined coefficient procedure requires only that the efficiency conditions be satisfied as an equality, as they are in the illustration and in the models of the paper. In particular, the problem need not be expressible as a social planning problem, as it is in the illustration. For example, the models in the paper cannot easily be expressed as social planning problems.

Third, when applied to growth models like the one in the illustration, the method yields exactly the same solution as the linear-quadratic method proposed in Kydland and Prescott 1982. Also, the log-linear variant of the undetermined coefficient method yields the same solution as the log-linear-quadratic version of the Kydland-Prescott method used in Christiano 1988.

Applying the Undetermined Coefficient Method

To get the models of the paper in shape for the undetermined coefficient method, their efficiency conditions and other restrictions, such as the resource constraint, must be expressed in a form analogous to (A3). Here I primarily describe how to do that in the Fuerst-Lucas model. Then I show how to modify things to accommodate the basic cash-in-advance and sluggish capital models.

The Fuerst-Lucas Model

In the paper, the efficiency conditions for the Fuerst-Lucas model are equations (18), (19), (24), and (31). It is convenient to eliminate R_t from (19). Accordingly, substituting from (18) and (19) into (24) and (31) gives[31]

$$E_t\{(P_t/W_t)^2 f^*_{H,t} u_{L,t} - \beta^* P_{t+1} f^*_{K,t+1}(u_{L,t+1}/W_{t+1})\} = 0 \qquad (A10)$$

$$E_{t-1}\{(u_{c,t}/P_t) + (P_t/W_t) f^*_{H,t}(u_{L,t}/W_t)\} = 0. \qquad (A11)$$

For convenience, a slightly rearranged version of (18) is reproduced here:

$$E_t\{u_{L,t} + W_t\beta^*(u_{c,t+1}/P_{t+1})\} = 0. \qquad (A12)$$

The efficiency conditions, (A10), (A11), and (A12), are not enough to solve the model. This is because these constitute only three restrictions, while we seek six objects: equilibrium decision rules for K_{t+1}, C_t, N_t, and L_t and market-clearing price rules for P_t and W_t. Three additional restrictions are given by the households' cash-in-advance constraint, (1); the loan market-clearing condition, (14); and the goods market-clearing condition, (16). I will show below how these restrictions can be used to substitute out for P_t, W_t, and C_t in (A10), (A11), and (A12). Then these three efficiency conditions, together with a transversality-type condition, will be enough to pin down approximate equilibrium decision rules for K_{t+1}, L_t, and N_t with a variant of the undetermined coefficient procedure just described. The equilibrium R_t rule can then be inferred from (19), while the rules for P_t, W_t, and C_t follow from (1), (14), and (16).

Scaling the Variables   All the variables in the model except L_t and R_t display growth in equilibrium. But the undetermined coefficient method requires that the variables display no growth. This is because the method involves approximating the efficiency conditions around a stationary point. (Recall step 1 above.) To meet the stationarity requirement of the solution method, I work with a version of the efficiency conditions, (A10)–(A12), and restrictions (1), (14), and (16) expressed in terms of variables that have been scaled appropriately to eliminate growth.

Define

$$c_t = \exp(-\mu t)C_t \qquad (A13)$$

$$k_{t+1} = \exp(-\mu t)K_{t+1} \qquad (A14)$$

$$n_t = N_t/M_t \qquad (A15)$$

$$w_t = W_t/M_t \qquad (A16)$$

$$p_t = P_t \exp(\mu t)/M_t. \tag{A17}$$

It turns out that c_t, k_{t+1}, n_t, w_t, and p_t converge to constants in the nonstochastic version of the model. This implies that C_t and K_t grow at the same rate, μ, as the state of technology, z_t, while W_t grows at the rate of money growth, x. Since K_t grows at the rate μ, it follows from the production function (5) that output, Y_t, does too. Finally, P_t's growth rate equals $x - \mu$, the rate of money growth less the rate of output growth.

Associated with the scaled variables in (A13)–(A17) are scaled marginal utilities and productivities. Consider the marginal utilities first. Replacing C_t by $\exp(\mu t)c_t$ in the partial derivative of (4) with respect to C_t gives

$$u_{c,t} \equiv u_c(C_t, L_t) = u_c(c_t, L_t) \exp\{\mu t[(1 - \gamma)\psi - 1]\}$$

$$\equiv \tilde{u}_{c,t} \exp\{\mu t[(1 - \gamma)\psi - 1]\} \tag{A18}$$

$$u_{L,t} \equiv u_L(C_t, L_t) = u_L(c_t, L_t) \exp\{\mu t(1 - \gamma)\psi\}$$

$$\equiv \tilde{u}_{L,t} \exp\{\mu t(1 - \gamma)\psi\}. \tag{A19}$$

Next consider the marginal productivities. Let

$$f(k_t, \theta_t, L_t) \equiv \exp(-\mu t) f^*(K_t, z_t L_t)$$

$$= \exp(-\alpha\mu) k_t^\alpha [\exp(\theta_t) L_t]^{(1-\alpha)} + (1 - \delta)k_t \tag{A20}$$

where $(1 - \delta) \equiv (1 - \delta^*) \exp(-\mu)$. If $f_{k,t}$ and $f_{H,t}$ denote the partial derivative of f with respect to its first and third arguments, then

$$f_{H,t}^* = \exp(\mu t) f_{H,t} \tag{A21}$$

$$f_{K,t}^* = \exp(\mu) f_{k,t}. \tag{A22}$$

(The variables H and L are interchangeable for my purposes at this point since the labor market-clearing condition requires that they be equal.) Substitute (A13)–(A22) into (A10)–(A12) and rearrange to get

$$E_t\{(p_t/w_t)^2 f_{H,t} \tilde{u}_{L,t} - \beta p_{t+1} f_{k,t+1}(\tilde{u}_{L,t+1}/w_{t+1})\} = 0 \tag{A23}$$

$$E_{t-1}\{(\tilde{u}_{c,t}/p_t) + (p_t/w_t) f_{H,t}(\tilde{u}_{L,t}/w_t)\} = 0 \tag{A24}$$

$$E_t\{\tilde{u}_{L,t} + w_t \beta^*(\tilde{u}_{c,t+1}/[p_{t+1}(1 + x_t)])\} = 0. \tag{A25}$$

Here $\beta \equiv \beta^* \exp[(1 - \gamma)\psi\mu]$. Equations (A23)–(A25) are a version of the Fuerst-Lucas model's efficiency conditions in which all variables have been scaled.

Next consider the scaled version of restrictions (1), (14), and (16). Dividing (1) by C_t and using the goods market-clearing condition, (16), gives

$$P_t = (M_t - N_t)/[f^*(K_t, z_t L_t) - K_{t+1}]. \tag{A26}$$

Multiplying both sides of (A26) by $\exp(\mu t)/M_t$ and using (A13)–(A17) yields

$$p_t = (1 - n_t)/[f(k_t, \theta_t, L_t) - k_{t+1}] \equiv p(k_t, k_{t+1}, n_t, L_t, \theta_t). \tag{A27}$$

Rearrange (14) as

$$W_t = (N_t + X_t - P_t I_t)/L_t. \tag{A28}$$

Divide both sides of this by M_t to get

$$w_t = [n_t + x_t - p_t \exp(-\mu t) I_t]/L_t$$
$$= \{n_t + x_t - p(k_t, k_{t+1}, n_t, L_t, \theta_t)[k_{t+1} - (1 - \delta)k_t]\}/L_t$$
$$\equiv w(k_t, k_{t+1}, n_t, L_t, \theta_t, x_t). \tag{A29}$$

In (A29), I have used (8), the definition of δ, and (A13)–(A17). Also, from the goods market-clearing condition,

$$c_t = f(k_t, \theta_t, L_t) - k_{t+1} \equiv c(k_t, k_{t+1}, \theta_t, L_t). \tag{A30}$$

Solving the Scaled System   The six restrictions (A23)–(A25), (A27), (A29), and (A30) can now be used to find the six objects: equilibrium decision rules for k_{t+1}, L_t, n_t, and c_t and equilibrium price rules for p_t and w_t. To translate these back into the unscaled counterparts that interest us involves a simple application of (A13)–(A17).

Replacing p_t, w_t, and c_t in the efficiency conditions, (A23)–(A25), by the functions $p(\cdot)$, $w(\cdot)$, and $c(\cdot)$, we can write

$$W(k_t, k_{t+1}, k_{t+2}, L_t, L_{t+1}, n_t, n_{t+1}, s_t, s_{t+1})$$
$$= (p_t/w_t)^2 f_{H,t} \tilde{u}_{L,t} - \beta p_{t+1} f_{k,t+1}(\tilde{u}_{L,t+1}/w_{t+1}) \tag{A31}$$

$$q(k_t, k_{t+1}, L_t, n_t, s_t) = (\tilde{u}_{c,t}/p_t) + (p_t/w_t) f_{H,t}(\tilde{u}_{L,t}/w_t) \tag{A32}$$

$$Q(k_t, k_{t+1}, k_{t+2}, L_t, L_{t+2}, n_t, n_{t+1}, s_t, s_{t+1}) = \tilde{u}_{L,t} + w_t \beta \tilde{u}_{c,t+1}/[p_{t+1}(1 + x_t)] \tag{A33}$$

where $s_t \equiv (\theta_t, x_t)'$ and obeys (12)–(13). In this notation, (A23)–(A25) can be written

$$E[W(k_t, k_{t+1}, k_{t+2}, L_t, L_{t+1}, n_t, n_{t+1}, s_t, s_{t+1})|k_t, s_{t-1}, s_t] = 0 \qquad \text{(A34)}$$

$$E[q(k_t, k_{t+1}, L_t, n_t, s_t)|k_t, s_{t-1}] = 0 \qquad \text{(A35)}$$

$$E[Q(k_t, k_{t+1}, k_{t+2}, L_t, L_{t+1}, n_t, n_{t+1}, s_t, s_{t+1})|k_t, s_{t-1}, s_t] = 0. \qquad \text{(A36)}$$

Define the following linear functions:

$$k_{t+1} = k^0 + k^1 k_t + k^2 s_{t-1} + k^3 s_t \qquad \text{(A37)}$$

$$L_t = L^0 + L^1 k_t + L^2 s_{t-1} + L^3 s_t \qquad \text{(A38)}$$

$$n_t = n^0 + n^1 k_t + n^2 s_{t-1} \qquad \text{(A39)}$$

where k^i, L^i, n^i are (undetermined) scalars for $i = 0, 1$ and 1×2 vectors for $i = 2, 3$.

These 16 undetermined coefficients can be computed by a suitably modified version of steps 1–3 above. In particular, first find the nonstochastic steady-state values of k_t, L_t, and n_t that obtain when x_t and θ_t are held fixed at x and θ. Then compute the first-order Taylor series expansion of W, q, and Q about the nonstochastic steady-state values of their arguments. (Here, it is understood that the nonstochastic steady-state values of x_t and θ_t are x and θ, respectively.) Finally, substitute (A37)–(A39) into the versions of (A34)–(A36) with W, q, and Q replaced by their linear expansions and solve for the undetermined coefficients subject to the transversality-type condition $0 \leqslant k^1 \leqslant \beta^{1/2}$. Here, it is useful to take advantage of the fact that, conditional on a value of k^1, the remaining undetermined coefficients may be found by solving a linear system of equations. For complete details of these computations, including steady-state formulas, see Christiano 1990b (sec. IX).

To simulate an artificial time series for the Fuerst-Lucas model, first draw a sequence of $\varepsilon_{\theta,t}$ and $\varepsilon_{x,t}$ from a random number generator. These, together with (12) and (13), can be used to generate a series of s_t's. Equations (A37)–(A39) can then be used to compute a sequence of k_t's, n_t's, and L_t's. Scaled prices, wages, and consumption may then be computed from $p(\cdot)$, $w(\cdot)$, and $c(\cdot)$ in (A27), (A29), and (A30). Unscaled variables may be obtained from (A13)–(A17). Finally, get R_t from (19).

The Other Cash-in-Advance Models
Solving the basic cash-in-advance and sluggish capital models requires only slight modifications to the preceding procedure. First, it is readily confirmed that those models' efficiency conditions are given by (A34)–(A36)

with minor changes in the conditioning set for the expectations operator. Second, the linearized versions of W, q, and Q are identical to those of the Fuerst-Lucas model, since all models share the same nonstochastic steady state.

The efficiency conditions for the basic cash-in-advance model are

$$E[W(k_t, k_{t+1}, k_{t+2}, L_t, L_{t+1}, n_t, n_{t+1}, s_t, s_{t+1})|k_t, s_t] = 0 \tag{A40}$$

$$E[q(k_t, k_{t+1}, L_t, n_t, s_t)|k_t, s_t] = 0 \tag{A41}$$

$$E[Q(k_t, k_{t+1}, k_{t+2}, L_t, L_{t+1}, n_t, n_{t+1}, s_t, s_{t+1})|k_t, s_t] = 0. \tag{A42}$$

Consider the following decision rules:

$$k_{t+1} = k^0 + k^1 k_t + k^3 s_t \tag{A43}$$

$$L_t = L^0 + L^1 k_t + L^3 s_t \tag{A44}$$

$$n_t = n^0 + n^1 k_t + n^3 s_t \tag{A45}$$

where k^i, L^i, n^i are scalars for $i = 0, 1$ and 1×2 vectors for $i = 3$. Values for k^i, L^i, n^i, $i = 0, 1, 3$, may be obtained by substituting (A43)–(A45) into the version of (A40)–(A42) with W, q, Q replaced by their linear expansions and imposing $0 \leqslant k^1 \leqslant \beta^{1/2}$. For details, see Christiano 1990b (sec. X.B).

The efficiency conditions for the sluggish capital model are

$$E[W(k_t, k_{t+1}, k_{t+2}, L_t, L_{t+1}, n_t, n_{t+1}, s_t, s_{t+1})|k_t, s_{t-1}] = 0 \tag{A46}$$

$$E[q(k_t, k_{t+1}, L_t, n_t, s_t)|k_t, s_{t-1}] = 0 \tag{A47}$$

$$E[Q(k_t, k_{t+1}, k_{t+2}, L_t, L_{t+1}, n_t, n_{t+1}, s_t, s_{t+1})|k_t, s_{t-1}, s_t] = 0. \tag{A48}$$

Consider the following decision rules:

$$k_{t+1} = k^0 + k^1 k_t + k^2 s_{t-1} \tag{A49}$$

$$L_t = L^0 + L^1 k_t + L^2 s_{t-1} + L^3 s_t \tag{A50}$$

$$n_t = n^0 + n^1 k_t + n^2 s_{t-1}. \tag{A51}$$

Here, as before, the coefficients are found by substituting the decision rules into the efficiency conditions with W, q, Q replaced by their linear expansions and imposing the constraint $0 \leqslant k^1 \leqslant \beta^{1/2}$. Details may be found in Christiano 1990b (sec. X.A).

The linear decision rules just discussed, and those underlying the quantitative analysis in the paper, involve approximation error, since they solve the linearized, not the actual, efficiency conditions. Methods for increasing the accuracy of the solution to the models of the paper are discussed in detail in Christiano 1990b. It would be of interest to investigate these to determine whether there is significant approximation error in the solution analyzed here.

Notes

The author thanks Martin Eichenbaum for drawing his attention to the Fuerst (1992) and Lucas (1990) work on which this paper builds and for many extensive discussions. The author is collaborating with Eichenbaum on further research on the topic of this paper. The author has also benefited from discussions with Gary Hansen and Finn Kydland.

1. For a discussion of the empirical evidence for this proposition, see the work by Friedman and Schwartz (1963), Cagan and Gandolfi (1969), Barro (1978b), Darby (1979a), Barro and Rush (1980), Melvin (1983), Mishkin (1983), Sims (1986), Cochrane (1989), Cook and Hahn (1989), Romer and Romer (1989), and King (1990).

2. My use of the terms *liquidity effect* and *anticipated inflation effect* depart very slightly from convention. In the literature, they refer exclusively to a money shock's impact on the interest rate, while I include its impact on employment and output.

3. I work with models in which wages and prices are perfectly flexible. See King 1990 for a discussion of the difficulties in accounting for the dominant liquidity effect in models in which prices or wages are inflexible.

4. Fuerst and Lucas build on previous work by Grossman and Weiss (1983) and Rotemberg (1984). For another model that displays a liquidity effect, see Baxter, Fisher, King, and Rouwenhorst 1990.

5. The conventional way to express the cash-in-advance constraint is as a weak inequality: $P_t C_t \leq M_t - N_t$. This version of the constraint allows the possibility that households could choose not to spend all the cash set aside for consumption purchases. I work with equation (1) because I only consider parameter values for which households make their cash constraint hold as an equality. That this is nonbinding can be verified ex post in simulations of the model by verifying that the marginal utility of money in each period is no less than the discounted expected marginal utility of money in the next period.

6. Suggested losses from getting by with low cash balances include lost leisure time (McCallum 1983, Kydland 1989, Den Haan 1991) and lost real resources (Marshall 1992, Sims 1989, Huh 1990).

7. The cash-in-advance approach has been pursued by Lucas (1984, 1990), Svensson (1985), Greenwood and Huffman (1987), and Lucas and Stokey (1987). The transaction cost approach has been pursued, in models closely related to those in this paper, by Marshall (1992), Kydland (1989), and Sims (1989). The pioneering studies of the transaction cost motive for holding money balances include those by Baumol (1952), Tobin (1956), and Miller and Orr (1966, 1968). An approach closely related to the transaction cost approach is the *cash-credit good* model studied by Lucas and Stokey (1983).

8. Note that I assume the number of shares in the firms and the financial intermediaries is fixed and the shares are not traded. Allowing shares to be traded would only complicate the notation without altering the substance of the analysis.

9. For example, if $r_t = 1.03$ and $\pi_{t+1} = 1.04$, then $r_t\pi_{t+1} = 1.0712 \cong 1 + 0.03 + 0.04$.

10. Other equilibrium models also imply an equation like (26); see, for example, Cooley and Hansen 1991, Lucas 1988b, and Chari, Christiano, and Kehoe 1991. Lucas (1988b) emphasizes the similarity between (26) and the money demand equations in the empirical literature. He also discusses the distinction between (26) and a demand equation in the price theory sense, which arises from the fact that one of the right-side variables, Y_t, is a choice variable from the point of view of firms.

11. For a further discussion of this point, see Goodfriend 1985. One caveat to this conclusion arises from the fact that (26) contains no error term, whereas empirical money demand equations do. Conceivably, a plausible theory of the error term exists which, in conjunction with (26), would imply the statistical significance of the lagged dependent variable.

12. For a further discussion of the impact of anticipated inflation on employment in a cash-in-advance economy, see B. Carmichael 1989.

13. For discussions of the impact of inflation on the capital stock when there is a cash-in-advance constraint on investment, see Stockman 1981 and Abel 1985.

14. In (24), after K_{t+1} is replaced by $I_t + (1 - \delta^*)K_t$, it is easy to see that the right side of this equation is decreasing in I_t because of diminishing returns to capital. Thus, if other variables remain fixed, the only way for I_t to rise and absorb more funds is for R_t to fall.

15. The condition $E_{t-1}\Lambda_t = 0$ uses the fact, known as the *law of iterated mathematical expectations*, that $E_{t-1}[E_t x_t] = E_{t-1}x_t$. For further discussion of this fact, see Sargent 1987a.

16. All calculations in this and the next section are based on model solutions obtained by a method that linearly approximates the efficiency conditions. That method is spelled out in the Appendix.

17. The data mnemonic for the monetary base is FMFBA. It is the sum of total reserves (member bank reserve balances plus vault cash) and currency outside the U.S. Treasury, the Federal Reserve Banks, and commercial banks. These data are averages of daily figures. This may introduce some bias into the analysis since the models speak to beginning-of-the-quarter, point-in-time money data. As Friedman (1983) has emphasized, time-averaged money growth figures are less volatile than point-in-time observations. This has been confirmed by Baxter, Fisher, King, and Rouwenhorst (1990).

18. In particular, from (8), the period t rate of capital depreciation is $\delta_t^* \equiv [(I_t - K_{t+1})/K_t] + 1$.

19. Formulas for the steady-state values of K/Y and $(1 - L)/L$ may be obtained by solving the nonstochastic steady-state versions of the efficiency and market-clearing conditions and budget constraints. Accordingly, substitute out for W_t/P_t in (18) from (19) to get $-u_{L,t} = (f_{H,t}^*/R_t)\beta^* u_{c,t+1}(P_t/P_{t+1})$. From (20) this becomes $-u_{L,t}/u_{c,t} = f_{H,t}^*/R_t^2$, or $[\gamma/(1 - \gamma)]C_t/(1 - L_t) = (1 - \alpha)(Y_t/L_t)/R_t^2$, which I'll call equation (†). Manipulating (16) gives $C_t/Y_t = 1 - (K_{t+1}/Y_t)[1 - (1 - \delta^*)K_t/K_{t+1}]$. In the steady state, L_t, C_t/Y_t, K_t/Y_t, and K_t/K_{t+1} converge to constants: L, C/Y, K/Y, and $\exp(-\mu)$. From this, (†) becomes

$$\exp(\mu)(K/Y)[1 - (1 - \delta^*)\exp(-\mu)] = 1 - (1/R)^2(1 - \alpha)[(1 - \gamma)/\gamma][(1 - L)/L].$$

Another equation that can be used to compute K/Y and L is (30), the nonstochastic steady-state version of (24):

$$Rr = \alpha(K/Y)^{-1} + (1 - \delta^*)R.$$

Here

$$R = (1 + x)\exp[-\mu(1 - \gamma)\psi]/\beta^*$$

$$r = \exp\{\mu[1 - (1 - \gamma)\psi]\}/\beta^*.$$

The variable r is the steady-state value of the real rate of interest, $u_{c,t}/[\beta^* u_{c,t+1}]$. (Note that the Fisher relation holds exactly here, since R is the product of r and the steady-state inflation rate.) The two equations above can be solved for K/Y and $(1 - L)/L$ given values for the following model parameters: δ^*, μ, α, γ, x, β^*, and ψ. Alternatively, for fixed values of K/Y and $(1 - L)/L$ [for example, the empirical sample averages of K_t/Y_t and $(1 - L_t)/L_t$], these equations can be used to solve for α and γ given δ^*, μ, x, β^*, and ψ.

20. Burnside, Eichenbaum, and Rebelo (1990) do not simply fit a first-order autoregression: they allow the possibility that there is classical measurement error in the hours-worked data used to construct z_t. The measurement error model they use is the one analyzed by Prescott [in Chapter 14 of this volume] and Christiano and Eichenbaum 1992.

21. In the computational results reported below, versions of the model with $(1 - \delta^*) \times (R_{t+1} - 1)$ deleted on the right side of (24) and (33) were solved. Professors Schlagenhauf and Wrase have redone the calculations with $(1 - \delta^*)(R_{t+1} - 1)$ included and report in a private communication that the computational results are not significantly different from what is reported here.

22. From (5), the marginal product of capital is $\alpha(z_t H_t/K_t)^{(1-\alpha)} + 1 - \delta^*$. Thus, dropping δ^* below unity introduces a linear term into the marginal product of capital, which makes it fall less quickly with expansions in K_t. The phenomenon identified here is also present in the real business cycle literature. For example, Long and Plosser's (1983) model assumes that $\delta^* = 1$ and, in equilibrium, investment is proportional to income. When the depreciation rate in that model is reduced, investment moves more than one-for-one with movements in income. The reason is that expansions in investment in response to a positive technology shock encounter diminishing returns less quickly when $\delta^* < 1$. Again, this reflects the addition of the linear term in the marginal product of capital.

23. Figure 21.9 highlights a distinction between the money transmission mechanism in the sluggish capital model and the one in other monetary rational expectations models. In those models (for example, Lucas 1973 and Sargent and Wallace 1975), a jump in the price level is instrumental in transmitting a surprise increase in money to an increase in output.

24. Christiano (1988) and Burnside, Eichenbaum, and Rebelo (1990) argue that, in a real business cycle model, reducing ρ_θ, the serial correlation in the technology shock, reduces the relative volatility of consumption and increases the relative volatility of labor. This suggests that the models' difficulties on these dimensions could be ameliorated by reducing ρ_θ to 0.8842, the lowest of the several point estimates reported by Burnside, Eichenbaum, and Rebelo. Doing so turns out to have a negligible effect on the dynamic properties of the models here. For example, the relative volatility of consumption in the basic, Fuerst-Lucas, and sluggish capital models is 0.53, 0.88, and 1.03, respectively. The corresponding results for the standard deviation of labor effort relative to that of output are 0.29, 0.30, and 0.55, respectively. These results are very close to those reported for the $\rho_\theta = 0.9857$ models in Table 21.3.

25. The Lucas and Stock-Watson numbers are long-run elasticities, which are the appropriate ones to compare with my models. The results in Goldfeld and Sichel's (1990) Tables 8.1 and 8.4 also support the view that my models' interest elasticity is considerably smaller than what is empirically plausible.

26. Although aggregate investment is roughly coincident with the cycle, this masks interesting dynamics that occur at a more disaggregated level. According to Kydland and Prescott [Chapter 17, Table 2], the nonresidential part of business fixed investment lags the cycle, while the residential part leads it. The lag in nonresidential investment may reflect the effects of the precommitment captured by the sluggish capital model.

27. My assumption about the nature of the money growth process, equation (13), deserves more attention. Although several other studies use this kind of model (Barro 1978b, Barro and Rush 1980, Cooley and Hansen 1989, and King 1990), it is by no means uncontroversial. For example, Sims (1986) and Bernanke and Blinder (1992) criticize this specification of policy on empirical grounds and suggest alternatives. It would be worth investigating these to see how they affect the relative magnitude of the anticipated inflation and liquidity effects.

28. My conclusions about the empirical plausibility of the various models and directions for future model modifications have been reached with relatively little use of the tools of formal statistical analysis. This reflects the preliminary stage of this work, in which mismatches between models and data are sufficiently blatant as to make a formal metric superfluous. In subsequent work, when comparisons between models and data involve greater subtleties, the tools of statistical sampling theory (for example, those discussed in Christiano and Eichenbaum 1992) will become necessary.

29. Our assumption about the time period of production closely resembles the technology assumption of Diamond and Dybvig (1983). They cite Friedman and Schwartz (1963) for evidence consistent with their technology assumption (Diamond and Dybvig 1983, p. 403).

30. One way to see why this modification might help is to recall the consumption response to a money shock in the sluggish capital model (Figure 21.6). It surges in the period of the shock and then immediately returns to its previous level. With a habit persistence utility function, consumption should instead come down slowly (as is empirically plausible, according to King 1990). Other things the same, a declining consumption trajectory implies a low interest rate.

31. The version of (24) considered here is the one with $(1 - \delta^*)(R_{t+1} - 1)$ deleted. To solve the version with $(1 - \delta^*)(R_{t+1} - 1)$ included requires trivial modifications to (A10), (A23), and (A31) below.

References

Abel, Andrew B. 1985. Dynamic behavior of capital accumulation in a cash-in-advance model. *Journal of Monetary Economics* 16 (July): 55–71.

Abreu, Dilip. 1988. On the theory of infinitely repeated games with discounting. *Econometrica* 56 (March): 383–96.

Adelman, Irma, and Adelman, Frank L. 1959. The dynamic properties of the Klein–Goldberger model. *Econometrica* 27 (October): 596–625.

Aiyagari, S. Rao. 1987. Overlapping generations and infinitely lived agents. Research Department Working Paper 328. Federal Reserve Bank of Minneapolis.

Altonji, Joseph G. 1982. The intertemporal substitution model of labour market fluctuations: An empirical analysis. *Review of Economic Studies* 49 (Special Issue): 783–824.

Altug, S. 1983. Gestation lags and the business cycle. Working Paper. Carnegie Mellon University.

Ando, Albert. 1977. A comment. In *New methods in business cycle research: Proceedings from a conference*, ed. C. A. Sims, pp. 209–12. Minneapolis: Federal Reserve Bank of Minneapolis.

Arrow, Kenneth J. 1964. The role of securities in the optimal allocation of risk-bearing. *Review of Economic Studies* 31 (April): 91–96.

Aschauer, David Alan. 1988. The equilibrium approach to fiscal policy. *Journal of Money, Credit and Banking* 20 (February): 41–62.

Ashenfelter, O. 1984. Macroeconomic analyses and microeconomic analyses of labor supply. In *Essays on macroeconomic implications of financial and labor markets and political processes*, ed. Karl Brunner and Allan H. Meltzer. Carnegie-Rochester Conference Series on Public Policy 21 (Autumn): 117–55. Amsterdam: North-Holland.

Auerbach, Robert D., and Rutner, Jack L. 1977. A negative view of the negative money multiplier: Comment. *Journal of Finance* 32 (December): 1814–17.

Azariadis, Costas. 1981. Self-fulfilling prophecies. *Journal of Economic Theory* 25 (December): 380–96.

Azariadis, Costas, and Guesnerie, Roger. 1986. Sunspots and cycles. *Review of Economic Studies* 53(5) (October): 725–38.

Backus, David K., and Kehoe, Patrick J. 1992. International evidence on the historical properties of business cycles. *American Economic Review* 82 (September): 864–88.

Bain, I. R. M. 1985. A theory of the cyclical movements of inventory stocks. Ph.D. dissertation. University of Minnesota.

Barro, Robert J. 1974. Are government bonds net wealth? *Journal of Political Economy* 82 (November/December): 1095–1117.

———. 1977. Unanticipated money growth and unemployment in the United States. *American Economic Review* 67 (March): 101–15.

———. 1978a. *The impact of Social Security on private saving: Evidence from the U.S. time series*. American Enterprise Institute Studies, No. 199. Washington, D.C.: American Enterprise Institute for Public Policy Research.

———. 1978b. Unanticipated money, output, and the price level in the United States. *Journal of Political Economy* 86 (August): 549–80.

———. 1979. On the determination of the public debt. *Journal of Political Economy* 87, Part 1 (October): 940–71.

———. 1981. Intertemporal substitution and the business cycle. In *Supply shocks, incentives and national wealth*, ed. Karl Brunner and Allan H. Meltzer. Carnegie-Rochester Conference Series on Public Policy 14 (Spring): 237–68. Amsterdam: North-Holland.

Barro, Robert J., and Gordon, David B. 1983. Rules, discretion and reputation in a model of monetary policy. *Journal of Monetary Economics* 12 (July): 101–21.

Barro, Robert J., and King, Robert G. 1984. Time-separable preferences and intertemporal-substitution models of business cycles. *Quarterly Journal of Economics* 99 (November): 817–39.

Barro, Robert J., and Rush, Mark. 1980. Unanticipated money and economic activity. In *Rational expectations and economic policy*, ed. Stanley Fischer, pp. 23–48. Chicago: University of Chicago Press/National Bureau of Economic Research.

Baumol, William J. 1952. The transactions demand for cash: An inventory theoretic approach. *Quarterly Journal of Economics* 66 (November): 545–56.

Baxter, Marianne; Fisher, Stephen; King, Robert G.; and Rouwenhorst, K. Geert. 1990. The liquidity effect in general equilibrium. Manuscript. University of Rochester.

Benhabib, Jess, and Nishimura, Kazuo. 1985. Competitive equilibrium cycles. *Journal of Economic Theory* 35 (April): 284–306.

Benhabib, Jess; Rogerson, Richard; and Wright, Randall. 1991. Homework in macroeconomics: Household production and aggregate fluctuations. *Journal of Political Economy* 99 (December): 1166–87.

Bernanke, Ben S. 1986. Alternative explanations of the money-income correlation. In *Real business cycles, real exchange rates and actual policies*, ed. Karl Brunner and Allan H. Meltzer. Carnegie-Rochester Conference Series on Public Policy 25 (Autumn): 49–100. Amsterdam: North-Holland.

Bernanke, Ben S., and Blinder, Alan S. 1992. The federal funds rate and the channels of monetary transmission. *American Economic Review* 82 (September): 901–21.

Berndt, Ernst R. 1980. Energy price increases and the productivity slowdown in United States manufacturing. In *The decline in productivity growth*, pp. 60−89. Conference Series 22. Boston: Federal Reserve Bank of Boston.

Bernheim, B. Douglas, and Bagwell, Kyle. 1986. Is everything neutral? *Journal of Political Economy* 96 (April): 308−38.

Bewley, T. F. 1972. Existence of equilibria in economies with infinitely many commodities. *Journal of Economic Theory* 4 (June): 514−40.

Blackburn, Keith, and Ravn, Morten O. 1991. Contemporary macroeconomic fluctuations: An international perspective. Memo 1991-12. University of Aarhus Center for International Economics.

Blinder, Alan S. 1974. Analytical foundations of fiscal policy. In *The economics of public finance*, essays by Alan S. Blinder, et al. Studies of Government Finance: 3−115. Washington, D.C.: Brookings Institution.

—————. 1986. Can the production smoothing model of inventory behavior be saved? *Quarterly Journal of Economics* 101 (August): 431−53.

Blinder, Alan S., and Solow, Robert M. 1973. Does fiscal policy matter? *Journal of Public Economics* 2 (November): 319−37.

Boldrin, Michele. 1989. Paths of optimal accumulation in two-sector models. In *Economic complexity: Chaos, sunspots, bubbles, and nonlinearity*, ed. William A. Barnett, John Geweke, and Karl Shell, pp. 231−52. New York: Cambridge University Press.

Braun, R. Anton. 1990. The dynamic interaction of distortionary taxes and aggregate variables in postwar U.S. data. Working Paper. University of Virginia.

Brayton, Flint, and Mauskopf, Eileen. 1985. The Federal Reserve Board MPS model of the U.S. economy. *Economic Modelling* 2 (July): 170−292.

Bresciani-Turroni, Costantino, 1937. *The economics of inflation*, tr. Millicent E. Sayers. London: Allen & Unwin.

Brock, William A., and Mirman, Leonard J. 1972. Optimal economic growth and uncertainty: The discounted case. *Journal of Economic Theory* 4 (June): 479−513.

Bryant, John B., and Wallace, Neil. 1980. A suggestion for further simplifying the theory of money. Research Department Staff Report 62. Federal Reserve Bank of Minneapolis.

—————. 1984. A price discrimination analysis of monetary policy. *Review of Economic Studies* 51 (April): 279−88.

Burns, Arthur F., and Mitchell, Wesley C. 1946. *Measuring business cycles*. New York: National Bureau of Economic Research.

Burnside, Craig; Eichenbaum, Martin; and Rebelo, Sergio. 1990. Labor hoarding and the business cycle. Manuscript. Northwestern University.

Cagan, Phillip. 1956. The monetary dynamics of hyperinflation. In *Studies in the quantity theory of money*, ed. Milton Friedman, pp. 25−117. Chicago: University of Chicago Press.

Cagan, Phillip, and Gandolfi, Arthur. 1969. The lag in monetary policy as implied by the time pattern of monetary effects on interest rates. *American Economic Review* 59 (May): 277−84.

Calvo, Guillermo A. 1978. On the time consistency of optimal policy in a monetary economy. *Econometrica* 46 (November): 1411–28.

Campbell, John, and Deaton, Augus. 1989. Why is consumption so smooth? *Review of Economic Studies* 56 (July): 357–73.

Campbell, John Y., and Mankiw, N. Gregory. 1987. Are output fluctuations transitory? *Quarterly Journal of Economics* 102 (November): 857–80.

————. 1989. International evidence on the persistence of economic fluctuations. *Journal of Monetary Economics* 23 (March): 319–33.

Carmichael, Benoit. 1989. Anticipated monetary policy in a cash-in-advance economy. *Canadian Journal of Economics* 22 (February): 93–108.

Carmichael, Jeffrey. 1982. On Barro's theorem of debt neutrality: The irrelevance of net wealth. *American Economic Review* 72 (March): 202–13.

Cass, David. 1965. Optimum growth in an aggregative model of capital accumulation. *Review of Economic Studies* 32 (July): 233–40.

Cass, David, and Shell, Karl. 1983. Do sunspots matter? *Journal of Political Economy* 91 (April): 193–227.

Chamberlain, Gary, and Wilson, Chuck. 1984. Optimal intertemporal consumption under uncertainty. Social Systems Research Institute Workshop Series 8422. University of Wisconsin, Madison.

Chari, V. V.; Christiano, Lawrence J.; and Kehoe, Patrick J. 1991. Optimal fiscal and monetary policy: Some recent results. *Journal of Money, Credit and Banking* 23, Part 2 (August): 519–39.

Chari, V. V., and Kehoe, Patrick J. 1988. Sustainable plans and debt. Research Department Working Paper 399. Federal Reserve Bank of Minneapolis. Forthcoming, *Journal of Economic Theory*.

————. 1990. Sustainable plans. *Journal of Political Economy* 98 (August): 783–802.

Chari, V. V.; Kehoe, Patrick J.; and Prescott, Edward C. 1989. Time consistency and policy. In *Modern business cycle theory*, ed. Robert J. Barro, pp. 265–305. Cambridge, Mass.: Harvard University Press.

Cho, Jang-Ok, and Cooley, Thomas F. 1989. Employment and hours over the business cycle. Working Paper 132. Rochester Center for Economic Research, University of Rochester.

————. 1990. The business cycle with nominal contracts. Working Paper 260. Rochester Center for Economic Research, University of Rochester.

Christiano, Lawrence J. 1987a. Dynamic properties of two approximate solutions to a particular growth model. Research Department Working Paper 338. Federal Reserve Bank of Minneapolis.

————. 1987b. Intertemporal substitution and the smoothness of consumption. Manuscript. Federal Reserve Bank of Minneapolis.

————. 1987c. Is consumption insufficiently sensitive to innovations in income? *American Economic Review* 77 (May): 337–41.

————. 1987d. Technical appendix to "Why does inventory investment fluctuate so much?" Research Department Working Paper 380. Federal Reserve Bank of Minneapolis.

————. 1988. Why does inventory investment fluctuate so much? *Journal of Monetary Economics* 21 (March/May): 247–80.

————. 1990a. Linear-quadratic approximation and value-function iteration: A comparison. *Journal of Business and Economic Statistics* 8 (January): 99–113.

————. 1990b. Computational algorithms for solving variants of Fuerst's model. Research Department Working Paper 467. Federal Reserve Bank of Minneapolis.

Christiano, Lawrence J., and Eichenbaum, Martin. 1992. Current real-business-cycle theories and aggregate labor-market fluctuations. *American Economic Review* 82 (June): 430–50.

Christiano, Lawrence J.; Eichenbaum, Martin; and Marshall, David. 1991. The permanent income hypothesis revisited. *Econometrica* 59 (March): 397–423.

Christiano, Lawrence J., and Ljungqvist, Lars. 1988. Money does Granger-cause output in the bivariate money-output relation. *Journal of Monetary Economics* 22 (September): 217–35.

Clark, Peter K. 1987. The cyclical component of U.S. economic activity. *Quarterly Journal of Economics* 102 (November): 797–814.

Cochrane, John H. 1988. How big is the random walk in GNP? *Journal of Political Economy* 96 (October): 893–920.

————. 1989. The return of the liquidity effect: A study of the short-run relation between money growth and interest rates. *Journal of Business and Economic Statistics* 7 (January): 75–83.

Cook, Timothy, and Hahn, Thomas. 1989. The effect of changes in the federal funds rate target on market interest rates in the 1970s. *Journal of Monetary Economics* 24 (November): 331–51.

Cooley, Thomas F., and Hansen, Gary D. 1989. The inflation tax in a real business cycle model. *American Economic Review* 79 (September): 733–48.

————. 1991. The welfare costs of moderate inflations. *Journal of Money, Credit and Banking* 23, Part 2 (August): 483–503.

Cooper, Richard N. 1985. Economic interdependence and coordination of economic policies. In *Handbook of international economics*, ed. Ronald W. Jones and Peter B. Kenen, vol. 2, pp. 1195–1234. Amsterdam: North-Holland.

Crawford, Robert G. 1973. Implications of learning for economic models of uncertainty. *International Economic Review* 14 (October): 587–600.

Danthine, Jean-Pierre; Donaldson, John B.; and Mehra, Rajnish. 1989. On some computational aspects of equilibrium business cycle theory. *Journal of Economic Dynamics and Control* 13 (July): 449–70.

Darby, Michael R. 1975. The financial and tax effects of monetary policy on interest rates. *Economic Inquiry* 13 (June): 266–76.

————. 1979a. *Intermediate macroeconomics.* New York: McGraw-Hill.

————. 1979b. *The effects of Social Security on income and the capital stock.* Washington, D.C.: American Enterprise Institute for Public Policy Research.

———. 1984. *Labor force, employment, and productivity in historical perspective.* Los Angeles: UCLA Institute of Industrial Relations.

Darby, Michael R., and Lothian, James R. 1983. British economic policy under Margaret Thatcher: A midterm examination. In *Money, monetary policy, and financial institutions,* ed. Karl Brunner and Allan H. Meltzer. Carnegie-Rochester Conference Series on Public Policy 18 (Spring): 157–207. Amsterdam: North-Holland.

David, Paul A., and Scadding, John L. 1974. Private savings: Ultrarationality, aggregation, and "Denison's Law." *Journal of Political Economy* 82 (March/April): 225–49.

Deaton, Angus. 1986. Life-cycle models of consumption: Is the evidence consistent with the theory? Working Paper 1910. National Bureau of Economic Research.

Debreu, Gerard. 1954. Valuation equilibrium and Pareto optimum. *Proceedings of the National Academy of Science* 70: 558–92.

———. 1959a. *The theory of value.* New York: Wiley.

———. 1959b. *Theory of value: An axiomatic analysis of economic equilibrium.* Cowles Foundation Monograph 17. New Haven: Yale University Press.

Den Haan, Wouter J. 1991. The term structure of interest rates in real and monetary production economics. Ph.D. dissertation. Carnegie Mellon University.

Diamond, Douglas W., and Dybvig, Philip H. 1983. Bank runs, deposit insurance, and liquidity. *Journal of Political Economy* 91 (June): 401–19.

Diamond, Peter A. 1984. *A search equilibrium approach to the micro foundations of macroeconomics: The Wicksell lectures, 1982.* Cambridge, Mass.: MIT Press.

Drazen, Allan. 1978. Government debt, human capital, and bequests in a life-cycle model. *Journal of Political Economy* 86 (June): 505–16.

Eckstein, Otto, and Sinai, Allen. 1986. The mechanisms of the business cycle in the postwar era. In *The American business cycle: Continuity and change,* ed. Robert J. Gordon, pp. 39–105. National Bureau of Economic Research Studies in Business Cycles, vol. 25. Chicago: University of Chicago Press.

Eckstein, Zvi; Eichenbaum, Martin; and Peled, Dan. 1982. Uncertain lifetimes and the welfare enhancing properties of annuity markets and social security. *Journal of Public Economics* 26 (April): 303–26.

Eckstein, Zvi, and Wolpin, Kenneth I. 1989. Dynamic labor force participation of married women and endogenous work experience. *Review of Economic Studies* 56 (July): 375–90.

The Economist. 1989. The business cycle gets a puncture. August 5, p. 57.

Eichenbaum, Martin S.; Hansen, Lars P.; and Singleton, Kenneth J. 1988. A time series analysis of representative agent models of consumption and leisure choice under uncertainty. *Quarterly Journal of Economics* 103 (February): 51–78.

Fama, Eugene. 1980. Banking in the theory of finance. *Journal of Monetary Economics* 6 (January): 39–57.

Fay, Jon A., and Medoff, James L. 1985. Labor and output over the business cycle: Some direct evidence. *American Economic Review* 75 (September): 638–55.

Federal Reserve Board of Governors (FR Board). 1983. Gross national product and income. *Federal Reserve Bulletin* 69 (February): A52.

Fischer, Stanley. 1976. Comments on Tobin and Buiter. In *Monetarism*, ed. Jerome L. Stein. Studies in Monetary Economics 1: 322–28. Amsterdam: North-Holland.

———. 1977. Long-term contracts, rational expectations, and the optimal money supply rule. *Journal of Political Economy* 85 (February): 191–205.

———. 1980. Dynamic inconsistency, cooperation, and the benevolent dissembling government. *Journal of Economic Dynamics and Control* 2 (February): 93–107.

Fisher, Irving. 1930. *The theory of interest*. New York: Macmillan.

Friedman, James W. 1971. A non-cooperative equilibrium for supergames. *Review of Economic Studies* 38 (January): 1–12.

Friedman, Milton. 1948. A monetary and fiscal framework for economic stability. *American Economic Review* 38 (June): 245–64.

———. 1960. *A program for monetary stability*. Millar Lectures No. 3, 1959. New York: Fordham University Press.

———. 1968a. *Dollars and deficits*. Englewood Cliffs, N.J.: Prentice-Hall.

———. 1968b. The role of monetary policy. *American Economic Review* 58 (March): 1–17.

———. 1983. Monetary variability: United States and Japan. *Journal of Money, Credit and Banking* 15 (August): 339–43.

Friedman, Milton, and Schwartz, Anna Jacobson. 1963. *A monetary history of the United States, 1867–1960*. Princeton, N.J.: Princeton University Press.

Friend, Irwin, and Blume, Marshall E. 1975. The demand for risky assets. *American Economic Review* 65 (December): 900–22.

Frisch, Ragnar. [1933] 1965. Propagation problems and impulse problems in dynamic economics. In *Readings in business cycles*, ed. R. A. Gordon and L. R. Klein. American Economic Association, 10: 155–85. Homewood, Ill.: Irwin.

Fudenberg, Drew, and Maskin, Eric. 1986. The Folk Theorem in repeated games with discounting or with incomplete information. *Econometrica* 54 (May): 533–54.

Fuerst, Timothy S. 1992. Liquidity, loanable funds, and real activity. *Journal of Monetary Economics* 29 (February): 3–24.

Gale, David. 1971. General equilibrium with imbalance of trade. *Journal of International Economics* 1 (May): 141–58.

———. 1974. The trade imbalance story. *Journal of International Economics* 4 (May): 119–37.

Geweke, John. 1977. The dynamic factor analysis of economic time series. In *Latent variables in socio-economic models*, ed. D. Aigner and A. Goldberger, pp. 365–83. Amsterdam: North-Holland.

Ghez, Gilbert R., and Becker, Gary S. 1975. *The allocation of time and goods over the life cycle*. New York: National Bureau of Economic Research.

Goldfeld, Stephen M., and Sichel, Daniel E. 1990. The demand for money. In *Handbook of monetary economics*, ed. Benjamin M. Friedman and Frank H. Hahn, vol. 1, pp. 299–356. Amsterdam: North-Holland.

Goodfriend, Marvin. 1985. Reinterpreting money demand regressions. In *Understanding monetary regimes*, ed. Karl Brunner and Allan H. Meltzer. Carnegie-Rochester Conference Series on Public Policy 22 (Spring): 207–41. Amsterdam: North-Holland.

Grandmont, Jean-Michel. 1985. On endogenous competitive business cycles. *Econometrica* 53 (September): 995–1045.

Green, Edward J. 1980. Noncooperative price taking in large dynamic markets. *Journal of Economic Theory* 22 (April): 155–82.

Green, Edward J., and Porter, Robert H. 1984. Noncooperative collusion under imperfect price information. *Econometrica* 52 (January): 87–100.

Greenwood, Jeremy; Hercowitz, Zvi; and Huffman, Gregory W. 1988. Investment, capacity utilization and the real business cycle. *American Economic Review* 78 (June): 402–17.

Greenwood, Jeremy, and Huffman, Gregory W. 1987. A dynamic equilibrium model of inflation and unemployment. *Journal of Monetary Economics* 19 (March): 203–28.

Greenwood, Jeremy; Rogerson, Richard; and Wright, Randall. Forthcoming. Household production in real business cycle theory. In *Frontiers of business cycle research*, ed. Thomas F. Cooley, Princeton, N.J.: Princeton University Press.

Grossman, Herschel I., and Van Huyck, John B. 1988. Sovereign debt as a contingent claim: Excusable default, repudiation, and reputation. *American Economic Review* 78 (December): 1088–97.

Grossman, Sanford. 1975. Rational expectations and the econometric modeling of markets subject to uncertainty: A Bayesian approach. *Journal of Econometrics* 3 (August): 255–72.

Grossman, Sanford, and Weiss, Laurence. 1983. A transactions-based model of the monetary transmission mechanism. *American Economic Review* 73 (December): 871–80.

Haberler, Gottfried. 1937. *Prosperity and depression: A theoretical analysis of cyclical movements.* Geneva: League of Nations.

Hall, Robert E. 1978a. The macroeconomic impact of changes in income taxes in the short and medium runs. *Journal of Political Economy* 86 (April): S71–S85.

————. 1978b. Stochastic implications of the life cycle–permanent income hypothesis: Theory and evidence. *Journal of Political Economy* 86 (December): 971–87.

————. 1982. *Monetary trends in the United States and the United Kingdom: A review from the perspective of new developments in monetary economics. Journal of Economic Literature* 20 (December): 1552–56.

Hansen, Gary D. 1984. Fluctuations in total hours worked: A study using efficiency units. Working Paper. University of Minnesota.

————. 1985a. Indivisible labor and the business cycle. *Journal of Monetary Economics* 16 (November): 309–27.

————. 1985b. Growth and fluctuations. Working Paper. University of California, Santa Barbara.

————. 1989. Technical progress and aggregate fluctuations. Department of Economics Working Paper 546. University of California, Los Angeles.

————. 1991. The cyclical and secular behavior of the labor input: Comparing efficiency units and hours worked. Manuscript. University of California, Los Angeles.

Hansen, Gary D., and Prescott, Edward C. 1991. Recursive methods for computing equilibria of business cycle models. Discussion Paper 36. Institute for Empirical Macroeconomics (Federal Reserve Bank of Minneapolis).

Hansen, Lars Peter. 1985. Econometric modeling of asset pricing under rational expectations. Paper presented to the Fifth World Congress of the Econometric Society, in Cambridge, Mass.

Hansen, Lars Peter, and Sargent, Thomas J. 1980. Formulating and estimating dynamic linear rational expectations models. *Journal of Economic Dynamics and Control* 2 (February): 7–46.

Hansen, Lars Peter, and Singleton, Kenneth J. 1982. Generalized instrumental variables estimation of nonlinear rational expectations models. *Econometrica* 50 (September): 1269–86.

————. 1983. Stochastic consumption, risk aversion, and the temporal behavior of asset returns. *Journal of Political Economy* 91 (April): 249–65.

Hayek, Friedrich August von. 1933. *Monetary theory and the trade cycle.* London: Jonathan Cape.

Heckman, James. 1984. Comments on the Ashenfelter and Kydland papers. In *Essays on macroeconomic implications of financial and labor markets and political processes,* ed. Karl Brunner and Allan H. Meltzer. Carnegie-Rochester Conference Series on Public Policy 21 (Autumn): 209–24. Amsterdam: North-Holland.

Hicks, J. R. 1935. A suggestion for simplifying the theory of money. *Economica,* n. s. 2 (February): 1–19.

Hodrick, Robert J.; Kocherlakota, Narayana R.; and Lucas, Deborah. 1991. The variability of velocity in cash-in-advance models. *Journal of Political Economy* 99 (April): 358–84.

Hodrick, Robert J., and Prescott, Edward C. 1980. Postwar U.S. business cycles: An empirical investigation. Discussion Paper 451. Carnegie Mellon University.

Hotz, V. Joseph; Kydland, Finn E.; and Sedlacek, Guilherme L. 1988. Intertemporal preferences and labor supply. *Econometrica* 56 (March): 335–60.

Huh, Chan G. 1990. Output, money and price correlations in a real business cycle model. Working Paper 90-02. Federal Reserve Bank of San Francisco.

Ibbotson, Roger G., and Sinquefield, Rex A. 1982. *Stocks, bonds, bills, and inflation: The past and the future.* Charlottesville, Va.: Financial Analysts Research Foundation.

Jump, Gregory V. 1980. Interest rates, inflation expectations, and spurious elements in measured real income and saving. *American Economic Review* 70 (December): 990–1004.

Juster, F. Thomas, and Stafford, Frank P. 1991. The allocation of time: Empirical findings, behavioral models, and problems of measurement. *Journal of Economic Literature* 29 (June): 471–522.

Kareken, John, and Wallace, Neil. 1977. Portfolio autarky: a welfare analysis. *Journal of International Economics* 7 (February): 19–43.

————. 1978a. Samuelson's consumption-loan model with country-specific fiat monies. Research Department Staff Report 24. Federal Reserve Bank of Minneapolis.

————. 1978b. International monetary reform: the feasible alternatives. *Federal Reserve Bank of Minneapolis Quarterly Review* 2 (Summer): 2–7.

————. 1981. On the indeterminacy of equilibrium exchange rates. *Quarterly Journal of Economics* 96 (May): 207–22.

Kehoe, P. J. 1984. Dynamics of the current account: Theoretical and empirical analysis. Working Paper. Harvard University.

Keynes, John Maynard. 1936. *The general theory of employment, interest, and money*. New York: Harcourt Brace.

King, Robert G. 1990. Money and business cycles. Manuscript. University of Rochester.

King, Robert G., and Plosser, Charles I. 1984. Money, credit, and prices in a real business cycle. *American Economic Review* 74 (June): 363–80.

————. 1985. Money, deficits, and inflation. In *Understanding monetary regimes*, ed. Karl Brunner and Allan H. Meltzer. Carnegie-Rochester Conference Series on Public Policy 22 (Spring): 147–95.

————. 1989. Real business cycles and the test of the Adelmans. Manuscript. University of Rochester.

King, Robert G.; Plosser, Charles I.; and Rebelo, Sergio T. 1987. Production, growth and cycles: Technical appendix. Manuscript. University of Rochester.

King, Robert G.; Wallace, Neil; and Weber, Warren E. 1992. Nonfundamental uncertainty and exchange rates. *Journal of International Economics* 32 (February): 83–108.

Kochin, Levis A. 1974. Are future taxes anticipated by consumers? *Journal of Money, Credit and Banking* 6 (August): 385–94.

Koopmans, Tjalling C. 1947. Measurement without theory. *Review of Economic Statistics* 29 (August): 161–72.

————. 1957. The interaction of tools and problems in economics. *Three essays on the state of economic science*, Chapter 3. New York: McGraw-Hill.

————. 1965. On the concept of optimal economic growth. In *The econometric approach to development planning*. Chicago: Rand-McNally.

Kormendi, Roger C., and Meguire, Philip G. 1987. The nonstationarity of aggregate output: A multicountry analysis. Manuscript. University of Michigan.

Kotlikoff, Laurence J., and Summers, Lawrence H. 1981. The role of intergenerational transfers in aggregate capital accumulation. *Journal of Political Economy* 89 (August): 706–32.

Kreps, David M.; Milgrom, Paul; Roberts, John; and Wilson, Robert. 1982. Rational cooperation in the finitely repeated prisoners' dilemma. *Journal of Economic Theory* 27 (August): 245–52.

Kreps, David M., and Wilson, Robert. 1982. Sequential equilibria. *Econometrica* 50 (July): 863–94.

Kydland, Finn E. 1983. Nonseparable utility and labor supply. Working Paper. Hoover Institution.

————. 1984. Labor-force heterogeneity and the business cycle. In *Essays on macroeconomic implications of financial and labor markets and political processes*, ed. Karl Brunner and Allan H. Meltzer. Carnegie-Rochester Conference Series on Public Policy 21 (Autumn): 173–208. Amsterdam: North-Holland.

————. 1989. The role of money in a business cycle model. Discussion Paper 23. Institute for Empirical Macroeconomics (Federal Reserve Bank of Minneapolis and University of Minnesota).

Kydland, Finn E., and Prescott, Edward C. 1977. Rules rather than discretion: The inconsistency of optimal plans. *Journal of Political Economy* 85 (June): 473–91.

————. 1980. Dynamic optimal taxation, rational expectations and optimal control. *Journal of Economic Dynamics and Control* 2 (February): 79–91.

————. 1982. Time to build and aggregate fluctuations. *Econometrica* 50 (November): 1345–70.

————. 1984. The workweek of capital and labor. Research Department Working Paper 267. Federal Reserve Bank of Minneapolis.

————. 1989. Cyclical movements of the labor input and its real wage. Research Department Working Paper 413. Federal Reserve Bank of Minneapolis.

————. 1991. Hours and employment variation in business cycle theory. *Economic Theory* 1 (January): 63–81.

Leamer, Edward E. 1983. Let's take the con out of econometrics. *American Economic Review* 73 (March): 31–43.

Leontief, W. 1965. Postulates: Keynes' *General Theory* and the classicists. In *The new economics: Keynes' influence on theory and public policy*, ed. S. Harris. Clifton, N. J.: Kelley.

Litterman, Robert B. 1979. Techniques of forecasting using vector autoregressions. Research Department Working Paper 115. Federal Reserve Bank of Minneapolis.

Long, John B., Jr., and Plosser, Charles I. 1983. Real business cycles. *Journal of Political Economy* 91 (February): 39–69.

Lucas, Robert E., Jr. 1972. Expectations and the neutrality of money. *Journal of Economic Theory* 4 (April): 103–24.

————. 1973. Some international evidence on output-inflation tradeoffs. *American Economic Review* 63 (June): 326–34.

————. 1975. An equilibrium model of the business cycle. *Journal of Political Economy* 83 (December): 1113–44.

————. 1976. Econometric policy evaluation: A critique. In *The Phillips curve and labor markets*, ed. Karl Brunner and Allan H. Meltzer. Carnegie-Rochester Conference Series on Public Policy 1: 19–46. Amsterdam: North-Holland.

————. 1977. Understanding business cycles. In *Stabilization of the domestic and international economy*, ed. Karl Brunner and Allan H. Meltzer. Carnegie-Rochester Conference Series on Public Policy 5: 7–29. Amsterdam: North-Holland.

————. 1980a. Methods and problems in business cycle theory. *Journal of Money, Credit and Banking* 12: 696–715. Reprinted in *Studies in business-cycle theory*, pp. 271–96. Cambridge, Mass.: MIT Press, 1981.

————. 1980b. Rules, discretion, and the role of the economic advisor. In *Rational expectations and economic policy*, ed. Stanley Fischer, pp. 199–210. Chicago: University of Chicago Press.

————. 1981a. Deficit finance and inflation. *New York Times* (August 26): 28.

————. 1981b. Inconsistency in fiscal aims. *New York Times* (August 28): 30.

————. 1984. Money in a theory of finance. In *Essays on macroeconomic implications of financial and labor markets and political processes*, ed. Karl Brunner and Allan H. Meltzer. Carnegie-Rochester Conference Series on Public Policy 21 (Autumn): 9–45. Amsterdam: North-Holland.

————. 1987. *Models of business cycles.* Yrjo Jahnsson Lectures Series. London: Blackwell.

————. 1988a. On the mechanics of economic development. *Journal of Monetary Economics* 22 (July): 3–42.

————. 1988b. Money demand in the United States: A quantitative review. In *Money, cycles, and exchange rates: Essays in honor of Allan H. Meltzer*, ed. Karl Brunner and Bennett T. McCallum. Carnegie-Rochester Conference Series on Public Policy 29 (Autumn): 137–67. Amsterdam: North-Holland.

————. 1990. Liquidity and interest rates. *Journal of Economic Theory* 50 (April): 237–64.

Lucas, Robert E., Jr., and Prescott, Edward C. 1971. Investment under uncertainty. *Econometrica* 39 (September): 659–81.

————. 1974. Equilibrium search and unemployment. *Journal of Economic Theory* 7 (February): 188–209.

Lucas, Robert E., Jr., and Sargent, Thomas J. 1981. eds. *Rational expectations and econometric practice.* Minneapolis, Minn.: University of Minnesota Press.

Lucas, Robert E., Jr., and Stokey, Nancy L. 1983. Optimal fiscal and monetary policy in an economy without capital. *Journal of Monetary Economics* 12 (July): 55–93.

————. 1987. Money and interest in a cash-in-advance economy. *Econometrica* 55 (May): 491–513.

McCall, John J. 1965. The economics of information and optimal stopping rules. *Journal of Business* 38 (July): 300–317.

McCallum, Bennett T. 1976. Rational expectations and the natural rate hypothesis: Some consistent estimates. *Econometrica* 44 (January): 43–52.

————. 1978. On macroeconomic instability from a monetarist policy rule. *Economics Letters* 4 (1): 121–24.

————. 1981. Monetarist principles and the money stock growth rule. *American Economic Review* 71 (May): 134–38.

————. 1983. The role of overlapping-generations models in monetary economics. In *Money, monetary policy, and financial institutions*, ed. Karl Brunner and Allan H. Meltzer. Carnegie-Rochester Conference Series on Public Policy 18 (Spring): 9–44. Amsterdam: North-Holland.

McGrattan, Ellen R. 1991. The macroeconomic effects of distortionary taxation. Discussion Paper 37. Institute for Empirical Macroeconomics (Federal Reserve Bank of Minneapolis).

Mankiw, N. Gregory. 1989. Real business cycles: A new Keynesian perspective. *Journal of Economic Perspectives* 3 (Summer): 79–90.

Mankiw, N. Gregory; Rotemberg, Julio J.; and Summers, Lawrence H. 1985. Intertemporal substitution in macroeconomics. *Quarterly Journal of Economics* 100 (February): 225–51.

Marimon, R. 1984. General equilibrium and growth under uncertainty: The turnpike property. Discussion Paper 624. Northwestern University, Center for Mathematical Studies in Economics and Management Science.

Marshall, David A. 1992. Inflation and asset returns in a monetary economy *Journal of Finance* 47 (September): 1315–42.

Meese, Richard. 1990. Currency fluctuations in the post–Bretton Woods era. *Journal of Economic Perspectives* 4 (Winter): 117–34.

Meese, Richard A., and Rogoff, Kenneth. 1983. Empirical exchange rate models of the seventies: Do they fit out of sample? *Journal of International Economics* 14 (February): 3–24.

Mehra, Rajnish, and Prescott, Edward C. 1985. The equity premium: A puzzle. *Journal of Monetary Economics* 15 (March): 145–61.

Melvin, Michael. 1983. The vanishing liquidity effect of money on interest: Analysis and implications for policy. *Economic Inquiry* 21 (April): 188–202.

Miller, Merton H., and Orr, Daniel. 1966. A model of the demand for money by firms. *Quarterly Journal of Economics* 80 (August): 413–35.

————. 1968. The demand for money by firms: Extensions of analytic results. *Journal of Finance* 23 (December): 735–59.

Miller, Preston J. 1981. Fiscal policy in a monetarist model. Research Department Staff Report 67. Federal Reserve Bank of Minneapolis.

————. 1982. A monetarist approach to federal budget control. Research Department Working Paper 210. Federal Reserve Bank of Minneapolis.

————. 1983. Budget deficit mythology. *Federal Reserve Bank of Minneapolis Quarterly Review* 7 (Fall): 1–13.

Mishkin, Frederic S. 1983. *A rational expectations approach to macroeconometrics: Testing policy ineffectiveness and efficient-market models.* Chicago: University of Chicago Press/National Bureau of Economic Research.

Mitchell, Wesley C. 1913. *Business cycles.* Berkeley: University of California Press.

————. [1923] 1951. Business cycles. In *Business cycles and unemployment.* New York: National Bureau of Economic Research. Reprinted in *Readings in business cycle theory,* pp. 43–60. Philadelphia: Blakiston.

————. 1927. *Business cycles: The problem and its setting.* New York: National Bureau of Economic Research.

Modigliani, Franco. 1977. The monetarist controversy or, should we forsake stabilization policies? *American Economic Review* 67 (March): 1–19.

Mortensen, Dale T. 1970. A theory of wage and employment dynamics. In *Microeconomic foundations of employment and inflation theory,* ed. E. S. Phelps, pp. 167–211. New York: Norton.

Muench, T.; Rolnick, A.; Wallace, N.; and Weiler, W. 1974. Tests for structural change and prediction intervals for the reduced forms of two structural models of the U.S.: The FRB-MIT and Michigan Quarterly models. *Annals of Economic and Social Measurement* 3 (July): 491–519.

Musgrave, John C. 1980. Government-owned fixed capital in the United States, 1925–79. *Survey of Current Business* 60 (March): 33–43.

Muth, John F. 1960. Optimal properties of exponentially weighted forecasts. *Journal of the American Statistical Association* 55 (June): 299–306.

Nickelsburg, Gerald. 1980. A theoretical and empirical analysis of flexible exchange rate regimes. Ph.D. dissertation. University of Minnesota.

Oi, Walter Y. 1962. Labor as a quasi-fixed factor. *Journal of Political Economy* 70 (December): 538–55.

Okun, Arthur, and Perry, George L., eds. 1973. *Brookings papers on economic activity*, vol. 3. Washington, D.C.: Brookings Institution.

Perron, Pierre. 1989. The Great Crash, the oil price shock, and the unit root hypothesis. *Econometrica* 57 (November): 1361–1401.

Phelps, E. S., ed. 1970. *Microeconomic foundations of employment and inflation theory*. New York: Norton.

Phelps, E. S., and Taylor, John B. 1977. Stabilizing powers of monetary policy under rational expectations. *Journal of Political Economy* 85 (February): 163–90.

Plosser, Charles I. 1982. Government financing decisions and asset returns. *Journal of Monetary Economics* 9 (May): 325–52.

Prescott, Edward C. 1977. Should control theory be used for economic stabilization? In *Optimal policies, control theory and technology exports*, ed. Karl Brunner and Allan H. Meltzer. Carnegie-Rochester Conference Series on Public Policy 7: 13–38. Amsterdam: North-Holland.

Ramsey, Frank. 1927. A contribution to the theory of taxation. *Economic Journal* 37 (March): 47–61.

Reischauer, Robert. 1990. Taxes and spending under Gramm-Rudman-Hollings. *National Tax Journal* 43 (September): 223–32.

Rogerson, Richard. 1984. Topics in the theory of labor markets. Ph.D. dissertation. University of Minnesota.

————. 1988. Indivisible labor, lotteries and equilibrium. *Journal of Monetary Economics* 21 (January): 3–16.

Rogerson, Richard, and Wright, Randall. 1988. Involuntary unemployment in economies with efficient risk sharing. *Journal of Monetary Economics* 22 (November): 501–15.

Romer, Christina D., and Romer, David H. 1989. Does monetary policy matter? A new test in the spirit of Friedman and Schwartz. In *NBER Macroeconomics Annual 1989*, ed. Olivier Jean Blanchard and Stanley Fischer, pp. 121–70. Cambridge, Mass.: MIT Press/National Bureau of Economic Research.

Romer, Paul M. 1986. Increasing returns and long-run growth. *Journal of Political Economy* 94 (October): 1002–37.

Rotemberg, Julio J. 1984. A monetary equilibrium model with transactions costs. *Journal of Political Economy* 92 (February): 40–58.

Samuelson, Paul Anthony. 1947. *Foundations of economic analysis*. Cambridge, Mass.: Harvard University Press.

————. 1958. An exact consumption-loan model of interest with or without the social contrivance of money. *Journal of Political Economy* 66 (December): 467–82.

Sargent, Thomas J. 1976a. A classical macroeconometric model for the United States. *Journal of Political Economy* 84 (April): 207–37.

————. 1976b. The observational equivalence of natural and unnatural rate theories of macroeconomics. *Journal of Political Economy* 84 (June): 631–40.

————. 1978. Estimation of dynamic labor demand schedules under rational expectations. *Journal of Political Economy* 86 (December): 1009–44.

————. 1979. *Macroeconomic theory*. New York: Academic Press.

————. 1981. Interpreting economic time series. *Journal of Political Economy* 89 (April): 213–48.

————. 1986. Equilibrium investment under uncertainty, measurement errors, and the investment accelerator. Manuscript. Hoover Institution, Stanford University, and University of Minnesota.

————. 1987a. *Macroeconomic theory*, 2nd ed. New York: Academic Press.

————. 1987b. *Dynamic macroeconomic theory*. Cambridge, Mass.: Harvard University Press.

Sargent, Thomas J., and Sims, Christopher A. 1977. Business cycle modeling without pretending to have too much a priori economic theory. In *New methods in business cycle research: Proceedings from a conference*, ed. C. A. Sims, pp. 45–109. Minneapolis: Federal Reserve Bank of Minneapolis.

Sargent, Thomas J., and Wallace, Neil. 1973. The stability of models of money and growth with perfect foresight. *Econometrica* 41 (November): 1043–48.

————. 1975. "Rational" expectations, the optimal monetary instrument, and the optimal money supply rule. *Journal of Political Economy* 83 (April): 241–54.

————. 1982. The real-bills doctrine versus the quantity theory: A reconsideration. *Journal of Political Economy* 90 (December): 1212–36.

————. 1983. A model of commodity money. *Journal of Monetary Economics* 12 (July): 163–87.

Scarth, William M. 1980. Rational expectations and the instability of bond-financing. *Economics Letters* 6 (4): 321–27.

Schinasi, Garry J., and Swamy, P. A. V. B. 1989. The out-of-sample forecasting performance of exchange rate models when coefficients are allowed to change. *Journal of International Money and Finance* 8 (September): 375–90.

Selten, Reinhard. 1975. Reexamination of the perfectness concept for equilibrium points in extensive games. *International Journal of Game Theory* 4 (1): 25–55.

Shell, Karl, and Wright, Randall. 1993. Indivisibilities, lotteries and sunspot equilibria. *Economic Theory* 3 (January): 1–17.

Simons, Henry C. 1936. Rules versus authorities in monetary policy. *Journal of Political Economy* 44 (February): 1–30.

Sims, Christopher A. 1972. Money, income, and causality. *American Economic Review* 62 (September): 540–52.

————, ed. 1977. *New methods in business cycle research: Proceedings from a conference.* Minneapolis: Federal Reserve Bank of Minneapolis.

————. 1980. Macroeconomics and reality. *Econometrica* 48 (January): 1–48.

————. 1986. Are forecasting models usable for policy analysis? *Federal Reserve Bank of Minneapolis Quarterly Review* 10 (Winter): 2–16.

————. 1989. Models and their uses. *American Journal of Agricultural Economics* 71 (May): 489–94.

Slutzky, Eugen. [1927] 1937. The summation of random causes as the source of cyclic processes. *Econometrica* 5 (April): 105–46.

Solow, Robert M. 1956. A contribution to the theory of economic growth. *Quarterly Journal of Economics* 70 (February): 65–94.

————. 1957. Technical change and the aggregate production function. *Review of Economics and Statistics* 39 (August): 312–20.

————. 1970. *Growth theory.* New York: Oxford University Press.

————. 1986. Unemployment: Getting the questions right. *Economica* 53 (Supplement): S23–S34.

Sonnenschein, Hugo. 1973. Do Walras' identity and continuity characterize the class of community excess demand functions? *Journal of Economic Theory* 6 (August): 345–54.

Steindl, Frank G. 1974. Money and income: The view from the government budget restraint. *Journal of Finance* 29 (September): 1143–48.

Stigler, Stephen M. 1978. Mathematical statistics in the early states. *Annals of Statistics* 6: 239–65.

Stiglitz, Joseph E. 1969. A re-examination of the Modigliani-Miller theorem. *American Economic Review* 59 (December): 784–93.

Stock, James H., and Watson, Mark W. 1991. A simple estimator of cointegrating vectors in higher order integrated systems. Manuscript. University of California, Berkeley.

Stockman, Alan C. 1981. Anticipated inflation and the capital stock in a cash-in-advance economy. *Journal of Monetary Economics* 8 (November): 387–93.

Strotz, R. H. 1955–56. Myopia and inconsistency in dynamic utility maximization. *Review of Economic Studies* 23: 165–80.

Summers, Robert, and Heston, Alan. 1984. Improved international comparisons of real product and its composition: 1950–1980. *Review of Income and Wealth* 30 (June): 207–62.

Svensson, Lars E. O. 1985. Money and asset prices in a cash-in-advance economy. *Journal of Political Economy* 93 (October): 919–44.

Swan, T. W. 1956. Economic growth and capital accumulation. *Economic Record* 32 (November): 334–61.

Tobin, James. 1956. The interest-elasticity of transactions demand for cash. *Review of Economics and Statistics* 38 (August): 241–47.

————. 1965a. Money and economic growth. *Econometrica* 33 (October): 671–84.

————. 1965b. Money wage rates and employment. In *The new economics: Keynes' influence on theory and public policy*, ed. Seymour E. Harris. Clifton, N.J.: Kelley.

————. 1977. How dead is Keynes? *Economic Inquiry* 15 (October): 459–68.

Tobin, James, and Buiter, Willem H. 1976. Long-run effects of fiscal and monetary policy on aggregate demand. In *Monetarism*, ed. Jerome L. Stein. Studies in Monetary Economics 1: 273–309. Amsterdam: North-Holland.

Tobin, J., and Dolde, W. 1971. Wealth, liquidity and consumption. In *Consumer spending and monetary policy: The linkages*. Monetary Conference Series 5: 99–146. Boston: Federal Reserve Bank of Boston.

U.S. Congress. 1984. Congressional Budget Office. Baseline budget projections for fiscal years 1985–1989. A report to the Senate and House committees on the budget—Part II. Washington, D.C.: U.S. Government Printing Office.

U.S. Council of Economic Advisers. 1983. *Economic report of the President, 1983*. Washington, D.C.: U.S. Government Printing Office.

Wallace, Neil. 1980. Integrating micro and macroeconomics: An application to credit controls. *Federal Reserve Bank of Minneapolis Quarterly Review* 4 (Fall): 16–29.

————. 1981. A Modigliani-Miller theorem for open-market operations. *American Economic Review* 71 (June): 267–74.

Watson, Mark W. 1986. Univariate detrending methods with stochastic trends. *Journal of Monetary Economics* 18 (July): 49–75.

West, Kenneth D. 1988. The insensitivity of consumption to news about income. *Journal of Monetary Economics* 21 (January): 17–33.

White, Betsy B. 1978. Empirical tests of the life cycle hypothesis. *American Economic Review* 68 (September): 547–60.

Wright, Randall. 1991. The labor market implications of unemployment insurance and short-time compensation. *Federal Reserve Bank of Minneapolis Quarterly Review* 15 (Summer): 11–19.

Zarnowitz, Victor. 1989. Facts and factors in the recent evolution of business cycles in the United States. Working Paper 2865. National Bureau of Economic Research.

Index